D0875172

Bad History, Worse Policy

Bad History, Worse Policy

How a False Narrative about the
Financial Crisis Led to the Dodd-Frank Act

Peter J. Wallison

The AEI Press

Publisher for the American Enterprise Institute

WASHINGTON, D.C.

Distributed by arrangement with the Rowman & Littlefield Publishing Group, 4501 Forbes Boulevard, Suite 200, Lanham, Maryland 20706. To order, call toll free 1-800-462-6420 or 1-717-794-3800. For all other inquiries, please contact AEI Press, 1150 Seventeenth Street, N.W., Washington, D.C. 20036, or call 1-800-862-5801.

Library of Congress Cataloging-in-Publication Data

Wallison, Peter J.
   Bad history, worse policy : how a false narrative about the financial crisis led to the Dodd-Frank Act / Peter J. Wallison.
     p.   cm.
   Includes bibliographical references and index.
   ISBN 978-0-8447-7238-7 (cloth) — ISBN 0-8447-7238-0 (cloth) — ISBN 978-0-8447-7239-4 (pbk.) — ISBN 0-8447-7239-9 (pbk.) — ISBN 978-0-8447-7240-0 (ebook) — ISBN 0-8447-7240-2 (ebook) 1. Finance—Government policy—United States. 2. United States. Dodd-Frank Wall Street Reform and Consumer Protection Act. 3. Federal National Mortgage Association. 4. Federal Home Loan Mortgage Corporation. I. Title.
   HG181.W283 2012
   332.7'20973--dc23

2012033490

Printed in the United States of America

Contents

Preface

The winners write the history, so a contemporary and contrary view is essential. With their victory in the elections of 2012, Barack Obama and the Democrats put themselves in a position to cement the Dodd-Frank Act into law. As this is written, more than two years after the act was passed, fewer than half of all the regulations required by the act had been finalized, but the election provided the Obama administration with four more years in which to get the job done. Sadly, the result will be much slower growth for the U.S. economy and a decline in the significance of the U.S. financial industry—formerly the world leader—in the global economy.

At some point in the future, scholars will wonder why the United States tied its own hands and limited its economic growth in the early 2000s. They will look back at the period after the second World War and note that until the second decade of the 21st century the United States led the world in innovation and economic growth, with startling advances particularly evident in the living standards of the middle class. Then, in 2008, there was a financial crisis, and in 2010 the Dodd-Frank Act, a financial reform law; after that, the wheels of the U.S. economy just turned more slowly.

I hope this book, made possible by a generous grant from the Templeton Foundation, will help future scholars sort it all out—that it will be seen as a chronicle of why and how the U.S. crushed the life out of one of its most successful industries, impeded the growth of its economy and hobbled improvement in the lives of its own citizens. It is made up principally of 30 essays, beginning in 2004 and extending through 2012, in which I chronicled the underlying causes of the crisis and how the left developed a false narrative both to deny the government's role in the crisis and to provide a foundation for legislation that would place the U.S. financial system under the government's control. These essays, called *Financial Services Outlooks,* are included in substantially the form in which they were originally published by the American Enterprise Institute.

I have tried to provide some context for these essays with accompanying commentary that places them in the political and economic background that existed at the time they were written. If, in retrospect, there are errors in the essays, I thought it best to leave them uncorrected, as evidence of what was known, or what I thought, at a particular time. Similarly, as I was writing the commentary, regulations were being proposed, modified and in some cases issued in final form; these changes could not be incorporated into the book before its publication in early 2013.

Introduction:
Obamacare for the Financial System

The Great Depression persuaded the public that private enterprise was a fundamentally unstable system, that the Depression represented a failure of free market capitalism, that the government had to step in. . . . The widespread acceptance of these views sparked the enormous growth in the power of government . . . that is still going on. We now know, as many economists knew then, that . . . the truth about the Depression was very different. The Depression was produced, or at the very least, made far worse by perverse monetary policies followed by the U.S. authorities. . . . Far from being a failure of free market capitalism, the Depression was a failure of government. Unfortunately, that failure did not end with the Great Depression. . . . In practice, just as during the Depression, far from promoting stability, the government has itself been the major single source of instability.

—Milton Friedman, *A Monetary History of the United States*

The 2008 financial crisis was the most serious shock to the U.S. economy since the Great Depression. It triggered a lengthy recession, deepened a painful housing market collapse, and set the stage for massive taxpayer bailouts. Perhaps most serious, the 2008 crisis triggered a view—never far below the surface on the left—that capitalism itself was at fault. Wall Street greed, private sector irresponsibility, and regulatory failure quickly became the heart of the narrative pushed by the left and embraced by the Obama administration and the mainstream media. This narrative helped to shackle public opinion behind the Dodd-Frank Act (DFA),[1] a modern analog of New Deal legislation like the National Industrial Recovery Act and the Agricultural Adjustment Act, both of which were eventually declared unconstitutional.

Instead of a thorough study of the causes of the financial crisis, we got the left's perennial prescription for the economy's ills—more government controls. Like its health care twin, popularly known as Obamacare, the DFA leaves the financial system nominally in private hands but subjects it to so many controls that it will no longer be able to function independently of the government. In this book, I will attempt to show how this was brought about through the development, propagation, and acceptance of false narratives—first about the government sponsored enterprises (GSEs) the Federal National Mortgage Association (Fannie Mae) and the Federal Home Loan Mortgage Corporation (Freddie Mac) and then about the financial crisis itself.

The DFA is yet another example of the aphorism that the speed and scale of a government prescription is directly proportional to the vapidity of its diagnosis. In effect, the most serious U.S. financial crisis in at least eighty years has never been thoroughly investigated, nor its causes fully debated. From the moment in the 2008 presidential debates that President Obama called it the result of "Republican deregulation," no serious consideration was given by his administration or the Democratic Congress to the real causes of the financial crisis. Together, in the DFA, they enacted far-reaching legislation that will likely hobble one of the most successful industries this country has ever produced, and they will have done it on the basis of nothing more substantive than a half-baked political slogan.

A challenge to this dominant narrative is now emerging. During the 2011 and 2012 Republican presidential debates, almost all the candidates—including the eventual victor, Mitt Romney—argued that the 2008 financial crisis was caused by U.S. government housing policy. Republicans in Congress have also introduced legislation to repeal the act in its entirety. These efforts are not necessarily driven solely by ideological considerations. There is strong evidence that the DFA has impeded recovery from the

---

1. Dodd-Frank Wall Street Reform and Consumer Protection Act, Public Law 111-203 (July 21, 2010).

recession that followed the financial crisis. Enacted in July 2010, the act started the gross domestic product (GDP)—including both the housing and manufacturing sectors—on a downward track from which it never fully recovered. Before the DFA, average GDP growth had been 2.5 percent. After, through the third quarter of 2012, it was 2 percent.

These results illustrate the underlying rationale for an exchange between Jamie Dimon, the chairman of JPMorgan Chase, the largest U.S. bank, and Fed chief Ben Bernanke on June 8, 2011: Dimon said, "I have a great fear that someone's going to write a book in 10 or 20 years and the book is going to talk about the things we did in the middle of the crisis that actually slowed down the recovery. . . . Has anyone bothered to study the cumulative effect of all these [regulations]? . . . Is this holding us back [from creating jobs] at this point?"[2] Bernanke's reply was candid: "Has anybody done a comprehensive analysis of the impact [of new regulations] on credit? I can't pretend that anybody really has. You know, it's just too complicated. We don't really have the quantitative tools to do that."[3]

Narratives and Policy

If government housing policy—and not lack of regulation—caused the financial crisis, more and tighter regulation as embodied in the DFA would be the wrong policy response. It will unnecessarily increase costs for the private sector and reduce economic growth and jobs. Instead, one would repeal Dodd-Frank, change government housing policy, and then evaluate whether any additional regulation is necessary.

These were ideas I had been pressing for many years through the *Financial Services Outlook* essays that form the heart of this book. Between 2004 and 2012, I had written more than seventy essays on the regulation of financial services. From these, with a generous grant to AEI from the John Templeton Foundation, I selected twenty-nine *Outlooks* that covered important aspects of three related topics Fannie Mae and Freddie Mac, the financial crisis of 2008, and the Dodd-Frank Act.

---

2. Quoted in Canfield and Associates, *GSE Report*, July 1, 2011, 1.
3. Ibid.

In reviewing these essays, I found that they reflect a common theme: the power of ideas—shaped into a narrative or description of an event—to affect public policy. Until 2004, when both GSEs were found to have manipulated their accounting, they were thought to be politically powerful but well managed and essentially harmless toilers in the housing finance vineyard. This image—the product of a well-tended narrative about their benign and helpful role in housing finance—protected them from serious challenge. After the financial crisis, despite a strong case that the government's housing finance policies were the principal cause of the breakdown, the left succeeded in constructing a counternarrative in which "unbridled free markets" were the principal culprits. This narrative was accepted uncritically by the media and became the conventional explanation for the crisis. With no other ideas admitted into the public square, the DFA was the inevitable result.

Accordingly, this book emphasizes the importance of narratives in shaping public policy. Before policies and laws can be changed, the narrative that gave rise to the existing policies must be challenged or shown to be wrongly founded or outdated. Obviously, this is not a new insight; it's always been clear that ideas have consequences. But in the case of the Dodd-Frank Act, it is possible to discern a clear line from the narrative about the GSEs, through the initial ideologically tinged narrative about the causes of the financial crisis, to the principal terms of the act. In order to repeal the act, then, it is necessary to show that its policy rationale—the underlying narrative—is false. That is the purpose of this book.

When I joined AEI in 1999, I had already decided that my first project would be to explore the role of Fannie Mae and Freddie Mac in the U.S. housing finance system. I'd had this idea in mind since my years as general counsel of the Treasury, when I'd first encountered these obscure but immensely powerful Washington institutions. In 1999 I knew relatively little about the two GSEs, but enough to recognize that they represented a peculiar and troubling business model—shareholder-owned private firms that were listed on the New York Stock Exchange, thinly capitalized, highly profitable, and the beneficiaries of what was then described by outside observers as "implicit" government backing. The companies denied that they had any such government support, implicit or otherwise, and of course the government—often through the Treasury Department—issued the same denial. But the markets refused to believe it and continued to provide Fannie and Freddie with rates on their debt securities that were better than AAA and only slightly higher than what Treasury itself was required to pay.

This structure worried me. It was not clear how their risk-taking could be controlled if creditors—the only group that doesn't benefit from risk-taking—have no incentive to care whether the two firms are taking risks. In other words, how could there be any form of market discipline if the credit markets were assured that they would be reimbursed by Uncle Sam if one or both of the GSEs were to fail? Here, undoubtedly, was the clearest and most troubling case of moral hazard in the U.S. financial system. Even government deposit insurance covers only a specified amount of bank deposits; Fannie and Freddie had accumulated liabilities of more than $5 trillion, and all of these obligations were implicitly on the government's books. If the markets were correct about the nature of this government backing, the taxpayers were eventually going to face substantial costs.

Fannie and Freddie were regulated, to be sure, but I am skeptical in general about the efficacy of regulation. Government employees, as diligent as they may be, simply do not have the incentives to be tough and thorough in supervising complex financial institutions. And if these incentives are absent, regulation itself creates moral hazard by providing an illusory sense that an objective third party is controlling a regulated firm's risk-taking. Indeed, the fact that they were regulated at all was a strong signal to the markets that the government was aware of its implicit obligations and would stand by them. Under these circumstances, weak regulation was the worst of all possible worlds, and the regulatory structure for the GSEs in 1999 was notoriously weak. For example, their regulator, the Office of Federal Housing Enterprises Oversight (OFHEO), did not even have the ability to increase their capital as their risks increased; their capital level had been set by statute at an appallingly low level—2.5 percent on their mortgage assets and forty-five basis points on their guarantees of mortgage-backed securities (MBS). Accordingly, my objective—as outlined in chapter 1—was to raise public awareness of the risks associated with these two firms in the hope that this would spur congressional action for tighter and more comprehensive regulation.

There is some irony associated with my view of the GSEs' potential risks for taxpayers; during the time I was studying the GSEs, I was largely unaware of the nature and scope of the risks they were actually taking.

This was not because of my own limitations as an analyst—limitations I readily admit—but because the same lack of disclosure that characterized the GSEs' financial statements also extended to their activities in buying and securitizing mortgages. Although their fraudulent accounting awakened Congress, the White House, and Fed chairman Alan Greenspan to the dangers they might potentially pose to the financial system and the taxpayers, by late 2004 few people had yet realized that the GSEs were also buying hundreds of billions of dollars of subprime and other low-quality mortgages in order to meet the affordable housing goals that had been imposed on them by Congress in 1992. It wasn't until shortly before they became insolvent and were taken over by their regulator—acting as a conservator—that the data began to come out in understandable form. These data made clear for the first time the poor quality of the mortgages the GSEs had been acquiring. It showed not only why they had become insolvent but why their activity was a primary element in the government housing policies that ultimately caused the 2008 financial crisis.

There is a sequel to all of this. In July 2009, I was appointed by John Boehner, then the House minority leader, as a member of the Financial Crisis Inquiry Commission (FCIC), a congressionally appointed ten-member group (six Democrats and four Republicans) that was to investigate the causes of the financial crisis and report to Congress, the president and the American people. Ultimately, for the reasons outlined below, I dissented from the commission's majority report.[4] In my dissent, I pointed out that by 2008, because of government housing policies, almost half of all mortgages in the United States were subprime or otherwise weak and that the vast majority of these mortgages were on the books of government agencies like Fannie and Freddie. The FCIC majority ignored these numbers. Nevertheless, in December 2011, the SEC sued some of the top officers of Fannie and Freddie during the period prior to their insolvency, alleging that they had failed to disclose the full scope of their purchases of subprime and other low-quality mortgages. The SEC had been able to conduct a thorough investigation of the books and records of the GSEs and had obtained nonprosecution agreements in which both firms admitted that

---

4. Peter J. Wallison, "Dissent from the Majority Report of the Financial Crisis Inquiry Commission," 23–28, http://www.aei.org/files/2011/01/26/Wallisondissent.pdf.

they had acquired and not disclosed the mortgages that ultimately caused their insolvency. These agreements showed that there were actually more subprime and low-quality mortgages on their books in 2008 than I had reported in my dissent.

Because Fannie and Freddie were hiding their subprime credit risks, I and others—including Alan Greenspan and economists at the Fed—were focused on the interest rate risk associated with their portfolios of mortgages and mortgage-backed securities. Together, the GSEs held mortgages and MBS with a value of more than $1.5 trillion. Their statutory capital was extremely thin, only 2.5 percent of their assets, and they were carrying these instruments with borrowed funds. If interest rates should rise above the rate on the funds they had borrowed, they would begin to suffer cash and accounting losses on the value of the instruments themselves. For example, if the GSEs were earning 5 percent on the mortgages in their portfolios but were required to pay 6 percent for the funds necessary to carry these portfolios, they would sustain significant losses. Because they were so thinly capitalized, it would not take long for them to become insolvent. In addition, their assets would have to be written down, causing a further decline in capital. These losses, in turn, could trigger much higher funding costs, eventually requiring the government either to come to their rescue or close them down. Ultimately, of course, it was their credit risk-taking and not their interest rate risk-taking that did them in. Their shares fell sharply in value in the summer of 2008, when investors realized that the unprecedented number of mortgage delinquencies and defaults would affect their profitability, even if the government protected their creditors.

This raises the legitimate question of whether it was the GSE form itself or government housing policy that caused the failure of these two firms and ultimately the financial crisis. The answer is: both. If it had not been for the GSE form, which allowed Fannie and Freddie to operate with the implicit backing of the U.S. government, they could never have grown as large as they did and could never have had such outsized influence on the U.S. housing market. In addition, it was the moral hazard associated with this implicit government backing—the belief in the credit markets that the government would never allow Fannie or Freddie to fail—that allowed them to operate without anyone's scrutiny. The fact is that no investor that was buying their securities—either their debt securities or the MBS they had guaranteed—cared what risks they were taking. In the end, everyone was confident that Uncle Sam would stand behind them, a confidence that was fully borne out. This enabled the U.S. Department of Housing and Urban Development (HUD) to raise the affordable housing goals over time—substantially increasing their risk-taking—without engendering any significant concern in the credit markets. To the extent that financial analysts were looking at Fannie and Freddie, they were equity analysts, who probably believed the narrative that Fannie and Freddie only bought prime mortgages. Even if housing prices stopped rising, they reasoned, the high quality of the GSEs' portfolios would keep them from suffering debilitating losses.

The Narrative on Fannie Mae and Freddie Mac

There was little support for tighter and more comprehensive regulation of Fannie and Freddie when I joined AEI in 1999. To the extent that they were known at all, the GSEs were seen as largely benign facilitators of an efficient housing market, and their soft-focus advertising emphasized their contributions to the American dream of homeownership. Americans generally thought of the U.S. housing finance system as efficient and effective, and the politicians who supported it called it "the envy of the world." Few Americans—or lawmakers for that matter—knew that the U.S. mortgage interest rates and homeownership rates were somewhere in the middle of the pack for developed countries, even though only the United States directly subsidized housing finance, allowed refinancing without penalty, and in many states allowed "nonrecourse" mortgages in which homeowners had no liability on the mortgage note beyond whatever value the lender received on foreclosure. With all this misplaced satisfaction, it was difficult for Congressman Richard Baker—then the head of the House subcommittee with jurisdiction over the GSEs—to find cosponsors for tougher regulation of the GSEs, even among Republicans.

Between 1999 and 2005, I sponsored seventeen AEI public conferences about the GSEs and the risks they posed to the taxpayers. But apart from raising interest in the GSEs in the Washington policy community, my efforts seemed to produce no significant additional support for regulatory legislation. During much of this period, when Alan Greenspan was asked in congressional testimony about Fannie and Freddie, he usually said that he thought they were well-managed institutions and didn't see any particular reason for the Fed to be concerned about them. This was essentially the conventional wisdom—the narrative—about the GSEs. They were seen as a necessary part of the plumbing of the housing finance system, and exploring what problems they might cause in the future was more trouble than it was worth. It seemed as though things would go on this way indefinitely, with the two firms skating by their critics on the strength of their unparalleled Washington networks, the narrative about their quietly helpful role in fostering homeownership, and (not coincidentally) the fact that they had made the realtors, homebuilders, and securities industry—three highly influential lobbying groups—into their cheerleaders, surrogates, and ardent backers in lobbying Congress.

But then, in 2003 and 2004, as recounted more fully in chapter 1, things went wildly off the rails for the GSEs. In the wake of the Enron scandal, their own manipulation of accounting standards challenged the conventional narrative that they were good corporate citizens and unlikely to be the source of financial problems. They were no longer the untouchables. A new narrative developed—that they were more concerned about their own profitability than advancing homeownership and were potentially problematic for the health of the economy. No one truly understood the scope of the dangers they posed. That did not become clear until the financial crisis. But under the new narrative, it was not safe for most lawmakers to be seen in public with them. Alan Greenspan, now awakened to the dangers they posed, was a powerful voice, calling for reform in almost every appearance before Congress. And Washington institutions such as the Fed's economic staff and the Congressional Budget Office began examining whether their shareholders—rather than homeowners—were really getting the benefit of the government subsidy they enjoyed.

Still, the GSEs were powerful enough to stymie moves by the Bush administration—even with a Republican Congress—to improve and tighten their regulation. Fannie and Freddie had lost their aura of invincibility and their reputation as good and honest corporate citizens, but their support by various important interest groups, and the formidable networks they had established in Washington, gave them sufficient raw power in Congress to prevent serious tightening of their regulation.

By 2005 the administration felt strongly enough about the need for tougher GSE regulation that it opposed House legislation—adopted by the Republican-led House Financial Services Committee (HFSC)—because it did not go far enough in controlling the two firms. When the Democrats took control of Congress in 2006, the chances for reform looked bleak, especially because Barney Frank—the GSEs' biggest booster in Congress— became the HFSC's chair. However, Frank was willing to work with Hank Paulson, Bush's new Treasury secretary, to develop fairly strong regulatory legislation, and Frank was able to move the legislation through the House. Frank's new openness to tighter regulation of the GSEs showed that conditions in Washington had indeed changed significantly, but it had taken a major and somewhat serendipitous event—the sudden dismissal of the top three officials of Freddie described in chapter 1—to make that change happen. Without the destruction of the GSEs' image as honest and well-managed firms—in other words, the destruction of the prevailing narrative about them in Washington—it is doubtful that Congress would have taken the steps to increase the power of their regulator before the financial crisis hit in September 2008.

The Narrative for the Financial Crisis

Unfortunately, as it turned out, this stitch was not in time. As outlined more fully in chapter 2, the first indications of a coming financial crisis appeared in 2007. Government officials who would be expected to have the best information about what was happening in the financial markets—particularly the new chairman of the Federal Reserve, Ben Bernanke, who replaced Greenspan in 2006—were unable to foresee what was coming. In March 2007, Bernanke told Congress that "at this juncture . . . the impact on the broader economy and financial markets of the problems in the subprime markets seems likely to be contained."[5] One year later, the problem that was likely to be contained had grown so serious that it induced the Fed to rescue Bear Stearns, one of the largest investment banks on Wall Street. By September 2008, in the midst of the presidential campaign, the subprime

---

5. Newsmax, March 27, 2007, http://archive.newsmax.com/archives/ic/2007/3/28/1107 09.shtml.

problem was out of control; virtually all of the world's largest financial institutions appeared to be in trouble, and Lehman Brothers—another large investment bank—was allowed to fail, shocking the market, causing banks and others to hoard cash, and bringing on a full-scale panic now known as the financial crisis.

From the beginning, the government blamed the private sector, and particularly Wall Street, for the financial crisis. Like the narrative for the Great Depression described in the Milton Friedman quote that keynoted this introduction, the financial crisis narrative was simple and wrong. In this telling, the crisis was caused by irresponsible private-sector risk-taking, greed on Wall Street, and predatory lending by unscrupulous and unregulated mortgage originators. To this, during the 2008 presidential debates, then-candidate Obama added "Republican deregulation," supplying both a partisan element and insufficient regulation as another cause. Blaming the private sector and the largest banks for the financial crisis absolved the government's housing policies—which had been initiated during the Clinton administration and actively pursued under George W. Bush—and created a foundation for the enactment of the DFA. Because it was accepted and propagated without serious examination by the media, this explanation for the crisis still has a tight hold on what Americans believe about the crisis that befell them in 2008.

In point of fact, the government itself was principally responsible for the crisis. Ill-considered housing policies, imposed on and implemented by Fannie Mae and Freddie Mac, fostered the creation of twenty-eight million subprime and other weak and risky mortgages[6]—half of all mortgages in the United States. Of these, by 2008, 74 percent were on the books of Fannie and Freddie or other government-controlled or regulated agencies—with

---

6. In my dissent and elsewhere, until December 2011, I used the number twenty-seven million to describe the number of subprime and other risky mortgages in the financial system in 2008. In December 2011, the SEC sued certain top officers of Fannie Mae and Freddie Mac, alleging that they failed to inform investors of the number of subprime loans they had acquired. Accompanying the SEC press release on the subject were nonprosecution agreements between the SEC and the two GSEs in which the GSEs agreed to the SEC's finding that the actual number of subprime and other low-quality loans that the GSEs held or had guaranteed in 2008 was closer to thirteen million, raising the total number of outstanding subprime and other nonprime loans to twenty-eight million.

about three-quarters of these on the books of the GSEs—showing irrefutably where the demand for these subprime mortgages originated. Beginning in 2007, these loans failed in massive numbers, driving down housing prices, weakening the financial institutions that held them, and causing the panic and the financial crisis

There was still a lot about the GSEs that was unknown, and a lot that was assumed to be true and was not. One of the most persistent myths, even today, is that Fannie and Freddie only bought prime loans.[7] This had been true before the 1990s, but because of a 1992 change in their governing law, it had not been true for the sixteen years leading up to the financial crisis. Unknown to me and to others who were following the GSE issue, since 1992 the GSEs had been acquiring increasing numbers of subprime and other weak and risky loans. The law that made this necessary was the Housing and Community Development Act of 1992,[8] which required that 30 percent of all loans the GSEs acquired had to be made to low- and moderate-income (LMI) borrowers, defined as borrowers with incomes at or below the median in the communities where they lived. The Department of Housing and Urban Development (HUD) had been given authority to administer the act, and through both the Clinton and Bush administrations it had expanded and tightened this quota so that, by 2007, 55 percent of all loans they acquired had to be LMI loans.[9]

Although it was possible to find prime loans among LMI borrowers, it was not easy; to meet a quota of 50 percent or more, the GSEs were required to substantially reduce their underwriting standards. However, they did not accurately report what they had done. For example, although they were acquiring large numbers of loans that would ordinarily be considered subprime because they were made to borrowers with FICO credit scores lower than 660, Fannie and Freddie did not use this common definition for

---

7. In an article in the *New York Times* on July 14, 2008, columnist Paul Krugman stated, incorrectly, that Fannie and Freddie were not allowed to acquire subprime loans and that this showed the value of regulation. Because of careless or ideologically driven columnists such as Krugman, who is widely read, the false narrative about Fannie and Freddie and ultimately the financial crisis was perpetuated.

8. Title XIII of the Housing and Community Development Act of 1992, Public Law 102-550, 106 Stat. 3672, H.R. 5334 (enacted October 28, 1992).

9. See http://www.aei.org/files/2011/01/26/Wallisondissent.pdf, 71, table 10.

determining whether a loan was subprime. Instead, they defined mortgages as subprime only if they had bought these loans from subprime originators. In their reports to firms that aggregated and published mortgage market data, the GSEs did not reveal this definitional sleight of hand, and thus almost all the GSEs' loans were recorded as prime when in fact substantial numbers—perhaps as much as 40 percent—were subprime or otherwise of low quality.

This was an extremely important fact and the reason why I and so many others—including Bernanke, other regulators, and most private sector observers—did not understand the true scope of the risks the GSEs were creating until their insolvency and the onset of the financial crisis. If they had fully disclosed their purchases of subprime loans and mortgage-backed securities based on subprime and other weak loans, investors, risk managers, analysts, and even regulators would have had a better understanding as the financial crisis approached of the riskiness of both the mortgage market and the assets of the largest financial institutions. In December 2011, the Securities and Exchange Commission (SEC) sued the former top officers of Fannie and Freddie for failing to disclose the full extent of the subprime and other risky loans they were acquiring.

The funds the government poured into the housing market helped to build a ten-year housing price bubble, extending from 1997 to 2007. Housing bubbles suppress delinquencies and defaults, because rising prices allow borrowers to refinance or sell the home before a default occurs. By 2002, investors around the world and on Wall Street began to believe that privately issued mortgage-backed securities—based on subprime loans— were good risk-adjusted investments; they were producing high yields but were not showing the losses that were normally associated with subprime loans. The boom in Wall Street activity extended from about 2004 to 2006, and by 2007—when the private MBS market collapsed in tandem with the housing bubble—there were about 7.8 million subprime loans outstanding in the form of privately issued mortgage-backed securities (PMBS)—less than 26 percent of the twenty-eight million outstanding.

When the great ten-year housing bubble deflated, it caused the collapse of the PMBS market as buyers were frightened off by an unprecedented number of delinquencies and defaults. This "mortgage meltdown," as it was called in the media, weakened the financial condition of all the institutions that had substantial investments in these instruments. An event of this kind, a weakening of an entire industry because of a sudden decline in the value of a widely held asset, is known to scholars as a common shock.[10]

The rescue of Bear Stearns in March 2008 temporarily calmed the markets; investors and creditors thought the U.S. government had signaled that it would rescue all large financial firms. But when Lehman was allowed to file for bankruptcy in September 2008, market participants were shocked, and a full-scale panic ensued. Banks and others, fearful of withdrawals by depositors and counterparties, hoarded cash, and the sudden evaporation of credit was what defined the financial crisis. Fannie and Freddie became insolvent and were taken over by the government only a week before Lehman Brothers' failure brought on the financial crisis. These two events were not unrelated. The GSEs had dominated the housing finance market ever since the savings and loan industry collapsed almost twenty years earlier. Moreover, a sharp decline in mortgage and housing values—the mortgage meltdown—is what precipitated the crisis. These related events should have been a powerful indicator that the GSEs' housing finance activities had some role in the financial crisis.

But it was not to be. The whole question of the government's responsibility for the crisis became enmeshed in the partisan and ideological struggles that were roiling the waters in Washington on the eve of the 2008 election. By characterizing the financial crisis as a result of Republican deregulation, President Obama made the crisis not only a partisan matter—a failure of the Bush administration—but also an ideological challenge to the Republicans' governing philosophy. Obama's statement was wrong, but neither John McCain nor his advisers were able to respond effectively. Indeed, McCain made things worse by saying on numerous occasions that the financial crisis was caused by "Wall Street greed." This became the accepted narrative—the conventional wisdom—asserted in news articles and dozens of books as though it were the uncontroverted truth. Any effort to show the GSEs' role, and the role of government housing policy, was denounced as a "loony" idea[11] or irredeemably partisan, if not ignored altogether. Accordingly, the

---

10. George Kaufman and Kenneth Scott, "What Is Systemic Risk and Do Bank Regulators Retard or Contribute to It?" *Independent Review* 7, no. 3 (Winter 2003): 3.

11. Joe Nocera, "Inquiry Is Missing a Bottom Line," *New York Times*, January 28, 2011.

most serious financial disaster since the Great Depression did not receive—and has never received—the careful study it deserved.

The effort to suppress a competing narrative—an alternative explanation of the financial crisis—reached the level of farce with the report of the Financial Crisis Inquiry Commission (FCIC), a group set up by Congress in 2009 to investigate and report on the causes of the 2008 crisis. With a government charter and government funding, one would expect that the commission would be duty-bound to consider every reasonable possibility. It didn't come close. Composed of ten members—six Democratic and four Republican appointees (I was one of the Republican appointees)—the commission was completely controlled by its chair, Philip Angelides, a Democrat who had run for governor of California and was a confidant of House Speaker Nancy Pelosi. Angelides appointed almost every member of the staff, decided what the commission would investigate, established a schedule of public hearings on what he thought were key topics before there had been any investigation, and reviewed and revised drafts of the report before the other commissioners saw them. The Republican vice chair, Bill Thomas, a former congressman with a populist streak who knew little about the financial markets, was ineffective in getting Angelides to look into anything other than the subjects the Democrats wanted to pursue.

As a result, the report's discussion of the GSEs' role in the financial crisis was almost completely perfunctory, and the whole report was a sad whitewash—nothing but a confirmation of the left's position that the crisis was the result of ineffective regulation of an irresponsible private sector. I wrote a one-hundred-page dissent that—in typical fashion for Angelides—was cut to nine pages in the version of the report that was commercially distributed through bookstores.

The irony is that this did not have to be a partisan dispute. The Bush administration was at least as culpable as the Clinton administration in pushing Fannie and Freddie to acquire the subprime and other low-quality mortgages that eventually drove them to insolvency, helped to build a gigantic ten-year housing bubble, and—as outlined in my dissent and discussed below—caused the financial crisis. It is, however, an ideological dispute. Even today, there is a frenzied effort on the left to counter any suggestion that the government had a role in the financial crisis, through the GSEs or otherwise.[12] Although there are no data that challenge the overwhelming evidence of the government's central role, the left apparently believes that implicating the government in the financial crisis is an impermissible heresy.

Nevertheless, scholars and others are gradually making an effort to ferret out and publish the facts about the financial crisis. In December 2011, for example, Gretchen Morgenson and Josh Rosner published *Reckless Endangerment*, in which they argued that Fannie Mae's efforts to solidify its political position by making subprime mortgages available to low-income borrowers had contributed to the financial crisis.[13] And in June 2012, Oonagh McDonald, a respected United Kingdom scholar and former Labour member of Parliament, published *Fannie Mae and Freddie Mac: Turning the American Dream into a Nightmare*.[14] This book indicts the U.S. government for causing the financial crisis by pursuing an ideologically based effort to foster loans to low-income borrowers, regardless of their ability to pay. Other books are also on the way, as scholars and others begin to question the underlying factual basis for the left's narrative.

The Narrative and the Dodd-Frank Act

The rescue of Bear Stearns in March 2008, based on a Fed loan to JPMorgan Chase, was a seminal event in the development of a narrative that would support the Dodd-Frank Act. There had been many rescues of banks over the years, and these could be explained by the fact that banks held government-insured deposits, were essential to the payment system, were government supervised, and were the institutions where many middle-class families kept their savings. In addition, the business of banking involves smaller banks holding deposits in larger institutions, permitting efficient transfers of funds through netting debits and credits. For this reason, the failure of a large bank could deprive many smaller institutions of necessary funds, with adverse effects throughout the financial system and the economy.

---

12. See, for example, Joe Nocera, "The Big Lie," *New York Times*, December 24, 2011, http://www.nytimes.com/2011/12/24/opinion/nocera-the-big-lie.html?_r=2.

13. Gretchen Morgenson and Joshua Rosner, *Reckless Endangerment: How Outsized Ambition, Greed, and Corruption Created the Worst Financial Crisis of Our Time* (New York: St. Martin's Griffin, 2011).

14. Oonagh McDonald, *Fannie Mae and Freddie Mac: Turning the American Dream into a Nightmare* (New York: Bloomsbury, 2012).

Bear Stearns involved none of these special factors, so the government's extraordinary use of its own resources to rescue Bear had to be justified in a different way. The justification used by the Bush administration and the Federal Reserve was that Bear was "interconnected" with other financial firms—especially through its activities in the credit default swap (CDS) market—and because of these interconnections Bear's failure would have brought down the entire financial system. Immediately after Lehman's bankruptcy, this interconnectedness theory was folded into the existing narrative about the causes of the crisis so that the narrative now explained why there had been a financial crisis (insufficient regulation) and why the government had to take extraordinary action (interconnections).

There is seldom an opportunity in social science to disprove ideas like this, since history seldom repeats itself without ambiguity, but in this case the failure of Lehman six months after Bear provides strong evidence that the interconnectedness theory is wrong.[15] Lehman was substantially larger than Bear, but it operated the same way. It financed itself in large part through repurchase agreements (known as "repos")—essentially very short-term collateralized loans—carried on a substantial business in derivatives, including CDSs, and was very active in trading and investing in MBS backed by subprime mortgages.

In other words, Lehman was just a larger version of Bear. Yet, with one exception (the Reserve Primary Fund, a money market mutual fund discussed below), when Lehman failed there were no knock-on effects—no instances where another firm was dragged into insolvency by the losses on its exposure to Lehman. For example, all CDSs written on Lehman—that is, insuring against Lehman's default—were settled with the exchange of $5.2 billion among hundreds of counterparties about five weeks after the bankruptcy petition was filed, and the overwhelming majority of CDSs to which Lehman itself was a party were canceled as provided in the CDS contracts. Those CDSs where Lehman counterparties were in the money (i.e., were owed something by Lehman) became creditors of the Lehman estate. There were losses, to be sure, but there is no record of any firm having failed as a result of Lehman's failure. This is extremely important in evaluating the

---

15. This conclusion, citing the relevant FSOs, is supported in an extensive analysis of the financial crisis by Hal Scott of Harvard Law School, "Interconnections and Contagion," November 20, 2012, http://www.capmktsreg.org/pdfs/2012.11.20_Interconnectedness_and_Contagion.pdf.

judgment of Paulson and Bernanke in rescuing Bear Stearns. If Lehman did not have any knock-on effects in the panicky market at the time, it is highly unlikely that Bear Stearns—a much smaller firm—would have had a more dramatic impact on the market when it had failed six months earlier.

Some analysts argue that the actions of the government after Lehman's bankruptcy prevented or mitigated Lehman's knock-on effects, but this seems implausible. The two principal government actions were the Troubled Assets Relief Program (TARP), which made available more than $800 billion for the acquisition of what the media had labeled "toxic assets"—principally the PMBS—that had weakened U.S. financial institutions, and an FDIC program that guaranteed loans by insured banks. TARP ultimately became a program for recapitalizing banks, but the first investments were not made until six weeks after Lehman's bankruptcy and were almost entirely repaid eight months later. Clearly, these capital injections were not necessary to fill holes in balance sheets caused by Lehman's inability to meet its obligations. The FDIC guarantee program also did not repair balance sheets. It simply gave institutions the confidence to continue lending. Indeed, both TARP and the FDIC's program had only one objective—restoring confidence, not repairing balance sheets weakened by the knock-on effects of Lehman's failure.

In other words, the interconnectedness theory is wrong; Lehman's failure might have had ill effects, but not because it dragged down other firms. None of the large firms that were either rescued or failed after Lehman—AIG, Wachovia, Washington Mutual, Merrill Lynch—was materially weakened because of its exposure to Lehman.

Why, then, were so many firms in financial trouble after Lehman? The short answer is that they were in trouble before Lehman, but the longer answer is our old friend, government housing policies. When the huge housing bubble created by these policies began to deflate in 2007, many banks and other financial institutions were holding PMBS backed by subprime loans. Although these were only 26 percent of the twenty-eight million low-quality mortgages outstanding, they represented almost $2 trillion.

When an unprecedented number of mortgages became delinquent or defaulted as the bubble deflated, investors fled the market for PMBS. Mark-to-market accounting, applicable for financial institutions virtually worldwide, then required these firms to write down the value of their PMBS assets to market values, which in a market without buyers were close to zero. The write-downs substantially reduced capital positions, making many of these institutions look unstable and perhaps insolvent. In addition, those that were using PMBS for liquidity purposes—something that was true of Bear and Lehman—found their liquidity drying up as creditors refused to take these instruments in repo transactions.

A broad weakening in the capital or liquidity of financial institutions because of a sharp decline in the value of a widely held asset, as noted earlier, is known as a common shock. Exactly this hit large numbers of financial institutions in the United States and around the world when what became known as the mortgage meltdown began in late 2006 and continued through 2007 and 2008. Even before the rescue of Bear and the bankruptcy of Lehman, the deteriorating financial condition of large numbers of financial institutions was setting the market up for a panic. All that was needed was a triggering event.

Lehman's bankruptcy was the trigger. It was part of an immense government blunder—one of the worst in all of financial history—in which the U.S. government first rescued Bear Stearns and then allowed Lehman, an even larger firm, to fail. The Bear rescue was the original sin; it suggested that the government had established a policy of rescuing all large financial institutions. But six months later, in what the market can only have considered an irrational act, the government reversed its policy and allowed Lehman to fail.

This was a classic case of moral hazard, where the government's actions distorted the normal response of the market. If Bear had been allowed to fail, market participants would have begun raising capital in order to persuade investors and others that they were strong enough to avoid a similar fate. Some capital was raised, but not enough; managements of the largest firms thought that the government's willingness to rescue large financial firms would keep their creditors and counterparties from running. After all, if they were going to be fully bailed out as Bear's creditors were, there would be no need to run. This prospect calmed the market for the six months between Bear's rescue and the Lehman collapse. Spreads on Lehman in the CDS market, which would be an expression of the market's fear of default, remained relatively steady from the time of Bear's rescue in March until just before the weekend of September 12–14, 2008. At that point, the spreads blew out when it became clear that the government had no potential buyers for Lehman and no apparent rescue plan.

The moral hazard created by the rescue of Bear had many other damaging effects. Although it kept the credit markets temporarily calm—despite a lot of bad news—the rescue probably also misled the managements of large firms such as Lehman into believing that they could avoid diluting their shares, and drive a harder bargain with potential acquirers, than the firm's financial condition would warrant. This discouraged purchasers, who saw these firms as potentially insolvent, and probably prevented an acquisition. In addition, although the government offered $30 billion in support for JPMorgan to acquire Bear, it was offering nothing to potential acquirers of Lehman. This alone would have prevented a deal; few acquirers want to look like suckers.

Finally, it is likely that the one firm that suffered a major loss because of Lehman's failure—the Reserve Primary Fund—was also a casualty of moral hazard. The fund had held a substantial amount of Lehman's commercial paper, which it could have sold in the weeks and months before the Lehman bankruptcy. It is possible that the fund's management declined to do so in the belief that eventually the creditors of Lehman, like the creditors of Bear, would be made whole. When Lehman failed, the commercial paper lost most of its value, and the fund was unable to redeem all its shares for $1 each. This is known as "breaking the buck," and in the panicky condition of market participants at the time it induced a run on other money market funds, requiring the Treasury to step in with a temporary guarantee. The Reserve Fund was the only firm seriously affected by Lehman's failure, and although the shareholder run on other funds was a serious matter, in the absence of a market panic it is highly unlikely that a single mutual fund breaking the buck—something that had happened only once before, with no adverse consequences—would induce a financial crisis.

If the Treasury and the Fed actually believed that there would be a systemic financial crisis if Bear was not rescued, the case for rescuing Lehman was even stronger. In reality, the failure to rescue Lehman—after rescuing Bear—was a world historical blunder by Treasury secretary Hank Paulson and Fed chair Ben Bernanke. The moral hazard created by the Bear rescue made it inevitable that there would be chaos if any other large financial institution was allowed to fail. However, when a financial crisis occurred after Lehman's bankruptcy, Secretary Paulson and Chairman Bernanke claimed that they had faced a Hobson's choice between bankruptcy and a government bailout, which they claimed was beyond the Fed's legal authority. The underlying implication of this argument was that if they hadn't been required to accept bankruptcy—if there had been another choice—a financial crisis could have been averted. In other words, it was the bankruptcy of Lehman that caused the chaos and panic that followed.

This notion eventually formed the conceptual underpinning for Title II of the Dodd-Frank Act, which established a government resolution system for financial institutions, separate from bankruptcy. Known as the Orderly Liquidation Authority (OLA), this title gives extraordinary power to the secretary of the Treasury, who can seize any financial firm he believes may cause instability in the U.S. financial system if it fails and turn it over to the FDIC for liquidation. If the firm challenges the secretary's judgment, the secretary can then take the issue to court, which is given only one day to decide the matter. If it doesn't make a decision in this time, the firm is consigned "by operation of law" to the FDIC, which must dismiss the management and liquidate the firm.

But as discussed in chapter 3, the underlying assumption of the OLA—that if the FDIC takes over a financial firm the outcome will be different from the chaos and panic that followed Lehman's bankruptcy—does not survive analysis. Three interrelated factors caused the panic after Lehman: (1) the moral hazard created by the earlier rescue of Bear; (2) the desire of investors to get their money out of a failing firm as quickly as possible, and (3) the weakening of virtually all large financial institutions at the same time as a result of the common shock associated with the mortgage meltdown.

There is nothing about the OLA that would have prevented any of these things from happening or would have resulted in a different outcome if—instead of filing for bankruptcy—Lehman had been seized by the FDIC under OLA authority. The shock to the market, and the resulting panic, would have been the same. In other words, the OLA would not be any improvement over bankruptcy.

The invalid interconnectedness theory and the mistaken view that the OLA would be better than bankruptcy are only two of the distorted facts that underlay the narrative for the Dodd-Frank Act. Others, also discussed in chapter 3, are the notion that the financial crisis was caused by predatory lending (the foundation for the Consumer Financial Protection Bureau in Title X and the Qualified Mortgage requirements in Title XIV), unregulated derivatives (the basis for new regulatory authority for the Commodity Futures Trading Commission and the Securities and Exchange Commission in Titles VII and IX), private mortgage securitization (the source of the Qualified Residential Mortgage and the 5 percent risk retention requirement of Title IX), or the proprietary trading by banks and other financial institutions (the conceptual underpinning of the Volcker Rule in Title VI).

The FCIC's investigation of predatory lending was never able to demonstrate with data that it was a significant factor in the financial crisis. There were plenty of anecdotes and much testimony, but never any numbers to suggest that predatory lending was so widespread as to require a whole new regulatory scheme at the federal level or the new rules for mortgage lending that imposed heavy penalties for making a loan that a borrower ultimately could not afford. It was clear that large numbers of mortgages went to people who ultimately could not meet their obligations, but it is far more likely that borrowers were taking advantage of the reduced underwriting standards produced by government policies than that originators were taking advantage of ignorant borrowers.

Although AIG got into serious trouble with its activities in the credit default swaps market, it was an outlier. There are no other examples of firms suffering the same debilitating losses. AIG's problems did not come from a lack of regulation in the market for credit default swaps or other derivatives. Instead, it is an example of bad management by a firm with a weak understanding of the risks it was assuming. This is no more a basis for regulating an entire market than imprudent lending by a single firm would justify regulating all lenders.

Mortgage securitization was mischaracterized in the left's narrative as an "originate to distribute" process, as though the supply produced the demand. This is exactly backward. As outlined above, initially government housing policies, and later private investor demand, created a market for subprime and other low-quality loans. Securitization was one way that this market was served, but securitization in itself was not the cause of the decline in underwriting standards. The notion that originators could create the demand for low-quality loans reflects a mistaken and naïve understanding of how markets work.

Finally, the Volcker Rule is based on the false idea that proprietary trading of securities by banks and their affiliates was somehow a cause of the financial crisis. There is simply no evidence of this and no evidence that this trading is riskier than lending. Prior to the crisis, trading activity by banks was a profitable business and added needed liquidity to the debt markets. The prohibition on proprietary trading will have serious adverse effects on the profitability of banks as well as issuers and buyers of debt instruments, who ultimately rely on market making by banks to keep their securities liquid.

Accordingly, almost nothing about the left's narrative for the financial crisis is correct. The crisis was not caused by lack of regulation, greed on Wall Street, or predatory lending by an irresponsible private sector; it was caused by the government's irresponsible and poorly conceived housing policy. The chaos and panic that occurred after Lehman's bankruptcy was not caused by the interconnectedness of large financial institutions or the knock-on effects of the Lehman failure; it was the result of a common shock that had weakened the financial condition of all large financial institutions that were holding PMBS assets when the mortgage meltdown occurred, together with the moral hazard created by the earlier rescue of Bear Stearns. Finally, there was no Hobson's choice between bankruptcy and a bailout for Lehman. Given the weakened financial condition of all large financial institutions at the time Lehman failed, together with government's irrational reversal of policy on financial rescues, a panic was inevitable when Lehman filed for bankruptcy and would have occurred even if Lehman had been taken over by the FDIC under the OLA established by the Dodd-Frank Act.

All of this makes clear that the Dodd-Frank Act is based on a false narrative of what caused the financial crisis and was not a legitimate response to the crisis. As former White House chief of staff Rahm Emanuel famously said, "You never want a serious crisis to go to waste. What I mean by that is an opportunity to do things you think you could not do before."[16] Instead, as Emanuel suggested, it represents a use of the financial crisis for ideological purposes—to enable the government to gain greater political control over the U.S. financial system. Under these circumstances, the act should be repealed.

In succeeding chapters of this book, I detail my efforts to combat the left's narrative through *Financial Services Outlooks* issued between 2004 and 2012. By 2012, I had made some progress; the Republican presidential candidate was arguing that the financial crisis was caused by the government's housing policies and that the Dodd-Frank Act should be repealed. But there still had been relatively few instances in which an alternative description of what had happened in the financial crisis appeared in the mainstream media. Until that occurs and the false narrative that underpins the Dodd-Frank Act is identified for the American people, any effort to repeal the act will be an uphill struggle.

---

16. See http://www.youtube.com/watch?v=1yeA_kHHLow.

1

Fannie Mae and Freddie Mac

Under the direction of James A. Johnson, Fannie Mae's calculating and politically connected chief executive, the company capitalized on its government ties, building itself in to the largest and most powerful financial institution in the world. . . . Fannie Mae led the way in relaxing loan underwriting standards, for example, a shift that was quickly followed by private lenders. . . . Eliminating the traditional due diligence conducted by lenders soon became the playbook for financial executives across the country.

— Gretchen Morgenson and Joshua Rosner,
Reckless Endangerment: How Outsized Ambition, Greed, and Corruption Led to Economic Armageddon

In 1999, when I started focusing my attention on the GSEs, the narrative about Fannie and Freddie was daunting. They were considered to be well-run and profitable institutions with a strong political base and were doing good work in promoting homeownership without any cost to the taxpayers. They could raise funds in the capital markets without increasing the national debt and spend money to increase homeownership without increasing the deficit. Although their actual function in the housing market—operating a secondary market in mortgages purchased from originators—was not widely understood by the public, their soft-focus advertising associated them with expanding the American dream of homeownership. It was a win-win all around. This narrative made the GSEs virtually impregnable in Washington.

There was, to be sure, a little-known seamier side. Fannie Mae controlled a foundation that it used to distribute grants to organizations and individuals who were in a position to provide it with political support or endorse its programs, and it maintained a network of local offices—often staffed with relatives of influential lawmakers—that encouraged political support for them among their constituents. Fannie, in particular, also had a reputation for thuggish behavior in which it threatened the livelihoods of its critics,[1] and both firms made substantial political contributions to their congressional supporters and occasionally hired away the best staffers of opponents who were not susceptible to other kinds of intimidation.

The GSEs' Narrative and the Sources of Their Power

Fannie's and Freddie's association with housing enabled them to attack any effort to restrain their activities as an attack on housing and the American dream. In this they were supported by three powerful interest groups, the National Association of Realtors, the National Association of Homebuilders, and the securities industry, which made substantial profits from underwriting and distributing their securities. Their own political contributions were supplemented by the considerable contributions of the realtors, homebuilders, and securities firms, which they were able to command and direct to favored lawmakers by sponsoring fundraisers. Most academics and other observers of the housing industry would agree that Fannie and Freddie were a long-term problem of some kind, but given all the other issues that were confronting Washington in 1999, taking on Fannie and Freddie was way down the list.

From the beginning, my opposition was based on the view that any government-sponsored enterprise would eventually self-destruct—with enormous costs to the taxpayers because its government backing allowed it to avoid the creditor oversight known as market discipline. Profit-making

---

1. In this connection, I have often told the humorous story of a conversation I had, shortly after joining AEI, with a friend wise in the ways of Washington. He was curious about what I was going to do in my new role as an aspiring scholar, and I told him that since my time as Treasury general counsel I had been interested in the power of the GSEs and the threat they posed to the taxpayers. There was a short silence on the other end of the phone. Then he asked, "Are you going to be criticizing Fannie Mae?" I said yes, another pause, and then he said, "Do you have someone to start your car in the morning?" That was my first inkling that it was somewhat naïve to assume that tackling Fannie and Freddie would be like tackling any other public policy issue.

firms such as Fannie and Freddie that were exempt from this kind of oversight would inevitably take excessive risks in order to boost their profits and the compensation of management. Fannie and Freddie were regulated by an office within the Department of Housing and Urban Development, but the regulator was woefully understaffed for dealing with two multi-trillion-dollar firms. Regulation itself is seldom effective in preventing risk-taking—witness the losses suffered by the regulated banks in the financial crisis—but in this case the regulator was overmatched by the GSEs, which also had the ability to discipline the regulator through their influence in Congress. The only real solution was privatization: persuading the GSEs that it was in their interests to privatize or persuading Congress to privatize them. But what really stood in the way was the narrative—the overwhelming sense in Washington that Fannie and Freddie were doing good and weren't asking for anything except to be left alone.

My interest in the GSEs had been stimulated when I was the general counsel of the Treasury between 1981 and 1985. Even then, during the Reagan administration, when the GSEs were much smaller, the political capital needed to confront them just wasn't there. It would have been fool-hardy to try to limit their activities when they had such powerful allies in and out of Congress and when the narrative about their good works undercut any policy basis for doing so. Could we really expect to control them or get them to privatize because of theoretical concerns about their lack of effective oversight?

Many people in Washington were concerned about their power, but few saw the point of taking on what was essentially a quixotic effort. Lawmakers and even think tanks and academics usually want to spend their reformist energy on something that might actually be achievable. Trying to gain control of the GSEs, by common agreement, was not. Even the largest banks, which were concerned that Fannie and Freddie would eventually manage to move into mortgage origination, were afraid to take them on directly. The banks had formed something called FM Watch (later FM Policy Focus), an organization in which the sponsors were unnamed, to avoid being identified as opponents. AEI promised at least one nervous contributor that its financial support would not be used to support my work.

There was even some opposition within AEI, but Chris DeMuth—then the president—was fully supportive from the beginning, and AEI never wavered, throughout those early years or since, even though many firms, foundations, and individuals would almost certainly have been afraid to become known as financial supporters of AEI while it provided a forum for criticism of the GSEs. Indeed, had it not been for my perch at AEI, I would probably not have been able to continue my criticism of the GSEs because of the considerable pressure they (and Fannie in particular) were willing to bring on Washington and other critics.

This was illustrated by personal experience. When I started my work at AEI, I had been a director of MGIC, a public company and the largest U.S. private mortgage insurer. At a board meeting in 1999 or 2000, the chairman of the firm reported on a meeting he had had at Fannie's offices in Washington. He had set up the meeting to find out why MGIC had not been named as one of the insurers for a new Fannie program. At the meeting, he was informed that "Fannie only wants to deal with its friends, and with Peter Wallison on your board we can't regard MGIC a friend." When that was reported to the board, I immediately resigned. This was how Fannie routinely operated in Washington, retaliating against its critics at every level. It was an effective strategy for a time. It intimidated many people, whether elected or unelected, but bought Fannie no goodwill. When Fannie began to fail, few in Washington would offer support.

AEI Conferences

The very fact that the GSEs had received so little attention over the years was something of an advantage for attracting interest in Washington. Media reporters who thought there might be a David-and-Goliath or hopeless-waste-of-time story, or had heard tales of the GSEs' power and thuggish behavior, attended the public conferences I organized at AEI. Also attending were numerous law firms and lobbying groups who were representing Fannie and Freddie and thought they had to keep up with even the slightest criticism of their client. I was delighted to think that many of them sitting out there in the audience taking notes were charging time to the GSEs. My strategy, through these public conferences, was to raise the profile of the GSEs on the Washington agenda—to bring these gigantic public liabilities out of the shadows—by providing new and credible information about the risks the GSEs created for the economy. Between 1999 and 2005, I organized seventeen of these conferences at which critics and supporters of the GSEs outlined their views.

Although it now seems obvious—after the GSEs were rescued by the government in 2008—that concern about the GSEs was a legitimate public policy issue, they had argued for many years that the GSEs had no government backing and should therefore be treated as any other private entity. Accordingly, in the first conference I noted that the question whether the GSEs were the recipients of government backing was not worth debating; it was clear from the extraordinarily low interest rates they were accorded by the capital markets. Then I continued:

> The apparent existence of a government benefit means that legitimate questions can be raised about Fannie and Freddie's activities: (i) whether they are achieving their public purposes; (ii) whether they should be allowed to enter businesses in competition with nonsubsidized companies; (iii) whether they are using their subsidy for the purposes for which it was intended; (iv) whether they should make political contributions; (v) whether they represent a significant financial risk to taxpayers; and ultimately (vi) whether they should retain their form as private companies with government support. These are the issues with which this and subsequent conferences will be concerned.[2]

The conferences that followed over several years largely pursued this initial agenda.

To be sure, providing a platform for academic and other critics of Fannie and Freddie was not a serious threat to their political and financial power. But Fannie's ultrasensitivity to any criticism required that they respond, and they did so by hiring their own academics—including a Nobel laureate, Joseph Stiglitz—to explain in widely circulated academic-style papers that the GSEs posed no risks at all.[3] Most of these experts probably now regret

---

2. Peter J. Wallison, "Public Purposes and Private Interests" (opening statement, AEI Conference on Fannie Mae and Freddie Mac, Washington, DC, March 24, 1999).

3. Joseph Stiglitz, Jonathan Orszag, and Peter Orszag, "Implications of the New Fannie Mae and Freddie Mac Risk-Based Capital Standard," *Fannie Mae Papers* 1, no. 2 (March 2002). Their conclusion was that "the risk to the government from a potential default on GSE debt is effectively zero." See http://www.pierrelemieux.org/stiglitzrisk.pdf.

writing those papers, which were collected and published by Fannie in a book titled *Housing Matters*.[4] In the end, however, it would be fair to say that there was very little movement in the Washington community's view of the GSEs or, more important, in Congress or the White House. For several years, the conferences seemed to be having little effect.

A Fortuitous Event Shifts the Narrative

All that began to change in June 2003, when Freddie Mac's board of directors suddenly dismissed its top three officers for manipulating the firm's accounting. This was a seminal event and materially remade the policy world surrounding the GSEs. The context is important. Enron's bankruptcy, and a frenzy about whether public companies had been accurately presenting their financial results, had recently seized the media and riveted Washington's attention. The Sarbanes-Oxley Act, another ill-considered piece of legislation like the Dodd-Frank Act, was moving through Congress as politicians sought to show that they were "doing something " about allegations in the media of false accounting by public companies. In the center of the scandal was Enron's auditor, Arthur Andersen, which also happened to be Freddie's auditor. In frenzied Washington, sharing an auditor with Enron was evidence enough for conviction, and when Freddie's board learned that its top three officers had been engaged in earnings management, it moved quickly to prevent further bad publicity for the company.

This somewhat fortuitous event broke the spell of indifference that had previously surrounded the GSEs. Another way to look at it was that the GSEs' protective narrative had been pierced. People no longer looked at these two firms in the same way. At first, when Fannie's share values fell on the news about Freddie, Franklin Raines, Fannie's CEO, asserted that Fannie could become "collateral damage"—implying that it was an innocent bystander to Freddie's accounting problems. But the Office of Federal Housing Enterprises Oversight, the GSEs' regulator, which had only days before declared both GSEs to be in good order, was severely embarrassed by Freddie's action. To recover its lost ground, OFHEO's director, Armando

---

4. Fannie Mae, *Housing Matters: Issues in American Housing Policy* (Washington, DC: Fannie Mae Papers, 2004).

Falcon, asked Congress for a special appropriation of $7.5 million to conduct a "forensic audit" of Fannie and Freddie. Given the circumstances, Congress had little choice, and the funds were approved. That audit, completed in 2004, showed that Fannie's accounting was worse than Freddie's and further weakened the GSEs' political position. Franklin Raines, the politically connected chairman of Fannie Mae, was compelled to resign.

Amazingly, by the end of 2004—despite the GSEs' extraordinary power—most of the policy issues I had set out as the objectives of the conferences were now seen as legitimate questions about the GSEs. The GSEs' business model was recognized as problematic, and further expansion of their activities was unlikely. The GSEs were also in an increasingly precarious political position. They were no longer looked on as untouchable. The prospects for their privatization had become promising enough that Thomas H. Stanton, Bert Ely, and I coauthored a book on how it might be done.[5]

Financial Services Outlooks on Fannie and Freddie

By 2004, the political process that the GSEs had dominated for so long had begun to work against them. Their accounting had been exposed as fraudulent, it was no longer cool to be seen with either of the firms, and the political system had begun to shake off its GSE shackles. There was little more I could do by holding conferences. Accordingly, I turned most of my attention to writing about the GSEs and providing a rationale for their privatization. The Financial Services Outlooks in this book are some of the products of that effort, and they record both the GSEs' gradual loss of political support and my frustration at the slow progress that was being made. My view then, as now, is that increased regulation—while better than the existing system for controlling them—was not ultimately going to protect the taxpayers. It never has, and as long as Congress is enthralled with regulation as a cure for moral hazard, it will continue to fail. The only true solutions, in my view, are privatization or liquidation. Nevertheless, as long as the GSEs opposed privatization, there was little chance that Congress would force it on them. Tougher regulation, at that point, was the only feasible

---

5. Peter J. Wallison, Thomas H. Stanton, and Bert Ely, *Privatizing Fannie Mae, Freddie Mac and the Federal Home Loan Banks: Why and How* (Washington, DC: AEI Press, 2004).

course. Accordingly, while privatization was my preferred remedy for the GSEs, many of the essays I wrote between 2004 and 2012 also focused on tightening their regulation. Because of their loss of political clout, it was no longer a fantasy to believe that the GSEs might one day be either better regulated or privatized.

The GSEs Lose Control of Their Political Risks. By the time the *Outlook* series began in 2004, it was possible to write, in my first piece on the GSEs, "In the past few months, Fannie Mae and Freddie Mac seem to have lost control of the one risk they really must control—their political risk."[6] In May 2004, in "The Case for Privatizing Fannie Mae and Freddie Mac Grows Stronger" (p. 38), I was able to list all the pressures they were facing and suggested that these pressures should be stimulating serious consideration of privatization. Among these pressures, the Bush administration seemed to be pursuing an effort to separate the government from the GSEs, rather than taking credit for what the GSEs were doing; the president announced that he would no longer appoint members of their boards, as permitted by their charters, and the administration and the Federal Reserve took a number of steps that seemed designed to loosen the GSEs' ties to the government or to deprive them of privileges that had previously functioned as indicia of government backing. At that point, I was looking at the affordable-housing goals like everybody else—as a cost to the GSEs that they could avoid by privatizing. What these pressures meant was that—at least when the Republicans controlled both the presidency and Congress—the GSEs had lost their most essential asset: their political invulnerability. Perhaps most important, Alan Greenspan—the widely respected chairman of the Federal Reserve Board—had become engaged in the issue. He now recognized the systemic threat they posed to the financial system and had begun to criticize them at almost every appearance before Congress.

Tighter Regulation. More pressures developed during 2005, with legislation to tighten their regulation finally moving in Congress. Although Congress could not yet bring itself seriously to consider privatization, it was

---

6. Peter J. Wallison, "The Case for Privatization of Fannie Mae and Freddie Mac Grows Stronger," *Financial Services Outlook*, May 2004.

willing to consider that old standby, tougher regulation. This could force privatization if it sufficiently cut back on the GSEs' profitability, but that required Congress to curb the GSEs' portfolios, which, by a wide margin, were the largest source of their profitability. With the low funding costs they could command as GSEs, Fannie and Freddie could profit handsomely by acquiring and holding mortgages and MBS that paid considerably more. As noted above, there was risk associated with this strategy, but only a GSE could make that a high profit activity. Other financial institutions had to pay too much for their funds and had to hold too much capital.

As I outlined in May 2005 in "Regulating Fannie Mae and Freddie Mac: Now It Gets Serious" (p. 48), the House Financial Services Committee actually took up and passed legislation that tightened the regulation of Fannie and Freddie—this in itself was remarkable given their unmatched political power only a few years earlier—but the final legislation failed to tackle the portfolio issue. For this reason, the administration eventually opposed it as too weak. But by September 2005 there was better news, recorded in "Regulating Fannie Mae and Freddie Mac: Now It Gets Serious (Continued)" (p. 63). The Senate Banking Committee, with a Republican majority, finally authorized the elimination of the GSEs' portfolios. However, the vote to send the legislation to the Senate floor was along party lines, which reduced the likelihood that it would be brought up for a vote without a compromise; the Democrats had sufficient votes to successfully filibuster the legislation, and it eventually died.

The Limitations of Regulation. In May 2006, the Office of Federal Housing Enterprises Oversight issued a scathing report on Fannie's accounting. OFHEO had found (as I reported in July 2006 in "Moral Hazard on Steroids: The OFHEO Report Shows That Regulation Cannot Protect U.S. Taxpayers," p. 73) that Fannie had not only manipulated its financial statements; it also had weak internal controls and inadequate accounting and computer systems, and had taken substantial business risks in order to improve its profitability and pay unearned bonuses to management. This was a big story in the press, but the real story—the failure of regulation involved here—did not get the attention it deserved. It is true that OFHEO was chronically understaffed, but it only had two firms to regulate. The failures it identified were huge, not technical issues that might have been overlooked. OFHEO's report was implicitly an indictment of its own regulation and of regulation itself. This regulator had missed everything of importance, and its reassuring reports about the condition of Fannie and Freddie over the years only increased the moral hazard that already flowed from their implicit government backing. It was another reason that outsiders never considered that Fannie and Freddie might be taking serious risks. After all, they had a regulator, who must be doing *something* to reduce their risk-taking.

At the time, those in Congress who wanted to prevent risk-taking by Fannie and Freddie were arguing for what was called "the gold standard"— regulation of the GSEs the way the banks are regulated. This *Outlook* argued, however, that bank regulation would not be enough. Banks, at least, were subject to some degree of market discipline because their deposits were only insured up to $100,000. But every dollar of the GSEs' debt was in effect fully insured. There was no market discipline. If regulation was what Congress wanted, it was not nearly stringent enough to protect the taxpayers. Accordingly, then, this *Outlook* was another argument for privatization. Realistically, there was no way to prevent risk-taking through bank-like regulation (this proved true even for banks when Wachovia, WaMu, and IndyMac—all insured and heavily regulated banks—failed in 2008); the correct answer for Fannie and Freddie was privatization.

What to Do about Insolvent GSEs. In August 2008, I took note of the fact that Fannie and Freddie were now acknowledged to be insolvent and likely candidates for a government takeover, through either a receivership or a conservatorship. In "Fannie and Freddie by Twilight" (p. 85), I explored the new landscape for the GSEs in their new weakened state and the five options that were available to them—muddling through (if the housing market suddenly stabilized), assisted survival, nationalization through a receivership, privatization, or liquidation. The actual takeover was not what I expected or wanted. The Treasury Department decided to use a conservatorship, which is still in existence more than four years later. This gave the GSEs an opportunity to survive for an indefinite period, and, as I'd feared, developments during this period made their chances of long-term survival greater. In particular, the enactment of the Dodd-Frank Act in 2010 made it very difficult for a private securitization market to revive and gave further advantages to FHA and the GSEs over private securitizers. By 2012, people on Wall Street were beginning to wake up to the fact that the common and preferred stock was still available in the market; although heavily discounted now, it could become very valuable if Congress could be persuaded to extend the life of one or both of the GSEs. This could mean that, without a decision on how to replace them, one day the GSEs could be freed from the conservatorship and could resume their former roles. As this is written, because of impediments to the revival of private securitization, there is no other way to fully finance the massive housing market in the United States.

The Causes of the GSEs' Insolvency. The enormous credit risks that Fannie and Freddie were assuming finally came to light after they were taken over by the government, but it took a while for the details to become clear. Now we know, because of the work of my AEI colleague Edward Pinto, that HUD's administration of the affordable-housing goals consisted of insistent and relentless demands that Fannie and Freddie reduce their underwriting standards in order to make more subprime and other risky loans available to low-income borrowers. But before these facts came to light, I and another AEI colleague, Professor Charles Calomiris of Columbia Business School, tried to explain why Fannie and Freddie would have taken on so much credit risk. In effect, their managements had put in jeopardy a hugely valuable franchise—an act that did not make rational sense.

In September 2008, in "The Last Trillion-Dollar Commitment: The Destruction of Fannie Mae and Freddie Mac" (p. 98), Calomiris and I suggested that Fannie and Freddie took these risks in order to retain the support in Congress necessary to fend off stringent regulation that would reduce their profitability and their management compensation. This effort increased after the accounting scandals, we posited, because those scandals weakened their political support in Congress and brought this regulation closer. This was the most plausible explanation available at the time, but as Pinto's work brought more information to light, it became clear that HUD was the principal source of the pressures for subprime and other risky lending by the GSEs.[7]

---

7. The relevant data on this question, and the role of HUD in administering the affordable-housing goals, are contained in my dissent from the majority report of the Financial Crisis Inquiry Commission, which can be downloaded from the AEI web site. See http://www.aei.org/docLib/Wallisondissent.pdf.

Nevertheless, retaining support in Congress might have been the reason Fannie originally agreed to the affordable-housing goals. In their book *Reckless Endangerment,* Gretchen Morgenson and Josh Rosner suggested that the key insight of James Johnson, Fannie's chairman during the period the affordable-housing goals were enacted, was to recognize that the GSEs' franchise would become incontestable if they were seen as bringing homeownership to people who previously could not get mortgage credit.[8] Ironically, while Johnson was correct to see that the goals would cement the GSEs' support in Congress, he did not see that HUD—under political pressure from the left and Congress—would eventually cause the destruction of the GSEs by pushing the affordable-housing idea beyond any reasonable limit.

Government Policies, the GSEs, and the Financial Crisis. The motives for the GSEs' activities in acquiring so many subprime and other low-quality loans had become clearer two months later, in November 2008, when I published "Cause and Effect: Government Policies and the Financial Crisis" (p. 116). At this point, the media and much of the left were engaged in the usual fibrillation about a "crisis of capitalism." Many of the major financial papers were running stories about how the financial crisis was a demonstration of the fundamental instability of a capitalist system. So I began this *Outlook* with the following statement: "The current financial crisis is not—as some have said—a crisis of capitalism. It is in fact the opposite, a shattering demonstration that ill-considered government intervention in the private economy can have devastating consequences." The piece went on to describe the ways in which government housing policies—primarily the affordable-housing goals implemented by HUD and the Community Reinvestment Act (CRA)—had caused a decline in underwriting standards and the propagation of risky mortgages throughout the financial system. The CRA in particular received coverage because so little was actually known about how it worked and what its effects might have been.

As to the GSEs and affordable-housing goals, I noted that in 1997 HUD had engaged the Urban Institute to study the GSEs' underwriting guidelines, and, sure enough, these guidelines were found to disqualify potential

---

8. Gretchen Morgenson and Joshua Rosner, *Reckless Endangerment: How Outsized Ambition, Greed, and Corruption Created the Worst Financial Crisis of Our Time* (New York: St. Martin's Griffin, 2011).

homebuyers with low incomes, low down payments, and poor credit histories. After the Urban Institute report, Fannie and Freddie modified their automated underwriting systems in order to allow many mortgages to qualify that they had previously rejected. By the year 2000, the GSEs were buying mortgages with zero down payments. Overall, the *Outlook* charted, for the first time, the gradual decline in underwriting standards. In addition, it focused on several other government policies—cash-out refinancing, loans without recourse, bank capital requirements, and tax policies that also contributed to the weakening quality of mortgages in the U.S. financial system.

The Future of Fannie and Freddie. In the January–February 2010 *Outlook,* titled "The Dead Shall Be Raised: The Future of Fannie and Freddie" (p. 133), I reviewed the GSE options available to Congress in early 2010 and concluded that there were very few. As this is written in mid-2012, not much has changed. The Republicans took over the House in November 2010, but have not yet moved any significant legislation. This is likely to be true for the reasons outlined in this *Outlook.* The housing market is still extremely weak, and the overwhelming majority of housing loans are ultimately being sold to the GSEs or to the FHA. There is little appetite in Congress for eliminating Fannie and Freddie until the housing market recovers, and nothing like that is currently in sight. In addition, there is the further problem that the private market will not recover as long as Fannie and Freddie are in place, because it is fruitless to try to compete with government-backed firms. This is a classic catch-22 problem.

In this *Outlook,* accordingly, I argued that continuing the conservatorship would give the government the greatest degree of flexibility for the future—particularly if the goal is, as it should be, to eliminate or privatize Fannie and Freddie. Three steps would be necessary: first, the sale or other liquidation of the GSEs' portfolios; second, the defeasing of the GSEs' existing MBS guarantees by placing them in a trust with U.S. government securities (the securities would be sold when and if necessary to meet the obligations on the guarantees); and third, the gradual reduction of the GSEs' conforming loan limits (the statutory limits on the size of mortgages that the GSEs can acquire), giving the private sector the opportunity to pick up the financing of mortgages in the areas from which the GSEs have been withdrawn. As far as I can tell, this was the first proposal along these lines that anyone had made, and it has since been adopted by many Republican law-makers as the preferred way for eliminating Fannie and Freddie over time.

Finally, in September 2010, I published "Going Cold Turkey: Three Ways to End Fannie and Freddie without Slicing Up the Taxpayers" (p. 147). In this *Outlook,* I reviewed seven of the most prominent plans for housing finance in the future. Not surprisingly, all of them contemplated a major government role. Most participants in Washington policy discussions are unable to conceive of housing finance or a housing market without a government presence. Many of these plans tried to deal with the obvious problem of moral hazard—excessive risk-taking by any government-backed entity because of the absence of market discipline—but all of them were doomed to failure. It's impossible to involve the government in any finan-cial system without creating moral hazard. The proposals that attempt to compensate the government for its risk-taking with some kind of insurance premium were the most pitiful. The framers of these ideas had learned noth-ing from all the failed efforts to combine insurance ideas with government risks. It won't work; the government cannot accumulate the funds necessary to meet the costs of the downturns, so the taxpayers are inevitably the losers. I reviewed the other advantages and disadvantages of government involve-ment in housing reform and concluded that the advantages were ephemeral, but the disadvantages would ultimately result in another financial crisis.

Accordingly, the narrative that supported the GSEs for many years was eventually torn apart by their own errors and arrogance. Their false aura of public service was broken when their accounting manipulations came to light. This in turn weakened their previously impregnable political posi-tion and allowed questions to be asked about the risks they were creating. Unfortunately, all this came too late. Although their first accounting scan-dal broke around Freddie Mac in 2003, their fortress narrative and their industry support still fended off serious reform until 2008, just before they were declared insolvent and taken over by the government. In my view, this shows the power of a narrative and why it is necessary to challenge and defeat the narrative before effective reform in Washington can be achieved.

The next chapter discusses the left's narrative for the financial crisis; it has thus far protected the government from blame for the financial crisis, and—through Dodd-Frank—advanced the ideological goals of its Demo-cratic Party sponsors in Congress and the administration.

"The Case for Privatizing Fannie Mae and Freddie Mac Grows Stronger"

Originally published May 2004

In the past few months, Fannie Mae and Freddie Mac seem to have lost control of the one risk they really must control—their political risk. As a consequence, their once impregnable position with investors has weakened substantially; now they are confronted with ugly choices that—only a few years ago—it did not seem likely they would ever have to make. A hard look at these choices suggests that privatization for these two government-sponsored enterprises (GSEs) has become an attractive option.

In late March, the Senate Banking Committee adopted tough new regulatory legislation despite Fannie and Freddie's tenacious opposition. To prevent the legislation from being tougher still, the two companies appeared to have called in all their Democratic markers, producing a rare partisan split in the committee. Under these circumstances, the enactment of new regulatory legislation this year is doubtful, but that is far from the end of the problems for these two government-sponsored enterprises.

No Longer a Political Juggernaut

Since last fall, Fannie and Freddie have been buffeted by an almost continuous barrage of bad news from government sources that once were afraid to stir up the GSEs' powerful network of support groups and lobbyists:

- The Treasury Department showed its determination to gain tougher regulation for Fannie and Freddie by opposing and ultimately dismembering a House Banking Committee bill that the Treasury considered too weak. This was the first sign that Fannie and Freddie, despite their massive network of lobbyists, would not have their usual way with the legislative process.

- The Office of Management and Budget, in an analysis that accompanied the president's 2005 budget, declared that Fannie and Freddie were undercapitalized, in need of serious new regulation, and failing to perform an important part of their mission: to provide affordable housing, especially for the minority community.

- At the request of the Office of Federal Housing Enterprises Oversight (OFHEO), the GSEs' regulator, Congress approved $7.5 million that would enable OFHEO to do a forensic audit of Fannie's accounting.

- With that audit underway, OFHEO suggested that it had already turned up accounting problems, warning the market that Fannie might have to restate its financial reports for previous years. When Fannie's spokesman denied that the company knew anything about this, OFHEO's director issued a statement calling Fannie's denial inaccurate and misleading.

- OFHEO proposed new corporate governance regulations that, among other things, would require Fannie and Freddie to split the offices of chairman and CEO and limit the terms of their directors.

- The White House let it be known that the president would no longer appoint the five directors of Fannie and Freddie that he is authorized to appoint, a clear effort to eliminate one of the links to the federal government that underpin Fannie and Freddie's status as "government sponsored."

- The Department of Housing and Urban Development (HUD), the GSEs' mission regulator, requested authority to levy $6.5 million in fees on the GSEs so it could better enforce its affordable and low-income housing regulations.

- HUD is now receiving public comments on significantly tougher regulations it has proposed in those areas, which if ultimately adopted will force Fannie and Freddie to devote more resources to the less profitable and riskier underserved market.

- The Federal Reserve Board announced that it would no longer permit Fannie and Freddie to borrow short-term from the Fed by incurring overdrafts in the course of making payments on their securities, a benefit some have calculated to be worth about $10 million per year.

FIGURE 1

FANNIE MAE P/E RELATIVE TO S&P FINANCIALS (SINCE JANUARY 1995)

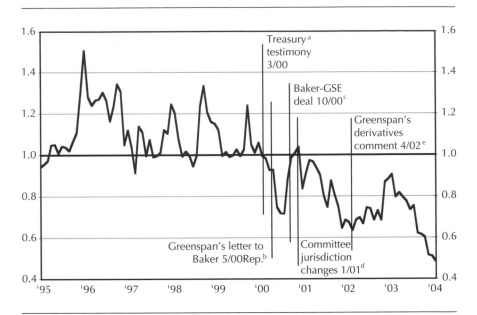

a. Under Secretary of the Treasury Gary Gensler testifies that the Clinton administration will support elimination of the Treasury "line of credit" to the GSEs.

b. Federal Reserve chairman Greenspan notes in a letter to Rep. Richard Baker (R-La.), chairman of the subcommittee with jurisdiction over the GSEs, that the GSEs distort allocation of funds within the financial markets and create risks.

c. Fannie and Freddie agree to issue subordinated debt and to hold ninety days' worth of liquidity.

d. House Financial Services Committee is established, with Rep. Michael Oxley (R-Ohio) as chair.

e. Chairman Greenspan comments that the GSEs create risk in the market through the use of derivatives.

- A Fed economic study concluded that the value of Fannie and Freddie's government subsidy was between $119 billion and $164 billion, far higher than earlier estimates by the Congressional Budget Office (CBO); that between 42 percent and 81 percent of the companies' market value is attributable to their government subsidy; and that the benefit homebuyers derived from this subsidy was only 7 basis points—less than a third of previous estimates.

- CBO announced that it had updated its 2001 study of Fannie and Freddie's subsidy and, using the same methodology, concluded that the subsidy had grown from $11 billion in 2000 to almost $20 billion in 2003. Of this amount, CBO estimated that Fannie and Freddie retained about one-third and passed the balance through to homebuyers. CBO also noted that its conclusions, although using a different methodology, were consistent with the Fed study.

- Gregory Mankiw, the chairman of the President's Council of Economic Advisers, declared in a speech that Fannie and Freddie posed risks to the economy and had to be reined in by stronger capital regulation and other restrictions. Speeches and testimony by Treasury officials also emphasized these concerns, and one Treasury official declared that if Congress wanted to eliminate the GSEs' $2.25 billion "line of credit" at the Treasury—another of the links that confer GSE status—the department would be willing to discuss doing so.

- The Organization for Economic Cooperation and Development (OECD), in a report on the U.S. economy, recommended that limits be placed on the growth of Fannie and Freddie.

- Last, but far from least, in testimony before the Senate Banking Committee, Fed chairman Alan Greenspan declared Fannie and Freddie a systemic danger to the economy and called for their privatization.

Declining Investor Support

Perhaps the most ominous signs of long-term trouble for Fannie and Freddie were not government actions at all, but changes in the way they are viewed in the private sector. Several examples suggest that their control over events is beginning to weaken. Wells Fargo, one of the nation's largest banks and a major player in the mortgage market, publicly challenged Fannie and Freddie's commitment to affordable and low-income housing. Only a few years ago, a public complaint about the GSEs by a participant in the housing markets would have been unthinkable.

Major media outlets began to assign reporters to the Fannie and Freddie "beat." The *Wall Street Journal, Washington Post, Financial Times,* Dow Jones Newswire, and Bloomberg News all designated specific reporters to follow events at or involving Fannie and Freddie. To call this a deathwatch would be an exaggeration, but it indicated that Fannie and Freddie had been recognized as a potential source of important developments in the future, virtually guaranteeing a flow of unfavorable publicity for two companies that had successfully flown under the media radar for many years.

Finally, and perhaps most important, investors and analysts began to draw attention to the severe decline in Fannie's price-earnings ratio (Freddie's is not available because it has not been able to publish audited financial statements for 2002 or 2003). Listed on the New York Stock Exchange, Fannie Mae has been consistently one of the most profitable public companies in the United States. The company boasts that it is one of only four or five companies in the S&P 500 that have had double-digit increases in profitability for fifteen straight years. Indeed, the company's profit has been doubling every five years since the beginning of the 1990s, and its return on equity has been consistently in the range of 23 to 26 percent.

With a success record like this, Fannie should have a price-earnings ratio well up into the 20s, but by mid-April 2004 its P-E was about 9.5. For comparison, the composite P-E ratio of the S&P 500 financials was twice as high (see figure 1). What this has meant for Fannie's shareholders is that the price of the stock has not participated at all in the recovery of the securities market since 2002. Although the Dow Jones Industrial Average has climbed almost 2,000 points since September 2002, Fannie's stock price is today almost exactly where it was when the market began its upward move. Moreover, as this *Outlook* goes to press, the price is lower than it was on January 4, 1999, the day that Franklin Raines became chairman and CEO of Fannie Mae.

The significance of this fact should not be underestimated. What it means is that investors have built into Fannie's stock price an enormous risk premium, perhaps anticipating that there will be some event—probably government action—that will seriously diminish the company's value. From the perspective of investors, the many events listed above constitute what analysts call "headline risk"—the downward pressure on a stock price that follows upon the disclosure of bad news.

If the Fannie Mae board is like other boards, this is their greatest concern. Fannie is not of course a takeover target, but since the takeover period of the 1980s corporate managements and boards have looked to a company's stock price as an indication of how investors view the quality of their stewardship. When a company's stock price is not increasing, at least when stock prices in general are rising, it is a vote of no confidence. On golf courses, around lunch and dinner tables, and in discussions with analysts, the company's directors and management are almost certainly being asked how the company plans to change this adverse trend.

Unfortunately for Fannie, this is a very difficult question. Quite apart from the headline risk created by the drumbeat of bad news coming from the administration and other government agencies, the legislation adopted by the Senate Banking Committee establishes a significant baseline for what Congress could do if a major event in the future stimulates a demand for new regulatory legislation. As long as this legislation is looming, it will be difficult for Fannie's stock price to recover. On the other hand, as the description of the legislation below might suggest, acceding to the bill and allowing it to become law would also be unpalatable to Fannie's management and investors. There are rumors in Washington that Franklin Raines, Fannie's chairman, told his board that agreeing to this bill would be tantamount to giving up Fannie's franchise. While this may be a bit of an exaggeration, the bill clearly has troubling elements for Fannie and Freddie.

The Senate Bill

Ever since it opposed a House bill that it characterized as too weak, the Treasury Department had been insisting that the administration had three bottom-line, nonnegotiable demands for any regulator of Fannie Mae and Freddie Mac: (1) the power to adjust the GSEs' capital requirements, including the imposition of a leverage ratio in addition to a minimum level of risk-based capital; (2) the authority to control the GSEs' mission—that is, to approve or disapprove of new activities; and (3) the ability to act as a receiver in the event of a GSE's insolvency, with the usual receiver's power to marshal assets and impose losses on classes of investors and creditors.

Although unusual in Washington, the administration's position does not appear to have been part of a bargaining process. When the legislation came before the Senate committee, the administration insisted on its minimum demands, and when the bill came out of committee with a weaker receivership provision than it wanted, the Treasury publicly opposed the bill. Fannie was not willing to compromise either. Despite statements by Franklin Raines that Fannie wanted a strong regulator—most recently at an AEI luncheon address in

February 2004[9]—the company implacably opposed almost every major provision of the Senate bill. Many observers saw Fannie's position as a product of the close presidential election: because of Fannie's close ties to the Democratic Party, a Kerry victory in November would likely end the threat of tougher regulation for the foreseeable future.

But in the absence of a Kerry victory, the Senate bill will hang over Fannie and Freddie like a dark cloud, until the extent of the new regulator's authority is determined. Not only was the new regulator given the power to increase minimum and risk-based capital, but under the Senate bill the same regulator would have the power to disapprove new activities if they were not deemed to be in "the public interest." This language would significantly impair the GSEs' ability to enter new activities by pointing to very broad language in their charters. The new regulator would also have receivership powers, but they would be subject to a forty-five-day period during which Congress could overturn the regulator's appointment of a receiver. The weakening of this provision caused the chairman of the committee, Senator Richard Shelby (R-Ala.), and the administration, to disavow the bill in the form that the committee has passed.

But the bill contains more unwelcome news for Fannie and Freddie. Among other things, it requires them to set aside 5 percent of their pretax earnings in an affordable housing fund, tightens the definition of low-income housing so that it applies to incomes that are 60 percent of median income (instead of 80 percent), and requires the GSEs to lead the market in extending credit to subprime borrowers and the manufactured housing market. All of these mandates will increase risks and reduce profitability. It is again important to note that demands of this kind, which were advanced by the Democrats on the committee and supported by the Republicans, would probably not have been politically possible as recently as last year and were most likely the price the Democrats extracted for their virtually unanimous support of the GSEs' position in opposition to the bill.

The Privatization Option

With all these wolves circling just outside their camp, it is no longer possible to dismiss the idea that Fannie and Freddie will opt for privatization. Indeed,

---

9. A summary, a transcript, and a video recording of the event are available online at www.aei.org/event742.

in comparison with the other courses available to them—accepting the Senate bill or continuing to oppose it—privatization is beginning to look attractive. If President Bush is reelected, the legislation adopted by the Senate Banking Committee this year will come back again in the next Congress, and probably in a stronger form. The regulatory portions will be difficult enough to accept, but it is almost impossible to imagine that the new affordable and low-income housing provisions—which will have significant adverse effects on the GSEs' profitability—can be eliminated from any new bill that passes Congress.

If Congress acts, the new law will increase the likelihood of regulatory action to raise the GSEs' capital levels, reduce their ability to expand their activities into new areas of the economy, and require costly support of affordable and low-income housing. If the bill is not passed, its potential impact will continue to depress their stock prices. When the board of directors asks Franklin Raines for the plan that will move the company's stock price out of the doldrums, it is hard to see any strategy that will work. Moreover, if things proceed as they have over the past three months, Fannie and Freddie will continue to look like the Bad News Bears, as government agencies, members of Congress, members of the mortgage industry, affordable and low-income housing groups, a range of independent analysts, their free market critics, and the press pummel them with complaints and charges. Investors, under these circumstances, will continue to build a risk premium into their stock prices that will drive their price-earnings ratios even lower.

Over against this is the example of the Student Loan Marketing Association, known as Sallie Mae, a GSE that privatized in the mid-1990s. Sallie's P-E is about 14, and it does not have to contend with regulation (the market sets its capitalization), restrictions on its activities (it can enter any business it wants), or meeting affordable and low-income housing goals. When Fannie and Freddie were free of criticism and threatening legislation, when they had convinced the markets that they had complete control of their political risk, it made a great deal of sense to remain as GSEs. In the circumstances they face today, the answer is no longer so clear.

If Fannie and Freddie's managements were to consider privatization, the most important question would be whether they would be able to obtain the highly favorable privatization framework Congress granted to Sallie Mae. In that case, Congress allowed Sallie to establish a private-sector holding company for the GSE, free of any controls or regulation and free to enter any business, and also permitted the original government-sponsored unit to continue functioning for an additional ten years, providing the parent company with a strong cash flow. If Fannie and Freddie could obtain similar treatment, they would be in a position to dominate the housing market while extending their activities into other areas of the financial economy. Because of their size and domination of a vital sector of the U.S. economy, the two companies as privatized entities might even be considered too big to fail and thus might continue to obtain the favorable financing they currently enjoy. For this reason, many have feared the possibility that the GSEs would seek privatization and obtain it in the form Congress granted to Sallie Mae.

This, however, is not the only way that privatization could occur, and a Congress worried about dropping two huge new unregulated financial companies into the competitive U.S. financial market has a number of alternatives. To demonstrate what possibilities are available, AEI recently sponsored the development by lawyer and consultant Thomas H. Stanton of a privatization plan for Fannie and Freddie that avoids the dangers implicit in the Sallie framework. The current version of the plan, along with a new system for financing housing, developed by Bert Ely, is posted in its entirety on the AEI website.[10]

The plan contains the following principal elements:

- Upon enactment, Fannie and Freddie must cease purchasing mortgages and mortgage-backed securities (MBSs) for their portfolios; existing mortgages and MBSs in their portfolios would be sold off and reduced to zero five years after the date of enactment.

- Fannie and Freddie could continue to securitize mortgages for a six-month period after enactment but at the end of that period would have to begin winding down that aspect of their operations; securitization activities would have to cease three years after enactment. As securitization by the GSE wound down it would gradually have to be transferred to a subsidiary of a private-sector holding company that Fannie and Freddie would be permitted to establish as described below.

---

10. Go to www.aei.org/event743.

- As in the case of Sallie Mae, Fannie and Freddie would be able to form holding companies that could engage in any business, but only if the GSEs maintained a capitalization equivalent to that required for a stand-alone AA rating (this will limit their ability to distribute cash from their GSE operations to the holding company as dividends), and only if they spin off to independent corporations their housing and mortgage databases and their automated underwriting systems. They would be able to continue to use both, but so could any other company that acquired a license from the spun-off company.

- At the end of five years, the GSE charters would be terminated, and any outstanding GSE obligations (including both debt and the guarantees of any remaining MBS) would be defeased (backed by U.S. Treasuries).

By requiring that they eliminate their portfolios of mortgages and MBSs over five years and their securitization activities over three, this plan would reduce the size of the companies that would succeed to the remaining business of Fannie and Freddie. They would no longer have size and data advantages over other mortgage market participants. In this way, the plan avoids the highly favorable framework adopted by Congress in the Sallie Mae privatization and should allay concern in the private sector that the privatization of Fannie and Freddie will free two gigantic financial companies—both of which could be considered too big to fail—to compete in any market they choose.

Nevertheless, while it must still be considered unlikely that Fannie and Freddie will seek privatization in the near future, it is no longer the wild long shot it once was. Although no one in Congress has joined Alan Greenspan's call for privatization, that is not the relevant test of likelihood. If there is to be a privatization initiative, it will come from Fannie or Freddie, or both, and if they are unable to increase their stock price significantly in any other way, privatization may be the best solution available.

At the pace that events are moving against Fannie and Freddie, it is entirely possible that within the next two years we will be discussing alternative privatization plans instead of new regulation.

"Regulating Fannie Mae and Freddie Mac: Now It Gets Serious"

Originally published May 2005

For well over a year, Congress has been toying with ever tighter regulation of Fannie Mae and Freddie Mac, while studiously avoiding the elephant in the living room—the companies' massive portfolios of mortgages and mortgage-backed securities (MBS). The stated rationale for the effort to create a "world-class regulator" is to reduce the risks—for the taxpayers and the economy generally—associated with these two huge companies. But since it is the portfolios themselves that engender those risks, all the activity in Congress to this point has seemed futile, like bailing furiously while ignoring the hole in the boat. But as the accounting misdeeds of Fannie and Freddie have come to light, and their aura of financial probity and political invincibility has begun to fade, Congress has been emboldened. The idea that the size of Fannie's and Freddie's portfolios might be limited or reduced has moved in from left field (well, maybe right field) and is now, appropriately, the central feature of the debate.

Fannie and Freddie are government-chartered, shareholder-owned public companies. Because of their government charters and many government-provided privileges, they are known as government-sponsored enterprises, or GSEs. The companies carry on their business in two ways. In a process known as a securitization, they buy mortgages from mortgage originators, place them in trusts, and issue securities from these trusts that are backed by the payments of principal and interest on the pooled mortgages. These transactions create what are called mortgage-backed securities (MBS). Fannie and Freddie only guarantee to the holders of MBS that the principal and interest on the mortgages in the trusts will be paid in full and on time. In other words, Fannie and Freddie take only the credit risk on these mortgages; the interest-rate risk—that interest rates will rise and the mortgages will become less valuable, or that interest rates will fall and the mortgages will be prepaid and disappear—is taken by the holders of the MBS. For their guarantee, Fannie and Freddie receive an annual fee as long as the pools remain in existence. In this segment of their business, Fannie and Freddie have guaranteed about $2.2 trillion in mortgages.[11]

In the other part of their business, Fannie and Freddie buy mortgages from originators and hold them in portfolio; they also repurchase for their portfolios some of the MBS that they have already issued. Because they are then the owners of these mortgages and MBS, they have assumed the credit risk, and because they have to borrow the funds to buy the mortgages and MBS, they assume the associated interest-rate risk. Of the two, interest-rate risk is far more significant, and Fannie and Freddie have to enter into large hedging transactions to mitigate it. They assume these substantial risks, and contract for hedging, because their portfolios of mortgages produce by far the greater part of their profits. This is true because, as GSEs, they are accorded favorable rates in the capital markets, and thus can arbitrage between their borrowing costs and the rate they will receive on the mortgages and MBS they hold. Their mortgages and MBS assets are currently worth approximately $1.5 trillion, and this is also approximately the aggregate amount of their borrowings.

To place this in some perspective, all Treasury debt held by the public totals $4.4 trillion, and all corporate bonds outstanding total $2.9 trillion. Fannie's and Freddie's liabilities—including both their MBS guarantees and their borrowings—come in right in the middle, at $3.7 trillion. Thus, only two companies—both of which are GSEs and implicitly backed by the U.S. government—account for more default risk than all other U.S. corporations combined. The risks for the taxpayers are obvious, but as many commentators have also pointed out, risk of this size, if concentrated in only two companies, poses a danger to the U.S. economic system as a whole—a danger known as systemic risk.

How Fannie and Freddie Lost Their Groove

Congressman Richard Baker (R-La.) has been concerned about the risks created by Fannie and Freddie since 2000, when he first introduced legislation to augment the powers of their regulator. However, the alignment of the political

---

11. These figures and those relating to the GSEs' portfolios of mortgages and MBS are from Dwight Jaffee, "On Limiting the Retained Mortgage Portfolios of Fannie Mae and Freddie Mac," preliminary draft of April 25, 2005, delivered at a conference at AEI on April 26, 2005 and available through www.aei.org/event1041.

stars was so unfavorable at the time that Baker—then the chairman of the House subcommittee that had jurisdiction over the GSEs—could not find sufficient support for his bill to bring it to formal consideration and possible amendment by the subcommittee (what is known as "mark-up"). Successive bills in 2002 and 2003 met similar fates, although the threat of legislation brought Fannie and Freddie to agree to modest changes in their financial procedures and voluntary registration of their equity securities under the Securities Exchange Act of 1934.

Then, in June 2003, came what in retrospect appears to have been the turning point. As part of the fallout from Enron and WorldCom, Freddie Mac decided to engage new auditors, replacing Arthur Andersen. The new auditors found discrepancies in the company's financial reports, and an independent counsel was engaged to do an investigation. The investigation showed that Freddie had manipulated its earnings in order to reduce reported volatility, and—perhaps more important—one of Freddie's senior managers seemed to have taken steps to obstruct the investigation. As a result, Freddie dismissed its three top officers, an action that apparently came as a complete surprise to the Office of Federal Housing Enterprise Oversight (OFHEO), the company's regulator. OFHEO was embarrassed by its failure to discover on its own the facts that led to the dismissal of Freddie's top officers—or even that there was an internal investigation that might lead to their dismissal—and its ability effectively to regulate the GSEs was publicly called into question.

This event seems to have precipitated major changes in the views and behavior of the three principal government groups that had the power to affect the future of Fannie and Freddie. The administration became engaged, seemingly for the first time, in considering the risks associated with both companies; OFHEO metamorphosed from a butterfly into a wasp; and members of Congress started to take Chairman Baker's legislation more seriously. The result was a complete change in the atmosphere surrounding the GSEs. Suddenly, administration figures—representatives of Treasury, the Department of Housing and Urban Development, the Council of Economic Advisers, and the Office of Management and Budget, among others—began making public statements criticizing the GSEs, questioning their role in the housing market and the risks they were creating for taxpayers and the economy. Federal Reserve chairman Alan Greenspan, citing these same risks, weighed in with letters to lawmakers and testimony supporting stricter regulation and even privatization. OFHEO vowed tougher regulation, and sought and received funds from Congress to do a forensic audit of Fannie, arguing that if Freddie had manipulated its financial results Fannie may also have done so. As a result of these steps and disclosures, the GSEs' share prices, which had been stable over several years, began a significant decline. Investors either were losing confidence in the companies, or were unwilling to absorb the constant headline risk to which the companies were subject.

By early 2004, lawmakers in both the Senate and House were saying that Fannie and Freddie needed a "world class" regulator, and the Treasury Department had formulated a three-part proposal that constituted what it called its minimum requirements for legislation: the new regulator should have authority to raise Fannie and Freddie's capital level, to control their mission, and to appoint a receiver to marshal their assets and pay off creditors in the event of a financial collapse. A weak bill developed by Michael G. Oxley (R-Ohio), the chairman of the House Financial Services Committee, was blown apart just before mark-up by administration opposition. Attention turned to the Senate.

In what turned out to be a huge strategic error, Fannie and Freddie chose to fight legislation in the Senate Banking Committee that embodied the administration's minimum requirements, particularly the receivership provision, in the late spring of 2004. The companies called in their chits and managed to obtain solid Democratic opposition to the bill crafted by the committee's chairman, Richard Shelby (R-Ala.). The committee also watered down the receivership provision. The partisan nature of the vote to send the bill to the floor virtually assured that it would not be taken up in the Senate unless Fannie and Freddie relented in their opposition, and the administration opposed the committee bill because of the weakened receivership language. Administration spokesmen warned the companies that if they continued to oppose the bill in 2004 there would be a tougher version in 2005, but Fannie and Freddie would not budge. It may be that the GSEs were banking on the defeat of President George W. Bush and on the assumption that a Democratic president would abandon the effort to pass tougher regulation. If that was their thinking, it was an exceedingly costly error.

In the fall of 2004, OFHEO reported that Fannie Mae had also manipulated its accounting, and to a degree far more significant than what Freddie had done. At a dramatic hearing in Richard Baker's subcommittee, Fannie's chair, Franklin Raines, stood by the company's accounting, claiming that Fannie was being victimized by an overzealous regulator and its accounting position would eventually be vindicated by the Securities and Exchange Commission (SEC), which had been asked to review the disputed accounting. The tenor of things in Congress was still so supportive of the GSEs that Armando Falcon, the director of OFHEO, received a far more hostile reception than Raines got in Baker's subcommittee. Nevertheless, most accounting specialists viewed Raines's position as unsupportable, and many questioned his judgment both in making a frontal assault on his regulator and in making statements under oath that might later put him in jeopardy. Weeks later, the SEC's chief accountant dismissed Raines's contentions, famously holding up a piece of paper and telling Raines to his face that Fannie's position on the relevant accounting was not even "on the page" of allowable interpretations. Shortly thereafter, Fannie announced that Raines had resigned as chairman and CEO. Both the Justice Department and the SEC have begun investigations of Fannie's accounting, and the company has dismissed its former auditors and retained an independent counsel to conduct an investigation of its own accounting.

Now, after these events as well as the results of the 2004 election, Fannie and Freddie would be delighted with the Senate committee bill, and as the new Congress began in January 2005, their managements both made statements that they were prepared to accept what they opposed in 2004—even receivership. But it was too late. The world had moved on. Today, the controversial issue before Congress is no longer receivership, but something far more significant.

Portfolio Size Limitations

In February 2005, the House Financial Services Committee heard testimony from Chairman Greenspan on the condition of the economy. After his prepared testimony, in response to a question about the GSEs' portfolios, Greenspan noted, "We have found no reasonable basis for that portfolio above very minimum needs." He then proposed "a $100 billion, $200 billion—whatever the number might turn out to be—limit on the size of the aggregate portfolios of those institutions—and the reason I say that is there are certain purposes which I can see in the holding of mortgages which might be helpful in a number of different areas. But $900 billion for Fannie and somewhat less, obviously, for Freddie, I don't see the purpose of it." Greenspan then articulated his reasons for limiting the GSEs' portfolios: "If [Fannie and Freddie] continue to grow, continue to have the low capital that they have, continue to engage in the dynamic hedging of their portfolios, which they need to do for interest rate risk aversion, they potentially create ever-growing potential systemic risk down the road." He added, "Enabling these institutions to increase in size—and they will, once the crisis, in their judgment, passes—we are placing the total financial system of the future at a substantial risk."[12]

The Fed chairman's statement drew substantial attention, but this was not the first time he had raised and discussed this issue. In February 2004 prepared testimony before the Senate Banking Committee, Greenspan emphasized the substantial interest-rate risk associated with the GSEs' large portfolios of mortgages and that concentrating that risk in only two companies raised issues of systemic risk. He pointed out that Fannie and Freddie could do everything they currently do for the mortgage market through securitization—issuing securities against pools of mortgages, the process by which they create MBS—without bearing any interest-rate risk. Then he continued:

> World class regulation, by itself, may not be sufficient and indeed, as suggested by Treasury Secretary Snow, may even worsen the situation if market participants infer from such regulation that the government is all the more likely to back GSE debt. . . . Most of the concerns associated with systemic risks flow from the size of the balance sheets that these GSEs maintain. *One way the Congress could constrain the size of these balance sheets is to alter the composition of Fannie and Freddie's mortgage financing by limiting the dollar amount of their debt relative to the dollar amount of mortgages securitized and held by other investors.* Although it is difficult to know how best to set such a rule, this approach would continue to expand the depth and liquidity of mortgage markets through mortgage securitization but would remove most of the potential systemic risks associated with these GSEs (emphasis added).[13]

Thus, as early as February 2004, Greenspan was telling the Senate committee members that their search for a world class regulator would not produce the reduction in systemic and other risk that they had identified as their goal.

---

12. Greenspan testimony, House Financial Services Committee, February 17, 2005, quoted in Canfield Associates, *GSE Report,* February 28, 2005, 3.

13. Senate Committee on Banking, Housing, and Urban Affairs, *Statement of Alan Greenspan,* 108th Congress, 1st session, February 24, 2004, 9–10 (available at http://banking.senate.gov/index.cfm?Fuseaction=Hearings.Detail&HearingID=92, as of May 12, 2005).

Indeed, tighter regulation might make the problem worse. The only way to reduce this risk, he pointed out, was to reduce the size of the GSEs' portfolios of mortgages and MBS.

The Serious Effects of Portfolio Limitations

The informal Greenspan statement in February 2005 got far more attention than his more complete and fully reasoned prepared testimony to the same effect a year earlier. Such are the ways of Washington. A lot had happened in the interim, including the OFHEO's critical report on Fannie's accounting, the SEC's confirmation of the OFHEO's position, and the resignation of Franklin Raines. In 2005, Greenspan's statement opened for debate an issue that Congress had, only a month before, not considered to be within the realm of political discussion. Thus, in January 2005, three Senators—Chuck Hagel (R-Neb.), John E. Sununu (R-N.H.), and Elizabeth Dole (R-N.C.)—had introduced tough new legislation to regulate Fannie and Freddie. The legislation was state-of-the-art at the time, and included a carefully developed "bright line" test that was intended to end Fannie's and Freddie's efforts to break out of the secondary mortgage market as their sole allowable field of operations. But the legislation made no mention of limiting the GSEs' portfolios. After the Greenspan testimony, however, that issue suddenly achieved currency, with lawmakers in both the House and Senate saying that they intended to look carefully at whether such a provision should be included in the legislation they were drafting.

The sudden appearance of this new threat changed the attitude of the GSEs toward the legislation. Although they had begun 2005 offering conciliatory statements and suggesting that they had no serious problems with the regulatory proposals that Congress was then contemplating, the GSEs were clearly alarmed by the idea that their portfolios might be limited or reduced. Fannie and Freddie and their constituent support groups—the homebuilders and the realtors, among others—made clear that they would fight limitations on GSE portfolios, and Senator Charles Schumer (D-N.Y.) and other Democrats made clear that they, too, would oppose any effort to limit this aspect of the GSEs' operations.

For the GSEs, this is clearly a kind of Armageddon. The legislation advanced in the past, no matter how "tough," posed no serious problem for Fannie and Freddie; indeed, although they made a show of opposing it, the legislation might well have improved their position by emphasizing their connection to the government and ending the headline risk they faced from the drumbeat of adverse commentary by members of the administration. With that criticism ended, and the uncertainty associated with the legislative drafting process out of the way, there was hope that their stock prices would revive. Over time, indeed, with their political muscle in Washington, there was a good chance that they would be able to gain control of their new regulator—no matter what its putative authority—as they had successfully controlled the OFHEO until Freddie's surprise disclosure of its accounting problems drove the agency to tough and decisive action.

But a serious proposal to limit the size of their portfolios is of a different order entirely than mere enhanced regulation. Although the exact number is difficult to determine, the GSEs' mortgage portfolios may provide as much as 85 percent of their profits. This seems to be a reasonable estimate, because their net interest income—the amount they earn on the difference between their borrowing costs and the yield on the mortgages and MBS they hold—is about $23 billion, while their fee income from the issuance of MBS is approximately $4 billion.[14] While the actual profit difference from each line of business may not be as great as the difference in the revenues from each line of business, the disparity between the two lines is so large that a serious limitation on the size of their portfolios will clearly cause a major reduction in the GSEs' earning potential and further depress their stock prices. In this sense, the long fight to control the GSEs has finally come to a point of real significance; if they lose this argument, they will no longer be the second and fourth largest financial institutions in the United States, or among the most highly profitable companies in the S&P 500. At the same time, they will no longer be creating major risks for the taxpayers and the economy.

Can Fannie and Freddie Win This Argument?

The reasons for limiting the GSEs' portfolios are easy to state. Their purpose is to create liquidity in the mortgage market by providing a means for mortgage originators to sell off their mortgages and thus make room in their portfolios for more mortgage loans. But they can do this solely through securitization, which does not involve the substantial interest-rate risk associated with holding a portfolio

---

14. These are 2004 numbers sourced to the OFHEO, Dwight Jaffee, "On Limiting the Retained Mortgage Portfolio of Fannie Mae and Freddie Mac," 6–7.

of mortgage assets. Under these circumstances, allowing Fannie and Freddie to continue on their present course is simply to create risks for the taxpayers, and to the economy generally, in order to improve the profits of their shareholders and the compensation of their managements. It is a classic case of socializing the risk while privatizing the profit. The Democrats and the few Republicans who oppose portfolio limitations could not possibly do so if their constituents understood what they were doing.

What, then, are the arguments advanced by the GSEs? Freddie Mac has been circulating on Capitol Hill a lobbying document that one should assume contains the best case the GSEs can make for retaining large portfolios of mortgages and MBS. The principal elements of this case are summarized in italics below, and counterarguments follow:

1. The accumulation of large portfolios adds liquidity and stability to the secondary mortgage market.

Fannie and Freddie currently hold more than a quarter of all MBS they have issued, and the idea that this level of accumulation is necessary to add liquidity to a market is, to say the least, highly counterintuitive. The essence of liquidity is supply—a large number of securities available for purchase or sale. When Fannie and Freddie acquire and hold mortgages and MBS, they reduce the supply available to the market, and hence reduce liquidity.

Moreover, as Chairman Greenspan noted in his February 24, 2004, Senate testimony, liquidity and stability in the mortgage markets can be achieved just as well through securitization, without the extraordinary taxpayer and systemic risks entailed in the GSEs' purchases of mortgages and MBS:

> Limiting the debt of Fannie and Freddie and expanding their role in mortgage securitization would be consistent with the original congressional intent that these institutions provide stability in the markets for residential mortgages and provide liquidity for mortgage investors. Deep and liquid markets for mortgages are made using mortgage-backed securities that are held by non-GSE private investors. *Fannie's and Freddie's purchase of their own or each other's securities with their debt do not appear needed to supply mortgage market liquidity or to enhance capital markets in the United States* (emphasis added).[15]

---

15. Senate Committee, *Statement of Alan Greenspan,* February 24, 2004, 10.

2. The GSEs' purchases of mortgages and MBS increases demand, which in turn lowers mortgage interest rates.

Here Freddie conveniently describes only one side of the transaction. Of course the purchase of mortgages or MBS would reduce rates, but since Fannie and Freddie must borrow virtually every dollar they spend to buy mortgages and MBS, their borrowing has the effect of increasing rates. In the end, it is a wash. As Chairman Greenspan noted in Senate Banking Committee testimony on April 6, 2005:

> A recent study by Federal Reserve Board staff found no link between the size of the GSE portfolios and mortgage rates. The past year provides yet more evidence, with GSE portfolios not growing and mortgage spreads, as well as the spread between yields on GSE debentures and Treasury securities, declining further.[16]

Both facts here are important. Slower mortgage purchases by the GSEs have coincided with lower rather than higher mortgage rates—again breaking any connection between the GSEs' portfolios and lower rates—and the decline in spreads between GSE securities and Treasuries, as GSE borrowing declined, shows that GSE borrowing to purchase mortgages and MBS has the effect of raising interest rates. Greenspan continues:

> Limiting the systemic risks associated with the GSEs would require that their mortgage holdings be significantly smaller. At the same time, reducing portfolios would have only a modest effect on financial markets. Currently, these portfolios are financed largely by the issuance of GSE debt, which, in turn is held by investors. . . . In the simplest outcome, the holders of GSE debt would be seen as exchanging their debt instruments for mortgage-backed securities previously held on GSE balance sheets. *As for homebuyers, whether GSE mortgage purchases are held in GSE portfolios or securitized and sold to investors appears to have no noticeable effect on mortgage rates* (emphasis added).[17]

---

16. Senate Committee on Banking, Housing, and Urban Affairs, *Statement of Alan Greenspan,* 109th Congress, 1st session, April 6, 2005, 3 (available at http://banking. senate.gov/index.cfm?Fuseaction=Hearings.Detail&HearingID=14, as of May 12, 2005).

17. Ibid, 4–5.

3. GSE purchases of mortgages and MBS stabilize the market during periods of stress. This is what occurred during the Asian debt crisis in 1998, when the GSEs continued buying mortgages and MBS while other buyers held back.

This is a slightly different claim from the argument covered in item 1 above, in which Freddie contends that in normal times GSE purchases create liquidity and stability in the market. Although a buyer of last resort can add liquidity to a market, this is not the function that Fannie and Freddie are performing. As profit-seeking entities, they buy mortgages when conditions are favorable, not when the market needs support. Although they make a claim to public-spirited motives when they are on Capitol Hill, it is unlikely that they tell their shareholders the same thing. Indeed, if they are in fact buying mortgages when conditions are unfavorable, their managements are violating their fiduciary duty to maximize profits.

In testimony before the Senate Banking Committee on April 21, 2005, Douglas Holtz-Eakin, director of the Congressional Budget Office, addressed the claim that the GSEs provide special assistance to the mortgage market in times of stress: "GSEs' purchases during periods of financial stress appear to have been in response to more profitable opportunities (such as wider interest-rate spreads), but in doing so, the GSEs are displacing other investors who would have responded to those opportunities."[18] In other words, the GSEs turn out to be just one more opportunistic buyer of mortgages when market conditions are right— just as one would expect of profit-seeking shareholder-owned companies—not public-spirited sources of credit in periods of stress. When, in a time of stress, market conditions are adverse, the GSEs will not be there buying mortgages.

4. Borrowing by the GSEs to create their portfolios is good because it brings capital from abroad into the U.S. residential mortgage market and thus lowers interest rates.

This is essentially an argument that foreign investors will prefer Fannie and Freddie debt to purchasing the MBS that the GSEs guarantee. Since both GSE debt securities and MBS have the same credit rating, the only reason foreign investors might prefer GSE debt is that they do not want to take the prepayment

---

18. Senate Committee on Banking, Housing, and Urban Affairs, *Statement of Douglas Holtz-Eakin: Aligning the Costs and Benefits of the Housing Government-Sponsored Enterprises,* 109th Congress, April 21, 2005, 8 (available at http://banking.senate.gov/index.cfm?Fuseaction=Hearings.Detail&HearingID=150, as of May 12, 2005).

risk associated with MBS. In fact, Freddie explicitly makes this argument in its lobbying material ("[Foreign] investors do not want the prepayment risk of MBS."[19]). As noted above, when Fannie and Freddie borrow to buy and hold mortgages and MBS, the GSEs are taking the interest-rate risk, a substantial part of which is prepayment risk. Fannie and Freddie hedge some, but not all, of this risk, which is by far the greatest element of the risk they create for taxpayers and the economy generally (also known as systemic risk). On the other hand, when Fannie and Freddie securitize mortgages, the interest-rate risk is taken by investors.

Accordingly, what Freddie is saying in its lobbying material is that it assists the mortgage markets by taking interest-rate risk on behalf of foreign investors who are reluctant to do so. And what this means is that, because of the implicit government backing of the GSEs, U.S. taxpayers are ultimately the ones taking this risk.

To be sure, there might be some justification for this if there were evidence that Fannie and Freddie were actually lowering mortgage interest rates by borrowing to accumulate their large mortgage portfolios. In that case, it might be argued that although taxpayers are taking a risk, they are benefiting as homebuyers. The trouble with this argument is that there is no evidence whatever that the GSEs' portfolios have any significant impact on mortgage rates. As Chairman Greenspan said in his testimony on April 6: "Fannie's and Freddie's purchases of their own or each other's mortgage-backed securities with their market-subsidized debt do not contribute usefully to mortgage-market liquidity, to the enhancement of capital markets in the United States, or to the lowering of mortgage rates for homeowners."[20]

Indeed, that statement sums up the economic arguments against the position Freddie Mac advances in its lobbying material. In exchange for enormous risks—risks for the taxpayer and risks to the economic system—the U.S. homeowner gains nothing from the accumulation of portfolios of mortgages and MBS by Fannie and Freddie. Under these circumstances, it seems clear that if the debate in Congress on limiting the GSEs' portfolio is determined solely by the merits of the arguments on each side, Fannie and Freddie will lose. Unfortunately, however, congressional decisions are not always determined on the

---

19. Freddie Mac, *Freddie Mac's Retained Portfolio: Key to Fulfilling Our Mission,* Mission Statement, April 2005.

20. Senate Committee, *Statement of Alan Greenspan,* April 6, 2005, 5.

merits, and there are disturbing signs that this may be the case with the GSE reform legislation now under consideration.

The Legislation

Shortly after Chairman Greenspan's House testimony in February 2005—in which he reiterated the view that the portfolios of the GSEs should be limited to reduce the risks they create—key lawmakers in both the Senate and House pledged that they would consider his idea seriously. However, the only legislation on this question thus far introduced in either house is seriously deficient. That bill, introduced by Congressman Baker and House Financial Services Committee chairman Michael Oxley early in April 2005, authorizes the GSEs' regulator "to dispose of or acquire any asset or obligation, if the Director determines that such action is consistent with the safe and sound operation of the enterprise or with the purposes of this Act."[21]

This language leaves the regulator with no useful standard, and arguably does not increase at all the authority, currently held by OFHEO, to force the GSEs to divest assets that threaten their safety or soundness. If this language were to be included in the final law, it would fail completely to provide a legal basis for the regulator to act unless he or she could show that the portfolios of the GSEs were a threat to their financial condition. Whatever its purpose, this initial draft was clearly not intended to implement the Greenspan recommendation.

In testimony before the House Financial Services Committee on April 13, 2005, Secretary of the Treasury John Snow found this language deficient and outlined the Bush administration's position on how the issue should be resolved. He proposed that the GSEs' regulator be directed by law to reduce the size of Fannie's and Freddie's portfolios, and he proposed a standard for the regulator to follow. Arguing that Fannie and Freddie could do everything they currently do for the mortgage market through securitization—without the risks created by their portfolios—the secretary suggested that their portfolios should be reduced to the level necessary to assure the effective functioning of their securitization activities, and no more. Although the administration has not advanced specific language to embody this approach, Congress would be well advised to adopt it.

---

21. *To Reform the Regulation of Certain Housing-Related Government-Sponsored Enterprises, and for Other Purposes,* HR 1461, 109th Congress, 1st session.

For one thing, it is important to recognize the enormous political power of Fannie and Freddie, and their ability to marshal support from constituent groups such as homebuilders and realtors. If Congress itself cannot summon the political will to overcome the resistance of the GSEs and their support groups, the regulator certainly will not be able to do so. Punting the decision to the regulator may get it off the congressional agenda, but it will leave a serious problem unresolved. Congress must recognize that in order to assure that the GSEs' regulator has the authority to act on an issue as important and controversial as the size of their portfolios, he or she must be given explicit legislative direction. A general statement such as that advanced in the Oxley-Baker bill will not provide this direction, and will leave the regulator essentially powerless to act in the face of massive political opposition. When the committee proceeds to mark up the Oxley-Baker bill, currently scheduled for May 25, it ought to strengthen the language in this portion of the bill so that it conforms to the administration's approach, which both directs the regulator to reduce the size of the portfolios and provides a useful and practical standard for how large the resulting portfolios should be.

The Senate Banking Committee has not yet acted, but one must hope that the committee will take the Greenspan proposal seriously and adopt the administration's approach. As outgoing regulator Armando Falcon said in what is likely to be his final appearance before this committee, "I believe the most prudent course of action would be for Congress to give the regulator explicit authority to regulate the size of the housing Enterprises' portfolios, accompanied by specific statutory guidance on the exercise of such authority."[22] That's exactly what the administration's proposal would do.

The Critical Final Step

After years of trimming around the edges of the GSE problem, Congress—with the help of Chairman Alan Greenspan—has finally come to the nub of the issue. If Congress can bring itself to overcome the furious political opposition of the

---

22. Senate Committee on Banking, Housing, and Urban Affairs, *Statement by Armando Falcon, Jr.: Regulatory Reform of the Housing Government-Sponsored Enterprises,* 109th Congress, April 21, 2005, 5 (available at http://banking.senate.gov/index. cfm?Fuseaction=Hearings.Detail&HearingID=150, as of May 12, 2005).

GSEs and their supporters, it will direct the new GSE regulator to reduce the size of Fannie's and Freddie's portfolios and endorse a workable standard by which to measure the proper size of the smaller portfolios that result. This will solve, finally, the problem of two entities using their implicit government backing to control the residential mortgage market, which creates massive risks for the taxpayers and the economy in general.

If Congress cannot take this essential step, however, no amount of additional authority—given to a purported "world class regulator"—will significantly change the course of events. Fannie and Freddie will continue to grow, and one day—as Alan Greenspan has predicted—there will be a massive default with huge losses to the taxpayers and systemic effects on the economy. We should be grateful that Congress finally has before it a serious proposal that is equal to the seriousness of the problem. But we should also worry about whether Congress can find within itself the political will necessary to see the task through to its logical conclusion.

"Regulating Fannie Mae and Freddie Mac: Now It Gets Serious (Continued)"

Originally published September 2005

The GSE regulatory reform bill reported out of the Senate Banking Committee in July 2005 included a provision that would virtually eliminate the authority of Fannie Mae and Freddie Mac to acquire and maintain portfolios of mortgages and mortgage-backed securities. If this provision becomes law, it will sharply reduce the risks associated with the GSEs, as well as their profitability. The conventional wisdom in Washington and on Wall Street is that a bill this controversial, adopted on a party-line vote, will quickly die in the Senate, and that tough restrictions on the GSEs' portfolios will not become law. But this view fails to reckon with the determination of the White House—demonstrated over several years—to limit the risks that Fannie and Freddie create for both the taxpayers and the economy.

In the last essay that dealt with the regulation of Fannie Mae and Freddie Mac ("Regulating Fannie Mae and Freddie Mac: Now It Gets Serious," May 2005),[23] we noted that the only legislation then under consideration in Congress was a deficient bill that emerged from the House Financial Services Committee in April 2005. When that committee acted, its members had before them a proposal from the administration that would have placed significant limitations on the size of the mortgage portfolios that Fannie Mae and Freddie Mac would be permitted to accumulate. Had this provision been adopted, it would have virtually eliminated the risk that these government sponsored enterprises (GSEs) create for the taxpayers and the economy. But the committee punted. Its bill, HR 1461, failed to provide the necessary authority for the new GSE regulator to limit or reduce the GSEs' portfolios, which at that point amounted to approximately $1.5 trillion.

---

23. Peter J. Wallison, "Regulating Fannie Mae and Freddie Mac: Now It Gets Serious," *Financial Services Outlook,* May 2005, available at www.aei.org/publication22514. (See p. 48 of this book.)

Nevertheless, because portfolio limitations were now on the table for dis-cussion, a serious legislative debate was taking shape. This meant for the first time that all the congressional posturing about creating a "world class regulator" might actually amount to something—not because Congress would actually cre-ate one (the House committee bill did not even give the new regulator all the authority of a bank regulator), but because if Congress actually managed to limit Fannie's and Freddie's portfolios it would finally have taken or authorized the one step that might reduce the risks associated with their operations.

Although the House committee whiffed, the Senate Banking Committee connected, adopting a bill (S 190) that actually contained tougher language on portfolios than what the administration had proposed. Now, Senate action is pending on a bill that would truly reform GSE regulation; undoubtedly—from the perspectives of Fannie and Freddie—things have gotten very serious indeed.

Limiting the GSE portfolios is serious business for the taxpayers and the economy, as well as for the GSEs. The taxpayers and the economy will benefit because they will be relieved of the risk of a GSE default, with a resulting taxpayer bailout and possible systemic effects. For the GSEs, however, the result will be a sharp reduction in profitability—perhaps as much as an 85 percent decline—as they are compelled to carry out their mission through the less risky technique of securitization and the issuance of mortgage-backed securities (MBS).

Interest-Rate Risk

It is not always understood how and why the GSE portfolios create risks. When Franklin Raines was the chairman of Fannie Mae, he used to make speeches in which he questioned how anyone could think that Fannie was in a risky business. After all, he would say, Fannie's assets are the home mortgages of Americans, and everyone knows that homeowners go to great lengths to pay their mortgages. Moreover, he would point out, underlying these mortgages are the homes themselves, which as collateral are further protection for Fannie.[24]

---

24. For example, see Franklin Raines, "Government Policy and Financial Market Stability: The Case of Fannie Mae" (luncheon address, AEI, Washington, D.C., February 6, 2004): "Our debt funds mortgages. And there's a home behind every one of Fannie Mae's mortgages. The $1.5 trillion in property value securing our debt represents some of the safest collateral in the world." The transcript of this address is available at www.aei. org/eventtranscript742.

This argument was so disingenuous that it is remarkable he was able to get away with it for so long.

The risks that Fannie and Freddie take on when they hold mortgages and MBS in their portfolios are of two kinds: credit risk and interest-rate risk. Of the two, credit risk—the risk Franklin Raines was talking about—is substantially the smaller. The real risk is interest-rate risk. In fact, savings and loans could have made the Raines argument before they collapsed in the 1980s; their principal assets were also home mortgages, but they were unable to cope with interest-rate risk.

Interest-rate risk arises from the unusual fact that U.S. mortgages, by law, may be refinanced at any time without penalty. As a result, holders of mortgages and MBS can be seriously hurt both when interest rates rise and when they fall. A simple example will show how this can be true. Fannie Mae must borrow to buy the mortgages it holds in its portfolio. If it borrows at 4 percent and buys mortgages that are paying 5.5 percent, it profits from the 1.5 percent spread. However, if interest rates later decline to 3.5 percent, many homeowners will refinance their 5.5 percent mortgages to the new lower rate, and the 5.5 percent assets simply disappear from Fannie's books. Fannie can then acquire the new 3.5 percent mortgages, but it will still owe the original 4 percent rate on the funds it borrowed. In other words, it will now lose 0.5 percent on every 3.5 percent mortgage it holds with 4 percent funding. If interest rates stay low long enough, Fannie can lose a great deal of money, unless it can refinance its debt at the lower rate.

On the other hand, if interest rates rise, homeowners will not refinance their mortgages, but Fannie's 4 percent borrowings will eventually come due, and it will have to roll over its liabilities at a much higher rate. Now it may be paying 6 percent when its portfolio is only yielding 5.5 percent. Again it is losing money. A rising interest-rate environment like this is what caused the savings and loan industry to collapse in the 1980s. Most of Fannie and Freddie's funding is short term, which makes the companies vulnerable to a sharp and prolonged interest-rate rise. With Fannie and Freddie now holding approximately $1.5 trillion in mortgages and MBS, it is easy to see that this risk is enormous. To be sure, it is possible to hedge these risks by buying derivatives of one kind or another, but this entails its own risks, and also creates risks for the other large financial institutions that are counterparties to these instruments.

What the Senate Bill Does to Eliminate This Risk

S 190 addresses this problem by requiring that the GSEs reduce their portfolios to near zero—permitting them only to accumulate mortgages for purposes of securitization. This single and simple step eliminates most of the risk that Fannie and Freddie create for the taxpayers and the economy, but this does not mean that they will no longer be able to assist the housing market. This they can do through securitization, which is likely to have the same effect on interest rates as their purchasing and holding of mortgages. In the securitization process, Fannie and Freddie create trusts that hold a portfolio of mortgages. The trusts then sell mortgage-backed securities to investors—banks, pension funds, mutual funds, and individuals—and Fannie and Freddie guarantee that the holders of the MBS will receive a stream of interest and principal payments on the mortgages.

In these transactions, the GSEs are guaranteeing only that the homeowners whose mortgages are in the pools will make their payments in full and on time. They do not guarantee that homeowners will not refinance their mortgages when interest rates fall. In other words, they are taking only credit risk—not the far more substantial interest-rate risk that comes from borrowing funds to buy and hold a mortgage portfolio. In securitizations, the interest-rate risk is borne by the MBS investors, and thus is spread throughout the economy—and to foreign investors[25]—rather than concentrated in Fannie and Freddie alone. It is the concentration of risk in Fannie and Freddie that worries the administration and the Federal Reserve. If either of the two GSEs should suffer serious losses because of large fluctuations in interest rates—up or down, as noted above—it could require a taxpayer bailout or, even more serious, create adverse effects throughout the economy.

Thus, if Fannie and Freddie are required to perform their mission through securitization rather than through buying and holding mortgages, taxpayer and systemic risks will be minimized, and there will be no significant adverse effect

---

25. In defending their accumulation of portfolios, Fannie and Freddie have argued that foreign investors will not take interest-rate risk on MBS, and thus that it is necessary for the GSEs to borrow and accumulate portfolios in order to bring funds from abroad into the U.S. mortgage markets. However, a recent front-page *Wall Street Journal* article described heavy foreign demand for MBS: Ruth Simon, James R. Hagerty, and James T. Areddy, "Housing-Bubble Talk Doesn't Scare Off Foreigners: Global Investors Gobble Up Mortgage-Backed Securities, Keeping Prices Strong," *Wall Street Journal*, August 24, 2005.

on interest rates or the mortgage finance system. In fact, it is unlikely that home-buyers will notice any change at all in how the mortgage market functions. Of course, Fannie and Freddie and their supporters disagree with this analysis. But, as outlined in the May 2005 *Financial Services Outlook*,[26] their arguments do not seem well-founded.

Prospects for the Senate Bill

The conventional wisdom in Washington and on Wall Street is that the GSE reform legislation is going nowhere in this session of Congress. To be sure, both the House and Senate bills face formidable obstacles. In the House, the bill is stalled because of Republican unhappiness about its general fecklessness and the fact that it contains provisions for a fund that would enable the two compa-nies to reward their friends under the guise of assisting affordable housing. The problem is the opposite in the Senate. There, the bill is said to be stalled because it was so tough that it came out of committee on a party-line vote; without bipar-tisan support, some argue, there will be no action in the Senate.

The conventional wisdom, however, is wrong in this case; it has not taken into account the position of the administration, which since 2003 has shown itself to be relentless in seeking the toughest possible regulation of Fannie and Freddie. The bill that emerged from the Senate Banking Committee is exactly what the White House wants, and it is doubtful that this administration—and this particularly determined president—will let the opportunity pass. An admin-istration that has gained some measure of tort reform, approval of the Central American Free Trade Agreement, bankruptcy reform, and an energy bill—none of which received significant bipartisan support—is unlikely to shrink from pushing through Congress a bill that achieves one of its most important govern-ment reform priorities.

In an essay in 2004,[27] we reviewed the many ways in which the adminis-tration had, since 2003, subjected Fannie and Freddie to a barrage of adverse

---

26. Wallison, "Regulating Fannie Mae and Freddie Mac."

27. Peter J. Wallison, "The Case for Privatizing Fannie Mae and Freddie Mac Grows Stronger," *Financial Services Outlook,* May 2004, available at www.aei.org/publication 20395. (See p. 38 of this book.)

action; this pattern has continued in 2005. A few of the most significant actions, among many others, are the following:

- The White House refused to appoint the five directors that the president is authorized by law to appoint to the boards of Fannie and Freddie;

- The administration opposed as too weak legislation that was adopted by the Senate Banking Committee in 2004, and on the same grounds severely criticized the bill that emerged from the House Financial Services Committee in 2005;

- The Office of Management and Budget (OMB), in analyses that accompanied the president's 2005 and 2006 budgets, declared that Fannie and Freddie were undercapitalized and were failing to perform their affordable housing mission;

- The Office of Federal Housing Enterprise Oversight (OFHEO), the GSEs' regulator, proposed tough new corporate governance rules, began a forensic audit of Fannie, imposed a 30-percent capital increase on Fannie, and ultimately forced Fannie to restate its financial reports;

- The Department of Housing and Urban Development (HUD) adopted substantially stronger affordable-housing regulations, which will force Fannie and Freddie to devote more resources to a riskier, underserved market;

- The chairman of the President's Council of Economic Advisers declared in a widely reported speech that Fannie and Freddie posed risks to the economy and had to be reined in with stronger capital regulations;

- Treasury officials expressed willingness to discuss the removal of the GSEs' so-called Treasury line of credit, one of the GSEs' key links to the government;

- The Department of Justice determined that the Treasury had the authority under existing law to restrict the GSEs' issuance of debt, and thus to stop by administrative means alone the accumulation of portfolios of mortgages and MBS;

- In a series of economic analyses, the Fed—obviously in tune with the administration—declared that the subsidy the GSEs receives from the government was considerably higher than previously estimated by the Congressional Budget Office, and that the benefit that Fannie and Freddie pass on to the market is only 7 basis points, considerably lower than any earlier estimate and the GSEs' claims; and

- Fed chairman Alan Greenspan called for the privatization of Fannie and Freddie, or—failing that—a limitation on the size of their portfolios of mortgages and mortgage-backed securities.

It would be naïve to believe that, after all these efforts to clip the wings of the GSEs, to question their contribution to housing, and to express alarm about the risks they are creating, the White House will give up and walk away simply because the Republican House and Senate are having difficulty enacting new legislation. As powerful as the GSEs and their constituent groups may be, regulation of the GSEs is really only an inside-the-beltway issue. Few lawmakers will hear anything on the subject from actual voters. A strong case can be made— and is being made regularly by economists in and out of government[28]—that home buyers and sellers will not see any difference in their mortgage rates if Fannie and Freddie are compelled to carry on their business through securitization rather than through the accumulation of mortgages and MBS. Lawmakers, in other words, need not fear retribution from back home if they vote to

---

28. See, for example, Dwight M. Jaffee, "On Limiting the Retained Mortgage Portfolios of Fannie Mae and Freddie Mac" (Working Paper 294, Fisher Center for Real Estate and Urban Economics, University of California, Berkeley, June 30, 2005), available at http://repositories.cdlib.org/cgi/viewcontent.cgi?article=1031&context=iber/fcreue (the same paper was presented at an AEI conference, "Should Fannie Mae's and Freddie Mac's Mortgage and MBS Portfolios Be Capped, Reduced, or Eliminated," April 26, 2005); Andreas Lehnert, Wayne Passmore, Shane M. Sherlund, "GSEs, Mortgage Rates, and Secondary Market Activities," June 7, 2005; Senate Committee on Banking, Housing, and Urban Affairs, *Statement of Alan Greenspan*, 108th Congress, 1st session, February 24, 2004, 9–10 available at http://banking.senate.gov/index.cfm?Fuseaction=Hearings.Detail&HearingID=92, as of May 12, 2005; Task Force on Housing and Infrastructure, House Committee on the Budget, *Statement of Barbara Miles: Implications of the Debt Held by Housing Related Government Sponsored Enterprises*, 106th Congress, 2nd session, July 25, 2000, available at http://financialservices.house.gov/banking/91200crs.pdf.

restrict the GSEs' portfolios. And while they will hear from the realtors and the homebuilders, they will get more intense pressure from the White House if they attempt to shrink from their responsibilities. They also know that if financial trouble at the GSEs actually does cause loss for the taxpayers and problems for the economy in general—which is what the administration and the Fed fear— they will face blistering criticism from their constituents.

White House pressure to get legislation that curbs the size and risk of these portfolios is especially likely in light of the bond market's remarkable reaction to the recent troubles of the GSEs. Although neither company has been able to publish current audited financial statements—Fannie having recently reported that it will not be ready to meet this obligation until 2006 at the earliest—the bond market has been treating both companies as though they present no sig- nificant default risk. This is even true of their so-called subordinated debt, which was initially hailed as a market-based mechanism that would reveal through a growing spread over treasuries when the GSEs' financial condition was weak- ening. However, figure 1, which shows the spread over treasuries for Fannie's senior and subordinated debt, demonstrates clearly that the market is not pric- ing in any significant default risk for either security. It is even more remarkable that the spreads over treasuries for the subordinated debt continued to decline after the rating agencies announced that they would put the securities on watch for a possible downgrade. Indeed, in the past year, despite all Fannie's troubles, the spread of its debt over treasuries has narrowed considerably. Meanwhile, as shown in figure 2, the stock market has sharply discounted lower earnings for Fannie, making clear that the company's financial troubles are well-recognized. It must be wholly unprecedented in the capital markets for the spread of a com- pany's subordinated debt over treasuries to fall even as its earnings prospects also decline, and if there were ever further evidence needed that the GSEs are deemed to be government-backed, this is it.

The necessary conclusion to draw from these data is that if Congress wants to reduce the government's liability in the case of a failure of Fannie and Fred- die, tougher regulation alone is not going to do it. Higher capital levels, closer scrutiny, and further restrictions on their business may reduce their profitability, but those measures will only convince the market that the two companies are even more tightly tied in to the government and will never be allowed to fail. In the end, then, those steps are self-defeating because they fail to eliminate the source of the risks that the GSEs create. Accordingly, the only way to reduce the

FIGURE 1

TEN-YEAR FANNIE MAE SUBORDINATED DEBT MINUS TEN-YEAR TREASURY AND TEN-YEAR FANNIE MAE BENCHMARK NOTE MINUS TEN-YEAR TREASURY

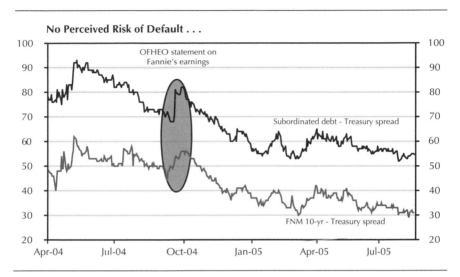

SOURCE: *Morning Political Report,* International Strategy & Investment, August 19, 2005.

FIGURE 2

FANNIE MAE STOCK PERFORMANCE

SOURCE: *Morning Political Report,* International Strategy & Investment, August 19, 2005.

systemic risk for taxpayers that is inherent in the GSEs' portfolios is substantially to reduce or eliminate the portfolios themselves.

The fact that no action has occurred thus far in either the House or Senate is not a sign that the legislation is in trouble. There are several ongoing government investigations of Fannie—by OFHEO, by the Justice Department, and by the Securities and Exchange Commission—and an internal investigation by an independent law firm retained by the Fannie board. Any of these could report dramatic new disclosures about Fannie's past behavior, and the repeated deferrals of the independent law firm's report suggest that serious issues have been encountered. The latest statement from the leader of that investigation, former senator Warren Rudman, is that the report for the Fannie board will not be completed until the late fall. Since an adverse report could give substantial new impetus to legislation, it only makes sense for the Senate and House leadership to await the outcome of one or more of these investigations before bringing legislation to the floor.

Nor is it reasonable to believe that Fannie and Freddie, no matter their political muscle, can avoid coming to terms with legislation—and the portfolio issue—at some point in the future. After the administration and the Fed have declared that the GSEs' portfolios are a dangerous source of taxpayer and systemic risk, the administration can hardly do nothing if Congress fails to act. In this respect, the administration always has a card to play—it can always use the Treasury's authority to restrict the GSEs' issuance of debt. The GSEs must realize this and must see that the only effective way to prevent the use of this authority in a wholesale manner is to reach a legislative compromise of some kind. Simply opposing any further action on legislation is a losing strategy. It is likely therefore that at some time in 2006 legislation will pass the House and Senate and the differences between the two bills will be considered in conference. Then the hard bargaining will begin, but in the end—given the administration's determination on this issue—it is highly likely that legislation limiting or eliminating the GSEs' portfolios will be sent to the president's desk.

"Moral Hazard on Steroids: The OFHEO Report Shows that Regulation Cannot Protect U.S. Taxpayers"

Originally published July 2006

No one should be surprised that the Office of Federal Housing Enterprise Oversight (OFHEO) found substantial risk-taking as well as accounting fraud at Fannie Mae. The combination of government backing and the opportunity for private profit invites both. Fannie's supporters argue that stronger regulation is enough to protect the taxpayers and the economy, but this ignores the unique characteristics of government sponsored enterprises (GSEs) as well as the inability of OFHEO itself to detect in advance the poor controls and false accounting at both Fannie Mae and Freddie Mac. Accordingly, the only sure way to eliminate the risk is to reduce the kinds of risky activities in which government-backed management can engage.

Many in Washington expressed surprise at the revelations in the May 2006 special OFHEO report on Fannie Mae. The report disclosed that the company had not only manipulated its financial statements, but also had weak internal controls, inadequate accounting and computer systems, and had taken substantial business risks in order to improve its profitability and pay unearned bonuses to its management.[29] But surprise was unwarranted; it is axiomatic that profit-making companies, when offered a subsidy in the form of government backing, will exploit the opportunity to its limit. Indeed, it can be argued that a board of directors and management of a shareholder-owned company have a fiduciary obligation to do so. Nor should it have been a surprise that OFHEO has now found Fannie Mae to be an entirely different company from the one on which it reported so favorably during the very years covered by the report. Regulation is

---

29. Office of Federal Housing Enterprise Oversight (OHFEO), *Report of the Special Examination of Fannie Mae* (Washington, D.C., May 2006), available at www.ofheo.gov/media/pdf/FNMSPECIALEXAM.PDF.

an inherently weak method of controlling risk-taking, especially when government backing—such as that enjoyed by the GSEs—encourages both risk-taking and weak controls.

The Absence of Market Discipline—and Its Consequences

One of the advantages of government support is that a government-backed management is permitted to take risks that are forbidden to others. This is true because government backing eliminates the restrictions—known as market discipline—imposed by wary creditors. Ordinary financial institutions such as banks borrow their raw material—money—and lend it to others. If creditors perceive that the risk of lending to a bank or other institution is rising, they will demand a higher rate of interest for any loan, increasing the institution's borrowing costs. Eventually, if the risk is not controlled, the institution will not be able to borrow at all, and thus will be prevented from expanding its operations. In this way, market discipline supplements bank regulation by signaling to regulators that there is something amiss, and limiting excessive risk. When large U.S. banks were deemed financially weak during the debt crisis involving Mexico, Brazil, and Argentina in the 1980s, the rates they had to pay for money rose substantially, and in some cases they were unable to access the credit markets at all without offering substantial collateral. Investors perceived a risk that these banks would default. Although bank deposits up to $100,000 are nominally insured by the Federal Deposit Insurance Corporation (FDIC), deposits are only a small proportion of the obligations of large banks; their other debt, consisting of commercial paper and longer term notes, is not seen as backed by the federal government—so market discipline continues to work to some degree, even for large banks.

But Fannie and Freddie are different from banks in one important way: despite the fact that their securities explicitly state that they are not backed by the federal government, their government charter and mission—plus the government's past behavior—have persuaded investors that neither company will be allowed to default. Thus, in a very practical sense, all their debt obligations—not just some limited amount corresponding to a bank's deposits—are seen by U.S. and foreign investors as nearly risk-free, and therefore are not subject to market discipline. In effect, they are given a free pass to take risk. The name for this phenomenon—in which government backing reduces market discipline—is moral hazard, and the GSEs represent moral hazard on steroids.

If there was ever any doubt about this, it has been erased since 2003, when first Freddie and then Fannie were forced to restate their financial reports because of false accounting and gross manipulation of their financial results. In the succeeding years, neither company has been able to file financial reports with the Securities and Exchange Commission or submit them to their shareholders or lenders. For ordinary corporations and banks, this would long ago have precipitated a plunge into bankruptcy—but not Fannie and Freddie. They have continued to operate normally, despite the fact that no one knows their true financial condition, and this has revealed a remarkable phenomenon. Because of their perceived government backing, the GSEs pay interest at a rate slightly higher than that of the U.S. Treasury. The difference between what they pay and what the Treasury pays is known as the "spread," and the width of the spread signals the degree of risk that the market sees in holding GSE debt. Figure 1 shows that after OFHEO reported in October 2004 that Fannie had falsified its financial statements, the spread of Fannie's debt over the Treasury's actually narrowed. In other words, Fannie's debt strengthened, rather than weakened, despite the financial scandals that then surrounded the company. And that was true not only of Fannie's senior debt; it was also true of its subordinated debt, which was originally created to provide an equity-like signal of the company's financial condition. But it now appears that Fannie's subordinated debt is also considered government-backed, and is therefore not subject to significant risk of default. In other words, investors have not lost any confidence in eventually getting paid by Fannie and Freddie, even though they can have no idea whether the two companies can repay their debts.

This privileged position was not lost on the management of Fannie Mae. The OFHEO report recounts in detail the sorry state of Fannie's risk controls, internal controls, staff competence, accounting systems, computer systems, compliance with accounting requirements, and corporate governance. A central element of the report is that Fannie and its management consistently misled investors, Congress, and the public about both its financial position and the risks it was taking. Thus, OFHEO noted in the special report: "Fannie was not 'one of the lowest risk financial institutions in the world' but was exposed to significant interest rate risk and quite large operational and reputational risks."[30] Indeed, Fannie's weakness in basic corporate and accounting controls was so serious that the

---

30. Ibid., 47.

FIGURE 1

**TEN-YEAR FANNIE MAE SUBORDINATED DEBT MINUS TEN-YEAR TREASURY AND
TEN-YEAR FANNIE MAE BENCHMARK NOTE MINUS TEN-YEAR TREASURY**

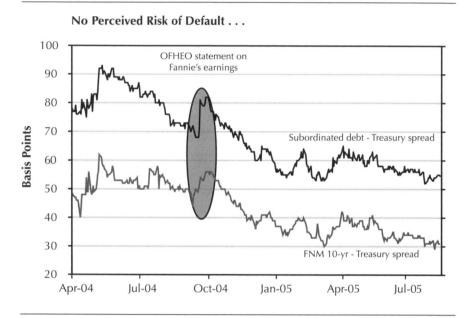

No Perceived Risk of Default . . .

SOURCE: *Morning Political Report,* International Strategy & Investment, August 19, 2005.

company has thus far been required to spend approximately $800 million on repairs of these systems, and both Fannie and Freddie (which has been at the repair process for three years) are said by the new director of OFHEO still to be years from adequacy.[31]

The fact that both Fannie and Freddie have had similar internal control and accounting problems makes it reasonable to assume that there is a similar cause, and that this cause can be found in their unique position as GSEs—privately-owned companies that are not subject to market discipline. They were not required to take the steps that all other companies must take to maintain their

---

31. James B. Lockhart III, Senate Committee on Banking, Housing, and Urban Affairs, *The OFHEO Report of the Special Examination of Fannie Mae,* 109th Cong., 2nd sess., June 15, 2006.

good credit standing, and so they did not take these steps. As long as the GSEs exist, they will always exhibit this tendency. Why indeed should any management spend money on all of the systems and controls that market discipline demands if they do not need these elements to persuade the market to lend to them?

Why Regulation Cannot Cut It

This presents a policy problem that is not just different in degree, but different in kind from the usual difficulties of supervising financial institutions. Solutions that might work for other kinds of financial firms and even banks will not work for the GSEs. It is clear that the capital markets cannot be induced to believe that the government will allow either Fannie or Freddie to fail. If investors will not lose confidence in the GSEs when neither of them can keep or publish accurate accounts, it is obvious that the capital markets will never believe the Treasury's traditional vow that Fannie and Freddie will not be bailed out if they encounter financial difficulty. Thus, without some kind of extraordinary action, the inducement to risk-taking by the managements of both companies will remain intact.

When the problems at the GSEs first came to light, however, the first instinct in Congress was not extraordinary at all: it was the reflexive effort to increase the degree and restrictiveness of regulation without questioning whether it is really a solution to the problem at hand. Thus, in the wake of the problems at Fannie and Freddie, the call in Congress was to create a new regulator with "world class" powers equivalent to those of a bank regulator.

The first problem with this idea was that, as Alan Greenspan pointed out, tighter regulation only increases the tendency of the markets to believe that Fannie and Freddie are wards of the government: "World-class regulation, by itself," said Greenspan, "may not be sufficient and indeed . . . may even worsen the situation if market participants infer from such regulation that the government is all the more likely to back GSE debt."[32] In addition, as noted above, bank regulators are assisted, at least to some degree, by the existence of market discipline, and the new GSE regulator will not have this vital support. So if it

---

32. Alan Greenspan, Senate Committee on Banking, Housing, and Urban Affairs, *Proposals for Improving the Regulation of the Housing Government Sponsored Enterprises,* 108th Cong., 2nd sess., February 24, 2004, available at www.federalreserve.gov/boarddocs/testimony/2004/20040224/default.htm.

were the intention of Congress to give the new regulator as much authority as a bank regulator wields, that would not have been enough. Given the complacent attitude of the capital markets, the new regulator would need more authority than a bank regulator in order to deal effectively with risk-taking by Fannie and Freddie. But the bill ultimately adopted by the House of Representatives in 2005 was deficient in this respect, as in many others. It did not even provide the new GSE regulator with all of the authority of bank regulators.[33]

Ultimately, however, there is this question: even if the new regulator were given extraordinary powers, beyond those of a bank regulator, would they be enough to protect the taxpayers or the economy against the incentives and opportunities for risk-taking and weak controls that government backing makes available to the GSEs' managements? The answer here appears to be no. Although there has been a great deal of talk about the weakness of OFHEO's authority, in the major respects necessary to prevent the risk-taking, financial manipulation, and false accounting at Fannie and Freddie, OFHEO has always possessed the powers necessary to do the job. Under its authority today, without any enhancement, it has the same examination authority as a bank regulator, complete access to the books, records, staff, and management of both GSEs, the power to request and review documents and internal memoranda, and subpoena power to back up its requests.[34] Indeed, the special OFHEO report itself, citing an earlier agency statement, notes that "OFHEO possesses supervisory responsibilities and powers 'essentially similar to those of Federal bank regulatory agencies.'"[35]

As much as Congress might wish it were not so, the problem was not and is not authority, but knowing what questions to ask. True, OFHEO has only limited cease-and-desist authority, and does not have the ability to put either of the GSEs into receivership, but neither of these customary bank powers would have been invoked by OFHEO against either Fannie or Freddie, simply because the agency lacked the necessary knowledge about what Fannie and Freddie were actually doing.

---

33. Peter J. Wallison and Thomas H. Stanton, *H.R. 1461: A GSE 'Reform' That Is Worse Than Current Law* (Washington, D.C.: AEI, June 17, 2005), available at www.aei. org/publication22705/.

34. The Federal Housing Enterprise Financial Safety and Soundness Act of 1992, *U.S. Code 12* (1992), chapter 46, available at http://uscode.house.gov/download/pls/12C46.txt.

35. OFHEO, *Report of the Special Examination of Fannie Mae*, 21.

Lack of knowledge—what is called actionable intelligence in warfare—is the Achilles' heel of regulation, and even if OFHEO had had extraordinary powers to intervene in the decision-making processes of Fannie and Freddie, it would not have been able to exercise that authority without the knowledge that excessive risk-taking or financial fraud was going on. The billions of dollars lost by Fannie Mae because of its excessive risk-taking and use of false accounting to hide its losses occurred while OFHEO was performing all the usual functions of a regulator—reviewing books and records, reading minutes of meetings, analyzing financial results, and interviewing employees. In its special report, OFHEO declared with appropriate rectitude that the company misled investors, Congress, and the public generally by falsely claiming that it was one of the best-run and least risky companies in the world. But if this was indeed false, why was OFHEO—exercising the usual authorities of bank supervisors—unable to discover any of these things in prior examinations? Thus, in a director's statement accompanying the agency's regular Report to Congress in 2002, Director Armando Falcon noted that in its supervision of the GSEs during the preceding year, OFHEO had found nothing amiss: "I am also pleased to report that OFHEO has found both Fannie Mae and Freddie Mac to be well-capitalized and operating in a safe and sound manner."[36] The similar message accompanying the 2003 report, in light of later events, rises to parody: "The Enterprises have remained safe and sound through another year of exceptional growth in the housing sector of our economy. In a year when more and more Americans have become homeowners, the public can take comfort in knowing that OFHEO is on the job, doing its part to ensure the strength and vitality of the nation's housing finance system."[37] The sad fact is that OFHEO was "on the job," but its assignment was beyond the capacity of any financial regulator or supervisor.

OFHEO's failure, unfortunately, is not something that can be cured by legislation; it is the result of the same deficiency shared by all regulators, and the reason why regulation should not be treated as a panacea. Risk-taking and fraud originate in the decisions of top management, in meetings to which no regulator

---

36. Office of Federal Housing Enterprise Oversight, "Director's Message," Report to Congress, June 15, 2002, available at www.ofheo.gov/Media/Archive/reports/ar61402.pdf.

37. Office of Federal Housing Enterprise Oversight, "Director's Message," Report to Congress, June 15, 2003, available at www.ofheo.gov/media/pdf/WEBsiteOFHEOREPto Congress03.pdf.

and few ordinary employees are ever privy. Were it not for the unusual events, outlined below, which put the OFHEO watchdog onto the scent, it is virtually certain that both Fannie and Freddie would still be manipulating their accounts and misleading investors, the public, Congress, and OFHEO itself.

It all goes back to Enron and WorldCom, and the fact that the auditor of both companies, Arthur Andersen, was in very bad odor after their collapse in 2002. It happened that Andersen was also the auditor for Freddie Mac, and in what might be called an act of caution, Freddie's board fired Andersen and engaged new auditors. In taking over the Freddie account, the new auditors discovered some troubling aspects of the company's accounting, which, in turn, moved the board to hire an independent counsel to look into the matter. The independent counsel found not only accounting problems, but also an apparent management cover-up, which precipitated the dismissal of the company's top three officers.

This event apparently came as a complete surprise to OFHEO, which had only days before released the Report to Congress cited above, in which it said that "the public can take comfort in knowing that OFHEO is on the job." The agency clearly had not been aware of the seriousness of the accounting problems at Freddie or perhaps even the existence of the independent counsel's investigation of the company. In its 2003 report, OFHEO dutifully reported only what it had apparently been told by Freddie's management—that there was a technical question of accounting interpretation, and that Freddie's management was "taking the appropriate action." Humiliated by the public disclosure of its cluelessness—the *Wall Street Journal* reported that "no one seemed more surprised [by the dismissal of Freddie's top officers] than the company's regulator"—OFHEO became far more aggressive toward both GSEs, eventually requesting and receiving from Congress a supplemental appropriation of $7.5 million to do a "forensic audit" of Fannie. The audit found evidence of false accounting. And the rest, as they say, is history.

The clear lesson here is that regulation has inherent limitations—and its first and most important limitation is what regulators and supervisors can actually know about the financial institutions they oversee. For this reason, regulation is highly overrated as a means of controlling risk. Risk is created at the top of an organization by management policies, in meetings that the regulators do not and never will be able to attend. The regulators, instead, are down at the grass roots, seeing the numbers but without understanding their meaning or the policies behind them. Like all financial supervisors, OFHEO was unable to obtain the essential knowledge about management's intent that was inevitably denied to it. Accordingly, placing confidence entirely in regulation as a protection for the taxpayers would be, in the end, an imprudent action for Congress, and even more so where the regulator's efforts are not supplemented by market discipline.

Reducing Risk by Eliminating Risky Activities

So if more and better regulation alone is not able to prevent a loss to the taxpayers and systemic risk to the economy, what will? The only sensible course is to reduce the risks that Fannie and Freddie are able to take. Fortunately, this is easy to do. The principal risk of the GSEs is what is known as interest rate risk, and comes from the fact that they have borrowed over a trillion dollars in order to buy and hold a portfolio of mortgages of roughly the same size. If interest rates rise or fall sharply, they can suffer huge losses. The bill passed almost a year ago by the Senate Banking Committee recognizes this fact and attempts to reduce the GSEs' retained portfolio to a minimum.[38]

The key and most significant element of the Senate bill would do just this. The reason is simple: carrying a portfolio of mortgages creates substantial interest rate risk—the same risk that destroyed the savings and loans a generation ago. Because of their government backing, the GSEs have the opportunity to make hefty profits from borrowing at a low rate of interest—only slightly more than the Treasury pays—and buying mortgages and MBS that pay considerably more. For this reason, over the last twenty-five years, the GSEs' portfolios of mortgages and MBS have increased from $60 billion to almost $1.5 trillion.[39] But the business of borrowing at low rates and buying higher yielding mortgages has its perils—principally interest rate risk.

A peculiar characteristic of interest rate risk is that it exists whether interest rates rise or fall. Two examples will show why this is true. Assume that a GSE borrows $1 million at 4 percent to buy a portfolio of mortgages that yields 5 percent. As long as it holds this portfolio, the GSE pockets the difference between

---

38. *Federal Housing Enterprise Regulatory Reform Act of 2005,* 109th Cong., 1st sess., S. 190, July 22, 2005, available at http://banking.senate.gov/_files/CommitteePrint.pdf.

39. Robert A. Eisenbeis, W. Scott Frame, and Larry D. Wall, "An Analysis of the Systemic Risks Posed by Fannie Mae and Freddie Mac and an Evaluation of the Policy Options for Reducing Those Risks" (working paper 2006-2, Federal Reserve Bank of Atlanta, April 2006), 55, available at www.frbatlanta.org/filelegacydocs/wp0602.pdf.

what it has to pay to its lenders (4 percent) and what it is receiving from the mortgages it is holding (5 percent). (This is only a simplified example; in reality, the GSEs' profits from holding mortgages and MBS are considerably higher. In a paper delivered at an AEI conference in 2004, Professor Dwight Jaffee of Berkeley estimated the average 2003 spread as 172 basis points for Fannie and 186 for Freddie.[40]) However, if interest rates fall to, say, 3 percent, many homeowners will refinance their 5 percent mortgages. The GSE will, of course, get the cash from this refinancing, but the mortgages it will be able to buy with this cash will then only pay 3 percent. Its profitable situation is now reversed; it is paying 4 percent to hold mortgages that are yielding 3 percent, and losing money on every one. That is exactly what OFHEO found had happened at Fannie: "Fannie Mae consistently took a significant amount of interest rate risk and, when interest rates fell in recent years, incurred billions of dollars in economic loss."[41]

But the GSEs can also lose if interest rates rise. Using the same hypothetical set of facts, what happens if interest rates rise to 6 percent? In that case, homeowners will hold onto their 5 percent mortgages, since refinancing will not pay, and the GSE has to worry about what it will do when its loans mature. If the loans are short-term, and about half of all GSE borrowings are contracted for a year or less, the GSE will be compelled to refinance its initial borrowing at 6 percent, and will again suffer a loss as it pays 6 percent to carry a mortgage portfolio that continues to pay only 5 percent. Thus, if its borrowings are short-term, a GSE will suffer a financial loss if interest rates rise, just as it will suffer a loss if interest rates decline while its liabilities are long-term.

To be sure, interest rate risk can be hedged—the risk can be shared with or transferred to others through various kinds of derivatives such as interest rate swaps. But swaps and other hedges are expensive, and to achieve higher levels of profitability, a GSE will not completely hedge its risk. In its report, OFHEO complained that in trying to hit the profit numbers that would have assured their bonuses, Fannie's management did not take the prudent steps necessary to hedge its interest rate risks. The report states: "During the period covered by this report, Fannie Mae's strategy was to match between 50 and 60 percent of the

---

40. Dwight Jaffee, "The Effects of Limiting the Retained Mortgage Portfolios of Fannie Mae and Freddie Mac" (speech, AEI, Washington, D.C., April 26, 2005), 5, available at www.aei.org/event1041.

41. OFHEO, *Report of the Special Examination of Fannie Mae*, 4.

[interest rate risk] of its mortgage assets."[42] Even this understates the degree of risk that Fannie was assuming. In his 2005 paper, Professor Jaffee notes that the GSEs hedge only the small, foreseeable interest rate risks, and that their hedging strategy "transfers the risk of unexpected, large, and future rate changes onto the U.S. Treasury based on the implicit guarantee . . . imposing on U.S. taxpayers the large and distant risks that would eventually require a U.S. Treasury bailout."[43] He concludes: "The firms are able to operate in this manner only because the purchasers of their agency debt and their MBS show little concern for the firms' riskiness, protected as they are by the implicit Treasury guarantee."[44] Moral hazard, again, flowing from the absence of market discipline.

There is no reason why Fannie and Freddie should be permitted to buy and hold large portfolios of mortgages. No less an authority than Alan Greenspan has testified to Congress that the portfolios seem to have no purpose other than to increase the earnings of the two companies.[45] As such, it is a classic example of privatizing profits while socializing risk and loss. Fannie and Freddie, in addition to their shareholders and managements, will profit from holding these portfolios, but if the risks they take cause them to suffer serious losses, the taxpayers will pick up the tab.

It is important to recognize that eliminating or severely restricting the size of their portfolios will not reduce the role of the GSEs in providing whatever assistance they are thought to give to the housing market. Indeed, most of what the GSEs do for the housing market today is done through what is known as securitization. In this process, Fannie and Freddie purchase mortgages from banks and other lenders and sell interests in these mortgages to investors. In this case, investors and not the GSEs take the interest rate risk. Because this process involves the purchase of mortgages by the GSEs, it adds the same amount of liquidity to the mortgage market as the GSEs' purchasing and holding mortgages

---

42. Ibid., 46.

43. Dwight Jaffee, "Effects of Limiting the Retained Mortgage Portfolios," 12.

44. Ibid.

45. "We have been unable to find any purpose for the huge balance sheets of the GSEs, other than profit creation through the exploitation of the market-granted subsidy." Alan Greenspan, Senate Committee on Banking, Housing, and Urban Affairs, *Reform of the Government-Sponsored Enterprises,* 109th Cong., 1st sess., April 6, 2005, available at www.federalreserve.gov/BoardDocs/Testimony/2005/20050406/default.htm.

in their portfolios—but with substantially less risk to them, to the taxpayers, and to the economy.

So the Senate Banking Committee has it right. By providing in its reform legislation for limiting the size of the GSEs' portfolios, it has adopted the one sure way to eliminate the threat that risk-taking by the GSEs poses to the taxpayers and the economy.

AEI staff assistant Daniel Geary and AEI editorial assistant Nicole Passan worked with Mr. Wallison to edit and produce this Financial Services Outlook.

"Fannie and Freddie by Twilight"

Originally published August 2008

Having now become explicitly government-backed entities, Fannie Mae and Freddie Mac (and their supporters in Congress) can no longer argue that they do not pose a risk to taxpayers. It is not politically feasible for the government to back private companies when their shareholders and managements keep the profits but the taxpayers cover the losses. Thus, even if they escape their current precarious financial straits, Fannie and Freddie are now operating in a kind of twilight before they will eventually have to be nationalized, privatized, or liquidated. In addition, the recent attention to covered bonds as a way to finance mortgages suggests that, in the future, Fannie and Freddie's traditional business—buying and holding or securitizing mortgages—will no longer be essential to U.S. housing finance. An analysis of the available options for policymakers suggests that the best course—from the standpoint of taxpayers—is not to keep Fannie and Freddie alive through the injection of government funds but to allow them to go into receivership. A receiver can continue their operations in the secondary mortgage market and—using the Treasury line of credit recently authorized by Congress—meet their senior debt and guarantee obligations as they come due. A decision to nationalize, privatize, or liquidate them can be made at a later time and can be implemented more simply and efficiently through a receivership than if the companies are helped to survive through government recapitalization.

It took a hair-raising crisis in the housing and international capital markets, but for Fannie and Freddie, the wondrously generous world of Washington— the world they have dominated for so many years with threats, intimidation, and sheer financial and political muscle—is at last coming to an end. Both companies are hovering near insolvency. Whether they can avoid eventual receivership will depend on how much further housing values fall. But even if they are lucky enough to survive this current crisis, their halcyon days will never return. This is not because Congress has learned any kind of lesson. Without question, the preferred position in Congress, especially on the Democratic side of the aisle, will be to reconstitute Fannie and Freddie as newly recapitalized government-sponsored enterprises (GSEs).

But this will not fly politically. The world was irretrievably changed by the Housing and Economic Recovery Act of 2008 (HERA) signed by President Bush on July 30, 2008. The act, in effect, authorized the bailout of the companies by giving the secretary of the treasury the authority to make unlimited loans to, and equity investments in, both GSEs. Thus, HERA resolved once and for all whether Fannie and Freddie were actually backed by the U.S. government; it provided the explicit backing that investors always believed would ultimately be there and that the enterprises themselves vigorously denied. But now that they are explicitly backed by the U.S. government, the GSEs can no longer claim that they represent no risk to taxpayers. As explicitly government-backed entities, they cannot deny the obvious: that their profits will go to their managements and shareholders while their losses will be picked up by taxpayers. This fact is crucial to their future.

The privatization of profit and the socialization of risk inherent in this new arrangement is politically untenable, even though it may take some time for Congress to see the substantial difference between their former status as merely government-sponsored and their new status as explicitly government-backed. Inevitably, however, the light will dawn and their form will have to be changed. The question, then, comes down to whether Fannie and Freddie will, in the future, become government agencies, private companies, or just unpleasant memories.

Moreover, there are strong indications that a far more efficient and sensible mechanism for financing home mortgages in the United States is about to be born. In mid-July, the Federal Deposit Insurance Corporation (FDIC) issued a final policy statement on how it would treat covered bonds in the event of a bank's failure,[46] and at the end of July, the Treasury issued a long statement on best practices for covered bonds.[47] In a covered bond transaction, mortgages remain on the books of the bank or other depository institution but serve as

---

46. Federal Deposit Insurance Corporation (FDIC), "Covered Bond Policy Statement," July 15, 2008, available at www.fdic.gov/ news/news/press/2008/pr08060a.html (accessed August 25, 2008).

47. Department of the Treasury, *Best Practices for Residential Covered Bonds* (Washington, DC: Department of the Treasury, July 2008), available at www.treas.gov/press/releases/reports/USCoveredBondBestPractices.pdf (accessed August 25, 2008).

collateral for bonds issued to finance the acquisition of the mortgages. If the mortgages in the covered bond pool default, the bank that established the pool has an obligation to replace the assets with performing mortgages that will continue to serve as collateral for the outstanding bonds.

In other words, this structure requires lending banks to retain an interest in the quality of the mortgages they make and addresses the problem that no one in the securitization process has a continuing interest in sound underwriting after the mortgages are sold to Fannie and Freddie. Trillions of dollars in covered bonds have been issued in Europe over many years without any substantial losses. There are, of course, issues associated with the widespread use of covered bonds in the United States—mostly in balancing the interests of the FDIC and bank depositors in gaining access to the assets of a failed bank—but if these can be balanced with the need for a strong residential finance system, covered bonds could, over time, make the Fannie and Freddie business model obsolete. This is one more indication that Fannie and Freddie, both as GSEs and as essential elements of the U.S. residential finance market, are on their way out.

The Gathering Storm

It is axiomatic that Congress only acts in a crisis, and this crisis was so serious that Congress was compelled to do three important things that under ordinary circumstances it would never have done: it adopted legislation, HERA, that significantly strengthened the regulation of Fannie Mae and Freddie Mac; it authorized the appointment of a receiver to take over either company if it becomes "critically undercapitalized"; and it gave the Treasury Department a blank check, limited only in time and by the U.S. debt limit, to make loans or equity investments in both companies. With its new powers, the regulator should be able to reduce the size of the GSEs and prepare them for one of the three fates: liquidation, privatization, or nationalization.

It need not have been this way. Congress was warned over two decades, by both Democratic and Republican administrations, about the dangers presented by Fannie and Freddie. But Congress, under both Democratic and Republican control, did nothing. The same process is now unfolding with respect to Social Security, Medicare, energy, securities class actions, and probably a dozen other long-term problems that Congress is seemingly unable to address. It makes you wonder why 98 percent of them are reelected.

Not that this and previous administrations are blameless. Although at their higher reaches—usually in the Treasury—they recognized the dangers, their bank regulatory arms continued to allow banks to invest in Fannie and Freddie securities without the percentage limitations normally applied to investments in privately owned business corporations. The regulators obviously believed that the government would eventually stand behind Fannie and Freddie and thus permitted U.S. banks to load up on Fannie and Freddie debt in preference to U.S. government securities. Now, thousands of banks hold more than their total Tier 1 capital in the form of Fannie and Freddie debt. A 2004 FDIC report showed that the holdings of GSE-related securities by commercial banks and savings associations aggregated more than 11 percent of the total assets of these institutions and more than 150 percent of their combined Tier 1 capital.[48] Holding Fannie and Freddie debt gave the banks some extra earnings over what they would receive from Treasuries, but it also sent signals to the capital markets that the government saw Fannie and Freddie as virtually risk-free. And when the prospect arose a few weeks ago that Fannie and Freddie debt might decline in value, Uncle Sam had to step in to prevent thousands of U.S. banks from becoming insolvent because of their GSE investments.

In any event, the Fannie and Freddie crisis has now arrived, and, in order to avert a disaster in the housing and financial markets, the United States government has been forced to put its credit behind these two ill-conceived and badly managed institutions. During the past month, as the dimensions of the problem have become clear, sensible people have actually wondered whether the credit of the United States might actually be impaired by the obligations it might be required to assume on Fannie and Freddie's behalf. That idea, previously unthinkable, is still highly unlikely, but what is clear is that the size of the taxpayers' losses will grow as housing prices continue to decline. There is no telling how deep into insolvency Fannie and Freddie might sink, and the further down they go, the more potential losses they will impose on the government and ultimately the taxpayers.

This, of course, is all water over the dam. The damage—allowing two privately owned companies to grow so large that they become both wards of the government and threats to the financial system—has been done. Now the only

---

48. FDIC, "Assessing the Banking Industry's Exposure to an Implicit Government Guarantee of GSEs," March 1, 2004, revised April 14, 2004, available at www.fdic.gov/bank/analytical/fyi/2004/030104fyi.html (accessed August 25, 2008).

relevant question is how we get out of this mess with minimal cost to taxpayers. In the end, the options available to the Treasury Department and the new GSE regulator, the Federal Housing Finance Agency (FHFA), are both unpleasant and few. They are outlined below.

Option 1: Muddling Through

This is not so much an option as a hope—one that seems increasingly distant as the housing market continues to decline and the GSEs continue to register losses. Nevertheless, under this scenario, the residential mortgage market stabilizes in a few months, Fannie and Freddie succeed in raising a few billion dollars in additional equity capital, and they survive the subprime meltdown. What happens then? As suggested above, it is not possible for Fannie and Freddie to continue as GSEs. There is no precedent for the U.S. government to back the obligations of private, shareholder-owned companies. The closest analogy is the FDIC's administration of the deposit insurance system, but this is inapposite for two reasons. First, taxpayers are not at risk in the deposit insurance system. The FDIC administers the program, but since the Federal Deposit Insurance Corporation Improvement Act of 1991, the FDIC has had the power to tax all insured banks in order to recover its losses from bailing out the depositors of any failed bank. Second, the deposit insurance system only covers deposits up to $100,000, and thus the total obligations of the FDIC (and the banking system that backs it) are substantially less than the total deposits in any single bank or in the banking system as a whole. However, the senior debt of the GSEs, which currently amounts to somewhat more than $5 trillion, is backed by taxpayers without limit. This does not mean that the losses will be anywhere near $5 trillion, but it does mean that the losses are potentially very large.

Accordingly, at some point, Congress—as much as it would like to let the whole issue drop and go back to business as usual—will have to address the future of Fannie and Freddie. In that event, if Fannie and Freddie survive, there will be two realistic choices: nationalization or privatization. If they do not survive and have to be taken over by a receiver, liquidation becomes an additional option.

Option 2: Assisted Survival

There has been a lot of speculation recently that Treasury Secretary Henry M. Paulson might use his new HERA authority to recapitalize Fannie and Freddie.

This seems highly unlikely. Most of this speculation assumes that the Trea-sury's investment will wipe out the existing shareholders or allow Paulson to take control of the companies, but he does not have the power to do either. HERA only authorizes the secretary to offer an equity infusion on terms he determines; the GSEs have no obligation to accept this offer and would prob-ably not do so if it means wiping out their shareholders or ceding control. The act's language in this respect is fairly explicit, and it was obviously intended to protect the enterprises from a government takeover: "Nothing in this sub-section requires the corporation [Fannie or Freddie] to issue obligations or securities to the Secretary without mutual agreement between the Secretary and the corporation."

Thus, if Paulson wants to recapitalize the GSEs, he will have to offer attrac-tive terms to the existing shareholders. The more attractive the terms, of course, the greater the adverse political fallout for the secretary. And justifiably so, because there is no good reason to use taxpayer funds to keep Fannie and Fred-die alive. Since they cannot remain as GSEs, they must either be nationalized or privatized at some point in the future. If nationalization is the choice, keeping them alive today only sets up a huge fight with the shareholders in the future over the value they should receive for the companies. In other words, if Paulson injects equity today to keep them operating, he would only be setting up condi-tions for more taxpayer funds to be used in the future to acquire them. A capital injection now would simply be a gift to the existing shareholders. This would be a serious mistake and thus is highly unlikely to occur.

In addition, there is the specter of the savings and loan (S&L) debacle of the late 1980s and early 1990s. In that case, failed institutions were allowed to keep operating, in part because the deposit insurance fund for the S&L industry was insufficient to bail them out and in part because it is always the inclination of regulators to forbear closing down the entities they supervise. As a result, the S&L managements—which were able to raise funds because of a government guarantee of their deposits—were able to take substantial risks in an effort to return to profitability. At the time, this was called "gambling for resurrection," and the same incentives would prevail for Fannie and Freddie's managements if—after a Treasury capital injection—they remained in control of the enter-prises. Indeed, in June, Fannie's mortgage portfolio expanded at an annualized rate of 23 percent, and Freddie's at a rate of 33.4 percent. The GSEs' portfolios are their most profitable activity, and also their riskiest. An expansion of their portfolios is exactly what one would expect to see when companies—with the benefit of government backing—are able to increase their risk-taking in an effort to recover their profitability and avoid receivership. Accordingly, unless a Treasury injection of capital enables the department to take full control of Fannie and Freddie and replace their managements, keeping them alive would simply result in a replay of the S&L debacle of twenty years ago—on a much larger scale.

Thus, the better policy for the Treasury by far will be to leave both enterprises to sink or swim on their own. If they succeed in raising sufficient capital from investors and if the housing market stabilizes in the next few months, they may be able to survive. At that point, nationalization or privatization will still be the only options, but the U.S. government will not have made it more expensive to do either by infusing them with taxpayer funds. If, on the other hand, they cannot survive through their own efforts or good fortune, nationalization can occur through a receivership, avoiding concerns about buying out existing shareholders.

Option 3: Nationalization through a Receivership

There are a number of wholly owned government corporations that could serve as models for the nationalization of Fannie and Freddie. The National Railroad Passenger Corporation (Amtrak), the Corporation for Public Broadcasting, and the Tennessee Valley Authority are three prominent examples. Assuming, then, that Fannie and Freddie survive, Congress could nationalize them if it believes they serve a necessary purpose in the mortgage markets. There are two ways for nationalization to occur: through the acquisition of all the outstanding shares of the GSEs if they weather the current storm, or through a receivership authorized under HERA if they do not.

Under HERA, if Fannie and Freddie are insolvent or are on the verge of insolvency—the statutory term is "critically undercapitalized"—the FHFA is authorized to appoint a receiver for each company. That would automatically wipe out the shareholders and replace the management. Given the current financial condition of the GSEs, the receivership provisions of HERA are among the most important elements of the new act. They consist of two parts, both of which come into effect if the GSE is critically undercapitalized: the director of FHFA has the discretion to appoint a receiver if, among many other things, it appears that the assets of the enterprise are less than its liabilities or if, in his judgment, neither enterprise will be able to meet its obligations as they come due; however, the director is required to appoint a receiver if he determines that for any period of sixty days the obligations of the enterprise have been greater than its assets. Thus, the director is *required* to appoint a receiver even if the GSEs are still able to borrow in the markets, as long as their assets are worth less than their liabilities for an extended period. No particular accounting methodology is specified, so it is worth noting in this connection that in their last financial reports, Fannie had net assets of $12.5 billion (a tiny amount in relation to its total assets of $2.5 trillion) on a fair value accounting basis, while Freddie had *negative* net worth of $5.6 billion on a fair value basis. Theoretically, then, the director of the FHFA could appoint a receiver for Freddie at the end of September (sixty days after he gained the authority).

Under these circumstances, it becomes even clearer that the Treasury should not try to keep the GSEs functioning by infusing capital into Fannie and Freddie—especially if the secretary cannot wipe out the shareholders by doing so. Since HERA authorizes the director of FHFA to appoint a receiver, the interests of the shareholders and management of either company may be eliminated without giving them a taxpayer-funded gift and without having to go through the arduous process of buying out the existing shareholders if, after the Treasury's infusion, one or both companies manage to survive.

After the enactment of HERA, everything necessary for a successful receivership appears to be in place. First, it is vitally important that the receiver have a source of financing. The holders of GSE debt must be paid in full as their debt matures. Any other policy will cause the value of the outstanding debt to decline, and, as noted above, this will impair the capital of the thousands of U.S. banks that have been allowed by their regulators to hold as much GSE debt as they want. Moreover, the mortgage markets must be kept functioning, and this too requires that Fannie and Freddie continue to operate normally under the receiver's control. Finally, unlike the normal insolvency, the receiver cannot sell Fannie and Freddie's assets in order to raise the funds to pay off their debt. Selling GSE assets would drive down the market value of the mortgages and mortgage-backed securities (MBS), weaken the financial condition of the financial intermediaries and banks that hold these assets, and drive up mortgage rates—probably bringing an already weak housing market to a dead halt.

Therefore, it is essential that the receiver be able to borrow from the Treasury for the working capital necessary to operate the receivership. This is made possible by section 1145 of the act, which authorizes the receiver to step into the shoes of the enterprises for all purposes: "The Agency shall, as conservator or receiver, and by operation of law, immediately succeed to—(i) all rights, titles, powers, and privileges of the regulated entity, and of any stockholder, officer, or director of such regulated entity with respect to the regulated entity and the assets of the regulated entity." This language also makes clear that the receiver can continue to carry on the business of the GSEs after they are taken over and thus continue to serve the mortgage markets as Fannie and Freddie do today. Accordingly, the receiver, acting in his Fannie or Freddie capacity, will be eligible to borrow from the Treasury, and the secretary, in effect, is authorized to lend to the receiver. Indeed, the availability of the Treasury line should enable the receiver, acting in his capacity as Fannie or Freddie, to continue to issue debt securities and guarantees of MBS, just as the two enterprises have done in the past. The existence of the Treasury line will reassure the markets that the receiver will be able to meet the obligations of the companies as they come due. Accordingly, with the line of credit available, it is possible that the receiver will never actually have to use it, since he can borrow in the name of Fannie or Freddie and have these borrowings credibly backed by the credit line at the Treasury.

There is, of course, the further question of whether nationalization would be good policy. That question involves issues beyond the scope of this *Financial Services Outlook,* but the answer does not depend on looking at the condition of the mortgage markets today. These markets have been grossly distorted over the years by the presence of Fannie and Freddie, which have driven out most of the competition for middle-class housing finance and forced most housing finance into the securitization mold. The likelihood is that the resulting lack of competition prevented innovation—such as covered bonds—and kept mortgage rates higher than they would otherwise have been. Studies by the Federal Reserve have shown that the maximum amount by which Fannie and Freddie might have lowered interest rates for home mortgages was seven basis points, with a strong possibility that they would have had no effect on interest rates whatsoever. The authors of the Fed study noted in summary: "We find that GSE portfolio purchases have no significant effects on either primary or secondary mortgage rate spreads. Further, we examine GSE activities and mortgage rate spreads in the wake of the 1998 debt crisis, and find that GSE portfolio pur-chases did little to affect interest rates paid by new mortgage borrowers."[49]

Accordingly, the argument for government intervention simply to lower mortgage rates through secondary market activity is weak. Although there is a possible role for government in subsidizing affordable housing, there is no par-ticular reason to use a nationalized Fannie or Freddie for this purpose. The same assignment could be given to Ginnie Mae and the Federal Housing Administra-tion. In addition, nationalization would prevent taxpayers from realizing what-ever inherent value remains in Fannie and Freddie's intangible assets—among other things, their relationships with other participants in the mortgage markets; their automated underwriting systems; and the information they have on home values, neighborhoods, and mortgagors. These assets, as discussed below, would be recoverable by the taxpayers if Fannie and Freddie were privatized or liquidated after a receivership but would be lost in a nationalization.

Option 4: Privatization

If Fannie and Freddie survive the current crisis, privatization would be a better policy choice than nationalization. Among other things, it would relieve tax-payers of the cost of buying the two enterprises from their existing sharehold-ers. There are a number of ways that privatization could be accomplished, but one certain condition must be that both companies be reduced in size. It will be very difficult for the private market to absorb two companies that each have obligations exceeding $2 trillion. In our book, *Privatizing Fannie Mae, Freddie Mac, and the Federal Home Loan Banks,*[50] Bert Ely, Thomas H. Stanton, and I proposed one approach to privatization. Briefly, we would require Fannie and Freddie to set up ordinary state-chartered corporate parent companies that

---

49. Andreas Lehnert, Wayne Passmore, and Shane M. Sherlund, "GSEs, Mortgage Rates, and Secondary Market Activities" (Finance and Economics Discussion Paper, Divi-sions of Research and Statistics and Monetary Affairs, Federal Reserve Board of Gover-nors, Washington, DC, September 8, 2006), 3, available at www.federalreserve.gov/pubs/feds/2006/200630/ 200630pap.pdf (accessed August 25, 2008).

50. Peter J. Wallison, Thomas H. Stanton, and Bert Ely, *Privatizing Fannie Mae, Fred-die Mac, and the Federal Home Loan Banks: Why and How* (Washington, DC: AEI Press, 2004), available through www.aei.org/book794/.

would acquire the GSEs. Over time, the GSE portfolios would be sold off and their new securitizations gradually transferred from the GSEs to private-sector subsidiaries of the new holding company. After a period of years, any remaining obligations on the GSEs' securitization guarantees would be defeased with U.S. government securities. We also recommended that their information and other intangible assets be licensed to all comers, so as to make available to their competitors the intangible assets that they were helped to acquire by their government backing.

The most serious technical obstacle to privatization will be the disposition of the GSEs' guarantees of MBS. There are currently about $3.7 trillion in such guarantees, and this obligation can only be eliminated when the mortgages in the securitization pool disappear through refinancing, payoff, or sale of the underlying residence. This could take as long as thirty years, so, if Fannie and Freddie are to be privatized, some way must be found to back the MBS with credit that is at least as good as that of Fannie and Freddie when they were still GSEs and implicitly backed by the U.S. government. One way to do this might be to keep the GSEs in being only for this purpose. They would not be able to engage in any new business and might be transferred as entities to Ginnie Mae for administration. Fannie and Freddie would have to indemnify the government for any losses incurred on these guarantees for as long as they remain in existence. This would be done most effectively by setting up a defeasement mechanism involving a deposit of U.S. government securities.

Apart from the financial difficulties of privatization, Congress in general will not want to see Fannie and Freddie disappear as GSEs. The two enterprises have been the source of considerable campaign funding for their supporters in Congress, lucrative jobs for congressional staffers, and good publicity for incumbents in their districts and states. The Democratic Congress, in particular, will prefer continued intervention in the mortgage market so that they can continue to establish priorities that will benefit favored groups in the Democratic political coalition. In addition, the banks and other mortgage lenders that might be compelled to compete with Fannie and Freddie will certainly oppose privatization. Other groups—home builders, the securities industry, realtors, and other traditional allies who profit from the activities of Fannie and Freddie—will also be in opposition. So, while nationalization will be expensive to accomplish if the government has to purchase the interests of the GSEs' shareholders, privatization will be politically difficult.

Option 5: Privatization through a Receivership

Privatization is less difficult, however, if Fannie and Freddie are taken over by a receiver. In that case, the receiver can trim them down to manageable size, isolate the bad assets in a good bank/bad bank structure, and sell shares in the good banks (i.e., what remains of Fannie and Freddie) to the public after organizing the good banks as ordinary state-chartered corporations with no continuing ties to the government. There have been a number of suggestions recently that in any privatization of this kind, Fannie and Freddie should be broken up into a number of smaller units. This may be good policy if they are to continue as GSEs—since the implicit government backing of GSEs allows them to grow without restraint while maintaining the fiction that taxpayers are not at risk for their losses. However, now that it is clear that Fannie and Freddie are explicitly backed by the U.S. government, the GSE structure—as discussed above—does not work politically. So the question is whether it is necessary to break Fannie and Freddie into smaller pieces when they are privatized without any connection to the U.S. government. In that case, it is likely that they will be more valuable as larger entities—thus returning more to the taxpayers who will bear the losses on the bad bank's assets—so it seems best not to break them up. The political difficulties associated with privatization through a receivership would be avoided because Congress would not have to participate in the process.

The receiver would also have more flexibility for dealing with the MBS guarantees. For one thing, under the receivership provisions in HERA, the receiver can repudiate all contracts entered by Fannie and Freddie before the receivership commenced. The receiver will certainly not want to repudiate the obligation on the guarantees since, again, these are held by thousands of U.S. banks, but the power to repudiate the guarantees themselves may enable the receiver to set up alternative defeasement structures that will adequately protect the MBS while reducing the administrative costs to the government. The receiver can determine, for example, whether the fees received from the securitized pools will be adequate to defray the government's risk on the guarantees or whether some supplemental payment from Fannie or Freddie's remaining assets is necessary to ensure that the government does not take any further losses in the future.

The central point, however, is that if Fannie and Freddie are eventually taken over by a receiver, the process of privatization is much easier than it would be if both companies had been kept alive by infusions of capital from the Treasury.

Option 6: Liquidation, Now or Never

The final option is liquidation. This would not be possible to achieve if Fannie and Freddie survive the current crisis. The political and financial pressure to keep them in being—either through nationalization or privatization—will be too great. Moreover, each of them will be too large for any single entity to acquire. So liquidation of Fannie and Freddie does not appear to be a viable option—if they remain going concerns by raising their own capital, by receiving a capital infusion from the Treasury, or because the housing market stabilizes before they become insolvent.

On the other hand, if they are taken over by a receiver, liquidation becomes a real possibility. The receiver will be able to marshal their assets and sell these assets over time for the maximum return. The proceeds of these sales could be used to pay off debt, defease the obligations on the MBS guarantees, and keep the losses to a minimum. This is approximately the same process that the FDIC used in resolving the thousands of failed S&Ls and commercial banks in the early 1990s. There is no time limit on the receiver's authority, so this process could take place over many years. During that time, the receiver could continue to operate both companies as they have been operated in the past, maintaining a functioning secondary market for mortgages until a functioning private secondary market has developed or until the covered bond financing system develops sufficiently to assume the largest role in residential finance.

"The Last Trillion-Dollar Commitment: The Destruction of Fannie Mae and Freddie Mac"

Originally published September 2008

The government takeover of Fannie Mae and Freddie Mac was necessary because of their massive losses on more than $1 trillion of subprime and Alt-A investments, almost all of which were added to their single-family book of business between 2005 and 2007. The most plausible explanation for the sudden adoption of this disastrous course—disastrous for them and for the U.S. financial markets—is their desire to continue to retain the support of Congress after their accounting scandals in 2003 and 2004 and the challenges to their business model that ensued. Although the strategy worked—Congress did not adopt strong government-sponsored enterprise (GSE) reform legislation until the Republicans demanded it as the price for Senate passage of a housing bill in July 2008—it led inevitably to the government takeover and the enormous junk loan losses still to come.

Now that the federal government has been required to take effective control of Fannie and Freddie and to decide their fate, it is important to understand the reasons for their financial collapse—what went wrong and why. In his statement on September 7 announcing the appointment of a conservator for the two enterprises, Treasury Secretary Henry M. Paulson pointed to their failed business models as the reason for their collapse. This was certainly a contributing element, but not the direct cause. The central problem was their dependence on Congress for continued political support in the wake of their accounting scandals in 2003 and 2004. To curry favor with Congress, they sought substantial increases in their support of affordable housing, primarily by investing in risky and substandard mortgages between 2005 and 2007.

As GSEs, Fannie and Freddie were serving two masters in two different ways. The first was an inherent conflict between their government mission and their private ownership. The government mission required them to keep mortgage interest rates low and to increase their support for affordable housing. Their shareholder ownership, however, required them to fight increases in their capital requirements and regulation that would raise their costs and reduce their risk-taking and profitability. But there were two other parties—Congress and the taxpayers—that also had a stake in the choices that Fannie and Freddie made. Congress got some benefits in the form of political support from the GSEs' ability to hold down mortgage rates, but it garnered even more political benefits from GSE support for affordable housing. The taxpayers got highly attenuated benefits from both affordable housing and lower mortgage rates but ultimately faced enormous liabilities associated with GSE risk-taking. This *Outlook* tells the disheartening story of how the GSEs sold out the taxpayers by taking huge risks on substandard mortgages, primarily to retain congressional support for the weak regulation and special benefits that fueled their high profits and profligate executive compensation. As if that were not enough, in the process, the GSEs' operations promoted a risky subprime mortgage binge in the United States that has caused a worldwide financial crisis.

The peculiar structure of the GSEs—shareholder-owned companies with a public mission—reflected a serious confusion of purpose on the part of the Lyndon Johnson administration and the members of Congress who created this flawed structure in 1968. In seeking to reduce the budget deficits associated with the Vietnam War and Great Society programs, the administration hit upon the idea of "privatizing" Fannie Mae by allowing the company to sell shares to the public. This, according to the budget theories of the time, would take Fannie's expenditures off-budget, while allowing it to continue its activities with funds borrowed in the public credit markets. But turning Fannie into a wholly private company was not acceptable either. Various special provisions were placed in Fannie's congressional charter that intentionally blurred the line between a public instrumentality and a private corporation. Among these provisions: Fannie was given a line of credit at the Treasury; the president could appoint five members of its board of directors; and its debt could be used, like Treasury debt, to collateralize government deposits in private banks.

Fannie's congressional charter and its unusual ties to the government ensured that the market would recognize its status as a government instrumentality: that despite its private ownership, the company was performing a government mission. Because it was highly unlikely that the U.S. government would allow one of its instrumentalities to default on its obligations, Fannie was perceived in the capital markets to have at least an implicit government backing and was thus able to borrow funds at rates that were only slightly higher than those paid by the U.S. Treasury on its own debt offerings. In 1970, the Federal Home Loan Bank Board created Freddie Mac to assist federal savings and loan associations in marketing their mortgages; Freddie was also allowed to sell shares to the public in 1989 and became a competitor of Fannie Mae under a congressional charter that established an identical special relationship with the government.

The special relationship, codified by these unique charters, required the GSEs to pursue another inherently conflicted mission that pitted their shareholders against the taxpayers. To the extent that their government backing allowed the GSEs to take excessive financial risks, it was the taxpayers and not the shareholders who would ultimately bear the costs. That result—the privatization of profit and the socialization of risk—has now come to pass. U.S. taxpayers are now called upon to fill in the hole that reckless and improvident investment activity—fueled by inexpensive and easily accessible funds—has created in the GSEs' balance sheets. The special relationship was also the GSEs' undoing, because it allowed them to escape the market discipline—the wariness of lenders—that keeps corporate managements from taking unacceptable risks. Normally, when a privately held company is backed by the government (for example, in the case of commercial banks covered by the Federal Deposit Insurance Corporation), regulation is the way that the government protects the taxpayers against the loss of market discipline. When Fannie Mae was privatized in 1968, however, no special regulatory structure was created to limit the taxpayers' exposure to loss. The Johnson administration officials who structured the privatization may not have realized that they were creating what we recognize today as a huge moral hazard, but when Fannie became insolvent (the first time) in the high-interest-rate environment of the early 1980s, policymakers recognized that the company represented a potential risk to taxpayers.

In 1991, as Congress finally began the process of developing a regulatory regime for the GSEs, congressional interest in supporting affordable housing was growing. At this point, Fannie Mae initiated its first foray into affordable housing—a relatively small $10 billion program, probably intended to show Congress that the GSEs would support affordable housing without a statutory mandate. Nevertheless, Congress added an affordable housing "mission" to the GSE charters when it created their first full-time regulator, the Office of Federal Housing Enterprise Oversight (OFHEO). The new agency had only limited regulatory authority. It was also housed in the Department of Housing and Urban Development (HUD), which had no regulatory experience, and it was funded by congressional appropriations, allowing the GSEs to control their regulator through the key lawmakers who held OFHEO's purse strings.

The new affordable housing mission further increased the congressional policy stake in the GSEs, but it also initiated a destructive mutual dependency: Congress began to rely on Fannie and Freddie for political and financial support, and the two GSEs relied on Congress to protect their profitable special privileges. In later years, attention to the political interests of Congress became known at the GSEs as "management of political risk." In a speech to an investor conference in 1999, Franklin Raines, then Fannie's chairman, assured them that "[w]e manage our political risk with the same intensity that we manage our credit and interest rate risks."[51]

Benefits to Congress

Managing their political risk required the GSEs to offer Congress a generous benefits package. Campaign contributions were certainly one element. Between the 2000 and 2008 election cycles, the GSEs and their employees contributed more than $14.6 million to the campaign funds of dozens of senators and representatives, most of them on committees that were important to preserving the GSEs' privileges.[52] And Fannie knew how to "leverage" its giving, not just its assets; often it enlisted other groups that profited from the GSEs' activities—the securities industry, homebuilders, and realtors—to sponsor their own fundraising events for the GSEs' key congressional friends. In addition to campaign funds, the GSEs—Fannie Mae in particular—enhanced their power in Congress by setting up "partnership offices" in the districts and states of important lawmakers, often hiring the relatives of these lawmakers to staff the local offices. Their lobbying activities were legendary. Between 1998 and 2008, Fannie spent

---

51. Quoted in Niles Steven Campbell, "Fannie Mae Officials Try to Assuage Worried Investors," *Real Estate Finance Today,* May 10, 1999. See also Binyamin Appelbaum, Carol D. Leonnig, and David S. Hilzenrath, "How Washington Failed to Rein in Fannie, Freddie," *Washington Post,* September 14, 2008.

52. Common Cause, "Ask Yourself Why . . . They Didn't See This Coming," September 24, 2008, available at www.commoncause.org/site/pp.asp?c=dkLNK1MQIwG&b=4542875 (accessed September 29, 2008).

$79.5 million and Freddie spent $94.9 million on lobbying Congress, making them the twentieth and thirteenth biggest spenders, respectively, on lobbying fees during that period.[53] Not all of these expenditures were necessary to contact members of Congress; the GSEs routinely hired lobbyists simply to deprive their opponents of lobbying help. Since lobbyists are frequently part of lawmakers' networks—and are often former staffers for the same lawmakers—these lobbying expenditures also encouraged members of Congress to support Fannie and Freddie as a means of supplementing the income of their friends.

In the same vein, Fannie and Freddie hired dozens of Washington's movers and shakers—at spectacular levels of compensation—to sit on their boards, lobby Congress, and in general help them to manage their political risk. (An early account of this effort was an article entitled "Crony Capitalism: American Style" that appeared in *The International Economy* in 1999.[54] A later version of the same point was made in *Investor's Business Daily* nine years later.[55]) The GSEs also paid for academic research to assure the public that the GSE mission was worthwhile and that the GSEs posed minimal risks to taxpayers. For example, Nobel laureate Joseph Stiglitz coauthored an article in 2002 purporting to show that the risk of GSE default producing taxpayer loss was "effectively zero."[56]

One of the most successful efforts to influence lawmakers came through community groups. Both Fannie and Freddie made "charitable" or other gifts

---

53. Center for Responsive Politics, "Lobbying: Top Spenders," 2008, available at www.opensecrets.org/lobby/top.php?indexType=s (accessed September 26, 2008).

54. Owen Ullmann, "Crony Capitalism: American Style," *The International Economy* (July/August 1999): 6.

55. Terry Jones, "'Crony' Capitalism Is Root Cause of Fannie and Freddie Troubles," *Investor's Business Daily,* September 22, 2008.

56. Joseph E. Stiglitz, Jonathan M. Orszag, and Peter R. Orszag, "Implications of the New Fannie Mae and Freddie Mac Risk-Based Capital Standard," *Fannie Mae Papers* 1, no. 2 (March 2002), available at www.sbgo.com/Papers/fmp-v1i2.pdf (accessed September 29, 2008). Interestingly, Stiglitz today is an outspoken critic of GSE risk-taking. According to Stiglitz, GSE risk-taking was a predictable consequence of the structure of the GSEs and their financial structure and compensation schedules. "We should not be worried about [GSE] shareholders losing their investments. In earlier years, they were amply rewarded. The management remuneration packages that they approved were designed to encourage excessive risk-taking. They got what they asked for. Nor should we be worried about creditors losing their money. Their lack of supervision fuelled the housing bubble and we are now all paying the price." (Joseph Stiglitz, "Fannie's and Freddie's Free Lunch," *Financial Times,* July 24, 2008.)

to community groups, which could then be called upon to contact the GSEs' opponents in Congress and protest any proposed restrictions on the activities or privileges of the GSEs. GSE supporters in Congress could also count on these groups to back them in their reelection efforts.

But these activities, as important as they were in managing the GSEs' political risks, paled when compared to the billions of dollars the GSEs made available for spending on projects in the congressional districts and states of their supporters. Many of these projects involved affordable housing. In 1994, Fannie Mae replaced its initial $10 billion program with a $1 trillion affordable housing initiative, and both Fannie and Freddie announced new $2 trillion initiatives in 2001.[57] It is not clear to what extent the investments made in support of these commitments were losers—the GSEs' profitability over many years could cover a multitude of sins—but it is now certain that the enormous losses associated with the risky housing investments appearing on Fannie and Freddie's balance sheet today reflect major and imprudent investments in support of affordable housing between 2005 and 2007—investments that ultimately brought about the collapse of Fannie and Freddie.

Even if the earlier affordable housing projects were not losers, however, they represented a new and extra-constitutional way for Congress to dispense funds that should otherwise have flowed through the appropriations process. In one sense, the expenditures were a new form of earmark, but this earmarking evaded the constitutional appropriations process entirely. An illustration is provided by a press release from the office of Senator Charles E. Schumer (D-N.Y.), one of the most ardent supporters of the GSEs in Congress. The headline on the release, dated November 20, 2006—right in the middle of the GSEs' affordable housing spending spree—was "Schumer Announces up to $100 Million Freddie Mac Commitment to Address Fort Drum and Watertown Housing Crunch." The subheading continued: "Schumer Unveils New Freddie Mac Plan with

---

57. Funding Universe, "Fannie Mae—Company History," available at www.funding universe.com/company-histories/Fannie-Mae-Company-History.html (accessed September 29, 2008); Funding Universe, "Freddie Mac—Company History," available at www. fundinguniverse.com/company-histories/Freddie-Mac-Company-History.html (accessed September 29, 2008); and Business Wire, "Fannie Mae's $2 Trillion 'American Dream Commitment' on Course with Over $190 Billion in Targeted Lending," news release, March 14, 2001, available at http://findarticles.com/p/articles/mi_m0EIN/is_2001_ March_14/ai_71707186/ (accessed September 29, 2008).

HSBC That Includes Low-Interest Low-Downpayment Loans. In June, Schumer Urged Freddie Mac and Fannie Mae Step Up to the Plate and Deliver Concrete Plans—Today Freddie Mac Is Following Through."[58] If this project had been economically profitable for Fannie or Freddie, Schumer would not have had to "urge" them to "step up." Instead, using his authority as a powerful member of the Senate Banking Committee—and a supporter of Fannie and Freddie—he appears to have induced Freddie Mac to make a financial commitment that was very much in his political interests but for which the taxpayers of the United States would ultimately be responsible.

Of course, Schumer was only one of many members of Congress who used his political leverage to further his own agenda at taxpayer expense and outside the appropriations process. The list of friends of Fannie and Freddie changed over time; while the GSEs enjoyed broad bipartisan support in the 1990s, over the past decade, they have become increasingly aligned with the Democrats. This shift in the political equilibrium was especially clear in the congressional reaction to the GSEs' accounting scandals of 2003 and 2004.

The Accounting Scandals

Fannie and Freddie reaped significant benefits from the careful management of their political risk. In June 2003, in the wake of the failures of Enron and WorldCom, Freddie's board of directors suddenly dismissed its three top officers and announced that the company's accountants had found serious problems in Freddie's financial reports. In 2004, after a forensic audit by OFHEO, even more serious accounting manipulation was found at Fannie, and Raines, its chairman, and Timothy Howard, its chief financial officer, were compelled to resign.

It is eloquent testimony to the power of Fannie and Freddie in Congress that even after these extraordinary events there was no significant effort to improve or enhance the powers of their regulator. The House Financial Services Committee developed a bill that was so badly weakened by GSE lobbying that the Bush administration refused to support it. The Senate Banking Committee,

---

58. Office of Senator Charles E. Schumer, "Schumer Announces up to $100 Million Freddie Mac Commitment to Address Fort Drum and Watertown Housing Crunch," news release, November 20, 2006, available at www.senate.gov/~schumer/SchumerWebsite/pressroom/record.cfm?id=266131 (accessed September 29, 2008).

then under Republican control, adopted much stronger legislation in 2005, but unanimous Democratic opposition to the bill in the committee doomed it when it reached the floor. Without any significant Democratic support, debate could not be ended in the Senate, and the bill was never brought up for a vote. This was a crucial missed opportunity. The bill prohibited the GSEs from holding portfolios of mortgages and mortgage-backed securities (MBS); that measure alone would have prevented the disastrous investment activities of the GSEs in the years that followed. GSE immunity to accounting scandal is especially remarkable when it is recalled that after accounting fraud was found at Enron (and later at WorldCom), Congress adopted the punitive Sarbanes-Oxley Act, which imposed substantial costs on every public company in the United States. The GSEs' investment in controlling their political risk—at least among the Democrats—was apparently money well spent.

Nevertheless, the GSEs' problems were mounting quickly. The accounting scandal, although contained well below the level of the Enron story, gave ammunition to GSE critics inside and outside of Congress. Alan Greenspan, who in his earlier years as Federal Reserve chairman had avoided direct criticism of the GSEs, began to cite the risks associated with their activities in his congressional testimony. In a hearing before the Senate Banking Committee in February 2004, Greenspan noted for the first time that they could have serious adverse consequences for the economy. Referring to the management of interest rate risk—a key risk associated with holding portfolios of mortgages or MBS—he said:

> To manage this risk with little capital requires a conceptually sophisticated hedging framework. In essence, the current system depends on the risk managers at Fannie and Freddie to do everything just right, rather than depending on a market-based system supported by the risk assessments and management capabilities of many participants with different views and different strategies for hedging risks.[59]

Then, and again for the first time, Greenspan proposed placing some limit on the size of the GSEs' portfolios. Greenspan's initial idea, later followed by

---

59. Alan Greenspan, "Proposals for Improving the Regulation of the Housing Government Sponsored Enterprises" (testimony, Committee on Banking, Housing and Urban Affairs, U.S. Senate, 108th Cong., 1st sess., February 24, 2004), available at www.federalreserve.gov/boarddocs/testimony/2004/20040224/default.htm (accessed September 29, 2008).

more explicit proposals for numerical limits, was to restrict the GSEs' issuance of debt. Although he did not call for an outright reduction in the size of the portfolios, limiting the issuance of debt amounts to the same thing. If the GSEs could not issue debt beyond a certain amount, they also could not accumulate portfolios. Greenspan noted:

> Most of the concerns associated with systemic risks flow from the size of the balance sheets that these GSEs maintain. One way Congress could constrain the size of these balance sheets is to alter the composition of Fannie and Freddie's mortgage financing by limiting the dollar amount of their debt relative to the dollar amount of mortgages securitized and held by other investors. . . . [T]his approach would continue to expand the depth and liquidity of mortgage markets through mortgage securitization but would remove most of the potential systemic risks associated with these GSEs.[60]

This statement must have caused considerable concern to Fannie and Freddie. Most of their profits came from issuing debt at low rates of interest and holding portfolios of mortgages and MBS with high yields. This was a highly lucrative arrangement; limiting their debt issuance would have had a significant adverse effect on their profitability.

In addition, in January 2005, only a few months after the adverse OFHEO report on Fannie's accounting manipulation, three Federal Reserve economists published a study that cast doubt on whether the GSEs' activities had any significant effect on mortgage interest rates and concluded further that holding portfolios—a far riskier activity than issuing MBS—did not have any greater effect on interest rates than securitization: "We find that both portfolio purchases and MBS issuance have negligible effects on mortgage rate spreads and that purchases are not any more effective than securitization at reducing mortgage interest rate spreads."[61] Thus, the taxpayer risks cited by Greenspan could not be justified by citing lower mortgage rates, and, worse, there was a strong

---

60. Ibid.

61. Andreas Lehnert, Wayne Passmore, and Shane M. Sherlund, "GSEs, Mortgage Rates and Secondary Market Activities" (Finance and Economic Discussion Series 2005-07, Divisions of Research & Statistics and Monetary Affairs, Federal Reserve Board, Washington, DC, January 12, 2005), 1, available at www.federalreserve.gov/Pubs/feds/2005/200507/200507pap.pdf (accessed September 29, 2008).

case for limiting the GSEs to securitization activities alone—a much less profitable activity than issuing MBS.

The events in 2003 and 2004 had undermined the legitimacy of the GSEs. They could no longer claim to be competently—or even honestly—managed. An important and respected figure, Alan Greenspan, was raising questions about whether they might be creating excessive risk for taxpayers and systemic risk for the economy as a whole. Greenspan had suggested that their most profitable activity—holding portfolios of mortgages and MBS—was the activity that created the greatest risk, and three Federal Reserve economists had concluded that the GSEs' activities did not actually reduce mortgage interest rates. It was easy to see at this point that their political risk was rising quickly. The case for continuing their privileged status had been severely weakened. The only element of their activities that had not come under criticism was their affordable housing mission, and it appears that the GSEs determined at this point to play that card as a way of shoring up their political support in Congress.

From the perspective of their 2008 collapse, this may seem to have been unwise, but in the context of the time, it was a shrewd decision. It provided the GSEs with the potential for continuing their growth and delivered enormous short-term profits. Those profits were transferred to stockholders in huge dividend payments over the past three years (Fannie and Freddie paid a combined $4.1 billion in dividends last year alone) and to managers in lucrative salaries and bonuses. Indeed, if it had not been for the Democrats' desire to adopt a housing relief bill before leaving for the 2008 August recess, no new regulatory regime for the GSEs would have been adopted at all. Only the Senate Republicans' position—that there would be no housing bill without GSE reform—overcame the opposition of Senators Christopher Dodd (D-Conn.), the banking committee chairman, and Schumer.

The GSEs' confidence in the affordable housing idea was bolstered by what appears to be a tacit understanding. Occasionally, this understanding found direct expression. For example, in his opening statement at a hearing in 2003, Representative Barney Frank (D-Mass.), now the chairman of the House Financial Services Committee, referred to an "arrangement" between Congress and the GSEs that tracks rather explicitly what actually happened: "Fannie and Freddie have played a very useful role in helping to make housing more affordable, both in general through leveraging the mortgage market, and in particular, they have a mission that this Congress has given them in return for some of the arrangements which are of some benefit to them to focus on affordable housing."[62] So here the arrangement is laid out: if the GSEs focus on affordable housing, their position is secure.

Increased Support for Affordable Housing

Affordable housing loans and subprime loans are not synonymous. Affordable housing loans can be traditional prime loans with adequate down payments, fixed rates, and an established and adequate borrower credit history. In trying to increase their commitment to affordable housing, however, the GSEs abandoned these standards. In 1995, HUD, the cabinet-level agency responsible for issuing regulations on the GSEs' affordable housing obligations, had ruled that the GSEs could get affordable housing credit for purchasing subprime loans. Unfortunately, the agency failed to require that these loans conform to good lending practices, and OFHEO did not have the staff or the authority to monitor their purchases. The assistant HUD secretary at the time, William Apgar, later told the *Washington Post* that "[i]t was a mistake. In hindsight, I would have done it differently." Allen Fishbein, his adviser, noted that Fannie and Freddie "chose not to put the brakes on this dangerous lending when they should have."[63] Far from it. In 1998, Fannie Mae announced a 97 percent loan-to-value mortgage, and, in 2001, it offered a program that involved mortgages with no down payment at all. As a result, in 2004, when Fannie and Freddie began to increase significantly their commitment to affordable housing loans, they found it easy to stimulate production in the private sector by letting it be known in the market that they would gladly accept loans that would otherwise be considered subprime.

Although Fannie and Freddie were building huge exposures to subprime mortgages from 2005 to 2007, they adopted accounting practices that made it difficult to detect the size of those exposures. Even an economist as seemingly sophisticated as Paul Krugman was misled. He wrote in his July 14, 2008, *New York Times* column that

---

62. Quoted in Gerald Prante, "Barney Frank on Fannie Mae and Freddie Mac in 2003," Tax Policy Blog, September 17, 2008, available at www.taxfoundation.org/blog/show/23617.html (accessed September 29, 2008).

63. Carol D. Leonnig, "How HUD Mortgage Policy Fed the Crisis," *Washington Post*, June 10, 2008.

Fannie and Freddie had nothing to do with the explosion of high-risk lending. . . . In fact, Fannie and Freddie, after growing rapidly in the 1990s, largely faded from the scene during the height of the housing bubble. . . . Partly that's because regulators, responding to accounting scandals at the companies, placed temporary restraints on both Fannie and Freddie that curtailed their lending just as housing prices were really taking off. Also, they didn't do any subprime lending, because they can't . . . by law. . . . So whatever bad incentives the implicit federal guarantee creates have been offset by the fact that Fannie and Freddie were and are tightly regulated with regard to the risks they can take. You could say that the Fannie-Freddie experience shows that regulation works.[64]

Here Krugman demonstrates confusion about the law (which did not prohibit subprime lending by the GSEs), misunderstands the regulatory regime under which they operated (which did not have the capacity to control their risk-taking), and mismeasures their actual subprime exposures (which he wrongly states were zero). There is probably more to this than lazy reporting by Krugman; the GSE propaganda machine purposefully misled people into believing that it was keeping risk low and operating under an adequate prudential regulatory regime.

One of the sources of Krugman's confusion may have been Fannie and Freddie's strange accounting conventions relating to subprime loans. There are many definitions of a subprime loan, but the definition used by U.S. bank regulators is any loan to a borrower with damaged credit, including such objective criteria as a FICO credit score lower than 660.[65] In their public reports, the GSEs use their own definitions, which purposely and significantly understate their commitment to subprime loans—the mortgages with the most political freight. For example, they disclose the principal amount of loans with FICO scores of less than 620, leaving the reader to guess how many loans fall into the

---

64. Paul Krugman, "Fannie, Freddie and You," *New York Times*, July 14, 2008.

65. Office of the Comptroller of the Currency, Federal Reserve Board, Federal Deposit Insurance Corporation, Office of Thrift Supervision, "Expanded Guidance for Subprime Lending Programs," 2001, available at www.federalreserve.gov/Boarddocs/SRletters/2001/sr0104a1.pdf (accessed September 29, 2008).

category of subprime because they have FICO scores of less than 660. In these reports, too, Alt-A loans—which include loans with little or no income or other documentation and other deficiencies—are differentiated from subprime loans, again reducing the size of the apparent GSE commitment to the subprime category. These distinctions, however, are not very important from the perspective of realized losses in the subprime and Alt-A categories; loss rates are quite similar for both, even though they are labeled differently. In its June 30, 2008, Investor Summary report, Fannie notes that credit losses on its Alt-A portfolio were 49.6 percent of all the credit losses on its $2.7 trillion single-family loan book of business.[66] Fannie's disclosures indicate that when all subprime loans (including Alt-A) are aggregated, at least 85 percent of its losses are related to its holdings of both subprime and Alt-A loans. They are all properly characterized as "junk loans."

Beginning in 2004, after the GSEs' accounting scandals, the junk loan share of all mortgages in the United States began to rise, going from 8 percent in 2003 to about 18 percent in 2004 and peaking at about 22 percent in the third quarter of 2006. It is likely that this huge increase in commitments to junk lending was largely the result of signals from Fannie and Freddie that they were ready to buy these loans in bulk. For example, in speeches to the Mortgage Bankers Association in 2004, both Raines and Richard Syron—the chairmen, respectively, of Fannie and Freddie—"made no bones about their interest in buying loans made to borrowers formerly considered the province of nonprime and other niche lenders."[67] Raines is quoted as saying, "We have to push products and opportunities to people who have lesser credit quality."

There are few data available publicly on the dollar amount of junk loans held by the GSEs in 2004, but according to their own reports, GSE purchases of these mortgages and MBS increased substantially between 2005 and 2007. Subprime and Alt-A purchases during this period were a higher share of total purchases than in previous years. For example, Fannie reported that mortgages and MBS of all types originated in 2005–2007 comprised 49.8 percent of its overall book of single-family mortgages, which includes both mortgages and MBS

---

66. Fannie Mae, "2008 Q2 10-Q Investor Summary," August 8, 2008, available at www.fanniemae.com/media/pdf/newsreleases/2008_Q2_10Q_Investor_Summary.pdf (accessed September 29, 2008).

67. Neil Morse, "Looking for New Customers," *Mortgage Banking,* December 1, 2004.

TABLE 1

SUBPRIME CHARACTERISTICS OF MORTGAGES ACQUIRED BY FANNIE MAE,
2005–2007

Subprime Characteristic	Percentage
Negative amortization (option ARMs):	62.2
Interest-only:	83.8
FICO scores less than 620:	57.5
Loan-to-value ratios greater than 90:	62.0
Alt-A:	73.0

SOURCE: Fannie Mae, "2008 Q2 10-Q Investor Summary," August 8, 2008, available at www.fanniemae.com/media/pdf/newsreleases/2008_Q2_10Q_Investor_Summary.pdf (accessed September 29, 2008).

retained in their portfolio as well as mortgages they securitized and guaranteed. But the percentage of mortgages with subprime characteristics purchased during this period consistently exceeded 49.8 percent, demonstrating that Fannie was substantially increasing its reliance on junk loans between 2005 and 2007. For example, in its 10-Q Investor Summary report for the quarter ended June 30, 2008, Fannie reported that mortgages with subprime characteristics comprised substantial percentages of all 2005–2007 mortgages the company acquired, as shown in table 1. Based on these figures, it is likely that as much as 40 percent of the mortgages that Fannie Mae added to its single-family book of business during 2005–2007 were junk loans.

If we add up all these categories and eliminate double counting, it appears that on June 30, 2008, Fannie held or had guaranteed subprime and Alt-A loans with an unpaid principal balance of $553 billion. In addition, according to the same Fannie report, the company also held $29.5 billion of Alt-A loans and $36.3 billion of subprime loans that it had purchased as private label securities (non-GSE or Ginnie Mae securities).[68] These figures amount to a grand total of $619 billion—approximately 23 percent of Fannie's book of single-family business on June 30, 2008—and reflect a huge commitment to the purchase of mortgages of questionable quality between 2005 and 2007.

Freddie Mac also published a report on its subprime and Alt-A mortgage exposures as of August 2008. Freddie's numbers were not as detailed as Fannie's,

---

68. Fannie Mae, "2008 Q2 10-Q Investor Summary," 20.

TABLE 2
SUBPRIME CHARACTERISTICS OF MORTGAGES ACQUIRED BY FREDDIE MAC, 2005–2007

Subprime Characteristic	Percentage
Negative amortization (option ARMs):	72
Interest-only:	90
FICO scores less than 620:	61
Loan-to-value ratios of greater than 90:	58
Alt-A:	78

SOURCE: Freddie Mac, "Freddie Mac Update," August 2008, 30, available at www.freddiemac.com/investors/pdffiles/investor-presentation.pdf (accessed September 29, 2008).

but the company reported that 52 percent of its entire single-family credit guarantee portfolio was from book years 2005–2007 (slightly more than Fannie) and that these mortgages had subprime characteristics, as shown in table 2. Based on these figures, it appears that as much as 40 percent of the loans that Freddie Mac added to its book of single-family mortgage business during 2005–2007 also consisted of junk loans.

Freddie's disclosures did not contain enough detail to eliminate all of the double counting, so it is not possible to estimate the total amount of its subprime loans from the information it reported. Nevertheless, we can calculate the minimum amount of Freddie's exposure. In the same report, Freddie disclosed that $190 billion of its loans were categorized as Alt-A and $68 billion had FICO credit scores of less than 620, so that they would clearly be categorized as subprime. Based on the limited information Freddie supplied, double counting of $7.6 billion can be eliminated, so that as of August 2008, Freddie held or had guaranteed at least $258 billion of junk loans. To this must be added $134 billion of subprime and Alt-A loans that Freddie purchased from private label issuers,[69] for a grand total of $392 billion—20 percent of Freddie's single-family portfolio of $1.8 trillion.

---

69. Freddie Mac, "Freddie Mac Update," August 2008, 30, available at www.freddiemac.com/investors/pdffiles/investor-presentation.pdf (accessed September 29, 2008).

A New Trillion-Dollar Commitment

Between 2005 and 2007, Fannie and Freddie acquired so many junk mortgages that, as of August 2008, they held or had guaranteed more than $1.011 trillion in unpaid principal balance exposures on these loans. The losses already recognized on these exposures were responsible for the collapse of Fannie and Freddie and their takeover by the federal government, and there are undoubtedly many more losses to come. In congressional testimony on September 23, James Lockhart, the director of their new regulator, the Federal Housing Finance Agency, cited these loans as the source of the GSEs' ultimate collapse, as reported in the *Washington Post:*

> Fannie Mae and Freddie Mac purchased and guaranteed "many more low-documentation, low-verification and non-standard" mortgages in 2006 and 2007 "than they had in the past." He said the companies increased their exposure to risks in 2006 and 2007 despite the regulator's warnings.
>
> Roughly 33 percent of the companies' business involved buying or guaranteeing these risky mortgages, compared with 14 percent in 2005. Those bad debts on mortgages led to billions of dollars in losses at the firms. "The capacity to raise capital to absorb further losses without Treasury Department support vanished," Lockhart said.[70]

Although a large share of the subprime loans now causing a crisis in the international financial markets are so-called private label securities—issued by banks and securitizers other than Fannie Mae and Freddie Mac—the two GSEs became the biggest buyers of the AAA tranches of these subprime pools in 2005–07.[71] Without their commitment to purchase the AAA tranches of these securitizations, it is unlikely that the pools could have been formed and marketed around the world. Accordingly, not only did the GSEs destroy their own financial condition with their excessive purchases of subprime loans in

---

70. Zachary A. Goldfarb, "Affordable-Housing Goals Scaled Back," *Washington Post,* September 24, 2008.

71. James Lockhart, "Reforming the Regulation of the Government Sponsored Enterprises" (testimony, Committee on Banking, Housing and Urban Affairs, U.S. Senate, 110th Cong., 2nd sess., February 7, 2008), 6, available at www.ofheo.gov/media/testimony/27 08LockharttestimonyWeb.pdf (accessed September 29, 2008).

the three-year period from 2005 to 2007, but they also played a major role in weakening or destroying the solvency and stability of other financial institutions and investors in the United States and abroad.

Why Did They Do It?

Why did the GSEs follow this disastrous course? One explanation—advanced by Lockhart—is that Fannie and Freddie were competing for market share with the private label securitizers and had to purchase substantial amounts of subprime mortgages in order to retain their position in a growing market. Fannie and Freddie's explanation is that they were the victims of excessively stringent HUD affordable housing goals. Neither of these explanations is plausible. For many years before 2004, Fannie and Freddie had followed relatively prudent invest-ment strategies, even with respect to affordable housing, but they suddenly changed their approach in 2005. Freddie Mac's report, for example, shows that the percentage of mortgages in its portfolio with subprime characteristics rose rapidly after 2004. Tables 1 and 2 show that for each category of mortgages with subprime characteristics, most of the portfolio of loans with those characteristics was acquired from 2005 to 2007. For example, 83.8 percent of Fannie's and 90 percent of Freddie's interest-only loans as of June 2008 were acquired from 2005 to 2007, and 57.5 percent of Fannie's and 61 percent of Freddie's loans with FICO scores of less than 620 as of June 2008 were acquired from 2005 to 2007. It seems unlikely that competing for market share or complying with HUD regulations—which contained no enforcement mechanism other than disclosure and delay in approving requests for mission expansions—could be the reason for such an obviously destructive course.

Instead, it seems likely that the event responsible for the GSEs' change in direction and culture was the accounting scandal that each of them encountered in 2003 and 2004. In both cases, they lost their reputation as well-managed companies and began to encounter questions about their contribution to reduc-ing mortgage rates and their safety and soundness. Serious observers questioned whether they should be allowed to continue to hold mortgages and MBS in their portfolios—by far their most profitable activity—and Senate Republicans moved a bill out of committee that would have prohibited this activity.

Under these circumstances, the need to manage their political risk became paramount, and this required them to prove to their supporters in Congress that they still served a useful purpose. In 2003, as noted above, Frank had cited an arrangement in which the GSEs' congressional benefits were linked to their investments in affordable housing. In this context, substantially increasing their support for affordable housing—through the purchase of the subprime loans permitted by HUD—seems a logical and even necessary tactic.

Unfortunately, the sad saga of Fannie and Freddie is not over. Some of their supporters in Congress prefer to blame the Fannie and Freddie mess on deregulation or private market failure, perhaps hoping to use such false diagnoses to lay the groundwork for reviving the GSEs for extra constitutional expenditure and political benefit in the future. As the future of the GSEs is debated over the coming months and years, it will be important to remember how and why Fannie and Freddie failed. The primary policy objective should be to prevent a repeat of this disaster by preventing the restoration of the GSE model.

Messrs. Wallison and Calomiris wish to thank Edward Pinto, a former chief credit officer of Fannie Mae, for his assistance in deciphering the GSEs' descriptions of their mortgage exposures. AEI research assistant Karen Dubas worked with the authors to produce this Financial Services Outlook.

"Cause and Effect: Government Policies and the Financial Crisis"

Originally published November 2008

Although the media are full of talk that we face a "crisis of capitalism," the underlying cause of the financial meltdown is something much more mundane and practical—the housing, tax, and bank regulatory policies of the U.S. government. The Community Reinvestment Act (CRA), Fannie Mae and Freddie Mac, penalty-free refinancing of home loans, tax preferences granted to home equity borrowing, and reduced capital requirements for banks that hold mortgages and mortgage-backed securities (MBS) have all weakened the standards for granting mortgages and the housing finance system itself. Blaming greedy bankers, incompetent rating agencies, or other actors in this unprecedented drama misses the point—perhaps intentionally—that government policies created the incentives for both a housing bubble and a reduction in the bank capital and home equity that could have mitigated its effects. To prevent a recurrence of this disaster, it would be far better to change the destructive government housing policies that brought us to this point than to enact a new regulatory regime that will hinder a quick recovery and obstruct future economic growth.

The current financial crisis is not—as some have said—a crisis of capitalism. It is in fact the opposite, a shattering demonstration that ill-considered government intervention in the private economy can have devastating consequences. The crisis has its roots in the U.S. government's efforts to increase homeownership, especially among minority and other underserved or low-income groups, and to do so through hidden financial subsidies rather than direct government expenditures. The story is an example, enlarged to an American scale, of the adverse results that flow from the misuse and manipulation of banking and credit by government. When this occurs in authoritarian regimes, we deride the outcome as a system of "policy loans" and note with an air of superiority that banks in these countries are weak, credit is limited, and financial crises are frequent. When the same thing happens in the United States, however, we blame "greedy" people, or poor regulation (or none), or credit default swaps, or anything else we can think of—except the government policies that got us into the disaster.

Expansion of homeownership could be a sound policy, especially for low-income families and members of minority groups. The social benefits of home-ownership have been extensively documented; they include stable families and neighborhoods, reduced crime and delinquency, higher living standards, and less depreciation in the housing stock. Under these circumstances, the policy question is not whether homeownership should be encouraged but how the government ought to do it. In the United States, the policy has not been pursued directly—through taxpayer-supported programs and appropriated funds—but rather through manipulation of the credit system to force more lending in support of affordable housing. Instead of a direct government subsidy, say, for down-payment assistance for low-income families, the government has used regulatory and political pressure to force banks and other government-controlled or regu-lated private entities to make loans they would not otherwise make and to reduce lending standards so more applicants would have access to mortgage financing.

The two key examples of this policy are the CRA, adopted in 1977, and the affordable housing "mission" of the government-sponsored enterprises (GSEs) Fannie Mae and Freddie Mac. As detailed below, beginning in the late 1980s—but particularly during the Clinton administration—the CRA was used to pressure banks into making loans they would not otherwise have made and to adopt looser lending standards that would make mortgage loans possible for individuals who could not meet the down payment and other standards that had previously been applied routinely by banks and other housing lenders. The same pressures were brought to bear on the GSEs, which adapted their underwriting standards so they could accept the loans made under the CRA and other loans that did not conform to what had previously been considered sound lending practices. Loans to members of underserved groups did not come with labels, and once Fannie and Freddie began accepting loans with low down payments and other liberalized terms, the same unsound practices were extended to bor-rowers who could have qualified under the traditional underwriting standards. It should not be surprising that borrowers took advantage of these opportunities. It was entirely rational to negotiate for a low-down-payment loan when that permitted the purchase of a larger house in a better neighborhood.

Many culprits have been brought before the bar of public humiliation as the malefactors of the current crisis—unscrupulous mortgage brokers, greedy investment bankers, incompetent rating agencies, foolish investors, and whiz-kid inventors of complex derivatives. All of these people and institutions played their part, of course, but it seems unfair to blame them for doing what the government policies were designed to encourage. Thus, the crisis would not have become so extensive and intractable had the U.S. government not created the necessary conditions for a housing boom by directing investments into the housing sector, requiring banks to make mortgage loans they otherwise would never have made, requiring the GSEs to purchase the secondary mortgage market loans they would never otherwise have bought, encouraging underwriting standards for housing that were lower than for any other area of the economy, adopting bank regulatory capital standards that encourage bank lending for housing in preference to other lending, and adopting tax policies that favored borrowing against (and thus reducing) the equity in a home.

As a result, between 1995 (when quotas based on the CRA became effective during the Clinton administration) and 2005, the homeownership percentage in the United States moved from 64 percent, where it had been for twenty-five years, to 69 percent; in addition, home prices doubled between 1995 and 2007. In other words, the government is responsible for the current crisis in two major respects: its efforts to loosen credit standards for mortgages created the housing bubble, and its policies on bank capital standards and the deductibility of interest on home equity loans made the current crisis inevitable when the bubble collapsed. This *Outlook* will explore the strong relationship between the intervention of the U.S. government in the housing market and the worldwide financial crisis that has resulted.

The Community Reinvestment Act

As originally enacted in 1977, the CRA was a vague mandate for regulators to "consider" whether an insured bank was serving the needs of the whole community it was supposed to serve. The "community" itself was not defined, and the act stated only that it was intended to "encourage" banks to meet community needs. It was enforced through the denial of applications for such things as mergers and acquisitions. The act also stated that serving community needs had to be done within the context of safe and sound lending practices, language that Congress probably inserted to ensure that the law would not be seen as a form of credit allocation. Although the act was adopted to prevent "redlining"—the practice of refusing loans to otherwise qualified borrowers in low-income areas—it also contained language that included small business, agriculture, and similar groups among the interests that had to be served. With the vague compliance standard that required banks only to be "encouraged" and their performance to be "considered," the act was invoked relatively infrequently when banks applied for permission to merge or another regulatory approval, until the Clinton administration.[72]

The decisive turn in the act's enforcement occurred in 1993 and was probably induced by the substantial amount of media and political attention that had been paid to the Boston Federal Reserve Bank's 1992 study of discrimination in home mortgage lending.[73] The study concluded that while there was no overt discrimination in the allocation of mortgage funds, more subtle forms of discrimination existed in which whites received better treatment by loan officers than members of minorities. The methodology of the study has since been questioned,[74] but it seems to have been highly influential with regulators and members of the incoming Clinton administration at the time of its publication. In 1993, bank regulators initiated a major effort to reform the CRA regulations. Some of the context in which this was occurring can be gleaned from the following statement by Attorney General Janet Reno in January 1994: "[W]e will tackle lending discrimination wherever and in whatever form it appears. No loan is exempt, no bank is immune. For those who thumb their nose at us, I promise vigorous enforcement."[75]

---

72. See the extensive discussion of the Community Reinvestment Act's development in A. K. M. Rezaul Hossain, "The Past, Present and Future of Community Reinvestment Act (CRA): A Historical Perspective" (working paper 2004-30, Department of Economics, University of Connecticut, Storrs, CT, October 2004), available at www.econ.uconn.edu/working/2004-30.pdf (accessed November 21, 2008).

73. Alicia H. Munnell, Lynn E. Browne, James McEneaney, and Geoffrey M. B. Tootell, "Mortgage Lending in Boston: Interpreting HMDA Data" (working paper 92-7, Federal Reserve Bank of Boston, 1992), available at www.bos.frb.org/economic/wp/wp1992/wp92_7.pdf (accessed November 21, 2008).

74. See discussion in Vern McKinley, "Community Reinvestment Act: Ensuring Credit Adequacy or Enforcing Credit Allocation?" *Regulation* 17, no. 4 (1994): 32, available at www.cato.org/pubs/regulation/regv17n4/vmck4-94.pdf (accessed November 21, 2008).

75. Ibid., 30.

The regulators' effort culminated in new rules adopted in May 1995 that would be phased in fully by July 1997. The new rules attempted to establish objective criteria for determining whether a bank was meeting the standards of the CRA, taking much of the discretion out of the hands of the examiners. "The emphasis on performance-based evaluation," A. K. M. Rezaul Hossain, an economist at Mount Saint Mary College, writes, "can be thought of as a shift of emphasis from procedural equity to equity in outcome. In that, it is not sufficient for lenders to prove elaborate community lending efforts directed towards borrowers in the community, but an evenhanded distribution of loans across LMI [low and moderate income] and non-LMI areas and borrowers."[76] In other words, it was now necessary for banks to show that they had actually made the requisite loans, not just that they were trying to find qualified borrowers. In this connection, one of the standards in the new regulations required the use of "innovative or flexible" lending practices to address credit needs of LMI borrowers and neighborhoods.[77] Thus, a law that was originally intended to encourage banks to use safe and sound practices in lending now required them to be innovative and flexible—a clear requirement for the relaxation of lending standards.

There is very little data available on the performance of loans made under the CRA. The subject has become so politicized in light of the housing meltdown and its effect on the general economy that most reports—favorable or unfavorable—should probably be discounted. Before the increases in housing prices that began in 2001, reviews of the CRA were generally unfavorable. The act increased costs for banks, and there was an inverse relationship between their CRA lending and their regulatory ratings.[78] One of the few studies of CRA lending in comparison to normal lending was done by the Federal Reserve Bank of Cleveland, which reported in 2000 that "respondents who did report differences [between regular and CRA housing loans] most often said they had lower prices or higher costs or credit losses for CRA-related home purchase and

---

76. A. K. M. Rezaul Hossain, "The Past, Present and Future of Community Reinvestment Act (CRA): A Historical Perspective," 54.

77. Ibid., 57.

78. See, for example, George J. Benston, "The Community Reinvestment Act: Looking for Discrimination That Isn't There" (Policy Analysis 354, Cato Institute, Washington, DC, October 6, 1999), available at www.cato.org/pub_display.php?pub_id=1213 (accessed November 21, 2008).

refinance loans than for others."[79] Much CRA lending after 2000 occurred during a period of enormous growth in housing values, which tended to suppress the number of defaults and reduce loss rates.

The important question, however, is not the default rates on the mortgages made under the CRA. Whatever those rates might be, they were not sufficient to cause a worldwide financial crisis. The most important fact associated with the CRA is the effort to reduce underwriting standards so that more low-income people could purchase homes. Once these standards were relaxed—particularly allowing loan-to-value ratios higher than the 20 percent that had previously been the norm—they spread rapidly to the prime market and to subprime markets where loans were made by lenders other than insured banks. The effort to reduce mortgage underwriting standards was led by the Department of Housing and Urban Development (HUD) through the National Homeownership Strategy published in 1994 in response to a request by President Clinton. Among other things, it called for "financing strategies, fueled by the creativity and resources of the private and public sectors to help homeowners that lack cash to buy a home or to make the payments."[80] Many subsequent studies have documented the rise in loan-to-value ratios and other indicators of loosened lending standards.[81]

After 1995 and the adoption of the new CRA regulations, homeownership in the United States grew rapidly. Having remained at 64 percent for almost twenty-five years, it grew to 69 percent between 1995 and 2005.[82] The increased availability of credit under CRA requirements probably also spurred housing

79. Robert B. Avery, Raphael W. Bostic, and Glenn B. Canner, "The Performance and Profitability of CRA-Related Lending," *Economic Commentary, Federal Reserve Bank of Cleveland* (November 2000), available at www.clevelandfed.org/research/Commentary/2000/1100.htm (accessed November 21, 2008).

80. Quoted in Joseph R. Mason, "A National Homeownership Strategy for the New Millennium." The National Homeownership Strategy, referred to in the Mason article, was removed from the Department of Housing and Urban Development website in 2007.

81. See, for example, Yuliya Demyanyk and Otto Van Hemert, "Understanding the Subprime Mortgage Crisis" (Social Science Research Network, August 19, 2008), available at http://ssrn.com/ abstract=1020396 (accessed November 21, 2008); and Robert Stowe England, "Giving It 100 Percent," *Mortgage Banking,* February 1, 2002.

82. Polina Vlasenko, "Home Ownership in the United States" (commentary, American Institute for Economic Research, Great Barrington, MA, September 2008), available at www.aier.org/research/commentaries/533-home-ownership-in-the-united-states (accessed November 21, 2008).

demand, which doubled home prices between 1995 and 2007.[83] The key question, however, is the effect of relaxed lending standards on lending standards in non-CRA markets. In principle, it would seem impossible—if down payment or other requirements were being relaxed for loans in minority-populated or other underserved areas—to limit the benefits only to those borrowers. Inevitably, the relaxed standards banks were enjoined to adopt under CRA would be spread to the wider market—including to prime mortgage markets and to speculative borrowers. Bank regulators, who were in charge of enforcing CRA standards, could hardly disapprove of similar loans made to better qualified borrowers. This is exactly what occurred. Writing in December 2007 for the Milken Institute, four scholars observed: "Over the past decade, most, if not all, the products offered to subprime borrowers have also been offered to prime borrowers. In fact, during the period from January 1999 through July 2007, prime borrowers obtained thirty-one of the thirty-two types of mortgage products—fixed-rate, adjustable rate and hybrid mortgages, including those with balloon payments—obtained by subprime borrowers."[84]

Sure enough, according to data published by the Joint Center for Housing Studies of Harvard University, from 2001 through 2006, the share of all mortgage originations that were made up of conventional mortgages (that is, the thirty-year fixed-rate mortgage that had always been the mainstay of the U.S. mortgage market) fell from 57.1 percent in 2001 to 33.1 percent in the fourth quarter of 2006. Correspondingly, subprime loans (those made to borrowers with blemished credit) rose from 7.2 percent to 18.8 percent, and Alt-A loans (those made to speculative buyers or without the usual underwriting standards) rose from 2.5 percent to 13.9 percent. Although it is difficult to prove cause and effect, it seems highly likely that the lower lending standards banks were required to adopt under the CRA influenced what they and other lenders were willing to offer to borrowers in prime markets. Needless to say, most borrowers

---

83. Economagic.com, "Economic Time Series Page: US: Average Price of Houses Actually Sold," available at www.economagic.com/em-cgi/data.exe/cenc25/c25q07 (accessed November 21, 2008). The average price of homes sold increased from $153,500 in the fourth quarter of 1995 to $322,100 in the first quarter of 2007.

84. James Barth, Tong Li, Triphon Phumiwasana, and Glenn Yago, "Surprise: Subprime Mortgage Products Are Not the Problem!" (Milken Institute, Santa Monica, CA, December 6, 2007), available through www.milkeninstitute.org/publications/publications .taf?function=detail&ID=38801030&cat=Papers (accessed November 21, 2008).

would prefer a mortgage with a low down payment requirement, allowing them to buy a larger home for the same initial investment. There is nothing immoral about this; if the opportunity is there, most families can think of better uses for their savings than making a large down payment for a home.

The problem is summed up succinctly by Stan Liebowitz of the University of Texas at Dallas: "From the current handwringing, you'd think that the banks came up with the idea of looser underwriting standards on their own, with regulators just asleep on the job. In fact, it was the regulators who relaxed these standards—at the behest of community groups and 'progressive' political forces. . . . For years, rising house prices hid the default problems since quick refinances were possible. But now that house prices have stopped rising, we can clearly see the damage done by relaxed loan standards."[85] The point here is not that low-income borrowers received mortgage loans that they could not afford; that is probably true to some extent but cannot account for the large number of subprime and Alt-A loans that currently pollute the banking system. It was the spreading of these looser underwriting standards to the prime loan market that encouraged the huge increase in credit availability for mortgages, the speculation in housing, and ultimately the bubble in housing prices.

Fannie Mae and Freddie Mac

Before they were taken over by a federal government conservatorship in September 2008, Fannie and Freddie had become two of the largest financial corporations in the world. In an important sense, the GSEs were the successors to the failed savings and loan associations (S&Ls) of the late 1980s and early 1990s. The fact that Fannie and Freddie were permitted—indeed encouraged—to grow after the S&Ls collapsed speaks volumes about the inability of congressional lawmakers to learn any lessons from the past. This discouraging conclusion comes into even sharper focus as we see policymakers developing solutions to the current crisis that will cause it to recur, just as the GSEs' supporters in Congress enabled them to repeat the policy mistakes that eventually, in the S&L fiasco, cost the taxpayers $150 billion.

---

85. Stan Liebowitz, "The Real Scandal: How Feds Invited the Mortgage Mess," *New York Post,* February 5, 2008.

By 2005, it had become clear that Fannie and Freddie were not materially assisting middle-class homebuyers by lowering interest rates.[86] Given the political basis for the existence of the GSEs, this is a significant fact. Both Fannie and Freddie had suffered major accounting scandals in 2003 and 2004, and their political support in a Republican Congress was shaky. Alan Greenspan, then at the height of his reputation for financial sagacity, had begun to campaign against them—particularly against their authority to hold the portfolios of mortgages and MBS that constituted their most profitable activity.

When the history of this era is written, students will want to understand the political economy that allowed Fannie and Freddie to grow without restrictions while producing large profits for shareholders and management but no apparent value for the American people. The answer is the affordable housing mission that was added to their charters in 1992, which—like the CRA—permitted Congress to subsidize LMI housing without appropriating any funds. As long as Fannie and Freddie could credibly contend that they were advancing the interests of LMI homebuyers, they could avoid new regulation by Congress—especially restrictions on the accumulation of mortgage portfolios, totaling approximately $1.5 trillion by 2008, that accounted for most of their profits. They could argue to Congress that if the mortgage portfolios were constrained by regulation, they could not afford to subsidize affordable housing.[87] In addition, the political sophistication of Fannie Mae's management enabled the company to serve the interests of key lawmakers who could and did stand in the way of the tougher regulation that might have made the current crisis far less likely.[88]

Although they were pressed by HUD's affordable housing regulations to buy increasing numbers of LMI loans, Fannie and Freddie appear to have willingly cooperated with the implementation of this policy. In 1994, HUD required that 30 percent of GSE mortgage purchases consist of affordable-housing mortgages,

---

86. See, for example, Andreas Lehnert, Wayne Passmore, and Shane M. Sherlund, "GSEs, Mortgage Rates, and Secondary Market Activities" (Finance and Economics Discussion Paper, Divisions of Research and Statistics and Monetary Affairs, Federal Reserve Board of Governors, Washington, DC, September 8, 2006), available at www.federal reserve.gov/pubs/feds/2006/ 200630/200630pap.pdf (accessed August 25, 2008).

87. See Peter J. Wallison and Charles W. Calomiris, "The Last Trillion-Dollar Commitment: The Destruction of Fannie Mae and Freddie Mac," *Financial Services Outlook* (September 2008), available at www.aei.org/publication28704/. (See p. 98 of this book.)

88. Ibid.

and requirements became tighter over the following years. But there was still doubt as to whether Fannie and Freddie were doing as much as they could to advance the administration's goals in this area. In 1997, for example, HUD commissioned the Urban Institute to study the GSEs' underwriting guidelines. The Urban Institute's report concluded: "The GSEs' guidelines, designed to identify creditworthy applicants, are more likely to disqualify borrowers with low incomes, limited wealth, and poor credit histories; applicants with these characteristics are disproportionately minorities. Informants said that some local and regional lenders serve a greater number of creditworthy low-to-moderate income and minority borrowers than the GSEs, using loan products with more flexible underwriting guidelines than those allowed by Fannie and Freddie."[89] Following this report, Fannie and Freddie modified their automated underwriting systems to accept loans with characteristics that they had previously rejected. This opened the way for the acquisition of large numbers of nontraditional and subprime mortgages. These did not necessarily come from traditional banks, lending under the CRA, but from lenders like Countrywide Financial, the nation's largest subprime and nontraditional mortgage lender and a firm that would become infamous for consistently pushing the envelope on acceptable underwriting standards.

By 1997, Fannie was offering a 97 percent loan-to-value mortgage, and by 2001, it was offering mortgages with no down payment at all. By 2007, Fannie and Freddie were required to show that 55 percent of their mortgage purchases were LMI loans and, within this goal, that 38 percent of all purchases were from underserved areas (usually inner cities) and 25 percent were purchases of loans to low-income and very-low-income borrowers.[90] Meeting these goals almost certainly required Fannie and Freddie to purchase loans with low down payments and other deficiencies that would mark them as subprime or Alt-A.

---

89. Kenneth Temkin, George Galster, Roberto Quercia, and Sheila O'Leary, "A Study of the GSEs' Single-Family Underwriting Guidelines" (executive summary, Urban Institute, Washington, DC, April 9, 1999), available at www.urban.org/url .cfm?ID=1000205&renderforprint=1 (accessed November 21, 2008).

90. Fannie Mae, *Fannie Mae's 2007 Annual Housing Activities Report* (Washington, DC: Department of Housing and Urban Development, March 17, 2008), 5, available at http://170.97.167.13/offices/hsg/gse/reports/2007aharfnmanarrative.pdf (accessed November 21, 2008).

There is no universally accepted definition of either subprime or Alt-A loans, except that neither of them is considered a prime loan (fifteen- or thirty-year amortization, fixed interest rate, good credit history) and both thus represent enhanced risk. The Federal Reserve Bank of New York defines a subprime loan as one made to a borrower with blemished credit or who provides only limited documentation. The federal bank regulators define a loan to a borrower with less than a 660 FICO score as subprime. Alt-A loans generally have a higher balance than subprime and one or more elements of added risk, such as a high loan-to-value ratio (often as a result of a piggyback second mortgage), interest-only payments, little or no income documentation, and the borrower as an investor rather than a homeowner. The term "subprime," accordingly, generally refers to the financial capabilities of the borrower, while Alt-A loans generally refer to the quality of the loan terms. Subprime and Alt-A loans are both defaulting at unprecedented rates and should be regarded together as the toxic loans that are currently on the books of banks and other troubled financial institutions around the world.

The decline in underwriting standards is clear in the financial disclosures of Fannie and Freddie. From 2005 to 2007, Fannie and Freddie bought approximately $1 trillion in subprime and Alt-A loans, amounting to about 40 percent of their mortgage purchases during that period. Freddie's data show that it acquired 6 percent of its Alt-A loans in 2004; this jumped to 17 percent in 2005, 29 percent in 2006, and 32 percent in 2007. Fannie purchased 73 percent of its Alt-A loans during these three years. Similarly, in 2004, Freddie purchased 10 percent of the loans in its portfolio that had FICO scores of less than 620; it increased these purchases to 14 percent in 2005, 17 percent in 2006, and 30 percent in 2007, while Fannie purchased 57.5 percent of the loans in this category during the same period.[91] For compliance with HUD's affordable-housing regulations, these loans tended to be "goal-rich." However, because they are now defaulting at unprecedented rates, the costs associated with these loans will be borne by U.S. taxpayers and are in large part the result of the failure of

---

91. See Fannie Mae, "2008 Q2 10-Q Investor Summary," August 8, 2008, 29–30, available at www.fanniemae.com/media/pdf/newsreleases/2008_Q2_10Q_Investor_Summary.pdf (accessed September 29, 2008); and Freddie Mac, "Freddie Mac Update," August 2008, 30, available at www.freddiemac.com/investors/pdffiles/investor-presentation.pdf (accessed September 29, 2008).

Congress to adopt an effective new regulatory structure for Fannie and Freddie. In this sense, the GSEs' extraordinary and devastating commitment to affordable housing loans was a tactical success.

All told, Fannie and Freddie probably hold or have guaranteed $1.6 trillion in subprime and Alt-A mortgages today. It is impossible to forecast the total losses they will suffer as a result, but if default rates on these loans continue at the unprecedented levels they are showing today, the losses could make the $150 billion S&L bailout in the late 1980s and early 1990s look small by comparison.

The GSEs' purchases of subprime and Alt-A loans affected the rest of the market for these mortgages in two ways. First, it increased the competition for these loans with private-label issuers. This competition had already existed, but the GSEs were not major buyers until late 2004. Prior to that, private-label issuers—investment and commercial banks for the most part—specialized in subprime and Alt-A loans because the financial advantages of the GSEs, including their access to cheaper financing, enabled them to exclude private-label competition from the conventional market. When the GSEs decided to ramp up their purchases of subprime and Alt-A loans, they began to take market share from the private-label issuers but also created greater demand for subprime and Alt-A loans from the mortgage brokers, mortgage bankers, and other members of the originator community. Second, the increased demand from the GSEs and the competition with private-label issuers drove up the value of subprime and Alt-A mortgages, reducing the risk premium that had previously suppressed originations. As a result, many more marginally qualified or unqualified applicants for mortgages were accepted, and these loans joined the flood of junk loans that flowed to both the GSEs and the private-label issuers beginning in late 2004. During this period, conventional loans (including jumbo loans) declined from 78.8 percent of all mortgages in 2003 to 50.1 percent at the end of 2006. During this same period, subprime and Alt-A loans increased from a 10.1 percent to a 32.7 percent share.[92] Since GSE purchases are not included in these numbers, in the years just before the collapse of home prices began, about half of all home loans being made in the United States were non–prime loans.

---

92. Joint Center for Housing Studies, *The State of the Nation's Housing 2008* (Cambridge, MA: Harvard University, 2008), 39, available through www.jchs.harvard.edu/publications/markets/son2008/index.htm (accessed November 21, 2008).

The GSEs' regulation-induced competition with private-label issuers almost certainly had the same effect on the quality of the mortgages the private-label issuers were securitizing. Since these mortgages aggregate more than $2 trillion, this accounts for the weakness in bank assets that is the principal underlying cause of the current financial crisis. In a very real sense, then, competition from Fannie and Freddie beginning in late 2004 caused both groups to scrape the bottom of the barrel—Fannie and Freddie in order to demonstrate to Congress their ability to increase support for affordable housing, and the private-label issuers trying to maintain their market share against the GSEs' increased demand for subprime and Alt-A products. Thus, the gradual decline in lending standards that began with the revised CRA regulations in 1993 and continued with the GSEs' attempts to show Congress that they were meeting their affordable housing mission came to dominate mortgage lending in the United States.

Homeowner Options under U.S. Law

State-based U.S. residential finance laws, accommodated by the national mortgage market system, give U.S. homeowners two free options that contributed substantially to the financial crisis we confront today. First, any homeowner may, without penalty, refinance a mortgage whenever interest rates fall or home prices rise to a point where there is significant equity in the home. The right to refinance is very rare in the commercial world because it increases the difficulty of matching assets and liabilities and thus places significant risks on financial intermediaries. Because home mortgages can be refinanced at any time, banks and others must engage in sophisticated hedging transactions to protect themselves against the disappearance of their mortgage assets if interest rates decline. More important for the purposes of this *Outlook,* the ability of homeowners to refinance their mortgages whenever they want also enabled them to extract any equity that had accumulated in the home between the original financing transaction and any subsequent refinancing. When combined with the gradual decline in lenders' demands for substantial down payments and the absence of any prepayment penalty, this option permitted homeowners to obtain in cash at the time of a refinancing a significant portion of the equity that had accumulated in the home up to that point. That equity, of course, could have been the result of a general increase in home prices rather than a homeowner's gradual amortization of principal under the mortgage loan.

The result was the so-called cash-out refinancing, in which homeowners treated their homes like savings accounts, drawing out funds through refinancing to buy cars, boats, or second homes, or pay for other family expenditures. By the end of 2006, 86 percent of all home mortgage refinancings were cash-out refinancings, amounting to $327 billion that year.[93] Unfortunately, this meant that when home prices fell, there was little equity in the home behind the mortgage and frequently little reason to continue making payments on the mortgage. This phenomenon, of course, applied to prime mortgages as well as subprime and Alt-A loans. The degree to which holders of prime mortgages might be willing to abandon their homes when the mortgage debt is greater than the home's value is one of the major unknowns of the current crisis.

The willingness of homeowners to walk away from their "underwater" mortgages is increased by the second element of the options that are routinely made available to U.S. homeowners and accommodated by the national mortgage system. In most states, either mortgages are "without recourse"—meaning that defaulting homeowners are not personally responsible for paying any difference between the value of the home and the principal amount of the mortgage obligation—or the process for enforcing this obligation is so burdensome and time-consuming that lenders simply do not bother to enforce it. Frequently, the mortgage note permits the lender to waive this burden in exchange for a quick foreclosure and sale. The homeowner's opportunity to walk away from a home that is no longer more valuable than the mortgage it carries exacerbates the effect of the cash-out refinancing that occurred throughout the bubble period.

There is a lot of discussion in Washington today about new regulations that will prevent the recurrence of today's crisis. The ideas are as far-reaching as regulating all financial intermediaries and as modest as providing better disclosure to homeowners when they take out a mortgage, but no one in Congress or elsewhere is considering or recommending that homeowners be required to pay a penalty for the privilege of refinancing their homes when mortgage rates decline or that state laws allowing for nonrecourse mortgages be preempted. These simple changes would go far toward rationalizing our mortgage system for the future, without the harmful effects on the whole economy that will result from new and unnecessary regulation of financial intermediaries.

---

93. Ibid, 37.

Tax Policies

The housing bubble, as well as the problem of homeowners extracting equity from their homes, was made considerably worse by tax laws. Two elements deserve particular mention: the deductibility of mortgage interest and the deductibility of interest on home equity loans. Of these two, the most influential by far is the general mortgage interest deduction. That provision substantially tilts the decision whether to rent or buy a home in favor of ownership. This might be a good idea if it encouraged low-income families to buy rather than rent their homes, but it does not. In general, low-income individuals do not pay any federal income taxes and thus get no benefit from the mortgage interest deduction. Even families with moderate incomes do not get a benefit from the mortgage interest deduction unless they itemize their tax returns.

But in terms of its effect on the current financial crisis, the deductibility of interest on home equity loans is far and away the most important provision in the tax laws. Interest on consumer loans of all kinds—for cars, credit cards, or other purposes—is not deductible for federal tax purposes, but interest on home equity loans is deductible no matter what the purpose of the loan or the use of the funds. As a result, homeowners are encouraged to take out home equity loans to pay off their credit card or auto loans, or to make the purchases that would ordinarily be made with credit cards, auto loans, or ordinary consumer loans. Under these circumstances, homeowners are encouraged not only to borrow against their homes' equity in preference to other forms of borrowing, but also to extract equity from their homes for personal and even business purposes. Again, the reduction in home equity has enhanced the likelihood that defaults and foreclosures will rise precipitously as the economy continues to contract.

Bank Capital Regulations

Under a 1988 international protocol known as Basel I, the bank regulators in most of the world's developed countries adopted a uniform system of assigning bank assets to different risk categories. The purpose of the system was to permit some flexibility in the allocation of capital, based on the perceived riskiness of various types of assets. Capital is viewed as a shock absorber, and thus more capital should be held against the possibility of losses from riskier assets. The general rule is that banks are required to hold 8 percent risk-weighted capital in order to be adequately capitalized and 10 percent in order to be well-capitalized, so that the riskiest assets have to be backed by no less than 8 percent capital, while the safest (sovereign debt) are assigned a risk weight of zero. In this system, commercial loans received a risk weight of 100 percent, meaning that a bank must have capital of at least 8 percent of the value of its portfolio of commercial loans. In the same system, residential mortgages are deemed to be half as risky as commercial loans and were assigned a 50 percent risk weight, so banks are required to hold only 4 percent capital against the value of a residential mortgage. In addition, asset-backed securities rated AAA were assigned a 20 percent risk weight, so only 1.6 percent capital is necessary for a bank to hold AAA-rated MBS.

Basel I is in the process of being replaced by Basel II, which generally permits banks to use more refined methods, including internal models, for determining the risk weight to be placed on their assets and the capital they will be required to hold. However, for the purposes of this *Outlook,* it is only necessary to consider the effects of Basel I, which has been in force for all relevant periods up through 2007. The risk weight for residential mortgages has not been changed in Basel II.

The 50 percent risk weight placed on mortgages under the Basel rules provides an incentive for banks to hold mortgages in preference to commercial loans. Even more important, by purchasing a portfolio of AAA-rated MBS, or converting their portfolios of whole mortgages into an MBS portfolio rated AAA, banks could reduce their capital requirement to 1.6 percent. This amount might have been sufficient if the mortgages were of high quality or if the AAA rating correctly predicted the risk of default, but the gradual decline in underwriting standards meant that the mortgages in any pool of prime mortgages—and this was certainly true of subprime and Alt-A mortgages—often had high loan-to-value ratios, low FICO scores, or other indicators of low quality. In other words, the effect of the Basel bank capital standards, applicable throughout the world's developed economies, has been to encourage commercial banks to hold only a small amount of capital against the risks associated with residential mortgages. As these risks increased because of the decline in lending standards and the ballooning of home prices, the Basel capital requirements became increasingly inadequate for the risks banks were assuming in holding both mortgages and MBS portfolios. Even if it is correct to believe that residential mortgages are less risky than commercial loans—an idea that can certainly be challenged in today's economy—the lack of bank capital behind mortgage assets became blazingly clear when the housing bubble deflated.

Conclusion

A review of the key housing, tax, and regulatory policies pursued by the U.S. government over many years connects these policies very directly to the rise of a housing bubble, a decline in the quality of mortgages, and a reduction in the home equity and bank capital that would have protected the economy in the event of a bubble's collapse.

Preventing a recurrence of the financial crisis we face today does not require new regulation of the financial system. What is required instead is an appreciation of the fact—as much as lawmakers would like to avoid it—that U.S. housing policies are the root cause of the current financial crisis. Other players—"greedy" investment bankers; foolish investors; imprudent bankers; incompetent rating agencies; irresponsible housing speculators; shortsighted homeowners; and predatory mortgage brokers, lenders, and borrowers—all played a part, but they were only following the economic incentives that government policy laid out for them. If we are really serious about wanting to prevent a recurrence of this crisis—rather than increasing the power of the government over the economy—our first order of business should be to correct the destructive housing policies of the U.S. government.

Mr. Wallison thanks Edward Pinto for his assistance in the preparation of this Outlook.

"The Dead Shall Be Raised:
The Future of Fannie and Freddie"

Originally published January–February 2010

The renewed interest in Fannie Mae and Freddie Mac is premature. They are currently the mainstays of the U.S. housing market—more important now than they were before being placed in a government conservatorship in September 2008. Many observers do not believe the two government-sponsored enterprises (GSEs) can survive the immense losses they will cause taxpayers, but this is far from true. For Fannie and Freddie to be eliminated, a new mortgage-financing system must take their place, but there is not even a hint of a replacement on the horizon. Once the housing market recovers, the GSEs will still be the only game in town, and supporting them will continue to be the course of least resistance for Congress. Moreover, it will not be easy to implement any of the alternatives to reestablishing Fannie and Freddie as GSEs. Nationalizing or reorganizing them as public utilities would both have significant drawbacks, while privatizing the GSEs—the most sensible approach—would require a major change in public attitudes about securitization. Sadly, in the absence of viable alternatives, their restoration as GSEs seems the most likely outcome.

It has been an interesting few weeks for the small band of stalwarts who have always followed the depredations of Fannie and Freddie. The Treasury's Christmas Eve action,[94] which removed the cap on the financial support it would provide the two companies, awakened renewed interest in what they will ultimately cost taxpayers. Then, in a surprise move, Representative Barney Frank (D-Mass.)—the GSEs' long-time sponsor-protector—announced that the House Financial Services Committee, which he chairs, would seek to abol-

---

94. U.S. Department of the Treasury, "Treasury Issues Update on Status of Support for Housing Programs," news release, December 24, 2009, available at www.treas.gov/press/releases/2009122415345924543.htm (accessed February 4, 2010).

ish them. All this interest—and certainly Barney Frank's promise—is probably premature, since the two companies, still under the control of the Obama administration's conservatorship, are the mainstays of the housing finance market in the United States today. Indeed, because they have securitized 75 percent of all mortgages originated in the United States in the first three quarters of 2009, the GSEs are playing a more prominent role in the U.S. housing market now than ever before.[95] It is unlikely, accordingly, that Congress will seriously tinker with the GSEs until the housing market stabilizes or another credible source of financing for middle-class homes capable of replacing them becomes available.

Still, it is not too early to review the options that will be available to policymakers when they consider the future of the GSEs. Given the sad history of these two companies, one might think they will be received as pariahs when Congress is again asked to look at them, but that is unlikely. The GSEs offer advantages to Congress that will be hard to replicate, and as policymakers weigh the alternatives, they will be under significant pressure to reestablish Fannie and Freddie as GSEs. This will be a huge policy mistake, but one that may yet be made if the public fails to understand how and why the GSEs contributed to the financial crisis and why they will do so again if they are restored to their former role in the housing finance system.

In their former lives, Fannie and Freddie were politically powerful shareholder-owned companies known as GSEs because they were established through congressional charters, had government "missions" to operate a secondary market in residential mortgages and support low- and middle-income housing, and were viewed in the financial markets as government-backed even though their debt securities and other obligations had no explicit government guarantee. Their implicit, or assumed, government backing enabled them to drive all competition out of the middle-class housing sector, permitting Fannie and Freddie to acquire over $5 trillion in mortgages, which they either held in portfolios totaling approximately $1.5 trillion or securitized as mortgage-backed securities (MBS). In pursuing their mission to support low- and middle-income

---

95. Dwight M. Jaffee, "The Future Role of Fannie Mae and Freddie Mac in the U.S. Mortgage Market" (paper presented at AEA/AREUEA session "The Future of the GSEs," Atlanta, GA, January 3, 2010), 2, available at www.aeaweb.org/aea/conference/program/retrieve.php?pdfid=299 (accessed February 4, 2010).

housing—also called affordable housing—Fannie and Freddie assumed the credit risk on almost 11 million subprime and other high-risk mortgages and contributed substantially to the growth of a housing bubble. When that bubble began to deflate in 2007, they began to suffer huge losses that resulted in their apparent insolvency and a government takeover in September 2008.[96]

Today, Fannie and Freddie are wards of the government, held in conservatorships established under the Housing and Economic Recovery Act of 2008 (HERA). Placing the GSEs in conservatorships rather than receiverships was an error.[97] A conservatorship is generally created for the purpose of restoring a failed company to health, while a receivership would have given the government the clear authority to close the GSEs when that became the appropriate course. The conservator exercises the powers of a board of directors and, thus, cannot terminate unfavorable contracts or wind up the firm's business; however, a receiver, like a trustee in bankruptcy, has the powers necessary to liquidate failed companies, pay off their creditors, and terminate their existence. Under HERA, the Treasury had a choice between a conservator and a receiver for the two GSEs. Choosing a receiver would have signaled that the GSEs were on their way out, although the receivership could have lasted for years while Congress debated and adopted an alternative means of financing mortgages. In contrast, a conservatorship is, at best, a temporizing mechanism; it has effectively put off the decision of what will actually be done with Fannie and Freddie, and it gives Congress a role in making that decision. Congressional involvement in this situation will not produce a good policy result; GSEs offer Congress great advantages—particularly opportunities to direct spending on housing without appropriations and to use the GSEs for political benefit.

This *Outlook* will outline and analyze the four possible outcomes for Fannie and Freddie—nationalization, reorganization as a public utility, restoration to GSE status, and privatization. Liquidation is another possible outcome, but its policy implications are not substantially different from privatization, so it will not be treated as a separate option in this *Outlook*.

---

96. See Peter J. Wallison and Charles W. Calomiris, "The Last Trillion-Dollar Commitment: The Destruction of Fannie Mae and Freddie Mac," AEI *Financial Services Outlook* (September 2008), available at www.aei.org/outlook/28704. (See p. 98 of this book.)

97. See, for example, Peter J. Wallison, "Fannie and Freddie by Twilight," AEI *Financial Services Outlook* (August 2008), available at www.aei.org/outlook/28517.

Nationalization

One option available to Congress is to nationalize the GSEs. This would entail merging Fannie and Freddie into a single government agency responsible for maintaining a secondary mortgage market. The new agency, like the GSEs themselves, would buy mortgages from banks and other originators, package them into MBS, and sell them to investors. Costs would, presumably, be kept low by the government's explicit backing of the agency's MBS and of its debt, as well as by the absence of any requirement for capital or profit. For this analysis, let us leave aside the usual concerns about government agencies as operating units—their inefficiency, resistance to change, and difficulty in recruiting high-quality staffs—because one overriding issue seems to disqualify nationalization as a realistic option for Congress. As a nationalized activity, the new combined agency would have to be included in the federal budget, which is already in serious deficit. In 1970, Congress "privatized" Fannie Mae—that is, sold it off to public shareholders—as a way of reducing Fannie Mae's budgetary impact. It may also be that the GSEs were given an affordable housing mission in 1992 because the Federal Credit Reform Act of 1990 (FCRA),[98] impaired the usefulness of the Federal Housing Administration (FHA) for this purpose. Even assuming the new agency did nothing more than securitize mortgages, maintaining a secondary mortgage market would have a significant budgetary effect. In a growing housing market, its outlays to acquire mortgages would always be larger than the revenues it would recoup by selling MBS, and there is always the chance the GSEs will suffer losses on the mortgages the government would then guarantee.

In addition, under the FCRA the subsidy value of explicit government guarantees of private debt must be recorded in the budget. The subsidy value associated with the guarantees of a nationalized entity performing a secondary market function could be quite high, especially because it is likely that Congress will require any such entity to accept loans for securitization that private insurers or securitizers could reject as too risky. For example, consider the loans requiring low down payments and loans to borrowers with blemished credit that Congress and the Clinton and Bush administrations wanted Fannie and Freddie to accept.

---

98. Federal Credit Reform Act of 1990, Public Law 101-508, *U.S. Statutes at Large* 104 (1990): 1388–609.

Further, a nationalized agency would be subject to periodic spurts of congressional generosity with the taxpayers' money. For example, Congress periodically directed the FHA to reduce the down payments required from borrowers. Under these congressional demands, mortgages with loan-to-value ratios of more than 90 percent went from less than 1 percent of FHA mortgages in 1956 to more than 85 percent of its guaranteed loans in 2008. As loan-to-value ratios rose, the FHA's financial condition deteriorated; today the agency is probably in need of a congressional bailout. In short, if nationalization is what Frank has in mind as his replacement for Fannie and Freddie, he will have a fight on his hands if budget projections remain as dire in the near future as they are today.

A Public-Utility Structure

Proposals to reorganize Fannie and Freddie as one or more public utilities rely on a model in which the GSEs would be privately owned by banks or other private shareholders but would function like public utilities under federal regulation. As Fannie and Freddie did when they were GSEs, the public-utility version would buy mortgages from originators and securitize them; the main difference is that as public utilities Fannie and Freddie would probably be prohibited from holding mortgage portfolios. In this model, their guarantee fee rates and costs would be limited so they would pay a steady dividend to their shareholders, allowing them to raise capital, and regulation would limit their risk-taking. Any borrowing would presumably not be backed by the government, but as discussed below it seems likely they would still require some government support to function effectively.

Special support from the government would be necessary because a utility model would have to be shareholder owned to keep it off-budget, but its rates would be regulated. Allowing it to set its own rates, or to function as an unregulated cooperative owned by banks or others, would amount to a privatization, which is not what the supporters of the utility model have in mind. Unlike an electric utility, however, mortgage securitization involves significant risk, and dealing with risk requires differential pricing. A utility subject to government rate regulation will generally not be permitted to charge differential rates on any but the most formulaic terms. Thus, a rate-regulated securitizer, the public-utility version of Fannie and Freddie, might be allowed to charge a higher rate for a low FICO score or a mortgage with a high loan-to-value ratio, but not for a mortgage that is subject to high risk because of the area in which it originated. Risk-based pricing is very difficult for the government to do. The Federal Deposit Insurance Corporation has never been successful, for example, with risk-based pricing for bank deposit insurance premiums. The likelihood, therefore, is that regulated rates will tend to be blended: higher-quality mortgages will subsidize the lower-quality ones that the entity is required to take on. Under these circumstances, an unregulated competitor could skim the cream of the best mortgages in the market and always charge a lower rate than its government-regulated competitor for the highest-quality mortgages. Over time, this would lead to the regulated utility holding a portfolio of securitized mortgages seriously skewed toward the risky end of the curve. The solution will be to give the utility some special advantage—guaranteeing its MBS or conferring a monopoly over a special section of the market, or both. The former would create automatic market acceptance of its MBS as against those of its competitors, while the latter would simply exclude competitors. Safety-and-soundness regulation would be relied on, in the absence of market discipline or competition, to prevent excessive risk-taking.

But these government-conferred advantages have their own problems. The most serious concern is the budgetary effect of such a measure, since the MBS guarantee would have to be scored under the FCRA. Again, the subsidy level would need to be high because a government-regulated utility would be expected to accept risky mortgages other securitizers would shun. In addition, unlike public utilities such as local electric or water companies, Fannie and Freddie as regulated utilities would be taking major risks with the taxpayers' credit card. They will need to set rates for their guarantee fees that will provide a safe return to the shareholders while at the same time covering the potential for losses, and this will be extremely difficult, especially when—as is true for all regulated entities—Congress will have a strong influence on the rates prescribed or approved by their regulator. As in the case of the FHA, political forces will suppress guarantee fees, thereby preventing the utilities from being compensated appropriately for the risks Congress will require them to take. Without a profit incentive, and under pressure from Congress, there would be little incentive on the part of management or creditors to raise guarantee fees to fully compensatory levels. With these fees too low for the risk involved, regulated utilities will eventually become insolvent, and, ultimately, the taxpayers will pick up the losses.

In other words, there are strong arguments against reorganizing Fannie and Freddie based on a public-utility model. Not only would doing so have an undesirable budgetary effect, but it would also likely be costly for taxpayers in the long run.

Restoration as Government Sponsored Enterprises

GSEs have always been popular in Congress because they appear to provide free money for purposes for which Congress would normally have to appropriate funds. Because GSEs can borrow with the implicit backing of the federal government and can be directed to spend their funds on policies and programs favored by Congress, lawmakers perceive them as an improvement over the well-known and much-vilified earmark. For GSEs to spend money for congressionally desired purposes, members of Congress do not need the agreement of other lawmakers as they do with appropriations, and GSEs can spend without the hassle of troublesome public reporting. Because of the power Congress has over GSEs—the continuing ability to affect the scope and value of the GSEs' franchise—GSEs are always willing to do favors for important members. In Fannie and Freddie's case, favors included absorbing the cost of unprofitable housing or other projects in states or districts of important lawmakers, raising campaign funds from industries dependent on a flow of funds from the GSEs (such as realtors and home builders), and even hiring the relatives of important congressional supporters for Fannie Mae's local offices. It was a form of corruption, certainly, but for many years it was impossible for anyone to do anything about it. Fannie and Freddie were too powerful in Congress, and Congress enjoyed the benefits of controlling GSEs too much. Restoring Fannie and Freddie as GSEs opens the door again to many of these same problems.

Given this history, what—other than nationalization—could Barney Frank have had in mind when he said his committee would seek to abolish Fannie and Freddie? One need not be particularly cynical to see this is not a sudden confession of error. Before the two GSEs can be eliminated, Frank said, Congress will have to come up with "a whole new system of housing finance."[99] Currently, Congress is not considering a new system of housing finance, nor does

_____

99. Nick Timiraos and Michael R. Crittendon, "Fannie Mae, Freddie Mac Should Be Eliminated, Frank Says," *Wall Street Journal*, January 22, 2010.

it appear to have conceived of one. Even if a new system were under consideration, it would take years to implement. Frank knows this as well as anyone; in all likelihood, his "new system" will turn out to be the same old system, but he can express regret as it happens. Schadenfreude perhaps. The administration promised to say something about its plans for Fannie and Freddie in the budget document it delivered February 1, but once again it had apparently overpromised: the budget document was silent on the future of the GSEs.

Under these circumstances—although I would like to be proven wrong—the restoration of Fannie and Freddie as GSEs seems the most likely direction Congress will take once the housing-finance market stabilizes. It has the benefit of being the course of least resistance—everything else will look like a leap into the unknown—and the lack of a prospective system to replace Fannie and Freddie will further buttress the arguments of the GSEs' supporters in and out of Congress. The advocates of restoration will have to overcome several obstacles, of course, such as the fact that the GSEs will have recently cost the taxpayers as much as $400 billion (and perhaps even more) before their losses were entirely taken into account. But it is likely that the GSEs' insolvency will be attributed to weak regulation before the adoption of HERA, and perhaps to the fact that their regulation was divided between the Department of Housing and Urban Development, which was their "mission regulator," and the Office of Federal Housing Enterprise Oversight, which was their safety-and-soundness regulator. Under HERA, it will be argued, a new agency, the Federal Housing Finance Agency, will have both responsibilities and will thus be able to assure that they do not take too many risks while pursuing their affordable housing mission.

Despite these modified arrangements, it is difficult to say anything has fundamentally changed. Congress will still be influential with both the GSEs and their regulator, insisting that underwriting standards be relaxed so their constituents will find it easier to get mortgages. These diminished standards will eventually result in losses. The example of the FHA, discussed above, is relevant here. Moreover, regulation itself is a weak reed. Considering how often it has failed, it is remarkable that regulation is still considered a protection for the taxpayers. After the savings and loan crisis in the late 1980s and early 1990s—when almost 1,600 commercial banks also failed—Congress adopted the Federal Deposit Insurance Corporation Improvement Act, which contained every tough provision Congress and the bank regulators could think of to prevent bank crises in the future. Yet, we have just come through the worst banking crisis since the Great Depression. Furthermore, the GSEs are far more difficult to control with regulation than banks. Because of their centrality to the housing system and the ability of Congress to affect their franchise directly, Congress is acutely interested in what they are doing and the GSEs are equally interested in retaining Congress's approval. This is not a healthy mix. Requests directly from Congress will trump the restrictions imposed by their regulator, or the regulator itself will get congressional signals to relax restrictions that might be impairing the ability of their constituents to buy homes.

From all indications, the Obama administration is not likely to include the revenues and expenses of the GSEs in the federal budget now or in the foreseeable future, and this will also increase their attractiveness to Congress. The Congressional Budget Office recently added $291 billion to its baseline 2009 deficit to account for Fannie and Freddie's operations, arguing that they were being used as instruments of federal policy and that the administration had promised to extend unlimited funds to support them.[100] However, the Office of Management and Budget controls the standards for what is included in the president's budget and continues to follow a policy of treating privately owned companies as outside the federal budget process. Thus, while the market will continue to perceive Fannie and Freddie as entities at least implicitly backed by the government—demonstrated most recently by the conservatorship and the Treasury's unlimited financial support—their activities will have no effect on the federal budget. If this policy holds, and it is certainly likely to continue when the housing market has stabilized and some federal support has been withdrawn, Fannie and Freddie and their congressional supporters will have the best of both worlds—the assurance of government backing and the freedom to operate without affecting the deficit.

But it is important to remember that GSEs are founded on a false premise: that private companies can perform a government mission. This cannot be true. Private shareholder-owned companies must seek profit, while a public mission assumes complete devotion to that public objective. Given a choice between

---

100. Congressional Budget Office (CBO), *CBO's Budgetary Treatment of Fannie Mae and Freddie Mac,* 111th Cong., 2nd sess. (Washington, DC, January 2010), 2, available at www.cbo.gov/ftpdocs/108xx/doc10878/01-13-FannieFreddie.pdf (accessed February 4, 2010).

the two, the public mission is inevitably slighted. The requirement that the GSEs support affordable housing certainly accelerated their demise, but even without that spur the GSEs had plenty of incentives to increase risk-taking. As long as the private capital markets were persuaded that creditors would be rescued if they ran into financial trouble, there was no effective check on the GSEs' risk-taking. Although they had a weak regulator, the GSEs would have evaded even a strong regulator. Much of the call for a stronger regulator was based on the idea that the new regulator of the GSEs should have bank-like regulatory authority; now we know, as noted above, that not even bank-like regulatory power over the banks could prevent banks from taking excessive risks. To be successful, regulation needs the assistance of effective market discipline. Where moral hazard has eroded market discipline, regulation will not be able to prevent excessive risk-taking. As Professor Dwight Jaffee has observed:

> The flaw—and I believe the fatal flaw—with any and all plans to reconstitute the firms as GSEs is that they leave unresolved the inherent incompatibility of a private firm with a public mission. We have learned from first-hand experience that the incentive of a GSE with a government guarantee, implicit or explicit, is to expand its size and risk-taking as much as possible, and that these incentives ultimately dominate any public mission. I believe that the reestablishment of new GSEs will inevitably end with a new government bailout.[101]

As an example, if we assume that the GSEs will no longer be able to hold portfolios—one of the sources of their risks—and will be functioning solely through securitization, what risks could they take? First, we have to assume they will operate by placing a guarantee on the MBS they issue and that this guarantee will be deemed in the market to be roughly the equivalent of a federal-government guarantee. As noted above, the market is likely to slip back into the habit of believing that Fannie and Freddie are backed by the government. After all, in bailing out Fannie and Freddie's creditors, the government did exactly what those who thought the GSEs were government-backed expected the government to do. The government did the same thing in 1987 when it bailed out

---

101. Dwight M. Jaffee, "The Future Role of Fannie Mae and Freddie Mac in the U.S. Mortgage Market," 21.

the Farm Credit System,[102] and it is useful to note that the Farm Credit System is now a fully functioning set of GSEs again and is still off-budget. We can expect, then, that Fannie and Freddie will be able to function as they have in the past: by placing their guarantee on a pool of mortgages. The credit risks they take, unless compensated by high rates, will eventually result in insolvency and another government rescue.

To be sure, Fannie and Freddie as GSEs could be compensated for their risk-taking and losses through their guarantee fees. If these fees are high enough, they could operate in a safe and sound manner. But as regulated entities, they are not likely to be able to exploit their franchise without some congressionally extracted cost. The choice Fannie and Freddie made the first time around was to increase market share by cross-subsidizing their subprime and Alt-A loans with the high profits thrown off by their portfolios. This pleased their congressional supporters and protected their franchise. The same strategy will seem appropriate if they are restored as GSEs. Even if they do not have the authority to hold mortgage portfolios, the dynamic is unlikely to change. Risk-taking through expanding their market share and reducing their lending standards will enable them to earn substantial profits while increasing their congressional support. This strategy, however, will eventually result in unmanageable losses. In the end, as always, the taxpayers will be handed the bill.

Congress should face the fact that the profit mission of a shareholder-owned company is simply incompatible with a government mission of any kind. Although restoring Fannie and Freddie to their former status may appear to be an attractive option, doing so will be like rolling a live grenade into the future.

A Sensible Approach to Privatization

Although it is the most sensible approach to take, privatizing Fannie and Freddie is an unlikely choice for Congress at this point. The principal reason for pessimism in this respect is that the deficiencies of securitization have received

---

102. Bert Ely, "The Farm Credit System, Reinvented and Mission-Challenged: How a Fortunate Few Receive a Benefit from the Farm Credit System That Congress Never Intended or Envisioned," Ely & Company Inc., November 2002, available at www.aba.com/NR/rdonlyres/05858407-284E-46CD-9443-38EB9601A25A/28165/Ely111809999997.pdf (accessed February 4, 2010).

much of the blame for the current financial crisis, and privatizing Fannie and Freddie would add two more players to a market many lawmakers already think should be supplanted by something else. However, the negative view of securitization—also known, tellingly, as the originate-to-distribute system—is undeserved. In reality, securitization is a financial technology that has consistently produced low-cost credit for consumers.

Although originators sell their mortgages to those higher up the chain, it is not true—as many observers seem to believe—that they have no further risks. The standard agreements in the securitization market allow buyers to put back to originators—or anyone lower in the chain than themselves—any mortgages not performing as promised. As a result of these arrangements, many banks tried to return faulty mortgages to their originators, only to find that the originators had gone out of business. Recently, there were reports in the press that Fannie and Freddie were trying to return some deficient mortgages to the banks from which they were purchased. Of course, banks and investment banks could have done many things to protect themselves from faulty mortgages—why they failed to do so in time is something of a mystery—but it is not true that the securitization system is inherently faulty because originators do not bear any responsibility once they sell the loans.

There is as yet no substitute for the securitization system, and the banks—without a secondary mortgage market into which to sell their loans—cannot likely produce enough lendable funds to keep the mortgage markets functioning at the level required for continued growth. The private securitization market will have to be restored before the housing markets can return to normal, but that will probably take several years. During that period, Fannie and Freddie and the implicit government guarantees they offer will be necessary to keep the housing market functioning. That is one of the reasons the markets will again become accustomed to dealing with Fannie and Freddie as restored GSEs, and why keeping them in existence will be the course of least resistance.

Ultimately, the best policy is still to privatize or liquidate Fannie and Freddie and leave the secondary mortgage market to a large number of competing private participants. A private competitive market would not require a taxpayer bailout, would price mortgages according to risk, and would display the innovation and efficiencies characteristic of private markets. While Fannie and Freddie existed, these private market characteristics were suppressed and the secondary markets were distorted. Because of their low-cost, government-backed financing, Fannie and Freddie were able to drive all competition from the secondary market for middle-class prime mortgages. Private participants were relegated to a relatively small jumbo market or the risky subprime market. Without Fannie and Freddie, a vigorously competitive secondary market for middle-class prime mortgages probably would have developed. For this reason, once the securitization market has returned to normal, privatizing Fannie and Freddie should be considered while they remain in the conservatorship.

As it happens, the current conservatorship offers unique opportunities for privatization that would not exist if the GSEs were operating normally. There are three key obstacles. The first is what to do about their portfolios of mortgages and MBS, which probably total about $1.5 trillion at this point. The second is how to deal with about $4 trillion in MBS that they have previously guaranteed. The third obstacle is how to privatize giant companies that—because of their centrality to the mortgage market—will immediately become too big to fail. In many ways, the third problem is the toughest.

First, addressing the GSEs' portfolios should not be a significant obstacle to privatizing or liquidating them. Their mortgages and MBS will have a continuous depressive effect on housing prices until they are put in private hands. For this reason, the conservator should begin selling them slowly over the next few years as the securitization market struggles to recover. As with the Resolution Trust's sale of the savings and loans' assets, the prices the government receives are not as important as removing the overhang of unsold assets.

The second problem is more complicated. If Fannie and Freddie are not to be GSEs anymore, how can the guarantees they have made continue to protect the holders of their MBS? Substituting a direct government guarantee will be a windfall, but removing the guarantee entirely will cause the MBS to plunge in value. This obstacle can also be overcome; it can be handled through a process known as defeasement, a structure commonly used in the private sector. At some point, the Treasury will have to absorb the losses associated with Fannie and Freddie; this will occur whether Congress decides to restore them to health as GSEs or to liquidate or privatize them. These losses could exceed $400 billion. Part of the recognition of these losses will be defrayed by the gain on the sale of the GSEs' portfolios, but the balance must be borne by the taxpayers. When the Treasury decides to recognize this loss, it should defease the continuing obligation on the GSEs' guarantees by placing them in a trust with a sufficient amount of risk-free Treasury securities to assure the holders of the MBS that there are funds available to compensate them for any losses they might suffer on the MBS previously guaranteed by Fannie and Freddie.

Finally, privatizing or liquidating Fannie and Freddie can be easily done under the conservatorship. Currently, the GSEs operate under a conforming loan limit that prescribes the maximum size of mortgages they are permitted to buy. The limit is currently $730,000 for a single-family home in an expensive area and substantially lower in lower-cost areas. To decrease the size of the GSEs so they will no longer be too big to fail, the Federal Housing Finance Agency can gradually reduce the conforming loan limit, thereby slowly exposing a larger proportion of the housing-finance market to private-sector securitization, including a private sector affiliate of Fannie and Freddie. If the private market seizes these opportunities, and if the market is functioning satisfactorily, the conforming loan limit eventually can be reduced to a very small number, even zero. If it reaches zero, they will have been privatized. At that point, all further securitization by Fannie and Freddie must be done through an ordinary corporation, and the government-chartered GSEs will become subsidiaries, operating until the last MBS has been redeemed.

Conclusion

Of the four methods for dealing with Fannie and Freddie, only privatization assures the existence of a competitive, innovative, low-cost market, without the danger of an eventual taxpayer bailout. Nationalization falls apart as an option because of its budgetary effects, and a public-utility model will not work because rates could not be regulated in a manner that would enable Fannie and Freddie to compete effectively with private-sector firms. In the absence of alternatives—and there are none currently on the horizon—the GSE form is likely to be the one Congress will turn to. However, if the securitization market returns to normal while the GSEs are still in the current conservatorship, they can easily be privatized by reducing the conforming loan limit over time.

"Going Cold Turkey:
Three Ways to End Fannie and Freddie
without Slicing Up the Taxpayers"

Originally published September 2010

Most of the plans put forward for replacing Fannie Mae and Freddie Mac involve some continuing role for the government in housing finance. The reasons behind these plans are less than persuasive, and recent experience has shown that the moral hazard created by the government's presence in the housing-finance market can produce catastrophic results for taxpayers. Instead of trying to find ways that government can remain involved in housing finance, the new Congress should consider how to withdraw the government from any role in financing prime mortgages and implement various promising private-financing mechanisms—covered bonds, the Danish system, and a more focused and regulated securitization system.

The key question about the future of Fannie and Freddie—or, more properly, of government involvement in the mortgage market—is not whether the government guarantee should be explicit or implicit, or whether it should apply to the firm that issues mortgage-backed securities (MBS) or to the securities themselves. The key question is whether any government support for the secondary mortgage market makes sense as a matter of policy. If we look at the recent history of government involvement in the housing field, the picture is not pretty. Just within the last twenty years, the savings and loan (S&L) industry collapsed, with a loss to taxpayers of approximately $150 billion. Now Fannie Mae and Freddie Mac are operating under government conservatorships, with estimates of losses running from $400 billion to $1 trillion. Is it possible that Congress simply cannot learn from its mistakes?

Both the S&L industry and Fannie Mae were the products of Depression-era legislation to assist the housing industry. Fannie began life as a government agency with a simple mission: to buy mortgages from banks and other mortgage originators, providing these institutions with the funds to make more mortgages.

Initially, Fannie was funded by appropriations, and its activities added to the federal deficit during the Vietnam period. To address this problem, Congress "privatized" Fannie in 1968, allowing it to sell its voting shares to the public. But Fannie retained its government charter and mission, and these—together with various tax and other benefits—gave it a credible claim to implicit government support and to designation as a government-sponsored enterprise (GSE). Freddie Mac, Fannie's smaller competitor, was chartered in 1970 with the same benefits, and the two GSEs were seen in the capital markets as backed by the government.

Federal S&Ls had government charters and a government mission to originate mortgages, and they were eligible for federal deposit insurance. Thriving in the postwar boom, by 1965 S&Ls controlled 26 percent of consumer savings and made 46 percent of all single-family mortgages.[103] In 1966, when the industry had assets of approximately $130 billion, the government placed ceilings on the interest rates that could be paid on insured accounts at banks and S&Ls, but it allowed S&Ls to pay one-quarter percent more, assuring the industry of a steady flow of insured deposits to support the long-term mortgage assets they were expected to hold. With this government assistance, by 1979 the S&L industry had more than quadrupled in size to almost $580 billion.[104]

But the S&Ls were taking massive interest-rate risks. Their government mission required them to fund their long-term mortgage assets with short-term deposit liabilities. This was possible as long as the government controlled interest rates on insured deposits, but if the cost of their deposits ever increased substantially, they could not survive. When money-market mutual funds were developed during the inflationary (and high-interest-rate) period of the late 1970s and early 1980s, the S&Ls and banks suffered huge losses of low-cost deposits, and the government had to abandon its deposit-interest controls. As a result, by the early 1980s, most S&Ls were insolvent; it was impossible to fund thirty-year fixed-rate mortgages, paying 5 or 6 percent, when short-term rates in the money markets were as high as 20 percent.

When the S&L industry collapsed in the late 1980s and early 1990s, Fannie and Freddie—with their implicit government backing—stepped in as two gigantic S&Ls and began a period of exceptional growth, doubling in size every

---

103. David Mason, "Savings and Loan Industry (U.S.)," available at http://eh.net/encyclopedia/article/mason.savings.loan.industry.us (accessed September 20, 2010).
104. Ibid.

five years. By 2008, they were responsible for the credit risk of mortgages with an unpaid principal of over $5.5 trillion. But while the S&Ls were destroyed by interest-rate risk, the GSEs were destroyed by credit risk. Beginning in 1992, they were required to purchase increasing numbers of subprime and Alt-A mortgages in order to meet the affordable-housing goals imposed by Congress and administered by the Department of Housing and Urban Development (HUD). When these high-risk loans defaulted as the housing bubble deflated in 2007, Fannie and Freddie suffered massive losses. By late 2008, they were insolvent and the government took them over; at that point, they held or had guaranteed 12 million high-risk loans, with an unpaid principal of $1.8 trillion.

Thus we have two business models, both operating in the housing field with government support, that eventually collapsed into insolvency with huge costs to taxpayers. What they had in common was their government backing, which substantially reduced market discipline, allowing them to grow at extraordinary rates and take risks that other financial intermediaries would not have been permitted to take—for far longer than other firms that are funded privately.

Neither the interest risks taken by the S&Ls nor the credit risks taken by the GSEs could have occurred if investors and lenders had been looking to the credit of these institutions—rather than the government's credit—when they provided them with funds. Moreover, it was government backing that allowed these institutions to continue operating and incurring losses long after ordinary private companies would have been shut down by their creditors. The ability of the GSEs to continue operating when firms without government backing would have been shut down was in itself a major contributor to the bubble's size and destructiveness when it began to deflate in mid-2007. As the bubble grew, rising home prices both disguised the risks that homeowners and lenders were taking and made greater risks necessary if homebuyers were to afford the higher housing prices.

Arguments in Support of a Government Role

Given this history, it is surprising that arguments for continued government involvement in the housing market are so resilient. Government support for housing resulted in two recent catastrophes for taxpayers, and the arguments in support of government involvement are remarkably thin. In effect, they boil down to three:

TABLE 1
SUBPRIME AND ALT-A LOANS BY TYPE, JUNE 30, 2008

Entity	Number of Subprime or Alt-A Loans	Unpaid Principal Amount
Fannie Mae and Freddie Mac	12 million	$1.8 trillion
Federal Housing Administration and Other Federal Agencies	5 million	$0.6 trillion
Community Reinvestment Act and HUD Programs	2.2 million	$0.3 trillion
Total, Federal Government	**19.2 million**	**$2.7 trillion**
Private-Label Issuers[a]	7.8 million	$1.9 trillion
Total	**27 million**	**$4.6 trillion**

NOTE: Countrywide and many others; Wall Street firms represent about 25 percent of the total.

SOURCES: See the following works by Edward Pinto: "Sizing Total Exposure to Subprime and Alt-A Loans in U.S. First Mortgage Market as of 6.30.08" (memorandum, updated April 21, 2010), available at www.aei.org/docLib/Pinto-Sizing-Total-Exposure.pdf, which accounts for all 27 million high-risk loans; "Sizing Total Federal Government and Federal Agency Contributions to Subprime and Alt-A Loans in U.S. First Mortgage Market as of 6.30.08" (memorandum, updated April 21, 2010), available at www.aei.org/docLib/Pinto-Sizing-Total-Federal-Contributions.pdf, which covers the portion of these loans that were held or guaranteed by federal agencies and the four large banks and Countrywide that made these loans under the Community Reinvestment Act; and "High LTV, Subprime and Alt-A Originations over the Period 1992–2007 and Fannie, Freddie, FHA and VA's Role" (memorandum, updated April 21, 2010), available at www.aei. org/docLib/Pinto-High-LTV-Subprime-Alt-A.pdf, which covers the acquisition of these loans by government agencies from the early 1990s, when the process of reducing underwriting standards began. See also Edward Pinto, "Government Housing Policies in the Lead-up to the Financial Crisis: A Forensic Study" (discussion draft, August 14, 2010), available at www.aei.org/docLib/ Pinto-Government-Housing-Policies-Crisis.pdf.

The Government Enables the Thirty-Year Fixed-Rate Mortgage. Frequently, supporters of government involvement in the mortgage market argue that only with the government's support can a thirty-year fixed-interest-rate mortgage be possible. This is a myth. Those who make this statement have apparently not bothered to check the market for mortgages larger than those the GSEs are permitted to buy (known as "jumbo" loans). Even today, when the private securitization market is still weak from the effects of the financial crisis, many lenders and brokers are offering thirty-year fixed-rate jumbo loans, which of course have no government backing.

Government Involvement Lowers Mortgage Rates. This issue was carefully explored by Federal Reserve economists before the financial crisis occurred; their summary was that the low funding rates that Fannie and Freddie received because of their implicit government backing did not result in reduced interest rates for homebuyers: "We find that GSE portfolio purchases have no significant effects on either primary or secondary mortgage rate spreads."[105] A more detailed description appears later in the paper:

> We estimate that if the GSEs unexpectedly increase their portfolio purchases by $10 billion (about 3.7 percent of average monthly originations during 2004), the primary and secondary mortgage rate spreads would increase 1.4 and 1.3 basis points after one month, respectively. But if the GSEs instead unexpectedly increased their securitization activity (that is, their gross issuance of MBS) by $10 billion, we estimate that primary and secondary mortgage rate spreads would decline 0.6 and 0.5 basis points, respectively. Note that none of these effects is statistically different from zero.[106]

The Housing Market Would Not Be Stable without Government Support. Finally, the argument is made that the housing market must have government support in order to remain stable in adverse financial conditions. This is a peculiar argument to make when the government's main efforts to promote housing—the S&Ls and the GSEs—have both collapsed with devastating consequences for taxpayers, and the government's own housing policies produced a vast number of high-risk mortgages that caused a 30 percent decline in housing prices when they defaulted. As shown in table 1, the government was the principal customer for these subprime and Alt-A loans.

The effect of such a large number of subprime and other nontraditional mortgages on the U.S. financial system is shown by data on foreclosure starts following

---

105. See, for example, Andreas Lehnert, Wayne Passmore, and Shane M. Sherlund, "GSEs, Mortgage Rates, and Secondary Market Activities" (working paper, Federal Reserve Board, Divisions of Research & Statistics and Monetary Affairs, Finance and Economics Discussion Series, Washington, DC, September 2006), available at www.federalreserve. gov/pubs/feds/2006/200630/200630pap.pdf (accessed September 20, 2010).

106. Ibid., 23.

the deflation of recent housing bubbles.[107] After the bubble that ended in 1979, when almost all mortgages were the traditional type, with substantial down payments and borrowers with good credit histories, foreclosure starts reached a high point of only 0.87 percent in 1982. After the next bubble, which ended in 1992 and in which the vast majority of loans were still the traditional type, foreclosure starts reached a high of 1.32 percent in 1994. After the bubble that ended in 2007, however, when almost half of all U.S. mortgages were subprime or otherwise high risk, foreclosure starts for all loans reached the (thus far) unprecedented level of 5.37 percent in 2009, despite government efforts to prevent or delay foreclosures. The lesson is that where residential mortgages are of good quality, the deflation of occasional bubbles will not cause a serious financial disruption—certainly not enough disruption to warrant continuous government involvement in the housing field—but if government policy or moral hazard erodes underwriting standards, the private housing-finance system can be devastated.

Certainly, the fact that Fannie and Freddie—even though insolvent—are today the mainstays of the housing-finance market will be used to support the view that the government needs to be involved in the housing market, if only to be there in the event of a colossal failure such as the 2008 financial crisis. If we leave aside the fact that the government's involvement in the housing-finance business actually caused the colossal failure, this argument is superficially attractive. However, the data in Figure 1 show that the prime residential MBS market was no more seriously affected by the deflation of the housing bubble in 2007 than any of the other securitized-asset classes. All these classes suffered losses in value as a result of the recession that followed the financial crisis, but prime residential MBS—which were almost entirely prime jumbo mortgages— declined and recovered along with all other asset-backed securities. The real losses were in the collateralized debt obligations (CDOs) and the mezzanine (BBB) asset-backed CDOs. These were the lowest-quality asset-backed securities available in the market and included mainly subprime and Alt-A mortgages. The fact that prime mortgages behaved the way all other assets behaved in the financial crisis and afterward is a significant observation; it shows that government involvement in the housing market is no more necessary for housing assets than

---

107. Mortgage Bankers Association, "National Delinquency Survey," available at www.mbaa.org/ResearchandForecasts/ProductsandSurveys/NationalDelinquencySurvey. htm (accessed September 22, 2010).

it is for any other asset class, and—perhaps more important—that if the assets themselves are high quality, like prime mortgages, a nongovernment market for these assets is as stable as any other asset market.

Still, some argue that only a government-backed organization will be able to keep interest rates stable when the private markets are disrupted. This, however, turns out to be another myth. Federal Reserve economists also reviewed this issue, by looking at what happened in an earlier financial crisis. They concluded that Fannie and Freddie did not add appreciably to the stability of interest rates:

> We examined the empirical connection between mortgage interest rates and GSE secondary market activities, especially GSE purchases of mortgages for their own portfolios. If GSE portfolio purchases affected mortgage rates, they could stabilize mortgage markets. This benefit would flow to all mortgage market participants, not just GSE share-holders. . . . We found that portfolio purchases have economically and statistically negligible effects on both primary and secondary mortgage rate spreads.[108]

More important, enlisting the government to keep money flowing to the housing market when it is tight elsewhere would be bad policy. If participants in the housing market are insulated from the vicissitudes of the market, they will take more risks and be less prudent in their investment decisions. This is what helped create housing bubbles in the past. The possibility that financing for housing could be subject to disruption or financing restrictions is, of course, one of the risks that the housing industry fears, but that fear itself will reduce the overbuilding and excessive leverage that have caused volatility and repeated housing bubbles in the past.

The Problem with Current Solutions

Despite these myths and potential policy errors, most of the proposals for replacing Fannie and Freddie involve a government role of some kind.[109] How many

---

108. Andreas Lehnert, Wayne Passmore, and Shane M. Sherlund, "GSEs, Mortgage Rates, and Secondary Market Activities," 34, note 5.

109. The following seven proposals, all involving some form of government support, are representative of many more: Donald Marron and Phillip Swagel, "Whither Fannie

times do these housing-based disasters have to happen before policy-makers realize that there is no way for the government to participate in the financing of mortgages without distorting the market and making it vulnerable to bubbles and collapses? To be sure, the taxpayer costs that resulted from the insolvency of Fannie and Freddie came from a very special kind of government support—an implicit guarantee of their obligations—that enabled them to function for many years with lower funding costs than any other market participants. For this reason, many of the plans that have been advanced to supplant Fannie and Freddie specifically avoid any guarantee of the firm or firms that would operate in their place. Instead, they propose only that the government guarantee the MBS that these privately funded firms would issue.

But would things have been different if the government had only guaranteed the GSEs' MBS? Not significantly. The GSEs needed government support to borrow the huge sums that were necessary to carry their portfolios, which amounted to about $1.5 trillion by 2008. If their activities had been limited to issuing and guaranteeing MBS, the mere fact that their government backing was limited to MBS would not have prevented the huge crash in home prices

---

and Freddie? A Proposal for Reforming the Housing GSEs," e21, May 24, 2010, available at www.economics21.org/commentary/whither-fannie-and-freddie-proposal-reforming-housing-gses (accessed September 20, 2010); James B. Lockhart, "Private Sector Should Take Over GSE Role," *American Banker,* September 14, 2010; Mortgage Finance Working Group, "A Responsible Market for Housing Finance" (white paper, Center for American Progress, Washington, DC, December 2009), available at www.americanprogress.org/issues/2009/12/pdf/housing_finance.pdf (accessed September 22, 2010); House Financial Services Committee, *Testimony of Rick Judson on Behalf of the National Association of Home Builders,* 111th Cong., 2d sess., April 14, 2010, available at www.house.gov/apps/list/hearing/financialsvcs_dem/judson_4.14.10.pdf (accessed September 20, 2010); House Financial Services Committee, *Testimony of Jack E. Hopkins on Behalf of the Independent Community Bankers of America,* 111th Cong., 2d sess., April 14, 2010, available at www.house.gov/apps/list/hearing/financialsvcs_dem/hopkins_testimony_4.14.10.pdf (accessed September 20, 2010); House Financial Services Committee, *Statement of Michael D. Berman, CMB, Chairman-Elect, Mortgage Bankers Association,* 111th Cong., 2d sess., March 23, 2010, available at www.house.gov/apps/list/hearing/financialsvcs_dem/berman_testimony.pdf (accessed September 20, 2010); and House Financial Services Committee, *Testimony of Anthony T. Reed on Behalf of the Housing Policy Council of the Financial Services Roundtable,* 111th Cong., 2d sess., April 14, 2010, available at www.house.gov/apps/list/hearing/financialsvcs_dem/reed_4.14.10.pdf (accessed September 20, 2010).

resulting from the default of the poor-quality mortgages they had guaranteed. It was not the failure of the GSEs to pay their investors that caused the financial crisis; it was the fact that they were able to make low-quality mortgages that drove down housing values when they failed. This was only possible because investors relied on the government's backing of the GSEs' guarantees; without that, no one would have taken these guarantees seriously. For good reason, none of the reform plans under consideration allow any of the replacements for Fannie and Freddie to accumulate large portfolios, but that does not mean that these plans eliminate the moral hazard the government guarantee creates.

Some plans recognize this and seek to address it with a fee or premium for the government's support. This has a nice private-sector ring, but it is not a solution. The government has no way to set a risk-based premium, and any premium it does set will be viewed as a tax on homebuyers and thus be subject to political control. If the premium is supposed to be risk based, the government agency that imposes it faces a difficult political problem because it will have to discriminate among specific borrowers, with low-income and other risky borrowers subject to the highest rates. This is politically infeasible, but it is also largely impractical; if there is any question about whether the government can set risk-based premiums, we need only look at the record of the Federal Deposit Insurance Corporation (FDIC), which has been required to do that with bank insurance premiums for years. It is questionable whether the agency has been able to develop a truly effective risk-based system, but the FDIC's current negative-capital position demonstrates that whatever premiums it thought it might have been setting were inadequate for the risk involved. Now is the time to be realistic about what government can and cannot do and what we can expect from a government role in the housing market.

If we are prepared to face facts, recent experience should tell us that there is no way to avoid the moral hazard arising from the government's involvement in housing finance. Housing risks will always gravitate to the place where they are covered by the government guarantee. If they do not start there, over time Congress will move them there, if only to benefit constituents. A good example is the increase in the conforming-loan limit (the maximum size of a mortgage that the GSEs can buy) that Congress adopted in 2008. There was then what seemed to be a quarter-point difference between the interest rates on mortgages within the conforming-loan limit and the interest rate on the jumbo mortgages outside it. This was unacceptable to Congress, even though the higher rates were applicable in communities where homes could cost upward of a million dollars. So as the GSE reform legislation moved through Congress, a higher conforming-loan limit was legislated for those areas where houses were expensive. That moved these higher-cost mortgages under the GSE guarantee that was ultimately backed by taxpayers. This process will never stop unless politics is taken out of housing finance, and that can only happen if the government's role is eliminated.

Options for the Private Financing of Mortgages

If we are serious about preventing another round of government-induced losses in the housing-finance system, we should begin to look seriously at wholly private-sector solutions. These fall into three categories: (1) those that rely on depository institutions, like covered bonds; (2) those that rely on a separation of the credit and interest-rate risks, like the Danish model; and (3) those that rely on a senior-subordinated or collateralized structure, like the securitization model.

Covered Bonds. In 2008, the Treasury Department developed a model covered-bond program. It was modest in size but was intended to demonstrate how such a system would work.[110] As proposed by the Treasury, banks would be authorized to sell bonds backed by a specified pool of mortgages. The mortgages would remain on the banks' balance sheets but would be segregated from their other assets. The banks would be able to use the bond proceeds for any banking purpose, but the principal and interest on the mortgages would flow to the investors. The key to the success of the program would be an obligation on the part of the banks to top up the mortgage pool (which would be overcollateralized in any event) whenever defaults or delinquencies jeopardized the quality or sufficiency of the collateral backing the bonds.

Structures like this have been used for many years in Europe and have largely succeeded in creating a high-quality debt security without any

---

110. The Treasury proposal was quite small, allowing covered bonds to form only 4 percent of the liabilities of a depository institution. This limitation might have been imposed to placate the FDIC, which does not like the idea that some of the assets of a bank might be placed beyond its reach in the event of the bank's insolvency.

government guarantee. One of their advantages is getting the incentives right: the banks that issue covered bonds have a strong incentive to make good-quality loans because they are ultimately required to keep replenishing high-quality collateral for the bonds. If they do not, the bondholders have a claim beyond the mortgages against the bank itself.

Shortly after the Treasury's proposal was advanced, Representative Scott Garrett (R-N.J.) reintroduced legislation he had previously sponsored to create a larger covered-bond program. The legislation was marked up in the House Financial Services Committee and sent to the House floor in July 2010 as HR 5823.[111] It emerged different from the Treasury's approach in several respects, the most significant of which allowed covered bonds to be issued by any financial firm, not just banks and other regulated depository institutions. This is potentially important because deposits in the U.S. banking system today are not large enough to provide funding for the U.S. housing market.[112] Whether other mortgage lenders will be able to compete with banks as covered-bond issuers is a question for the future, but permitting nondepositories to issue covered bonds may increase their usefulness as a funding mechanism for mortgages.

While covered bonds do not require any direct or indirect government support, the issuers under both the Treasury and Garrett proposals would be regulated by a covered-bond regulator, and each issuance of covered bonds would have to be approved by the regulator. The Treasury proposal requires, among other things, that the mortgages in the cover pool have a loan-to-value ratio of 80 percent at the time they are included in the pool. The Garrett plan only requires that the mortgages be in compliance with supervisory guidance at the time the loan is originated.

The Danish Mortgage System. This system is unique in the world, although Mexico appears to be adopting the same structure, and whether it would be compatible with the way mortgages originate in the United States remains to be seen. One of the distinguishing features of the Danish system is that it separates the credit and interest-rate risk on a mortgage. This permits some interesting

---

111. *United States Covered Bond Act of 2010,* HR 5823, 111th Cong., 2d sess., July 22, 2010. The bill was considered in committee on July 28, 2010.

112. Deborah Solomon and Nick Timiraos, "New Fees Weighed for Mortgage Industry," *Wall Street Journal,* August 24, 2010.

options for mortgage borrowers. In Denmark, mortgages are arranged with a small group of specialized mortgage banks. When the terms are settled, the mortgage is added to a pool of mortgages all issued at the same interest rate, so all the mortgages in the pool are identical (except for size). For example, on any given date, a hypothetical issue of thirty-year fixed-rate callable bonds will go to market at whatever the market rate for mortgage bonds with these terms is on that day. Borrowers who want thirty-year fixed-rate loans will authorize the mortgage bank to add their loan to the pool backing the bonds. Loans can also be added to the pool after it is established. Interests in the pool are purchased by capital-markets participants, which of course could be investors from anywhere in the world. The specialized mortgage bank that arranges the mortgage is responsible only for the credit risk, and in effect functions like a mortgage insurer. If the mortgage defaults, the mortgage bank must buy it back from the pool. Again, as with covered bonds, the incentives are well aligned. The mortgage bank has a strong interest in assuring that the mortgages it adds to any given pool are of good quality, since it is bearing the risk of default. It also earns a fee for its services in arranging for the mortgage and placing the mortgage in the pool. Under this system, there have been no mortgage-bank defaults in Denmark in the past two hundred years.

One of the most interesting elements of the Danish system is that the issuance of identical mortgages at the same interest rate makes it possible for homeowners to buy the bonds that are backed by their mortgages, or any portion of them, and thus create equity in the home that did not exist when the mortgage was issued. This becomes an attractive option, for example, if market interest rates rise. In that case, the market value of the mortgage bonds falls. The homeowner can then enter the market and—by arranging for a new mortgage at the higher rate—purchase at a discount any principal amount of the bonds backed by the pool of which his mortgage is a part. This portion of the mortgage obligation is then canceled. In effect, he is refinancing as someone might do in the United States, but with a major difference. Although he will be paying a higher interest rate for the new mortgage, he has in effect reduced the principal amount of the debt on his home by acquiring—at a discount—all or a portion of the debt represented by his original mortgage.

It is also possible for the homeowner to have his mortgage included in an issue of callable bonds. In this case, he also has the option of calling the debt on his home at par when interest rates fall. This transaction is then identical to

FIGURE 1
PRICE MOVEMENTS OF SELECT SECURITIZED-ASSET CLASSES

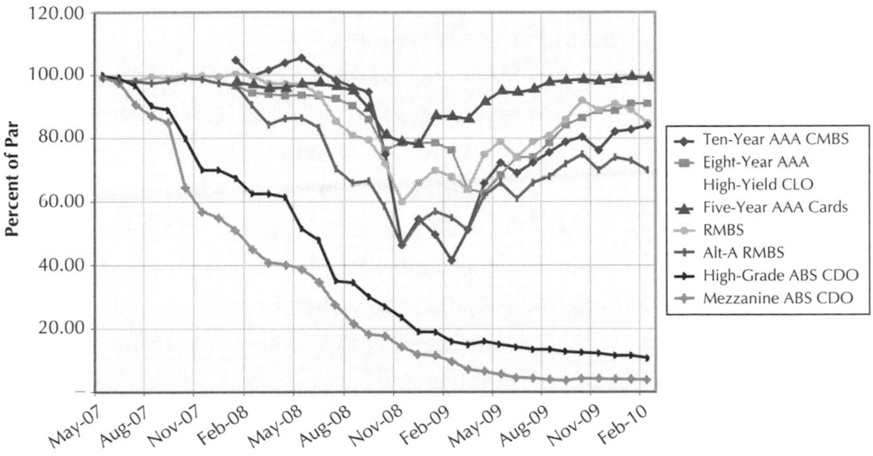

Abbreviations for the key: CMBS = Commercial Mortgage-Backed Securities; CLO = Collateralized Loan Obligation; RMBS = Residential Mortgage-Backed Securities; ABS = Asset-Backed Securities; CDO = Collateralized Debt Obligation

what occurs in the case of a U.S. mortgage refinancing. So the Danish system offers the homebuyer the same opportunity to refinance as occurs in the United States when interest rates fall, but it also offers the unique opportunity to buy down the loan when interest rates rise. The use of a market rate also makes the Danish system completely transparent; homeowners know the interest rate they have received is the market rate at the time their mortgage was financed.

Again, like covered-bond systems, the Danish mortgage system is highly regulated but does not require any government financial support. All loans are made with recourse to the borrower, loan-to-value ratios may not exceed 80 percent, and mortgage banks are also regulated.[113] However, the Danish system could be adapted to provide a wider variety of options for U.S. homebuyers through, among other things, the use of supplemental mortgage insurance, improved disclosure to investors, and higher capital requirements for mortgage banks.

---

113. A good summary of the Danish system can be found in Linda Lowell, "Can a Danish Import Fix U.S. Housing Finance?" *HousingWire Magazine*, June 2010, 32–38.

Securitization. Figure 1 shows that a securitization market for *prime* mortgages can survive even in the most adverse financial conditions in seventy years. The key is to make sure that the system securitizes mortgages of high quality. In one sense, securitization is inferior to both covered bonds and the Danish system because it does not align incentives as well as they do. The credit support in the securitization system comes not from a pool of mortgages backed by a well-capitalized issuer as in the covered-bond system or a well-capitalized financial institution as in the Danish system. Instead, it comes from a senior-subordinate credit structure that in effect—by requiring lower tranches to take the first losses in any mortgage pool—reduces the likelihood that the senior tranches will suffer losses. In this way, the senior tranches can reach investment grade. The failure of the securitization system in 2007 may lead some observers to believe that it does not have a future, but that judgment is highly premature. It occurred almost entirely in the securitization of subprime and Alt-A mortgages; as shown in the figure, securitizations of prime-quality mortgages performed as well as any other asset-backed security in the recessionary period that followed the deflation of the housing bubble.

Securitization has some distinct advantages. In addition to using proven technology and structures that are already in place, securitization is not subject to size limits. As the mortgage market grows, a soundly based securitization market grows with it; the capitalization of the mortgage insurer (the mortgage bank in Denmark or the covered-bond issuer in Europe or the United States) is not an issue. Finally, the securitization market has functioned satisfactorily for thirty or forty years, produces interest rates that Fed economists found to be competitive with those offered by the GSEs, and is still working well for many types of assets.

The principal deficiency of private securitization as a replacement for Fannie and Freddie is the absence of proper incentives. This, however, does not mean that the whole securitization system has to be discarded. The recently adopted Dodd-Frank Act requires that participants in a securitization chain divide up (as the regulators decide) a 5 percent retention amount on any securitization; this is intended to make them hold "skin in the game." The system is probably unworkable, but it is unlikely to be used in any event; there is a statutory provision that permits the Securities and Exchange Commission and other regulators to eliminate any retention if the mortgages involved in the securitization meet certain quality tests that the regulators themselves are authorized to establish. This provides a lot of leeway, for good or ill. But assuming that the regulators can establish strong quality standards—including a substantial down payment, good credit from the borrower, adequate documentation, mortgage insurance, adequate disclosure to investors, strong reps and warranties, and required terms for put-backs to earlier participants in the securitization chain—requirements such as these could cure many of the inherent ills of the securitization structure.

Of course, at this point, investors are still avoiding the mortgage-securitization market because of their experience during the financial crisis, but other asset-backed markets are beginning to function normally. This means that Fannie and Freddie will continue to be the mainstay of residential-mortgage finance until investors have the confidence to return to the mortgage-securitization market. The recoupment of some of the value of prime mortgages initially lost in the financial crisis, as shown in the figure, suggests that the jumbo securitization market is gradually returning to normal, although it might take several more years to reach the level of operation common before 2007.

The Transition to a Private Market

If we assume that during this period the GSEs remain under government control, there is time to make the transition from a government-dominated housing-finance system to one that relies principally on the private financial markets. As the securitization market for mortgages gradually returns to normal, Congress could authorize the GSEs' regulator, the Federal Housing Finance Agency, to reduce the conforming-loan limit in incremental steps. As this limit declines, the private securitization market should enter the newly vacant space, while Congress and others watch to make sure that adequate funds are available for mortgages. This process could be continued until the conforming-loan limit is so low that virtually all mortgages are being financed privately. At this point, the GSEs could be either closed down or allowed to restructure into fully private firms. Ideally, the government would no longer be in the business of financing prime mortgages.

Of course, there is no reason for securitization to be the only nongovernmental system for financing mortgages. Congress can always adopt legislation authorizing covered bonds, the Danish system, or any other financing system it can agree on. However, in the absence of such congressional action, securitization is a satisfactory fallback option so Fannie and Freddie can be eliminated or privatized.

What to Do about Affordable Housing

Affordable housing is one other alleged benefit of government involvement in the housing-finance market. It was not discussed earlier for two reasons. First, there now seems to be a recognition, even among some of the most ardent supporters of affordable housing in Congress, that imposing an affordable-housing mission on the GSEs was a mistake. In an interview on Larry Kudlow's television program in late August, Representative Barney Frank (D-Mass.)—the chair of the House Financial Services Committee and previously the strongest congressional advocate for affordable housing—conceded that he had erred: "I hope by next year we'll have abolished Fannie and Freddie . . . it was a great mistake to push lower-income people into housing they couldn't afford and couldn't really handle once they had it." He then added, "I had been too sanguine about Fannie and Freddie."[114] Accordingly, most of the groups submitting plans for the reform of the housing-finance system do not cite affordable housing as a reason for government involvement.

Second, there is no reason why policies on affordable housing should be introduced into the conventional market. The idea that low-income groups should have access to mortgage credit makes sense for many reasons, but this is social policy, not economic policy. It was the confusion of the two that led Congress in 1992 to adopt legislation that added an affordable-housing mission to the GSEs' existing obligation to foster and maintain a liquid secondary market in conventional (that is, nongovernment) mortgages. The government already had an affordable-housing agency, the Federal Housing Administration (FHA), which was authorized to insure mortgages for borrowers who could not meet the standards for prime loans. The problem was that FHA was an on-budget agency and thus was limited in how much credit it could provide to underserved groups. The affordable-housing mission for Fannie and Freddie put them into competition with FHA—as well as one another—for high-risk mortgages. The result was

---

114. Larry Kudlow, "Barney Frank Comes Home to the Facts," GOPUSA, August 23, 2010, available at www.gopusa.com/commentary/2010/08/kudlow-barney-frank-comes-home-to-the-facts.php#ixzz0zdCrWpCY (accessed September 20, 2010).

that millions of these mortgages were made and insured or guaranteed, with immense losses for taxpayers.

The right decision, if Congress wants to pursue a social policy in the housing field, would have been to provide the necessary funds to FHA, rather than distorting the conventional market by hiding the subsidies in the GSEs' off-budget activities. There are certainly reasons for encouraging homeownership, and Congress may want to subsidize the purchase of homes by individuals who cannot meet the standards for prime loans. But as shown by the experience with Fannie and Freddie, mixing social policy with what is essentially economic policy for improving housing finance was a costly mistake that should not be repeated.

Conclusion

The policy case for government involvement in housing finance is weak. All the major arguments in its favor have little or no merit. Moreover, recent history provides two examples of colossal losses for taxpayers coming directly from the moral hazard that government support of the housing market inevitably engenders. Instead of looking at more plans and proposals to replace Fannie and Freddie with another government-backed vehicle, Congress should begin to look seriously at ways to withdraw the government from the housing-finance market and rely solely on the private market.

2

The Financial Crisis

*The bedrock question then is: Why did so many monthly mortgage pay-
ments stop coming? And the bedrock answer is: Because mortgage loans
were made to more people whose prospects of repaying them were less
than in the past. Nor was this simply a matter of misjudgment by banks
and other lenders. The political pressures to meet arbitrary lending
quotas, set by officials with the power of economic life and death over
banks and over Fannie Mae and Freddie Mac, led to riskier lending
practices than in the past.*

—Thomas Sowell, *The Housing Boom and Bust*

The financial crisis struck in earnest in September 2008 with the failure of
Lehman Brothers, but conditions in the financial markets had been deteriorating long before that. In fact, many economists date the beginning of the
financial crisis to a specific date, August 9, 2007, when the French bank
BNP suddenly announced that it would no longer accept redemptions of
shares in a fund that invested in PMBS because it could not be sure of their
value. This was a recognition that the market for PMBS—especially PMBS
backed by subprime mortgages—was no longer functioning properly. An
unprecedented number of mortgage delinquencies and defaults had begun
to show up in the United States, and investors had fled the market for
mortgage-backed securities. On that day, the three-month London Interbank Offered Rate (LIBOR) over the overnight index swap (OIS) rate—or
the LIBOR-OIS spread—a measure of the rate at which banks lend to one
another, jumped from about eight basis points to about eighty basis points
and stayed at elevated levels through the financial crisis. Close observers of

the financial markets argue that this increase meant that there was a steady level of anxiety underlying trading in the money markets, as though a terrifying specter was out there somewhere but couldn't yet be seen.

The Financial Crisis Inquiry Commission Absolves the Government

The left's narrative for this period, as outlined in the introduction, focused on the errors of the private sector. The majority report of the FCIC is the best source for this narrative, but many books and probably thousands of newspaper and magazine articles and commentary make the same assertions—almost all without any data at all. The FCIC majority relied on what it called "millions of pages of documents" and interviews with "over 700 witnesses," but the citations to documents in the report are very limited, and the interviews with witnesses were almost entirely done by the staff without the knowledge or the participation of the commissioners. Except for the eight public hearings and a few private meetings with administration officials and academics, the members of the commission had no opportunity to question witnesses. For that reason, the quotes throughout the report from witness testimony are almost uniformly unreliable, since no commissioner, other than the FCIC's Philip Angelides, had an opportunity to cross-examine witnesses or even to see the testimony in context.[1]

The majority's conclusions followed the left's narrative—the crisis could have been prevented by more effective regulation; there was a failure of risk management in the private sector, including risky investments and excessive leverage; the private sector was guilty of predatory lending and "a willful disregard for a borrower's ability to pay," which fed a "securitization pipeline that transported toxic mortgages from neighborhoods across America to investors around the globe." In addition, the report cited an over-the-counter derivatives market, including credit default swaps, that involved "uncontrolled leverage; lack of transparency, capital, and collateral requirements; and concentrations of risk."[2] Finally, "without the active

---

1. Financial Crisis Inquiry Commission, *The Financial Crisis Commission Report* (Washington, DC: Government Printing Office, 2011), xi.

2. Ibid., xxiv.

participation of the rating agencies, the market for mortgage-related securities could not have been what it became."[3]

If this sounds like phrases you have heard repeatedly in the media over the last four years, it is not a coincidence. The FCIC, controlled by its chairman, Angelides, set out to validate the left-wing narrative that the media had already adopted. Indeed, Congress did not even wait for the commission to report before enacting the Dodd-Frank Act, which was based on the narrative the left had already established as the story of the financial crisis. Virtually all of the ideas in the FCIC's majority report were easily disproved by a clear-eyed view of the role of government housing policies in creating the demand for subprime and other low-quality mortgages and by a close analysis of what actually happened after the Lehman Brothers bankruptcy. But the FCIC attempted neither. It was an ideologically motivated whitewash on an issue of vital national importance.

On the GSEs and government housing policies, the commission majority said: "The GSEs participated in the expansion of subprime and other risky mortgages, but they followed rather than led Wall Street. . . . They relaxed their underwriting standards to purchase riskier loans and related securities in order to meet stock market analysts' and investors' expectations for growth, to regain market share, and to ensure generous compensation for their executives and employees." On government housing policies in general, the report had only this to say: "Finally, as to the matter of whether government housing policies were a primary cause of the crisis: for decades, government policy has encouraged homeownership through a set of incentives, assistance programs, and mandates. These policies were put in place and promoted by several administrations and Congresses—indeed, both Presidents Bill Clinton and George W. Bush set aggressive goals to increase homeownership." Although a non-sequitur, this language suggests that the authors of the report thought the answer was yes—that government housing policies had something to do with the financial crisis—but the rest of the report was virtually silent on what exactly that was.[4]

No explanation was ever given for the decline in underwriting standards, although that was the key reason for the growth of the housing

---

3. Ibid.
4. Ibid., xxvii.

bubble and the twenty-eight million subprime and other weak mortgages in the financial system by 2008. The GSEs were absolved of any major responsibility, as required by the left's narrative, with the following language:

> The GSEs participated in the expansion of subprime and other risky mortgages, but they followed rather than led Wall Street and other lenders in the rush for fool's gold. They purchased the highest rated non-GSE mortgage-backed securities and their participation in this market added helium to the housing balloon, but their purchases never represented a majority of the market. Those purchases represented 10.5% of non-GSE subprime mortgage-backed securities in 2001, with the share rising to 40% in 2004, and falling back to 28% by 2008. They relaxed their underwriting standards to purchase or guarantee riskier loans and related securities in order to meet stock market analysts' and investors' expectations for growth, to regain market share, and to ensure generous compensation for their executives and employees—justifying their activities on the broad and sustained public policy support for homeownership.[5]

It is worthwhile to review this paragraph in detail to see how it evades the facts about the role of the GSEs in the buildup of subprime and other low-quality mortgages. First is the statement, adopted early and repeated frequently in the left's narrative, that the GSEs "followed rather than led Wall Street." This notion is supposedly supported by the succeeding sentences in the same paragraph, which point out that the two GSEs were major purchasers of the PMBS that Wall Street was producing, having purchased as much as 40 percent of Wall Street's production in 2004 and almost 30 percent in succeeding years. The suggestion is that if the GSEs were purchasing PMBS from Wall Street in 2004, then Wall Street was in the business first. However, this is a false inference. First, if two GSEs could be relied on to purchase 30 to 40 percent of Wall Street's production, they were building Wall Street's business, providing the economies of scale that made Wall Street's outreach to the rest of the market likely to be highly

---

5. Ibid., xxvi.

profitable. In addition, and more important, the paragraph ignores completely the activities of Fannie and Freddie before 2004 in acquiring whole subprime and other nonprime loans directly from originators, which they themselves either securitized or held in portfolio.

As I reported in my dissent, the GSEs began acquiring high loan-to-value (LTV) mortgages as early as 1994 and by 2001 had already acquired at least $700 billion in subprime and other risky loans. In that year, on the other hand, Wall Street's full production of PMBS based on these loans had not yet reached $100 billion. So it is clear that the GSEs, because of the affordable-housing goals, were well ahead of Wall Street in the subprime business. In fact, as described earlier, their purchases built the enormous housing bubble that attracted investors to the PMBS backed by subprime loans. Before the bubble, subprime lending had been a niche business, and there was only a small market for PMBS based on these low-quality and risky mortgages. All these data were in two memoranda submitted to the FCIC early in its inquiry by my AEI colleague Edward Pinto. Despite my many requests, Pinto was never given an opportunity to meet with the members of the commission, and his data—which have since been validated by the SEC in a suit against various senior officials of Fannie and Freddie—were never seriously considered by the FCIC, sent by the staff to the members of the commission, or described in its report. As part of the suit, both Fannie and Freddie signed nonprosecution agreements with the SEC in which they admitted to acquiring even more subprime and other low-quality mortgages than Pinto had initially estimated.[6]

Finally, the report states, relying on testimony not subject to independent review or cross-examination, that the GSEs relaxed their underwriting standards in order to meet the expectations of analysts and investors, to regain market share, and to assure their managements of high levels of compensation. This approach again tends to support the idea that the private sector—or at least private sector incentives such as profits, market share, and compensation—were the cause of the financial crisis. For some reason,

---

6. See Securities Exchange Commission Non-Prosecution Agreements with Fannie Mae (www.sec.gov/news/press/2011/npa-pr2011-267-fanniemae.pdf) and Freddie Mac (www.sec.gov/news/press/2011/npa-pr2011-267-freddiemac.pdf).

however, the commission majority failed to include in their analysis the following statement by Fannie Mae in its 2006 10-K:

> We have made, and continue to make, significant adjustments to our mortgage loan sourcing and purchase strategies in an effort to meet HUD's increased housing goals and new subgoals. These strategies include entering into some purchase and securitization transactions with *lower expected economic returns than our typical transactions*. We have also relaxed some of our underwriting criteria to obtain goals-qualifying mortgage loans and increased our investments in higher-risk mortgage loan products that are more likely to serve the borrowers targeted by HUD's goals and subgoals, *which could increase our credit losses.*[7]

Financial Services Outlooks and the Left's Narrative

This analysis demonstrates that the FCIC simply attempted to support the conventional left-wing narrative for the financial crisis rather than discharge its responsibility to consider all potential causes. The *Financial Services Outlooks* written after the financial crisis were intended to challenge this narrative, showing the key areas in which the FCIC story and many others propagated through the media after the 2008 financial crash did not align with the facts.

This effort began in April 2008, one month after the rescue of Bear Stearns, which stimulated the usual chorus for more regulation—especially for investment banks like Bear. The arguments in favor of this course have now become well worn: these institutions were engaged in what was called "shadow banking" but were not regulated like banks. Bear's rescue had been unprecedented; never before had the government—in this case the Fed—put up cash to assist a bank holding company, JPMorgan Chase, to acquire a troubled nonbank financial institution. Later, it would become clear that this was a huge error. If Bear Stearns had been allowed to fail, it is unlikely that anything significant would have occurred. There would have been losses for its counterparties, of course, but Lehman Brothers' failure

---

7. Fannie Mae, *2006 10-K,*146 (emphasis added).

six months later showed that these counterparty losses were not likely to be the cause of a systemic breakdown. If necessary, the Fed had authority to provide liquidity support to the market in general and—for good collateral—to institutions such as investment banks and could have done so for financial institutions shaken by the collapse of Bear.

The Original Sin: The Bear Rescue. My April 2008 essay "Bear Facts: The Flawed Case for Tighter Regulation of Securities Firms" (p. 184) argued against a rush to judgment on the question of whether investment banks required regulation like commercial banks. I pointed out that despite the claim that they were engaged in shadow banking, investment banks like Bear were very different business models from commercial banks. Among other things, investment banks borrowed short to hold and trade portfolios of liquid securities—thus closely matching their assets and liabilities—while commercial banks had inherently mismatched assets and liabilities because they used short-term deposits to make long-term and largely illiquid loans. Anyway, bank regulation had not been particularly successful, a fact that was becoming quite plain as the mortgage meltdown weakened commercial banks as profoundly as it weakened the lightly regulated investment banks. I also noted that there was something very special about this crisis, the first in more than eighty years to adversely affect virtually all financial institutions. It would be sensible to understand why this had happened now before deciding to regulate the entire financial system.

Later, after the bankruptcy of Lehman Brothers, it would become clear that the Bear rescue was more than simply a misjudgment about whether investment banks should be allowed to fail. By seeming to establish a policy that the U.S. government would not allow large nonbank financial institutions to fail, the rescue of Bear created substantial moral hazard. Market participants now assumed that the creditors of other large nonbank financial institutions would also be protected. This appears to have changed the way managements functioned as the mortgage meltdown continued to evolve. First, many seemed to assume that they did not have to raise large amounts of additional capital in order to reassure creditors. Second, those who might be in danger of runs as financial conditions worsened assumed that they could drive harder bargains with potential acquirers because their creditors were not likely to fear that the firm would fail. And third, some managements—notably the asset managers at the Reserve Primary Fund—seemed to assume that they could hold their Lehman Brothers commercial paper to maturity because even if Lehman failed, they as creditors would be bailed out. In the end, Lehman's bankruptcy upset all these expectations, caused a market panic, and caused the Reserve Fund to "break the buck" (fail to maintain its share value at $1 per share).

The Role of Mark-to-Market Accounting. After the rescue of Bear, I began to look more closely at why the mortgage meltdown was having such a severe effect on all financial institutions. There seemed to be two principal reasons. First, most of the affected firms were subject to accounting rules—established by the Financial Accounting Standards Board (FASB)—that required securities to be carried on balance sheets at market value, except in special circumstances. Known as fair value accounting, and more descriptively as mark-to-market accounting, these rules may have been as destructive as the mortgage meltdown itself. As mortgage losses continued, there were very few buyers in the market for PMBS, so market prices were almost entirely distress prices, but it seemed that accountants were still requiring write-downs in the value of these assets—in some cases to the values established in distress sales by firms that were trying to raise cash—even though it was not yet clear that these instruments had sustained or would sustain losses.

This seemed unwarranted. There was no reason to suppose that, because investors were hanging back in the midst of a panic-like atmosphere, these assets had no value. Many of them were still flowing cash, and it seemed as though a discounted cash flow valuation would make more sense than market value at a time like this. These thoughts were expressed in my essay titled "Fair Value Accounting: A Critique" (p. 199), published in July 2008. Many months afterward, the Securities and Exchange Commission made some moves to correct this problem, but they were too little and far too late. Finally, the House Financial Services Committee threatened the FASB with legislation to resolve the problem, and to avoid this outcome the FASB retreated somewhat. It would not be unreasonable to trace the recovery of financial institutions to the FASB's retreat. In 2011, banks began to supplement the income in their financial reports by removing reserves they had taken under accounting pressures in 2008 and 2009. It had turned out that the drastic write-downs were unnecessary—indeed, many AAA–rated PMBS pools returned to 95 percent of their face value by 2012—but the damage had already been done.

Second, all of the financial institutions that were in trouble were holding large amounts of PMBS. Later, it would turn out that most of the private sector losses were in PMBS or collateralized debt obligations (CDOs) that were backed by or based on subprime or other low-quality mortgages. These came to be known in the media as "toxic assets." The fact that these assets were so widely held, and formed a significant part of the assets of the affected financial institutions, suggested strongly that the cause of the crisis was a "common shock" rather than a kind of contagion in which one failing institution drags down others. That, however, was not a term I used in this *Outlook*. It came later and, as I noted in the introduction, assumed great importance in my analysis of the financial crisis.

The "Interconnections" Theory. The chaos that developed after the Lehman bankruptcy in September 2008 raised a new and related set of issues. The question was no longer why Bear had been rescued, but why Lehman's bankruptcy seemed to trigger a financial crisis. This issue was covered in an *Outlook* titled "Systemic Risk and the Financial Crisis" (p. 213) in October 2008, only a month after the Lehman bankruptcy. The post-Lehman chaos had been traumatic; the financial system simply ground to a halt, and banks and other financial institutions hoarded cash. No one had ever seen anything like this. At the time, much discussion about systemic risk took place in the media and among academics and government officials. The notion seemed to be that large financial institutions like Lehman create systemic risk because of their interconnections with other firms; because of these interconnections, the failure of one of these firms could bring down the entire financial system.

The systemic risk idea was not new. I and many others had argued that the failure of Fannie or Freddie would be a systemic event; given their centrality to the housing finance system, that seemed plausible to me, but it did not seem likely that the bankruptcy of a single large nonbank financial institution like Lehman could produce the same result. What was new at this point, however, was the idea that financial institutions were "interconnected," leaving the inference that if one failed, it would drag down others.

It was already clear to me where all this was going. The fundamental question would be whether the market had been brought down by "interconnectedness" between Lehman and others. In this *Outlook,* I argued that there was no evidence of contagion caused by interconnectedness. The more likely cause of the crisis was the fact that commercial banks and investment banks all held the same assets—assets that declined sharply in value. Shortly after the Lehman bankruptcy, then, I was already questioning the narrative about the crisis that was beginning to form. Its central elements—apart from the claim that regulation had been insufficient—was that the interconnections between large financial institutions made it necessary to regulate them more stringently, lest the failure of one bring down the others.

There was little evidence for this interconnectedness idea, but it had arisen shortly after the rescue of Bear Stearns six months earlier. Treasury Secretary Paulson and Fed Chairman Bernanke had been pressed to explain the unprecedented rescue of an uninsured financial institution like Bear. Their argument, impossible to test at that point, was that all these large financial institutions were interconnected—especially through the mysterious new instruments known as credit default swaps—and that the failure of one would bring the others down. This, in their view, made the saving of Bear mandatory. Perhaps they really believed this, but it was made to order for the media, which immediately fell for the idea that CDSs were—in Warren Buffett's words—"financial weapons of mass destruction." In any event, it was obvious that the systemic risk concept—coupled with the interconnection idea—would now be used to argue for a much more intrusive and comprehensive regulation of the financial system than then existed.[8]

In this *Outlook,* then, I argued that in the case of Lehman there was no evidence of "contagion"—by which I meant one firm infecting another through interconnectedness—even when the effects of CDSs were considered. At this point, I hadn't yet recognized that a common shock had been the cause of the crisis, but I was getting close. I concluded, "The fact that the current financial crisis is caused by doubts about the solvency of almost

---

8. When I was able to question Buffett at a public FCIC hearing, he admitted that the firms he controlled also used these financial weapons of mass destruction. What he was objecting to was that others—presumably not as smart as he—were taking these risks.

all of the world's major financial institutions sets it apart from any other financial crisis in history."

Although the common shock idea was to come later, at this point it seemed clear that the interconnectedness concept was going to be a central element of the narrative about the financial crisis. I argued that to sustain this view, interconnectedness had to be apparent in the chaos after Lehman. It turned out, as I argued later, that Lehman proved interconnectedness was a myth. Nevertheless, the interconnectedness idea— although clearly wrong—became part of the left's narrative and the basis for the stringent regulation of "systemically important financial institutions" (SIFIs) under the Dodd-Frank Act.

The Role of Credit Default Swaps. I followed this *Outlook* with another in November 2008, titled "Cause and Effect: Government Policies and the Financial Crisis." This was a transitional piece, and so it is also summarized in chapter 1, which covers Fannie and Freddie. At this point, the media were seriously engaged with the idea that the financial crisis was a "crisis of capitalism." To many writers, such as George Soros, it was long-awaited evidence that the capitalist system was inherently unstable and had to be radically reformed. To them, the irresponsibiliity of the banks and Wall Street was the cause of the financial crisis, and in this they were cheered on by government officials, who were eager to avoid blame for their own actions.

I saw things differently. By this time, working with Edward Pinto, I had found enough information to be able to link the affordable-housing requirements imposed by Congress in 1992 to the large numbers of subprime and other risky loans that were in the financial system in 2008. I hadn't put all the pieces together—that would not come until after I'd been appointed to the FCIC and begun to see additional evidence that confirmed my initial view—but this essay contains the seeds of the positions I was able to establish, with more data, later on.

As noted above, one of the government's key arguments for the Bear rescue, and the subsequent bailout of the giant insurance holding company AIG, was that Bear, AIG, and many other large financial firms were "interconnected" through CDSs. Huge numbers—like $600 trillion in outstanding derivatives, including $60 trillion in CDSs—were thrown around as though they meant something. Brooksley Born, a Washington lawyer who had tried unsuccessfully to regulate the derivatives market, including CDSs, when she was head of the Commodity Futures Trading Commission (CFTC) during the Clinton administration, was "lionessed" by the left as someone who could have saved the financial system if she'd only been able to gain control over the CDS market. In a typical move, Bill Moyers devoted his public television show, *Frontline,* to Born's courageous effort to regulate CDSs.

I was suspicious of this story. It seemed to me that most people who were frightened about CDSs couldn't explain what they were and how exactly they could cause a systemic breakdown. In a December 2008 *Outlook* titled "Everything You Wanted to Know about Credit Default Swaps—But Were Never Told" (p. 223), I described how CDSs worked and what risks they did or did not create. Briefly, CDSs are an insurance-like product in which one counterparty promises another, in exchange for a regular premium, to make up any loss that might arise from the failure of a third party to meet a specified financial obligation. Almost every player in the market hedges the risk it assumes in writing this CDS protection, and this spreads the risk of losses widely. All these hedging transactions multiply the number of parties on the same risk, and that accounts for the very large overall number—like $60 trillion—but there can be only one actual loss: the amount of the original obligation that has defaulted. Everything else sums to zero.

It became clear to me in writing this essay that CDSs—far from being a dangerous instrument—were a very valuable way to diversify and limit risks. It also became clear that the failure of a large firm that was engaged in the CDS market would not bring down others. This was another thing that was proved by Lehman's failure. Lehman was a big player in the CDS market, but its inability to meet its CDS obligations had no major effect on other market participants. Ultimately, even the FCIC (of which Brooksley Born was also a member) could not substantiate any significant losses in the financial crisis that came from the widespread use of CDSs, concluding instead that they were the cause of government "concerns" about losses—because of lack of transparency—rather than actual losses. That seemed accurate to me, but I couldn't tell whether Paulson and Bernanke, who had been propagating the interconnectedness idea, really believed that CDSs were a problem or whether they simply found it convenient to let the media—which understood nothing about the issue—continue to believe that these mysterious new instruments were "financial weapons of mass destruction."

Stress Tests. Further proof of my general view of the importance of accounting in the financial crisis came forward in May 2009, when the bank regulators completed their "stress tests" of the nineteen largest financial institutions. These tests, described in an *Outlook* that month titled "Stress for Success: The Bank Stress Tests Buy Time" (p. 243), showed that most of the largest institutions were adequately capitalized for the risks that might lay ahead of them. A few required additional capital, but none was likely to fail. This obviously relieved the financial markets, and although my essay suggested that the tests only bought time, it became clear later that they were a turning point for market confidence. From that point on, the share prices of most of these institutions began to rise—later to fall when the scope of the new regulations they would face became clear.

Glass-Steagall and the Myth of Deregulation. Once the idea that the private sector had caused the financial crisis became the accepted view, it was a simple step from there to claim that the crisis occurred because of insufficient regulation. One false idea was that deregulation in the past had made the financial system vulnerable to the financial crisis. The so-called repeal of the Glass-Steagall Act, it was said, allowed financial institutions to take the risks that allegedly caused their weakness or insolvency. I tried to bring some light to this subject in the October 2009 *Outlook,* titled "Deregulation and the Financial Crisis: Another Urban Myth" (p. 255). There, I showed that there had been relatively little deregulation in the financial sector over the last thirty years and what little deregulation had occurred—especially the changes in the Glass-Steagall Act—could not have had any bearing on the financial crisis. Indeed, I pointed out, if Glass-Steagall had been completely untouched, the financial crisis would have unfolded exactly as it had. Far from deregulation, the most important law applicable to banking during this period was the FDIC Improvement Act of 1991, which imposed strong new regulations on banks and savings and loans after the S&L collapse of the late 1980s and early 1990s. At the time, Congress hailed this law as a source of such tough new regulations that banking crises would not occur again.

Ideas Have Consequences. In several *Outlook* essays in 2010 I began to address an issue that was of increasing interest to me and became the theme of this book—the effect of narratives on policymaking, and especially the narrative that the left developed to explain the financial crisis. This story was a combination of the Bush administration's rationale for bailing out Bear Stearns (primarily on the basis of "interconnectedness" among financial institutions) and Barack Obama's blaming the crisis on "Republican deregulation." It ignored any significant government role and focused solely on the greed and irresponsibility of private financial institutions, which it claimed were allowed to take inordinate risks by deregulation, ineffective regulation, or simple lack of regulation. This view was pursued in many books about the crisis, became the only description of the crisis in the media, and drove the legislative process in Congress. The remarkable thing about this narrative was that it was either false or shockingly incomplete in almost every major respect.

For example, it was obvious to all observers that the buildup of subprime mortgages in the U.S. financial system was the source of the mortgage meltdown that weakened all financial institutions, but the left's narrative paid no serious attention to why this had happened—why so many subprime and other weak mortgages were created. A common explanation, often provided by bank regulators, was that these mortgages were created by "unregulated mortgage brokers" or because of "originate-to-distribute securitization." These ideas were accepted uncritically, but even a little thought would have raised questions about their validity. Clearly, it is not possible simply to create and sell a shoddy product like a subprime mortgage unless there is a willing buyer. The left's narrative never sought to determine who the principal buyers were and why.

This, however, was not difficult to determine: the buyers were the institutions that ended up holding or guaranteeing most of these mortgages, and that pointed to government policies—not unregulated mortgage brokers or securitization—as the reason for the growth in subprime mortgages. As noted earlier, 74 percent of the subprime and other low-quality mortgages were on the books of government agencies such as Fannie Mae and Freddie Mac, FHA, and other government or government-controlled entities. Only 26 percent of these mortgages were on the books of banks or other private sector investors. This is not to excuse the unregulated mortgage brokers or securitizers, but only stupidity or willful blindness would blame them for arranging or selling the mortgages that others were eager to buy.

Once it was clear who bought or guaranteed most of these mortgages, the next question would be, why did they want to acquire these shoddy mortgages? This question also has an obvious answer: there were laws and regulations that required government agencies to buy these loans. Although these policies were well known, they were not explored or considered relevant to the financial crisis, even though it was the delinquency and failure of subprime and other low-quality loans—most of which were on the books of government agencies—that drove down housing prices in the United States, created the mortgage meltdown, and led to the financial crisis. Indeed, the GSEs alone bought or guaranteed so many of these loans that they became insolvent, so it should not have been difficult for observers to determine the immediate effect of the government policies with which Fannie and Freddie were complying. Yet, these facts were ignored as all of the blame for the financial crisis in the left's narrative fell on the private sector, which was responsible for only a minority of all the subprime and low-quality mortgages in the U.S. financial system.

Exactly why this reporting failure happened is still unclear to me. I am not one to believe in conspiracies, but there was a remarkable parallelism in the way the media handled facts and news about the financial crisis. In almost every FCIC public meeting, well covered by the media, I stated that there were at least 25 million subprime or other low quality loans outstanding in the United States—a truly shocking number since it was almost half of all mortgages outstanding. Yet I am not aware that this number was ever reported in a news article about an FCIC open meeting, nor did I ever get a call from a member of the media inquiring about where that number came from and how it could be justified. We are supposed to have an independent media in this country, and there are probably thousands of people regularly commenting on public affairs, but ideas that should have been easily dismissed came to be accepted as the only valid explanations of the financial crisis, and ideas that should have received attention were ignored. Whatever the reason, the dominance of the left's narrative led directly to the adoption of the Dodd-Frank Act—proof of the proposition that ideas have consequences.

Operating under the left's narrative about the financial crisis, Congress continued the legislative process that ultimately resulted in the Dodd-Frank Act. Noting this, in May 2010, I published an *Outlook* titled "Ideas Have Consequences: The Importance of a Narrative" (p. 273). At the outset of this essay, I used a quote from Tolstoy that seemed to me to have particular relevance to what I was seeing in Congress: "The most difficult subjects can be explained to the most slow-witted man if he has not formed any idea of them already; but the simplest thing cannot be made clear to the most intelligent man if he is firmly persuaded that he knows already, without a shadow of doubt, what is laid before him." The left's narrative had taken control of the process despite the fact that it bore very little relationship to what had actually happened in the financial crisis. In this essay, I focused on the interconnections theory, pointing out that events after the Lehman bankruptcy showed clearly that interconnections among large financial firms had nothing to do with the financial crisis. Nevertheless, Congress was proceeding as though these facts had never come to light. Again, the narrative was the determining factor.

The Real Lessons from *The Big Short*. One of the key notions underlying the left's narrative was the irresponsibility of the private sector, supposedly demonstrated by the fact that private sector firms knew the mortgages they sold were toxic but continued to sell them anyway. In this connection, it seemed to me that a best-selling book at the time, *The Big Short,* by Michael Lewis, was instructive on this issue. Many readers interpreted this book as a story about a few guys who were clever enough to see that there was a bubble in housing and figure out a way to exploit their perception. But to me it demonstrated something else—that most people on Wall Street, even those who were engaged in selling so-called toxic mortgage-backed securities, did not realize that these securities were going to default. They were offered the opportunity to bet against the housing bubble that was developing, but almost everyone refused, although the profits they could have made were enormous. Thus, in June 2010, I published "Missing the Point: Lessons from *The Big Short*" (p. 284), in which I noted: "Rather than being greedy and aware of the poor quality of the CDOs they were selling, the traders and their managers on Wall Street consistently resisted the idea that it would be profitable to bet against these instruments, even though the returns from such a bet could be astoundingly high."

The notion that the banks were motivated by greed and took excessive risks was also neatly undercut by observing what they bought. Although in many cases the PMBS that were eventually labeled toxic assets were indeed of poor quality, they were rated AAA at the time they were issued and thus were thought to be the safest—and certainly the lowest-yielding—securities in a particular pool. If the banks were really greedy risk takers, they would have bought lower-rated tranches, which reflected more risk and bore higher yields. The likelihood is that the banks, as well as everyone else—including the rating agencies—were misled by the growth of the bubble into thinking that "this time it's different," that subprime mortgages were not as risky as everyone had previously thought. Whatever the reason, it contradicted the element in the left's narrative that the private sector acted irresponsibly and was motivated by greed.

Alternative Narratives. In looking at narratives and their role in policy development, I reviewed an interesting paper by two Brookings Institution scholars, Martin Neil Baily and Douglas J. Elliott, who had proposed a narrative for the financial crisis that differed from the left's version as well as my own. In my October–November 2010 essay, "Slaughter of the Innocents: Who Was Taking the Risks That Caused the Financial Crisis?" (p. 296). I summarized their proposal and considered whether it better explained the financial crisis than my view that the crisis was the result of government housing policy. The Baily-Elliott narrative was that the twenty-five-year period of relative quiet in the financial markets—known as the "great moderation"—had lulled market participants into believing that the business cycle had been conquered and hence that the risks of investing were much lower than previously believed. As a result, risk management was reduced in importance, investors believed that home prices would always continue to rise, and government regulators did not foresee the dangers in unregulated investment banks or the weak regulation of Fannie and Freddie. The interesting element of this analysis is that it avoided the cop-out of so many other narratives—I called them "perfect storm narratives"—that blamed dozens of elements all coming together at the same time to explain the financial crisis.

However, what the Baily-Elliott narrative could not explain was the unprecedented size of the great housing bubble that developed between 1997 and 2007. They saw that bubble as a natural result of the loss of risk aversion during the great moderation. However, that bubble was nine times larger than any previous bubble and—when it deflated—was a major factor in the mortgage meltdown and the financial crisis. The only plausible explanation for a bubble of this size was the government's involvement. Fannie and Freddie and other government agencies not only increased the size of the bubble with their massive investments in low-income housing but also reduced the quality of the mortgages they were willing to buy, so by 2007 and 2008 half the mortgages in the bubble were subprime or otherwise risky. The enormous government investments in low-income lending through Fannie and Freddie and other vehicles show that more than merely the loss of risk aversion—posited by Baily and Elliott—was at work. If the government's activity had not occurred, accordingly, it is doubtful that the loss of risk aversion in the great moderation would have produced a housing bubble half full of subprime loans.

The Failure of the FCIC Commission. The FCIC majority report was published in January 2011, accompanied by my dissent and a different dissent by the three other Republicans on the panel. I thought it would be useful to outline the major differences, as I saw them, among these three views. Accordingly, for my January–February 2011 *Outlook* essay I wrote "The Lost Cause: The Failure of the Financial Crisis Inquiry Commission" (p. 312). The commission majority had done the predictable thing, producing a report that was nothing more than an endorsement of the left's narrative and thus a failure as an inquiry. It failed to consider all the available evidence—specifically passing over Pinto's data on the number of subprime mortgages in the financial system before the crisis—and even missed its statutory deadline. There was not an original thought or a new probative fact about the financial crisis in its five hundred pages. Although everyone agreed that the financial crisis was triggered by the meltdown of a vast number of subprime and other weak mortgages, the commission never tried to explain why underwriting standards had declined so significantly as to produce this outcome.

The separate dissent by the other Republicans was also troubling for a similar reason. It argued that ten things came together to cause the crisis, and—implausibly—if they all hadn't occurred together, there would not have been a crisis. Government housing policy during the Clinton and Bush administrations, in their view, was not a factor. This "perfect storm" analysis made their dissent useless as a guide to policy. It seemed to me that they did not want to support an analysis that indicted the Bush administration, but at the same time did not want to sign whatever it was that the Democrats had produced. That, to me, was a disappointment. We were appointed to tell the American people, Congress, and the president why the United States had a devastating financial crisis, and we owed them the truth as we saw it—no matter who might be at fault. Their refusal to blame government housing policy as the cause of the crisis made it more difficult for me, in the succeeding years, to get my dissent established as a valid alternative to the left's narrative. Whenever he had the opportunity, Angelides would point out that nine of the ten commissioners disagreed with my analysis. Nevertheless, by the fall of 2011, as I noted in the introduction, virtually all the Republican candidates for president were saying in debates and elsewhere that the financial crisis was caused by government housing policy, with Fannie and Freddie at its heart.

In my dissent, I presented evidence—developed largely through Pinto's work—that in 2008 there were twenty-seven million subprime and other risky mortgages in the U.S. financial system (updated from the twenty-five million I cited in 2009). After the SEC sued the top officers of Fannie and Freddie for failing to disclose the number of subprime and other risky mortgages they had acquired, we were able to update the total to twenty-eight million, using information the SEC had forced the companies to divulge. This was half of all mortgages outstanding, and 74 percent of these low-quality loans were on the books of government agencies such as Fannie Mae and Freddie Mac. The FCIC never challenged this number, or produced any other number, yet the data told the story about what happened in 2008. More important, although the FCIC touched all the bases of the left's narrative, they simply asserted connections between these elements and the financial crisis; they were never able to connect the dots to make a persuasive case. In the end, I concluded, the FCIC had written a long and politically motivated story *about* the financial crisis rather than about the *causes* of the crisis. Even though the Dodd-Frank Act had already been enacted when the FCIC issued its report, an historic opportunity to be honest with the American people had been lost.

Despite a number of *Financial Services Outlook*s questioning the conventional narrative, much congressional testimony, and many speeches and articles making the same point, the legislative process on what was to become the Dodd-Frank Act had moved relentlessly on. Although the

Wall Street Journal carried my op-eds, and Fox News invited me for an occasional interview, the mainstream media—ABC, CBS, NBC, CNN, the *New York Times,* the *Washington Post,* and others—showed no interest. This meant that the public only heard that the financial crisis was caused by errors of the banks and the private sector, for which sweeping regulation was to be the remedy.

Although the problems of Fannie Mae and Freddie Mac were recognized, these were seldom connected in any way to the financial crisis. I don't think this was political bias, although it certainly was a politically congenial position for the left-leaning media. Instead, I believe it reflects the pressures of the 24/7 news cycle and perhaps a dollop of laziness on the part of reporters, editors, and producers. Once a narrative gets established, it becomes a consensus in the media and, as Tolstoy noted, is exceedingly difficult to dislodge. In this case, the left's narrative for the financial crisis was easy to understand. It explained what reporters saw happening in the economy generally and in the political process. To get reporters to go back and raise questions about a prior consensus meant that they would not be spending time on reporting what was happening currently.

The corollary, unfortunately, is that if one wants to repeal a law such as the Dodd-Frank Act, one needs to show that the underlying narrative for the law was wrong. This requires changing many minds that have already accepted and acted on a different view of the world. It can be done, but it takes a great deal of time. Tolstoy didn't even believe it was possible. In the 1930s, for example, most people assumed that the Depression was caused by excessive and destructive competition; accordingly, commerce and competition had to be restrained and directed by government. Only later did academic work show that competition promotes innovation, reduces prices, and extends the benefits of economic growth throughout society. Subsequently, deregulation of communications, air transportation, truck and rail transportation, securities trading, and many other fields lowered prices and spurred growth in the U.S. economy. The fact that this took forty years is disheartening but true. It increases my sense of urgency to gain the repeal of Dodd-Frank before it is fully implemented by regulation. Once that occurs, we will experience generations of slow growth and crony capitalism before it is undone. The place to start is to show that the law, configured in the image of a false narrative, is illegitimate.

"Bear Facts: The Flawed Case for Tighter Regulation of Securities Firms"

Originally published April 2008

One of the best titles ever devised for a book about Washington was Lawrence F. O'Brien's *No Final Victories*. That's the way Washington really is; nothing is ever finally settled. The latest example of this phenomenon comes in the wake of the Bear Stearns bailout. Those who have always argued for more regulation now see a new day dawning, with an opportunity to impose greater controls on the securities industry and to ensure an enhanced role for the Fed. This is the only significant flaw in the Treasury plan for reorganization of the financial regulatory agencies. Regulating securities firms the way we regulate banks, and giving them routine access to the Fed's discount window, makes no practical or policy sense. Unlike banks, securities firms have no regular or inherent need for liquidity, and their failure—no matter how large they are—will not ordinarily cause a systemic event. Bear Stearns was bailed out because of the unprecedented fragility—indeed panic—in the world credit markets in mid-March. The fact that this has not happened in seventy years should tell us something. Accordingly, those who understand the failures and costs of regulation (to paraphrase the late William F. Buckley) should stand athwart the path to needless controls yelling "Stop!"

There is no question that the Fed's rescue of Bear Stearns was a bailout. Yes, the shareholders received only a fraction of the value they probably expected for the firm—and it is plausible that this very low price was intended to discourage others from seeking the Fed's assistance in the future—but the transaction was a bailout because the creditors and counterparties of Bear Stearns were protected against loss, and that is the significant fact about this extraordinary event. By enabling Bear Stearns to be acquired by JPMorgan Chase, the Fed made sure that Bear Stearns's creditors and counterparties would be paid. The protection of these counterparties against loss is what creates the principal problem associated with bailouts—moral hazard.

The Fed, however, had no choice. The financial markets depend on confidence among counterparties in each other's solvency, and the collapse of Bear Stearns and losses suffered by its counterparties—even though those losses are still speculative today—would have spread new doubts through the financial system about other securities firms and banks. Once again, as with the collateralized-debt obligations that began this downward spiral, no one would have known where the losses were and which firms had been fatally weakened. The cascading losses—and the cascading fear of losses—would have been too much for the market to absorb at a time when it was already so fragile that the largest banks were afraid to lend to each other.

Instead of arguing about whether a bailout occurred, the ensuing debate should be about where we go from here. Headlines such as "Ten Days That Changed Capitalism"[9] are overwrought, and those that announced "Political Pendulum Swings toward Stricter Regulation"[10] are premature. It is important to keep these events in perspective. This is the first time in seventy years that the Fed has assisted a nonbank through the discount window. That should tell us that the turmoil in the financial markets that gives rise to genuine systemic risk is very rare. The current difficulties, then—unless there is a gross overreaction in Congress—should be considered neither a turning point in the capitalist system nor a basis for establishing a new, more comprehensive regulatory structure for the large investment banks. It should also be obvious that the Fed acted as it did—and with the approval of the Treasury—because of the fragility of the markets at the time. As Fed chairman Ben Bernanke himself said, "Under more robust conditions, we might have come to a different decision about Bear Stearns."[11] Broad statements that this changed the world or was made necessary because investment banking firms have become too big to fail are nonsense. There is no reason in principle that the failure of a securities firm—no matter how large—should be a systemic event. Securities firms and investment banking firms are different from banks, and people who believe that size alone is what determines whether a firm is too big to fail do not understand this difference.

---

9. David Wessel, "Ten Days That Changed Capitalism," *Wall Street Journal*, March 27, 2008.

10. Elizabeth Williamson, "Political Pendulum Swings toward Stricter Regulation," *Wall Street Journal*, March 24, 2008.

11. "Bear's Market," editorial, *Wall Street Journal*, April 4, 2008.

Still, what happened with Bear Stearns is important. The markets learn not by what the government says but by what it does. The fact that the Fed and Treasury bailed out the creditors of Bear Stearns will leave a mark. For many years to come, market discipline of securities firms will be impaired, as some market participants will persist in believing that the largest securities firms have or will have the backing of the Fed when they need it and hence that they are less risky as borrowers than their true financial condition might warrant. The only way that this belief can be effectively countered is for a large securities firm to be allowed to fail. For better or for worse, these opportunities do not come along very often; Drexel Burnham and Kidder Peabody are two examples from the 1990s in which large securities firms were allowed to fail. A new and tighter regulatory structure for the largest securities firms will send exactly the wrong signal—that these firms are somehow under government protection. There is no doubt that if securities firms were to get regularized access to the Fed's discount window, some special degree of regulation by the Fed would be appropriate, but there is no good reason in policy or otherwise for that predicate to be established.

The argument that large securities firms should have regularized access to the Fed's discount window ultimately rests upon the erroneous notion that they are too big to fail. While this could conceivably be true for some banks, it is clearly not true for securities firms. As discussed below, there are key differences between commercial banks and securities firms that warrant a lender of last resort for the former but not the latter. As noted above, the Fed's actions in the Bear Stearns case were situation-related and not a judgment about the securities industry in general. Under these circumstances, the rationale for Fed regulation of investment banks (as opposed to commercial banks) falls apart.

Although there are some in Congress and elsewhere who propose regulation for every ill, regulation has not proven to be an effective way to promote financial market stability in the past. In the modern history of the United States, there have only been two cases in which substantial portions of an industry have collapsed, and both were depository institutions that were heavily regulated. In the late 1980s and early 1990s, 1,600 banks and roughly one third of all savings and loan associations (S&Ls) failed.[12] It is no coincidence that wholesale collapses occur in regulated industries: by increasing moral hazard—the sense

---

12. Federal Deposit Insurance Corporation (FDIC), *Managing the Crisis: The FDIC and RTC Experience, 1980–1994* (Washington, DC: FDIC, 1998), 493.

that the regulators have things under control—regulation gives investors and creditors a false sense of security and increases the likelihood of excessive risk-taking, instability, and failure among regulated entities. Indeed, the current market turmoil that forced the Fed's hand on Bear Stearns began in the banking system, despite the pervasiveness of bank regulation. When we consider whether extensive new regulation should be extended to investment banks, especially if the objective is to create stability, we should consider these factors and others discussed below.

The (Lack of) Success of Bank Regulation

Any objective look at bank regulation in the United States would have to conclude that it has been unsuccessful in a number of important respects. First, it has certainly not created stability. Banks have been regulated at the state level since they began as state-chartered institutions two hundred years ago and at the federal level since the establishment of the national bank system in 1863 under the Office of the Comptroller of the Currency. Despite this oversight, there were repeated bank panics and widespread failures throughout the nineteenth and twentieth centuries.[13] The Federal Reserve System was established in 1913 to mitigate or prevent these panics, but it was not successful in preventing massive numbers of bank failures before and during the Depression.[14] In 1933, a deposit insurance system was established that was intended to bring stability to the banking system, but, as noted above, the failure of large numbers of banks and S&Ls during the late 1980s and early 1990s resulted in a bailout that cost the taxpayers about $150 billion.

Moreover, regulation has bureaucratized the banks and sapped their entrepreneurial and innovative spirit. The banking system was once by far the largest and most important financial industry in the U.S. economy, but it failed to adapt sufficiently to changes in the economy and technology to retain its advantage over other competing forms of financial intermediation. Securities

---

13. Charles W. Calomiris, *U.S. Bank Deregulation in Historical Perspective* (Cambridge: Cambridge University Press, 2000), 3–4, available through www.aei.org/book272/.

14. Allan H. Meltzer, *A History of the Federal Reserve, Volume 1: 1913–1951* (Chicago: University of Chicago Press, 2003), 332, 367–68, 374.

firms grew as large as they did in part because the banks were not as aggressive or innovative. Mutual funds, hedge funds, and private equity firms are also supplanting banks as the agents of change in finance. It should not be a surprise that none of the major securities firms are affiliated with banks—and that none of the securities firms acquired by banks after the Gramm-Leach-Bliley Act of 1999 permitted these affiliations—became or continued to be key players in the U.S. securities business.

This is not to say that banks should not be heavily regulated. There is no choice as long as the government operates a deposit insurance system through the Federal Deposit Insurance Corporation. Deposit insurance creates moral hazard by eliminating or severely reducing the incentive of depositors and creditors to follow with care the activities and risks of a financial institution to which they have advanced credit—a process known as market discipline. The power of market discipline to prevent excessive risk-taking and leverage should not be underestimated. During 2007, after months of punishing turmoil in the financial markets, the hedge fund industry—which many people had thought would be responsible for market instability because of its secretiveness and lack of regulation—was still remarkably stable. The industry consists of thousands of funds, managing almost $2 trillion in assets,[15] but during 2007, only forty-nine funds, representing $18.6 billion in assets, closed their doors. That was a smaller number of closures than in 2006, when the financial markets were functioning smoothly; in that year, eighty-three funds managing $35 billion closed down. Thus far in 2008, there have been a few hedge fund closures, representing $3.9 billion in assets.[16] The activities and strategies of hedge funds are completely unregulated, so their risks and leverage are controlled by nothing more than the wariness of and close observation by their investors—in other words, by market discipline.

In accepting deposit insurance in 1933, banks effectively became wards of the government. That has restrained their growth, flexibility, and responsiveness to change. Accordingly, the first question one should ask about extending

---

15. U.S. Government Accountability Office (GAO), *Hedge Funds: Regulators and Market Participants Are Taking Steps to Enhance Market Discipline, but Continued Attention Is Needed* (Washington, DC: GAO, January 2008), 5, available at www.gao.gov/new. items/d08200.pdf (accessed April 8, 2008).

16. *Wall Street Journal*, "Fund Closures Dropped in 2007," March 27, 2008.

bank-like regulation to the securities industry is whether it makes sense to place bureaucratic and regulatory restraints on a part of our financial industry that has been successful in dominating the global financial markets through their extraordinary innovativeness and entrepreneurial skill. This is especially questionable when the record of bank regulation has not produced the stability that the supporters of regulation expect.

Why the Securities Industry Doesn't Need Bank-Like Regulation

Commercial banks make loans, which can be difficult to sell when they need cash to meet depositors' demands. In addition, when depositors generally want to hold cash instead of bank deposits, the need for a large number of banks to sell assets at the same time can drive down market prices and weaken the financial condition of the banks. This is exactly the same process that is causing turmoil in today's markets, although the reason is more complicated than a simple demand for cash by depositors. The Fed's discount window was established in order to address this problem. It allowed banks to pledge their best and most liquid assets to the Fed as collateral for loans, with the assurance that they could redeem the assets when the deposit withdrawals have ended and the loans are repaid.

In principle, then, discount window access should not be required for securities firms. Unlike commercial banking, in which the essence of the business is to acquire assets—loans—that are inherently difficult to liquidate, the securities industry presents a completely different pattern. Virtually all the assets of securities firms are securities, not commercial loans, and are thus inherently more liquid than the assets of banks. Securities can be sold or pledged for financing without difficulty when markets are functioning normally. Thus, if one were designing a system from scratch in, say, 2005, there would have been no reason to assume that any financial institutions other than commercial banks would need a facility like the Fed's discount window.

The reason that the usual liquidity of securities firms could not save Bear Stearns is that markets have not been functioning normally since the subprime meltdown began in June 2007. This has occurred for two principal reasons. First, the default rate on subprime loans made in 2006 and 2007 was well beyond any previously experienced, and many of these subprime loans were mixed in with prime loans in pools that were serving as collateral for mortgage-backed securities (MBS). Moreover, these MBS were themselves backing other collateralized debt obligations, so it became difficult for anyone to determine exactly where the losses were actually located. Under these conditions, the markets where these instruments were normally bought and sold virtually closed down, and Bear Stearns's collateral—the source of the firm's liquidity—lost much of its value. Second, the concurrent fall in housing sales, prices, and values—following the development of a huge bubble in housing prices—added further uncertainty to the task of determining which financial institutions were healthy and which were sick, and which pools of asset-backed securities were safe and which were not. As housing prices continued to fall, pools that had previously seemed strong began to look weaker, and it was impossible to make an estimate of risk until the full extent of the housing price decline became known. The loss of confidence thus far peaked in mid-March, when rumors spread through the market that Bear Stearns was going to fail. In normal times, Bear would have been able to borrow against its securities holdings, or sell securities to raise the cash necessary to instill confidence in its creditors and counterparties, but because of doubts about the quality of these assets, Bear was apparently unable to find counterparties who would accept these securities as collateral for financing.

There is no reason to believe that this unusual set of circumstances will occur again, just as it has not occurred in the last seventy years. As was true of the dot-com bubble, a new technology—in this case securitization—attracted a lot of enthusiasm and investment before all the pitfalls and risks were fully understood. In the future, participants in the securitization market will be more cautious; market participants, after all, learn from experience. It is important to note that bank regulators themselves neither understood the risks that were building up in the banking system nor warned the banks or the public about the dangers associated with dividing and subdividing payment streams from mortgages. Regulators, too, learn from experience, but what that means is that establishing a regulatory structure now to deal with today's problem will not protect us from tomorrow's. This is characteristic of regulators, who are fully capable of understanding risks and problems that occurred in the past but who, like the rest of us, cannot foresee the consequences of changes in the market or technology. "Omniscience," as Alan Greenspan said recently, "is not given to us. There is no way to predict how innovative markets will develop."[17]

---

17. Greg Ip, "His Legacy Tarnished, Greenspan Goes on Defensive," *Wall Street Journal,* April 8, 2008.

The collapse of Bear Stearns was an unfortunate event, but it is wrong to believe that the Fed would have stepped in if conditions in the financial markets at that moment were not so dire. The collapse and bankruptcy of Drexel Burnham and Kidder Peabody, as noted above, occurred without any substantial market impact. At the time of its collapse in 1990, Drexel was one of the most powerful firms on Wall Street, with 5,300 employees (compared with Bear's 14,000 employees seventeen years later), and it dominated the junk bond market with about 50 percent of all junk bond transactions. Drexel had asked the Fed for support, but was refused.[18] Extending bank-like regulation to the securities industry rests upon the false assumption that Bear Stearns would have been bailed out regardless of market conditions simply because it was a large financial player. To be sure, Bear Stearns was one of the major securities firms, but its failure under normal market conditions would not have caused systemic risk—no matter what its size.

The reason for this is another difference between commercial banks and investment banks. Commercial banks do not collateralize their borrowings. They borrow on the basis of their balance sheets. In addition, the business of banking requires that banks hold deposits from other banks, and banks are always in the process of clearing payments and deposits on which other banks may already have paid out funds. As an example, if a check drawn on bank A is deposited in bank B, it would not be unusual for bank B to allow its customer to use the funds before they have actually been collected from bank A. Multiplied millions of times a day, it is obvious that large sums are always in the process of collection between banks. If a large bank were to fail, its inability to meet its payment obligation would cascade down through the banking system, jeopardizing the ability of other banks down the line to make their own payments. That is why a large bank could be too big to fail.

Securities firms, also called investment banks, are entirely different. They do not borrow on the basis of their balance sheets. Instead, their borrowing is generally collateralized by the securities they hold. If they fail, their counterparties can sell the collateral, which is generally highly liquid, to make themselves whole. The problem that Bear Stearns and other investment banks have encountered in the recent market turmoil is that their collateral was no longer

---

18. Brett Duval Fromson, "Did Drexel Get What It Deserved?" *Fortune,* March 12, 1990.

acceptable, or was not acceptable for the funding they needed. For this reason, it is incorrect to say that securities firms—simply because they are large or connected to many other firms—have become too big to fail. When markets are functioning normally, the failure of a securities firm does not have anything like the market effect of the failure of a bank, because the lenders and counterparties of securities firms are generally protected by collateralization of the obligations they hold. It was the fact that markets were not functioning normally that made the possible failure of Bear Stearns a systemic event. The collateral that would normally have protected the firm's counterparties could not be marketed, and the psychological effect of the failure would have seriously worsened the loss of market confidence that then prevailed.

At this point, it is worth saying a word about credit default swaps (CDS), because many people who favor regulation have cited CDS as a source of new risks in the financial economy. In a recent article in the *Financial Times*, for example, George Soros wrote: "There is an esoteric financial instrument called credit default swaps. The notional amount of CDS contracts outstanding is roughly $45,000 billion. . . . To put it into perspective, this is about equal to half the total US household wealth."[19] This is a highly misleading statement. It sounds like a scary number, as intended, but it bears no relationship to the actual amount of liability that a CDS—or all CDSs combined—might represent.

A CDS is a kind of financial guarantee or insurance, and in a CDS transaction, a protection buyer purchases protection against the default on an obligation (like a loan) by a borrower. The "notional amount" of a CDS is generally the principal amount of the loan on which the CDS is written, not the actual loss that might be incurred if there is a default. In effect, a CDS is a kind of insurance policy, with a purchaser of protection and a seller of protection. Like most insurance, it covers losses to property, but the property is seldom a total loss. For example, if a bank has made a loan to company A in the amount of $1 million (this is the notional amount), it might purchase protection against loss on the loan by entering a CDS with an insurance company. In this way, the bank converts its risk on company A into a risk on an insurance company, which is probably a net reduction in the bank's credit risk. As long as the loan is outstanding, the bank makes payments to the insurance company. If company A defaults, the

---

19. George Soros, "The False Belief at the Heart of the Financial Turmoil," *Financial Times,* April 3, 2008.

insurance company pays the bank the $1 million and collects what it can from company A. The "default" could be a missed payment or something more serious, but the loss suffered by the insurance company is usually a fraction of the notional amount. Thus, the insurance company would carry its CDS obligation on its balance sheet at its fair value, which would be considerably less than the notional value of $1 million. As an example, in Bear Stearns's unaudited financial statements for the quarter ended August 31, 2007, the company reported derivative contracts including CDSs with a notional value of $2.2 trillion, but this notional value was carried on the firm's books at $40.3 billion, or about 2 percent of the notional amount. Similarly, the notional amount of Merrill Lynch's payout obligations under derivative contracts was $4 trillion, which the firm was carrying (according to its unaudited financial statements as of September 27, 2007) at $111 billion, or approximately 2.5 percent.

When any firm is selling credit protection in the form of a CDS, its counterparty looks to the seller's financial strength. This is true in any insurance or guaranty transaction. Counterparty risk is always present and often hedged. But if the protection seller defaults, as might have occurred with Bear Stearns, the losses suffered by its CDS counterparties are not direct losses on the loans or other obligations insured by the CDS but the loss of the insurance they had purchased. In the worst case, the buyers of protection from Bear Stearns would have had to put the full principal amount of the original loans back on their balance sheets. Alternatively, they could have entered new CDSs with more stable counterparties. Bear Stearns's failure would have exposed many counterparties to serious losses, but only if the underlying loans or securities—which Bear Stearns was insuring—themselves went into default. Of course, those who had sold protection against a Bear Stearns default would have been required to pay up, but in the normal case this risk would have been spread widely throughout the markets. Again, in the fragile and panicked markets of mid-March this might have been a problem; in normal markets—what Bernanke called more "robust" markets—that is not likely.

From this discussion, it should be obvious that CDSs are not the scary instruments that the proponents of regulation, such as George Soros, would have people believe. The existence of CDSs is not a reason for adopting stronger regulation, and the growth of CDSs has not changed the financial world or made it riskier. On the contrary, as shown by the hypothetical CDS transaction between the bank and the insurance company outlined above, CDSs can represent an efficient way for companies to hedge their risks or (in the case of the insurance company) to take on risks that give them valuable diversification and a cash flow.

Would Regulation Be a Cure?

Despite its repeated failures, the continued faith in financial regulation as a way to prevent future instability, or to protect against the recurrence of the current market problems, is somewhat touching. We have already seen that regulation did not prevent instability in the heavily regulated banking industry; did not prevent the banks from leading the financial parade that eventually gave rise to the subprime meltdown and the current worldwide financial turmoil; and oversaw the decline of the banking industry as an innovative, entrepreneurial, and aggressive competitor in the financial markets. These outcomes demonstrate that regulators do not have foresight or skills superior to those of market participants themselves.

In addition, although we would like regulators to act countercyclically, they are unable to do so because they operate in a political system. Many in Congress are now blaming the regulators for not acting to prevent the subprime meltdown and are devising schemes to enhance regulatory authority in the future, but the reaction in Congress would have been entirely different if—say, in 2006—the Fed or some other bank regulator had imposed restrictions on bank financing of adjustable-rate mortgages or mortgages with small or no down payments. In that case, the outcry in Congress would have been enormous, with lawmakers claiming that this action was interfering with the hopes of ordinary Americans to achieve the American dream of homeownership. Hearings would have been scheduled, as they are now scheduled to second-guess the Fed and the Treasury about the Bear Stearns bailout, and the regulators would have been called on the carpet in front of television cameras to explain why they were interfering with a market that was providing what all Americans want. The regulators know this. Their very human reaction is to hope for the best and leave the problems for someone else's watch.

Finally, one has to ask which firms will be regulated by any more comprehensive system of regulation applicable to the securities industry. Those who are promoting regulation seem to be thinking that it will be applicable to the largest firms in the securities industry—Merrill Lynch, Morgan Stanley, Goldman Sachs,

Lehman Brothers, and perhaps a few others. But there is a difficult line-drawing problem here. The securities industry consists of over 5,000 broker-dealers, large and small, engaged in all aspects of the securities business. Are all of these to be more heavily regulated because a few of the largest ones might one day ask for access to the Fed's discount window? On the other hand, if only the largest are to be heavily regulated, on what basis will they be selected? One can be sure that because of its costs—tangible and intangible—additional regulation will be resisted by all firms that are threatened with heavier regulation, even those that are among the largest. The rationale for imposing heavier regulation on small securities firms is weak—unlike banks, the securities business does not by its nature require the holding of illiquid assets—and the opposition of the industry as a whole will be strong.

But a compromise in which only the largest firms will be subjected to regulation will not work either. If these firms alone are made eligible for Fed discount window access, they will have a significant competitive advantage over their smaller rivals. Creditors and counterparties will prefer to deal with firms that are more heavily regulated and have the potential to borrow from the Fed, rather than those that do not. And that additional regulation and access will not only upset the competitive balance within the industry, but it will also go some distance toward creating moral hazard and reducing market discipline. In other words, greater regulation and discount window access will create a competitive imbalance within the securities industry, while diminished market discipline for the largest players will ensure that the securities industry will see greater instability in the future.

The Treasury Plan

In announcing the Treasury plan, Secretary Henry M. Paulson made some sensible statements that seem to have been lost in the media frenzy that followed:

> Some may view these recommendations as a response to the circumstances of the day; yet, that is not how they are intended. This Blueprint addresses complex, long-term issues that should not be decided in the midst of stressful situations. . . .
>
> These long-term ideas require thoughtful discussion and will not be resolved this month or even this year. . . . I am not suggesting that more

regulation is the answer, or even that more effective regulation can prevent the periods of financial market stress that seem to occur every ten years. . . . This is a complex subject deserving serious attention. Those who want to quickly label the Blueprint as advocating "more" or "less" regulations are over-simplifying this critical and inevitable debate.[20]

The Treasury plan is divided into three parts—short-term, intermediate-term, and long-term recommendations. The intermediate-term ideas are all sensible. They involve the merger of the Securities and Exchange Commission (SEC) and the Commodity Futures Trading Commission, the establishment of an optional federal charter for insurance companies (which are now regulated only at the state level), and the phaseout of the thrift charter. These are not particularly adventurous or bold ideas—as hard as they will be to achieve in today's Washington—but they are sound steps in the right direction.

The heart of the Treasury plan is the long-term restructuring. As Secretary Paulson indicated, these proposals are intended to be debated over time and are not designed specifically for the problems of today. They are both innovative and bold. With one major exception and one minor one, they deserve serious consideration, and because of their underlying logic, they will probably set the direction that reform will ultimately take. Although everyone who has a stake in the current structure, who lacks imagination, or who fears change is now taking potshots at this portion of the plan, the Treasury staff members who worked so hard on it should not be discouraged. During the Reagan administration, the Treasury proposed a plan for bank deregulation that would have eliminated the affiliation restrictions of the Glass-Steagall Act and many other restrictions on affiliations between banks and other financial services providers. That plan was also attacked from all sides and never received more than a courteous nod from a Republican Senate. But the idea kept coming back because it was the only idea that made sense, and it was finally adopted eighteen years later as the Gramm-Leach-Bliley Act of 1999.

The foundational idea in the Treasury plan is that banks, securities firms, and insurance companies represent a single financial services industry—not

---

20. Henry M. Paulson, "Remarks by Secretary Henry M. Paulson, Jr. on Blueprint for Regulatory Reform" (remarks, Department of the Treasury, Washington, DC, March 31, 2008), available at www.treas.gov/press/releases/hp897.htm (accessed April 9, 2008).

three separate industries—and ought to be regulated that way. In reality, these firms are all competing with one another, and as long as this is true it makes no sense to regulate them separately. The Treasury plan proposes to set up two regulatory agencies—one to regulate the safety and soundness of the companies that make up these three industries and the other to regulate business conduct, which probably means consumer protection. A variation of this structure was adopted in the United Kingdom several years ago and has since functioned well. Importantly, the Treasury plan would take holding company regulation away from the Fed and place it where it belongs—at the level of the bank or prudential regulator. However, two agencies seem unnecessary. The reasons given for two agencies in the plan discussion were weak, and everything we know about bureaucracies tells us that two agencies with jurisdiction over the same entities will fight endlessly over jurisdiction; some business conduct rules will affect safety and soundness and vice versa. The Financial Services Authority in the U.K. combines both functions in one agency, and that seems to make more sense.

A major objection is the proposed role for the Fed. Despite Secretary Paulson's statement, establishing the Fed as an anti–systemic risk SWAT team looks suspiciously like something that was added to compensate the Fed for depriving it of holding company supervision. If this was the reason, it was one of the few concessions that the long-term elements of the plan made to interagency politics, and it is a bad idea. As discussed above, regulators do not have the ability to spot and prick incipient bubbles, and, in any event, Congress will step in to stop any actions that interfere with the party that is going on as a bubble is growing. There were plenty of indications before the subprime meltdown that the housing economy was overheating, but no regulator felt that it had sufficient clout to stand up to Congress and call a halt. As for sniffing out innovations that might one day lead to systemic risk, that is simply a fantasy. Innovations like asset-backed securities, CDSs, and dividing and subdividing MBS into increasingly complex assets—all market developments that have been charged with responsibility for the subprime crisis of today—have good elements as well as bad. Among the good are the spreading of risk beyond depository institutions and market efficiencies that substantially lower consumer costs for credit. It is doubtful that any human being, let alone a bureaucracy like the Fed, could have predicted that these instruments, when combined with an unprecedented subprime default rate and fair value accounting, would cause the market turmoil we are experiencing today. Worse still, if the Fed actually tries to shut down market innovations it fears, we will see the destruction of the kinds of innovation that have driven financial market progress over the last quarter century.

It does not appear that the Treasury plan envisions regularized access to the Fed's discount window by securities firms, although one of the short-term elements of the Treasury plan contemplates cooperation between the Fed and the SEC in providing the Fed with the necessary information about the securities firms that might be potential discount window borrowers during the current period of market turmoil. That is the good news. The bad news is that many in Congress believe that regulation creates stability, that CDSs are creating new and unmanageable risks in the financial markets, that the failure of a large securities firm can cause systemic risk, and that regulators have foresight superior to market participants. As long as these ideas are current, there will always be a threat of increased government control of the financial markets.

AEI research assistant Karen Dubas worked with Mr. Wallison to produce this Financial Services Outlook.

"Fair Value Accounting: A Critique"

Originally published July 2008

Fair value accounting, introduced formally in 1993 by the Financial Accounting Standards Board (FASB), was intended to make financial statements easier to compare and balance sheets more reflective of real values. Instead, as applied by accountants in the current credit crunch, it has been the principal cause of an unprecedented decline in asset values and an unprecedented rise in instability among financial institutions. The system has to be rethought, not only because of its contribution to financial instability but also because its procyclicality tends to create asset bubbles and exacerbate the effects of their collapse.

This is an essay about accounting, but that is not a good reason to stop reading. It has been more than a year since the credit crisis began, and it is now becoming clear that accounting—specifically, what is called fair value accounting—is at the core of it. If you think accounting is simply a way of recording numbers, think again. Accounting is a highly conceptual art in which many objectives compete for priority. And as in politics, appearance is often the same thing as reality. The financial condition of a company may appear strong or weak depending on the accounting theory that is used to value its assets. Trillions of dollars in worldwide investor losses—and the immense losses perhaps still to come—testify to the power of accounting concepts to shape reality.

A wide range of culprits has been implicated in the conventional analysis of today's credit crisis. Subprime mortgage brokers unconcerned about the quality of their loans, subprime borrowers taking loans they knew they could not repay, sloppy underwriting by lenders, condo-flippers hoping to sell their properties before the mortgage reset, impenetrably complex securitized instruments created by financial whiz kids, poor rating agency models, shoddy risk management at banks, laziness or inattention by investors, irresponsible sales practices by securities firms, and ineffective supervision by regulators are all elements that are properly cited as contributing causes. But for $500 billion in bad subprime debt to cause a year-long crisis in a financial market with global assets of $140 trillion, something else had to be at work.

That something else is fair value accounting—a sensible system in some respects and for some limited purposes, but not well designed for the challenges it has faced in the subprime meltdown, when it has been applied woodenly and without concern for the larger issues of systemic effect. FASB, the private group that establishes financial accounting policy, introduced the basic elements of fair value accounting in 1993 and currently has underway a long-term project, known as the "measurement framework," to determine how the various ways to measure asset values should apply to different types of business activities. It might have been better if this study had been completed before fair value accounting was offered as the conventional way to value assets.

Fair value accounting rests on two underlying concepts: first, asset valuations should be consistently applied across industries so that companies can be more easily compared, and second, where there is a market price for an asset, it should under ordinary circumstances be carried on a company's balance sheet at that price. As general rules, these are unexceptionable, but in practice they are in conflict and in some cases unworkable. Not all companies follow the same business model, even within the same industry. Some primarily hold assets to maturity, while others actively trade assets and liabilities. These different business models can result in significantly different asset valuations, and in some cases similar valuations for widely different business models. This can make companies in the same industry difficult to compare, especially because there is currently no way to make clear to investors or analysts what percentage of a company's assets are valued under each method. In addition, market-based movements in asset values can create substantial volatility in balance sheets and earnings reports—again, depending on a company's business model. Finally, where there is no observable market price, other valuation methods must be used, and these can vary from company to company—again, calling comparability into question.

The key underlying issue—which should be addressed in FASB's measurement framework—is the reason for fair valuing assets. Why, for example, is market price important? What does it tell investors or creditors if there is no intention to sell an asset at that price? It is clear that some nonmarket valuation method must be used when there are no observable market prices for an asset, but what rule applies when there is a limited market for an asset or when the market is not functioning normally? In the limited or abnormal market case, as discussed below, a strong argument can be made that the market price is misleading rather than informative. It is true that valuations based on the initial cost of an asset—although simple to apply—can be misleading as conditions change over time, but it appears that the mark-to-market approach favored by fair value accounting can be equally misleading in some circumstances and, in the market conditions today, affirmatively harmful to a full understanding of a company's financial condition.

The Basics of Fair Value Accounting

The foundational ideas associated with fair value accounting were adopted by FASB in Statement of Financial Accounting Standards (FAS) 115.[21] The rule divided financial assets into three categories—those held "to maturity," those held "for trading purposes," and those "available for sale." Each of these categories is treated slightly differently. Assets held to maturity are valued at amortized cost; assets held for trading are marked to market, with unrealized gains or losses included in earnings; and assets deemed available for sale are marked to market, with unrealized gains or losses excluded from earnings but included in shareholders' equity.

Obviously, these three categories provide many opportunities for the manipulation of earnings. For example, a management that wanted to increase earnings during a reporting period could transfer appreciated assets from the available-for-sale category to the trading category, where the appreciation would add to the bottom line; in the same way, moving a depreciated asset from the trading category to the available-for-sale group would reduce reported losses. To prevent this kind of manipulation, FAS 115 contains a number of rules about how assets are to be valued when moved from one category to another. The held-to-maturity category is particularly difficult for accountants and auditors to police because its key element is an assessment of management's intent, which is always difficult to determine. For that reason, FAS 115 contains a number of stringent rules about when an asset may not be treated as held-to-maturity; these prohibit held-to-maturity treatment, for example, if the asset might be sold to

---

21. Financial Accounting Standards Board, *Statement of Financial Accounting Standards No. 115, Accounting for Certain Investments in Debt and Equity Securities,* May 1993.

meet the company's need for liquidity or if there were changes in funding terms or currency risk. If an asset is excluded from the held-to-maturity category, it is automatically carried in the available-for-sale group—and in that case it is supposed to be marked to market.

Because of the restrictive rules on when an asset could be considered held to maturity, it is likely that many commercial banks carried large portfolios of asset-backed securities as available for sale, even though the purpose of these assets was to produce cash flows. Investment banks, on the other hand, because their business model involved trading, probably carried proportionately more assets in their trading accounts, where the rise or fall in market value directly affected their earnings. In both cases, how to mark these assets to market became a highly complex and controversial matter, especially when increases or decreases in value on a mark-to-market basis could directly affect earnings. Accordingly, in 2006, FASB adopted FAS 157 in order to provide accountants and preparers with more guidance on how marking to market was supposed to be done.

FAS 157 formally defines "fair value" as "the price that would be received to sell an asset[22] . . . in an orderly transaction between market participants at the measurement date."[23] In other words, fair value is, theoretically, a quoted price for an asset in a properly functioning market. To implement the mark-to-market valuation regime, the rule established three categories or levels of certainty, a structure known as the "fair value hierarchy." Level 1 covers those assets for which there is an observable—that is, quoted—price in the market. This is not as easy as it sounds, since for many debt and asset-backed securities there may not be a liquid and functioning market in identical assets. Where there is no market for identical assets, Level 2 in the hierarchy applies. This category describes how to use quoted prices for similar assets in active markets or other observable prices such as yield curves for the same or similar assets.

---

22. FAS 157 applies also to the fair valuing of liabilities, which is beyond the scope of this essay. However, many critics of the fair value system have noted the bizarre fact that a company's earnings may be increased under fair value principles when the rating on its liabilities is reduced.

23. Financial Accounting Standards Board, *Statement of Financial Accounting Standards No. 157, Fair Value Measurements,* September 2006.

Finally, there are Level 3 assets. In the words of FAS 157, Level 3 covers assets for which there is "little, if any, market activity." There is much confusion about Level 3 assets, primarily because this level can only be understood by deciphering the obscure language that FASB used to describe this category. Level 3 makes extensive use of the terms "observable inputs" and "unobservable inputs" in describing the valuation process. Observable inputs appear to be market prices, although why FAS 157 did not simply call them so is unclear. Unobservable inputs are "the reporting entity's own assumptions about the assumptions market participants would use in pricing the asset." Unobservable inputs are disfavored: "Unobservable inputs shall be used to measure fair value to the extent that observable inputs are *not available*."[24] It appears that, with this language, FASB was attempting to create a kind of sliding scale on which greater weight in valuation would be placed on market prices when these are available. Confirming this interpretation, FAS 157 states: "Valuation techniques used to measure fair value shall maximize the use of observable inputs"—that is, market prices—"and minimize the use of unobservable inputs." In other words, FAS 157 requires reporting companies and their auditors to give greater weight to market prices, where they are available, than to any other method of valuing assets. Nevertheless, there are many cases in which observable inputs are not available in any sense; in these cases, it appears, companies use cash flow estimates and expectations to value their asset-backed portfolios and other assets.

With this background, it becomes clear why and how fair value accounting has had such a profound effect on the financial reports of banks and securities firms. The stringent rules on when assets can be considered held to maturity forced most debt and asset-backed securities into the two accounts that are required to be marked to market under FAS 115. Then, although FAS 157 allows the use of a model of some kind under Level 3, it disfavors this method if market prices are available. FAS 157's bias toward the use of market prices—which continued, as described below, even where the market was not functioning normally—had a predictable effect on how auditors interacted with reporting companies; in general, it appears that auditors have given substantial weight to market prices in valuing assets, despite the condition of the market, and this in turn has had a highly adverse effect on the apparent financial condition of companies.

---

24. Ibid., paragraph 21a and b. Emphasis added.

The Effect of Mark-to-Market Accounting on Asset Values

As losses mounted in subprime mortgage portfolios in mid-2007, lenders demanded more collateral. If the companies holding the assets did not have additional collateral to supply, they were compelled to sell the assets. These sales depressed the market for mortgage-backed securities (MBS) and also raised questions about the quality of the ratings these securities had previously received. Doubts about the quality of ratings for MBS raised questions about the quality of ratings for other asset-backed securities (ABS). Because of the complexity of many of the instruments out in the market, it also became difficult to determine where the real losses on MBS and ABS actually resided. As a result, trading in MBS and ABS came virtually to a halt and has remained at a standstill for almost a year. Meanwhile, continued withdrawal of financing sources has compelled the holders of ABS to sell them at distressed or liquidation prices, even though the underlying cash flows of these portfolios have not necessarily been seriously diminished. As more and more distress or liquidation sales occurred, asset prices declined further, and these declines created more lender demands for additional collateral, resulting in more distress or liquidation sales and more declines in asset values as measured on a mark-to-market basis. A downward spiral developed and is still operating.

The Institute of International Finance (IIF) concisely described this process in a report issued in April 2008:

> [O]ften-dramatic write-downs of *sound* assets required under the current implementation of fair-value accounting adversely affect market sentiment, in turn leading to further write-downs, margin calls and capital impacts in a downward spiral that may lead to large-scale fire-sales of assets, and destabilizing, pro-cyclical feedback effects. These damaging feedback effects worsen liquidity problems and contribute to the conversion of liquidity problems into solvency problems.[25]

The unending writedowns have produced a number of similar statements by analysts to the effect that things have gone too far—that assets have been written down well below their real value. Statements of this kind have been made by

---

25. Institute of International Finance, "IIF Board of Directors: Discussion Memorandum on Valuation in Illiquid Markets," April 7, 2008, 1. Emphasis in original.

S&P analysts,[26] the Bank of England,[27] the Financial Stability Forum,[28] and, most recently, the Bank for International Settlements.[29]

It is through this mechanism that the decline in market values—and its recognition in the mark-to-market valuation required by fair value accounting—has had its most significant effect on the balance sheets of financial intermediaries such as commercial and investment banks. These entities were likely holding large amounts of MBS and ABS, many of them rated AAA and thus initially thought to be of high quality. Because of the difficulty in meeting the standards for assets held to maturity (carried at amortized cost) under FAS 115, most of these assets were probably carried on balance sheets either as trading assets or assets available for sale—both of which are subject to mark-to-market rules under fair value accounting principles. By many accounts, the cash flows associated with these assets have generally continued to meet expectations, but the market values of the assets themselves have continued to fall. Under fair value accounting principles, then, these commercial and investment banks have been required to continue to write down the value of the asset-backed securities on their books, producing large and continuing operating and capital losses and making them appear weaker than they would if their assets were valued on the basis of the cash flows these assets produce.

In an effort to shore up their balance sheets, these organizations were compelled to sell shares at much reduced values, causing substantial losses to their shareholders. Bear Stearns, the first victim of this process because it had been unable or unwilling to raise sufficient new equity in time, had to be rescued by the Federal Reserve. Its failure would likely have created panic among the millions of investors around the world who—in mid-March—had

---

26. Standard & Poors, "More Subprime Write-Downs to Come, but the End Is Now in Sight for Large Financial Institutions," March 13, 2008, available at www2.standard andpoors.com/portal/site/sp/en/us/page.article/4,5,5,1,1204834028416.html (accessed July 17, 2008).

27. Sean O'Grady, "Banks Are Overstating Losses, Says King," *Independent,* May 1, 2008.

28. Financial Stability Forum, "Report of the Financial Stability Forum on Enhancing Market and Institutional Resilience," April 7, 2008, 31, available at www.fsforum.org/publications/r_0804.pdf?noframes=1 (accessed July 17, 2008).

29. Richard Barley, "ABX May Overstate Likely Subprime Bond Losses—BIS," Reuters, June 8, 2008.

doubts about the financial stability of most of the world's major financial institutions. Without this rescue, these investors and creditors might have rushed
for the doors in all the great commercial and investment banks, producing a
worldwide financial collapse. It seems an unavoidable conclusion, however,
that the doubts about the financial stability of these institutions were sown by
the drastic cuts in asset prices required by the mark-to-market valuations of fair
value accounting, instead of a fair appraisal of the value of the cash flows their
assets were producing.

This was not a necessary outcome. FAS 157 contains language that—if
properly and reasonably applied—might have prevented this outcome. It should
be recalled that FAS 157 requires market prices to be used for the valuation of
assets when they are sold in an "orderly transaction" and that Level 3 valuations (unobservable inputs, like models) may be used when there is "little, if any,
market activity." In discussing the meaning of "orderly transaction," the rule's
language is important:

> A fair value measurement assumes that the asset or liability is exchanged
> in an orderly transaction between market participants to sell the asset
> . . . at the measurement date. An orderly transaction is a transaction that
> assumes exposure to the market for a period prior to the measurement
> date to allow for marketing activities that are usual and customary for
> transactions involving such assets or liabilities; *it is not a forced transac-
> tion* (for example, a forced liquidation or distress sale).[30]

This language would have made it possible for FASB or accountants themselves to adjust their implementation of FAS 157 so that preparers could take
account of the fact that the market prices they were seeing were the result of
"a forced liquidation or distress sale." It was also possible that the Securities
and Exchange Commission (SEC)—which has delegated financial rulemaking
authority to FASB—would step in and clarify FAS 157 so that the market prices
of distressed and liquidation assets did not become the basis for the values
that accountants would require that their clients use. But that is not what happened. In early March 2008, the SEC sent a letter to the chief financial officers
of public companies, commenting on FAS 157 and its applicability in current
market conditions:

---

30. FAS 157, 3, paragraph 7. Emphasis added.

Fair value assumes the exchange of assets or liabilities in orderly trans-actions. Under SFAS 157, it is appropriate for you to consider actual market prices, or observable inputs, even when the market is less liquid than historical market volumes, *unless prices are the result of a forced liquidation or distress sale.* Only when actual market prices, or relevant observable inputs, are not available is it appropriate for you to use unobservable inputs which reflect your assumptions of what market participants would use in pricing the asset or liability.[31]

The letter gave no useful guidance whatsoever to companies or accountants about the effect of market conditions on asset values. It avoided completely the central question—whether market values were the result of distress sales and liquidations—and probably made things worse by saying that "actual market prices" had to be used as long as they are available, unless of course these "actual market prices" are the result of a forced liquidation or distress sale. Moreover, the last sentence of the quoted paragraph also discouraged the use of Level 3 valuation methods under FAS 157—which applies when there is "little, if any market activity"—by stating that this was possible "only when actual market prices, or relevant observable inputs, are not available." If Level 3 valu-ations had been permitted, companies might have been able to use discounted cash flow for valuing their assets, thus avoiding the writedowns associated with marking their assets to distressed market prices. All the SEC had to do in this connection was note that, even though some prices were available in the mar-ket, there was actually "little . . . market activity"—a fact everyone in the market was pointing out at the time.

As for FASB and the accounting profession, they resisted any change in the wooden application of mark-to-market accounting to asset values. Their representatives continued to insist that if a market price was available, no mat-ter what the condition of the market, it was to be preferred to any other way of establishing asset values. Thus, at an AEI conference on fair value accounting in April 2008, an FASB representative responded as follows to a question about

---

31. Securities and Exchange Commission, "Sample Letter Sent to Public Companies on MD&A Disclosure Regarding the Application of SFAS 157 (Fair Value Measurements)," March 2008, available at www.sec.gov/divisions/corpfin/guidance/fairvalueltr0308.htm (accessed July 17, 2008). Emphasis added.

whether companies are being compelled to use distressed or liquidation prices to value their assets:

> Are there many willing buyers of those assets? That might suggest that it is not a distressed sale even though the seller is in distress. So it's a very judgmental question, and just to sort of complete the loop, even in those rare circumstances where we would say, that's a distressed sale, it does not mean that you ignore it.[32]

A representative of an accounting firm expressed the same view:

> Fewer or even a lack of any transactions in a debt security or similar debt security makes it much more challenging to determine fair value. But, again, even with fewer transactions, less liquidity in the marketplace, I don't think that would lead you down the path that fair value is still not the most relevant measurement to users of the financial statements.[33]

These responses simply read out of FAS 157 the language that creates an exception for markets that reflect distress or liquidation sales. If this language was intended to have any meaning, it would certainly apply in the financial market we have been experiencing since the summer of 2007. The failure of the SEC, FASB, and the accounting profession to accept responsibility for adjusting the rule to take account of a truly unprecedented and still-dangerous situation for the financial markets is difficult to understand. All that can be said with certainty is that this failure occurred and is continuing, with huge resulting losses to investors and unnecessary jeopardy to the stability of financial institutions.

Fair Value Accounting and Asset Bubbles

Fair value accounting must be fixed, and quickly—not just because of its strongly adverse impact on financial institutions in today's market, but also

---

32. Leslie Seidman, "What Is Fair Value Accounting and Why Are People Concerned about It?" (presentation, American Enterprise Institute, Washington, DC, April 8, 2008), available through www.aei.org/event1704/.

33. Mark Scoles, "What Is Fair Value Accounting and Why Are People Concerned about It?" (presentation, American Enterprise Institute, Washington, DC, April 8, 2008), available through www.aei.org/event1704/.

because it is highly procyclical. In other words, it tends to exacerbate current financial trends, whatever they are. It may well be, for example, that fair value accounting was in substantial part responsible for the residential real estate bubble that collapsed—with devastating consequences—over a year ago.

We can now see how the mark-to-market effect of fair value accounting has caused a downward slide in asset values and how this decline has evolved into a dangerous downward spiral. But it is important to note that rising asset prices have the opposite—and equally procyclical—effect. As market values rise for homes, stocks, commodities, or any item that has a readily available price, more and more credit becomes available to carry these assets. As more credit is available, more money is chasing fewer assets and prices rise. From the standpoint of institutions, a rise in the value of assets is recognized in earnings under fair value principles if the assets were held for trading and recognized in the institution's capital or equity position if the assets were treated as available for sale. In both cases, the growing earnings and strengthening capital induces more borrowing and the acquisition of more assets, so the upward spiral—also known as a bubble—continues.

It is no answer to say that bubbles and collapses of all kinds are ultimately the result of the human tendency to think that trends at any given moment will continue. Of course this is true, but the object of policy design is to adopt those policies that will counteract and ameliorate what we know to be the normal failures in human activities and perceptions.

Procyclicality is obviously an unintended consequence of fair value accounting, but nonetheless an issue for policymakers. The central purposes of fair value accounting were good—to make financial statements easier to compare and to bring asset values more in line with reality—but these goals, even if they had been achieved, are not as important as avoiding or reducing asset bubbles, producing steady growth in the economy, and encouraging stability in our financial institutions. That is why, to paraphrase Georges Clemenceau on war and generals, accounting is too important to be left to accountants. Someone with a broader perspective than the accuracy of financial statements has to take control of the process of reforming fair value accounting. This would normally be a task for the SEC, but the agency, with its March 2008 letter to chief financial officers, indicated that it is not prepared to take on this task.

If some policymaker takes charge, reform will mean curbing its effect in causing bubbles when assets are rising in value and the instability of financial institutions when asset values are falling. It will also mean giving the term "forced liquidation or distress sale" its obviously intended meaning as a protection against requiring financial institutions and others to use market prices that are not a true reflection of asset values. In a properly functioning market, asset values reflect the discounted value of cash flows. In a market that is not functioning normally, as is true today, market prices—affected by liquidity considerations and distress sales—can diverge from the values derived from cash flows. This point was made well in the discussion memorandum published by IIF in April 2008:

> There is of course no question that actual or reasonably likely losses or deterioration of underlying cash flows on assets should be reflected in valuations. However, under conditions since July 2007, lack of market activity, expectations of continued downward pressures, extremely high risk premia, uncertainty, and sometimes irrational results . . . have created a situation where it has become obvious that the market has failed to produce pricing inputs that reflect actual default probabilities of sound assets.[34]

It is also no answer to say that assets are worth "whatever someone else will pay for them." In one sense that is a truism, but in a deeper sense it only reflects reality at one moment in time and only if the assets are in fact for sale at that time. As accountants look at the issue, the value of something is its value in the market on the "measurement date." That is perhaps true in the artificial world created by having to complete and publish a financial statement as of a particular date. But, with the exception of assets actually held for trading purposes, the true value of an asset such as an asset-backed security is far more likely to be the cash flow it produces than its price in the market on an arbitrary measurement date.

Any reform of fair value accounting must also recognize that there is more at stake in accounting than financial reports. Companies exist to create value, not financial reports. The true value of a going concern is not what the market would pay for its assets, one by one, on a particular day, but—as IIF correctly noted—the cash flows that it can generate. Similarly, especially in the case of

---

34. Institute of International Finance, "IIF Board of Directors: Discussion Memorandum on Valuation in Illiquid Markets," 1.

financial institutions—the assets of which are particularly subject to market volatility—the importance of stability must be taken into account. All this appears to have been abandoned in the interest of creating a reference number for accountants on a particular "measurement date."

What Now?

Assets held for trading should be valued at the market, even if the market is weak, illiquid, or not functioning normally. That is one of the risks a company takes in holding assets for trading purposes. But assets held for sale—that is, not held to maturity—are a different matter. There is no good reason to mark these assets to market, even if there is a market. A better means of valuation—one more in line with what investors want to know about companies—is to value these assets for balance sheet purposes based on the discounted value of their cash flows. To be sure, there are opportunities here for manipulation by managements. The choice of a discount rate can have important effects, as well as other factors, but every system—including the system set up by FAS 115—presents opportunities for management manipulation. Indeed, each major element of an income statement—as most accountants will admit—is nothing more than an estimate by management about the future.[35]

What we should be looking for in an accounting system is a regime that represents reality, not one that is easy for accountants to administer. If asset-backed securities and loans, even those held for sale, were valued on the basis of their cash flows, there would be elements of contention between auditors and managements, but there would also be far less procyclicality in the result. Cash flows do not change as rapidly as market values, and asset valuations based on cash flows would not foster bubbles as rapidly as a valuation system based on marking to market. Gains and losses in this category would, as today, be reflected in the equity account and not in earnings, as is currently the rule under FAS 115. This would also have a salutary effect in reducing the procyclicality of fair value accounting.

---

35. See Peter J. Wallison, "Hostages to Fortune: A Change in the Audit Certification Can Reduce Auditors' Risks," *Financial Services Outlook* (April 2007), available at www.aei.org/publication25915.

Finally, the standards for counting assets as held to maturity should be eased so that financial institutions could hold more assets in this category. This would also significantly reduce the procyclicality problem associated with fair value accounting. It will be objected that this opens a large loophole for management manipulation, because assets that are falling in value have less of an impact on a company's financial position if they are deemed to be held to maturity and thus not marked to market. Our first objective here, however, should not be preventing manipulation but instead making sure that our accounting system does not foster destructive financial bubbles. If manipulation is occurring—and even if it is not—it would be good policy for financial disclosure to include a footnote in which management records the transfers of assets among the various FAS 115 categories—trading, held-for-sale, and held-to-maturity—and the effect these have had on the financial statements.

Research assistant Karen Dubas worked with Mr. Wallison to produce this Financial Services Outlook.

"Systemic Risk and the Financial Crisis"

Originally published October 2008

The current financial crisis has sharpened interest—on the part of both the public and policymakers—in both stronger regulation and the extension of regulation to new areas. One of the theories for doing so is concern that the failure of one institution can, by passing its losses to others, create systemic risk. In this analysis, the current crisis is presented as an example of systemic risk becoming reality. To prevent a recurrence, greater regulation, covering a wider range of participants in the financial markets, is necessary. However, there is as yet no evidence that the current crisis was the result of systemic risk, which is characterized by a kind of contagion. Instead, the crisis appears to have arisen from the failure of traditional regulated institutions—in a particularly dramatic case of herd behavior—to limit their risk-taking. The result has been a mammoth solvency and stability problem, but one without any apparent contagion. Accordingly, the current crisis provides support for better supervision of traditionally regulated industries, but no warrant either for a systemic risk regulator or for the supervision of other participants in the financial markets that have not previously been regulated.

With the financial crisis now in full flower, many policymakers assume that new regulation is necessary to prevent "systemic risk." For example, Barney Frank (D-Mass.), chairman of the House Committee on Financial Services, has endorsed a "systemic risk regulator" to "act when necessary to limit risky practices or protect the integrity of the financial system." The systemic risk regulator would apparently oversee a far broader regulatory system than exists anywhere today: "To the extent that anybody is creating credit they ought to be subject to the same type of prudential regulation that now applies to commercial banks."[36] This idea makes sense only if one assumes—as Frank apparently does—that the

---

36. Stephanie Baum, "Congressman Frank Urges Creation of Risk Regulator," Dow Jones Financial News Online, March 20, 2008, available at www.efinancialnews.com/usedition/index/content/2350130123 (accessed October 27, 2008).

losses of a single firm engaged in a credit-granting activity can somehow be transmitted to others and thus engender systemic risk. But there is no reason to believe that the current crisis, as bad and as widespread as it is, resulted from systemic risk, or would be addressed by new regulation specifically directed at preventing systemic risk.

What is systemic risk? Is the current financial crisis an example of systemic risk becoming a reality? Policy development, like the practice of medicine, is a process of diagnosis and prescription. First we have to understand what exactly we are dealing with, and then we must adopt solutions that are tailored to address it. If we want to prevent another crisis like this one in the future, we should adopt policies that are directed at that goal, not at problems we do not have. If the current crisis is not the result of systemic risk, it would do no good—and might do substantial harm—to adopt policies designed to curb or control it. This *Outlook* will attempt to define what is meant by systemic risk and will compare that definition to what we know thus far about the causes of the financial crisis. This is only a preliminary and tentative effort; there is much still to be learned about the causes of the crisis, but it is useful to establish a framework for judging whether what we are facing today is the result of a failure of our current regulatory system to address and contain systemic risk.

The classic case of systemic risk arises in the banking system and has been defined as "the probability that cumulative losses will occur from an event that ignites a series of successive losses along a chain of institutions or markets."[37] It envisions a cascade of losses flowing from the failure of a single large bank, brought on by the interconnections of the banking and payment systems. If a large bank cannot meet its obligations at the end of a business day, other banks—awaiting a payment from the failing bank—cannot meet their own obligations, and so on down the chain. Unless the supervisors act quickly, the result could be losses throughout the banking system and the economy; hence, a systemic event.

There is also a broader concept of systemic risk, focusing on markets rather than institutions. The Commodity Futures Trading Commission defines it as "the risk that a default by one market participant will have repercussions on other participants due to the interlocking nature of financial markets. For example,

---

37. George G. Kaufman, "Bank Failures, Systemic Risk, and Bank Regulation," *Cato Journal* 16, no. 1 (Spring/Summer 1996): 20.

Customer A's default in X market may affect Intermediary B's ability to fulfill its obligations in Markets X, Y and Z."[38]

What these concepts have in common is their assumption that systemic risk is a kind of contagion—that the failure of one institution or market participant is transmitted to other institutions and other markets in somewhat the same way that a disease is transmitted through contact.

The concept of contagion radiating from a single default is central to any understanding of systemic risk. Without contagion—losses cascading from one entity to many others—any economic downturn in which many businesses collapse from lack of sales could be called a systemic event, and the danger of this happening could be called systemic risk. If so, there would be a basis for regulating every business to prevent its failure from causing losses to and the failure of others.

Similarly, if there is evidence that today's financial crisis is not the result of contagion—if it arose independently of whatever connections might exist between and among the affected institutions—it would be a great policy mistake to impair the interconnections. For example, credit default swaps (CDSs) have been blamed by many commentators—including some as sophisticated as George Soros[39]—for creating "interconnectedness" among financial institutions that has made it possible to transmit losses from one institution to others. If this interconnectedness is in fact a significant contributing factor to current market conditions, then serious consideration should be given to regulations that control or limit it. But if interconnectedness is not a causal factor in the current crisis, it would be a serious error to restrict the use of CDSs, which are also very important and effective hedging and risk management tools for financial institutions and others.[40] In fact, if the transmission of losses from one institution or market to another is not a factor in the current crisis, restricting the use of CDSs would, on the whole, increase rather than reduce the risks of financial

---

38. This is the definition used by the Commodity Futures Trading Commission, available at www.cftc.gov/educationcenter/glossary/glossary_s.html.

39. George Soros, "The False Belief at the Heart of the Financial Turmoil," *Financial Times*, April 3, 2008.

40. See, for example, discussion of credit default swaps in Peter J. Wallison, "For Financial Regulation, the Era of Big Government Really Is Over," *Financial Services Outlook* (June 2008), available at www.aei.org/publication28152/.

institutions—without doing anything to reduce significantly the likelihood of similar financial crises in the future.

The same analysis applies to the regulation of companies and institutions that are not currently regulated. If there is evidence that their default will have a sufficiently large adverse effect on others to be considered systemic, then regulation might be appropriate. But if there is no evidence of this effect—or likelihood that it will occur—then it would be a mistake to regulate companies that do not otherwise require it and for which the tangible and intangible costs of regulation would be an unnecessary burden. For example, Frank seems to believe that all credit-granting entities should be regulated like commercial banks. This seems to have some relationship to his concern about systemic risk. Retailers routinely grant credit to customers, but it is hard to imagine that the failure of a retailer—no matter how large—would create systemic risk in any sense that that term is generally understood. In view of his position in Congress, however, Frank's position on this question must be taken seriously. The balance of this *Outlook* will consider the causes of the current crisis and whether it is an instance of the contagion between institutions and markets that characterizes systemic risk—or something else.

Solvency, Not Liquidity

The current crisis has three noteworthy elements: It is worldwide, engulfing the economies of nearly all the developed countries. It is comprehensive in that it involves financial institutions of all kinds. And it is characterized by doubts about the stability and solvency of most of the world's major financial institutions. The first two of these elements fit within the conventional notion of systemic risk—a widespread adverse financial or economic result springing from a default or a shock to the markets. The pervasive nature of the crisis—both geographically and in terms of the number of institutions it affects—is certainly consistent with the contagion metaphor that underlies systemic risk. But the third element is unusual and, perhaps, unprecedented. With the possible exception of the Great Depression of the 1930s, no prior financial crisis appears to have had its origin in doubts about the solvency—rather than the liquidity—of a substantial number of the largest financial institutions in the United States and other developed countries. Many scholars and market observers have blamed the apparent intractability of the current crisis on the failure of the Treasury and the Fed to recognize that it was a problem of solvency rather than of illiquidity.[41] As long as there are questions about the solvency of banks and other financial intermediaries, no amount of liquidity is likely to induce depositors and counterparties to feel comfortable about making long-term commitments to them. And without these commitments, banks and others will continue to be vulnerable to runs by their depositors and counterparties.

The Troubled Assets Relief Program (TARP) was the first major effort by the government to deal with the turmoil in the financial markets as a solvency rather than a liquidity problem. By proposing to buy distressed mortgage assets from banks and others, the Treasury and the Fed apparently hoped to improve the balance sheets of these institutions and thus their capital positions. In its first use of the TARP funds, the Treasury went at this issue even more directly, requiring nine of the largest U.S. financial institutions to accept infusions of capital in the form of preferred stock. Whether any of these moves will slow the deterioration of prices or encourage banks to lend is unknown at this point.

Understanding the current crisis as a solvency problem seems correct. The underlying cause was the collapse of the housing bubble in the United States, aggravated by the fact that weak subprime and Alt-A loans were major constituents of the housing-related assets held by banks and other financial intermediaries around the world. These mortgage loans, which are held mostly in the form of mortgage-backed securities (MBS) and collateralized debt obligations (CDOs), are defaulting at unprecedented rates. The difficulty of determining the value of the underlying mortgages has caused the market for these instruments to come to a virtual halt, and it has also engendered uncertainty about the solvency of the financial institutions that hold them. Until investors and counterparties are persuaded that these institutions are solvent, they will not be stable.

Seeing the crisis as a solvency problem rather than a liquidity problem also clarifies a lot about the major events of the last six months, beginning with the bailout of Bear Stearns. According to the testimony of SEC chairman Christopher Cox, the firm was solvent and had sufficient liquid resources to continue operations only days before its imminent collapse resulted in its forced sale to

---

41. See, for example, Vincent R. Reinhart, "A Bill That Deserved to Pass," *The American*, October 6, 2008, available at www.aei.org/publication28743/.

JPMorgan Chase.[42] However, in the three days from March 12 to March 14, Bear was unable to borrow funds through the collateralization of assets that had previously been acceptable for short-term loans, and the firm's liquidity position declined by almost $17 billion[43] as clients and counterparties withdrew their funds. This market behavior is consistent with the view that doubt about the quality of the firm's assets—and hence its long-term solvency—was the ultimate cause of its collapse.

After Bear Stearns, the Fed opened the discount window to all four remaining large investment banks—Lehman Brothers, Merrill Lynch, Morgan Stanley, and Goldman Sachs—enabling these institutions to meet whatever liquidity needs occurred. Nevertheless, in early September, Lehman encountered the same market resistance that had destroyed Bear Stearns and, without a similar rescue effort by the government, filed for bankruptcy. The Lehman bankruptcy caused the remaining investment banks to seek shelter—Merrill Lynch in a merger with Bank of America and Morgan Stanley and Goldman Sachs as financial services holding companies supervised by the Federal Reserve. In other words, in a little over six months, all five members of the rich and independent investment banking community in New York were in bankruptcy, controlled by others, or functioning under the bank-like supervisory regime of the Fed.

These events were not precipitated by a lack of liquidity. All the investment banking firms, to the extent that they could not use their assets for collateral in the market, had the option of borrowing from the Fed through the discount window, but the failure of Lehman showed that liquidity itself was not the problem; investors did not have enough confidence in the solvency of these firms to treat them as suitable counterparties. Following the collapse of Lehman, the Fed was compelled to bail out AIG, the world's largest insurance holding company, and the London Interbank Offer Rate (LIBOR) rose to unprecedented levels. Banks began hoarding cash, not only to meet customer withdrawals but also because of fear about the solvency of their bank counterparties. This condition has eased somewhat only because governments agreed to guarantee loans between banks.

---

42. Christopher Cox, "Testimony Concerning Recent Events in the Credit Markets" (U.S. Senate, Committee on Banking, Housing and Urban Affairs, April 3, 2008), available at www.sec.gov/news/testimony/2008/ts040308cc.htm (accessed October 27, 2008).

43. Stephen Labaton, "SEC's Role in Wall Street Crisis," *New York Times,* October 5, 2008.

The market reaction to the Lehman collapse is itself a demonstration of the fact that contagion or systemic risk is not a factor in the current financial crisis. The sudden rise in LIBOR and the freezing of the credit markets that followed immediately thereafter had nothing to do with contagion. Banks did not stop lending to one another because Lehman filed for bankruptcy. This reaction ensued because the underlying problem is not contagion or illiquidity but rather fear that others are not or will not be solvent or stable counterparties.

No Evidence of Contagion

If the current crisis is indeed caused by counterparty and investor doubts about the solvency of most of the world's major financial institutions, it cannot at the same time be the result of systemic risk as that idea is generally understood. There is no apparent contagion. The crisis instead arose from the fact that all these institutions invested heavily in the same weak assets—primarily MBS and CDOs backed in whole or in part by subprime and Alt-A mortgages. Whatever one may call this—herd behavior is one explanation—it is not the result of contagion. There is further evidence for this conclusion in the recent settlement of CDS obligations arising out of the collapse of Lehman. The reason for the bailout of Bear Stearns is still debated, as is the reason for not bailing out Lehman, but recent events cast doubt on the claim that the Treasury and Fed pressed for Bear to sell itself to JPMorgan Chase because of fear that the CDSs on Bear's debt would cause massive counterparty losses if Bear were to default. Two potential problems were cited: losses on the CDSs written on Bear (which might cause other firms to go over the brink) or chaos associated with unwinding these losses (which might create substantial additional market instability).[44]

Bear's acquisition by JPMorgan Chase obviated the need to account for any losses on the CDSs written on Bear's outstanding debt, so we will never know whether Bear's default might have directly threatened other financial institutions. However, Lehman was a larger firm than Bear, with $600 billion in outstanding debt on which CDSs with a notional amount totaling $400 billion had been written. Last week, all $400 billion in claims were settled among the

---

44. See, for example, Shah Gilani, "The Real Reason for the Global Financial Crisis . . . the Story No One's Talking About," Money Morning, September 18, 2008, available at www.moneymorning.com/2008/09/18/credit-default-swaps (accessed October 27, 2008).

CDS counterparties for a total payment of $5.2 billion. This does not mean that $5.2 billion was the total extent of the losses but only that the vast majority of the losses were settled among the participants through the sale of collateral or the netting of claims on one another. The settlement was completely orderly, almost humdrum. Perhaps more important was the fact that AIG's CDS losses on Lehman's debt—also settled at the same time—were only $6.2 million. AIG had been a major participant in the CDS market, and many market observers had attributed its need for a bailout immediately after the Lehman bankruptcy to the losses AIG would suffer because of CDSs it had written to back Lehman's debt. However, a spokesman for AIG noted after the settlement that the company had hedged its Lehman obligations and that these hedges almost canceled one another out.[45] There is much more to learn about the role of CDSs in the financial crisis, but it is altogether clear, even now, that whatever role they played, it was a tiny one when compared to the contribution of imprudent investments in junk mortgages and MBS.

Despite their relative newness on the financial scene, CDSs are nothing more than insurance contracts or indemnification agreements. In exchange for a regular premium payment, the party that sells protection is in effect assuming its counterparty's risk on a loan or other obligation. If A lends money to B, A bears the risk of B's default. If A wants to be protected against B's default, A enters a CDS with C, who promises to pay A if B defaults. There is nothing mysterious about this transaction. Since C is now bearing the risk of B's default, it is functionally the same transaction as if C had made the loan to B. No new risk is created; the same risk—B's obligation to A—has simply been transferred to C by contract. Financial institutions lend to one another all the time, and these loans are routinely transferred or sold. A CDS transaction is a substitute for the sale of a loan.

Why is it thought that a simple transaction like this—when called a CDS—creates some special kind of "interconnectedness" that had not existed before? If B defaults, C indemnifies A and tries to recover from B. If C hedges its risk by buying protection from D, and D does the same with E, and so on, that creates a large "notional" amount as all the obligations are added up, but in the end there is only one true loss—B's default on the loan from A. Arrangements like

---

45. Mary Williams Walsh, "Tracking Firm Says Bets Placed on Lehman Have Been Quietly Settled," *New York Times,* October 23, 2008.

this have been going on in finance for hundreds of years; the CDS is simply a new way of transferring a risk without actually selling the loan. The presence of CDSs, as shown by the Lehman settlement, does not necessarily create any market disruption or do more to create interconnectedness or risk than ordinary loan arrangements.

Conclusion

The fact that the current financial crisis is caused by doubts about the solvency of almost all of the world's major financial institutions sets it apart from any other financial crisis in history. It also casts doubt on the notion that the crisis is the result of systemic risk. There is no evidence of the contagion that is the hallmark of a systemic risk event. Instead, the world's financial institutions got into trouble the old-fashioned way: by taking unnecessary risks when acquiring assets—in this case MBS and CDOs backed in whole or in part by subprime and Alt-A loans—and not through a cascade of losses transmitted from one failing firm to another.

This suggests that to the extent that greater regulation is in prospect, it should focus on limiting the risk-taking of regulated institutions such as insured commercial banks and savings and loan associations. The failure of a large number of insured depository institutions shows that better regulation and better regulatory tools are warranted. The failure of at least two investment banks raises the question of whether investment banks should be regulated. The answer to this question would be yes, if there is evidence that the failure of a large investment bank such as Lehman caused others to fail or even to become substantially weaker. If so, that could—if large enough in effect—be an example of systemic risk. Thus far, however, there is no evidence that Lehman's failure has had any substantial adverse effect—there has been no contagion—even though a market panic resulted. If there had not been widespread concern about the financial stability of most of the world's major financial institutions, it seems highly likely that the panic itself could easily have been addressed by the Fed's action in making large amounts of liquidity available—as it has done in similar circumstances in the past—on a temporary basis.

Thus, unless there is compelling evidence of contagion, the current financial crisis does not furnish any support for regulating institutions such as investment banks, securities firms, hedge funds, private equity firms, finance companies, leasing companies, retailers, or the myriad other financial players that currently grant credit or otherwise participate in the financial markets in one way or another. Nothing that has happened thus far in the financial crisis suggests that the failure of these organizations has had or would have any significant effect on the financial institutions—primarily insured depository institutions—for which the federal government is responsible and whose failure could result in costs for the taxpayers.

"Everything You Wanted to Know about Credit Default Swaps— But Were Never Told"

Originally published December 2008

Credit default swaps (CDSs) have been identified in media accounts and by various commentators as sources of risk for the institutions that use them, as potential contributors to systemic risk, and as the underlying reason for the bailouts of Bear Stearns and AIG. These assessments are seriously wide of the mark. They seem to reflect a misunderstanding of how CDSs work and how they contribute to risk management by banks and other intermediaries. In addition, the vigorous market that currently exists for CDSs is a significant source of market-based judgments on the credit conditions of large numbers of companies—information that is not publicly available anywhere else. Although the CDS market can be improved, excessive restrictions on it would create considerably more risk than it would eliminate.

There are so many potential culprits in the current financial crisis that it is difficult to keep them all straight or to assess their relative culpability. Greedy investment banks, incompetent rating agencies, predatory lenders and mortgage brokers—even the entire system of asset securitization—have all been blamed for the current condition of the financial markets. The oddest target, however, is CDSs. Almost every media report and commentary about the collapse of Lehman Brothers in September and the ensuing freeze in the credit markets mentions CDSs as one of the contributing causes, just as similar reports and commentary accompanied the government's decision to rescue Bear Stearns in March and AIG in September. One conventional explanation for the Bear rescue has been that CDSs made the financial markets highly "interconnected." It is in the nature of credit markets to be interconnected, however: that is the way money moves from where it is less useful to where it is most useful, and that is why financial institutions are called "intermediaries." Moreover, there is very little evidence that Bear was bailed out because of its involvement with CDSs—and some good evidence to refute that idea. First, if the government rescued Bear because of CDSs, why did it not also rescue Lehman? If the Treasury Department and the Federal Reserve really believed that Bear had to be rescued because the market was interconnected through CDSs, they would never have allowed Lehman—a much bigger player in CDSs than Bear—to fail. In addition, although Lehman was a major dealer in CDSs—and a borrower on which many CDSs had been written—when it failed there was no discernible effect on its counterparties. Within a month after the Lehman bankruptcy, the swaps in which Lehman was an intermediary dealer were settled bilaterally, and the swaps written on Lehman itself ($72 billion notionally) were settled by the Depository Trust and Clearing Corporation (DTCC). The settlement was completed without incident, with a total cash exchange among all counterparties of $5.2 billion. There is no indication that the Lehman failure caused any systemic risk arising out of its CDS obligations—either as one of the major CDS dealers or as a failed company on which $72 billion in notional CDSs had been written.

Nevertheless, Securities and Exchange Commission (SEC) chairman Christopher Cox was quoted in a recent *Washington Post* series as telling an SEC roundtable: "The regulatory black hole for credit-default swaps is one of the most significant issues we are confronting in the current credit crisis . . . and requires immediate legislative action. . . . The over-the-counter credit-default swaps market has drawn the world's major financial institutions and others into a tangled web of interconnections where the failure of any one institution might jeopardize the entire financial system." Readers of this *Outlook* should judge for themselves whether this is even a remotely accurate portrayal of the dangers posed by CDSs.[46]

The fact that AIG was rescued almost immediately after Lehman's failure led once again to speculation that AIG had written a lot of CDS protection on Lehman and had to be bailed out for that reason. When the DTCC Lehman settlement was completed, however, AIG had to pay only $6.2 million on its Lehman exposure—a rounding error for this huge company. As outlined in a recent *Washington Post* series on credit risk and discussed below, AIG's exposure was not due to Lehman's failure but rather the result of the use (or misuse)

---

46. Robert O'Harrow Jr. and Brady Dennis, "Downgrades and Downfall," *Washington Post,* December 31, 2008.

of a credit model that failed to take account of all the risks the firm was taking.[47] It is worth mentioning here that faulty credit evaluation on mortgage-backed securities (MBS) and collateralized debt obligations (CDOs) have also been the cause of huge losses to commercial and investment banks. As I argue in this *Outlook,* there is no substantial difference between making a loan (or buying a portfolio of MBS) and writing protection on any of these assets through a CDS. Faulty credit evaluation in either case will result in losses.

If CDSs did not trigger the rescue of Bear and AIG, what did? The most plausible explanation is that in March, when Bear was about to fail, the international financial markets were very fragile. There was substantial doubt among investors and counterparties about the financial stability and even the solvency of many of the world's major financial institutions. It is likely that the government officials who decided to rescue Bear believed that if a major player like Bear were allowed to fail, there would be a run on other institutions. As Fed chairman Ben Bernanke said at the time, "Under more robust conditions, we might have come to a different decision about Bear Stearns."[48] When the markets are in panic mode, every investor and counterparty is on a hair-trigger alert because the first one out the door is likely to be repaid in full while the latecomers will suffer losses. The failure of a large company like Bear in that moblike environment can be responsible for a rush to quality; in a normal market, there would have been a much more muted reaction. For example, when Drexel Burnham failed in 1990, there was nothing like the worldwide shock that ensued after Lehman's collapse, although Drexel was as large a factor in the market at that time as Lehman was before its failure.

After the Lehman bankruptcy, there was a market reaction much like what would have happened if Bear had failed. The markets froze, overnight interbank lending spreads went straight north, and banks stopped lending to one another. In these circumstances, the rescue of AIG was inevitable, although it is likely that the company would have been allowed to fail if the reaction to the Lehman failure had not been so shocking. The Fed's statement on its rescue of AIG pointed to the conditions in the market—not to CDSs or other derivatives—as the reason for its actions: "The Board determined that, in current circumstances, a disorderly failure of AIG could add to already significant levels of financial

---

47. Ibid.
48. Editorial, "Bear's Market," *Wall Street Journal,* April 4, 2008.

market fragility and lead to substantially higher borrowing costs, reduced household wealth, and materially weaker economic performance."[49] Indeed, the sensitivity of the markets and the government in September is shown by the reaction of the Treasury and the Fed when the Reserve Fund, a money market mutual fund, "broke the buck"—that is, allowed the value of a share to fall below one dollar. The fund had apparently invested heavily in Lehman commercial paper and thus suffered a loss that the manager could not cover. Treasury moved immediately to guarantee the value of money market fund shares, apparently for fear that the Reserve Fund's losses would trigger a run on all money market funds. Needless to say, money market funds are not "interconnected." The Treasury's action in backing money market mutual funds after Lehman's failure was another response to the market's panic.

So, if CDSs are not responsible for the financial crisis or the need to rescue financial companies, why are they so distrusted? Some observers may simply be drawing a causal connection between the current financial crisis and something new in the financial firmament that they do not fully understand. Misleading references to the large "notional amount" of CDSs outstanding have not helped. This *Outlook* will outline how CDSs work and explain their value both as risk management devices and market-based sources of credit assessments. It will then review the main complaints about CDSs and explain that most of them are grossly overblown or simply wrong. Improvements can certainly be made in the CDS market, but the current war on this valuable financial innovation makes no sense.

How Credit Default Swaps Work

Figure 1 shows a series of simple CDS transactions. Bank B has bought a $10 million bond from company A, which in CDS parlance is known as "the reference entity." B now has exposure to A. If B does not want to keep this risk—perhaps it believes A's prospects are declining, or perhaps B wants to diversify its assets—it has two choices: sell the bond or transfer the credit risk. For a variety of tax and other reasons, B does not want to sell the bond, but it is able to eliminate most or all of the credit risk of A by entering a CDS. A CDS is nothing more than a contract in which one party (the protection seller) agrees to reimburse another party (the protection buyer) against a default on a financial

---

49. Robert O'Harrow Jr. and Brady Dennis, "Downgrades and Downfall."

FIGURE 1
How Credit Default Swaps Operate

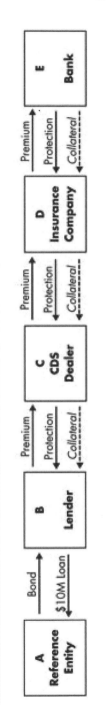

Source: Peter J. Wallison.

obligation by a third party (the reference entity). In figure 1, the reference entity is A, the protection buyer is B and the protection seller is C. Although figure 1 shows B purchasing protection against its entire loan to A, it is important to note that B also could have purchased protection for a portion of the principal amount of the $10 million bond. The amount of protection that B purchases is called the "notional amount."

The CDS market is a dealer market, so transactions take place through dealers, over the counter rather than on an exchange. Accordingly, in purchasing protection against A's default, B's swap is with C, a dealer—one of many, including the world's leading banks, that operate in this market. The structure of the CDS is simple. C agrees to pay $10 million (or whatever notional amount the parties negotiate) if A defaults, and B agrees to make an annual premium payment (usually paid quarterly) to C. The size of this payment or premium will reflect the risk that C believes it is assuming in protecting B against A's default. If A is a good credit, the premium will be small, and correspondingly the premium would be larger when the market perceives greater credit risk in A. Under the typical CDS contract, B is entitled to request collateral from C in order to assure C's performance. As a dealer, C generally aims to keep a matched book. For every risk it takes on, it typically acquires an offsetting hedge. So C enters a CDS with D, and D posts collateral. The transfer of B's risk to C and then to D (and occasionally from D to E and so on) is often described by many CDS critics as a "daisy chain" of obligations, but this description is misleading. Each transaction between counterparties in figure 1 is a separate transaction, so B can look only to C if A defaults, and C must look to D. B will not usually deal directly with E. However, there are now services, such as those of a firm called Trioptima, that are engaged in "compressing" this string of transactions so that the intermediate obligations are "torn up." This reduces outstandings and counterparty risk.

Does this hypothetical string of transactions create any significant new risks that go beyond the risk created when B made its loan to A? In the transaction outlined in figure 1, each of the parties in the chain has two distinct risks—that its counterparty will be unable to perform its obligation either *before* or *after* A defaults. If C becomes bankrupt *before* A defaults, B will have to find a new protection seller; if C defaults *after* A defaults, B will lose the protection that it sought from the swap. The same is true for C and D if their respective counterparties default. In the CDS market, in which premiums are negotiated based on current views of the risk of A's default, the premium—also known as the spread—for new protection against A's default could be more costly for B, C, and D than the original premium negotiated. Although this might mean a potential loss to any of these parties, it is likely—if the risk of a default by A has been increasing—that the seller of protection will have posted collateral so that each buyer will be able to reimburse itself for the additional premium cost for a new CDS.

It is important at this point to understand how the collateral process works. Either the buyer or the seller in a CDS transaction may be "in the money" at any point—that is, the CDS spread, which is moving with market judgments, may be rising or falling, depending on the market's judgment of the reference entity's credit. At the moment the CDS transaction was entered, the buyer and seller were even, but if the credit of the reference entity begins to decline, the CDS spread will rise, and at that point the buyer is "in the money"—it is paying a lower premium than the risk would warrant. Depending on the terms of the original agreement, the seller then may have to post collateral—or more collateral. But if the reference entity's credit improves—say, its business prospects are better   then the CDS spread will fall and the seller is in the money. In this case, the buyer may have to put up collateral to ensure that it will continue to make the premium payments.

What happens if A defaults? Assuming that there are no other defaults among the parties in figure 1, there is a settlement among the parties, in which E is the ultimate obligor (conceptually, C has paid B, D has paid C, and E has paid D. But if E defaults, D becomes the ultimate payer, and if D defaults, C ends up holding the bag. Of course, D then would have a claim against E or E's bankrupt estate, and the same for C if D defaults. Critics of CDSs argue that this "daisy chain" is an example of interconnections created by CDSs that might in turn create systemic risk as each member of the string of transactions defaults because of the new liability it must assume. But this analysis is superficial. If CDSs did not exist, B would suffer the loss associated with A's default, and there is no reason to believe that the loss would stop with B. B is undoubtedly indebted to others, and its loss on the loan to A might cause B to default on these obligations, just as E's default might have caused D to default on its obligations to C. In other words, the credit markets are already interconnected. With or without CDSs, the failure of a large enough participant can—at least theoretically—send a cascade of losses through this highly interconnected structure. CDSs simply move the risk of that result from B to C, D, or E, but they do not materially increase the risk created when B made its loan to A. No matter how many defaults occur in the series of transactions presented in figure 1, there is still only one $10 million loss. The only question is who ultimately pays it.

The Role of Credit Default Swaps in the Financial Economy

Financial regulators have few resources that will materially reduce risk-taking. They can insist on more capital, which both provides a cushion against losses and a nest egg that management has an incentive to protect, and they can clamp down on innovation, which can always be a source of uncertainty and therefore risk. But beyond that, they are limited to ensuring that banks, securities firms, and insurance companies—to the extent that they are regulated for safety and sound-ness—carefully review the risks they take and have the records to show for it. The current credit crunch is testimony to the ineffectiveness of regulation. Despite the most comprehensive oversight of any industry, the banking sector is riddled with bad investments and resulting losses. In fact, by creating moral hazard, it is likely that the regulation of banks has reduced the private-sector scrutiny that banks would have received as part of a fully operating system of market discipline.

In light of the consistent failure of traditional regulation, a sophisticated and intelligent regulatory process should now foster risk-management innovations that have been developed by the private sector, especially the derivative instru-ments that have greater potential to control risk than government oversight. CDSs are one of these instruments, but not the only one. A simple example of effective risk-shifting is the interest rate swap, which—like the CDS—was developed by financial intermediaries looking for ways to manage risk. The documentation for interest rate swaps, as well as for CDSs, was developed by the International Swaps and Derivatives Association (ISDA). Interest rate swaps have been an important and useful risk-management device in the financial markets for at least twenty-five years. The value of an interest rate swap is that it allows financial intermediaries to match their assets and their liabilities and thus to reduce their interest rate risks. Say that a bank has deposits on which it must pay a market or "floating" rate of interest, but it also holds mortgages on which it receives only a fixed monthly interest payment. This is a typical position for a bank—but a risky one. If interest rates rise, it may be forced to pay more interest to its depositors than it is receiving from the mortgages it holds, and thus would suffer losses. Ideally, it would want to trade the fixed rate it receives on its mortgage portfolio for a floating rate that will more closely match what it has to pay its depositors. That way, it is protected against increases in market rates. An interest swap, in which the bank pays a fixed rate to a counterparty and receives a floating rate in return, is the answer; it matches the bank's interest rate receipts to its payment obligations.

But what kind of entity would want to do such a swap? Consider an insurance company that has fixed obligations to pay out a certain sum monthly on the fixed annuities it has written. Insurance companies try to match this obligation with bonds and notes that are the ultimate source of the funds for meeting its fixed obligations, but these do not necessarily yield a fixed return for periods long enough to fully fund its annuity commitments. Instead, they mature well before its annuity obligations expire, and may—if interest rates decline—yield less than it is required to pay out to annuitants. The insurance company, then, would be able to avoid risk with a swap that is the exact mirror image of what the bank needs. Into this picture steps a swap dealer, which arranges a fixed-for-floating interest rate swap between the bank and insurance company. The notional amount can be set at any number—its purpose in an interest rate swap is simply to provide the principal amount on which the interest will be paid—so the parties agree on $100 million. The bank agrees to pay the insurance company a fixed amount—say, 5 percent—on the notional amount of $100 million, and the insurance company agrees to pay the bank a floating rate of interest on the same notional amount. If interest rates rise to 6 percent, the bank is "in the money" and the insurance company pays the bank the 1 percent difference, and, if they fall to 4 percent, the bank pays the insurance company 1 percent.

The important thing to notice about this transaction is that both the bank and the insurance company are better off—both have reduced their risks. The bank now gets a floating payment that assures it of the funds necessary to pay its depositors no matter how high interest rates rise, and the insurance company is better off because it gets a fixed payment from the bank that allows it to pay its annuitants no matter how far interest rates fall. Both parties have hedged their interest rate risk through use of a derivative. The notional amount of interest rate swaps currently outstanding grew to $464.7 trillion by June 30, 2008.[50] This is a frighteningly large number, but—as discussed below—its only reality is as the

---

50. International Swaps and Derivatives Association, "ISDA Mid-year 2008 Market Survey," news release, September 24, 2008, available at www.isda.org/press/press092508.html (accessed December 30, 2008).

basis on which counterparties are exchanging fixed for floating rates. No one actually owes anyone any portion of this $464.7 trillion. The payment obligations are only interest. The interest rate swap is a classic example of a private-sector mechanism for risk management that could not have been developed or implemented by a regulatory agency. It is also a good way to think about CDSs, which have risk-management characteristics much like interest rate swaps.[51] Let's assume that a bank holds a loan to a corporate customer that makes oil field equipment. The bank is receiving a stream of payments on the loan with which it is satisfied, but it concludes as a matter of risk management that it has too much credit exposure to the oil business. If oil prices fall, its loans to the industry may be in jeopardy. One of the objectives of risk management is diversification, but even better is holding uncorrelated assets—that is, assets that do not rise or fall in value or marketability at the same time. Still better, from the risk-management standpoint, are assets that are negatively correlated—that rise in value when the others are falling. For example, a bank would like to hold loans to both an auto manufacturer and an oil company; as oil prices rise, the auto manufacturer becomes weaker but the oil company becomes stronger; other things being equal, the bank's risks are balanced.

Using this strategy, the hypothetical bank we are discussing would like to divest some of its oil industry exposure and instead balance its portfolio with exposure to the risk of, say, auto sales. In a world where CDSs are available, this is easily done. The bank enters a swap with an intermediary CDS dealer in which the dealer promises to reimburse the bank if the oil field services company defaults. The dealer must now find a hedge in the form of a company that is willing to sell protection on the oil services company. A logical protection seller might be an insurance company. The insurance company has substantial outstanding loans on commercial real estate. Taking on the risk of an oil service company would provide needed diversification and could be uncorrelated—or even negatively correlated—with the places where the insurance company's commercial real estate is located. Through this transaction, the bank has reduced or eliminated the credit risk of a loan to the oil industry, but the loan remains

---

51. An excellent discussion of the role of credit default swaps appears in David Mengle, "Credit Derivatives: An Overview" (paper, 2007 Financial Markets Conference, Federal Reserve Bank of Atlanta, May 15, 2007), available at www.frbatlanta.org/news/conferen/07fmc/07FMC_mengle.pdf (accessed December 30, 2008).

on its books and it keeps the oil company's stream of interest and principal payments, as well as its commercial relationship with this client. Now the bank enters another CDS, this time with a hedge fund, in which the bank promises to indemnify the fund against losses on a portfolio of loans to auto dealers. For this protection, the hedge fund makes a monthly payment to the bank (for simplicity, we are disregarding the intermediary dealer). After these two transactions, the bank has somewhat diversified and balanced its portfolio by substituting the credit risk of a portfolio of auto loans for an oil industry loan. Because the portfolio of auto loans may be negatively correlated with the oil industry risks, the bank's portfolio is now likely to be more stable. The insurance company has done the same. Once again, a derivative has operated as an effective risk management tool, reducing the credit risk profile of two financial intermediaries.

It is also important to note that the same risk-management purposes can be served by a bank or any other financial intermediary taking on a risk that diversifies its portfolio, even if it has no relation at all to a reference entity. Because the party writing the protection is paid for assuming the credit risk, the CDS functions in much the same way, from a risk management perspective, as an actual loan. This issue is discussed more fully below in the section on whether CDSs represent "gambling" or "betting."

CDSs also offer an increasingly important window into risk-taking that has not previously existed. In this, CDSs can help both investors and regulators. On November 25, for example, a newswire reported: "Credit default swaps protection generally narrowed Tuesday amid improvement in key spread product markets such as the commercial mortgage-backed securities and asset-backed arena."[52] Similarly, on December 10, the interim assistant treasury secretary for financial stability, Neel Kashkari, told the House Financial Services Committee that "one indicator that points to reduced risk of default among financial institutions is the average credit default swap spread for the eight largest U.S. banks, which has declined more than 200 basis points since before Congress passed the [Emergency Economic Stabilization Act]."[53]

---

52. Market News International, November 25, 2008.

53. Neel Kashkari (testimony, House Financial Services Committee, December 10, 2008), available at www.treasury.gov/press/releases/hp1322.htm (accessed December 30, 2008).

The fact that CDSs are available as an indicator of risk in the financial markets generally, and with respect to particular institutions, is vastly important. Up to now, there has been no generally available, market-based source of credit assessments about financial institutions. Interest rate spreads and stock prices are not as valuable because they are influenced by many factors other than risk-taking and creditworthiness. If properly used, the data on CDS spreads for reference entities can alert regulators to problems at individual banks, securities firms, or insurance companies. Even more important, it can assist investors and creditors in exerting market discipline over financial institutions. In light of the general failure of regulation for controlling risk-taking, the enhancement of market discipline is extremely important. A widening of a reference entity's CDS spread will alert investors that they should investigate risk-taking more fully before advancing funds. Even if CDSs were not important for risk management, the existence of the information generated by the CDS market would alone provide economic justification for allowing this market to operate freely and without restrictions. The importance of this development cannot be overstated. Virtually since their inception, banks have been the repositories of credit information about borrowers. As the securities market grew and public disclosure became more complete, banks lost some of their role as the preferred intermediaries between investors and borrowers; many public companies went to the securities market for credit financing. At the same time, rating agencies began to substitute for credit analysis by some institutional lenders and bond buyers. The growth of CDSs provides for the first time a market-based credit assessment available to all institutional lenders and bond buyers. At a time when the value of rating agencies is being questioned,[54] the CDS market offers critical new information to use in credit assessment.

Myths about Credit Default Swaps

Despite these significant benefits, criticism of CDSs is widespread. It is not uncommon to find statements by market observers that CDSs have no economic purpose, create enormous risks for the financial economy, create systemic risks, are little more than irresponsible gambling by market participants, and create

---

54. Alex J. Pollock, "How to Improve the Credit Rating Agency Sector" (testimony, Committee on Banking, Housing, and Urban Affairs, U.S. Senate, March 7, 2006), available at www.aei.org/publication24011/.

hidden liabilities that do not appear in financial statements. Almost all of these claims are either grossly exaggerated or wrong.

Claim: The Notional Amount of CDSs Outstanding Represents a Huge Risk for the World's Financial System. One of the most striking elements associated with credit default swaps is the notional amount outstanding at any one time. As a measure of the growth of CDSs, the aggregate notional amount is of some use, but as a measure of the risk in the market, it is meaningless. Nevertheless, critics of CDS use the aggregate notional amount number to suggest that huge risks are being created in some mysterious way. Shortly after Bear Stearns was rescued, George Soros wrote: "There is an esoteric financial instrument called credit default swaps. The notional amount of CDS contracts outstanding is roughly $45 [trillion]. . . . To put it into perspective, this is about equal to half the total US household wealth."[55] This is not putting CDSs "into perspective." Coming from a sophisticated financier, it seems more like a deliberate attempt to mislead. The notional amount of CDSs outstanding—although suitable for scaring people—is not in any sense relevant to the size of the risks associated with CDSs.

Returning again to the hypothetical transaction in figure 1, we can calculate the notional amount that comes out of the reporting of the transaction by the various participants. B reports that it is paying a premium for protection on a notional amount of $10 million (the loan to A), C reports that it has sold protection for this amount, as have D and E and the dealer intermediary between D and E. Thus, the total notional amount arising from this series of transactions is $50 million, or five times the actual potential loss in the event that A defaults. The DTCC recently began publishing data on CDSs from its Trade Information Warehouse, which gathers about 90 percent of all CDS transactions.[56] The DTCC's data eliminate the multiple-counting in each swap transaction and report that as of the week ending December 12, what the DTCC calls the "gross notional amount" of CDSs outstanding was $25.6 trillion.[57]

55. George Soros, "The False Belief at the Heart of the Financial Turmoil," *Financial Times,* April 3, 2008.

56. Bradley Rogoff and Michael Anderson, "DTCC Data Show Corporate CDS Fears Overblown," Barclays Capital Credit Strategy, November 6, 2008.

57. Depository Trust and Clearing Corporation, "Trade Information Warehouse Data," week ending December 12, 2008, available through www.dtcc.com/products/derivserv/data_table_i.php (accessed December 30, 2008).

This amount is many times the actual potential loss on all CDSs outstanding at any time because the protection sold must be reduced by the protection bought. The result is called the net notional amount and has been estimated at 10 percent of the gross notional amount in the market.[58] Accordingly, using the gross notional figure reported by the DTCC, we can estimate that the net notional amount is about $2.5 trillion (a total of $2.75 trillion with the additional 10 percent not reported by DTCC), a sum that is a fraction of the figure Soros used. These are not small numbers, of course, but they are far less than the number usually used to describe the total risk in the CDS market. And even these numbers are only "real" if every reference entity were to default and if sellers' recoveries after these defaults were zero.

Claim: CDSs Are Written by or between Parties That Do Not Understand the Risks They Are Assuming. In one sense, this statement is true. There are always lenders who lose money because they do not understand the risk they are assuming, and there are undoubtedly writers of CDS protection who also do not understand the credit risk to which they are exposed. If the statement is meant to communicate the idea that a CDS risk is different from or more complex than a loan (or the acquisition of a portfolio of MBS), however, it is wrong. First, almost all swaps are negotiated through dealers, who serve as the actual counterparties. Dealers typically carry matched books, which means that they hedge their risks by entering offsetting CDSs. To remain in business, they must be sure of the quality of the counterparties they choose. In figure 1, for example, B buys protection from C, a dealer. C then enters a corresponding swap with D, which sells protection to C to cover C's exposure to B. If D does not have a AAA credit rating (and maybe even if it does), it probably has to post collateral to protect C, and C may have to post collateral to assure B that it is protected. In fact, 63 percent of all CDSs—and 65 percent of the dollar exposure—are collateralized,[59] precisely

---

58. Bradley Rogoff and Michael Anderson, "DTCC Data Show Corporate CDS Fears Overblown."

59. International Swaps and Derivatives Association, "ISDA Margin Survey 2008," available at www.isda.org/c_and_a/ pdf/ISDA-Margin-Survey-2008.pdf (accessed December 30, 2008). See also Michael S. Gibson, "Credit Derivatives and Risk Management" (Finance and Economics Discussion Series 2007-47, Divisions of Research & Statistics and Monetary Affairs, Federal Reserve Board of Governors, Washington, DC, May 22, 2007), available at www.federalreserve.gov/pubs/feds/2007/200747/200747pap.pdf (accessed December 30, 2008).

because the parties that are paying for protection want to make sure it is there when they need it. In addition, recalling the earlier discussion of counterparties moving in and out of the money, a protection buyer and a protection seller may have obligations to post collateral if the spread on a particular reference entity rises or falls. No institution that enters this market does so lightly.

The AIG case is a good illustration of the CDS process and was covered extensively in the *Washington Post* series cited above. Initially, AIG's counterparties generally agreed that AIG would not be required to post collateral because it was rated AAA, but when it was downgraded by the rating agencies, it was immediately required by its swap agreements to post collateral. In addition, AIG had written a lot of protection on MBS and CDO portfolios, and, as these declined in value, it was again required by its counterparties to post collateral to cover its increased exposure. When AIG could not do so, it was threatened with bankruptcy, and that is when the Fed stepped in with a rescue. The rescue of AIG, as noted above, had nothing to do with Lehman's failure, but it did have a lot to do with AIG's failure to assess the risks of MBS and CDOs. Does this sound familiar? Of course it does—it is the same problem faced by many banks that also failed to assess properly the risk of these assets. Apparently, AIG relied excessively on a credit risk model that did not adequately account for both the sharp decline in the mortgage market or a downgrade of AIG's credit rating.

This points up a fact that gets too little attention in the discussion of CDSs: that the best analogy for these instruments is an ordinary commercial loan. A seller of protection is taking on virtually the same risk exposure as a lender. It is no more mysterious than that. Successful lending requires expertise in assessing credit—the same skill required for writing CDS protection. AIG, like many banks, misjudged the riskiness of a portfolio of MBS and CDOs. That does not mean that CDSs are any riskier than loans; if AIG, instead of selling protection on various portfolios of MBS and CDOs, had bought the portfolios themselves, there would have been very little commentary other than clucking about the company's poor credit judgment. For some reason, the fact that it did substantially the same thing by selling protection on these instruments through CDSs has caused commentators to see the issue as a problem created by the swaps rather than as a simple example of poor credit assessment.

Recently, in order to eliminate the constant calls for more collateral, the Fed purchased the portfolios of MBS and CDOs on which AIG had written protection. An article in the *Wall Street Journal* then noted that this was a "blessing" for the banks that had bought protection from AIG. Indeed it was; that is why the banks bought the protection. If AIG had not covered this liability, the banks would have taken these losses. This illustrates another central point about CDSs: one institution's loss is another's gain. The risk was already in the market. It was created when some bank or investment bank borrowed the funds necessary for assembling a portfolio of MBS or CDOs. The fact that AIG was the final counterparty and suffered the loss means that someone else did not. Ultimately, there is only one real risk, represented by the original loan or purchase transaction (in the case of an asset like an MBS portfolio). CDSs, to the extent that they are initiated by parties that are actually exposed to a risk, merely transfer that risk, for a price, to someone else.

A recent article in the *Wall Street Journal* focused on an instrument called a synthetic CDO and noted that many buyers of these instruments suffered losses because of the meltdown in the U.S. mortgage market.[60] Because a CDS is a part of a synthetic CDO, the article once again raised the question of whether protection sellers in the CDS transaction understand the risks they are assuming. However, the writers of the article did not make clear (or failed to understand) that, despite a fancy name and the presence of a CDS, the buyers of these instruments were taking a risk that was essentially identical to investing in a portfolio of loans. In an ordinary CDO, a number of loans are bundled into a pool, and debt instruments are sold to investors backed by the assets in the pool. A CDO, then, is just a generalized term for the same process in which the more familiar MBS are created. The investor in a CDO takes the risk that the instruments in the pool will not lose value or default. In a synthetic CDO, an investor buys a security issued by a special purpose vehicle (SPV) and becomes the seller of protection in a CDS in which the SPV is the protection buyer. The SPV is usually created by a bank that is seeking CDS protection on a portfolio of loans it intends to continue to hold. The SPV uses the cash investment to buy a portfolio of high-quality debt securities. The low yield on the high-quality debt securities is supplemented by the premium on a CDS, and two yields in effect replicate the yield that the investor would have received—and the risk it would have taken—if it had invested in the same portfolio of loans that the bank is holding. Once

---

60. Mark Whitehouse and Serena Ng, "Insurance Deals Spread Pain of U.S. Defaults World-Wide," *Wall Street Journal,* December 23, 2008.

again, there is no essential difference between investing in the actual loans or investing in the synthetic CDO. The credit risk and the yield are the same.

The *Journal* story noted that "towns, charities, school districts, pension funds, insurance companies and regional banks" have taken on the risk of these synthetic CDOs and that some have suffered losses as a result of the weakening credit markets. Of course, many (maybe most) have profited from the premiums they have received over time for taking this risk. Two things should be noted at this point. The first is that while synthetic CDOs replicate the risks associated with a portfolio of loans, they are complex investments; there is a question whether they are suitable investments for towns, school districts, and other investors that may not be able properly to evaluate the risks. To the extent that this happened, it would be a violation of the "investor suitability" rules applicable in the United States and any equivalent rules in the countries where these investments were sold. The second point is that the fault in this process was not with the CDSs that were part of the synthetic CDOs, any more than a corporation would be at fault if a bond dealer sold one of its bonds to an investor who could not understand the risks. The role of the CDS is to replicate the risk of owning a portfolio of loans, and the risk they create is not any greater than that.

Writing CDS protection is much the same as making a loan or buying a bond. In order to participate in this market, an institution must have the capability to evaluate credit risk. It is not a market for individuals or even institutions that do not have credit-evaluation skills or access to them. Even institutions with credit-evaluation skills suffer losses on some risks they acquire—as shown by the AIG case—but it is certainly not true that, in general, those institutions that buy and sell CDSs are not aware of the risks they are assuming.

Claim: Transactions between Parties That Have Nothing to Do with the Reference Entity Are Simply Gambling and Have No Independent Value. Because CDSs are much like loans, they can be used to take on the same risk as a loan or a bond. If an institutional investor believes that an issuer will grow stronger over time, it can buy the company's bonds and profit from the strengthening of the issuer's credit position. Alternatively, the investor can sell protection on the same notional amount as the bond—that is, taking on the same exposure without actually buying the bond—and profit in the same way. If the issuer's prospects improve, the CDS rises in value because the premium received is now greater than it would need to be for the lower risk involved. The seller of protection is now "in the money" in the sense that it has an asset that has appreciated in value.

The risk management benefits of CDSs exist independently of whether a lender has any financial interest in a particular reference entity. Thus, the bank that bought protection on its loan to an oil service company could achieve the same risk management purposes—reducing its exposure to the oil industry—by buying protection on an equivalent notional amount of an oil company's outstanding obligations, even though it does not have any direct exposure to the oil company. If the risk is highly correlated with the oil service company's risk, the bank can nearly duplicate the same risk management result. Just as an investor can do this for risk management or hedging purposes, it can also do it as speculation, without having any direct financial interest in the issuer that is the reference entity. Indeed, when a dealer is approached by an institution to buy or sell protection, it is impossible to tell whether the purpose is hedging an existing risk or speculating on the change in the risk profile of the reference entity. Is this simply betting, as some suggest, or does it have a value apart from its value to the two parties involved?

In discussing this subject, it would be useful to avoid the pejorative terms "betting" or "gambling" and use the term "speculation," which more closely approximates what is happening when a party buys or sells protection without any connection to the reference entity involved. Speculation is frequently denounced, while "hedging" is considered good and prudent, yet it is very difficult to tell the difference between the two. Commodity futures have for a long time permitted farmers to protect themselves in the event of a decline in prices when their crop is ready for market. Most people would call this prudent hedging, but what are the investors on the other side of the futures trade doing? In effect, they are selling protection, just like the seller in the CDS transaction. Some observers might call this speculation because the seller of protection to the farmer is speculating (others might call it "gambling" or "betting") that the price will be higher than what he has agreed to pay the farmer. Thus, speculation can have an important role in making markets work.

It may be objected, however, that in hedging or speculation transactions, real things like wheat or loan exposure are involved, while buying or selling CDSs without any connection to the reference entity is different. Consider then puts and calls—options to sell or buy stocks—that are traded regularly on the Chicago Board Options Exchange. These are an accepted part of equity markets and are known as equity derivatives. They can be used for hedging a stock position without selling or buying the stock, or they can be used—without owning the stock—simply to speculate that a stock's price will go up or down. The function of puts and calls is exactly the same as the role played by those who buy or sell CDSs without any connection to a reference entity. The transaction adds to the liquidity and the total information in the market. That is in part why the buying and selling of CDSs provides a continuous, market-based assessment of the credit of a large number of commercial or industrial companies and financial institutions. Some people consider speculation in a security or a commodity to be betting, but economists recognize that this activity provides benefits to a market through added market liquidity and mitigation of bubbles. In the case of CDSs, however, the exogenous benefits of speculation are particularly strong because it provides a market-based credit judgment about the financial position of individual issuers that is not available anywhere else.

Claim: There Is No Way to Know by Looking at a Company's Balance Sheet How Much CDS Exposure It Has Taken On. Exposures to CDS transactions as a protection seller are shown on all balance sheets where that exposure is deemed to be material. The exposure is shown in the aggregate, without listing particular transactions or risks, just as a bank would show its commercial and industrial loans in the aggregate. Normally, parties selling protection have hedged themselves, and it is very unlikely that all, or even most, exposures will result in liability at the same time. So, for the most part, CDS liabilities are carried on balance sheets at somewhere between 1 and 2 percent of their notional amount, reflecting both hedges and the likelihood of losses on a diversified portfolio. Of course, as risks rise or fall, these values are adjusted. The nature of these liabilities is then described in a footnote.

Because CDSs sold or bought by dealers are marked to market every day, it is possible that the risk associated with protecting a counterparty will increase as the financial condition of the reference entity deteriorates. This may require the liability of the protection seller to be written up on its balance sheet, and will almost certainly require more collateral. The opposite is also true. If the reference entity's financial condition markedly improves—perhaps its business prospects are better—the liability on the protection seller's balance sheet will diminish and the collateral requirement could be reduced, eliminated entirely, or moved to the buyer of protection if the seller is now "in the money." This also means that a CDS can move from a liability to an asset on the balance sheet of the buyer or seller, depending on whether the spread on the reference entity has risen (advantage to the buyer) or declined (advantage to the seller) since the CDS was contracted.

Conclusion

Although the Lehman failure demonstrated that the CDS market works well even under severe stress, there are proposals for improvements and reforms. These reforms—including a clearinghouse or an exchange for CDSs and perhaps some additional form of regulation for the CDS market as a whole—are beyond the scope of this *Outlook*. However, because CDSs and their value are not well understood, there is a serious danger of excessive regulation that will impair the value of CDSs for risk management and credit assessment purposes. As reform proposals take shape, I may revisit this issue in a subsequent *Outlook*.

Far from creating new or significant risks, CDSs simply move risks that already exist from one place to another. For this reason, they are a major advance in risk management for all financial intermediaries, and restrictions on their use will create more risk in the financial system than it will eliminate. In addition, the vigorous and liquid current market in CDSs provides a market-based reading of the risks of companies that is not available from any other source and that can be of major assistance to regulators, as well as investors and creditors.

"Stress for Success:
The Bank Stress Tests Buy Time"

Originally published May 2009

The stress tests of the nineteen largest U.S. banks, finally made public in early May, turned out to be a successful effort to instill market confidence. If the assumptions underlying the tests prove accurate, it will be a turning point in the economic recovery, and Treasury Secretary Timothy Geithner will have won a high-stakes bet. But if, as some contend, the stress tests were not stressful enough, there will be renewed doubts about the health of the banks, and the credibility of the Treasury Department and the administration will be severely eroded. Whatever happens, the publication of detailed information about the condition of the major banks changes market expectations for the future; throws light on prior Treasury decisions; and raises questions about the efficacy of mark-to-market accounting, the way the Troubled Assets Relief Program (TARP) was used and not used, and the prospects for the Public-Private Investment Program (PPIP) that has been proposed to purchase so-called toxic assets. Most significantly, the stress tests strongly suggest that greater and earlier disclosure by the supervisors about the financial conditions of the largest banks might have prevented a substantial amount of investor losses.

On May 7, Secretary Geithner revealed the results of the stress tests of nineteen major bank holding companies. To the surprise of many, the results showed that the banks were not near insolvency and that massive injections of capital would not be required to enable them to get through the difficult financial times that are likely to lie ahead. Instead, the report suggested that almost half of the group required no additional capital at all, and the remaining eleven required only $75 billion, most of which could be made up by converting to common stock some or all of the preferred stock they had issued to the government in exchange for investments under TARP. There was some skepticism among observers about whether the stress tests were sufficiently stressful. "It sure sounds to me like they are designing this to make it sound like the banking system is in great shape," Paul J. Miller, a respected bank analyst, said.[61] News stories after the report indicated that final negotiations between the banks and the supervisors who conducted the tests resulted in a reduction in the size of the expected losses,[62] but overall, the stock market viewed the results positively, with large gains for many of the institutions that were given the tests—including those shown to need more capital.

Assuming that the likely outcome was not known in advance, the stress test results amounted to a major winning bet for Geithner and the administration. At the time the testing process began, in February 2009, many informed observers predicted a disastrous outcome. As a *New York Times* news analysis put it, "Some of the nation's large banks, according to economists and other financial experts, are like dead men walking. A sober assessment of the growing mountain of losses from bad bets, measured in today's marketplace, would overwhelm the value of the banks' assets, they say. The banks, in their view, are insolvent."[63] Many pundits, such as the *Times'* Paul Krugman, had predicted that the major banks were so insolvent that they would have to be nationalized.[64] Nouriel Roubini, who had established himself as a credible forecaster of disaster, estimated that the entire U.S. banking system was already insolvent, with $1.4 trillion in new capital necessary to bring the system back to where it was before the financial crisis.[65] With these predictions representative of what was common in the media and the blogosphere, it seemed to be a huge gamble to set up the stress tests without having funds at the ready to keep the banks solvent if the tests showed large gaps in their capitalization.

The stress tests were designed to determine the conditions of the banks under two differing scenarios—a base case that the Fed called a "consensus forecast" at the time the stress testing process began and a "more adverse scenario" that envisioned a deeper and more protracted downturn than the consensus. Both

61. Edmund L. Andrews and Eric Dash, "Government Offers Details of Bank Stress Test," *New York Times,* February 26, 2009. See also "Buffett Criticizes Bank Stress Tests," *Reuters,* May 4, 2009.

62. David Enrich, Dan Fitzpatrick, and Marshall Eckblad, "Banks Won Concessions on Tests," *Wall Street Journal,* May 9, 2009.

63. Steve Lohr, "Ailing Banks May Require More Aid to Keep Solvent," *New York Times,* February 13, 2009.

64. Paul Krugman, "Wall Street Voodoo," *New York Times,* January 19, 2009.

65. Nouriel Roubini, "Nationalize Insolvent Banks," *Forbes,* February 12, 2009.

these terms are taken from a Federal Reserve paper that summarizes the tests and the results (both generally and with respect to each of the participating bank holding companies individually).[66] Given the secrecy with which bank financial data had previously been treated, this is a remarkable document. However, as discussed below, it probably raises market expectations that will not necessarily be fulfilled in the future and significant questions about the assumptions and the decisions that have propelled the financial crisis for the last year.

The Results

Several things about the tests, as described in the Fed paper, are noteworthy. First, each participating institution was instructed to estimate its own potential credit losses over a two-year period, beginning with the year-end 2008 financial statement data. This means that all the losses that were taken by the end of 2008 had already been incorporated in the financial baseline. Second, with respect to their securities losses, the banks were asked to estimate "cash flow losses" instead of discounts arising from mark-to-market valuations. Third, the participants were provided with the supervisors' own estimates of the likely range of losses for major asset classes (mortgages, commercial loans, commercial real estate, et cetera) for both the base case and the more adverse case. For example, the Fed's estimates for credit card losses were 12–17 percent in the base case and 18–20 percent in the more adverse scenario. Most of the participants exceeded the Fed's estimates for credit card and first lien mortgage losses under the more adverse test but were in the range suggested by the supervisors for the commercial real estate and commercial loan losses under that set of assumptions. The losses estimated by the institutions are not expected losses, for which they might create reserves, but only losses that might be expected under the scenarios proposed. Moreover, and most important, the stress tests purported to cover only a two-year period—2009 and 2010, including reserves for anticipated losses in 2011—and say nothing about what might happen after that. Presumably, if the forecasts and the estimates of capital needs are correct, an anticipated upturn in the economy in and after 2010 will put the banks out

---

66. Board of Governors of the Federal Reserve System, "The Supervisory Capital Assessment Program: Overview of Results," May 7, 2009, available at www.federalreserve. gov/newsevents/press/bcreg/bcreg20090507a1.pdf (accessed May 29, 2009).

of range of any difficulty, but, if actual conditions are materially worse than the forecast, most or all of these institutions could be in serious trouble.

Overall, the participants as a group estimated losses of $600 billion over the next two years under the more adverse scenario. This amount is roughly consistent with the International Monetary Fund's (IMF) estimate that U.S. banks could face collective writedowns of $550 billion in 2009 and 2010.[67] The banks as a group estimated heavy losses on single-family mortgages. According to the report, "Expected loss rates on first-liens and second/junior liens are well outside the historical experience of commercial banks." This result is consistent with the fact that subprime and Alt-A loans constitute such a large proportion—probably 40–45 percent—of total single-family mortgages outstanding. "Together," the Fed observed, "residential mortgages and consumer loans (including credit card and other consumer loans, not shown) account for $332 billion, or 70 percent of the loan losses projected under the more adverse scenario." Interestingly, commercial real estate is not, according to the participating institutions, the problem many have expected: the anticipated losses come in below the supervisors' indicative estimates of 9–12 percent. Table 1 illustrates the dollar amounts that make up the $600 billion estimated loss under the more adverse scenario, with related percentages of losses in each category.

One of the surprising elements of the Fed's report was the discussion of securities. The participating institutions were reported to hold only $200 billion in nonagency (that is, "private label") mortgage-backed securities (MBS), "and only a portion of these were recent vintage or were backed by riskier nonprime mortgages. Remaining material exposures included corporate bonds, mutual funds, and other asset-backed securities." This amount is much smaller than most analysts had assumed because these MBS were considered to be the toxic assets that were driving down bank capital positions. The reason may be that substantial portions of the original holdings had been written down or written off, as noted below. If so, some of the most problematic bank assets—the ones that are supposed to be sold in the PPIP—have been eliminated as sources of uncertainty on the balance sheets of the largest banks. The supervisors reviewed whether there was adequate asset backing for these remaining MBS and ultimately concluded that only $35 billion in charges to the banks was appropriate—"equal

---

67. Mark Landler, "I.M.F. Puts Bank Losses from Global Financial Crisis at $4.1 Trillion," *New York Times*, April 22, 2009.

TABLE 1
ESTIMATED LOSSES FOR **2009** AND **2010** FOR THE MORE ADVERSE SCENARIO

Loan Category	Estimated Loss (in billions of dollars)	Percentage of Losses within Category
First lien mortgages	102.3	8.8
Second/junior lien mortgages	83.2	13.8
Commercial and industrial loans	60.1	6.1
Commercial real estate loans	53.0	8.5
Credit card loans	82.4	22.5
Securities (AFS and HTM)	35.2	N/A
Trading and counterparty	99.3	N/A
Other[a]	83.7	N/A
Total Estimated Losses (before purchase accounting adjustments)	$599.2 billion	

SOURCE: Board of Governors of the Federal Reserve System, "The Supervisory Capital Assessment Program: Overview of Results," May 7, 2009, available at www.federalreserve.gov/newsevents/press/bcreg/bcreg20090507a1.pdf (accessed May 29, 2009).

NOTE: a) Includes other consumer and nonconsumer loans and miscellaneous commitments and obligations.

to the difference between book and market value, with almost one-half of the estimated losses coming from the non-agency MBS." Nonagency MBS are the private label securities, many of them based on subprime or other weak loans, that have been considered the central cause of the banks' financial weakness. Here, the Fed report is saying that less than $17.5 billion on the books of these nineteen banks had to be written down to market value.

All told, the Fed estimated that the nineteen institutions had written down or taken losses equal to $400 billion by the end of 2008. "They include charge-offs, write-downs on securities held in the trading and in the investment accounts, and discounts on assets acquired in acquisitions of distressed or failed financial institutions." After giving the institutions credit for the losses already recorded in assets they acquired, the Fed estimated that the total losses of the nineteen institutions since the middle of 2007 (when the mortgage meltdown began) through the end of 2010 would be $935 billion under the more adverse scenario. This, too, is roughly consistent with the IMF estimate that U.S. banks would have to take losses of about $1.05 trillion over the same period.

Parameters of the Stress Tests

Despite doubts about the quality of the stress test, it was certainly not a sham. As the Fed paper noted, "the estimated loan loss rates under the more adverse scenario are very high by historical standards. The two-year cumulative loss rate on total loans equals 9.1 percent in the more adverse scenario. . . . [T]his loss rate is higher than two-year loss rates observed for commercial banks from 1920 to 2007/2008. In addition to the sharpest two-year drop in residential house prices since then . . . the rise in the unemployment rate in the scenario would be more severe than any U.S. recession since the 1930s." This scenario may not reflect what will actually happen, but it was not a six-inch hurdle. The baseline forecast used the forecasts of well-known groups of forecasters; the more adverse forecast was intended to be somewhat worse, but still plausible. It was not intended to be a "worst-case" scenario, just a "plausible" one that was worse than the base case. The elements of the two forecasts are summarized in table 2.

Nevertheless, concerns about the assumptions used in the test are justified. For example, an unemployment rate of 10.3 percent in the more adverse scenario is actually what forecasters are now expecting for a base case in 2010. Indeed, the unemployment rate for May 2009 was already 8.9 percent—0.5 percent above the base case for all of 2009 used in the stress test assumptions and equal to the estimated level of 2009 unemployment used in the more adverse scenario. House prices are much more difficult to predict because they vary widely from market to market, but both scenarios are predicting a bottoming out in 2010, with the more adverse scenario less optimistic about how fast that bottoming may occur. GDP forecasts also vary widely, but *The Economist*'s estimate of a 3.2 percent decline in U.S. GDP, for example, is higher than the baseline contraction used in the stress test assumptions and very close to the more adverse scenario.[68]

Overall, it appears that the more adverse scenario is—as advertised—"plausible" but that it did not put the tested banks under stress significantly greater than today's economic conditions. This and other elements of the tests raise a number of questions.

---

68. "Outlook for 2009–10," Economist Intelligence Unit, available at www.economist. com/countries/USA/profile.cfm?folder=Profile-Forecast (accessed May 29, 2009).

TABLE 2
ECONOMIC SCENARIOS: BASELINE AND MORE ADVERSE ALTERNATIVES

	2009	2010
Real GDP[a]		
Average baseline[b]	−2.0	2.1
Consensus Forecasts	−2.1	2.0
Blue Chip	−1.9	2.1
Survey of Professional Forecasters	−2.0	2.2
Alternative more adverse	−3.3	0.5
Civilian Unemployment Rate[c]		
Average baseline[b]	8.4	8.8
Consensus Forecasts	8.4	9.0
Blue Chip	8.3	8.7
Survey of Professional Forecasters	8.4	8.8
Alternative more adverse	8.9	10.3
House Prices[d]		
Baseline	−14	−4
Alternative more adverse	−22	−7

SOURCE: Board of Governors of the Federal Reserve System, "The Supervisory Capital Assessment Program: Design and Implementation," April 24, 2009, available at www.federalreserve. gov/newsevents/press/bcreg/bcreg20090424a1.pdf (accessed May 29, 2009).

Notes: a) Percent change in annual average.

b) Baseline forecasts for real GDP and the unemployment rate equal the average of projections released by Consensus Forecasts, Blue Chip, and Survey of Professional Forecasters in February.

c) Annual average.

d) Case-Shiller 10-City Composite, percentage change, fourth quarter of the previous year to fourth quarter of the year indicated.

Were the Tests a Legitimate Inquiry or a Public Relations Effort?

The stress tests accomplished at least one objective that the administration dearly wanted: they persuaded investors, at least for a while, to believe that the banks are in better financial condition than the most widely quoted commentators had suggested. The fact that the tests succeeded as public relations does not mean they were not serious and valid inquiries that might turn out to be correct. There are two unknowables about the tests: whether reality will match the assumptions used in the scenarios and whether the supervisors and banks correctly estimated how their asset values would respond if the stress assumptions were correct.

There is also a question about the process. If Secretary Geithner went into these tests without having any idea how they would come out, he was engaged in an irresponsible gamble. The test results could conceivably have demonstrated that most of the major banks were deeply insolvent and triggered another heart-stopping sell-off in the equity markets. The notion that the Treasury might have risked this possibility as a way of forcing Congress to appropriate more funds for TARP seems highly implausible. That would not have been the only result of yet another meltdown; the others could have included a complete loss of confidence in the financial system and the U.S. government, both of which could have led to chaos. On the other hand, the bank supervisors were in the best position to know the actual condition of the banks. It is not implausible to think that they advised Geithner that the banks would survive adversity that was greater than the base case but not as adverse as some forecasters were suggesting. Under those circumstances, it would make sense for Geithner to order the stress tests as a way of cooling off the rampant speculation that was growing in the media in early 2009.

Accordingly, it is reasonable to believe (and hope!) that Geithner and Obama were not taking such serious risks when the stress tests were begun; that, in effect, they already knew the likely results. This is not a bad thing. Until the results of the tests were revealed, information about the actual condition of the banks was only known to the supervisors, and by tradition, this information has been considered highly confidential. The result was widespread speculation and fear. If, in these conditions, the supervisors can offer a bit more information, the market's outlook can clearly be improved. And in this case it was. However, all these actions have consequences. The next time there is doubt about the condition of the banks, the market will expect more information from the supervisors and the Treasury, and if it is not forthcoming, the market participants will draw negative conclusions. In other words, this particular ploy will work once, but it narrows the administration's options in the future. This was indeed a gamble, but not of the kind many thought. It was unlikely that the stress tests would produce a sharply negative outcome, but if the tests do not produce a return of confidence that stimulates an economic recovery and the resulting economic downturn is significantly worse than the more adverse scenario, the credibility of the administration and the Treasury will have been seriously damaged.

What Do the Tests Say about Mark-to-Market Accounting?

As noted above, the stress tests did not generally value the banks' assets by suggesting that they be marked to market. Only a small portion of the total of $200 billion in MBS were marked down to market levels, and then only if the supervisors did not believe that these assets had sufficient collateral backing to avoid further credit losses. The rest were valued on the basis of their cash flows. As many commentators had been arguing over the course of the mortgage melt-down, it was the process of marking bank securities assets to market that made them appear so weak. By valuing MBS on the basis of their cash flows, the stress tests made the consequences of this difference in treatment abundantly clear. If all the securitized assets had been valued at what they could be sold for in the market, the banks would indeed have looked seriously troubled. Instead, the overwhelming majority were treated as temporarily impaired. In addition, the Fed reported that a significant portion of the $400 billion in losses that the nineteen banks recognized in the last six quarters were securities assets that had already been written down or written off. We do not know whether those write-downs—which were probably consistent with the requirements of fair value accounting at the time they occurred—covered securities holdings that were still receiving significant cash flows. If so, they might have received much higher values if the supervisors had stepped in earlier to require cash flow–based valuation. There is no way of knowing at this point whether the supervisors would have made the same judgments about write-offs or write-downs that the banks themselves made under the accounting rules in place at the time. However, the decision of the supervisors to ask for cash flow valuations could be one reason that the banks look healthier than many analyst estimates, and the fact that these assessments were accepted as valid by the market suggests that investors do not require mark-to-market valuations in order to consider banks financially sound.

It has never been clear why marking assets to market made any sense for financial institutions such as commercial banks. Their depositors and counter-parties want to know the value of their cash flows and how those cash flows contribute to their long-term stability, not what their assets could be sold for if they had to liquidate at a given point in time. The fact that the securities markets took the stress test cash flow valuations in stride—and in fact reacted positively with a sharp rise in the valuations of the banks involved—suggests that the

Financial Accounting Standards Board should revise its requirements for bank accounting so that bank securities assets can be valued on the basis of cash flows rather than market values. This would also have salutary countercyclical effects when the economy returns to growth in the future. At that time, asset prices in the market may rise again on the usual exuberance, and banks that mark their assets to market will look healthier than they really are.

Why Did Current and Former Treasury Secretaries Back Away from Valuing Bank Assets?

When former treasury secretary Henry Paulson went to Congress with his initial request for $700 billion in TARP funds in September 2008, he apparently intended to use the funds to buy bad or doubtful assets from the banks and in this way restore confidence in their financial condition. But after the appropriation was voted, he moved instead toward recapitalizing the banks with preferred stock investments. Similarly, while recognizing the need to buy the bad assets from the banks, Geithner developed the PPIP structure, which provides financing to private groups that would purchase the assets after negotiating prices with the banks. Since the taxpayers would be taking most of the risk in these arrangements, but splitting the profits with the private groups, the natural question is why the Treasury did not decide to purchase the assets itself.

One of the theories for why this did not occur either under Paulson or Geithner is that neither official wanted to pay more for the assets than market prices and then be accused of subsidizing the big Wall Street banks at the expense of the taxpayers. Another view was that the process was too complex and time-consuming to be done by the Treasury. After the stress tests, neither of these arguments seems to justify the Treasury's refusal to use the TARP funds as originally intended. It could well be true that neither Paulson nor Geithner wanted to be accused of subsidizing the banks with taxpayer funds, but if so, it reflects not only a want of political courage to do the right thing but a mistaken judgment about how such an action would be viewed in the markets. Of course, there would be some who would have claimed that the taxpayers were ripped off, but the market reaction to the stress test valuations suggests that most analysts would have seen the pricing at cash flow values as justifiable. Similarly, the argument about complexity does not seem valid after the stress tests, in which the supervisors simply asked the banks to value their securities assets, including their MBS, at their cash flow values and then made independent valuations of those cases in which the credit losses were likely to exceed the value of the collateral. Apparently, it could be done by the supervisors in two months without the need to engage outside consultants.

What Did We Learn about the Banks' MBS Holdings?

The fact that there are only $200 billion of MBS on the books of the nineteen participating banks—and that much of that is not made up of the subprime loans that were presumably the "toxic assets" we have heard so much about—was another surprise of the Fed's stress test report. What it means is that between mid-2007 and the end of 2008, the nineteen largest banks had substantially written off or written down most of their most problematic assets—the assets that analysts cited as the source of their financial problems. This was a very important fact and would have gone a long way toward restoring confidence in the markets if it had been made public by the supervisors. Instead, by establishing PPIP, the Treasury implied that these assets were still a problem.

Moreover, with the MBS no longer a significant source of weakness, the vast majority of the questionable assets of the largest banks are quite conventional items, like first and second lien mortgages, commercial and industrial loans, commercial real estate loans, and credit card loans. Losses can and will occur in all these areas, of course, but bank analysts are quite capable of estimating these losses based on past history. What we had been told that was different and more problematic about this banking crisis was that the losses were in MBS and collateralized debt obligations that were so complex that they were impossible to value. Now we find that even if they all had been written down to zero, the big banks would still have sufficient capital to carry them through a normal downturn—and maybe even the more adverse downturn used by the supervisors in the stress tests.

This, too, raises a question about why all this information was not made public while the market was led to believe that things were far worse than they turned out to be. Like the stress tests themselves, information of this kind could have calmed the fear in the markets and given analysts the information they needed to better assess the condition of the banks. Without it, everyone was left guessing, and some of the guessing was counterproductive to the recovery of the economy.

It will also tell us something if the PPIP proceeds. After successfully passing the stress tests, the banks will have much less incentive to sell the securities assets that supervisors have seen fit not to criticize or write down. These assets are probably producing significantly more cash than they cost to carry. Accordingly, since it is doubtful that there are an abundance of new profitable loans to make in a recessionary economy, these holdings can probably be excluded from the securities the banks are going to be willing to sell at this point. On the other hand, the assets that have been written down, which could be close to $400 billion in original value, might be candidates for sale. They may still remain on bank balance sheets (it is unlikely that they have actually been sold) but substantially written down. If the banks can get prices for these that reflect the value of their continuing cash flows, it will improve their capital position and could be a windfall. If the PPIP actually gets off the ground—that is, if there is sufficient interest in the private sector and the banks to enter these transactions—we will have an interesting test. If the banks will not sell their written-down assets at the prices the private groups are willing to pay, it will mean that the cash flows on these assets are strong enough that they remain profitable assets. That in itself will be a signal that the write-downs have been excessive.

Conclusion

If we take the stress test report seriously, and we should, it is difficult to avoid the conclusion that a lot of losses—for bank shareholders as well as investors generally—could have been avoided if bank supervisors had provided more information, sooner, about the financial condition of the largest banks. The Fed and the Treasury have taken many unprecedented steps to stem the steep economic decline that began with the mortgage meltdown almost two years ago. The one unprecedented thing they did not do—disclosing more fully the information they as supervisors had about the financial condition of the largest banks—would likely have been the cheapest and most effective.

"Deregulation and the Financial Crisis: Another Urban Myth"

Originally published October 2009

What caused the financial crisis? The widely accepted narrative, prominent in the media and pressed by the Obama administration, is that the crisis was caused by deregulation—the "repeal" of the Glass-Steagall Act and the failure to regulate both derivatives and mortgage brokers—which allowed excessive financial innovation, risk-taking, and greed among financial players from mortgage brokers to Wall Street bankers. With this diagnosis, the proposed remedy is more regulation and government control of the financial system, from the over-the-counter derivative markets to mortgage brokers and the compensation of CEOs. The alternative explanation is that the crisis was caused by the government's own housing policies, which fostered the creation of 25 million subprime and other low-quality mortgages—almost 50 percent of all mortgages in the United States—that are now defaulting at unprecedented rates. In this narrative, the fact that two-thirds of all these weak mortgages are now held by government agencies, or were produced by government requirements, shows that the demand for these mortgages—and the financial crisis itself—originated in Washington. The problem for the administration's narrative is that its principal examples do not stand up to analysis: the repeal of a portion of the Glass-Steagall Act did not eliminate the restrictions on banks' securities activities (they were left unchanged), the mortgage brokers were responding to demand created by the government, and, there is no evidence that the failure to regulate credit default swaps (CDS) had any effect in causing or enhancing the financial crisis. Without a persuasive explanation for the cause of the financial crisis, the administration's regulatory proposals rest on a mythic foundation.

The administration's proposals for regulatory reform in the financial industry are based on the notion that the financial crisis was caused by too little regulation, and perhaps by inherent flaws in the financial system. To explain why a worldwide crisis occurred now, and not at some earlier time during the seventy years since the Great Depression, the administration's defenders claim that deregulation or nonregulation during the last twenty years allowed banks and other financial institutions to take risks that resulted in their near-insolvency, while the large number of weak mortgages in our financial system is explained by a failure to regulate mortgage brokers.

Since the administration and Congress are proceeding as though deregulation caused the financial crisis, it is appropriate—indeed necessary—to ask: what deregulation? We have all heard it many times: the financial crisis was caused by the "repeal" of the Glass-Steagall Act in 1999,[69] although even a small amount of research would have shown that the relevant provisions of Glass-Steagall were not repealed. Another bit of mythmaking is the claim that the prohibition on regulating CDS and other derivatives in the Commodity Futures Modernization Act of 2000 was a cause of the financial crisis.[70] It is not unusual to see statements by otherwise knowledgeable people that the CDS "brought the financial system to its knees."[71] Recently, President Barack Obama justified the need for a Consumer Financial Protection Agency by claiming that predatory lending by unregulated mortgage brokers was a cause of the financial crisis:

> Part of what led to this crisis were not just decisions made on Wall Street, but also unsustainable mortgage loans made across the country. While many folks took on more than they knew they could afford, too often folks signed contracts they didn't fully understand offered by lenders who didn't always tell the truth.[72]

Unfortunately for the administration and its supporters, these examples of "deregulation" or nonregulation do not support the argument they are making

---

69. See Thomas R. Keene and Andrew Frye, "Dinallo Says Problem Is Regulatory Structure, Not Pay," Bloomberg.com, October 23, 2009, available at www.bloomberg.com/apps/news?pid=20601087&sid=aNrJwDBv5jYU (accessed November 2, 2009).

70. *Commodity Futures Modernization Act of 2000,* Public Law 106-554, U.S. Statutes at Large 114 (2000): 2763, appendix E.

71. Lynn Stout, "Regulate OTC Derivatives by Deregulating Them," *Regulation* 32, no. 3 (Fall 2009): 30–41.

72. White House, "President Obama Promotes Tougher Rules on Wall Street to Protect Customers," news release, September 19, 2009, available at www.whitehouse.gov/the_press_office/Weekly-Address-President-Obama-Promotes-Tougher-Rules-on-Wall-Street-to-Protect-Consumers (accessed November 2, 2009).

for broader regulation of the financial system. The so-called repeal of Glass-Steagall was not a repeal of the restrictions on banks' securities trading—so banks are still subject to the prohibitions in Glass-Steagall; there is no evidence that credit default swaps or other derivatives had anything to do with the financial industry's losses or the financial crisis; and, as outlined below, the government itself—or government requirements—appear to be the source of most of the funds and the demand for the deficient loans that were made by the unregulated mortgage brokers.

Thus, a more compelling narrative than the administration's deregulation hypothesis would focus on the effect of over 25 million subprime and Alt-A (that is, nonprime) mortgages that are pervasive in the mortgage system in the United States. These junk loans, amounting to almost 50 percent of all mortgages, began defaulting at unprecedented rates in 2007, and the resulting losses caused the collapse of the asset-backed financing market in 2007, the near collapse of Bear Stearns in March 2008, and the bankruptcy of Lehman Brothers the following September. Perhaps more important than these events, the loss of the asset-backed securitization market—where receivables from credit cards, consumer loans, and mortgages were financed—caused a huge reduction in financing for businesses and consumers, precipitating the current recession.

Although the administration blames the production of these deficient loans primarily on unregulated mortgage brokers, many of whom it calls "predatory lenders," this turns the mortgage market on its head. Mortgage brokers—even predatory ones—cannot create and sell deficient mortgages unless they have willing buyers, and it turns out that their main customers were government agencies or companies and banks required by government regulations to purchase these junk loans. As of the end of 2008, the Federal Housing Administration held 4.5 million subprime and Alt-A loans. Ten million were on the books of Fannie Mae and Freddie Mac when they were taken over, and 2.7 million are currently held by banks that purchased them under the requirements of the Community Reinvestment Act (CRA). These government-mandated loans amount to almost two-thirds of all the junk mortgages in the system, and their delinquency rates are nine to fifteen times greater than equivalent rates on prime mortgages. In addition to destroying companies and neighborhoods and causing a severe recession, the accumulation of these loans on government-backed balance sheets will result in enormous losses for taxpayers in the future.

There is empirical evidence to support the idea that defaults of junk loans caused the financial crisis. In his book *Getting Off Track,* Stanford University economist John Taylor notes that on August 9, 2007, the spread between the London Interbank Offer Rate (LIBOR) and Overnight Index Swap (OIS) rates rose abruptly, indicating that concern about counterparty risk had suddenly taken hold among the world's major internationally active banks. Before August 9, the LIBOR rate was usually about ten basis points higher than the OIS rate, which is a rate-free rate that reflects what the market anticipates the federal funds rate will be over the next three months. On August 9, the spread suddenly jumped to approximately sixty basis points and still remains elevated over two years later. A reasonable interpretation of this change is that information about defaulting U.S. mortgages—and ignorance about who was actually holding these loans— caused this sudden expression of counterparty risk.[73]

The "Repeal" of Glass-Steagall

The law known popularly as the Glass-Steagall Act initially consisted of only four short statutory provisions. Section 16 generally prohibits banks from underwriting or dealing in securities,[74] and Section 21 prohibits securities firms from taking deposits.[75] The remaining two sections, Section 20[76] and Section 32,[77] prohibit banks from being affiliated with firms that are principally or primarily engaged in underwriting or dealing in securities. In 1999,

---

73. John B. Taylor, *Getting Off Track: How Government Actions and Interventions Caused, Prolonged, and Worsened the Financial Crisis* (Stanford: Hoover Institution Press, 2009), 15–21.

74. *See Banking Act of 1933,* Public Law 73-89, *U.S. Statutes at Large* 48 (1933) 162. Section 16, as incorporated in 12 U.S. C 24 (Seventh), both prohibits banks from underwriting and dealing in securities and permits them to act as brokers, as follows: "The business of dealing in securities and stock by the association shall be limited to purchasing and selling such securities and stock without recourse, solely upon the order, and for the account of, customers, and in no case for its own account, and the association shall not underwrite any issue of securities or stock."

75. *U.S. Code 12* § 378.

76. Ibid., 12 § 377.

77. Ibid., 12 § 78.

the Gramm-Leach-Bliley Act (GLBA)[78] repealed Sections 20 and 32, so banks could thereafter be affiliated with securities firms, but Sections 16 and 21 were left intact, so that whatever banks were forbidden or permitted to do by Glass-Steagall—before the enactment of GLBA—remains in effect. In other words, after GLBA, banks were still prohibited from underwriting and dealing in securities, although they were now permitted, under very restrictive rules discussed below, to be affiliated with investment banks.

An investment bank is a securities firm—a firm specializing in the business of trading securities of all kinds. These firms are not backed by the government in any way, and—unlike commercial banks—are intended to be risk takers. The Glass-Steagall Act was designed to separate commercial banks from investment banks; it did that simply by prohibiting affiliations between the two and by prohibiting commercial banks from engaging in the business of underwriting and dealing in securities. After sixty-five years and many academic studies showing this separation was unnecessary and ill-advised,[79] GLBA repealed the affiliation prohibition but—as noted above— it left the restrictions on banks' securities activities untouched.

Glass-Steagall in the Context of Banking Law

Most U.S. banks are subsidiaries of bank holding companies (BHCs), ordinary corporations that have controlling positions in banks but are also permitted to engage in or control firms engaged in other financial activities. BHCs do not have the advantages available to banks—unquestioned access to the Fed's discount window, the ability to offer insured deposits, or participation in the nation's payment system—but they are free to engage in activities such as securities underwriting and dealing that are not permitted to banks. No one quarrels with the proposition that banks should not be able to use their insured deposits to engage in risky or speculative activities. For one thing, government-insured deposits give banks a source of funds that is lower cost than what is available

---

78. *Gramm-Leach-Bliley Act,* Public Law 106-102, *U.S. Statutes at Large* 113 (1999): 1338.

79. See, for example, the work cited in James R. Barth, R. Dan Brumbaugh Jr., and James A. Wilcox, "The Repeal of Glass-Steagall and the Advent of Broad Banking," *Journal of Economic Perspectives* 14, no. 2 (Spring 2000), 191–204.

to others, and thus would permit banks to compete unfairly with many other financial institutions that must raise their funds in the capital markets without government assistance. But more important than that, U.S. banking laws are designed to separate banks from the risks that might be created by the activities of their holding companies and other affiliates. This is done for two reasons: to ensure the so-called safety net (deposit insurance and access to the discount window) is not extended beyond banks to their holding companies or their nonbank affiliates, and to protect the banks' financial positions from exposure to the risks their affiliates take, including those affiliates engaged in securities activities. Insofar as possible, the banking laws are structured to allow a holding company—and even a bank securities subsidiary—to fail without endangering the health of any related bank. This separation is effected by severely restricting the transactions between banks and their affiliates, and thus the risks that banks might take on the activities of their affiliates or subsidiaries.

In order to reduce the range of bank risk-taking, banking laws and regulations also limit the activities in which banks themselves are permitted to engage. That is the context in which the Glass-Steagall Act should be viewed. As noted above, Glass-Steagall continues to prohibit banks from underwriting or dealing in securities. "Underwriting" refers to the business of assuming the risk that an issue of securities will not be fully sold to investors, while "dealing" refers to the business of holding an inventory of securities for trading purposes. Nevertheless, banks are in the business of making investments, and Glass-Steagall did not attempt to interfere with that activity. Thus, although Glass-Steagall prohibited underwriting and dealing, it did not interfere with the ability of banks to "purchase and sell" securities they acquired for investment. The difference between "purchasing and selling" and "underwriting and dealing" is crucially important. A bank may purchase a security—say, a bond—and then decide to sell it when the bank needs cash or believes the bond is no longer a good investment. This activity is different from buying an inventory of bonds for the purpose of selling them, which would be considered a dealing activity and involves considerable market risk because of the volatility of the securities markets.

Nor did Glass-Steagall ever prohibit banks from buying and selling whole loans, even though a loan could be seen as a security. When securitization was developed, banks were permitted—even under Glass-Steagall—to securitize their loan assets and sell their loans in securitized form. Similarly, banks were always permitted to buy and sell securities based on assets, such as mortgages, that they could otherwise hold as whole loans. Glass-Steagall did not affect this authority, but the act was interpreted to make clear that banks could not deal in or underwrite these or other nongovernment securities. Under this interpretation, banks could not underwrite or deal in mortgage-backed securities (MBS), but they were free to buy these securities as investment securities and sell them when they believed that would be appropriate. Again, these restrictions remained in force after GLBA; the only difference was that GLBA now permitted banks to be affiliated with firms that engaged primarily or principally in underwriting or dealing in securities, and this affiliation could be through a subsidiary of the bank's holding company (both the bank and the securities firm would then be under common control) or through a subsidiary of the bank itself. In both cases, whether the securities firm is a holding company affiliate or a subsidiary, there are severe restrictions on transactions—outlined below—between the bank and the securities firm.

Finally, Glass-Steagall permitted banks to underwrite and deal in government securities, or securities backed by a government, and this was also unaffected by GLBA. For example, both before and after Glass-Steagall and GLBA, banks have been able to underwrite and deal in U.S. government securities, the securities of Fannie Mae and Freddie Mac, and the general obligation bonds of states and municipalities. This exemption applies mostly to securities backed by the U.S. government or by a state or municipality, although it also applies in cases where the issuer of the security is performing a government mission but is not strictly backed or guaranteed by a federal, state, or municipal government— such as with Fannie Mae and Freddie Mac.

From this analysis, it should be clear that the GLBA's repeal solely of the affiliation provisions of the Glass-Steagall Act did not permit banks to do anything that they were previously prohibited from doing. Accordingly, it is incorrect to suggest that Glass-Steagall's repeal had any effect whatever on the ability of banks to engage directly in the risky business of underwriting and dealing in securities.

Nevertheless, it is reasonable to ask whether the repeal of the affiliation provisions of Glass-Steagall could have caused banks to suffer the losses that were a prominent feature of the financial crisis and whether the possibility of affiliation with banks could have caused the losses to the large securities firms—also known as investment banks—that drove one of them into bankruptcy (Lehman Brothers), two of them into becoming subsidiaries of banks (Merrill Lynch and Bear Stearns), and two more into recasting themselves as BHCs under the supervision of the Fed (Goldman Sachs and Morgan Stanley). The remaining portions of the Glass-Steagall discussion in this *Outlook* will review the specific restrictions that Glass-Steagall imposes on banks, the restrictions on transactions between banks and their securities affiliates and subsidiaries, and the possibility that affiliations with a bank—permissible after GLBA—might have caused the losses suffered by the large investment banks.

Regulation of the Securities Activities of National Banks

Almost all the big banks—including Citibank, Wachovia, Bank of America, JP Morgan Chase, and Wells Fargo—are national banks, chartered, regulated, and supervised by the Office of the Comptroller of the Currency (OCC), an office within the Treasury Department. OCC regulations allow banks to underwrite or deal only in securities backed by federal, state, or local government, and the securities of companies like Fannie Mae and Freddie Mac that are deemed to be performing a government mission.[80] Other types of securities, such as corporate bonds, municipal bonds that are not general obligations of municipalities, small-business-related securities that are investment grade, and securities related to commercial or residential mortgages, may be bought and held by banks in limited amounts, but banks may not underwrite or deal in them.[81]

Accordingly, under OCC regulations, before and after GLBA, banks could not underwrite or deal in MBS or other nongovernmental securities. They could, of course, invest in MBS, but they could do this before and after the adoption of both Glass-Steagall and GLBA, just as they were permitted to invest in the whole loans that the MBS represented. In other words, to the extent that banks suffered losses on MBS, collateralized debt obligations, or other instruments that were securitized versions of whole loans, their losses came not from underwriting or dealing in these securities, but from imprudent investments. It would be correct to say, therefore, that banks suffered losses on these securities by acting as banks—as lenders—and not as the securities traders that some commentators seem to imagine.

---

80. Office of the Comptroller of the Currency, "Investment Securities," *Code of Federal Regulations 12,* § 1.2(a), 1.2(b), available at http://www.occ.gov/fr/cfrparts/12CFR01.htm#%C2%A7%201.02%20Definitions (accessed November 2, 2009).

81. Ibid.

Bank Affiliations with Securities Firms

Although banks themselves could not underwrite or deal in MBS or other nongovernmental securities under Glass-Steagall, GLBA permitted banks to be affiliated with securities firms that were engaged in this activity. Did this newly permitted affiliation cause banks to take losses they would not have sustained if GLBA had not repealed the affiliation prohibitions in the Glass-Steagall Act? The answer again is no. Banking law and regulations prevent the activities of a bank securities affiliate or subsidiary from adversely affecting the financial condition of a related bank.

As noted above, these laws and regulations are designed to separate a bank as fully as possible from the risks its holding company takes, or by any affiliate that is a subsidiary of the holding company. Although it is possible after GLBA for a bank to hold a securities firm as a subsidiary, OCC regulations require that this subsidiary be treated like a subsidiary of the holding company, rather than like a subsidiary of the bank. The principal statutory provisions that wall off the bank from its holding company affiliates and from its own securities subsidiary are sections 23a and 23b of the Federal Reserve Act, which are applicable to all banks, whether chartered by federal or state governments.[82]

Section 23a limits the financial and other transactions between a bank and its holding company or any holding company subsidiary. For extensions of credit, the limit is 10 percent of the bank's capital and surplus for any one holding company affiliate and 20 percent for all affiliates as a group. All such lending or extensions of credit must be collateralized with U.S. government securities up to the value of the loan, and must be overcollateralized if other types of marketable securities are used as collateral.[83] All transactions between a bank and its affiliates must be on the same terms as the bank would offer to an unrelated party.[84] Other restrictions also apply, including prohibitions on the bank's purchase of a low-quality asset from an affiliate,[85] or the bank's issuance of a guarantee, acceptance, or letter of credit on behalf of an affiliate.[86] All these

---

82. *U.S. Code 12* § 371c and 371c-1.
83. Ibid., 12 § 371c(c)(1).
84. Ibid., 12 § 1(a)(1).
85. Ibid., 12 § 371c(a)(3).
86. Ibid., 12 § 371c(b)(7).

restrictions are applied by the Comptroller of the Currency to a national bank's relationship with a securities subsidiary and by the Federal Deposit Insurance Corporation as the federal regulator of state-chartered insured banks.[87]

Of course, if the securities firm is a subsidiary of the bank rather than a holding company affiliate, the bank will have an investment in the subsidiary that could be lost if the subsidiary fails. However, OCC regulations require that the bank "must deduct the aggregate amount of its outstanding equity investment, including retained earnings, in its [securities subsidiary] from its total assets and tangible equity and deduct such investment from its risk-based capital . . . and . . . may not consolidate the assets and liabilities of [the securities subsidiary] with those of the bank."[88]

These restrictions substantially reduce any likelihood that the business of a securities affiliate or subsidiary will have an adverse effect on the bank. The bank's lending to a securities affiliate or subsidiary is severely limited, must be collateralized, and must be made on the same terms the bank would offer to an unrelated third party. In addition, the bank's investment in a securities subsidiary is not recorded as an asset on its balance sheet. In other words, the bank's investment in its securities subsidiary is effectively written off at the time it is made. Accordingly, if the securities subsidiary should fail, there will be no impact on the bank's regulatory capital position. Under these circumstances, it is highly unlikely that any activity carried on in a securities affiliate or securities subsidiary of a bank could have an adverse effect on the capital position of the bank.

It is also very doubtful that the restrictions of sections 23a and 23b would be ignored either by a bank as an institution or by any director, officer, or employee of a bank or its holding company. The law permits civil and criminal penalties for knowing violations of sections 23a, 23b, or any other regulation, and the civil fines can be enormous. For example, banking regulators can impose on any bank director or officer a personal, civil money penalty of up to $1 million for every day a violation continues.[89]

It thus seems clear that GLBA's repeal of the affiliation provisions of the Glass-Steagall Act did not and could not have had any adverse effect on the

---

87. *Code of Federal Regulations 12* § 5.39(h)(5).
88. *Code of Federal Regulations 12* § 5.39(h)(1)(i) and (ii).
89. *U.S. Code 12* § 1818(i).

financial condition of any related bank, and thus did not contribute, and could not have contributed in any way, to the financial crisis.

What Caused the Problems of the Largest Banks?

Since banks' securities activities were not affected in any way by the GLBA repeal of the affiliation provisions of Glass-Steagall, one must look elsewhere for the causes of the financial weakness that many U.S. banks suffered. As noted above, there is strong evidence that despite heavy regulation, many of the banks that got into trouble did so by failing to act prudently in their investment or lending activities—in other words, in their capacity as banks—and not because they engaged in securities trading or were affiliated with investment banks that were underwriting and dealing in securities. Many banks and other financial institutions bought and held MBS that were rated AAA but performed very poorly. Others, and particularly the very large banks, in order to gain regulatory approval for expansions and mergers, committed themselves to make mortgage loans that would comply with the requirements of the CRA. These regulations, enforced by the bank regulators, required loans to borrowers at or below 80 percent of the median income, and in many cases these borrowers did not have the financial resources to meet their obligations, especially when housing prices stopped rising in late 2006 and early 2007. There are data to support this hypothesis.

In spring 2008, at the request of the Treasury Department, the Fed and the Comptroller of the Currency supervised a special process of stress testing by the nineteen largest U.S. financial institutions (most of which were bank holding companies with large subsidiary banks). Table 1 is taken from a report by the Fed on the stress tests and shows the aggregate projected losses for all nineteen institutions in an economically adverse scenario.[90] For purposes of this discussion, two items in this table stand out—the very large projected losses on first and second lien mortgages and the projected trading and counterparty losses. The former is consistent with the hypothesis advanced at the outset of this *Outlook*—that the largest banks committed themselves to make large numbers of

---

90. Board of Governors of the Federal Reserve System, "The Supervisory Capital Assessment Program: Overview of Results," news release, May 7, 2009, available at www.federalreserve.gov/newsevents/press/bcreg/bcreg20090507a1.pdf (accessed November 4, 2009).

TABLE 1
ESTIMATED LOSSES FOR 2009 AND 2010 FOR THE MORE ADVERSE SCENARIO

Loan Category	Estimated Loss (in billions of dollars)	Percentage of Losses within Category
First lien mortgages	102.3	8.8
Second/junior lien mortgages	83.2	13.8
Commercial and industrial loans	60.1	6.1
Commercial real estate loans	53.0	8.5
Credit card loans	82.4	22.5
Securities (AFS and HTM)	35.2	N/A
Trading and counterparty	99.3	N/A
Other[a]	83.7	N/A
Total Estimated Losses (before purchase accounting adjustments)	599.2 billion	

SOURCE: Board of Governors of the Federal Reserve System, "The Supervisory Capital Assessment Program: Overview of Results," news release, May 7, 2009, available at www.federal reserve.gov/newsevents/ press/bcreg/bcreg20090507a1.pdf (accessed November 4, 2009).

NOTE: (a) Other category includes other consumer and nonconsumer loans and miscellaneous commitments and obligations.

CRA-qualifying loans in order to gain regulatory approval for expansions in the late 1990s and 2000s. The total projected residential mortgage losses for Bank of America, Citibank, JP Morgan Chase, and Wells Fargo are $167 billion out of a total for all nineteen institutions of $185 billion. The mortgage losses of the other banks in the survey were negligible.

In the case of counterparty and trading losses, the projected total is also consistent with the hypothesis that banks themselves did little trading of securities after GLBA—either directly (which continued to be prohibited by Glass-Steagall) or indirectly through affiliates or subsidiaries. The relatively high level of trading and counterparty losses in the table—still a relatively small portion of the total—is probably attributable to including the holdings of the independent investment banks (Goldman Sachs and Morgan Stanley) among the nineteen institutions and the consolidation of the assets of the investment banks acquired in 2008 by JP Morgan Chase (Bear Stearns) and Bank of America (Merrill Lynch). The projected aggregate trading and counterparty losses for those four institutions alone were over $80 billion of the total of $99 billion for all nineteen institutions as a group. Similar losses for all the other banks in the survey were again negligible.

Equally important, what is clearly visible in Table 1 is that all nineteen institutions—most of which were banks—were projected to suffer losses on what anyone would consider traditional bank assets: residential and commercial mortgages, commercial loans, credit card receivables, and the like.

Accordingly, the enactment of GLBA—to the extent that it allowed banks to affiliate with securities firms—did not result in major bank losses from their own or their affiliates' securities or trading activities. On the contrary, it seems clear that the banks got into trouble and precipitated the financial crisis and the recession by doing exactly the things we expect them to do by making loans and holding normal and traditional financial assets. The absence of any major source of projected losses coming from securities and trading activities shows that the repeal of the affiliation provisions of the Glass-Steagall Act did not induce the banks to take on unusual amounts of trading assets. Nor was trading a significant source of their projected financial losses.

Was Bank Affiliation the Problem?

There is still one possibility—that GLBA's repeal of the affiliation provisions in Glass-Steagall enabled securities firms to establish relationships with banks— and these relationships caused the near-insolvency of Merrill Lynch, Goldman Sachs, and Morgan Stanley and the bankruptcy of Lehman Brothers. However, this seems highly unlikely. Each of these investment banking firms had a subsidiary bank—something that would not have been possible before the repeal of the affiliation provisions of Glass-Steagall—but these bank affiliates were far too small to cause any serious losses to their massive parents. Table 2 shows the relative size of the parent and the subsidiary bank for each of the four major securities firms.

In light of the huge disparities between the size of each major investment bank and the size of its depository institution subsidiary, it is highly unlikely that the insured bank subsidiary could cause any serious financial problem for the parent investment bank or significantly enhance the financial problems the parent company created for itself through its own operations.

Accordingly, the banks that encountered financial problems got into trouble the old-fashioned way—by making imprudent loans or taking imprudent

TABLE 2
RELATIVE SIZE OF INVESTMENT BANKS AND THEIR BANK SUBSIDIARIES

Investment Bank	Investment Bank Assets (est.)	Subsidiary Bank's Assets
Goldman Sachs	$800 billion	$25.0 billion[a]
Morgan Stanley	$660 billion	$38.5 billion[b]
Merrill Lynch	$670 billion	$35.0 billion[c]
Lehman Brothers	$600 billion	$4.50 billion[d]

SOURCE: Author calculations.

NOTES: (a) Board of Governors of the Federal Reserve System, "Order Approving Formation of Bank Holding Companies," news release, September 22, 2008, available at www.federalreserve.gov/newsevents/press/orders/orders20080922a1.pdf (accessed November 4, 2009); (b) Ibid; (c) iBanknet, "Merrill Lynch Bank & Trust Co, FSB," available at www.ibanknet.com/scripts/callreports/getbank.aspx?ibnid=usa_2577494 (accessed November 4, 2009); (d) iBanknet, "Woodlands Commercial Bank," available at www.ibanknet.com/scripts/callreports/getbank.aspx?ibnid=usa_3376461 (accessed November 4, 2009).

financial risks. There is no evidence of significant amounts of risky securities activities. Similarly, the investment banks got into trouble in their own way and not because of their affiliations with small banks. Thus, the repeal of the affiliation provisions of the Glass-Steagall Act had no significant effect whatever in triggering or enhancing the financial crisis.

Credit Default Swaps

What about the other claimed "deregulation" that is alleged to have caused the financial crisis? Here the culprits are derivatives, and particularly credit default swaps (CDS). These instruments are not as well understood, so they have given rise to wild and truly absurd claims about their responsibility for the financial crisis.

Routinely, the media contains unchallenged statements to the effect that CDS "brought the banking system to its knees."[91] Dozens of articles have been written about the supposed dangers of CDS, without anyone having to explain how, exactly, CDS would or could have such a dire effect.[92] Two *Outlooks* have outlined how CDS work and questioned how they could have the key role in

---

91. Lynn Stout, "Regulate OTC Derivatives by Deregulating Them," 30.
92. Ibid.

the financial crisis so readily assigned to them.[93] I will not repeat the analysis in those pieces but instead will focus on two cases—the bankruptcy of Lehman Brothers and the Fed's rescue of AIG. Between them, they tell us a lot about whether CDS are the dangerous instruments they are made to appear.

Lehman Brothers was a major player in the CDS market, but there is no indication that Lehman was forced into bankruptcy by its CDS obligations. Instead, the most thorough accounts of the Lehman crisis in 2008 attribute the company's collapse to its funding sources' lack of confidence in the firm's viability.[94] When Lehman went into bankruptcy, the firm had over 900,000 outstanding derivative contracts.[95] This would not be unusual for a dealer, which usually tries to hedge all its CDS obligations with an offsetting contract, thus doubling the number of its contracts. Once in bankruptcy, Lehman has not been able to perform on any of its CDS obligations, and many of them may have been canceled by Lehman's trustee, yet there have been no reports of any counterparties being forced into bankruptcy because Lehman was unable to perform. This is not surprising, given how CDS work. A CDS can be viewed as an insurance or guarantee contract. Where Lehman was functioning as the guarantor, it promised its counterparty that if a company we shall call A defaults on its obligations, Lehman will pay the counterparty a notional amount specified in the guarantee contract. In return, Lehman would receive a quarterly payment from its counterparty known as a premium.

What happened when Lehman failed? Clearly, its counterparty in the CDS on A would not be paid, but what loss had the counterparty suffered? The answer is that Lehman's counterparty has suffered no significant loss unless company A has also defaulted. In that case, Lehman would have owed its counterparty the notional amount, but was unable to pay. In the absence of a default by company

---

93. See Peter J. Wallison, "Everything You Wanted to Know about Credit Default Swaps—But Were Never Told," AEI *Financial Services Outlook* (December 2008), available at www.aei.org/outlook/29158; and Peter J. Wallison, "Unnecessary Intervention: The Administration's Effort to Regulate Credit Default Swaps," AEI *Financial Services Outlook* (August 2009), available at www.aei.org/outlook/100065. (See pp. 223 and 409 of this book.)

94. See, for example, David Wessel, *In Fed We Trust: Ben Bernanke's War on the Great Panic* (New York: Crown Business, 2009).

95. Subcommittee on Commercial and Administrative Law of the House Committee on the Judiciary, "Too Big to Fail: The Role for Bankruptcy and Antitrust Law in Financial Regulation Reform," 111th Cong., 1st sess., 2009, 1–13, available at http://judiciary.house.gov/hearings/pdf/Miller091022.pdf (accessed November 4, 2009).

A, Lehman's counterparty had a simple remedy—it could go back into the market and purchase another CDS to cover its exposure to company A, agreeing to pay the necessary premium to that new guarantor. It is similar to what would have happened if a homeowner's fire insurer had failed before the homeowner had a fire. The homeowner would simply call his broker and buy another policy. The loss, if any, would have been negligible. In other words, Lehman's failure to perform on its CDS would only have been significant if many companies whose obligations Lehman was covering through CDS had defaulted before or simultaneously with Lehman's default. That apparently did not happen in September 2008, when Lehman went into bankruptcy. Although many markets froze at that moment, the CDS market continued to function, and most, if not all, of Lehman's counterparties probably covered their exposures with new CDS.

This was the state of things when Lehman was the party that had issued CDS guarantees to protect the exposures of others. What happened when it was Lehman's debt itself that was protected by CDS written by other CDS market participants? There were CDS in the notional amount of approximately $72 billion written on Lehman, and Lehman's bankruptcy meant that all the parties that had written protection on Lehman were now obligated to pay their counterparties. Within a month of the Lehman bankruptcy, however, all of these obligations had been settled by the exchange of $5.2 billion among hundreds of counterparties. The relatively small amount that was ultimately necessary to settle the CDS on Lehman probably reflects in part the fact that the CDS market naturally disperses risks among many counterparties—just as the advocates of the CDS system have claimed—and also the fact that the notional amount outstanding on any reference entity (the issuer of the obligation that is covered—in this case Lehman) is always many times the actual amount of the loss. Moreover, there is no indication that the bankruptcy of Lehman—a firm with assets of about $600 billion— resulted in such large losses for any of the guaranteeing parties that their solvency or stability was threatened. One would imagine that, if CDS are the source of such a dangerous "interconnectedness" in the financial system, the bankruptcy of a major player like Lehman would have had a greater effect on the CDS market than it did. Yet that market apparently took the Lehman bankruptcy in stride.

AIG, which was rescued by the Fed with loans that totaled over $175 billion, also offers some important perspective. AIG got into serious trouble because a substantial portion of the CDS it wrote were guaranteeing collateralized debt obligations (CDOs) backed by pools of MBS that were in turn backed by pools of subprime and Alt-A mortgages—the toxic assets that later drove many large banks and other financial institutions to the brink of insolvency. Although the exact terms of these CDS are not known, AIG was probably guaranteeing to the holders of these CDOs that it would reimburse their losses if the securities lost value. In addition, AIG apparently did not hedge its risks—a very unusual and risky approach to writing swaps. Thus, AIG is a kind of worst-case example; it wrote swaps without hedging, and it wrote them on the instruments that had caused the worst losses to hundreds (if not thousands) of other financial institutions. In other words, it is not an example of what would generally happen in the CDS market, but rather what would and should almost never happen. Lawyers often note that hard cases make bad law, and in the same sense, basing policy on a worst-case scenario like AIG would also produce a bad set of rules.

Nevertheless, it is worth considering what actually would have happened if AIG had been allowed to fail. In this thought experiment, we will assume that AIG is different from Lehman because its obligation to reimburse its counterparties had already in a sense matured; the CDOs it was covering had already lost value when its problems arose. As a result, as contemplated in almost all CDS contracts, its counterparties were seeking collateral from AIG to assure themselves that when they made a claim for their losses AIG would be able to pay. AIG did not have sufficient funds to provide collateral and thus would have defaulted on its obligations if the Fed had not stepped in. If AIG had been allowed to fail, and had not performed under its CDS obligations, its counterparties would have suffered real losses. This is different from the hypothetical circumstance of the homeowner and the fire insurance company. In this case, the "fire" has occurred—at least in part—before the insurance company has failed, and the homeowner has suffered a real loss that the failed insurance company cannot cover. René M. Stulz quantifies the potential loss to AIG as follows:

> By August 2008, AIG had a total amount of unrealized losses on its credit default swaps of $26.2 billion and had posted collateral worth $16.5 billion. . . . On September 16, after having been downgraded by S&P and Moody's, AIG had to post $14.5 billion additional collateral. It could not meet these collateral requirements without a bailout.[96]

---

96. René M. Stulz, "Credit Default Swaps and the Credit Crisis," (Working Paper 15384, National Bureau of Economic Research, Cambridge, MA, September 2009), available at www.nber.org/papers/w15384 (accessed November 4, 2009).

This implies that AIG's total uncollateralized CDS obligations on the CDOs were somewhere between $25 billion and $41 billion. It is doubtful that this loss, spread among what were probably hundreds of counterparties world-wide, would have caused a systemic breakdown. In any event, it is important to recognize what an outlier AIG was in the swap market. It doubled down by taking only one side of swap contracts and did so massively, losing billions of dollars, covering an instrument that had been rated AAA—MBS backed by U.S. subprime mortgages—but which turned out to be a disastrous investment for virtually every financial institution that touched it.

Apart from AIG, it is difficult to find an example of a participant in the CDS market whose activities might have led to its insolvency. That was certainly not true of Lehman, which was a major market player. The fact that Lehman's failure did not seriously disrupt the CDS market, or cause serious losses for its CDS counterparties, strongly suggests that the dangers of CDS are wildly exagger-ated. Under these circumstances, it is not at all clear that the failure to impose regulation on the derivative markets in 2000 was the deregulatory blunder it has been made out to be.

Conclusion

The causes of the financial crisis remain a mystery for many people, but certain causes can apparently be excluded. The repeal of Glass-Steagall by GLBA is certainly one of these, since Glass-Steagall, as applied to banks, remains fully in effect. In addition, the fact that a major CDS player like Lehman Brothers could fail without any serious disturbance of the CDS market, any serious losses to its counterparties, or any serious losses to those firms that had guar-anteed Lehman's own obligations, suggests that CDS are far less dangerous to the financial system than they are made out to be. Finally, efforts to blame the huge number of subprime and Alt-A mortgages in our economy on unregulated mortgage brokers must fail when it becomes clear that the dominant role in creating the demand—and supplying the funds—for these deficient loans was the federal government.

"Ideas Have Consequences: The Importance of a Narrative"

Originally published May 2010

There is substantial evidence that the cause of the financial crisis was nothing more complicated than a buildup of weak and high-risk mortgages in the U.S. financial system—mostly the result of U.S. government policy to expand homeownership.[97] Too little regulation was not a major factor. Under these circumstances, substantial changes in U.S. government housing policy—particularly with respect to Fannie Mae and Freddie Mac—would have been the most effective way to prevent a recurrence of a financial crisis. Yet the debate over financial regulation in Congress became a contest between those who want the government to have more control of the financial system and those who want it to have less. Considering the legislation that came out of both houses, the United States is well on its way to taking down the most innovative and successful financial system the world has ever known. This happened because an erroneous idea—that large, nonbank financial institutions are too "interconnected" to fail—initially adopted by the Bush administration as the rationale for the rescue of Bear Stearns, evolved into the narrative for explaining the chaos that followed Lehman's collapse. With this narrative generally accepted, the Obama administration's regulatory plan inevitably followed.

In his bestselling book *The Big Short*, Michael Lewis begins his description of the derivatives market with this quote from Leo Tolstoy: "The most difficult subjects can be explained to the most slow-witted man if he has not formed any idea of them already; but the simplest thing cannot be made clear to the

---

97. See Peter J. Wallison, "Deregulation and the Financial Crisis: Another Urban Myth," AEI *Financial Services Outlook* (October 2009), available at www.aei.org/outlook/100089; and Peter J. Wallison, "Cause and Effect: Government Policies and the Financial Crisis," *Critical Review* 21, no. 2–3 (June 2009): 365–76, available at www.aei.org/article/101071. (See pp. 255 and 116 of this book.)

most intelligent man if he is firmly persuaded that he knows already, without a shadow of doubt, what is laid before him."[98]

Although Lewis did not cite it for this purpose, Tolstoy's remark is a perfect description of the power of narrative in the modern day. Once a narrative about a public issue becomes accepted, it is virtually impossible to change; facts that support it are reported by the media, but contrary facts are ignored. So it has been with the notion that large, nonbank financial institutions like Bear Stearns, Lehman Brothers, and American International Group (AIG) cannot be allowed to fail—that is, declare ordinary bankruptcy—because their "interconnections" with other financial institutions will drag the others down. There is literally no evidence for this notion other than government statements that it is so, yet the claim—first advanced to justify the rescue of Bear Stearns—has evolved into the conceptual foundation for the regulatory regime developed by the Obama administration, passed by the House of Representatives, and now adopted in the Senate. This *Outlook* is about how this narrative was formed and how it has influenced policy even though it has no basis in fact.

Original Sin: The Rescue of Bear Stearns

The narrative's roots are entwined with the rescue of Bear Stearns, which involved a government-assisted sale of the company to JP Morgan Chase in March 2008. In recent public testimony before the Financial Crisis Inquiry Commission (FCIC), Christopher Cox, chairman of the Securities and Exchange Commission (SEC) in 2008, noted that during the week prior to its rescue, Bear—with over 10 percent capital under the Basel II standards that the SEC applied—was solvent and well capitalized.[99] Bear's top management testified in the same hearing that while the firm had lost money in the last quarter of 2007, it would have reported a profit in the first quarter of 2008 if it had not been taken over.[100] These claims need not be taken entirely at face value. It is possible that the firm's capital had been eroded by the time it was rescued on March 14, and the firm certainly would have been

---

98. Michael Lewis, *The Big Short: Inside the Doomsday Machine* (New York: W. W. Norton, 2010), ix.

99. Financial Crisis Inquiry Commission, *The Shadow Banking System—Day 1*, 111th Cong., 2d. sess., May 5, 2010, available at www.fcic.gov/hearings/05-05-2010. php (accessed May 20, 2010).

100. Ibid.

worth more as a going concern than as a bankrupt entity. It is also possible that the management's view about Bear's profitability in the first quarter was overly optimistic. The FCIC's own investigation found that Bear was legally solvent—its assets exceeded its liabilities—at the end of its first fiscal quarter in 2008 (which ended in February). But even if we discount these statements, it is unlikely that the market would have suffered a systemic breakdown if Bear Stearns had been allowed to fail. The firm clearly was not a hollow shell; its creditors would have recovered much, if not all, of their advances in the bankruptcy proceeding. What is more, most of Bear's short-term creditors had advanced their funds under repurchase, or "repo," agreements—a form of collateralized borrowing that the firm had begun to emphasize several years before because it was thought to be more stable than unsecured borrowing. The repo lenders would have been able to recover most, if not all, of their losses by selling the collateral underlying the repos.

In testimony before the FCIC, Bear's management officials said they were baffled by the creditor and counterparty run (withdrawals of funds or refusals to renew even secured financing) that the firm suffered in the week that began on March 10, 2008. The most they could offer was that the firm had simply lost the confidence of the market.[101] This explanation would not justify a rescue by the government, and indeed neither the firm's management nor Cox—speaking as a former member of Congress rather than SEC chair—thought the firm (the smallest of the big five investment banks) should have been considered too big to fail or otherwise systemically significant.

Why, then, did the government rescue Bear Stearns? The unprecedented nature of the action and its implications for moral hazard in the future certainly required a robust rationale. Federal Reserve Board of Governors minutes from March 14, 2008—just before the rescue—record the Board's agreement that "given the fragile condition of the financial markets at the time, the prominent position of Bear Stearns in those markets, and the *expected contagion* that would result from the immediate failure of Bear Stearns," the Fed should extend a loan to JP Morgan, which would eventually be passed along to Bear Stearns.[102]

---

101. Ibid.

102. Minutes of the Board of Governors of the Federal Reserve System, March 14, 2008, quoted in Greg Robb, "Bear Stearns Too Interconnected to Fail, Fed Says," MarketWatch, June 27, 2008, available at www.marketwatch.com/story/fed-believed-bear-stearns-was-too-interconnected-to-fail (accessed May 19, 2010) (emphasis added).

An idea similar to contagion—that Bear was too "interconnected" to fail—first appeared in the media in a *Wall Street Journal* article on March 17, 2008, and was loosely attributed to unnamed "government officials." According to the article, "Officials have been scrambling to come up with new tools because the old ones aren't suited for this 21st-century crisis, in which financial innovation has rendered many institutions not 'too big to fail' but '*too interconnected* to be allowed to fail suddenly.'"[103] Thereafter, the idea that Bear was too interconnected to fail was used regularly by Bush administration and Fed officials to justify their rescue,[104] and it appeared dozens of times in media stories.[105] The most complete statement of the "interconnectedness" theory was contained in Federal Reserve chairman Ben S. Bernanke's prepared testimony to the Senate Banking Committee on April 3, 2008:

> Our financial system is extremely complex and interconnected, and Bear Stearns participated extensively in a range of critical markets. The sudden failure of Bear Stearns likely would have led to a chaotic

103. Robin Sidel, Dennis K. Berman, and Kate Kelly, "J.P. Morgan Buys Bear in Fire Sale, as Fed Widens Credit to Avert Crisis," *Wall Street Journal,* March 17, 2008 (emphasis added).

104. See Federal Reserve chairman Ben S. Bernanke: "Our financial system is extremely complex and interconnected, and Bear Stearns participated extensively in a range of critical markets," and Robert Steel, undersecretary of the Treasury for domestic finance: "The failure of a firm at that time that was so connected to so many corners of our markets would have caused financial disruptions beyond Wall Street," quoted in Associated Press, "Quotes from Bear Stearns Hearing," FoxNews.com, April 3, 2008, available at www.foxnews.com/wires/2008Apr03/0,4670,Congress BearStearnsQuotes,00.html (accessed May 19, 2010). See also Michael M. Grynbaum, "Paulson Urges Americans to be Patient on the Economy," *New York Times,* July 23, 2008; "'Too Big to Fail' Is Too Expensive by Half," ChiefExecutive.net, November/ December 2009, available at www. chiefexecutive.net/ME2/dirmod.asp?sid=&nm=&type=Publishing&mod=Publications%3 A%3AArticle&mid=8F3A7027421841978F18BE895F87F791&tier=4&id=FA948EDD2F 744208935FAE67A5001184 (accessed May 19, 2010); Jeffrey E. Garten, "Yet Another Domino Falls," *Newsweek,* July 28, 2008; and Gretchen Morgenson, "Do You Have Any Reforms in Size XL?" *New York Times,* April 23, 2010.

105. See, for example, John Waggoner and David J. Lynch, "Red Flags in Bear Stearns' Collapse," *USA Today,* March 19, 2008; and Matthew Goldstein, "Bear Stearns' Big Bailout," Bloomberg Businessweek, March 14, 2008, available at www.businessweek. com/bwdaily/dnflash/content/mar2008/db20080314_993131.htm?campaign_id=rss_ daily (accessed May 19, 2010).

unwinding of positions in those markets and could have severely shaken confidence. *The company's failure could also have cast doubt on the financial positions of some of Bear Stearns' thousands of counterparties* and perhaps of companies with similar businesses.[106]

Part of this statement cannot be challenged; there is no question that financial institutions are interconnected. That is how a financial system performs its function; through these interconnections, money is transferred from a place where it is not being used efficiently to a place where it will be. The real question, however, is whether this interconnectedness is so substantial that the failure of one such institution will bring down others—whether, in Bernanke's words, Bear's failure could "have cast doubt on the financial positions of some of Bear Stearns' thousands of counterparties." If so, then its interconnectedness would have had significant implications for the financial system as a whole.

But if Bear was indeed solvent at the time—something the Fed and Treasury must have known from discussions with the SEC—it is highly implausible that its failure would have dragged down its counterparties. If a firm is solvent, all its creditors will be paid in due course. Although Bear had become illiquid when many counterparties withdrew their financing, bankruptcy is designed for firms that are solvent but illiquid; it provides temporary protection and allows a creditor panic to subside while the firm marshals its resources and makes arrangements for orderly payment. That is what Bear would have been able to do if it had been allowed to file for bankruptcy. Its rescue short-circuited that process, and thus we will never know whether Bear's filing would have brought about the systemic event that Bernanke feared by dragging down its counterparties.

What Lehman's Failure Demonstrated

However, a partial but persuasive answer to whether Bear's bankruptcy filing would have caused a systemic disruption is provided by the failure of Lehman Brothers that occurred six months later. Unlike Bear, Lehman was likely not

---

106. Senate Committee on Banking, Housing, and Urban Affairs, *Statement of Ben S. Bernanke, Chairman, Board of Governors of the Federal Reserve System,* 110th Cong., 2d sess., April 3, 2008, 3–4, available at http://banking.senate.gov/public/index. cfm?FuseAction=Files.View&FileStore_id=0a0ec016-ad61-4736-b6e3-7eb61fbc0c69 (accessed May 19, 2010) (emphasis added).

solvent, and it had certainly become illiquid by the time it filed for bankruptcy. Nevertheless, despite all the market turmoil that followed Lehman's bankruptcy filing, there was only one case of a Lehman counterparty or creditor failing *because* of Lehman's inability to meet its financial obligations. That case was the Reserve Fund, a money-market fund that held a substantial amount of Lehman's commercial paper. The Reserve Fund's losses caused it to "break the buck"—in other words, it failed to maintain a $1 per share redemption value—and triggered runs at other money-market funds where investors felt they might be at risk of a similar loss. The threat to "thousands of counterparties" that Bernanke envisioned occurring if Bear had not been rescued never materialized after Lehman filed for bankruptcy.

Even Lehman's credit default swap (CDS) obligations, and the CDSs written specifically on Lehman by others, did not cause any substantial disruption in the CDS market when Lehman collapsed. Within a month after the bankruptcy, all of the CDSs specifically written on Lehman were settled through the exchange of approximately $6 billion among hundreds of counterparties, and while Lehman had over nine hundred thousand derivatives contracts outstanding at the time it filed for bankruptcy, these did not give rise to any known insolvency among those of its counterparties that were protected by a Lehman CDS. In cases where Lehman's derivatives counterparties suffered losses, the counterparties filed appropriate claims in the Lehman bankruptcy proceeding, which are being adjudicated in the ordinary course. In other words, Lehman—a larger firm than Bear and one that had more "interconnections"—had no significant effect in dragging down its counterparties. This suggests that the rationale given for Bear's rescue—its extensive "interconnections"—was erroneous. If Lehman's interconnections did not drag down its counterparties, Bear's certainly would not have done so.

Lehman's Role in Creating the Financial Crisis

The turmoil and freeze-up in lending that followed Lehman's bankruptcy was unprecedented and frightening to all observers. However, there is a substantial likelihood that the moral hazard created by the rescue of Bear was the reason Lehman's bankruptcy precipitated a crisis. A review of the CDS spreads on Lehman shows that they moved within a relatively narrow range as Lehman's condition continued to weaken through the summer and into the fall of 2008.

It was not until just before the fateful weekend of September 13–14, 2008, that the spreads blew out, indicating that despite Lehman's deteriorating condition, those who were seeking to protect themselves against Lehman's failure were finding ready counterparties in the CDS market. This suggests strongly that the market was expecting a rescue until the very last minute, which would be entirely rational; no sensible person could have imagined that the U.S. government would rescue Bear but not Lehman. Lehman was much larger, more interconnected, and a major player in the CDS market—one of the markets where interconnections were supposed to be most troublesome. If, as government officials were arguing, Bear's interconnections were really the basis for Bear's rescue, it would have been completely irresponsible for officials to have allowed Lehman to fail. Indeed, it would not be surprising to learn that the managers of the Reserve Fund decided to hold the fund's Lehman commercial paper because they expected that Lehman would also be rescued and they could then avoid a loss on the paper's reduced value. This conclusion would be consistent with the CDS market's judgment about the likelihood of a government rescue for Lehman. Thus, when Lehman filed for bankruptcy, the markets were shocked. The result—hoarding cash and freezing lending—was the rational response to a sudden realization that the world's governments were not going to rescue all large firms. Now it was necessary to know the financial condition of all counterparties and to hold cash in case depositors and other funding sources were to withdraw funds or cut off lending. This produced the freeze-up in lending that most people now regard as the financial crisis.

In addition, the rescue of Bear probably made it more difficult to find a buyer for Lehman. After Bear, it was rational for Lehman's management to expect a rescue, and that would have reduced their interest in selling the firm or diluting the stockholders; it would also have kept the firm's selling price higher than it might otherwise have been. Potential buyers, like the Korean Development Bank or Barclays Bank, would likely have expected some U.S. government support, just as JP Morgan Chase had received in buying Bear. When this was not offered, it is likely that they backed away from the acquisition to put pressure on U.S. officials to come forward with financial assistance. Like other market participants, it was probably difficult for potential acquirers to believe that the U.S. government would have rescued Bear because it was supposedly too interconnected with others in the financial system, but would be willing to allow Lehman to fail.

These are all the likely consequences of the moral hazard created by the rescue of Bear, which increasingly—with the passage of time—seems to be the central policy error in the U.S. government's response to the financial-market weakness that was coming to light in early 2008. Thus, the rescue of Bear—which was probably unnecessary in the first place—reduced Lehman's incentive to want or to find a buyer, reduced the incentives of potential acquirers to make offers for Lehman without government support, and caused a catastrophic freeze-up in the market when it became clear that the U.S. government would not carry out with Lehman the logical implications of its claim that Bear was too interconnected to be allowed to fail.

The Bear Rescue Narrative Evolves

Nevertheless, by the time Lehman filed its bankruptcy petition in the fall of 2008, the idea that Bear had to be rescued because of its "interconnectedness" was the unquestioned explanation for the actions of the Treasury and Fed, regularly used by members of the Bush administration and repeated in virtually every media account of the Bear rescue.[107] Given this acceptance, and recalling the Tolstoy observation, it is not surprising that the turmoil following Lehman's bankruptcy was not examined for what it showed about the rescue of Bear; nor was Bear's rescue examined for what it likely contributed to the turmoil that occurred after Lehman's collapse. Instead, the post-Lehman chaos was interpreted as confirmation that Lehman *as well as* Bear should have been rescued. This is characteristic of narratives. Once they are established, subsequent events that are thought to confirm the narrative are reported in the media, while those that challenge the narrative are ignored or explained away. Thus, one commentator saw interconnectedness as the cause of the post-Lehman chaos even though it was largely imaginary:

---

107. See, for example, Mark Gongloff, "Street's Fate Is in Hands of Uncle Sam," *Wall Street Journal,* September 18, 2008; Stephen Labaton, "Trying to Rein in 'Too Big to Fail' Institutions," *New York Times,* October 26, 2009; Caroline Baum, "Ask Bear Stearns Stockholders about Moral Hazard," Bloomberg.com, March 18, 2008, available at www.sddt.com/Search/article.cfm?SourceCode=20080318fm (accessed May 19, 2010); and Irwin Stelzer, "Banking Crisis: It's Déjà Vu All Over Again," *Sunday Times* (London), March 23, 2008.

For many, the lesson of Lehman Brothers is that a financial firm had to fail in order to demonstrate how interconnected the entire financial system was, often at levels that even top U.S. market players and government officials could not have foreseen. . . . However painful Lehman's financial and economy effects was on the market [sic] experts said the bankruptcy provided the political will necessary to begin serious discussions about the country's need for a financial super regulator.[108]

Through interpretations like this, the explanation for why Bear was rescued evolved into a conclusion with far greater policy significance; under the new interpretation of Lehman, all large financial firms—because of their purported interconnectedness—were inherently a danger to financial-system stability. This provided a rationale for extensive government regulation, since regulation was believed (again, without much evidence) to be effective in reducing the likelihood of a financial institution's failure and thus the chances of another financial crisis. Writing in the *Journal of Credit Risk,* one commentator made this connection explicit: "This crisis—and the cases of firms like Lehman Brothers and AIG has made clear that certain large, interconnected firms and markets need to be under a more consistent and more conservative regulatory regime. It is not enough to address the potential insolvency of individual institutions—we must also ensure the stability of the system itself."[109]

That is exactly the approach the Obama administration adopted upon taking office. Through use of the interconnectedness idea, it became possible for the administration to propose a comprehensive system of regulation for the largest nonbank financial firms, going far beyond any regulatory regime ever envisioned in the past. This extensive regulation was justified by arguing that if one of these large firms were to fail it could—like Lehman—cause instability in the financial system, just as Bernanke had argued that the failure of Bear Stearns could have undermined the financial condition of "thousands" of its counterparties. The fact that this never occurred when Lehman failed was ignored. For

---

108. Ken Sweet, "Lehman's Harsh Lesson to the Global Economy," FoxBusiness.com, September 14, 2009, available at www.foxbusiness.com/story/markets/industries/finance/lehmans-harsh-lesson-global-economy (accessed May 19, 2010).

109. Jeffrey Rosenberg, "Toward a Clear Understanding of the Systemic Risks of Large Institutions," *Journal of Credit Risk* 5, no. 2 (Summer 2009).

example, in a statement on September 15, 2009, the anniversary of Lehman's bankruptcy, President Barack Obama stated:

> While holding the Federal Reserve fully accountable for regulation of the largest, most interconnected firms . . . we'll also require these financial firms to meet stronger capital and liquidity requirements and observe greater constraints on their risky behavior. That's one of the lessons of the past year. The only way to avoid a crisis of this magnitude is to ensure that large firms can't take risks *that threaten our entire financial system,* and to make sure they have the resources to weather even the worst of economic storms.[110]

This statement says it all: interconnected financial firms require regulation or they will, by taking risks, bring down the financial system again. Similar declarations—implicating interconnectedness in the financial crisis—were made in the white paper the administration issued in June 2009 as a prelude to the introduction of its regulatory legislation,[111] and thereafter by Treasury Secretary Timothy F. Geithner,[112] presidential adviser Paul Volcker,[113] and many others in the administration and Congress.[114] The beauty of it was that they could make these statements without fear of contradiction because the underlying idea— that large firms were so interconnected that the failure of one would bring down others—had now become not only an explanation for the rescue of Bear, but

---

110. Barack Obama, "Text of Obama's Speech on Financial Reform," *New York Times,* September 15, 2009 (emphasis added).

111. The white paper says, "All large, interconnected firms whose failure could threaten the stability of the system should be subject to consolidated supervision by the Federal Reserve regardless of whether they own an insured depository institution." See U.S. Department of the Treasury, *Financial Regulatory Reform: A New Foundation; Rebuilding Financial Supervision and Regulation,* 111th Cong., 1st sess. (Washington, DC, June 17, 2009), 6, available at www.financialstability.gov/docs/regs/FinalReport_web.pdf (accessed May 19, 2010).

112. FinancialStability.gov, "Treasury Secretary Tim Geithner Written Testimony House Financial Services Committee Hearing," news release, March 24, 2009, available at www.financialstability.gov/ latest/tg67.html (accessed May 19, 2010).

113. Paul Volcker, "How to Reform Our Financial System," *New York Times,* January 30, 2010.

114. Benton Ives, "Kanjorski Unveils Proposal to Break Up Risky Firms," *Congressional Quarterly Today,* November 18, 2009.

also, because of the chaos that followed Lehman's bankruptcy, the accepted narrative for what caused the financial crisis itself.

As Tolstoy observed, even intelligent people, once they have accepted an idea, cannot be persuaded to reexamine their position. That is the power of a narrative.

"Missing the Point:
Lessons from *The Big Short*"

Originally published June 2010

Although it has a valuable endorsement from an important Democratic senator, Michael Lewis's best-selling book *The Big Short* raises questions about the
validity of the ideas underpinning the financial regulation legislation Congress
is now considering.

During the first week of June, the press reported that Senator Dick Durbin
(D-Ill.) had interrupted a speech on the Senate floor to recommend a book to
his colleagues. That book is Michael Lewis's *The Big Short*,[115] which documents
some of the events on Wall Street leading up to the financial collapse of 2008.
It is a bit puzzling that Durbin chose to single out this book, which describes
how several neophyte money managers used credit default swaps (CDSs) to
make substantial profits by speculating against the value of collateralized debt
obligations (CDOs) and mortgage-backed securities (MBS) based on subprime
mortgages. Given that Durbin endorsed it, one might suppose that the book supports the narrative that underlies the financial regulatory legislation now before
the House and Senate: that CDSs and Wall Street greed were major causes of
the financial crisis. But the events that Lewis documents in *The Big Short* actually contradict the idea that Wall Street greed caused the financial crisis and
cast doubt on whether restrictions on the use of CDSs—a major element of the
Democratic plan for regulating the financial industry—would be good policy.

Credit Default Swaps. CDSs are not as mysterious as they seem and can most
easily be understood as a form of credit insurance.[116] The buyer of a CDS pur-

---

115. Michael Lewis, *The Big Short: Inside the Doomsday Machine* (New York:
W. W. Norton, 2010).

116. Although they can be understood as insurance, CDSs are not true insurance and
are not regulated as such. Insurance is an actuarial system in which protection is written
on a large pool of insured parties. It is not known in advance which of the insured parties

chases something like insurance coverage (called protection) against a loss he will suffer if a particular company (known as the reference entity) defaults on an obligation.[117] For this protection, the buyer pays an annual premium to the seller of protection who, in turn, promises to reimburse the buyer in a fixed amount (the "notional amount") if the reference entity defaults. This kind of contract is not new; for many years, banks have been writing contracts like this, called standby letters of credit, which often back municipal or other securities. For purposes of this discussion, the difference between CDSs and bank letters of credit is that CDSs are bought and sold in an over-the-counter market, in which the price of the coverage fluctuates with the market's assessment of the risk of default associated with the reference entity, while bank letters of credit are negotiated between the bank and the issuer, without reference to a prevailing market assessment about the issuer's credit. In a typical CDS transaction, the holder of, say, a $10 million IBM bond may want to be protected against IBM's default. To gain this protection, he buys a CDS from a dealer, usually a bank or other financial institution, in which he agrees to pay an annual premium for a predetermined period. The dealer, in turn, will usually attempt to hedge the obligation it has assumed by purchasing an offsetting obligation from another party, perhaps another dealer or a third party hoping to earn the premium by taking on this exposure. Banks and other financial institutions use CDSs as risk-management tools to reduce concentration in their portfolios and to take on risk that adds to their diversification. An important element of the CDS market is that participants can buy CDS coverage on the same IBM bond even if they do not actually own the bond. In effect, this transaction—called a "naked swap"—is roughly equivalent to a short sale in an equity market. They are speculating that IBM will default, or that its credit will weaken so that the short position becomes

---

will suffer a loss, and when a loss occurs the insured party is reimbursed only for the amount of the loss. A CDS is a contract that provides protection against a specific entity's default on its credit obligations; in the event of a default, the protected party receives a stated value independent of its actual loss.

117. For a more complete description of CDSs and related issues, see Peter J. Wallison, "Everything You Wanted to Know about Credit Default Swaps—but Weren't Told," AEI *Financial Services Outlook* (December 2008), available at www.aei.org/outlook/29158; and Peter J. Wallison, "Unnecessary Intervention: The Administration's Effort to Regulate Credit Default Swaps," AEI *Financial Services Outlook* (August 2009), available at www.aei.org/outlook/100065. (See pp. 223 and 409 of this book.)

more valuable. Naked swaps are a major feature of the transactions described in *The Big Short.*

Collateralized Debt Obligations. CDOs are also not complicated to understand, but they can be difficult to value. In a CDO, pools of various kinds of debts— auto loans, boat loans, retail-credit loans of various kinds, and mortgages—are aggregated and used to provide a stream of cash payments to the holders of securities backed by the pool. The CDOs that are the subject of *The Big Short* were mostly composed of subprime mortgages. The securities that are backed by the pool of loans have different priorities—called tranches—for receiving the cash that is paid into the pool. The group with the highest priority usually gets all the cash before any of the lower tranches are paid anything. Because of this priority, credit-rating agencies generally rate the top tranches AAA. Lower tranches, which are in effect subordinated, are rated AA, A, BBB, and so on. Because they have prior rights to the cash received by the pool, the AAA and other higher tranches take less risk than the others and are paid a lower return. The lower tranches, correspondingly, take more risk and receive a higher return. The CDOs that are the subject of *The Big Short* largely consisted of subprime mortgages, but with an additional twist; many of them were composed of the lower tranches—the BBB tranches—of MBS assembled previously by their Wall Street sponsors. The fact that cash receipts first have to reach the BBB tranches in the prior MBS makes the valuation of the CDO very complex.

Most of *The Big Short* focuses on several newly minted money managers who thought early in 2005 that in the relatively near future large losses would occur in the CDOs based on subprime mortgages and that they could profit from these defaults by purchasing CDS protection. This would be similar to believing that IBM will suffer losses and selling IBM stock short. The opportunity for profit existed because most people on Wall Street at the time seemed to believe a number of things that turned out to be wrong: (1) that the rating agencies' models accurately reflected the risks of the MBS and CDOs, (2) that housing prices never fall on a national basis (and thus that there was little correlation between housing prices in different regions), and (3) that if the housing bubble began to deflate the losses would not exceed historic levels. Because of these assumptions, the premiums required to purchase CDSs on the AAA and other top tranches of CDOs were extremely low—only twenty basis points (0.2 percent, or one-fifth of a penny) for each dollar of coverage on the AAA tranches of a CDO. Thus, in an extreme example, where the cost of a CDS is twenty basis points, an annual premium of $100,000 will enable the buyer of the CDS to obtain protection against the failure of the AAA tranch of a CDO with a value (before any default) of $50 million—a payoff of five hundred to one if a default occurs.

Persuading Wall Street That AAA CDOs Would Fail Was a Tough Sell

We now know that all of the assumptions of most investors and Wall Street experts turned out to be wrong, but the interesting thing about the Lewis book is how difficult it was to get Wall Street traders and investors to abandon their initial beliefs about subprime loans and CDOs. The money managers Lewis follows throughout the book—the people who saw the possibilities of failure even in the topmost tranches of CDOs—tried to persuade others to make the same bets or at least to understand why the traders and others continued to dismiss the possibility that a major mortgage meltdown could happen. In quoting the money managers with whom he talks, Lewis notes their amazement that none of the people they spoke to could even present rational counterarguments to the proposition that CDO defaults were inevitable: "Nobody we talked to," said one of the money managers, "had any credible reason to think this [the failure of subprime CDOs] was going to become a big problem. . . . No one was really thinking about it."[118] As Lewis notes, "The catastrophe was foreseeable, yet only a handful noticed."[119]

Here we come, then, to the first lesson of *The Big Short:* the inconsistency between events recounted in the book and the narrative about the financial crisis that powered the regulatory legislation that Congress is considering. Among many in Congress, it is widely held that the financial crisis was caused by reckless Wall Street players selling low-quality financial products like CDOs, despite knowing that these securities were bound to default and cause losses to their customers. As Senator Carl Levin (D-Mich.) described the results of his committee's investigation: "[W]e learned that . . . Goldman Sachs repeatedly put its own interests and profits ahead of its clients . . . and when the system finally collapsed under the weight of those toxic mortgages, Goldman profited from

---

118. Michael Lewis, *The Big Short: Inside the Doomsday Machine,* 147.
119. Ibid., 105.

the collapse."[120] This and statements like it promoted the idea that Wall Street financial institutions were at least reckless, and probably worse, in selling CDOs and MBS based on subprime mortgages.

But the real story, as Lewis tells it, is virtually the opposite. Rather than being greedy and aware of the poor quality of the CDOs they were selling, the traders and their managers on Wall Street consistently resisted the idea that it would be profitable to bet against these instruments, even though the returns from such a bet could be astoundingly high. In other words, far from being greedy and dishonest, these traders would be more easily characterized as dumb or deluded. Not only were they unwilling to bet against the subprime-mortgage market through CDSs when the profit possibilities were enormous, but they also continued to hold onto the very assets that others were telling them were almost certain to default when the housing bubble came to an end. As Lewis describes it, until actual losses were staring them in the face in late 2007 and early 2008, they even resisted the idea that they should hedge against the subprime-mortgage risks in their own portfolios. Only when the scale of defaults on the CDOs became obvious did the major institutions, in an attempt to reduce their losses, suddenly begin to buy the CDS protection that they had previously spurned.

The Wall Street crowd is not the only group that acted this way. Lewis recounts the difficulties the money managers faced for having speculated against the subprime market by investing in what ultimately became highly profitable CDSs. Many of these positions had been purchased in 2005, when the housing market was still strong and CDSs were very cheap, but the subprime losses did not begin to show up until late 2007. In the meantime, the investors in these funds grew restless; they saw money being paid out in premiums but did not see any gains. They began to clamor for their investments back, which would have required the sale of the CDSs well before the subprime mortgages lost value and the CDS speculations became valuable.

This is fully consistent with testimony given before the Financial Crisis Inquiry Commission, of which I am a member. The chief executive officers of the major banks, senior officials of Citigroup who were responsible for the bank's mortgage business and risk management, the top officers of Fannie Mae, the

---

120. Senator Carl Levin, "Statement of Sen. Carl Levin, D-Mich., on Senate Passage of the Restoring American Financial Stability Act of 2010," news release, May 20, 2010, available at http://levin.senate.gov/newsroom/release.cfm?id=325147 (accessed June 28, 2010).

ratings specialists at Moody's, and even Warren Buffett all admitted that they could not imagine losses on subprime mortgages on the scale reached in 2007 and 2008. Even the most informed financial regulators seemed unaware of the potential losses right in front of them. As late as May 17, 2007, Federal Reserve chairman Ben Bernanke reinforced the beliefs of all those who thought the possibility of a major meltdown in the mortgage market was overblown. "Given the fundamental factors in place that should support the demand for housing," he said, "we believe the effect of the troubles in the subprime sector or the broader housing market will be limited, and we do not expect significant spillovers from the subprime market to the rest of the economy or to the financial system."[121]

Although it may be unsatisfying to blame the financial crisis on something as mundane as human pigheadedness, that should be the conclusion of any careful reader of The Big Short. The book certainly does not validate the views of those in Congress and elsewhere who place the blame on "Wall Street greed."

Asset Bubbles and Public Policy

Nevertheless, there is a major public policy issue implicit in The Big Short, and it is probably not one that Durbin or other supporters of the new legislation intended to endorse. Bubbles have always been a feature of economies and financial systems, including the huge housing bubble that drove and was driven by the origination and sale of subprime mortgages between 1997 and 2007. As Carmen M. Reinhart and Kenneth S. Rogoff outline in their recent, widely acclaimed work, This Time Is Different, financial and other bubbles are caused by wishful thinking and delusion, features of human nature.[122] When prices for assets are rising, they tend to feed on themselves. Soon, the true value of an asset—what can be earned from its possession—is subordinated to the fact that it can be sold for more in the future. In the stock market, this is called "the greater fool theory": optimists believe there will always be a greater fool than themselves to buy the stock they bought in the hope that, against all reason, its price would continue to rise.

---

121. Ben S. Bernanke (speech, Federal Reserve Bank of Chicago's Forty-third Annual Conference on Bank Structure and Competition, Chicago, Illinois, May 17, 2007).

122. Carmen M. Reinhart and Kenneth S. Rogoff, This Time Is Different: Eight Centuries of Financial Folly (Princeton, NJ: Princeton University Press, 2009).

As the data in Reinhart and Rogoff's book imply, there are very few defenses against this market behavior. They cite hundreds of events over the past eight hundred years involving financial assets of all kinds. Nonfinancial assets—tulip bulbs in Holland in the 1600s are the classic case—are also subject to bubbles and crashes. In the classic work *Manias, Panics, and Crashes,* Charles Kindleberger and Robert Aliber attempt to find and describe the common elements in these events, including how and why they begin, develop, and ultimately crash.[123] In reality, there are only two viable defenses against bubbles: effective government regulation and short selling. Effective government regulation is easy to conceptualize but difficult to implement. In theory, a government agency could decide that a bubble is developing and use its regulatory authority to reduce or deflate it. In practice, it is not easy to recognize bubbles, as Bernanke's 2007 comment on the subprime bubble demonstrates; even if recognized, regulators may be reluctant to act against them.

The current financial crisis is a case in point. The subprime and other weak mortgages that were at the heart of the crash in housing and mortgage values enabled large numbers of people to buy homes who previously had not had access to housing credit. The infusion of government funds into this market through Fannie Mae, Freddie Mac, and other government housing programs drove a ten-year housing bubble from 1997 to 2007 that grew to unprecedented size. Even if banking regulators recognized that a bubble was developing—a point that is still unclear—they would have been powerless to stop it. Attempts to do so would have met with universal disapproval in a Congress that, along with the Bush administration, was delighted with the growth in homeownership that resulted from these programs. (For the thirty years between 1964 and 1994, homeownership in the United States remained at about 64 percent, but by the time the bubble burst in 2007, the homeownership rate had hit a record high of over 69 percent.) Whether it was the same blindness to reality that afflicted Wall Street, or timidity in the face of congressional opposition, U.S. regulators did not act to arrest the largest housing bubble in U.S. history, and the outcome was a worldwide financial crisis.

Although regulators cannot be relied upon to act against bubbles, at least one group—short sellers—has a real financial incentive to do so. Short sellers

---

123. Charles Kindleberger and Robert Aliber, *Manias, Panics, and Crashes: A History of Financial Crises,* 5th ed. (Hoboken, NJ: Wiley, 2005).

are those pessimistic folks who see opportunities in others' wishful thinking. In the equity markets, they borrow shares and sell them, hoping to reap a profit when share prices decline; if that happens, they buy the shares at the lower price, return the borrowed shares, and pocket the difference. They are active daily in the stock market but always under fire from those—especially corporate managements—who are both sensitive to criticism about the true value of their firm's shares and beneficiaries of rising share values. Whatever one thinks of short selling, there can be no question that it adds to selling pressure and thus tends to suppress the optimism that leads to the development of bubbles. In response to any concern about the growth of bubbles, short selling should be encouraged in all markets, not hindered.

The Big Short and the Importance of Short Selling

Herein lies another lesson of *The Big Short*. The book focuses on a group of short sellers in a debt market. Lewis does not point this out, but he is describing a new phenomenon. Until CDSs became available, it was not possible to sell short—to speculate against the prices of debt securities—in a debt market. In general, debt markets are too thin (that is, they do not have enough buyers and sellers) and buying and selling a debt security is too costly to permit active short selling. The advent of CDSs, which permit the risk of a debt exposure to be transferred apart from the debt security itself, changed those limitations. In the CDS market, a participant can easily sell short by contacting a market maker or dealer and negotiating a price for protection against the default of any publicly available security. This is possible—as it is in the equity markets through short selling—even if the buyer does not own the security he is speculating against and is not actually exposed to the risk. The money managers in *The Big Short* were, in effect, selling short through naked swaps by purchasing protection against defaults on various tranches of CDOs.

A CDS-based naked swap in a debt market has the same function and effect as a short sale of a stock in an equity market. In each case, it adds to the selling pressure on a security and—most importantly—supplies new information that aids in what is called price discovery. The most important function of any market is price discovery. Without markets, we would have no way of placing a value on a tangible or intangible asset. To decide, for example, that a barrel of oil is worth $50 or $80 today requires knowledge about its use, its transportation costs, its quality, its likely future availability, and dozens of other elements. These are all composed into a single price by supply and demand at a given moment in time. The more efficiently markets do this—that is, the more opinions about value that are included in a given offer to buy or to sell—the better the price discovery. In effect, greater liquidity reduces the spread between bid and asked prices. As the Squam Lake Working Group on Financial Regulation—a group of leading academic scholars in finance—stated in a recent report, "Buying and selling credit default swaps without the underlying bond is like buying and selling equity or index options without the underlying security. The advantages of these activities are well understood. Eliminating this form of speculation would make CDS markets less liquid, increasing the cost of trading and making CDS rate quotes a less reliable source of information about the prospects of named borrowers."[124]

In the CDS market, as in any market, the presence of as many buyers and sellers as possible improves the price of the credit protection that is purchased. For example, the fact that someone wants to buy protection against the default of IBM means that the dealer must go into the market and find a counterparty willing to take that exposure. The price (the premium) at which the CDS contract is written communicates information about the confidence that the market has in IBM. If many buyers suddenly appear in the market looking to buy CDS protection on IBM, supply and demand alone—apart from other factors, including news about IBM—will cause the premium to rise. The opposite is also true; the fact that many market participants are offering to sell protection on IBM will cause the premium—known as the spread—to fall.

The ability to speculate against the value of subprime MBS and CDOs in the CDS market played a major role in *The Big Short*. The main individuals whom Lewis follows in the book made enormous profits by purchasing CDSs—in the form of naked swaps—as protection against the losses they thought would occur when the bubble deflated. Lewis describes how easy this was. In some cases, the cost of protection was considerably less than 1 percent, implying that market makers thought the likelihood of losses on these securities was substantially less than one in one hundred. Of course, this seems ridiculous now, but that is the

---

124. Squam Lake Working Group on Financial Regulation, "Credit Default Swaps, Clearinghouses, and Exchanges" (working paper, Council on Foreign Relations, Center for Geoeconomic Studies, Washington, DC, July 2009), available at www.cfr.org/publication/19756/credit_default_swaps_clearinghouses_and_exchanges.html (accessed June 22, 2010).

nature of bubbles. When a bubble is developing, the vast majority of people believe that—as Reinhart and Rogoff put it—this time is different. There are always reasons prices, although inflated, do not seem out of line. Some participants in a bubble know it is going to deflate at some point, but they believe they can get out before this occurs. Others may believe the bubble is based on fundamentals and thus is not a bubble at all.

How to Defeat Bubbles

Given these human tendencies, the following policy question remains: how can we best protect against the growth of bubbles? Bubbles are harmful and destructive. When they deflate, they cause arbitrary losses and disrupt the economy, although few do the enormous harm of the mortgage meltdown of 2007 and 2008. Clearly, regulation has not worked to prevent bubbles, and there is good reason to believe it never will. The Fed had the authority to raise margin requirements on stocks during the dot-com bubble in the late 1990s and the authority to clamp down on subprime lending during the 2000s, but it did not act in either case. Perhaps the reasons for inaction were conceptual (like so many other market observers, the Fed simply did not recognize that a bubble was developing) or political (the Fed did not want to rile Congress by clamping down on markets in which constituents were prospering), but either way, actions that could have prevented those bubbles were not taken. The regulatory legislation now before Congress would set up a systemic risk council made up of the principal financial regulators and headed by the secretary of the Treasury. The purpose of the council would be to identify the bubbles as they are developing and to take the necessary action to deflate them or reduce their rate of growth. This might or might not work, but based on the track record of regulators in the past, this new plan for regulation does not seem promising.

The Big Short, however, points the way to a more effective system for combating bubbles. Future credit bubbles can be kept in check—or at least reduced in size before they collapse and cause major losses—if individuals and institutions are able to go short in the credit markets through the use of CDSs. For this to work, however, naked swaps would have to be permitted, even encouraged. Ordinary selling by those who already hold a particular debt security or are seeking only to hedge would not produce enough liquidity in a debt market to affect the price of protection substantially. Bid and ask spreads would remain wide, and the market would lack price discovery and would not give efficient signals about the credit quality of particular companies. Because neither party must actually own the debt security in a naked swap transaction, there is no necessary limit on the amount of liquidity and trading activity that could occur. Some traders will be speculating that the market's estimate of a company's risk is too great (they will sell CDS protection), while others will be speculating that it is not great enough (they will buy CDS protection). Naked swaps—and naked swaps alone—can make the CDS market efficient, liquid, and capable of producing credible market-based assessments of credit quality. By using naked swaps, the money managers in *The Big Short* demonstrated that there is financial opportunity in speculating against bubbles in debt markets, just as there is in selling short in equity markets. Unfortunately, too few individuals were willing to bet against the bubble in the years from 2005 to 2007, and when they finally began to recognize the losses that were occurring, they were too late to prevent the meltdown that caused the financial crisis.

Largely because of a limited understanding of the functions of markets, naked CDSs are under attack in both Europe[125] and the United States.[126] Many proposing to ban or limit naked CDSs claim that this activity is simply gambling, even though the benefits of short selling in equity markets—an analogous activity—are well understood. Beyond improvements in price discovery, naked swaps—if given the latitude to flourish—can offer significant protection against the development of future bubbles. As Professor René Stulz observes, short sales and naked CDSs are "critical to create conditions that make it more difficult for bubbles to emerge. . . . Investors help [bring] prices back into line with fundamentals through their speculation. So rather than forbid or restrain short-sales and naked CDS positions we should instead make them easier and less expensive. Derivatives that allow individuals to hedge risks that matter to them in their

---

125. Ben Moshinsky, "Emergency Bans on Naked CDS Trades Considered by EU," Bloomberg.com, June 14, 2010, available at www.bloomberg.com/news/2010-06-14/naked-credit-default-swap-trades-should-be-banned-eu-lawmaker-report-says.html (accessed June 22, 2010).

126. Lynn A. Stout, "Regulate OTC Derivatives by Deregulating Them," *Regulation* (Fall 2009): 30, available at www.cato.org/pubs/regulation/regv32n3/v32n3-1.pdf (accessed June 22, 2010).

daily life have to be encouraged, . . . [as should] derivatives that allow investors to take bets against what they think is a bubble."[127]

Fortunately, the legislation now in the House and Senate does not contain overt restrictions on naked CDSs. However, the legislation would place significant burdens on those who might function as buyers or sellers of protection in the CDS market and, thus, on those who might be willing to sell short in the midst of a bubble by purchasing protection against losses when the bubble deflates. For example, the legislation defines a "major swap participant" as one who maintains a "substantial position" in swaps, creates "substantial counterparty exposure," or is "highly leveraged." Major swap participants are ultimately going to be defined by regulations of the Commodity Futures Trading Commission (CFTC) and the Securities and Exchange Commission (SEC). Major swap participants are required to have particular capital levels and provide margin (collateral) for trades. What these terms will eventually mean will also be determined by the SEC and CFTC. Given the suspicions in Congress about CDS activity, it is likely that the regulations will impose heavy costs on the market participants, such as hedge funds, that are most likely to act as short sellers. This would encourage, not prevent, the growth of bubbles in the future. As Stulz notes, "In terms of market regulations, the focus should be on helping markets do their job rather than limiting their scope."[128]

Although regulations that severely restrict CDS activity would be consistent with the views of the senators and representatives who designed the regulatory legislation now under consideration, such regulations ignore the policy lesson implicit in The Big Short—that to reduce or prevent bubbles, we need more, not fewer, market participants willing to take positions contrary to the prevailing views of the majority. Before voting to impose these restrictions, it would be a good idea for Senators Durbin and Levin and their House and Senate colleagues to read The Big Short.

---

127. René Stulz, "What Should We Do about Bubbles?" Harvard Business Review blog Finance: The Way Forward, June 8, 2010, available at http://blogs.hbr.org/finance-the-way-forward/2010/06/what-should-we-do-about-asset.html (accessed June 28, 2010) (emphasis added).

128. Ibid.

"Slaughter of the Innocents: Who Was Taking the Risks That Caused the Financial Crisis?"

Originally published October–November 2010

What caused the financial crisis? Even though the Dodd-Frank Act (DFA) has been signed into law, this is still an important question. If we do not attribute the crisis to the right cause, we could well stumble into another crisis in the future; and if the DFA was directed at the wrong cause, we should consider its repeal. A Brookings Institution paper issued in late 2009 develops an interesting and plausible idea: the "great moderation"—the quiet period of almost continuous growth between 1982 and 2007—caused investors, managers, and regulators to believe that we had come to understand how the economy worked and how to tame the business cycle. This mistaken view in turn caused a decline in the normal aversion to risk, creating a housing bubble and the financial crisis. This is a compelling narrative and accounts for much of the risk-taking that was observed in the period leading up to the crisis, but in the end it is no more than an interesting theory. The reality is that, in pursuit of a social policy to increase homeownership, the U.S. government became a willing buyer of an unprecedented number of subprime and other high-risk mortgages. This created a housing bubble of unprecedented size and duration, but only the taxpayers were taking the risks necessary to create this financial disaster.

Last November, two highly respected Brookings Institution scholars, Martin Neil Baily and Douglas J. Elliott, published a paper entitled "Telling the Narrative of the Financial Crisis: Not Just a Housing Bubble."[129] It is an important paper for two reasons. First, it recognizes that a narrative—a story that explains

---

129. Douglas J. Elliott and Martin Neil Baily, "Telling the Narrative of the Financial Crisis: Not Just a Housing Bubble," Brookings Institution, November 23, 2009, available at www.brookings.edu/papers/2009/1123_narrative_elliott_baily.aspx (accessed October 27, 2010).

an event—influences the legislation or other public policy actions that follow. Second, as implied by the title of their paper, Baily and Elliott developed their own narrative for what caused the financial crisis, and they use it to argue that the crisis was not caused by government housing policies.[130] This *Outlook* considers whether the Baily-Elliott narrative is a better explanation of the financial crisis than the housing policies of the U.S. government.

Three Narratives

Writing in 2009, before the enactment of the DFA, Baily and Elliott began their essay by recognizing the importance of narratives. "Major crises," they note, "such as the recent financial crisis, usually end up being understood by the public in terms of some simple narrative, which then heavily influences the choices politicians make. We believe there are three major story lines still vying for acceptance by the public and that whichever one comes to dominate could strongly affect public policy."[131] They observe in particular that "one of the earliest theories of the Great Depression was that it sprang from the crash on Wall Street, which came to be associated with financial manipulation by bankers and rich speculators. This created much of the impetus for the separation of commercial and investment banking and the creation of the Securities and Exchange Commission and associated laws to protect investors." These words are a reminder, not only of the importance of narratives in shaping policy responses, but also that certain impulses and ideas are carried forward over generations and resurface when those who have accepted them find the right opportunity.

Baily and Elliott identify three distinct narratives that have been used to explain the financial crisis. The first is the view that government housing policies caused the crisis "by inflating a housing bubble and mismanaging the resulting

---

130. See, for example, Peter J. Wallison, "Deregulation and the Financial Crisis: Another Urban Myth," AEI *Financial Services Outlook* (October 2009), available at www.aei.org/outlook/100089; Peter J. Wallison, "The Dodd-Frank Act: Creative Destruction, Destroyed," AEI *Financial Services Outlook* (July–August 2010), available at www.aei.org/outlook/100983; and Peter J. Wallison, "Going Cold Turkey: Three Ways to End Fannie and Freddie without Slicing Up the Taxpayers," AEI *Financial Services Outlook* (September 2010), available at www.aei.org/outlook/100993. (See pp. 255, 439, and 147 in this book.)

131. Douglas J. Elliott and Martin Neil Baily, "Telling the Narrative of the Financial Crisis: Not Just a Housing Bubble," 1.

risks and problems, especially in regard to Fannie Mae and Freddie Mac. This narrative is popular among conservatives, particularly since it argues for a scaling back of government interventions in the economy and suggests less regulation, not more."[132]

The second narrative is that "Wall Street created the crisis by reckless behavior, greed, and arrogant belief in its own ability to understand and manage excessively complex investments. . . . This narrative is popular with the left, but is accepted much more widely than that, including by a broad populist sentiment that sees large banks and large corporations as at the root of many of the country's economic problems. Many in the media have also adopted this position. . . . The housing part of the crisis is viewed as principally resulting from financiers pushing naïve consumers into taking on mortgages bigger than they could handle and which were structured to hide large fees and interest rates that would jump after a few years."[133] This narrative, one might add, is easily recognizable as a lineal descendant of the ideas that motivated the New Deal.

The third narrative, and the one Baily and Elliott endorse, is that "the crisis was a very broad-based event with a wide range of people and institutions bearing responsibility, including many outside the United States. . . . Wall Street financial institutions failed to put in place or enforce the sound risk management processes and restraints that were needed . . . [and] government regulators did not adequately oversee these institutions, including, importantly, Fannie Mae and Freddie Mac. . . . Some of the federal government's actions to encourage home ownership also overshot and provided incentives for reckless behavior."[134]

The DFA, adopted after the Baily-Elliott paper was published, demonstrates that they were correct about the importance of narratives. Congress enacted and the president signed legislation that rather faithfully reflected a combination of narratives 2 and 3. Anyone who followed the debate that preceded the enactment of the DFA saw Congress directly responding to elements of both narratives. The Consumer Financial Protection Bureau was certainly written into the act because the Democrats who controlled the process believed—or said they did—that "naïve consumers" were duped into buying homes they could not afford to create fees for the mortgage originators and the "financiers" (this

---

132. Ibid., 2.
133. Ibid., 3.
134. Ibid., 4.

closely follows narrative 2). This is clearly the modern analogue of the New Deal–era view that the Great Depression was caused by financial manipulation and the abuse of investors. Similarly, the stringent regulation and supervision prescribed by the DFA for the largest bank holding companies and other systemically relevant firms were a reaction to the view that regulation had not been tough enough and had allowed too much risk-taking to occur. This response can be seen as the result of the general view that private decision making and markets need some government supervision or they will veer into crisis (basically, narrative 3).

There are, of course, elements of truth in both these narratives, but that will not be discussed here. This *Outlook* simply argues that narrative 1 is a better explanation of the financial crisis than narratives 2 and 3. In other words, government housing policy caused the financial crisis, not too little regulation, not predatory lending, and not excessive risk-taking. To be sure, all those things occurred—they always will—but none of them was significant enough to cause a worldwide financial crisis. If we come to believe that these were the causes of the crisis, we will simply be inviting another crisis to creep up on us while we are looking the wrong way. A strikingly clear example of this possibility is the introduction in Congress in late September 2010 of a bill to extend the Community Reinvestment Act (CRA)—which currently applies only to insured banks and savings and loans (S&Ls)—to the rest of the financial system.[135] The CRA requires insured banks and S&Ls to make loans (primarily mortgages) to borrowers in their service areas who are at or below 80 percent of the median income where they live. Banks must show that they are making such loans irrespective of whether the loans meet the bank's usual credit standards. As I will discuss later in this *Outlook,* that requirement contributed to the large number of subprime and other risky loans that failed in the financial crisis. If the narrative we adopt for what caused the financial crisis does not regard these loans as contributing factors—and narratives 2 and 3 certainly do not—then the conditions that gave rise to the crisis will eventually be repeated.

There is much more to narrative 1 than Baily and Elliott describe, but before introducing those points I will first outline in detail the case that Baily and

---

135. *To Amend the Community Reinvestment Act of 1977 to Improve the Assessments of Regulated Financial Institutions, and for Other Purposes,* 111th Cong., 2d sess. (September 29, 2010).

Elliott make for their narrative 3, which I believe is the most sophisticated and important alternative to the idea that government housing policies created the financial crisis.

Narrative 3: The Decline in Risk Aversion

The principal characteristic of narrative 3 is its comprehensiveness. All the main actors in the financial system are implicated:

- Wall Street did not put in place sound risk-management processes;

- Government regulators did not properly or effectively oversee these processes or the banks, investment banks, and Fannie Mae and Freddie Mac;

- The rating agencies' models were flawed and the agencies themselves had conflicts of interest, allowing complex and ultimately toxic instruments to be released into the financial market;

- Borrowers obtained mortgages under false pretenses, and unregulated mortgage brokers took advantage of unsophisticated buyers; and

- Homebuyers mistakenly believed housing prices would always go up.[136]

This approach—that virtually everyone was responsible for the financial crisis—is susceptible to the objection that it is blaming the crisis on a lot of random errors that all happened to occur at the same time. This is the central conceptual problem with narratives that cite multiple factors as causes: as "perfect storm" descriptions, they do not explain why all the various errors occurred together, except by chance, and what would have happened if they had not. Other perfect-storm explanations are unsatisfactory for this reason. However, Baily and Elliott introduce a new idea that addresses this problem rather neatly and distinguishes narrative 3 from many others. Their idea is this: "the principal underlying cause of the behaviors listed above was a major reduction in the risk premium [the additional interest rate required because of additional risk]

---

136. Douglas J. Elliott and Martin Neil Baily, "Telling the Narrative of the Financial Crisis: Not Just a Housing Bubble," 4.

resulting from 25 years of strong performance by the financial markets, encouraged by and associated with the 'great moderation' in the macro-economy, whereby business cycles seemed almost to vanish."[137]

Thus, Baily and Elliott are identifying a deeper cause of the financial crisis than has generally been outlined in conventional perfect-storm explanations, an element that in effect underlies the more superficial actions that have been cited as causes. That cause, explained in narrative 3, was a general relaxation in the usual fear of risk; this was induced by the "great moderation"—a period of general prosperity and growth that prevailed with few interruptions for the quarter century from 1982 to 2007.

During this period, they argue, "[m]any people, both experts and non-experts, believed that central banks and governments around the world had learned the secrets necessary to tame the business cycle. . . . People learned to take risks. Not only would one expect on average to be rewarded, as the textbooks tell us, but actual experience showed it almost always paid off much more handsomely and with less pain than the theories said. Individuals learned a similar thing with housing. . . . Since homeowners were usually highly levered through mortgage debt [that is, they made low downpayments when they bought their homes], a fairly steady and decent return [on a home investment] became a very attractive levered return. . . . This increased willingness to take risks worked in dangerous combinations with the 'easy money' conditions of the mid-2000s."[138]

So the heart of the argument for narrative 3 is that the long period of growth in the economy, without any serious financial crises, taught investors, corporate managers, and consumers that the risks of excessive leverage were limited; they could acquire assets and make investments with very little money of their own and profit a lot when the assets appreciated in value. This unhealthy process was exacerbated by Federal Reserve policies that made large amounts of credit available to support risk-taking. These elements account for most if not all of the errors made by banks, rating agencies, investors, and consumers in narrative 3.

---

137. Ibid., 5. Baily and Elliott are not the only ones to make this argument. Raghuram G. Rajan, a professor of finance at the Chicago Booth School of Business, makes the same general argument in his book *Fault Lines: How Hidden Fractures Still Threaten the World Economy* (Princeton, NJ: Princeton University Press, 2010).

138. Douglas J. Elliott and Martin Neil Baily, "Telling the Narrative of the Financial Crisis: Not Just a Housing Bubble," 12.

A major implication of this argument is that it turns the housing bubble into just one of a number of bubbles that could have, and probably would have, developed if the housing bubble had not deflated first. "A key policy question," Baily and Elliott write, "is whether the housing bubble was the unique driver of the crisis or whether we might have had a damaging crisis even if housing had played a more minor role. . . . Few would dispute that other bubbles existed and could have burst in a painful way—the argument is whether those bubbles would have been more like the stock market crash of 1987 or the Long-Term Capital [Management] failure, both of which hurt, but neither of which dramatically damaged the economy. . . . However, we believe there would have been a painful recession due to the bursting of the more comprehensive financial bubble, even if housing had played a significantly more minor role."[139]

In other words, the housing bubble was not unique; it was caused by the same underlying problem—the failure of nearly everyone to perceive the risks of high leverage. Rather than blaming the government for creating a huge housing bubble, Baily and Elliott blame investors, corporate managers, regulators, and homebuyers for failing to understand the risks involved when investors and consumers used high leverage to carry assets or buy homes with low downpayments or adjustable-rate mortgages.

After laying this foundation, the Baily-Elliott paper provides a number of examples that are intended to demonstrate that the general perception of risk had fallen to unprecedented lows by 2006 and 2007, before the financial crisis. They note the many credit losses that occurred after the housing bubble burst, including commercial real estate, ordinary business loans, and credit cards. "This does not rule out the possibility," they write, "that housing started the problem and the blow was so strong that it took down the other sectors. However, it is strongly suggestive that the imbalances in the other sectors were also very large prior to the housing bubble bursting, reinforcing the notion of a more comprehensive bubble made up of many sectoral bubbles. . . . [T]he problem did not have to begin with housing."[140]

Moreover, if housing was the precipitating cause of the crisis, Baily and Elliott argue, sectors of the economy unrelated to housing would not have been among the first to fall. One example is the leveraged loan market, which had

---

139. Ibid., 7.
140. Ibid., 8.

no apparent exposure to housing. If the housing bubble had not burst when it did, they argue, other bubbles would have grown so large that they would have been equally destructive when they ultimately burst.

Finally, according to Baily and Elliott, it is not clear that government policy was a necessary element of the housing bubble; conditions in the credit markets were sufficiently lax that the housing bubble could have grown to the size it did without any government help. Using market data, Baily and Elliott show, among other things, that price-to-earnings ratios of U.S. stocks were very high by historical standards in 2006–2007, that spreads over treasury rates of the sovereign bonds of emerging-market countries and U.S. high-yield corporate bonds were at historic lows, and that the International Monetary Fund's calculation of the average volatility forecast built into option pricing for a wide range of assets was at a low point in the 2003–2007 period.[141] All of these data support the key point of the Baily-Elliott argument that the housing bubble—which appears to have been at least a trigger for the crash that became the financial crisis—was only one aspect of a much broader economy- and society-wide increase in leverage and risk-taking. Accordingly, the government's role in promoting homeownership, whatever it was, was not the central cause of the financial crisis.

"Put another way," the authors write, returning the question to its public policy focus, "if we find ourselves in the future in another situation of widespread, excessive risk-taking, preventing problems in the housing sector is unlikely to be enough to prevent severe financial and economic problems when the bubble bursts."

In the next section, I will outline why the housing bubble was not just any bubble, why it was a sine qua non—a "but for" cause—of the financial crisis, and why it was sufficient to cause the crisis without any excessive risk-taking by market participants.

Narrative 1: The Role of Government Housing Policy

Since much of the Baily-Elliott paper is about bubbles, and whether the recent housing bubble was any more significant than other bubbles that might have been created by a market that had lost its fear of risk, any response should begin by examining the dimension of the housing bubble that began to deflate

---

141. Ibid., 8–11.

FIGURE 1
A HISTORY OF HOME VALUES

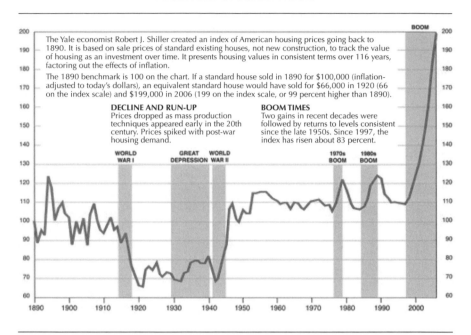

The Yale economist Robert J. Shiller created an index of American housing prices going back to 1890. It is based on sale prices of standard existing houses, not new construction, to track the value of housing as an investment over time. It presents housing values in consistent terms over 116 years, factoring out the effects of inflation.

The 1890 benchmark is 100 on the chart. If a standard house sold in 1890 for $100,000 (inflation-adjusted to today's dollars), an equivalent standard house would have sold for $66,000 in 1920 (66 on the index scale) and $199,000 in 2006 (199 on the index scale, or 99 percent higher than 1890).

DECLINE AND RUN-UP
Prices dropped as mass production techniques appeared early in the 20th century. Prices spiked with post-war housing demand.

BOOM TIMES
Two gains in recent decades were followed by returns to levels consistent since the late 1950s. Since 1997, the index has risen about 83 percent.

SOURCE: *New York Times.*

in 2007. Figure 1 is a chart prepared by the *New York Times* and based on the work of Robert J. Shiller. It shows the extraordinary growth of the 1997–2007 bubble, especially when compared to previous bubbles.

Two things stand out about the most recent bubble: it was much larger in real terms than any previous housing bubble, and it lasted more than twice as long as any previous bubble, especially the two that occurred before 1980 and 1990. The most recent bubble involved increases in real (not nominal) home prices of 80 percent over ten years, while the earlier ones involved increases of about 10 percent before they deflated. Asset bubbles in other sectors might be comparable, but none is likely to involve an asset that is one-sixth of the U.S. economy, and none—as I will show—was composed to such a large degree of weak and high-risk assets.

Why did this bubble last so long? This is an important question; bubbles get more destructive the longer they last because people who believe that prices will continue to rise stretch further and take more risks (use more leverage) to acquire assets that they believe will increase in value. This is exactly what happened in housing, as more and more people took out adjustable-rate mortgages with low "teaser" rates, or mortgages with low or no downpayments, so they could afford the monthly payment on homes that they thought were going to rise in value. A bubble, as Baily and Elliott point out in their paper, feeds on itself because as long as it lasts it disguises the risks that are being taken by those buying the inflating asset. In the housing bubble, for example, there were few losses from this risk-taking until the bubble burst because those who could not afford to pay for their homes could always refinance by using the higher appraised value of the home in a rising market. When the music stopped, these people were left without a method of refinancing, and the delinquencies and defaults began. As Warren Buffett said, "when the tide goes out, you can see who's swimming naked."

Baily and Elliott describe how a bubble finally collapses as follows: "The work on bubbles by Shiller and others makes clear that a bubble can grow for a very long time before it hits a natural limit. Such a limit will always be reached, because a key part of the dynamic of a bubble, like a Ponzi scheme, is that it needs to suck in increasing amounts of money in order to continue . . . leaving the bubble vulnerable to any piece of bad news that causes questions about the excessive valuation."[142] This is an accurate portrayal, and it emphasizes the fact that bubbles naturally end when those who are adding funds become nervous about excessive valuations.

In the case of the 1997–2007 bubble, however, one of the major contributors was not motivated by profit or concerned about risk. It was the U.S. government, following a social policy—using government's financial and regulatory power to boost homeownership by increasing the credit available to low-income borrowers. This was done, first, by requiring Fannie Mae and Freddie Mac to acquire increasing numbers of "affordable"-housing loans. An affordable-housing loan was one made to a borrower at or below the median income in the area where the borrower lived. This was required in legislation that Congress adopted in the early 1990s, the Housing and Community Development Act of 1992.[143] Ini-

---

142. Ibid., 15.

143. *Housing and Community Development Act,* Public Law 102-550, 102d Cong., 2d sess. (October 28, 1992).

tially, the act required that 30 percent of all loans Fannie and Freddie acquired had to be affordable, but the Department of Housing and Urban Development (HUD) was given authority under the act to increase these requirements. It did so repeatedly from 1995 until 2007, so that by 2007, 55 percent of all loans Fannie and Freddie acquired had to be affordable, with a subgoal of 25 percent for low-low income borrowers who were at or below 60 percent of the area median income (see table 1).

In effect, Fannie and Freddie were put into competition with the Federal Housing Administration (FHA), which also was required to insure mortgages for borrowers at or below the median income, and with insured banks, which were required under CRA to make loans to borrowers who were at or below 80 percent of the median income in the banks' service areas. It should be obvious that when Fannie and Freddie, FHA, and all insured banks are trying to find the same borrowers—those who are at or below the median income (or 80 percent of the median income in the case of CRA) where they live—borrowers who could meet the standards for prime loans (a substantial downpayment, unblemished credit, a steady job, and an income that would support a mortgage) might be difficult to find. But all these lenders were required by law or regulation to make the loans, so they had to settle for lower-quality loans than they would prefer or had customarily required. Moreover, in competing with one another, they paid more for these loans than they were worth on a risk-adjusted basis and thus underpriced the risks. The result by 2008, according to research by my AEI colleague Edward Pinto, was a telling distribution of subprime and other high-risk loans in the U.S. financial system.

As shown in table 2, two-thirds of the subprime and other high-risk loans were held or guaranteed by government entities or entities required by the government to acquire, guarantee, or insure the loans. This makes it very clear that the great bubble of 1997–2007 did not develop naturally as an ordinary bubble; it was driven by a government social policy intended to increase homeownership in the United States. For this reason, that bubble cannot be classified as just another bubble among many that the Baily-Elliott paper describes. Not only was it larger than any other known bubble in its dollar amount, but because of its provenance as an artifact of government policy it lasted well beyond the time when other bubbles would naturally have collapsed. For this reason alone, it was more destructive than any other bubble in history when it finally burst and, because of the low quality of the mortgages it contained, resulted in an

TABLE 1
HOUSING GOALS FOR FANNIE MAE AND FREDDIE MAC, 1996–2008 (PERCENT)

	1996	1997	1998	1999	2000	2001	2002	2003	2004	2005	2006	2007	2008
Low & Moderate Housing Goal	40	42	42	42	42	50	50	50	50	52	53	55	56
Fannie Actual	45	45	44	46	50	51	52	52	53	55	57	56	54
Freddie Actual	41	43	43	46	50	53	50	51	52	54	56	56	51
Special Affordable Goal	12	14	14	14	14	20	20	20	20	22	23	25	27
Fannie Actual	15	17	15	18	19	22	21	21	24	24	28	27	26
Freddie Actual	14	15	16	18	21	23	20	21	23	26	26	26	23
Underserved Goal	21	24	24	24	24	31	31	31	31	37	38	38	39
Fannie Actual	25	29	27	27	31	33	33	32	32	41	43	43	39
Freddie Actual	28	26	26	27	29	32	31	33	34	43	44	43	38

SOURCE: Federal Housing Finance Agency, *The Housing Goals of Fannie Mae and Freddie Mac in the Context of the Mortgage Market: 1996–2009* (Washington, DC, February 1, 2010), available at www.fhfa.gov/webfiles/15408/Housing%20Goals%201996-2009%2002-01.pdf (accessed November 1, 2010).

TABLE 2

SUBPRIME AND ALT-A LOANS BY TYPE, JUNE 30, 2008

Entity	Number of Subprime or Alt-A Loans	Unpaid Principal Amount
Fannie Mae and Freddie Mac	12 million	$1.8 trillion
Federal Housing Administration and Other Federal Agencies	5 million	$0.6 trillion
Community Reinvestment Act and HUD Programs	2.2 million	$0.3 trillion
Total, Federal Government	**19.2 million**	**$2.7 trillion**
Private-Label Issuers*	7.8 million	$1.9 trillion
Total	**27 million**	**$4.6 trillion**

NOTE: *Countrywide and many others; Wall Street firms represent about 25 percent of the total.

SOURCES: See the following works by Edward Pinto: "Sizing Total Exposure to Subprime and Alt-A Loans in U.S. First Mortgage Market as of 6.30.08" (memorandum, updated April 21, 2010), available at www.aei.org/docLib/Pinto-Sizing-Total-Exposure.pdf, which accounts for all 27 million high-risk loans; "Sizing Total Federal Government and Federal Agency Contributions to Subprime and Alt-A Loans in U.S. First Mortgage Market as of 6.30.08" (memorandum, updated April 21, 2010), available at www.aei.org/docLib/Pinto-Sizing-Total-Federal-Contributions.pdf, which covers the portion of these loans that were held or guaranteed by federal agencies and the four large banks and Countrywide that made these loans under the Community Reinvestment Act; and "High LTV, Subprime and Alt-A Originations over the Period 1992–2007 and Fannie, Freddie, FHA and VA's Role" (memorandum, updated April 21, 2010), available at www.aei.org/docLib/ Pinto-High-LTV-Subprime-Alt-A.pdf, which covers the acquisition of these loans by government agencies from the early 1990s, when the process of reducing underwriting standards began. See also Edward Pinto, "Government Housing Policies in the Lead-up to the Financial Crisis: A Forensic Study" (discussion draft, August 14, 2010), available at www.aei.org/docLib/Pinto-Government-Housing-Policies-Crisis.pdf.

unprecedented number of delinquencies and defaults. Table 3 shows the delinquency rates on the 27 million subprime and Alt-A mortgages that were in the bubble before the financial crisis.

The bubble was more destructive than others for yet another reason. While it is certainly true that as bubbles grow older their asset quality declines, this phenomenon is seldom forced and exacerbated by government policy. Without the government's active involvement, it is doubtful that the 1997–2007 bubble would have contained as many as 27 million subprime and Alt-A loans. If the bubble had developed naturally, in the ordinary way, it could conceivably have contained the 7.8 million loans that were eventually securitized by Countrywide (the largest originator and issuer of securities backed by subprime mortgages,

TABLE 3
DELINQUENCY RATES FOR SUBPRIME AND ALT-A MORTGAGES

Loan Type	Estimated Number of Loans	Total Delinquency Rate (Thirty-Plus Days and in Foreclosure)
High-Rate Subprime (including Fannie/Freddie private MBS holdings)	6.7 million	45.0%
Option ARM	1.1 million	30.5%
Alt-A (including Fannie/Freddie/FHLBs private MBS holdings)	2.4 million	23.0%
Fannie Subprime/Alt-A/Nonprime	6.6 million	17.3%
Freddie Subprime/Alt-A/Nonprime	4.1 million	13.8%
Government (FHA, VA FHLBs)	4.8 million	13.5%
Nonagency Subprime and CRA Type Loans (not high rate)	1 million	N/A
Total Number of Loans	**26.7 million**	

SOURCE: Derived from chart 53 in Edward Pinto, "Government Financial Policies in the Lead-up to the Financial Crisis: A Forensic Study" (Washington, DC: AEI, November 2010), available at www.aei.org/paper/100155.

or PMBS), as well as other originators and the Wall Street banks. But even then the quality of the mortgages in these PMBS issuances would have been higher than those that Countrywide and the others ultimately contributed to the recent bubble. This is because the government agencies or government-regulated entities like Fannie and Freddie could afford to pay more than their private-sector competitors for the subprime mortgages they needed; they acquired the cream of a bad crop, and that drove Countrywide and other securitizers further out on the risk curve to find mortgages they could securitize. Without competition from Fannie and Freddie and the banks under CRA, the PMBS ultimately securitized would have been far less "toxic" when the bubble collapsed.

In any event, these PMBS were less than one-third of the high-risk mortgages outstanding. If the FHA is included, because its role was to make subprime loans, we can increase the total to almost half of all the high-risk loans—still only 25 percent of all mortgages outstanding in the United States in 2008. There is clearly a relationship, as one would expect, between the quality of the mortgages in the bubble and the bubble's destructiveness when it deflates. With-out Fannie and Freddie and the CRA obligations of insured banks, the number of subprime and other high-risk mortgages in the financial system would have been, at most, only half the 27 million it eventually became.

It is impossible to know what would have happened if the bubble had burst when only 25 percent of the mortgages in the United States were subprime or otherwise high-risk, but clearly the damage to the financial system and the economy would have been much lower. For example, in the housing bubble that ended in 1979, when almost all loans were traditional mortgages, foreclo-sure starts in the ensuing slump peaked at just 0.87 percent in 1983. In the next bubble, which ended in 1989 and primarily involved traditional mortgages, foreclosure starts reached 1.32 percent in 1994. But in 2009, when half of all outstanding mortgages were subprime or otherwise high-risk, foreclosure starts jumped to a record of almost 5 percent by the middle of 2010.[144] And this was at a time when the banks were going slow on foreclosures because govern-ment programs were encouraging the renegotiation of delinquent mortgages, and banks did not want either the capital writedowns or the bad publicity that comes with large numbers of foreclosures.

What we know is that almost 50 percent of all mortgages outstanding in the United States in 2008 were subprime or otherwise deficient and high-risk loans. The fact that two-thirds of these mortgages were on the balance sheets of gov-ernment agencies, or firms required to buy them by government regulations, is irrefutable evidence that the government's housing policies were responsible for most of the weak mortgages that became delinquent and defaulted in unprec-edented numbers when the housing bubble collapsed. Under these circum-stances, one does not have to reach for reduced fear of risk as the explanation for the financial crisis. It is right there in the housing data.

Conclusion

Baily and Elliott make a strong case for explaining the financial crisis as the result of a general decline in risk aversion because of the effect of the great

---

144. Mortgage Bankers Association, *National Delinquency Survey* (Washington, DC, 2010), available through www.mbaa.org/ResearchandForecasts/ProductsandSurveys/NationalDelinquencySurvey.htm (accessed November 1, 2010).

moderation—the period from 1982 to 2007 when it seemed that we understood the causes of financial crises and had found a way to avoid or mitigate them. The evidence for a general weakening in risk aversion coming out of this period is plausible. But the Baily-Elliott narrative assumes that the 1997–2007 housing bubble was also caused by this factor, and that seems implausible. The extraordinary lengths to which the government went to force private-sector lending that would not otherwise have occurred—through affordable-housing requirements for Fannie and Freddie as well as demands on FHA and on the banks under CRA—shows that the housing bubble that ended in 2007 was not a natural occurrence or the result of mere risk aversion. If it had been, there would have been no need for these government programs.

The housing bubble that finally burst in 2007 was driven by a U.S. government social policy that was intended to increase homeownership in the United States and was thus not subject to the usual limits on the length and size of asset bubbles. As such, it was far larger and lasted far longer than any other bubble in modern times, and, when it deflated, the vast number of poor-quality mortgages it contained defaulted at unprecedented rates. This drove down U.S. housing values and caused the weakening of financial institutions around the world that we know as the financial crisis.

Market participants were certainly taking risks as the bubble grew, and it may well be, as Baily and Elliott posit, that this private risk-taking was greater than in the past. But the facts show that the bubble was inflated by a government social policy that created a vast number of subprime and Alt-A mortgages that would not otherwise have existed. And the risks associated with this policy—which could produce losses of more than $400 billion at Fannie and Freddie alone—were being taken by only one unwitting group: the taxpayers.

"The Lost Cause:
The Failure of the Financial
Crisis Inquiry Commission"

Originally published January–February 2011

It should not have been difficult for the Financial Crisis Inquiry Commission to identify the causes of the financial crisis. Everyone on the commission, and everyone interviewed, believed that the crisis was caused largely by the losses to financial institutions arising from the high rates of delinquency and failure among subprime and other low-quality mortgages in the 1997–2007 housing bubble. Where the commission lost its way was in its refusal to inquire why so many subprime and other weak mortgages were created in the first place—why, in other words, there was such a significant deterioration in mortgage underwriting standards in the years before the bubble's collapse. Without an answer to this question, the commission could only produce a narrative about the financial crisis, not a coherent description of what caused the financial crisis.

In late January 2011, the Financial Crisis Inquiry Commission issued its report on the 2008 financial crisis.[145] I was one of ten members on this commission and wrote a dissenting statement that is available online through AEI[146] or through the commission's website.[147] It is also available in hard copy, together with the full report and the other dissents, through the Government Printing

---

145. Financial Crisis Inquiry Commission, *Final Report of the National Commission on the Causes of the Financial and Economic Crisis in the United States* (Washington, DC, January 2011), http://c0182732.cdn1.cloudfiles.rackspacecloud.com/fcic_final_report_full.pdf (accessed February 4, 2011).

146. Peter J. Wallison, *Dissent from the Majority Report of the Financial Crisis Inquiry Commission* (Washington, DC: AEI, January 26, 2011), www.aei.org/paper/100190.

147. Peter J. Wallison, *Financial Crisis Inquiry Commission Dissenting Statement* (Washington, DC, January 2011), http://c0182732.cdn1.cloudfiles.rackspacecloud.com/fcic_final_report_wallison_dissent.pdf (accessed February 4, 2011).

Office.[148] Three other Republicans on the commission—Bill Thomas (who was also the commission's vice chair), Keith Hennessey, and Douglas Holtz-Eakin—also dissented, and their dissent (the THH dissent) can be found on the commission's website.[149] In this *Outlook*, I summarize my dissent and the logic on which it rested, offer a brief description of the deficiencies of the five-hundred-page majority report, and explain why I could not join in the dissent of the three other Republicans.

Since the commission's mandate was to explain what caused the financial crisis, my dissent focuses almost entirely on that question. George Santayana is often quoted for the aphorism that "those who cannot remember the past are condemned to repeat it." Attempting to identify the causes of the financial crisis, however, shows that Santayana's idea was a bit facile. Even if we know what happened in the past, there is still debate about its causes. The continuing appearance of revisionist histories about important events, such as our own Civil War or the Great Depression, testifies to the protean quality of the past. The difficult task for historians, economists, and public policy specialists is to discern which, among a welter of possible causes, were the significant ones—the ones without which history would have been different.

Using this standard, I believe that the sine qua non of the financial crisis was the U.S. government's housing policies; these fostered the creation of 27 million subprime and other risky loans—half of all mortgages in the United States—which were susceptible to default when the massive 1997–2007 housing bubble began to deflate. If the U.S. government had not chosen this policy path—feeding the growth of a bubble of unprecedented size and an equally unprecedented number of weak and high-risk residential mortgages—I do not believe that the great financial crisis of 2008 would have occurred. What follows is a brief summary of the argument in my dissenting statement.

The U.S. government's housing policies were intended to increase home-ownership by providing low-income borrowers with increased access to mortgage credit. Under legislation adopted by Congress in 1992, the Department of

---

148. See http://bookstore.gpo.gov.

149. Keith Hennessey, Douglas Holtz-Eakin, and Bill Thomas, *Dissenting Statement of Commissioner Keith Hennessey, Commissioner Douglas Holtz-Eakin, and Vice Chairman Bill Thomas* (Washington, DC, January 2011), http://c0182732.cdn1.cloudfiles.rackspacecloud.com/fcic_final_report_hennessey_holtz-eakin_thomas_dissent.pdf (accessed February 4, 2011).

Housing and Urban Development (HUD) in both the Clinton and George W. Bush administrations carried on an intensive effort to reduce mortgage underwriting standards. HUD used (1) the affordable-housing requirements imposed by Congress in 1992 on the government-sponsored enterprises (GSEs) Fannie Mae and Freddie Mac, (2) its control over the policies of the Federal Housing Administration (FHA), and (3) a "Best Practices Initiative" for subprime lenders and mortgage banks such as Countrywide, to encourage greater subprime and other high-risk lending.

Ultimately, all these entities, as well as insured banks covered by the Community Reinvestment Act (CRA), were compelled to compete for mortgage borrowers who were at or below the median income in the areas where they lived. This competition caused underwriting standards to decline, increased the numbers of high-risk loans far beyond what the market would have produced without government influence, and contributed importantly to the growth of the housing bubble.

When the bubble began to deflate in mid-2007, the millions of low-quality loans produced by this competition began to default in unprecedented numbers. The effect of these defaults was exacerbated by the fact that few if any investors—including housing-market analysts—understood at the time that Fannie Mae and Freddie Mac had been acquiring large numbers of subprime and other high-risk loans to meet HUD's affordable-housing goals. Thus, when so many mortgages began to default in 2007, investors were shocked and fled the multitrillion-dollar market for private mortgage-backed securities (MBS), dropping MBS values—and especially those MBS backed by subprime and other risky loans—to fractions of their former prices. Mark-to-market accounting then required financial institutions to write down the value of their assets, reducing their capital and liquidity positions and causing great investor and creditor alarm.

In this environment, the government's rescue of Bear Stearns in March 2008 temporarily calmed investor fears but created significant moral hazard; investors and other market participants reasonably believed after the rescue of Bear that all large financial institutions would also be rescued if they encountered financial difficulties. However, when Lehman Brothers—an investment bank even larger than Bear—was allowed to fail, market participants were shocked; suddenly, they were forced to consider the financial health of their counterparties, many of which appeared weakened by losses and the capital writedowns required by mark-to-market accounting. This caused a halt to lending and a hoarding of cash—a virtually unprecedented period of market paralysis and panic that characterized the financial crisis.[150]

Finding the Cause

Many commentators, as well as the commission majority and the THH dissenters, have expressed disagreement with my view of the causes of the financial crisis; they argue that the crisis was more complex and cannot be explained by any single cause. However, everyone agrees that the financial crisis had a single cause: the mortgage meltdown in late 2007 and the resulting delinquency and default of an unprecedented number of U.S. mortgages. As the commission majority said, "While the vulnerabilities that created the potential for crisis were years in the making, it was the collapse of the housing bubble—fueled by low interest rates, easy and available credit, scant regulation, and toxic mortgages—that was the spark that ignited a string of events, which led to a full-blown crisis in the fall of 2008." Indeed, most of the commission majority's report was taken up with anecdotes about how financial-institution managers and regulators failed to recognize the growth of the housing bubble and prevent the buildup of subprime and other weak mortgages in the U.S. financial system.

Since this was the acknowledged cause of the financial crisis, a commission charged with determining what caused the crisis should want to find out why there was such a massive accumulation of subprime and other risky loans—the "toxic mortgages" described above—that defaulted in the mortgage meltdown. Why, for example, did the underwriting standards that had prevailed for many years in the U.S. mortgage market suddenly begin to deteriorate in the early 1990s? If the financial crisis was in fact caused by the default of these mortgages, why these weak and risky mortgages were created was clearly a key question for the commission's inquiry. Unfortunately, neither the commission majority nor the THH dissenters made any significant effort to address this central issue.

For example, the majority's report says only that the "toxic mortgages" were "fueled by low interest rates and easy and available credit." Exactly how low interest rates and easy and available credit caused a decline in underwriting

---

150. Peter J. Wallison, *Dissent from the Majority Report of the Financial Crisis Inquiry Commission.*

standards is never explained. Similarly, the THH dissent says that "tightening credit spreads, overly optimistic assumptions about U.S. housing prices, and flaws in primary and secondary mortgage markets led to poor origination practices." How tightening credit spreads and the other factors led to "poor origination practices" is never addressed. In effect, both the majority report and the THH dissent treat the existence of 27 million weak loans as a "given"—a starting point for which no explanation is required.

This is not a minor flaw in their arguments. It is a serious failure to address the one aspect of the financial crisis that distinguishes it from all previous financial disruptions and crises. Before the 2008 crisis, the United States had frequently experienced extended periods of low interest rates, large flows of funds from abroad, and excessive optimism about the future of housing prices (housing bubbles). We also had the same general regulatory and financial structure and a private financial system in which managements were expected to anticipate and act on risks to their firms. None of these conditions or factors, separately or together, had ever before resulted in a mortgage-based financial crisis. The one element in the 2008 financial crisis that was completely unprecedented was the presence of 27 million subprime and other risky mortgages; never in the past were half of all mortgages in the United States in danger of delinquency and default when a housing bubble deflated. Treating this factor as a given is a classic case of ignoring the elephant in the room, and it prevented the commission majority and the THH dissenters from gaining a clear understanding of the mechanism through which the 2008 crisis came about.

My dissent addresses this error. It attempts to explain why there were so many subprime and other risky loans in the U.S. financial system in 2008, how the massive number of these loans caused the extraordinary size and longevity of the 1997–2007 bubble, and how the collapse of the bubble and the private MBS market caused the weakness of financial institutions in the United States and around the world.

The Deterioration of Underwriting Standards

It seems obvious that such a large number of subprime and other risky mortgages could not have accumulated in the U.S. financial system unless there had been a serious decline in mortgage underwriting standards, and why that decline occurred is a major piece of the crisis puzzle. For fifty years following World

War II, U.S. residential mortgages were solid assets, bought and held as investments by banks and other financial institutions in the United States and around the world. During this period, there were two major U.S. housing bubbles—in 1979 and 1989—but when they deflated they resulted only in local losses. If housing prices ever fell nationally—and this is a debated question—it was never more than by a small percentage. Mortgage defaults themselves, under the worst conditions, and in the localities hardest hit by the deflation of a bubble, never resulted in losses of more than 4 percent. It again seems obvious that the reason for this stability was the existence of strong underwriting standards, requiring down payments and good credit records for those who wanted to buy homes.

Why were previous underwriting standards abandoned? As I discuss in my dissent, the deterioration of mortgage underwriting standards began in 1992, when Congress adopted legislation that imposed what were called "affordable housing" requirements on Fannie Mae and Freddie Mac. Under these requirements, a certain percentage of mortgages purchased by Fannie and Freddie had to be loans to low- and moderate-income (LMI) borrowers—home buyers whose income was at or below the median income in the areas where they lived. This was an initial step in a U.S. government social policy that eventually had the desired effect: it made substantial amounts of mortgage credit available to LMI borrowers for the first time, and it succeeded in increasing the homeownership rate in the United States from 64 percent (where it had been for thirty years) to more than 69 percent in 2004. However, this policy also created a ten-year housing bubble of unprecedented size, and the growth of the bubble—by suppressing delinquencies and defaults as housing prices climbed[151]—fostered a large market for securitized subprime mortgages held by financial institutions in the United States and around the world. When the bubble collapsed, these subprime and other risky loans became the toxic assets that endangered

---

151. Although not the focus of this *Outlook*, the effect of the bubble's growth on the development of a huge market in MBS backed by subprime loans is important to note. As a housing bubble grows, it tends to suppress delinquencies and defaults. Homeowners who cannot meet their mortgage obligations can refinance or sell the home for more than the mortgage obligation. As the U.S. bubble grew, investors around the world saw that MBS backed by subprime mortgages were producing high yields but not showing losses commensurate with the risk. Thus, government policies, in stimulating the growth of the bubble, also were responsible for the development of the private market in MBS backed by subprime loans.

the stability and solvency of many financial institutions and caused others to become insolvent or illiquid.

Initially, Congress set the affordable-housing requirement at 30 percent—30 percent of the loans the GSEs bought from originators had to be loans to LMI home buyers. In the succeeding fifteen years, HUD tightened and extended these requirements so that by 2007, 55 percent of all loans had to qualify as affordable-housing loans to LMI borrowers. HUD also added various subgoals that required loans to borrowers at or below 80 percent and 60 percent of area median income.

HUD's increasingly aggressive affordable-housing requirements put Fannie and Freddie into competition with FHA, the banks that were subject to the CRA, and a group of subprime lenders who had pledged to HUD that they would reduce underwriting standards to make mortgage financing more available for low-income borrowers. With all these entities competing for the same borrowers, it was simply not possible to find enough prime borrowers among the targeted LMI group to meet HUD's demands. To find goals-eligible loans, the GSEs and others had to reduce their mortgage underwriting standards. In my view, this is the only plausible explanation for why mortgage underwriting standards declined so significantly between 1992 and 2007.

To illustrate what happened to mortgage underwriting standards during this fifteen-year period, consider down-payment requirements. By 2000, Fannie Mae was offering to buy loans with zero down payments. As described below, originators found that they could make loans to people with little or no down-payment resources and still sell those loans to Fannie or Freddie. Between 1997 and 2007, Fannie and Freddie bought over $1 trillion in mortgages with down payments of 5 percent or less. In 1990, only one in two hundred purchase money mortgages (that is, not refinances) had a down-payment requirement of less than 3 percent, but by 2007 almost 40 percent of all purchase money mortgages had down payments of that size. The credit quality of borrowers also declined. Between 1997 and 2007, Fannie and Freddie bought $1.5 trillion in subprime loans and over $600 billion in loans with other deficiencies that would have made them unsalable in 1990,[152] and officials of Fannie and Freddie attended meetings of mortgage originators to ask for more subprime loans.[153]

---

152. Peter J. Wallison, *Dissent from the Majority Report of the Financial Crisis Inquiry Commission,* 65.

153. Ibid., 60.

HUD's Role

Although there might be some question about whether HUD intended this result, and thus whether the decline in underwriting standards was a deliberate policy of the U.S. government, HUD made no effort to hide its purposes. In statements over several years, the department made clear its intent to reduce mortgage underwriting standards. I have included three of these statements below, the first made in 2000 when HUD was increasing the affordable-housing goals for Fannie and Freddie:

> Lower-income and minority families have made major gains in access to the mortgage market in the 1990s. A variety of reasons have accounted for these gains, including improved housing affordability, enhanced enforcement of the Community Reinvestment Act, *more flexible mortgage underwriting,* and stepped-up enforcement of the Fair Housing Act. *But most industry observers believe that one factor behind these gains has been the improved performance of Fannie Mae and Freddie Mac under HUD's affordable lending goals. HUD's recent increases in the goals for 2001–03 will encourage the GSEs to further step up their support for affordable lending.*[154] (emphasis mine)

Similarly, in 2004, when HUD was again increasing the affordable-housing goals for Fannie and Freddie, the department stated:

> Millions of Americans with less than perfect credit or *who cannot meet some of the tougher underwriting requirements of the prime market* for reasons such as inadequate income documentation, limited downpayment or cash reserves, or the desire to take more cash out in a refinancing than conventional loans allow, rely on subprime lenders for access to mortgage financing. *If the GSEs reach deeper into the subprime market, more borrowers will benefit from the advantages that greater stability and standardization create.*[155] (emphasis mine)

---

154. US Department of Housing and Urban Development, *HUD's Affordable Housing Goals for Fannie Mae and Freddie Mac,* Issue Brief No. V (Washington, DC, January 2011), 5, www.huduser.org/Publications/PDF/gse.pdf (accessed February 4, 2011).

155. US Department of Housing and Urban Development, *HUD's Housing Goals for the Federal National Mortgage Association (Fannie Mae) and the Federal Home Loan Mortgage Corporation (Freddie Mac) for the Years 2005–2008 and Amendments to*

Finally, the following statement appeared in a 2005 report commissioned by HUD:

> More liberal mortgage financing has contributed to the increase in demand for housing. During the 1990s, lenders have been *encouraged by HUD and banking regulators* to increase lending to low-income and minority households. The Community Reinvestment Act (CRA), Home Mortgage Disclosure Act (HMDA), government-sponsored enterprises (GSE) housing goals, and fair lending laws have strongly encouraged mortgage brokers and lenders to market to low-income and minority borrowers. *Sometimes these borrowers are higher risk, with blemished credit histories and high debt or simply little savings for a down payment. Lenders have responded with low down payment loan products and automated underwriting, which has allowed them to more carefully determine the risk of the loan.*[156] (emphasis mine)

These statements are strong evidence that the decline in mortgage underwriting standards between 1992 and 2007 did not just happen; nor was it the result of low interest rates, flows of funds from abroad, or any of the other events or conditions suggested by the commission majority and the THH dissenters. HUD intended the direct effect of its policies, which placed Fannie and Freddie into competition with other government agencies and other financial institutions that were effectively under the government's control—all of which were seeking loans to the same LMI borrowers. Because there were only a limited number of prime borrowers among the low-income groups targeted by government social policies, all these competing entities had to lower their underwriting standards to find the borrowers they needed to meet their government-imposed

---

HUD's Regulation of Fannie Mae and Freddie Mac, Document 04-24101 (Washington, DC, November 2, 2004), www.govpulse.us/entries/2004/11/02/04-24101/hud-s-housing-goals-for-the-federal-national-mortgage-association-fannie-mae-and-the-federal-home-lo (accessed February 8, 2011).

156. US Department of Housing and Urban Development, Office of Policy Development & Research, *Recent House Price Trends and Homeownership Affordability* (Washington, DC, May 2005), 85, www.huduser.org/Publications/pdf/RecentHousePrice.pdf (accessed February 4, 2011).

quotas. That, in summary, is the discussion in my dissent on why there were so many subprime and other high-risk mortgages in the U.S. financial system when the housing bubble deflated in 2007. In contrast, neither the majority report nor the THH dissent had a plausible explanation for the decline in underwriting standards. In both cases, this decline was treated as something that happened as a result of low interest rates or greater capital availability, without any explanation of why these factors would have that effect. With that view, they could only—at best—tell half the story of the financial crisis.

The Majority Report

Because of its refusal to consider the reasons for the decline in underwriting standards, the commission majority was forced to argue that the low quality of so many loans in the U.S. financial system resulted from a failure to regulate loan originators, especially mortgage brokers. As is true throughout the majority report, the discussion in this area is critical of certain practices in the market but educes no data on how widespread these practices were or how significant they might have been in contributing to the financial crisis.

In any event, what the majority report failed to recognize or communicate is that brokers do not finance mortgages. Before they make a mortgage, they must have a buyer to provide the financing. The reason that brokers were so active during the housing boom is that they could always find a buyer for the mortgages they were originating—and most of the time that buyer was Fannie, Freddie, FHA, a subprime lender involved in a HUD program, or a bank that needed certain kinds of mortgages to comply with the CRA. If those government mandates had not existed—if the GSEs and others had not been required by law to buy affordable-housing loans—many fewer subprime and other risky mortgages would have been originated. Subprime lending would have remained what it was before 1992, a niche business. Instead, the commission majority argued that the brokers were the source of the problem—as though regulating their activities was the solution to excessive subprime lending rather than ending the government mandates that made it possible for brokers, whether unscrupulous or honest, to find buyers for the subprime or other risky mortgages they originated.

The commission majority ended this portion of its report by concluding that "there was untrammeled growth in risky mortgages. Unsustainable, toxic loans polluted the financial system and fueled the housing bubble."[157] This statement is correct if one considers the 27 million subprime and other risky loans that existed in the U.S. financial system before the financial crisis. However, the commission majority failed to produce data that connect the abusive practices the report condemns, such as yield-spread premiums, to any given number of subprime or otherwise risky loans. Without this data, it is impossible for any-one to conclude that abusive lending practices or predatory lending had any significant effect on the financial crisis. This is true throughout the commission majority's report. Because the majority refused to do a thorough analysis of why and how so many subprime and other risky loans were originated, they were left to claim that "toxic loans polluted the financial system and fueled the housing bubble" without any supporting evidence.

There is some irony here. Although no statistics for the prevalence of predatory lending were ever produced, the commission majority identified it as a cause of the housing bubble and, presumably, the financial crisis; yet, even though the commission had data showing that Fannie and Freddie had made 12 million subprime and other risky loans—enough to drive them into insolvency—it concluded that the role of these two GSEs in the crisis was only "marginal." The political bias in this conclusion is clear.

Sometimes, the commission majority's efforts to protect Fannie and Freddie were unintentionally humorous. One example involves piggyback loans. Fannie and Freddie were required by their charters to limit their purchases to mortgages with loan-to-value ratios of no more than 80 percent, unless the borrower paid for mortgage insurance. "Worried about defaults," the commission majority intones, "the GSEs would not buy mortgages with downpayments below 20% unless the borrower bought mortgage insurance." By 2000, however, as I report in my dissent, Fannie was offering to buy loans with *no* down payment and no mortgage insurance. How did it do this? The commission report is a bit cagey: "Unluckily for many homeowners, for the housing industry, and for the finan-cial system, *lenders* devised a way to get rid of the [insurance requirement] that had added to the cost of homeownership" (emphasis mine). The answer that the lenders purportedly thought up was the piggyback mortgage in which, as the commission reports, "[t]he lender offered a first mortgage for perhaps 80% of the home's value and a second mortgage for another 10% or even 20%. . . .

---

157. Ibid., 101.

Lenders liked them because the smaller first mortgage—even without mortgage insurance—*could potentially be sold to the GSEs*"[158] (emphasis mine).

The commission makes clear that piggyback loans were risky: "[T]he piggybacks added risks. A borrower with a higher combined [loan-to-value ratio] had less equity in the home. In a rising market, should payments become unmanageable, the borrower could always sell the home and come out ahead. However, should the payments become unmanageable in a falling market, the borrower might owe more than the home was worth. Piggyback loans—which often required nothing down—guaranteed that many borrowers would end up with negative equity if house prices fell."[159] So the commission majority starts its discussion with a statement that suggests the GSEs were cautious and conservative (they were "worried about defaults" and so "would not buy mortgages with downpayments below 20%"), but ends with a description of a common transaction—the piggyback loan—in which Fannie and Freddie bought loans with no down payment and no mortgage insurance, loans the commission majority itself characterizes as risky. Given that Fannie was offering a zero down payment mortgage in 2000, without any mortgage insurance, it is obvious that the firm knew it was buying loans with piggyback mortgages and no down payment at all. In fact, in 2008, both Fannie and Freddie disclosed in their 10-K forms that they had made sizable purchases of piggyback loans that had materially added to their exposure of loans with down payments of 5 percent or less.

This example confirms several important points in my dissent: the GSEs bought risky loans that were bad for borrowers because they had no down payment and that led to defaults when the bubble deflated; they both hid and enhanced their risk-taking by evading the mortgage-insurance requirement through piggyback loans; and the commission majority was not candid about the GSEs' role in the financial crisis—in this case, suggesting that "lenders" made up the whole piggyback idea so they could sell the loans to Fannie and Freddie, as if Fannie and Freddie did not realize what they were buying. Despite this inculpatory discussion, the commission majority was still able to claim that the role of Fannie and Freddie in the financial crisis was "marginal." There is little doubt that the affordable-housing requirements impelled Fannie and Freddie

---

158. Ibid., 110.
159. Ibid.

to enter into these risky transactions; apparently, the commission majority was unable to accept this fact.

The THH Dissent

The errors in the THH dissent are of a different order. I will not make any overall judgment about that dissent, but simply explain why I could not join it. This discussion will consider an op-ed the THH dissenters published in the *Wall Street Journal*[160] on the same day that the majority report was released, as well as their dissent itself. In the *Journal* article, they argue that both the majority report and my dissent are too simple as explanations of the financial crisis. Instead, they "subscribe to a third narrative—a messier story that emphasizes both global economic forces and failures in U.S. policy and supervision. Though our explanation of the crisis doesn't fit conveniently into the political order in Washington, we believe that it is far superior to the other two."[161]

Both the *Journal* article and the THH dissent say that "the crisis was the product of ten different factors. Only when taken together can they offer a sufficient explanation of what happened." This is a "perfect storm" analysis, in which the event in question—the financial crisis—only occurred because the stars were aligned in a particular way. If all ten factors were really necessary for the financial crisis to occur, however, we need not worry about another crisis. The statistical likelihood that all these elements will again come together at the same time is vanishingly small. This explanation is not only inherently implausible but also provides no guidance to policymakers about what actions they should take to prevent a recurrence.

There are several respects in which this dissent is similar to the majority report. First, it has no explanation to support its assertion that "tightening credit spreads, overly optimistic assumptions about U.S. housing prices, and flaws in primary and secondary mortgage markets led to poor origination practices." Since poor origination practices—that is, low mortgage underwriting standards— were the principal reason that the U.S. financial system was weighed down with subprime and other risky loans, it was incumbent on the THH dissenters

---

160. Bill Thomas, Keith Hennessey, and Douglas Holtz-Eakin, "What Caused the Financial Crisis," *Wall Street Journal,* January 27, 2011.

161. Ibid.

to explain how these factors led to low underwriting standards. They never do. Second, in attempting to explain the proliferation of low-quality mortgages in the U.S. financial system, they identify "easy financing," "ineffective regulatory regimes," "irresponsible lenders," and "lenient regulatory oversight" of mortgage originators—all ideas that dominated the commission majority's report—but do not explain why mortgage underwriting standards declined in the first place. As noted above, none of these elements would have resulted in a proliferation of low-quality loans unless there were *buyers* with reduced mortgage underwriting standards. There were such buyers: government agencies, GSEs, and banks subject to the CRA, all of which were operating under government-mandated requirements that forced them to reduce their underwriting standards.

Finally, and most troubling, is the THH dissent's focus on risk management, which also parallels the commission majority's report. As they put it, "An essential cause of the financial and economic crisis was appallingly bad risk management by the leaders of some of the largest financial institutions in the United States and Europe." This idea was supplemented in the *Journal* article with this statement: "Managers of many large and midsize financial institutions amassed enormous concentrations of highly correlated risk . . . and they amplified this risk by holding too little capital relative to the risks and funded these exposures with short-term debt. . . . They assumed such funds would always be available. Both turned out to be bad bets." No data are presented for these statements.

As it happens, there are data on the question of asset concentrations, and they seem to contradict the statement that financial institutions held "enormous concentrations" of high-risk mortgages. *Inside Mortgage Finance,* a major source for data on mortgages and MBS, publishes an annual report on mortgage-related holdings of financial institutions. These data show that in December 2008 all U.S. financial institutions (excluding Fannie and Freddie and the Federal Home Loan Banks) held a total of $951 billion in MBS not guaranteed by Fannie or Freddie.[162] The Fed's flow of funds data indicate that the assets of all these institutions at that time totaled $40 trillion.[163] Accordingly, the

---

162. Inside Mortgage Finance, *The 2009 Mortgage Market Statistical Annual,* Volume II (Bethesda, MD, 2009), 277.

163. Board of Governors of the Federal Reserve System, *Flow of Funds Accounts of the United States* (Washington, DC, 2010), tables L.109, L.114–23, www.federalreserve.gov/releases/z1/current/z1.pdf (accessed February 9, 2011).

nonagency MBS held by all U.S. financial institutions was about 2.4 percent of their total assets. That does not sound like an "enormous concentration." If we just look at commercial banks, they had $13 trillion in assets and held $210 billion in MBS,[164] again representing 1.6 percent of assets and roughly 20 percent of capital. Inside Mortgage Finance also has data for the top twenty-five bank holding companies. If we look just at the top four bank holding companies, we get the same result ($5 trillion in assets and $110 billion in nonagency MBS again equals approximately 2 percent of assets and 20 percent of capital).[165] In contrast, during the early 1980s, the major U.S. banks held debt of Brazil, Argentina, and Mexico—all of which were unable to meet their dollar obligations, which were 147 percent of the capital of the eight largest U.S. banks.[166] Moreover, the total bank holdings include all MBS, not just those backed by subprime or other risky mortgages; accordingly, the holdings of the so-called "toxic assets" would have been smaller. But going beyond data, it is troubling that the THH dissenters believe that a generalized failure of risk management was a cause of the crisis. First, the idea is inherently implausible. Given the widespread nature of the financial crisis, a very large number of financial institutions in all developed countries would be subject to this criticism. Since virtually all of them were in trouble in the crisis, there would have been what might be called a universal failure of proper risk management throughout the financial markets. Needless to say, it is highly unlikely that the managements of all the world's major financial institutions would become incompetent at the same time. In the real world, some banks and financial institutions fail, but others are better managed and survive. This suggests that something happened to create the financial crisis that was beyond the experience and expectations of the managements of all these institutions. My dissent suggests what that was: the collapse of the U.S. housing bubble and the sudden appearance in late 2007 of an unprecedented number of delinquencies and defaults among the 27 million subprime and other high-risk loans outstanding in the United States. This caused the collapse of the MBS market. Criticizing the managements of all the world's

---

164. Inside Mortgage Finance, *The 2009 Mortgage Market Statistical Annual,* Volume II, 2.

165. Ibid., 283.

166. Federal Financial Institutions Examination Council, *Country Exposure Report* (Washington, DC, December 1982), 2; and FDIC, *Reports of Condition and Income* (Washington, DC, December 31, 1982).

major financial institutions without understanding the facts of which they were aware at the time is the purest hindsight.

Second, by suggesting—along with the commission majority—that a major cause of the financial crisis was the wholesale failure of bank and financial-institution managements, the THH dissent endorsed a policy foundation for more regulation as well as the underlying rationale for the Dodd-Frank Act. After all, if the managements of virtually all the world's financial institutions cannot be trusted to manage their firms, then—to protect the public—governments must oversee them. Yes, it is all hindsight, and highly implausible, but that is exactly the rationale that the Democratic Congress used in designing and enacting the Dodd-Frank Act—and, unfortunately, the implicit policy message of the THH dissent.

Conclusion

There is powerful evidence that the financial crisis was caused by government housing policies and not by a lack of regulation or the simultaneous failures of risk management among the world's largest financial institutions. Under these circumstances, as I state in my dissent, there is reason to doubt that the Dodd-Frank Act was necessary to prevent another financial crisis. It is more likely that a change in government housing policy would provide greater protection against another financial crisis than the Dodd-Frank Act, with none of the adverse effects that the act is likely to have on economic growth in the United States.

3

The Dodd-Frank Act

It is the character rather than the volume of government activity that is important. A functioning market economy presupposes certain activities on the part of the state; there are some other such activities by which its functioning will be assisted; and it can tolerate many more, provided they are of the kind which are compatible with a functioning market. But there are those which run counter to the very principle on which a free system rests and which must therefore be altogether excluded if such a system is to work. In consequence, a government that is comparatively inactive but does the wrong things may do much more to cripple the forces of a market economy than one that is more concerned with economic affairs but confines itself to actions which assist the spontaneous forces of the economy.

— Friedrich A. Hayek, *The Constitution of Liberty*

The Dodd-Frank Act began its journey to eventual enactment in March 2009, with Treasury's unveiling of a plan for a new regulatory structure. The plan was prefigured by various proposals that were circulating in Washington and elsewhere—all of them based on the left's government-absolving narrative that the financial crisis was caused by private greed and risk-taking, insufficient regulation, and particularly the notion—first articulated by Treasury Secretary Paulson and the Bush administration—that the largest financial institutions were so interconnected that the failure of one would bring many of the others down. As long as these ideas were the only ones in general circulation, the enactment of the administration's plan was foreordained.

The Dodd-Frank Legislative Process

As the specific provisions of the act were unfolded, I criticized them in testimony before the relevant committees or in op-eds and *Financial Services Outlooks*. The final act adopted by the House and Senate after a conference of several weeks was well over 2,000 pages. The enrolled version of the act was 849 densely-packed pages, consisting of fifteen titles. According to Davis Polk, a law firm that had closely followed the legislative process, the final act mandated 398 new regulations—many of them to be adopted jointly by two or more agencies—and 67 studies. In many important respects the act was little more than a series of directions to the regulators to come up with specific definitions of statutory terms. By September 2012—more than two years after enactment—regulators have completed only 131 final rules (32.9 percent) and have proposed 135 more (33.9 percent) which have not yet been finalized. No regulations have been proposed for the remaining one-third of the required rules required by Congress. Even where final rules have been adopted, only 38.8 percent were issued within the deadline Congress had established.[1] The act was so open-ended that many constitutional specialists argued that it amounted to an unconstitutional delegation of legislative authority. Eventually, a number of plaintiffs filed a suit making exactly this claim, among others, and many lawyers argued that the act would be tied up in the courts for many years as firms challenged the final regulations that emerge from the agency process and are actually applied to them.

It was remarkable how little serious work on the language of the act was done in committee hearings. Ideally, committee hearings would delve deeply into the specific language of a proposed law, allowing those testifying to inform the committee about potential unintended consequences or practical pitfalls that would impair the purposes of a proposed law. But almost all hearings that were held before the act was passed in both houses were exploratory; there was no specific legislative language to react to, just concepts—questions such as how would one define and control systemic risk. There was

---

1. David Polk, *Dodd-Frank Progress Report*, September 2012, 2, http://www.davispolk .com/files/Publication/2de563f3-93a9-40c4-bb57-04e90d534b58/Presentation/Publication Attachment/209a8a98-285b-4eba-b217-05c5511d2f48/Sept2012_Dodd.Frank.Progress. Report.pdf.

little opportunity to respond to actual language, and often the feeling that the hearings were to build a record of having held hearings without actually accepting advice. In at least one case, witness objections to a specific provision of the act, seemingly accepted by the committee chair, was eventually ignored when the legislative language actually emerged. This occurred in the House Financial Services Committee, where I and other witnesses expressed strong opposition to the idea that specific firms would be designated as systemically important financial institutions (SIFIs)—on the ground that it would give these firms an aura of government backing that would provide them with funding advantages over smaller competitors. In the course of the hearing, the chairman, Barney Frank, said that there "would be no list," but when the bill actually emerged from the committee it authorized a new agency, the Financial Stability Oversight Council (FSOC) to designate specific firms as SIFIs; there was no doubt that these firms would be publicly named.

In all, this massive act, with far-reaching consequences for the U.S. financial system was adopted in less than 18 months from the time it was rolled out as a draft by the Treasury Department. It passed the House without a single Republican vote, and the Senate with only two Republican votes. It is an indication of the complexity of the law, and the difficulty of the assignment Congress gave the regulatory agencies that (according to Davis Polk) two years after the act was signed by President Obama only 123 rules had been finalized, 134 rules had been proposed but not finalized and 141 rules had not yet even been proposed.[2]

Financial Services Outlooks on Dodd-Frank

It is possible to connect every major portion of the Dodd-Frank Act with one or more elements of the left's narrative about the causes of the financial crisis, indicating once again the close relationship between narratives and the policies that result. This point will be illustrated as I discuss the *Financial Services Outlooks* that I wrote as the legislative process on the Dodd-Frank Act moved along.

---

2. Davis Polk, Dodd-Frank Progress Report, 2, July 18, 2012. http://www.davispolk.com/files/Publication/15a76992-d82a-4d15-a2db-fcde9effc3d0/Presentation/PublicationAttachment/b82f9d23-0edc-49eb-af02-ff97ff34bd56/071812_Dodd.Frank.Progress.Report.pdf.

The Group of Thirty Report. One of the first confirmations of the tight connection between the narrative about the financial crisis and the underlying concepts in the Dodd-Frank Act came from the so-called Group of Thirty, a private group of financial experts headed by former Fed chairman Paul Volcker. The group's report was a down-the-line endorsement of the notion that the financial crisis was caused by the errors of the private sector and could only be addressed by handing the government more regulatory authority—in this case, authority to regulate all "systemically significant" financial institutions, not just banks. In January 2009, I reviewed what was known as the G30 report in an essay titled "Regulation without Reason: The Group of Thirty Report" (p. 345). The "without reason" part of the title came from the observation that the group never thought it was necessary to explain why it was proposing more regulation of financial institutions when the financial crisis had shown that the regulation of banks had been a failure. Instead, its report simply assumed that in light of the financial crisis more regulation was necessary. This was a good deal less than one might expect from a group of financial experts, but it was much in tune with the tenor of the times and a confirmation that the false narrative about the causes of the financial crisis had already taken hold.

The Fed as Systemic Regulator. By February 2009, the idea began to circulate in Washington that the Fed should become the regulator of the major financial institutions that were eventually to be classified as systemically significant. In an *Outlook* dated February 2009, "Risky Business: Casting the Fed as a Systemic Risk Regulator" (p. 361), I pointed out that the Fed—as the regulator of the largest bank holding companies in the United States, many of which had insurance and securities subsidiaries—had already been, in effect, a systemic regulator for major portions of the financial system; in that capacity it had failed to spot the growing housing bubble or to prevent the risk-taking that was alleged to have caused the financial crisis. Moreover, this idea meant that the Fed—at most a bank regulator—would also have to become a regulator and supervisor of insurers, finance companies, securities firms, hedge funds, and possibly others. The idea that one regulator could take the place of the market in sorting out the competitive conflicts among all these different businesses was in my view massively naïve.

The fact that this idea was gaining such currency in Washington accurately reflected the slap-dash nature of the legislation that was then under development in the Obama administration. A similar decision later put the FDIC—an agency wholly unprepared for this responsibility—in the role of resolving the largest financial institutions if they were to fail. If one thought that a new and more effective regulatory structure was necessary after the financial crisis, the responsible thing would have been to build one from scratch. That, of course, would have taken time, and the Obama administration wanted to take advantage of the sense of urgency that prevailed at the time to push through new regulatory legislation.

The Financial Stability Oversight Council and the Designation of SIFIs.
When the administration's plan was finally made public in March 2009, it proved to be everything that I and others had feared. There were many troubling provisions, but the one element that seemed to me the most disturbing was the proposal to create a body (the FSOC) that would designate certain institutions as SIFIs (as noted in the previous chapter) and subject them to special regulation on that account. This was a reflection of the invalid "interconnections" idea that was part of the left's narrative, and it fit in well with the Obama administration's apparent desire—also expressed through its health care legislation—to place large portions of the private sector under government control. In the March–April 2009 *Outlook,* "Reinventing GSEs: Treasury's Plan for Financial Restructuring" (p. 377), I argued that designating these institutions as "systemically important" would amount to a declaration that they were too big to fail and—as had happened with Fannie Mae and Freddie Mac and the largest banks—give them funding advantages over others in their industry.

As this is written, in the summer of 2012, the agency that was given this authority, the Financial Stability Oversight Council—made up of all the federal financial regulators—had completed a regulation that describes the standards it will use to designate a particular financial institution as systemically important. As might be expected, "interconnections" had become the major element of this regulation—in addition, of course, to size—but that had clarified nothing. What these interconnections were and how they were to be measured had not been specified, so the entire FSOC effort had been an exercise in "sconking"—the scientification of non-knowledge. In the end, the FSOC would be making a completely arbitrary determination based on a collection of meaningless standards. It would be funny if it weren't so dangerous to the survival of a competitive financial system.

In my view, although there are exceedingly dangerous provisions in the Dodd-Frank Act—many of them discussed below—this is the worst. By providing funding advantages to the largest firms, it has the potential to force consolidation in what are now highly diversified and competitive industries. Just as Fannie and Freddie were able to drive all competition out of the secondary mortgage market because of their funding advantages, so would the largest insurers, finance companies, hedge funds, and others come to dominate their markets, creating massive, government-supported, sclerotic firms that would depend for their continuing dominance on good crony-capitalist relationships with whoever was in power at the Fed and Treasury.

Consumer Financial Protection Bureau. In keeping with the notion that the financial crisis was caused in part by predatory lending—an idea also suggested in the FCIC's majority report, again without any significant data—the administration also needed a strong element of consumer protection in the Dodd-Frank Act. It brought this in with a proposal for an agency that would have unprecedented authority to control financial transactions with consumers.

In July 2009, in "Unfree to Choose: The Administration's Consumer Financial Protection Agency" (p. 396), I summarized the proposal as containing unprecedented regulatory authority along three dimensions. First, it would cover financial transactions with consumers down to the street level all over the country—taking the place of state and local regulation where it existed and imposing federal regulation for the first time where states and localities had not seen fit to impose it. Second, it extended to virtually all firms that had financial dealings with consumers the same general rules that had previously applied only to banks. Every firm of whatever size that had financial dealing with consumers—from check cashers to retailers—would be covered by a federal regulator. And third, and by far the most radical, was a proposal that allowed this new agency to forbid transactions that it deemed "abusive" (a particularly difficult idea to define), including transactions where the consumer involved did not understand the transaction.

In other words, a business could be in violation of the law and the agency's regulations if it sold a product to a consumer who did not fully understand the nature of the transaction. To implement this idea, the agency was to be authorized to approve "plain vanilla" or less risky products for consumers, putting the business in the position of deciding in individual cases whether a consumer had the sophistication or intelligence to understand a particular product. This, the brainchild of a group who call themselves behavioral economists, could be a catastrophically bad idea for consumers. Behavioral economics posits that consumers often make irrational choices and can be misled by advertising that is not necessarily deceptive but relies on the consumer's lack of sophistication.

At this writing the Consumer Financial Protection Bureau (CFPB) is up and running, with a large staff that (according to reports) includes a strong complement of behavioral economists. It would not be surprising if the "plain vanilla" product is all that financial institutions offer in the future. That way, they can protect themselves against consumer or CFPB lawsuits alleging that they misled consumers who didn't understand the financial products they were offered. If, as anticipated, the burden will fall on the provider to show that he or she properly presented a non-plain vanilla product only to consumers who could understand it, adopting only the plain vanilla product will be the only mechanism for escaping these attacks. If the agency's powers are not modified in some way, that's the plain vanilla future American consumers can expect. The originator of this concept was a Harvard Law School professor and now a Democratic candidate for the Senate from Massachusetts named Elizabeth Warren. In pushing for the idea, she had analogized it to the Consumer Products Safety Commission, but that agency only responds when a product has been shown to be unsafe in some way; it has no prior approval function. Because of the "abusive" standard, however, the CFPB has put itself in a position where it must approve financial products before they can be offered. This will substantially raise the costs of businesses and consumers and of course crush innovation in financial services products.

In addition, the substantial costs of regulation will be felt for the first time by small financial firms such as check cashers, currency exchangers, and payday lenders, and will require these industries to consolidate and reduce the availability of services that consumers regularly use. Those services that survive will be more costly.

Credit Default Swaps. Another major element of the administration's regulatory plan was its proposal to regulate derivatives and, in particular, credit default swaps. The connection to the left's narrative in this case is obvious. Even though the FCIC was unable to find any specific causal relationship between derivatives and the financial crisis, it remained a totem of the left that the use of derivatives had to be controlled by regulation. In response, in August 2009 I published "Unnecessary Intervention: The Administration's Effort to Regulate Credit Default Swaps" (p. 409), which showed that the frenzy about the dangers of derivatives, particularly CDSs, was wildly out of proportion to the actual harm they could do. The key points in the piece were that (1) the default of a firm that had written CDS protection did not cause a loss to any of the firms that had bought protection unless there had been a prior default by the reference entity—the firm whose default was covered by the CDS, and (2) no matter how many CDSs had been written to protect against the default of a single firm, there was only one loss.

To illustrate, let's assume that A bought protection from B against a default by C, and that B—to hedge its risk—then bought protection from D and D protection from E, and so forth. This would produce a daisy chain of transactions, each of which would be counted for the total amount at risk, but there would be no losses to anyone in the chain unless C defaulted. In that case, someone—usually the last person in the chain—would suffer a loss, but everyone else would recover from a counterparty. The important points are that there is no loss (other than the cost of the premium to pay for the protection) until there is a default, and then there is only one real loss; all the other payments between the CDS counterparties sum to zero. Thus, the numbers thrown around about the trillions of dollars at risk were only scare tactics. The real potential losses to the financial system in the event of a failure are single-digit fractions of the total.

This point was demonstrated by Lehman's failure. The firm was a big player in the CDS market, but the losses on its collapse did not threaten any counterparty's solvency and were all settled in five weeks at an auction in which $5.2 billion was exchanged among hundreds of counterparties. In addition, Lehman's failure as a counterparty on CDSs did not cause any losses itself unless the reference entities against whose default Lehman had written CDS protection had previously failed. If that hadn't happened, those who had bought protection from Lehman simply went back into the market and bought new protection—which of course might have been more expensive at that time. I also noted that AIG was the only firm seriously damaged by its involvement in CDSs and that this damage occurred primarily because it had sold credit protection to counterparties without hedging its position.

That was seldom done by the firms that actively bought and sold protection in the CDS market. Accordingly, to regulate an entire market because of the failure of a single firm would be like regulating all lending because a single firm made bad loans. I argued that if AIG had been allowed to fail instead of being rescued, no serious harm would have come to its counterparties, most of which had already hedged their exposure to AIG.

The legislation eventually passed, of course, and along the way was made even more burdensome. As this is written in the summer of 2012, the Commodity Futures Trading Commission (CFTC) and the SEC, which were given the authority in the Dodd-Frank Act to regulate derivatives, are both struggling with the complexities of regulating this market and have not yet formulated their most important implementing regulations.

The proposal to regulate derivatives was introduced in August 2009, at a time when it looked as though the whole Dodd-Frank project was in trouble. Even the Democrats were wary of some provisions, and Senator Dodd (the chairman of the Senate Banking Committee) was openly skepti-cal about the idea that the Fed—which in light of the financial crisis had already failed as a systemic supervisor—might be the systemic regulator. At that point, Dodd was talking about a consolidation of the regulatory agencies—a worthwhile step but one that would involve considerable time and controversy to achieve. I was becoming optimistic, accordingly, that the legislation could be sidetracked until after the election of 2010, when there was a chance that the Republicans would take over the House.

Some of this optimism comes through in the *Outlook* on derivatives and CDSs, but Senator Dodd did not follow through. By early 2010, after his deci-sion not to run for reelection to the Senate, Dodd had backed away from the idea of setting up a consolidated regulator and from other objections he had raised, clearing the way for the legislation to be completed by the following July. Apparently, Senator Dodd wanted to get the legislation done while he was still in the Senate, putting him on the same page as an administration that did not want a good crisis to go to waste. Later, of course, the legisla-tion was named after Senator Dodd and his coauthor, Congressman Barney Frank, which is as good an image as any for the way the country's business is manipulated for the benefit of public officials. Although this is speculation, it seems plausible that Senator Dodd abandoned the effort to take authority from the Fed and consolidate the regulatory agencies because he realized that this would prevent the enactment of the legislation while he was still in the Senate, making it unlikely that the new and landmark law would bear his name.

Orderly Liquidation Authority. One of the most significant elements of the Dodd-Frank Act is its provision for the orderly resolution of large "systemically important financial institutions." Indeed, when it became clear that the designation of SIFIs could create a too-big-to-fail (TBTF) problem, the administration's response was not to deny that the problem exists, but to claim that it is solved by the Orderly Liquidation Authority, also called the Orderly Resolution Authority (ORA), in Title II of the act. Whether this is an accurate assessment was addressed in an *Outlook* written in September 2009 as this provision was being framed by the administration and Congress. Titled "TARP Baby: The Administration's Resolution Authority for Nonbank Financial Firms" (p. 422), this essay questioned whether events in the financial crisis supported the idea that the ORA was necessary and whether it actually provided a cure for the too-big-to-fail problem.

Conceptually, the provision appears to be based on the interconnectedness idea—that the failure of one large systemically significant firm will bring down others—a central notion in the left's narrative for the financial crisis. Accordingly, if a large failing firm of this kind can be prevented from going into bankruptcy—placed instead in an orderly liquidation vehicle run by the FDIC—knock-on effects such as those supposedly experienced when Lehman filed for bankruptcy can be avoided. Therefore, the argument runs, with an OLA in place officials will not be afraid in the future to resolve these failing firms by handing them over to the FDIC; ipso facto, no more TBTF.

However, as noted above, Lehman did not have any knock-on effects. To be sure, there was chaos after Lehman Brothers went into bankruptcy, but the important point is that Lehman's failure did not cause any other major financial institution to fail (the one exception, as noted in the introduction, was the Reserve Primary Fund, a money market mutual fund that held onto its Lehman commercial paper, apparently in the belief that Lehman, like Bear Stearns, would be rescued). Under those circumstances it simply cannot be contended that the failure of a large financial institution—because of its interconnections—will cause instability in the financial system if it fails.

By this time, I had more fully developed the common shock idea—that virtually all financial institutions had been weakened before the financial crisis by the mortgage meltdown. As noted in the introduction, the common shock concept had been described by two scholars, George Kaufman and Kenneth Scott, who are also my colleagues on the Shadow Financial Regulatory Committee. In the 2003 article I mentioned earlier, they had defined "common shock" as a phenomenon in which virtually all financial institutions are weakened at the same time by the decline in the value of a widely held asset:

> When one [firm] experiences adverse effects from a shock—say, the failure of a large financial or nonfinancial firm—that generates severe losses, uncertainty is created about the values of other [firms] potentially also subject to adverse effects from the same shock. To minimize additional losses, market participants will examine other [firms], such as banks, in which they have economic interests to see whether and to what extent they are at risk. The more similar the risk-exposure profile to that of the initial [firm] economically, politically, or otherwise, the greater is the probability of loss, and the more likely it is that participants will withdraw funds as soon as possible. This response may induce liquidity problems and even more fundamental solvency problems. This pattern is referred to as a "common shock" or "reassessment shock" effect and represents correlation without direct causation.[3]

This description perfectly matches what happened after Lehman's bankruptcy. When Lehman failed, because of the mortgage meltdown that had weakened virtually all large financial institutions, a market panic was a foregone conclusion. Many market participants reasoned that if Lehman was driven into bankruptcy, firms that looked like Lehman were likely also to be near bankruptcy. This in itself was obvious, but it produces a different remedy from the left's narrative. By accepting the interconnections concept, the left's narrative was moving debate toward a new and highly intrusive regulatory system that would focus on individual systemically important firms and attempt through stringent regulation to keep them from failing. However, if the crisis was caused by a common shock, there was little point in regulating individual large institutions; if financial policy again allowed

---

3. George Kaufman and Kenneth Scott, "What Is Systemic Risk and Do Bank Regulators Retard or Contribute to It?" *Independent Review* 7, no. 3 (Winter 2003), 3.

virtually all institutions to hold the same assets, a crisis will occur again if those assets lose substantial value. The correct policy would be to prevent common shocks, not to focus on more stringent regulations of large firms.

Accordingly, in this *Outlook* I pointed out for the first time that the chaos that followed Lehman's decline was caused by a common shock, not by the Lehman failure itself. If there were no knock-on effects of Lehman's failure in the midst of the financial crisis—when investors were in a state of panic and all financial institutions were seen as weak because of mark-to-market accounting—then there was certainly no need for an orderly resolution authority in times when the market was stable. In those difficult times, as Lehman showed, other firms were still able to survive the failure of a large nonbank financial institution. Accordingly, the Lehman event actually shows the opposite of what it is frequently cited for; instead of demonstrating the need for an OLA, it shows that in a stable market any large nonbank financial institution can go into bankruptcy without jeopardizing the financial condition of others. In other words, this *Outlook* demonstrates that nonbank financial firms should never be considered too big to fail and hence that there was no need for an orderly resolution process for these firms outside bankruptcy.

The FSOC and Crony Capitalism. This, however, is a separate question from the moral hazard that is created when certain firms are designated as SIFIs. In such cases, the firms so designated have been given an aura of government concern for their safety and soundness that will inevitably result in their appearing to be less risky credits than firms that have not received a SIFI designation. Imagine, for example, how a pension fund manager would distinguish between two firms, one of which has been designated as a SIFI and the other not. Buying a bond issued by the former rather than the latter would be much easier to justify, and that will give firms designated as SIFIs large funding advantages in comparison to their smaller competitors.

When the Dodd-Frank Act finally passed in July 2010, I published an *Outlook* that summarized my bleak view of its long-term effects. In that July–August 2010 issue, "The Dodd-Frank Act: Creative Destruction, Destroyed" (p. 439), I saw the legislation as installing a corporatist structure on the previously competitive financial industry. The authority of the FSOC to designate certain firms as SIFIs was, to me, the single most troubling thing about the act. SIFIs were to be considered systemically important because—under the invalid "interconnections" idea in the left's narrative—if one of these SIFIs failed, it would drag down others. Once designation occurs, the firm is turned over to the Fed for what the DFA called "stringent" regulation.

In the interests of creating a doubtful stability, accordingly, the act had created a structure that could eventually place all the sectors of the financial industry under the government's control, primarily by empowering the Fed to regulate all the largest firms in each industry. The kind of creative destruction that is brought about by innovation and change will be made far more difficult, as smaller firms are unable to compete effectively with the large government-backed firms. The Fed, with authority to control the capital, liquidity, leverage, and activities of all these firms—insurers, securities firms, finance companies, hedge funds, and others, in addition to bank holding companies and banks—will have the power of life and death over SIFIs; an increase in the capital required of one industry will provide competitive advantages to others; permitting one firm to enter a new business will disadvantage others.

All these factors will place the Fed and to some extent the secretary of the Treasury, as the head of the FSOC, at the center of the concerns of the managements of these large financial firms. Rather than focusing their attention where it should be placed—how they can develop new products or outrun their competition—they will be worrying about how their regulator will view their actions. In the end, what this will create is a kind of partnership between the government and the largest financial institutions in which there will be an implicit bargain: we'll protect you if you behave as we want. This is the essence of the corporatist or crony capitalist economy, where the most successful firms will be those that can navigate the politics of Washington rather than the challenges of the competitive market. What this will produce over time is a different kind of U.S. economy, one with less innovation and competition, higher consumer prices, and slower economic growth.

Comparing the New Deals of FDR and Obama. As the year after the enactment of Dodd-Frank wore on, it became apparent that the economy was not recovering as it had from recessions in the past. The housing market was still weak, and the unemployment rate was not improving. It occurred to me that this slow recovery had some resemblance to the 1930s—and this raised a question whether both the Obama economy and the New Deal had something in common. I explored this issue in the June–July 2011 *Outlook*, which was titled "Is Obama's New Deal Better Than the Old One?" (p. 452), and I concluded that the similarities came from common factors—primarily legislation and regulations that created uncertainties for business, discouraging investment and hiring. The Dodd-Frank Act and the health finance legislation known as Obamacare were compared to the New Deal's National Industrial Recovery Act and the Agricultural Adjustment Act, both of which were eventually struck down by the Supreme Court. Those acts raised questions about the future for the business community and slowed the New Deal recovery substantially. From the time of Roosevelt's election in 1932, through the year 1940, the unemployment rate never sank below 14.5 percent, and there was a double-dip recession in 1937. This history suggests that the business uncertainties created by Dodd-Frank and Obamacare could be having similar effects today. The Dodd-Frank Act seems to be having exactly the same effect on the economy as the early enactments of FDR's New Deal.

The Orderly Liquidation Authority and Too-Big-to-Fail. When the regulations under the Dodd-Frank Act began to appear in 2011, I returned to some of the ideas I had written about earlier. The increasing dissatisfaction with the Dodd-Frank Act caused many observers to look, perhaps for the first time, at whether the act addressed many of the issues raised by the 2008 financial crisis. One element that continued to be politically salient in Washington was the issue of too big to fail. Both Democrats and Republicans opposed the notion that any firm should be TBTF, so the Democrats and the administration were on the defensive about the FSOC's authority to designate certain firms as SIFIs. This seemed to be a clear case in which the act had fostered TBTF and moral hazard. In defending the act, its supporters claimed that while the designation of firms could make them TBTF, there were two countervailing elements. The first was that the OLA eliminated the possibility that any firm might be considered TBTF by the regulators because the regulators would no longer be afraid of closing down a large firm; by turning the firm over to the FDIC for liquidation, none of the problems with a bankruptcy would arise. The second argument was that designation as a SIFI would not confer any benefits because stringent regulation by the Fed would be so costly that it would overwhelm whatever funding benefits the agency might receive because it was perceived as TBTF.

Both arguments are without foundation and implausible. The first was addressed in August–September 2011 in "The Error at the Heart of the Dodd-Frank Act" (p. 470), which concluded not only that the orderly resolution provisions of the act would not prevent a similar chaotic event if conditions in the market were the same as those in 2008, but also that the existence of an orderly resolution process would create affirmative harm to the financial system. I noted, first, that it was a common shock—combined with mark-to-market accounting—that caused the weakness and instability that characterized the period before Lehman's bankruptcy in 2008. When the market for MBS collapsed in 2007, financial firms could no longer use their MBS for financing and were required to write down the value of their holdings on their balance sheets, reducing their regulatory capital as well as their liquidity. This caused deep anxiety among investors and market participants, so when Lehman was allowed to fail, a full-scale panic erupted.

I then asked whether things would have been different if the OLA had actually been in effect at the time. The answer was no. The seizure of a firm by the secretary of the Treasury—the mechanism set up by the act as the first step in the OLA process—would not be any less shocking to the market than the firm's bankruptcy filing. In 2008, with the financial system already ripe for panic because of the common shock, the takeover of Lehman by the FDIC would have induced the same panic as had occurred after Lehman's bankruptcy. Investors and market participants would have run on other firms that seemed to present the same risks as Lehman. On the other hand, the Lehman case also shows that there are likely to be very few, if any, knock-on effects even where there *is* common shock. Together these facts demonstrate, as I argued in this *Outlook,* "that in the absence of a common shock that weakens all or most financial institutions, the bankruptcy of one or a few firms would not cause a financial crisis; on the other hand, given a similarly severe common shock in the future, subjecting a few financial firms to the act's orderly resolution process will not prevent a crisis." In other words, the correct policy, as I had observed before, was to prevent common shocks, not to set up an elaborate regulatory structure to prevent failures.

This *Outlook* also demonstrated that the orderly liquidation process in the act was not just useless but affirmatively harmful. It is applicable to any financial firm that the government believes might cause a financial crisis when it fails, and since the act's resolution process is an alternative to bankruptcy, it throws into question whether any creditor of a financial firm can know what law will govern the borrower's insolvency. If it is the bankruptcy system, the creditor will be able to predict the likely outcome of the firm's failure, but in the OLA the FDIC is given enormous discretionary powers to prefer some creditors over others. There is no way to know in advance which of the two systems will apply, and the uncertainties this will produce will inevitably raise the cost of financing for all financial firms of any size. Moreover, the OLA introduces another destructive issue—the politics that will be involved as powerful figures and interests in Washington seek to improve the outcome for their constituents in any case the FDIC is handling.

Would SIFIs' Costs Exceed Their Benefits? On the question whether SIFIs would face such costly additional regulation that they would not get any net benefit out of their more favorable funding, I argued in my October–November 2011 *Outlook*, "Magical Thinking: The Latest Regulation from the Financial Stability Oversight Council" (p. 488), that this defied logic. It would only work if the additional cost of regulation exactly balanced the funding advantages—a wholly implausible outcome. Nevertheless, if it were to happen—if the cost of regulation were actually to exceed the funding benefits, then all these SIFIs would be out-competed by their smaller and more nimble competitors. What we would have then was a group of large failing firms being kept alive by the Fed to avoid its own embarrassment if they failed. In the end, they would fail, and the taxpayers would have to pick up the pieces.

Housing Finance. Another area where the act was having an adverse effect was in the housing field, which continued to be historically weak almost four years after the financial crisis. Again, the reason for this was perfectly clear: following the left's narrative about the financial crisis, the act had imposed so many poorly thought-out regulations on the financial system—particularly in housing finance—that credit for mortgages was unavailable even though rates were at historic lows. Accordingly, in the February 2012 *Outlook*, "Empty Promise: The Holes in the Administration's Housing Finance Reform Plan" (p. 502), I reviewed how the Dodd-Frank Act had made it difficult, perhaps impossible, for there to be a revival of a private housing finance system in the United States. Not only did the act provide substantial competitive advantages to the FHA and the GSEs—which will keep private sector securitizers out of the largest sectors of the housing market—but it also imposed numerous restrictions on mortgage lending that would have to be eliminated before a robust private housing finance system could reemerge.

One key provision of the act that caused particular trouble was the so-called Qualified Mortgage, or QM. This idea, like the others in the DFA, came right out of the left's narrative, which held that homebuyers had been deceived into taking favorable mortgages that they did not understand. When the collapse came, these homebuyers lost their homes. Accordingly, the QM provides that the originator of a mortgage had to be sure that the homebuyer could afford it. If it were to turn out that the borrower could not afford the mortgage, the borrower could use that as a defense to foreclosure. Obviously, it's virtually impossible to be sure that someone can afford a mortgage—even at the moment the purchase is closed—and this has made lenders very cautious about making mortgages, even before the QM is in effect. The CFPB now has jurisdiction over this matter, and as this book is written it has not yet decided whether there should be a safe harbor—a series of tests that will be considered a sufficient showing that the borrower could afford the mortgage—or whether a demonstration that the lender attempted to determine the financial capacity of the borrower would create a rebuttable presumption in favor of the lender. Obviously, a rebuttable presumption is not going to be much legal protection in the future. If there is no safe harbor, getting a mortgage will be much tougher and more expensive in the future than it was in the past.

The QM is perhaps the clearest example of the absurdity of the results produced by the left's false narrative about the financial crisis. Adopting the idea that mortgage defaults were caused by lenders rather than borrowers could only be dreamed up by a professor somewhere; no one else could be so driven by ideology and so fully adrift from reality. Yet the DFA is suffused with other examples, large and small, of an ideologically driven effort to control the U.S. financial system instead of a clear-eyed view of what caused the financial crisis.

The conceptual flaws in the DFA, outlined in this chapter, are attributable to the fact that it is based almost entirely on a false narrative about what caused the financial crisis. For this reason, it has impeded the economic recovery and placed the reelection of President Obama in jeopardy. When the Supreme Court upheld the constitutionality of Obamacare in late June 2012, Republicans vowed to work for its repeal in the next session of Congress. In the next chapter, I review why the Dodd-Frank Act—which has perhaps caused even more economic uncertainty than Obamacare—deserves at least similar attention.

"Regulation without Reason: The Group of Thirty Report"

Originally published January 2009

For months, the media have been predicting that a strong new regulatory flux would emerge from the financial crisis. Now, with a new report by the dirigiste wing of the Group of Thirty (G30), we know what the future could look like. A good summary is that bank-like regulation would be spread beyond the banking industry. But there's a problem: banks have been tightly regulated for years, both in the United States and Europe, and of all the institutions hurt by the financial crisis, they are in the most trouble. How do the bankers, academics, and financial policymakers who make up the G30 deal with this? They don't. In the wake of this report, the principal question that Congress, the Obama administration, and the American people should ask is why regulation should be extended to most of the major players in the financial system when it has been a consistent failure for banks.

Just before the inauguration of President Barack Obama, a subcommittee of the G30, a private organization of international financial experts, published a report setting out a series of recommendations for regulatory reform in the wake of the financial crisis.[4] Because the head of the subcommittee was Paul Volcker, an adviser to President Obama, the *Washington Post* immediately suggested that its recommendations were a forerunner to what the Obama administration would propose, calling it "the first hint of the kind of changes to the financial system President-elect Barack Obama might push for in the coming weeks and months."[5] We should all hope that greater thought and imagination

---

4. See Working Group on Financial Reform, *Financial Reform: A Framework for Financial Stability* (Washington, DC: Group of Thirty, January 15, 2009), available at www.group30.org/pubs/recommendations.pdf (accessed January 21, 2009).

5. Anthony Faiola, "Obama Adviser Presents Plan to Alter Global Financial System," *Washington Post,* January 15, 2009.

goes into the Obama administration's proposals on financial regulation, whatever they may be.

The report is unusual in that it consists almost entirely of background discussion and recommendations, without any underlying analysis or justification for its proposals. The idea that far-reaching recommendations can be made without any analytical support—based, apparently, solely on the credentials of the authors—is disconcerting. And the recommendations are indeed far-reaching. Among them:

- Special regulation of "systemically important banking institutions"

- "A framework for national-level consolidated prudential regulation and supervision over large internationally active insurance companies"

- Reorganization of money market funds as "special purpose banks" if they offer transaction features

- Special prudential regulation of "systemically significant" private pools of capital (such as hedge funds and private equity)

- A special legal regime that would provide regulators with "authority to require early warning, prompt corrective actions, and orderly closings of regulated banking organizations, and other systemically significant regulated financial institutions"

These are recommendations that could profoundly reshape the U.S. financial system—and not for the better.

The Elephant in the Room: The Failure of Bank Regulation

The weakness of the banking industry—the most heavily regulated part of the financial system—is the central and most obvious problem in the current financial crisis. This is not a new development. The current regulatory regime for commercial banks and savings and loans (S&Ls) was substantially tightened after the S&L debacle in the late 1980s, in which the S&L industry collapsed and 1,600 commercial banks also failed. This gave rise to the Federal Deposit Insurance Corporation Improvement Act of 1991 (FDICIA), which significantly increased the powers of bank and S&L regulators. FDICIA was adopted to make sure, as is always said, "this won't happen again." Yet, only a few weeks ago, the federal government had to commit several hundred billion dollars for a guarantee of Citigroup's assets, despite the fact that examiners from the Office of the Comptroller of the Currency (OCC) have been inside the bank full-time for years, supervising the operations of this giant institution under the broad powers granted by FDICIA to bank supervisors.

Ordinarily, confronted with this dismal narrative, anyone recommending more regulation—covering yet more of the financial system—would at least feel the need to explain why the new regulation would be different and better than before. To be sure, there is an effort to advance "improvements" in prudential regulation and supervision, but these are weak and pedestrian. There are also some vague recommendations for reducing regulation's obvious procyclicality, but for the most part, these are superficial and unimaginative. Fundamentally, the report seems to reflect a judgment that the financial crisis makes the need for new and broader regulation self-evident. In reality, however, the opposite is true; the financial crisis shows that regulation is no better than market discipline at preventing the failure of financial institutions and that even in the dire circumstances of the current crisis, systemic risk—the only justification for extending regulation beyond banks—has not appeared.

Apart from its multinational approach, the report's recommendations for improving regulation and supervision have all been around the track in ages past: "Countries should reevaluate their regulatory structures with a view to eliminating unnecessary overlaps and gaps in coverage" (there were no "gaps" in coverage, however, in the OCC's unsuccessful supervision of Citi); countries should "reaffirm the insulation of national regulatory authorities from political and market pressures" (it is doubtful that this means freedom from congressional oversight, but if not, it has no meaning at all); the central bank should have supervisory responsibility over systemically significant firms (the Federal Reserve has had such authority over the holding companies of all the major U.S. banks since the 1970s, to no apparent effect); and there should be more international cooperation and coordination (the Basel Committee on Banking Supervision, consisting of the bank regulators of all the developed countries, has also been operating without notable success since the 1970s).

The recommendations for how supervisors are supposed to deal with procyclicality are somewhat more insightful. There is a recommendation for increasing bank capital requirements in periods of exuberance and a recommendation for greater risk disclosures, but no discussion of how procyclicality might have contributed to the failure of bank regulation in the current crisis or in the past. There is veiled criticism of Basel II's new model-based approach to credit risk ("Benchmarks for being well capitalized should be raised, given the demonstrable limitations of even the most advanced tools for estimating firmwide risk."), and there is an important gesture toward changing the focus of fair value accounting so that it more closely aligns with an institution's intermediary role ("[T]he accounting principles and approaches applicable to regulated financial institutions whose primary purpose is to intermediate credit and liquidity risk need to be better aligned with the firm's business model. A pure mark-to-market accounting model is generally preferred for trading activities and most elements of market risk."). The balance of the recommendations, however, is uninspiring. For example: "conducting periodic reviews of a firm's potential vulnerability to risk arising from credit concentrations, excessive maturity mismatches, excessive leverage, or undue reliance on asset market liquidity" (If this has not been part of regular bank supervision, it is unclear what the regulators have been doing.); "international capital standards should be enhanced" (The Basel Committee spent the last ten years trying to develop an enhanced international capital standard for banks, which went into effect just before the collapse.); and "supervisory guidance for liquidity standards should be based on a more refined analysis of a firm's capacity to maintain ample liquidity under stress conditions" (According to the chairman of the Securities and Exchange Commission [SEC], two days before its rescue, Bear Stearns had $12 billion in liquid securities;[6] how would "refinements" have addressed this?). In other words, there are few new ideas underlying the G30's move to impose more and broader regulation on the financial system—just the same old impulse for more regulation when the regulation already in place has failed once again.

The Deficiencies of Financial Regulation—and When It Is Needed

Even if regulation had been successful in the past, there would be many reasons not to impose it more widely—none of which can be found in the report:

---

6. Christopher Cox (address, Security Traders Twelfth Annual Washington Conference, Washington, DC, May 7, 2008), available at www.sec.gov/news/speech/2008/spch050708cc.htm (accessed January 27, 2009).

- The very existence of regulation—especially safety-and-soundness regulation, with which the report primarily deals—creates moral hazard and reduces market discipline. Market participants believe that if the government is looking over the shoulder of the regulated industry, it is able to control risk-taking, and lenders are thus less wary that regulated entities are assuming unusual or excessive risks.

- Regulation creates anticompetitive economies of scale. The costs of regulation are more easily borne by large companies than by small ones. Moreover, large companies have the ability to influence regulators to adopt regulations that favor their operations over those of smaller competitors, particularly when regulations add costs that smaller companies cannot bear.

- Regulation impairs innovation. Regulatory approvals necessary for new products or services delay implementation, give competitors an opportunity to imitate, and add costs to the process of developing new ways of doing business or new services.

- Regulation adds costs to consumer products. These costs are frequently not worth the additional amount that consumers are required to pay.

- Safety-and-soundness regulation in particular preserves weak managements and outdated business models, imposing long-term costs on society.

These deficiencies—together with its regular failure as a protection for the taxpayers or the economy—suggest that regulation should be a last resort, employed only when absolutely required. There are several circumstances that may meet this standard:

- When a company or an industry has the backing—implicit or explicit—of the government. Explicit backing exists, for example, with commercial banks. Implicit backing existed when Fannie Mae and Freddie Mac were allowed to continue operating with government charters and other benefits that signaled to the market that they would never be allowed to fail. In these cases, the wariness of creditors is impaired, and market discipline is reduced, allowing more risk-taking than would normally occur. Because of its adverse effect on competition and its tendency to create taxpayer liabilities, government backing—explicit or implicit—should be avoided. But where it occurs, regulation is the only option.

- When the failure of a particular company or financial institution will have systemic effects by weakening or causing defaults by its counterparties, depositors, or creditors. As discussed below, there are elements here of self-fulfilling prophecy. If we designate companies as "systemically significant," we will certainly make them so. The designation itself reduces or eliminates market discipline and enables them to grow faster than their competitors. In normal markets, it is very difficult for companies without government backing to become systemically significant, and currently, the only companies that can be so considered are already regulated as banks. As discussed below, a designation as "systemically significant" operates as government backing.

- When there is a significant asymmetry of knowledge between a supplier of services and its customers. Personal insurance lines—such as homeowners, auto, or life—are frequently cited as examples of this. The complex contracts required for this service are beyond the ability of most consumers to understand. State or federal regulation is necessary in this case for consumer protection. The same may be true of mortgage loans. It may well be that some homebuyers do not understand the commitments they are making when they sign up for mortgages with low teaser rates and high resets. In these cases, regulation may be required to assure that the risks are made known to them in clear and simple language. Regulation of this kind does not necessarily involve safety and soundness.

- When there is a market failure of another kind, such as a harmful pharmaceutical product that could be sold to consumers before the dangers are known.

One of the deficiencies of the report is that it does not appear to recognize that a decision to regulate more fully involves a weighing of any of these considerations. It nods in this direction with the statement that "care must be taken not to extend the reach of regulations too far or too deeply," but it never explains why the broader safety-and-soundness regulation it recommends is not extending regulation "too far or too deeply" or why it is necessary. There is no suggestion that regulation has any costs or deficiencies or that it has failed in specific instances, nor is there an argument that despite these deficiencies and failures, regulation is necessary in certain cases. Without this kind of policy analysis, it is difficult to see why extending regulation beyond commercial banks, S&Ls, and government-sponsored enterprises (GSEs) like Fannie Mae and Freddie Mac—all of which have some form of government backing that diminishes the effect of market discipline—would be productive or useful. As noted above, experience with regulation shows that it impairs competition and innovation, raises consumer and social costs, and interferes with the market discipline that holds risk-taking in check.

Is There Any Policy Basis for Extending Regulation?

Since the advent of the financial crisis, many observers have argued that it resulted from excessive trust in the ability of markets to regulate themselves. Occasionally, these critiques go so far as to claim that this has been the prevailing theory of the last thirty years and has thus been proven wrong. The fact that some unregulated or largely unregulated institutions have failed during the financial crisis is cited as evidence that there is a need for greater government oversight of the financial system. This formulation misstates the history of financial regulation, ignores the fact that the most regulated institutions in the economy—commercial banks—are in the most financial trouble, and fails to explain why it is necessary for the federal government and taxpayers to prevent the failure of any company (or failures within any industry) that is currently not regulated.

In reality, there has been no "theory" during the last three decades that private markets and private financial institutions could largely be trusted to regulate themselves. The adoption of FDICIA in 1991 proves that the contrary is actually true. The theory that has prevailed over the last three decades is the same one that has governed U.S. government policy on financial regulation for the last two hundred years—that there is no sound policy reason for the federal government to regulate or protect the safety and soundness of any financial institution for which it has not assumed financial responsibility. The idea that the federal government has in some sense withdrawn its regulation of financial institutions over the last thirty years—or that a different theory about financial regulation prevailed in the past—is entirely fallacious. Yet, by proposing regulation that goes beyond the traditional role of the federal government, the report does not seem to recognize that it is breaking new policy ground or that there is any need to justify such an expansion of government control and responsibility.

With the limited exception of the five largest investment banks, federally backed commercial banks, S&Ls, and GSEs are the only financial institutions that have ever been regulated for safety and soundness at the federal level. In 2004, in response to a demand by the European Union (EU) that securities firms operating in the EU have a consolidated home-country safety-and-soundness regulator, the SEC assumed this role for the five largest investment banks then doing business in the EU. This proved disastrous, as all five took advantage of the moral hazard thus created to overleverage themselves.

Assuming, however, that we treat the investment banks as unregulated, there has been only one total failure among these institutions—Lehman Brothers—while four others have either been rescued (Bear Stearns and Merrill Lynch) or sought shelter with the Fed by becoming bank holding companies (Morgan Stanley and Goldman Sachs). It may well be that all these institutions would have ultimately failed, but this result must be compared with the failures of the many heavily regulated banks and S&Ls that have failed thus far, and particularly with the multibillion dollar rescue of at least one bank—Citibank—that was overseen continuously for years by the OCC. The argument that the failure of unregulated financial institutions was the result of their lack of regulation is clearly unsustainable; it completely ignores the fact that many more fully regulated entities have suffered the same fate. If regulation does not produce a better result than nonregulation, there is no reason to impose it.

Why might the government want to regulate the safety and soundness or—more specifically—the leverage of financial institutions for which it has no financial responsibility? Although they are painful when they occur, the failures of companies are a good thing from the standpoint of the overall health and productivity of the economy. Bad managements or bad business models are eliminated from the market, making room for good managements and better business models. The losses by investors and creditors make them cautious about their investments and loans in the future, enhancing market discipline. Why would the government want to prevent these salutary results? Among the reasons for regulation cited above, the only one that seems plausible as a basis for safety-and-soundness regulation is the government's interest in preventing systemic risk—that is, the possibility that the failure of one institution, through contagion, would cause other failures throughout the economy.

This, however, has never happened. There is no example in all of U.S. history in which the failure of an unregulated financial entity—securities firm, hedge fund, insurance company, finance company, or private equity fund—caused a systemic breakdown. In 1990, for example, when the investment bank Drexel Burnham failed, there was no systemic result. Occasionally, the example of the hedge fund Long-Term Capital Management (LTCM) is cited. What we know of that event is that the Fed—fearful that a systemic event would ensue if LTCM failed—convened a number of large LTCM lenders and suggested that they rescue the fund, which they did. We do not know what would have happened if they had not, and many scholars believe that the Fed overreacted.[7] In any event, LTCM never failed, and there was no systemic event. In order to maintain that there is now a policy basis for regulating firms and industries that have not previously been regulated, there must be a demonstrated change in market conditions. There is simply no evidence of this—no evidentiary basis whatsoever for arguing that the financial market is any different today than it has always been or that the failure of an unregulated entity today would have a systemic effect on the economy as a whole. Since the beginning of the financial crisis, many hedge funds have suffered major losses and have closed their doors, but in no case has the failure of a hedge fund had a systemic effect. The same thing is true of insurance companies. The G30's recommendation for hedge fund or insurance company regulation is thus without empirical justification. If, in the current panicky market, hedge fund failures have not brought down other financial institutions, what justification can there be for regulating their safety and soundness or their activities in the future, when market conditions will have returned to normal?

Reports in the media that the financial markets are now more "interconnected" are also not evidence of any change in market structure. Financial markets have always been interconnected; that is how they perform their primary function of moving money from places where it is not useful to places where it is.

---

7. Shadow Financial Regulatory Committee, "The Issues Posed by the Near-Collapse of Long-Term Capital Management," September 28, 1998, available at www.aei.org/docLib/20051114_ShadowStatement151.pdf.

Financial institutions are called "intermediaries" because they are interconnected, and nothing about the financial markets today makes them more interconnected than they were before. It is true that money moves faster in the electronic markets we have today and that this makes it possible for investors and counterparties to move their funds more quickly from institutions that they regard as troubled, but this is not an indication that the markets are more interconnected.

This is demonstrated by the failure of Lehman Brothers. At the time Lehman failed, there was a strong reaction of panic in the financial markets. Banks stopped lending to one another, and the credit markets froze. We are still living with the results of that event. However, Lehman's inability to meet its obligations did not result in the "contagion" that is the hallmark of systemic risk. No bank or any other Lehman counterparty seems to have been injured in any major respect by Lehman's failure, although of course losses occurred. The market freeze was caused not by these relatively minor losses but by a recognition on the part of banks and other financial institutions that their counterparties could be weak and neither they nor their counterparties would be bailed out by the government. Knowing that they would have to close if they could not meet depositor or investor demands for cash, their hoarding of cash after Lehman's failure was wholly rational. Although there were media reports that AIG had to be rescued shortly after Lehman's failure because it had been exposed excessively to Lehman through credit default swaps (CDSs), these were inaccurate. When all of the CDSs on Lehman were settled about a month later, AIG's exposure turned out to be only $6.2 million. Moreover, although Lehman was one of the largest players in the CDS market, all its CDS obligations were settled without incident, and all the CDSs written on Lehman itself were settled for a cash exchange of only $5.2 billion among hundreds of counterparties. There is no indication that any financial institution became troubled or failed because of the failure of Lehman, and hence no systemic risk arose out of the failure of one of the largest dealers in the CDS market.[8] This casts considerable doubt on

---

8. As an aside, credit default swaps (CDSs) are no different from loans. If a company writes protection on a loan, as AIG did, what it has done is not essentially different from making the loan itself. The widely bruited concerns about CDSs are unfounded. There is no evidence that they create any more risks than lending itself. See Peter J. Wallison, "Everything You Wanted to Know about Credit Default Swaps—but Were Never Told," *Financial Services Outlook* (December 2008), available at www.aei.org/publication 29158. (See p. 223 of this book.)

the notion that CDSs have made the market more "interconnected" or that they somehow increased aggregate market risks.

Reasons for Financial Regulation

The G30 report seems to rely on two ideas as the basis for the extension of regulation beyond institutions that have some form of government backing: that regulation will produce more "transparency" for stakeholders in financial institutions and that systemic risk in the future can only be prevented if a government agency is empowered to identify "systemically significant" financial institutions and regulate them accordingly.

Transparency. Transparency is important in fostering market discipline, and one of the goals of regulation—where regulation is required because of government backing—should be to develop metrics or indicators of risk-taking that will better inform creditors and counterparties about the risks that financial institutions have assumed.[9] Is the same requirement necessary for unregulated entities? No; transparency for its own sake, while an attractive ideal, is not worth the costs and deficiencies of regulation unless there is a sound policy rationale for regulation. That policy basis for transparency exists in securities regulation, in which disclosure is required for companies and others that seek investments from the general public. Here, there is a genuine asymmetry of knowledge: managements of companies know far more about their companies than ordinary retail investors. Beyond disclosure to investors, is there a reason for insisting on transparency elsewhere? The G30 report describes the market for CDSs as one for which regulation of some kind is necessary to assure transparency. The CDS market, like the foreign exchange and the interest-rate swap markets, is a dealer market; trades occur over the counter and are not visible until reported. The interest-rate swap market has been functioning for twenty-five years without serious mishap, and the foreign exchange market much longer, also without serious breakdowns. Would it be useful to disrupt these markets in order to achieve transparency? The fact that the CDS market is functioning well, even at

---

9. Shadow Financial Regulatory Committee, "An Open Letter to President-Elect Obama," December 8, 2008, available at www.aei.org/docLib/20081208_Statement No.264.pdf.

a time when many other markets—many of them more transparent—are virtually shut down, suggests that transparency is not necessary to serve the needs of those who participate in this market. This does not mean that improvements in the infrastructure of the CDS market are unnecessary, but these can be achieved by the participants in the market without government involvement. If there were a genuine concern about systemic risk arising out of transactions in the CDS market, that might put a different cast on the question, but since the Lehman bankruptcy, it has been very difficult to argue that the CDS market is a source of systemic risk.

The quality and tone of the G30 report is captured well in its discussion of CDSs. After noting that efforts are underway to "address infrastructure weaknesses," the report states: "For most of the past 30 years, the markets developed in something of a regulatory vacuum, being regarded legally as neither securities nor futures contracts. Innovations were widespread and the markets grew explosively, suggesting that, beyond serving a valuable risk transfer function, a large speculative element has emerged." Note the circular logic. The CDS market should be regulated because it has not been regulated. No reason is given for why "speculation" among sophisticated consenting adults should be curbed by regulation.

"Systemically Significant" Institutions. The final question, then, is whether—as proposed in the G30 report—a government agency should be empowered to identify "systemically significant" institutions and regulate them specially. The basis for this proposal appears to be a desire for stability and a fear of systemic risk. It is important to note, however, that there is no evidence that the failure of an institution that is currently unregulated poses any kind of threat to the financial system. As noted above, no hedge funds, for example, have needed a rescue by the government. And although many have closed their doors, none of these closures has created a systemic event.

Moreover, the suggestion that a government agency should be empowered to designate systemically significant institutions and regulate them more fully than others is a particularly troubling idea for industries—such as hedge funds, insurance companies, securities firms, and private equity groups—for which the G30 report suggests that safety-and-soundness regulation is necessary to avoid systemic risk. The recommendation seems to ignore the obvious consequences of such a policy. Even assuming that it is possible to identify systemically significant institutions in advance of their failure—which itself is difficult to believe—what would such a designation mean? Clearly, the institutions involved would not be allowed to fail—that is the reason they are being designated as systemically significant. And if these institutions are not going to be allowed to fail, they will have substantial competitive advantages over institutions that are not so designated. They will have easier access to capital and loans and will grow faster. Other, presumably smaller, competitors seeking the same advantages will consolidate in order to be considered within the category of the select few that will not be allowed to fail. In other words, designating institutions as systemically significant will have essentially the same result as creating a new crop of GSEs like Fannie Mae and Freddie Mac. But this new category would be open-ended, so virtually any company could join by proving to the designating agency that its failure could be a threat to the system. The effect on our competitive system would be dire.

Far from making the financial system more stable, the designation of certain companies or financial institutions as systemically significant would have the effect of increasing the number of failures. In his famous book *Manias, Panics, and Crashes,* Charles Kindleberger recognizes this problem:

> When asset prices tumble sharply, the surge in the demand for liquidity may drive many individuals and firms into bankruptcy, and the sale of assets in these distressed circumstances may induce further declines in asset prices. At such times a lender of last resort can provide financial stability or attenuate financial instability. The dilemma is that if investors knew in advance that government support would be forthcoming under generous dispensation when asset prices fall sharply, markets might break down somewhat more frequently because investors will be less cautious in their purchases of assets and of securities.[10]

It is not possible to cure moral hazard by injecting more of it into the economy. Systemic risk is context-specific. As noted above, when Drexel Burnham failed in 1990, the markets were stable and functioning normally. There was very little reaction and no systemic problems that arose because of this failure. However, in 2008, when there was doubt about the solvency and stability of

---

10. Charles Kindleberger and Robert Alibar, *Manias, Panics, and Crashes: A History of Financial Crises,* 5th ed. (Hoboken, NJ: Wiley, 2005), 14.

most of the world's major financial institutions, the failure of Lehman produced a significant effect, even though there is no evidence that Lehman's failure to meet its obligations resulted in any contagion to or substantial adverse effects on any other financial institution. For this reason, it is impossible to know in advance when the failure of a particular institution will have a systemic effect and when it will not. The effect of a failure will depend on the nature of its relationships with other institutions and on the financial condition of those institutions at some future time. For these reasons, the decision of the systemic regulator or designating agency will be wholly arbitrary, although of course erring on the side of caution so as to increase its bureaucratic reach.

The Lehman example also seems to demonstrate that even when a major institution fails at a time of profound market panic, the actual systemic risks are minimal or nonexistent. Other institutions come to fear runs by their depositors and counterparties and hoard cash for that reason, but they do not suffer life-threatening losses as a result of the failure. Nor is it possible to argue that regulation is necessary in order to prevent the failure of systemically significant institutions; if there were ever a systemically significant institution, it was Citibank, and of course the government had to step in to rescue it despite the fact that the bank was heavily and continuously regulated. So even if it were possible to identify systemically significant institutions, and even if we were willing to bear the competitive and moral hazard consequences of designating these institutions as too big to fail, we would still not be able to avert their failure through regulation.

Sometimes it is argued that the government has created so much moral hazard by rescuing some financial institutions during the current crisis that we now have no choice but to regulate systemically significant firms. However, even if the firms rescued during the financial crisis are seen by some in the future as too big to fail—or an indication that others will be so considered in the future—that is still not a good reason for removing all doubt by declaring any firm to be systemically significant and thus too big to fail. Any uncertainty about what the government will actually do, especially when the market is functioning normally, will preserve some element of market discipline. The appropriate policy response in the future is to adopt procedural restrictions on the government's use of its rescue authority so that some question remains about whether the government will exercise this option when the market is in a more normal condition. This was done in FDICIA, which requires the secretary of the treasury to consult with the president before the FDIC is permitted to bail out a large failing institution. In addition, of course, if financial institutions are allowed to fail, that would go some way toward restoring market discipline. Allowing Lehman to fail would have had this effect, but it was premature. There was still too much fear in the market. Finally, it would make sense to adopt policies that will limit the growth of institutions that might be considered too big to fail, including added capital charges for growth beyond a certain size. A policy of this kind might induce large companies to reduce their size in order to avoid the capital penalty involved. In the end, it is important to recall that—with the exception of AIG and GMAC—virtually all the institutions that have received assistance from the government are within the banking sector, which is already heavily regulated. These rescues do not provide a rationale for extending regulation to areas of the economy that are currently not regulated for safety and soundness, especially if regulation will create within these industries preferred players that will be considered too big to fail.

Conclusion

The G30 report falls far short of a reasonable prescription for the future. Without acknowledging and explaining the failure of bank regulation—or at least proposing new methods of regulation that overcome the deficiencies of the current regulatory system—the report cannot really be taken seriously as a public policy document.

Unfortunately, that does not mean that many in Congress, and maybe many in the Obama administration, will not use the credentials of the report's authors as a basis for adopting its recommendations. The report, however, discourages this until

> [t]he financial crisis . . . fully run[s] its course. Financial markets and institutions have yet to reengage in a healthy process of risk intermediation. Real economies around the world are experiencing sharp contraction, which is likely to lead to additional credit defaults. Governments and central banks are stretching to their limits with programs to stabilize both financial systems and real economies.
>
> *Initiatives to address these immediate challenges must take precedence over even the most pressing agendas for financial regulatory*

reform. Moreover, until the full costs of the current crisis are known—including the financial costs from its economic fallout—there will not be clarity on the extent of needed reforms and a sensible timetable for implementing them and for rolling back of greatly extended safety nets.

This is sound advice. But if members of Congress and the administration decide to go forward with regulatory reforms, they should consider why it is that bank regulation has been such a consistent failure and what that says about extending similar regulation to other sectors of the financial system. The lodestar in any such inquiry should be economic growth, not government growth.

"Risky Business:
Casting the Fed as a
Systemic Risk Regulator"

Originally published February 2009

Conventional wisdom in Washington is coalescing around the idea that the Federal Reserve should be empowered as a systemic risk regulator to supervise all "systemically significant" financial institutions. Last month's *Outlook*[11] contended that the failure of banking regulation argues strongly against extending safety-and-soundness regulation beyond the banking sector and that designating some firms as systemically significant would create another class of companies—like Fannie Mae and Freddie Mac—that are implicitly backed by the federal government. This *Outlook* examines the notion that the Fed should be the systemic regulator, pointing out that the agency has for many years had all the powers of a systemic regulator for banks and has failed to use them effectively; that supervising industries other than banking requires skills and knowledge that the Fed does not have and probably could not acquire in any reasonable amount of time; and that a role as systemic regulator would impair the Fed's independence and create conflicts with its more important function as the nation's monetary authority. Finally, this *Outlook* questions whether systemic risk itself can be defined—and whether the commonly accepted notion of systemic risk supports the creation of a systemic risk regulator.

Although there is no draft legislation yet available, the broad outlines of what the Obama administration is likely to propose in the wake of the financial crisis are becoming clear. The Group of Thirty report,[12] the report of

---

11. Peter J. Wallison, "Regulation without Reason: The Group of Thirty Report," *Financial Services Outlook* (January 2009), available at www.aei.org/publication29285.

12. Working Group on Financial Reform, *Financial Reform: A Framework for Financial Stability* (Washington, DC: Group of Thirty, January 15, 2009), available at www.group30. org/pubs/recommendations.pdf (accessed January 21, 2009). (See p. 361 of this book.)

the Congressional Oversight Panel that followed,[13] and statements by Barney Frank,[14] the influential chairman of the House Financial Services Committee, indicate that there is substantial support for a plan that would extend prudential (that is, safety-and-soundness) regulation beyond banking to hedge funds, securities firms, insurance companies, private equity firms, and other financial intermediaries. Not all members of these industries will be regulated for safety and soundness, only those that are deemed to be systemically significant by a new regulator of systemic risk. The agency that Frank seems determined to invest with this authority is the Federal Reserve.

There are a number of reasons to be concerned about extending safety-and-soundness regulation beyond banking to other sectors of the financial system, and particularly doing so by designating certain companies as systemically significant. But empowering the Fed as the systemic risk regulator raises several major issues:

- The Fed has been aware of the problem of systemic risk for at least thirty years and has had the power to control it through its regulation of bank holding companies (BHCs) for at least that long. If the Fed has made any efforts to control the risk-taking of the largest banks—the financial institutions that might cause systemic risk—those efforts have failed.

- The Fed is a bank regulator; it has no expertise in regulating or understanding the details of businesses like hedge funds, securities firms, or insurance companies. Yet, as the regulator of systemically significant companies, the Fed would be required to make important decisions about such things as appropriate capital levels, leverage, products, and risk management that require deep understanding of any industry in which a systemically significant firm is located.

- There are inherent conflicts between the role of the Fed as the nation's central bank and its potential role as a regulator of systemically

---

13. Congressional Oversight Panel, *Special Report on Regulatory Reform* (Washington, DC: Government Printing Office, January 2009), available at http://cop.senate.gov/documents/cop-012909-report-regulatoryreform.pdf (accessed February 19, 2009).

14. Stacy Kaper, "Fed First as Hill Tackles Reg Reform in 2 Parts," *American Banker,* February 4, 2009.

significant companies. The United States is one of only a few major developed countries that have authorized a monetary authority to take a role in bank regulation, and the trend in the last quarter century has been to separate monetary policy from financial regulation.

- To maintain its credibility for monetary policy purposes, the Fed must be independent of the political organs of government. But, as systemic risk regulator, it would inevitably be drawn into the politics of regulation, adversely affecting the credibility of its efforts to maintain price stability.

- As the lender of last resort, the Fed is in a particularly good position to provide financing to nonbank financial institutions that encounter financial difficulties. This will spread the federal safety net beyond banking and raise questions about whether there should be restrictions on commercial ownership of all systemically significant companies.

- There is no accepted definition of systemic risk and no generally understood idea—other than size itself—for how the potential for systemic risk might be identified before a systemic event actually occurs. The widely accepted view that systemic risk results from an external shock as well as simple contagion raises questions about the efficacy of regulating systemically significant firms. Granting to any agency the authority to determine whether a company is systemically significant or whether any activity would pose a systemic risk would be a blank check.

The Fed and Systemic Risk

In 1970, Congress granted the Federal Reserve the power to regulate and supervise BHCs. This power is extensive, and it has allowed the Fed to regulate BHCs in the same way that a bank supervisor can regulate a bank. The Fed regulates the capital of BHCs, limits their nonbanking activities, and, through the BHC, is able to influence the lending policies of the underlying bank. Although the term "systemic risk" is not used in the Bank Holding Company Act, the Fed has all the powers under the act that it might conceivably be given in any legislation in which the Fed is constituted as a systemic regulator. Nevertheless, the Fed never used these powers to stem the problems at Citigroup, Wachovia, or the other banking institutions that have had to be rescued in the current financial crisis.

It is not as though the Fed is unfamiliar with the concept of systemic risk. In 1998, the Federal Reserve Bank of New York (with the acquiescence of the Federal Reserve Board) stepped in to prevent the collapse of the hedge fund Long-Term Capital Management when it thought that the collapse would have far-reaching systemic effects. There is some question whether this was the correct judgment,[15] but there is no question that the Fed was sensitive to the issue of systemic risk. Nor is there any question that if the Fed wanted to control the risk-taking of the largest banks—the institutions most likely to be declared systemically significant—it could have done so through its control over their holding companies. Accordingly, before handing the power to control systemic risk to the Fed, Congress should want to know why the Fed has not exercised its existing power to control systemic risk in the banking system—and why it was unable to prevent the near failure of Citibank, the principal subsidiary of Citigroup and an institution that everyone would define as systemically significant.

The Fed's Expertise

The Fed is a bank regulator. It goes without saying that banking is a completely different business from insurance, which is different from securities trading, which, in turn, is different from the risk-taking and arbitrage transactions of hedge funds. The regulation of each company must take account of these differences. In order to decide on such issues as the appropriate amount of capital or leverage, the systemic regulator or supervisor of each form must have a detailed knowledge of the business practices, accounting standards, and taxation of each business model.

Accordingly, in order to be a systemic risk regulator for industries and business sectors other than banks, the Fed or some other institution would have to acquire a great deal of expertise in other fields of finance. It would be required to understand how these industries function and why they function the way

---

15. See Shadow Financial Regulatory Committee, "The Issues Posed by the Near-Collapse of Long-Term Capital Management," September 28, 1998, available at www.aei.org/docLib/20051114_ShadowStatement151.pdf.

they do. Every change in capital or leverage would have an effect not only on the competition within the industry in which the particular firm is located, but also on the ability of the firm to compete with other members of the financial services field. In today's financial services sector, banks, insurers, securities firms, hedge funds, mutual funds, finance companies, leasing companies, and even private equity firms compete for business, for capital, and for credit. Any significant mandated change in how the largest firms in each of these financial services industries do business will have an impact—positive or negative—on firms in every other financial services industry. It is for this reason that the Senate report on the Gramm-Leach-Bliley Act did not give the Fed the authority to supervise the nonbanking subsidiaries of financial holding companies. "It is inefficient and impractical," the report noted, "to expect a regulator to have or to develop expertise in regulating all aspects of financial services."[16] This was the judgment of Congress when securities and insurance were the only activities that were subject to any form of safety-and-soundness regulation (which, in the case of securities firms, was regulation intended primarily to protect customer accounts). If the legislation under consideration ultimately authorizes the Fed (or some other regulator) to supervise every financial intermediary that is systemically significant, it will create a giant regulator that will be required to understand in detail how each of these businesses operates and how a change in its capital, leverage, or business model will affect every other member of the financial services industry.

The underlying theory of the proposal to constitute the Fed as a systemic risk regulator is that the agency will not only be able to supervise the systemically significant members of the financial services industry—no matter what business form they take—but will also be able to recognize the development of systemic risks before they place the financial system in jeopardy. Thus, the Fed would have to be able to forecast the effect of new products and business activities on future financial health. Not only will the agency be required to know what is the best capital level for these companies in many different businesses and with many different risk profiles, but it will also need to understand what particular activities or investments present excessive risks when undertaken by such a business. The answers to these questions for hedge funds and insurance

---

16. *Financial Services Act of 1998,* 105th Cong., 2nd sess., September 18, 1998, S. Rep. 105-336.

companies, for example, are quite different from one another and quite different from those for banks. Hedge funds are traders and risk-takers; insurance companies are specialists in pooling risks. Hedge funds are financed by equity; insurance companies are generally corporations with capital ratios and long-term assets. Banks are part of a global payment system. Can any one agency make these varied judgments effectively—more effectively than the market itself?

Conflicts among the Fed's Roles

As the U.S. central bank, the Fed is responsible for maintaining price stability while fostering economic growth and employment. To a large extent, these roles are in conflict. As Robert E. Litan and Charles W. Calomiris noted in a 2000 article: "[W]eakness in the financial sector can tempt a central bank with supervisory authority over financial institutions to pursue a looser monetary policy than it would otherwise follow, imparting an inflationary bias."[17] For example, it might be that at a time of bank weakness, a tight monetary policy would have an adverse effect on the health of the financial institutions under the Fed's supervision. Instead of considering the overall health of the economy when it makes its monetary policy decisions, the Fed as bank supervisor or systemic regulator could defer a necessary rate increase in order to reduce the pressure on the institutions it supervises. This danger would be particularly acute if the Fed were the systemic regulator because systemically significant financial institutions are—by definition—too big to fail; they must be kept healthy lest their failure cause an adverse systemic event. The Fed would certainly be tempted in these circumstances to hold off on an interest rate increase in hopes of preserving the health of the systemically significant firms it is supervising. An opposite outcome is also easily imaginable; imagine that the Fed decides not to invoke its power to close down a weak institution because it fears that such an action will then require it to increase market liquidity in order to prevent further financial institution defaults.

Ideally, if there were to be a systemic regulator, it should have the health of the institutions it supervises solely in mind when it makes its decisions. However,

---

17. Charles W. Calomiris and Robert E. Litan, "Financial Regulation in a Global Marketplace," in *Brookings-Wharton Papers on Financial Services: 2000,* ed. Anthony M. Santomero and Robert E. Litan (Washington, DC: Brookings Institution Press, 2000), 292.

the Fed's interest in promoting market stability can lead it to encourage— rather than discourage—risk-taking by the banks it supervises. One example of this phenomenon in action was the Fed's successful effort in 1982 to get various U.S. banks to extend loans to Mexico at a time when Mexico was unable to meet its foreign exchange obligations. Although the banks themselves were threatened by losses on their Mexican loans, they followed the Fed's direction and made new loans to Mexico. At the time, Fed chairman Paul Volcker assured the banks that these risky loans would not be held against them: "[W]here new loans facilitate the adjustment process and enable a country to strengthen its economy and service its international debt in an orderly manner, new credits should not be subject to supervisory criticism."[18] This is not to say that Volcker's decision was wrong in that instance, but only to point out a clear example of the conflict of interest that affects the Fed's administration of its bank regulatory functions.

It is perhaps for this reason that central banks in almost all developed countries have no role other than that of monetary policy. The European Central Bank was established with only a monetary policy role, and only the United States and Israel give their monetary authorities any role in financial system regulation. Elsewhere—Switzerland, Canada, Australia, Germany, Sweden, Spain, the United Kingdom, and Japan, to name just a few—banks are regulated by other government entities. And the trend has been strongly in this direction, with the United Kingdom, Japan, and Australia having taken bank regulation away from their central banks in recent years.

The traditional position of the Fed has been that its bank regulatory activities assist it in keeping tabs on the economy. The theory is that the examination of banks and reports from banks provide a source of confidential information, not available elsewhere, for judging the health of the overall economy. This would, in turn, contribute to the Fed's role as systemic regulator. This argument has always had a make-weight aspect to it. There is no reason for the Fed to have to examine banks or other institutions to get this information, even on a confidential basis. In reality, the Fed does not examine many banks; almost all the large banks are nationally chartered and examined and regulated by the Comptroller of the Currency (OCC). The Fed regulates and supervises BHCs, the companies that control banks. Most of the day-to-day supervisory work on BHCs is done

---

18. Quoted in Bernard Shull, *The Fourth Branch: The Federal Reserve's Unlikely Rise to Power and Influence* (Santa Barbara, CA: Praeger, 2005), 150.

by the regional Federal Reserve banks and not the Federal Reserve Board itself. If necessary, both the OCC and the Federal Deposit Insurance Corporation receive reports from banks and could furnish the confidential information in these reports to the Fed.

Threats to the Fed's Monetary Policy Role

The Federal Reserve System was designed to be independent of both Congress and the executive branch. The seven members of the Board of Governors of the Federal Reserve System are appointed by the president for fourteen-year staggered terms—by far the longest in the federal government—and the agency is independent of the congressional appropriations process. The chairman is appointed by the president for a four-year term, but his term is not coextensive with the election of the president, so that the Fed chair remains in office for at least the first two years of the new president's term.

This extraordinary insulation from the elected branches gives the Fed credibility with the financial markets, which are justifiably concerned that the Fed's policies on price stability will eventually start to follow election returns, allowing the dollar to devalue for political rather than economic reasons. As Laurence Meyer, a former Fed governor, observed: "The motivation for granting independence to central banks is to insulate the conduct of monetary policy from political interference, especially interference motivated by the pressures of elections to deliver short-term gains irrespective of longer-term costs . . . [and] to provide a credible commitment of the government, through its central bank, to achieve . . . price stability."[19]

The Fed's independence has spawned a great deal of controversy, as it should in a democracy. The question is whether an organization that has the power to affect the economy in such substantial ways—resulting in more growth or less in both the economy and employment—should be able to function without accountability to the elected branches. The agency's independence has been repeatedly challenged by powerful members of Congress, usually when

---

19. Laurence H. Meyer, "The Politics of Monetary Policy: Balancing Independence and Accountability" (speech, University of Wisconsin, La Crosse, WI, October 24, 2000), available at www.federalreserve.gov/BOARDDOCS/SPEECHES/2000/20001024. htm (accessed February 20, 2009).

it tightens monetary policy and suppresses economic growth in the interest of maintaining stable prices. This conflict springs from important political interests. Price stability—that is, a stable currency value—favors lenders; inflation in currency values favors borrowers because they are able to repay their loans with inflated dollars. The tribunes of the common man, like William Jennings Bryan, opposed the "cross of gold" because they saw the tight money policies implied by the gold standard as a burden on the working man (now called "working families"). This controversy continues into the modern era. In 1989, for example, then-representatives Lee Hamilton (D-Ind.) and Byron Dorgan (D-N.D.) introduced legislation intended to make the Fed "more accountable" for its decisions, a move described as follows in the New York Times: "The Midwestern farmers and businessmen whom Mr. Hamilton and [Mr. Dorgan] represent often favor lower interest rates or 'easy money' to make borrowing easier. . . . But the Federal Reserve has traditionally agreed with bankers and bond dealers, who typically advocate 'hard money,' or higher rates, to prevent the inflation that can devalue the loans they make and the securities in which they deal."[20]

Today, the question of the Fed's independence does not revolve around hard money versus easy money but instead around the credibility of the Fed's policies. For the past twenty-five years, with the exception of a few years after the dot-com collapse in the early 2000s and current efforts to address the financial crisis, the Fed has followed a policy of keeping inflation low by controlling the money supply or otherwise attempting to limit price increases. This has resulted in a slow rate of inflation (1 or 2 percent a year) and relatively stable long-term interest rates. Long-term rates, which are essential for investment planning by business, will remain stable as long as the credit markets believe that the Fed will continue to follow a stable price policy in the future. In the late 1970s, the Fed's commitment to price stability had lost credibility, and long-term rates rose to historic highs. It took several years of painful Fed money supply management to win back the credibility that was required to bring these rates down. The credit markets understand that the political pressures in a democracy favor inflation—there are simply many more borrowers than lenders—and so they watch carefully to determine if the Fed is buckling under pressure from Congress and the president. Thus, while the Fed's independence is inconsistent with

---

20. Louis Uchitelle, "Moves On in Congress to Lift Secrecy at the Federal Reserve," New York Times, August 24, 1989.

democracy, it reflects a practical judgment that the nation's economy would be better off if its monetary policy is determined by economic rather than political considerations. A similar judgment, as noted above, has been made in many other major developed countries. Indeed, at least one study has shown that in countries where the central bank is also engaged in bank regulation, inflation rates tend to be higher.[21] This is what would be expected if the central bank is under pressure to put off credit-tightening in order to make sure that the banks it supervises are stable.

Nevertheless, the cooperation between the Fed and the Treasury in the last year—as the financial crisis has deepened—has been unprecedented. Although there has been relatively little commentary about this in the media, it raises serious questions about the Fed's long-term independence from the elected branches and hence the credibility of its stable price policies. When the crisis comes to an end, this will surely be one of the major issues that the financial markets will worry about. Will the Fed simply have become an arm of the Treasury Department, or will it be able to separate itself in the future from Treasury policies that it has had a major role in creating and implementing? Will the Fed sop up the liquidity that it has poured into the economy, or will it again cooperate with the Treasury at least through the election of 2012? It is through this lens that the Fed's power over systemically significant companies should be viewed. Giving the Fed the power to regulate all the key financial firms in the U.S. economy would involve the agency in major decisions about how business is carried out by whole industries. Unlike monetary policy—which depends for its success on the financial markets' belief that the Fed is making its decisions on the basis of economic rather than political factors—there is no practical or policy basis for insulating the Fed's control over systemically significant companies from political influence. These decisions would be so important that they should be subject to political influence.

Fortunately, there seems to be some recognition of the importance of this issue on the part of Senate Banking Committee chairman Christopher Dodd (D-Conn.). At a hearing on regulatory reform on February 4, 2009, Dodd noted

---

21. Carmine Di Noia and Giorgio Di Giorgio, "Should Banking Supervision and Monetary Policy Tasks Be Given to Different Agencies?" (Working Paper 411, Department of Economics and Business, Universitat Pompeu Fabra, Barcelona, October 19, 1999), 8, available at www.econ.upf.edu/docs/papers/downloads/411.pdf (accessed February 19, 2009).

the danger associated with giving the Fed a major regulatory role: "We must be mindful of ensuring the independence and integrity of the Fed's monetary policy function."[22] In the same hearing, Volcker was asked about the broad authority some have talked about giving to the Fed. In response, he pointed out that there are dangers in loading up the Fed with responsibilities: "You will have a different Federal Reserve if the Federal Reserve is going to do all the regulation from a prudential standpoint. . . . You have to consider whether that's a wise thing to do when their primary responsibility is monetary policy."[23]

Use of the Discount Window

The Fed has one authority that no other regulator possesses—the ability to create and lend money without an appropriation from Congress. The flexibility of the Fed's authority as lender of last resort has been demonstrated in the current financial crisis by the agency's willingness to lend on an emergency basis to companies and organizations that are not banks or BHCs. The continued availability of this authority raises troubling questions if the Fed is to become the regulator of all systemically significant financial institutions. The Group of Thirty report[24] contains a recommendation that, in whatever form regulation might take, it should preserve the restriction in current law that prevents the commercial firms from acquiring control of insured depository institutions.

Ironically, this restriction, known as the separation of banking and commerce, has contributed substantially to the financial crisis by depriving the banking industry of the capital that could come in from outside the industry. In the past year, the Fed has made efforts to loosen its rules on what constitutes a controlling position in a bank, but there is still very little capital coming into the industry. The longstanding reason for the separation of banking and commerce has been a fear (wholly unwarranted, in my view) that if commercial firms were to control banks, the government "safety net"—which includes the Fed's discount window lending facility—would be spread beyond the banking industry.

---

22. Christopher Dodd, "Modernizing the U.S. Financial Regulatory System" (remarks, Committee on Banking, Housing, and Urban Affairs, U.S. Senate, February 4, 2009), available at http://dodd.senate.gov/?q=node/4752 (accessed February 19, 2009).

23. Quoted in Steven Sloan, "Dodd Voicing Doubt on Fed Systemic Role," *American Banker,* February 5, 2009.

24. See Peter J. Wallison, "Regulation without Reason: The Group of Thirty Report."

That spreading, of course, has already occurred as a result of the Fed's efforts to keep many financial institutions afloat during the current financial crisis, but the proposal to make the Fed the regulator of systemically significant financial firms threatens to institutionalize a substantial broadening of the Fed's lender-of-last-resort functions. As discussed more fully below, the underlying reason for regulating systemically significant firms is concern that their failure will cause failures elsewhere in the economy—that is why they are called "systemically significant." Under these circumstances, giving the Fed authority to regulate and supervise these firms is essentially the same thing as giving it authority to use its lender-of-last-resort facility to provide them with the liquidity necessary to prevent their failure. The effect, of course, will be to extend the safety net far beyond the banking industry and, to the extent that the policy of separating banking and commerce is intended to prevent the spread of the safety net to commercial firms, to raise a question of whether there should be restrictions on commercial ownership of any firm that is deemed to be systemically significant. For this reason, if any agency were to be given authority to regulate all systemically significant firms, the Fed should be the last agency on the list.

Defining Systemically Significant Institutions

There is a certain glibness in the reports, papers, and proposals that recommend the regulation of systemically significant financial institutions. The idea completely avoids the difficult question of how to identify these institutions. This is not an unimportant omission. Because the notion of systemic risk has so little content, any systemic regulator is far more likely to err on the side of broadening than narrowing the range of firms it chooses to regulate. This is because of the criticism it will receive if a systemic event occurs because of the failure of an institution that was not previously designated as systemically significant.

But the far more difficult problem will be identifying what is meant by systemically significant and the relationship of this term to the concept of systemic risk. Since the beginning of the financial crisis, there has been increasing attention to the concept of systemic risk. Some commentators have noted that conceiving of systemic risk as arising from contagion—the cascade of losses coming from the failure of one institution—is obsolete at a time when assets are marked to market.[25] In that case, the losses of one or a few institutions because of some external shock can be transmitted to others without any connection between them. That would be a fairly good description of what happened to most of the world's financial intermediaries in the current crisis—when the external shock was a sudden recognition among investors that asset-backed securities of various kinds might be far less safe as investments than the ratings on them might have implied. When this occurred in the summer of 2007, the asset-backed securities market suddenly dried up. Funding for portfolios of such securities could not be found, and intermediaries were compelled to sell these assets at distress prices. The substantially reduced market prices caused the write-down of the same or similar assets on the balance sheets of other financial intermediaries, and what has been called the mortgage meltdown began. Various academic papers have referred to this sequence of events as an example of systemic risk—the danger of widespread losses coming from a systemic shock.[26]

The difficulty this raises is that systemic risk arises not from the failure of a large institution, or even a small group, but from an exogenous event—a shock to the system—that can come from a potentially infinite number of sources. Looking at the current financial crisis, its origin can be found in the combination of a deflating housing bubble in the United States, an unprecedented number of subprime and other nonprime mortgages, an originate-to-distribute securitization system, poor analysis by rating agencies, low costs for borrowed money, and a mark-to-market accounting system that caused asset values (and hence bank capital) to spiral down as distress sales occurred. In the current case, virtually all financial intermediaries were overleveraged in light of the rapid decline in the liquidity of their assets. Accordingly, one of the ways to prevent this ever happening again might be to regulate the various financial intermediaries in such a way as to prevent them from becoming overleveraged again. However, the next crisis may come from an entirely different combination of circumstances—one

25. See, for example, Markus Brunnermeier et al., *The Fundamental Principles of Financial Regulation,* Geneva Reports on the World Economy, preliminary conference draft (Geneva: International Center for Monetary and Banking Studies, 2009), 14–15, available at www.voxeu.org/reports/Geneva11.pdf (accessed February 19, 2009).

26. Ibid.; see also Philip F. Bartholomew, "Banking Consolidation and Systemic Risk," in *Brookings-Wharton Papers on Financial Services: 2000,* ed. Anthony M. Santomero and Robert E. Litan (Washington, DC: Brookings Institution Press, 2000), 373.

for which regulation of leverage or capital will not have prepared the regulated institutions. In fact, since regulation will force all the regulated institutions into the same approved mode of regulation, it might weaken the system by reducing the diversity that would allow some financial firms to survive the next shock. So if we do not know exactly how systemic risk will next manifest itself, how can we rely on the regulation of systemically significant institutions to protect us? Moreover, if systemic risk comes from an external shock, there is no reason to regulate only the systemically significant institutions—whatever they are—when virtually all financial institutions are likely to be affected. Why create the problems that come from differential regulation when it will not create any material difference in the outcome?

Even if we think of systemic risk in the traditional way—as the result of a cascade of losses coming from the failure of a large and interconnected institution—how would we identify such an institution? One way, of course, is by size, but is that likely to be sufficient? The interbank payment system is one clear potential source of systemic risk. If one bank in the system were to fail to meet its payment obligations to the others, there could be a cascade of losses as the recipient banks would be unable to meet their own obligations at the end of the day. The trouble with this is that relatively small institutions can have outsized effects on the payment system if they fail to meet their payment obligations, and these institutions are unlikely to be considered systemically significant. An example is the failure of Herstatt Bank in 1974. That failure caused a systemic breakdown, even though no one would have considered Herstatt to have been a systemically significant bank.

Finally, there is the fact that what might be considered systemically significant is highly context-specific. Comparing the failure of the securities firm Drexel Burnham Lambert in 1990 with the failure of Lehman Brothers in 2008 makes this point. Drexel was a very large firm in the context of the market at the time, but its failure did not cause any systemic distress. On the other hand, Lehman's failure in September 2008, when everyone in the market was jittery, caused a worldwide freeze of interbank lending.

This analysis suggests that it is difficult to define systemic risk and what institutions can legitimately be considered systemically significant. Those who argue for regulating systemically significant institutions have not defined them, and until that happens, the suggestion that the Fed or any other agency should regulate this imaginary group has no sound basis.

The Problem of Differential Regulation

Even assuming that we can identify systemically significant institutions, what would be the consequences of regulating them—as opposed to regulating the entire industry of which they are a part? Such a step would have a disastrous effect on the competitive financial system in the United States. If a financial institution is designated as systemically significant, the financial markets will see it as a declaration that the institution is too big to fail. After all, the whole purpose of regulating systemically significant firms is to prevent them from failing, since, by definition, their failure would have an adverse systemic effect on the financial system or the economy generally.

As we have seen with Fannie Mae and Freddie Mac, any indication that a private firm has the implicit backing of the government—especially if the backing comes from an agency like the Fed, with the power to extend financing—would persuade the markets that extending credit to this institution would involve less risk than extending credit to an institution that is operating without this special designation. For this reason, a firm that is designated as systemically significant would be able to raise funds at lower cost than its competitors, would be likely be more profitable than its competitors, and would have greater access to capital. In industries such as insurance, in which the financial soundness of the company could make a competitive difference, the companies that were able to boast of implicit government backing would be the most successful in attracting customers. Overall, the systemically significant firms would grow larger in relation to others in the same industry and would gradually acquire more and more of their less successful competitors. Eventually, we would see a market much like the housing market that Fannie and Freddie have come to dominate, with a few giant companies, chosen by the government, that have pushed out all competition.

It is, of course, possible that the opposite could occur. The companies that are designated as systemically significant could face so much costly regulation that they become less profitable than their competitors. They might even weaken financially as their competitors took away more of their business by operating more efficiently and offering lower prices. However, implicit government backing, as demonstrated by Fannie Mae and Freddie Mac, can enable companies to drive all competition from their markets. The likelihood is that if the systemically significant companies encountered competitive difficulties, the

Fed or any other regulator would be compelled at some time to provide them with financial assistance or regulatory forbearance.

Conclusion

The case for creating a systemic risk regulator has not been made. There is no clear definition of systemic risk, and specially supervising companies arbitrarily designated as systemically significant would seriously disrupt competition in every field in which a systemically significant company were to operate. In addition, even if it were possible to identify systemically significant companies and to overcome the competitive problems such a policy would entail, the Federal Reserve would be a very poor choice for the systemic supervisor. Such an assignment for the Fed would create significant conflicts with its monetary policy role and impair the independence that the agency needs to carry out that role effectively.

"Reinventing GSEs: Treasury's Plan for Financial Restructuring"

Originally published March–April 2009

In late March—timed to impress the G20—the Obama administration revealed its plan for regulating and restructuring the U.S. financial system. There were no surprises; its approach, presented by Treasury Secretary Timothy Geithner, endorsed both a single powerful systemic regulator, with authority to designate and regulate "systemically important" institutions in every financial sector, and a system for liquidating or bailing out financial firms that might cause a systemic breakdown if they failed. Although presented as a way to prevent a repeat of the current financial crisis, the proposals will, if implemented, seriously impair competitive conditions in all U.S. financial markets—enhancing the power of large companies that are designated as systemically important and threatening the survival of those that do not receive that endorsement. Underlying the plan is the erroneous belief—shattered by the catastrophic condition of the heavily regulated banking sector—that regulation can prevent risk-taking and failure. Although the plan could get through Congress if the financial industry remains inert and apathetic, the weakness of the administration's case suggests that it is vulnerable to determined opposition.

The Obama administration and Congress are now filling in the details of a long-anticipated plan for reorganizing and restructuring financial regulation. It is no exaggeration to say that the proposal will create what are essentially government-sponsored enterprises (GSEs) like Fannie Mae and Freddie Mac in every sector of the financial economy.

The principal elements of the administration's plan are these:

- Establishing a federal agency as the systemic regulator of the financial system

- Giving that agency the authority to designate "systemically important" financial institutions and establish a special regulatory structure for these firms

- Providing a mechanism for the government to take control of financial institutions when and if it decides that their failure will create "systemic risk"

To be sure, there are differences between the implicit government backing that Fannie and Freddie exploited and a designation as a "systemically important" firm, but in competitive terms, these differences are minor. Designation as a systemically important firm is, in effect, a certification by the government that a firm is too big to fail—its failure, in theory, will create systemic risk—and this status will be seen in the markets as lowering its risk as a borrower. Lower risk will translate into lower funding costs, exactly the advantage that allowed Fannie and Freddie to drive all competition from their market. Indeed, it may well be that the systemically important firms will be more formidable competitors than Fannie and Freddie, which were restricted by their charters from expanding beyond their secondary market role. There is no indication that systemically important firms will be similarly restricted.

In light of the competitive danger that the administration's proposal creates for smaller firms, the lack of any adverse reaction thus far in the financial services sector is surprising. It is also surprising that the administration would back a plan that will inevitably create more firms—rather than fewer—that are too big to fail. It is not hard to understand why the largest firms might not see the plan as a threat; they might believe that the government support they receive will be more helpful than harmful in the future. But it is harder to understand why there seems to be so little vocal opposition at this point from the many smaller firms—insurance companies, securities firms, hedge funds, and finance companies—that will be forced to face government-aided competition. Perhaps they believe that these changes are inevitable. There is little else to explain the support for the idea from such organizations as the U.S. Chamber of Commerce and the Securities Industry and Financial Markets Association—two organizations that are normally skeptical about excessive regulation and object to the government picking winners and losers. This *Outlook* will review the administration's plan in detail, show the weakness of the administration's argument, and outline why and how it will make major changes in the structure of and competitive conditions in the financial sector of the economy.

The Administration's Plan

In congressional testimony on March 26, 2009, Secretary Geithner described the major features of the administration's plan:

> To ensure appropriate focus and accountability for financial stability we need to establish a single entity with responsibility for consolidated supervision of systemically important firms. . . . That means we must create higher standards for all systemically important financial firms regardless of whether they own a depository institution, to account for the risk that the distress or failure of such a firm could impose on the financial system and the economy. . . .
>
> [W]e must create a resolution regime that provides authority to avoid the disorderly liquidation of any nonbank financial firm whose disorderly liquidation would have serious adverse consequences on the financial system or the U.S. economy. . . . Depending on the circumstances, the FDIC and the Treasury would place the firm into conservatorship with the aim of returning it to private hands or a receivership that would manage the process of winding down the firm.[27]

The last sentence makes clear that this is not simply a proposal for winding down failed financial institutions in an orderly way; instead, it contemplates a "conservatorship," which would allow the government to take control of a failing company and restore it to financial health. This approach complements the idea that systemically important firms are too big to fail and creates the vehicle that would actually prevent their failure. Underlying the plan, of course, is the glaringly false assumption that regulation can prevent excessive risk-taking and failure by financial firms. One glance at the catastrophic condition of the heavily regulated banking industry should convince anyone who thinks about it objectively that regulation is not the panacea its proponents suggest. The

---

27. Timothy F. Geithner, written testimony (Committee on Financial Services, U.S. House of Representatives, March 26, 2009), available at www.house.gov/apps/list/hearing/financialsvcs_dem/geithner032609.pdf (accessed April 8, 2009).

administration has not yet decided what agency would be the systemic regulator, and it has not formally named the agency that would have the authority to take over and resolve or rescue failing or failed nonbank financial firms. The Federal Deposit Insurance Corporation (FDIC) seems to be the frontrunner for the resolution agency; the Federal Reserve has been mentioned frequently as the likely systemic regulator,[28] but this raises serious policy issues.[29]

The Consequences of Designating Firms as Systemically Important

The dangers to competition inherent in the administration's plan arise in two ways: direct benefits to firms that offer products enhanced by the apparent financial soundness of the firm that offers them, and indirect benefits through a lower cost of funds for firms that are perceived to be less risky than their competitors. In insurance, for example, where the financial soundness of a company could make a competitive difference, the companies that can boast that they are too big to fail are likely to be more successful in attracting customers than their smaller competitors. Similarly, but more indirectly, firms that can boast that they are systemically important and thus too big to fail would—like Fannie Mae and Freddie Mac—appear less risky as borrowers than firms that are not protected by the government, and this will produce lower financing costs. Eventually, these firms will be able to use their superior financing opportunities to drive competition from their markets. Overall, the systemically significant firms will be subject to less market discipline, will be able to take more risks than others, will grow larger in relation to others in the same industry, and will gradually acquire more and more of their less successful competitors. Eventually, we will see a market much like the housing market that Fannie and Freddie came to dominate, with a few giant companies, chosen by the government, that have pushed out all significant competition.

It is, of course, possible that the opposite could occur. The companies that are designated as systemically significant could face so much costly regulation

---

28. See Damian Paletta, "U.S. to Toughen Finance Rules," *Wall Street Journal,* March 16, 2009.

29. See, for example, Peter J. Wallison, "Risky Business: Casting the Fed as a Systemic Risk Regulator," *Financial Services Outlook* (February 2009), available at www.aei.org/publication29439. (See p. 361 of this book.)

that they become less profitable than their competitors. Indeed, some supporters of designating systemically significant firms have argued that systemically important firms will face such onerous regulation that no firm will want the honor. But this seems unlikely. Yes, it is possible to regulate systemically important companies so strictly that they are not able to compete effectively with others, but such a policy would be self-defeating. If regulation so impairs the operations of systemically important companies that they cannot carry on their businesses efficiently, that will only mean they will have to be bailed out sooner. The failure of companies under regulatory supervision is a serious indictment of the regulator's effectiveness, and regulators try hard to avoid it. Regulatory forbearance—refusal to step in and close failing institutions—is a product of this tendency and one of the most significant causes of the savings and loan (S&L) and banking crisis of the late 1980s and early 1990s. So pervasive was regulatory forbearance for S&Ls and banks during that period that a policy called "prompt corrective action" was written into the Federal Deposit Insurance Corporation Improvement Act of 1991 (FDICIA), the tough banking legislation that was supposed to prevent future widespread bank losses. As discussed below, it has not worked as hoped. Regulatory forbearance seems to continue. The twenty-one banks that have been resolved by the FDIC over the past year have averaged losses on assets of 24 percent,[30] even though prompt corrective action was intended to enable institutions to be closed before they had suffered any losses. Contrary to the notion that regulators could be tough on systemically important firms, experience shows that they try to help their regulated clients succeed.

The Administration's Plan for Resolving or Rescuing Failing Financial Firms

The extraordinary FDIC losses on failing banks should be a warning to anyone who contemplates a nonbankruptcy system for resolving failed or failing financial institutions. In the few cases in which regulators will actually close institutions under the administration's plan, the losses will be expensive for taxpayers. In most cases, however, regulatory forbearance will ensure that excuses will

---

30. Calculation by the author, based on Federal Deposit Insurance Corporation press releases and available upon request.

be found to rescue most financial firms, also at taxpayer expense. A rescue not only avoids embarrassment for the regulator but is also generally approved by Congress because it saves jobs and avoids financial disruption. It can be safely predicted, accordingly, that for the largest institutions—those designated as systemically important—the new resolution system will simply become a bailout system, with the taxpayers handed the bill. The capital markets understand this tendency on the part of regulators. That is why the administration's proposal for a special resolution system for failing financial firms increases the likelihood that the capital markets will see systemically important firms as less likely than others to be allowed to fail, and thus less risky as borrowers.

Secretary Geithner defended this portion of his plan by suggesting that it is merely doing for nonbanks what the FDIC already does for banks. This argument omits the key reasons for FDIC's resolution process—why it exists and who pays for it. Commercial banks and other depository institutions perform a special role in our economy. They offer deposits that can be withdrawn on demand or used to pay others through an instruction such as a check. If a bank should fail, its depositors are immediately deprived of the ready funds they expected to have available for such things as meeting payroll obligations, buying food, or paying rent. Because of fear that a bank will not be able to pay in full on demand, banks are also at risk of "runs"—panicky withdrawals of funds by depositors. Although runs can be valuable and efficient market discipline for insolvent banks, they can be frightening experiences for the public and disruptive for the financial system. The unique attribute of banks—that their liabilities (deposits) may be withdrawn on demand—is the reason that banks, and only banks, are capable of creating a systemic event if they fail. If a bank cannot make its payments to other banks, the others can also be in trouble, as can their customers. That is systemic risk, but it is unlikely to be caused by any other kind of financial institution because these financial institutions—securities firms, hedge funds, insurance companies, and others—tend to borrow for a specific term or to borrow on a collateralized basis. Their failures, then, do not cause any immediate cash losses to their lenders or counterparties. Losses occur, to be sure, but those who suffer them do not lose the immediate access to cash that they need to meet their current obligations. It is for this reason that describing the operations of these nondepository institutions as "shadow banking" is so misleading. It ignores entirely the essence of banking—which is not simply lending—and how it differs from other kinds of financial activity.

Because of the unique effects that are produced by bank failures, the Fed and the FDIC have devised systems for reducing the chances that banks will not have the cash to meet their obligations. The Fed lends to healthy banks (or banks it considers healthy) through what is called the discount window—making cash available for withdrawals by worried customers—and the FDIC will normally close insolvent banks just before the weekend and open them as healthy, functioning institutions on the following Monday. In both cases, the fears of depositors are allayed and runs seldom occur. Although Secretary Geithner is correct that the administration's plan would, in effect, extend FDIC bank resolution processes to other financial institutions, for the reasons outlined above, there is much less reason to do so for financial institutions other than banks. Indeed, as discussed below, if the market had been functioning normally in September 2008, both AIG and Lehman Brothers could have been allowed to fail without severe market disruption.

There is also the question of funding. Funds from some source are always required if a financial institution is either resolved or rescued. The resolution of banks is paid for by the premiums that banks pay for deposit insurance; only depositors are protected, and then only up to $250,000. Unless the idea is to create an industry-supported fund of some kind for liquidations or bailouts, the Geithner proposal will require the availability of taxpayer funds for winding up or bailing out firms considered to be systemically important. If the funding source is intended to be the financial industry itself, it would have to entail a very large tax. The funds used to bail out AIG alone are four times the size of the FDIC fund for banks and S&Ls when that fund was at its highest point—about $52 billion in early 2007. If the financial industry were to be taxed in some way to create such a fund, it would put all of these firms—including the largest—at a competitive disadvantage vis-à-vis foreign competitors and would, of course, substantially raise consumer prices and interest rates for financial services. The 24 percent loss rate that the FDIC has suffered on failed banks during the past year should provide some idea of what it will cost the taxpayers to wind up or (more likely) bail out failed or failing financial institutions that the regulators flag as systemically important. The taxpayers would have to be called upon for most, if not all, of the funds necessary for this purpose. So, while it might be attractive to imagine the FDIC resolving financial institutions of all kinds the way it resolves failed or failing banks, it opens the door for the use of taxpayer funds to protect the regulators of all financial institutions against charges that they failed to do their jobs properly.

Sometimes it is argued that bank holding companies (BHCs) must be made subject to the same resolution system as the banks themselves, but there is no apparent reason why this should be true. The whole theory of separating banks and BHCs is to be sure that BHCs could fail without implicating or damaging the bank, and this has happened frequently. If a holding company of any kind fails, its subsidiaries can remain healthy, just as the subsidiaries of a holding company can go into bankruptcy without implicating the parent. If a holding company with many subsidiaries regulated by different regulators should go into bankruptcy, there is no apparent reason why the subsidiaries cannot be sold off if they are healthy and functioning, just as Lehman's broker-dealer subsidiary was sold to Barclays Bank immediately after Lehman declared bankruptcy. If there is some conflict between regulators, these—like conflicts between creditors—would be resolved by the bankruptcy court. Moreover, if the creditors, regulators, and stakeholders of a company believe that it is still a viable entity, chapter 11 of the Bankruptcy Code provides that the enterprise can continue functioning as a "debtor in possession" and come out of the proceeding as a slimmed-down and healthy business. Several airlines that are functioning today went through this process, and—ironically—some form of prepackaged bankruptcy that will relieve the auto companies of their burdensome obligations is one of the options the administration is considering for that industry. (Why bankruptcy is considered workable for the auto companies but not financial companies is some-thing of a mystery.) In other words, even if it were likely to be effective and efficient—which is doubtful—a special resolution procedure for financial firms is unlikely to achieve more than the bankruptcy laws now permit.

In addition to increasing the likelihood that systemically important firms will be bailed out by the government, the Geithner resolution plan will also raise doubts about priorities among lenders, counterparties, shareholders, and other stakeholders when a financial firm is resolved or rescued under the government's control, rather than in a bankruptcy proceeding. In bankruptcy, a court decides how to divide the remaining resources of the bankrupt firm. Even in an FDIC resolution, insured depositors have a preference. It is not clear who would get bailed out and who would take losses under the administration's plan. In any event, the current bankruptcy system is regarded as potentially "disorderly," although why a resolution by a government agency will be more orderly has not been specified. In any event, it is likely that favored constituencies will seek, and probably get, more of the available funds in a windup or a bailout carried out by a government agency than they would in a normal bankruptcy. Given that bailouts are going to be much more likely than liquidations, especially for systemically important firms, a special government resolution or rescue process will also undermine market discipline and promote more risk-taking in the financial sector. In bailouts, the creditors will be saved in order to prevent a purported systemic breakdown, reducing the risks that creditors believe they will be taking in lending to systemically important firms. Over time, the process of saving some firms from failure will weaken all firms in the financial sector. Weak managements and bad business models should be allowed to fail. That makes room for better managements and better business models to grow. Introducing a formal rescue mechanism will only end up preserving bad managements and bad business models that should have been allowed to disappear while stunting or preventing the growth of their better-managed rivals. Finally, as academic work has shown again and again, regulation suppresses innovation and competition and adds to consumer costs.

With all these deficiencies in the administration's plan for creating systemically important companies—together with a special liquidation or bailout system as an alternative to bankruptcy—it is useful to consider the administration's rationale for such an extraordinary change in the financial sector's structure and competitive conditions. It appears, in this connection, that the administration is resting its case on only two events—the failure of Lehman Brothers and the rescue of AIG—as the reasons for advancing its extraordinary plan. Both examples, as discussed below, are inapposite. AIG should not have been rescued—saving the taxpayers $200 billion—and Lehman's failure was not the disruptive incident that has been portrayed in the media and elsewhere. Indeed, if the market had been functioning normally when Lehman failed, its failure, like Drexel Burnham Lambert's in 1990, would have caused little market disruption.

The Exaggerated Significance of AIG and Lehman

Secretary Geithner has defended his proposal by arguing that, if it had been in place, the rescue of AIG last fall would have been more "orderly" and the failure of Lehman Brothers would not have occurred. Both statements might be true, but would that have been the correct policy outcome? Recall that the underlying reason for the administration's plan to designate and specially regulate systemically important firms is that the failure of any such company would cause a systemic event—a breakdown in the financial system and perhaps the economy as a whole. Using this test, it is clear at this point that neither AIG nor Lehman is an example of a large firm creating systemic risk.

In a widely cited paper, John Taylor of Stanford University concluded that the market meltdown and the freeze in interbank lending that followed the Lehman and AIG events in mid-September 2008 did not begin until the Treasury and Fed proposed the initial Troubled Asset Relief Program funding later in the same week, an action that suggested (along with then–treasury secretary Henry M. Paulson's warnings of imminent doom) that financial conditions were much worse than the markets had thought.[31] Taylor's view, then, is that AIG and Lehman did not have any causal relationship to the meltdown that occurred later that week.

Since neither firm was a bank or other depository institution, this is highly plausible. Few of their creditors were expecting to be able to withdraw funds on demand to meet payrolls or other immediate expenses, and later events and data have cast doubt on whether the failure of Lehman or AIG (if it had not been bailed out) would have caused the losses many have claimed. Advocates of broader regulation frequently state, and the media dutifully repeat, that the financial institutions are now "interconnected" in a way that they have not been in the past.

This idea reflects a misunderstanding of the functions of financial institutions, all of which are intermediaries in one form or another between sources of funds and users of funds. In other words, they have always been interconnected in order to perform their intermediary functions. The right question is whether they are now interconnected in a way that makes them more vulnerable to the failure of one or more institutions than they have been in the past, and there is no evidence of this. The sections below strongly suggest that there was no need to rescue AIG and that Lehman's failure was problematic only because the market was in an unprecedentedly fragile and panicky state in mid-September 2008.

AIG Should Have Been Sent to Bankruptcy. AIG's quarterly report on Form 10-Q for the quarter ended June 30, 2008—the last quarter before its bailout

---

31. John B. Taylor, "The Financial Crisis and the Policy Responses: An Empirical Analysis of What Went Wrong" (Working Paper 14,631, National Bureau of Economic Research, Cambridge, MA, January 2009), 25ff, available at www.nber.org/papers/w14631 (accessed April 8, 2009).

in September—shows that the company had borrowed, or had guaranteed subsidiary borrowings, in the amount of approximately $160 billion, of which approximately $45 billion was due in less than one year.[32] Very little of this $45 billion was likely to be immediately due and payable, and thus, unlike a bank's failure, AIG's failure would not have created an immediate cash loss to any significant group of lenders or counterparties. Considering that the international financial markets are more than $12 trillion, the $45 billion due within a year would not have shaken the system. Although losses would eventually have occurred to all those who had lent money to AIG, they would have occurred over time and been worked out in a normal bankruptcy proceeding, after the sale of its profitable insurance subsidiaries.

Many of the media stories about AIG have focused on the AIG Financial Products subsidiary and the obligations that this group assumed through credit default swaps (CDSs). However, it is highly questionable whether there would have been a significant market reaction if AIG had been allowed to default on its CDS obligations in September 2008. CDSs—although they are not insurance—operate like insurance; they pay off when there is an actual loss on the underlying obligation that is protected by the CDS. It is much the same as when a homeowners' insurance company goes out of business before there has been a fire or other loss to the home. In that case, the homeowner must go out and find another insurance company, but he has not lost anything except the premium he has paid. If AIG had been allowed to default, there would have been little if any near-term loss to the parties that had bought protection; they would simply have been required to go back into the CDS market and buy new protection. The premiums for the new protection might have been more expensive than what they were paying AIG, but even if that were true, many of them had received collateral from AIG that could have been sold in order to defray the cost of the new protection.[33] CDS contracts normally require a party like AIG that has sold protection to post collateral as assurance to its counterparties that it can meet its obligations when they come due.

---

32. American International Group, 10-Q filing, June 30, 2008, 95–101.

33. A full description of the operation of credit default swaps appears in Peter J. Wallison, "Everything You Wanted to Know about Credit Default Swaps—but Were Never Told," *Financial Services Outlook* (December 2008), available at www.aei.org/publication29158. (See p. 223 of this book.)

This analysis is consistent with the publicly known facts about AIG. In mid-March, the names of some of the counterparties that AIG had protected with CDS became public. The largest of these counterparties was Goldman Sachs. The obligation to Goldman was reported as $12.9 billion; the others named were Merrill Lynch ($6.8 billion), Bank of America ($5.2 billion), Citigroup ($2.3 billion), and Wachovia ($1.5 billion).[34] Recall that the loss of CDS coverage—the obligation in this case—is not an actual cash loss or anything like it; it is only the loss of coverage for a debt that is held by a protected party. For institutions of this size, with the exception of Goldman, the loss of AIG's CDS protection would not have been problematic, even if they had in fact already suffered losses on the underlying obligations that AIG was protecting. Moreover, when questioned about what it would have lost if AIG had defaulted, Goldman said its losses would have been "negligible." This is entirely plausible. Its spokesman cited both the collateral it had received from AIG under the CDS contracts and the fact that it had hedged its AIG risk by buying protection against AIG's default from third parties.[35] Also, as noted above, Goldman only suffered the loss of its CDS coverage, not a loss on the underlying debt the CDS was supposed to cover. If Goldman, the largest counterparty in AIG's list, would not have suffered substantial losses, then AIG's default on its CDS contracts would have had no serious consequences in the market. This strongly suggests that Secretary Geithner's effort to justify the need for a systemic regulator is based on very weak or exaggerated data. AIG could have been put into bankruptcy with no costs to the taxpayers. A systemic regulator would have rescued AIG—just as the Fed did—amounting to an unnecessary cost for U.S. taxpayers and an unnecessary windfall for AIG's counterparties. We will probably never know why the Fed decided to bail out AIG, but the most likely reason is that it simply panicked at the market's reaction to the Lehman failure.

Lehman's Failure Did Not Cause a Systemic Event. Despite John Taylor's analysis, it is widely believed that Lehman's failure proves that a large company's default, especially when it is "interconnected" through CDSs, can cause a

---

34. Mary Williams Walsh, "A.I.G. Lists Banks It Paid with U.S. Bailout Funds," *New York Times,* March 16, 2009.

35. Peter Edmonston, "Goldman Insists It Would Have Lost Little if A.I.G. Had Failed," *New York Times,* March 21, 2009.

systemic breakdown. For that reason, Secretary Geithner contends, there should be some authority in the government to seize such a firm and keep its failure from affecting others. Even if we accept, contrary to Taylor, that Lehman's failure somehow precipitated the market freeze that followed, it does not support the proposition that, in a normal market, Lehman's failure would have caused a systemic breakdown. In fact, analyzed in light of later events, it is evidence for the opposite conclusion. First, after Lehman's collapse, there is only one example of any other organization encountering financial difficulty because of Lehman's default. That example is the Reserve Fund, a money market mutual fund that held a large amount of Lehman's commercial paper at the time Lehman defaulted. This caused the Reserve Fund to "break the buck"—to fail to maintain its share price at exactly one dollar—and it was rescued by the Treasury. The fact that there were no other such cases, among money market funds or elsewhere, demonstrates that the failure of Lehman in a calmer and more normal market would not have produced any significant knock-on effects. In addition, when Lehman's CDS obligations were resolved a month after its bankruptcy, they were all resolved by the exchange of only $5.2 billion among all the counterparties, a minor sum in the financial markets and certainly nothing that in and of itself would have caused a market meltdown.[36]

So, what relationship did Lehman's failure actually have to the market crisis that followed? The problems that were responsible for the crisis had actually begun more than a year earlier, when investors lost confidence in the quality of securities—particularly mortgage-backed securities (MBS)—that had been rated AAA by rating agencies. As a result, the entire market for asset-backed securities of all kinds became nonfunctional, and these assets simply could not be sold at anything but a distress price. Under these circumstances, the stability and even the solvency of most large financial institutions—banks and others that held large portfolios of MBS and other asset-backed securities—were in question.

In this market environment, Bear Stearns was rescued through a Fed-assisted sale to JPMorgan Chase in March 2008. The rescue was not necessitated because failure would have caused substantial losses to firms "interconnected" with Bear, but because the failure of a large financial institution in this fragile market environment would have caused a further loss of confidence—by

---

36. See Peter J. Wallison, "Everything You Wanted to Know about Credit Default Swaps—but Were Never Told."

investors, creditors, and counterparties—in the stability of other financial institutions. This phenomenon is described in a 2003 article by George Kaufman and Kenneth Scott, who write frequently on the subject of systemic risk. They point out that when one company fails, investors and counterparties look to see whether the risk exposure of their own investments or counterparties is similar: "The more similar the risk-exposure profile to that of the initial [failed company] economically, politically, or otherwise, the greater is the probability of loss and the more likely are the participants to withdraw funds as soon as possible. The response may induce liquidity and even more fundamental solvency problems. This pattern may be referred to as a 'common shock' or 'reassessment shock' effect and represents correlation without direct causation."[37] In March 2008, such an inquiry would have been very worrisome; virtually all the large financial institutions around the world held the same assets that drove Bear toward default.

Although the rescue of Bear temporarily calmed the markets, it led to a form of moral hazard—the belief that in the future governments would rescue all financial institutions larger than Bear. Market participants simply did not believe that Lehman, just such a firm, would not be rescued. This expectation was shattered in September 2008 when Lehman was allowed to fail, leading to exactly the kind of reappraisal of the financial health and safety of other institutions described by Kaufman and Scott. That is why the market froze at that point; market participants were no longer sure that the financial institutions they were dealing with would be rescued, and thus it was necessary to examine the financial condition of their counterparties much more carefully. For a period of time, the world's major banks would not even lend to one another. So what happened after Lehman was not the classic case of a large institution's failure creating losses at others—the kind of systemic risk that has stimulated the administration's effort to regulate systemically important firms. It was caused by the weakness and fragility of the financial system that began almost a year earlier, when the quality of MBS and other asset-backed securities was called into question and became unmarketable. If Lehman should have been bailed out, it was not because its failure would have caused losses to others—the reason for

---

37. George G. Kaufman and Kenneth Scott, "What Is Systemic Risk and Do Regulators Retard or Contribute to It?" *The Independent Review* 7, no. 3 (Winter 2003). Emphasis added.

the designation of systemically important firms—but because the market was in an unprecedented condition of weakness and fragility.

Thus, the two examples that Secretary Geithner has used to push his plan are inapposite. AIG should clearly have been sent to bankruptcy court, and Lehman's failure was only important because it caused market participants to reappraise the risks of dealing with one another in an unprecedented market environment—in which almost every large financial institution was already weak and possibly insolvent. Regrettably, the administration is using these two inapposite examples—its only examples—to set in place an entirely new, broader, and wholly unnecessary system of regulation and resolution. In the unlikely event that the worldwide financial markets in the future were to again become fragile and fearful, it would be far better to have an ad hoc response from the U.S. government than to establish a vast new regulatory structure today for an event that is a wildly remote possibility.

The Weak Case for Designating Systemically Important Firms

Even if there were facts that made it sensible to designate systemically important companies today and create a special system of resolution for them, major questions would still be unresolved.

How Would Systemically Important Firms Be Identified? Even if a systemic event could be caused by the failure of a systemically important firm, how would we identify such a firm in advance? Secretary Geithner has cited numerous criteria in addition to size, including reliance on short-term funding or whether it is a source of credit for households.[38] There are no examples of a large financial institution's failure actually causing a systemic event for the simple reason that, in every case of a large bank's failure, it has been bailed out. When other kinds of financial institutions have failed, no systemic disruption has occurred. In theory, for the reasons outlined earlier, the failure of a large bank could result in a systemic breakdown, but on what basis would nonbanks be designated as systemically important? Experience provides no answer. Making things tougher for the proponents of the administration's plan is the fact that the only examples we have contradict their assumptions. Not only have large

---

38. Timothy F. Geithner, written testimony, March 26, 2009.

nonbank financial institutions such as Drexel Burnham failed without causing a systemic event, but the failure of quite small firms have caused what some might consider systemic events, even though no one would have classified them as systemically important in advance. For example, when two tiny securities dealers—Bevill, Bresler and ESM—failed in the mid-1980s, Paul Volcker, then chairman of the Federal Reserve Board, told Congress: "The failure of some dealers operating at the periphery of the market . . . did have severe repercussions for some customers. The insolvency of a number of thrift institutions was precipitated, while other institutions involved in financing or servicing the fringe dealers were placed in some jeopardy. In our highly interrelated and interdependent financial markets, these developments carried at least the seeds of more widespread systemic problems."[39] This comment provides an indication of how malleable the concept of systemic risk can be. In another well-known case, the 1976 failure of Herstatt Bank, a small German bank, caused a breakdown in the international payment system, although Herstatt would not have been on anybody's list of systemically important institutions when it failed.[40] What the Herstatt case shows is that regulating systemically important firms does not provide any assurance that systemic risk will be avoided. It creates the dangers to competition discussed above, suppresses innovation, and raises costs, but it does not make the financial system materially safer.

Anyway, Would Regulation Work? Even if we assume that it is possible to determine in advance which firms will cause systemic risk, would regulation prevent it? Although this idea is central to the administration's case, all the evidence we have points the other way: regulation is simply not effective in preventing risk-taking and failure. The evidence is too clear to be ignored. After the S&L debacle in the late 1980s and early 1990s—a financial crisis in which most of the S&L industry as well as almost 1,600 commercial banks failed—Congress adopted FDICIA. At the time, this legislation was considered extremely tough banking legislation—so much so that, in a speech to a conference at the Federal

---

39. Paul A. Volcker, statement (Subcommittee on Telecommunications, Consumer Protection and Finance, Committee on Energy and Commerce, U.S. House of Representatives, June 26, 1985), 1–2.

40. George G. Kaufman and Kenneth Scott, "What Is Systemic Risk and Do Regulators Retard or Contribute to It?" 11–12.

Reserve Bank of Chicago in 1992, Alan Greenspan, then chairman of the Federal Reserve Board, complained that the law created too many restrictions on banks.[41] Greenspan might have had it right; sixteen years after the adoption of FDICIA, we entered the worst U.S. banking crisis since the Depression, and perhaps the worst of all time.

This does not say much for the effectiveness of regulation, and it certainly does not provide a basis for believing that if we were to extend safety-and-soundness regulation beyond banks to other areas of the financial sector, we would be doing anything to prevent another crisis in the future. Indeed, there is significant evidence that regulation introduces moral hazard and makes the failure or weakness of regulated entities more likely. One example of this is the contrast between hedge funds—unregulated as to safety and soundness—and commercial banks, which are heavily regulated for this purpose. Hedge funds have long been targets for lawmakers looking for opportunities to impose new regulations.[42] Yet, the current crisis was caused by regulated banks, not hedge funds, and although some hedge funds have failed, no hedge funds have had to be bailed out by the government because they might create systemic risk. Moreover, hedge funds have performed much better than regulated banks in protecting their investors against losses. As Houman Shadab testified recently before Congress: "Even throughout 2008, while hedge funds have experienced the worst losses in their entire history as an industry, they have still managed to shield their investors' wealth from the massive losses experienced by mutual funds and the stock market more generally. From January through October 2008, the U.S. stock market lost 32 percent of its value while the average hedge fund lost approximately 15.48 percent."[43] Bank stocks, of course, have performed worse than the stock market as a whole.

---

41. Alan Greenspan, remarks (Twenty-Eighth Annual Conference on Bank Structure and Competition, Federal Reserve Bank of Chicago, May 7, 1992), available at http://fraser.stlouisfed.org/historicaldocs/ag92/download/27852/Greenspan_19920507.pdf (accessed April 8, 2009).

42. See, for example, Senate Finance Committee, "Grassley Seeks Multi-Agency Response on Lack of Hedge Fund Transparency, Expresses Alarm at Risk to Pension-Holders," news release, October 16, 2006, available at www.senate.gov/~finance/press/Gpress/2005/prg101606.pdf (accessed February 4, 2008).

43. Houman B. Shadab, testimony (Committee on Oversight and Government Reform, U.S. House of Representatives, November 15, 2008).

It is difficult, then, to escape the conclusion that regulation would not achieve any of the objectives that the administration has set out for it and that the motivation to broaden regulation and extend it to other areas of the financial economy is ideological, rather than based on facts, evidence, or even experience. Regulation adds costs and reduces competition and innovation. If it does not produce outcomes that are better than market discipline—and it certainly has not when we compare unregulated hedge funds and regulated banks—it should not be imposed on industries in which government backing is not present.

Finally, the proponents of systemic regulation argue that the administration's plan should be adopted because we have already bailed out so many firms that it is impossible to return to a world in which there is no systemic regulation. In other words, the moral hazard already created by the bailouts that have occurred justifies new and broader regulation. The cat, as they say, is out of the bag. Leaving aside the absurdity of the government getting more power because it made errors in the use of the power it had already been given, the trouble with this argument is that it treats the current financial crisis as an event that is likely to recur in the future. However, this crisis—involving as it does all developed countries and virtually all major financial institutions—is an unprecedented event that has required unprecedented actions by the government. To use the current crisis as a basis for a major policy change like that which the administration has proposed, it is necessary to believe that a worldwide meltdown of financial institutions will be a routine event in the future. But given the fact that nothing like this has ever happened before, there is no reason to believe that after the current crisis is over the financial markets will continue to expect bailouts of large nonbank financial institutions.

A useful analogy is the Fed's current role in addressing the problems of the financial sector. Because of the severity of the crisis, the Fed has been working hand in glove with the Treasury Department to provide funds for bank rescues and bailouts. If the markets were to take this cooperation as a precedent for the way the Fed will act in the future, they could well conclude that the Fed is no longer a truly independent central bank. However, most people in the financial markets probably understand that the Fed's extraordinary actions today will not create precedents for the future and that, when the current crisis is over, the Fed will act to show its independence of the Treasury, with its reputation for objectivity in its decision-making undiminished.

The Fed and Treasury are well aware of this problem and recently issued a joint statement pointing out that "[a]ctions that the Federal Reserve takes, during this period of unusual and exigent circumstances, in pursuit of financial stability . . . must not constrain the exercise of monetary policy."[44] In other words, the mere fact that some extraordinary and unprecedented actions had to be taken to deal with this crisis does not mean that everything in our financial system has changed. The same is true for the structure of the financial system itself. It should be designed for what is likely to occur in the future, not for a situation like the current unprecedented crisis.

Conclusion

The administration is attempting to build a case for a wholesale restructuring of the financial markets on the basis of two inapposite examples—AIG and Lehman. The fundamental changes its plan entails—the establishment of a powerful regulator with the authority to designate certain firms as systemically important and a system for resolving or rescuing financial institutions other than banks—will seriously impair competition in the financial sector and threaten to create large companies that are not significantly different in their competitive effect from Fannie Mae and Freddie Mac. Up to now, there has been little resistance from the financial sector, but the administration's case for this vast change in financial regulation is so weak—and the result of implementing its plan so troubling—that concerted financial industry opposition is likely to develop.

---

44. Board of Governors of the Federal Reserve System and U.S. Department of the Treasury, "The Role of the Federal Reserve in Preserving Financial and Monetary Stability," news release, March 23, 2009, available at www.federalreserve.gov/newsevents/press/monetary/20090323b.htm (accessed April 2, 2009).

"Unfree to Choose: The Administration's Consumer Financial Protection Agency"

Originally published July 2009

The administration's proposal for a Consumer Financial Protection Agency (CFPA) promises to be one of the most comprehensive and controversial pieces of regulatory legislation ever presented to Congress. In addition to extending the government's regulatory reach deep into areas now regulated by the states, the proposal would—for the first time—set up a statutory system for denying some financial products and services to consumers who are considered to lack the sophistication or experience to understand them. This is a sharp and unprecedented turn from the traditional disclosure approach to consumer protection, which punished fraud or deception but otherwise assumed that with adequate disclosure all Americans could make their way in a consumer economy. In a real sense, with this proposal, the administration has validated the conservative case that liberalism seeks to control the lives of ordinary Americans but does not interfere with the privileges of the educated elites. Finally, in proposing that the CFPA pursue the "rigorous application" of the Community Reinvestment Act (CRA), the administration has shown that it does not understand how that act contributed to the current financial crisis.

In late June, the administration circulated a white paper outlining its ideas for regulating the financial system. Most of the content simply repeated ideas presented to Congress in late March by Treasury Secretary Timothy Geithner.[45] The only real surprise in the white paper was the inclusion of the CFPA, a new federal-level agency to focus entirely on consumer protection. Because it

---

45. For commentary on these earlier proposals, see Peter J. Wallison, "Risky Business: Casting the Fed as a Systemic Regulator," *Financial Services Outlook* (February 2009), available at www.aei.org/outlook/100006; and Peter J. Wallison, "Reinventing GSEs: Treasury's Plan for Financial Restructuring," *Financial Services Outlook* (March/April 2009), available at www.aei.org/outlook/100027. (See pp. 361 and 377 of this book.)

was new and dramatically framed, the CFPA immediately drew the attention of the press and the concerns of a financial industry that was already feeling beleaguered by the prospect of broad new government regulation. The legislation that followed two weeks later was consistent with the white paper, but the white paper is more descriptive about the administration's intentions than the dry legislative language.

"We propose," said the white paper, "the creation of a single federal agency . . . dedicated to protecting consumers in the financial products and services markets, except for investment products and services already regulated by the SEC [Securities and Exchange Commission] or CFTC [Commodity Futures Trading Commission]. We recommend that the CFPA be granted consolidated authority over the closely related functions of writing rules, supervising and examining institutions' compliance, and administratively enforcing violations. The CFPA should reduce gaps in federal supervision; improve coordination among the states; set higher standards for financial intermediaries; and promote consistent regulation of similar products."[46] The jurisdiction of the new agency is intended to be broad, covering "credit, savings and payment products," according to its mission: "to help ensure that . . . consumers have the information they need to make responsible financial decisions . . . [and] are protected from abuse, unfairness, deception or discrimination."[47]

Hidden in these generalities are powers likely to make the CFPA one of the most controversial proposals ever put forward by an administration. Although the underlying idea of the CFPA probably springs from a well-meaning intention to protect consumers, many Americans—including those the agency intends to protect—will see a reduction in their options as consumers, while the privileges of the more sophisticated and better-educated elites will remain unimpaired.

The Basics

The CFPA is intended to be an independent agency with sole rule-making and enforcement authority for all federal consumer financial protection laws (with

---

46. U.S. Department of the Treasury, *Financial Regulatory Reform: A New Foundation* (June 30, 2009), 55–56, available at www.financialstability.gov/docs/regs/FinalReport_web.pdf (accessed July 6, 2009).

47. Ibid., 57.

the exception of those covered by the SEC and the CFTC). The draft legislation gives the agency jurisdiction over all companies, regardless of size, that are engaged generally in providing credit, savings, collection, or payment services. This is accomplished by transferring to the CFPA most or all of the authorities in sixteen federal statutes—ranging from the CRA to the Truth in Savings Act—that cover lending, mortgage financing, fair housing, credit repair, debt collection practices, fair credit reporting, and a multitude of other consumer financial products and services. The agency will be funded by fees imposed on the thousands of companies—from banks and credit card companies to local finance companies and department stores—that are subject to the legislation.[48] In many cases, the agency's jurisdiction will be concurrent with the jurisdiction of state agencies, but the CFPA will not preempt state law.

The white paper refers to the agency's regulations as "a floor not a ceiling," thus making room for states to impose regulations that go beyond those of the CFPA. State agencies will be permitted to enforce the CFPA's regulations, and vice versa.

In some ways, the plan is self-contradictory. The white paper speaks of the need for consistent standards, but the draft legislation leaves untouched the jurisdictions of the SEC, the CFTC, and the jurisdiction of the states with respect to insurance. Thus, the draft legislation sets up the possibility that inconsistent consumer protection standards will apply to products that compete directly with one another. In addition, given the administration's constant refrain about using its regulatory reforms to prevent regulatory arbitrage—in which a regulated entity seeks the most favorable jurisdiction under which to offer its products—it is odd that the legislation creates these arbitrage opportunities by placing the banks under the CFPA while leaving insurance regulation to the states and securities regulation under the SEC.

As might be expected, the new agency will have jurisdiction over disclosure to consumers. This is the customary way that consumer protection has proceeded at the federal level. In the past, consumers were generally expected to have the ability to make decisions for themselves if they were given the necessary information. The securities laws, for example, are largely consumer

---

48. *Consumer Financial Protection Agency Act of 2009*, § 1018, as proposed by the U.S. Department of the Treasury, June 30, 2009, available at www.financialstability.gov/docs/CFPA-Act.pdf (accessed July 6, 2009).

protection laws, developed during the New Deal period. In selling a security, an issuing company and any underwriter or dealer must supply investors with all material facts, including any additional facts needed to ensure that the information disclosed is not misleading. This approach has worked well for seventy-five years.

The material facts standard of the SEC is of course subject to interpretation, but it is possible to give it some content by imagining what an investor would want to know about the risks a company faces and its financial and business prospects. The white paper states that the CFPA will use a "reasonableness" standard, which it defines as "balance in the presentation of risks and benefits, as well as clarity and conspicuousness in the description of significant product costs and risks."[49] The draft legislation follows this pattern, so that disclosure to consumers must—perhaps like a drug label or a securities prospectus—include both the benefits and the risks of a product or service. These will be difficult guidelines for the regulated industry to follow, especially because enforcement actions and lawsuits may result from violations. Despite substantial disclosure on drug labels and in securities prospectuses—in some cases ordered by the regulatory agency—successful law-suits in both areas have claimed that the disclosure was not sufficient.

The Suitability Problem

The real trouble begins, however, when the administration's plan gets beyond the relatively simple issue of disclosure and proposes that the CFPA define standards for what the white paper calls "plain vanilla" products and services. The draft legislation describes them as "standard consumer financial products or services" that will be both "transparent" and "lower risk." According to the white paper, the CFPA will have authority "to require all providers and intermediaries to offer these products prominently, alongside whatever other lawful products they choose to offer."[50] This idea, seemingly quite simple, raises a host of significant questions. If there is a plain vanilla product, who is going to be eligible for the product that has strawberry sauce? In other words, once the baseline is

---

49. U.S. Department of the Treasury, *Financial Regulatory Reform: A New Foundation*, 64.

50. Ibid., 15.

established for a product that can or must be offered to everyone, who is going to be eligible for the product that, because of its additional but more complex features, offers financial advantages? This is the suitability problem—requiring providers to decide whether a particular product or service is suitable for a particular customer—and the administration's plan is caught in its web.

As an example, consider a mortgage with a prepayment penalty. The white paper notes that the "CFPA could determine that prepayment penalties should be banned for certain types of products, because penalties make loans too complex for the least sophisticated consumers or those least able to shop effectively."[51] This seems logical if one assumes—as the administration seems prepared to do—that some consumers can be denied access to products they want. As the white paper notes, "[t]he CFPA should be authorized to use a variety of measures to help ensure alternative mortgages were obtained only by consumers who understood the risks and could manage them."[52] So, what about the husband and wife who intend to keep their home until their children are grown and are willing, for this reason, to accept a prepayment penalty in order to get a lower rate on their fixed-rate mortgage? The administration is suggesting that this option might not be available to them if the mortgage provider (and ultimately the CFPA) does not consider them "sophisticated" consumers. This kind of discrimination between and among Americans is something new and troubling. The administration's plan clearly intends for some consumers to be denied access to certain products and services. "As mortgages and credit cards illustrate," the white paper declares, "even seemingly 'simple' financial products remain complicated to large numbers of Americans. As a result, in addition to meaningful disclosure, there must also be standards of appropriate business conduct and regulations that help ensure providers do not have undue incentives to undermine those standards."[53] In other words, by requiring that all providers offer plain vanilla products and services in addition to other products, the administration is creating a regime in which providers must keep "complicated" products out of the hands of Americans who may not be able to understand them. Although no specific regulation forbids offering an unsophisticated customer a product that is more complex than the plain vanilla baseline

---

51. Ibid., 68.
52. Ibid., 66.
53. Ibid., 67.

product, the possibility of enforcement actions by the CFPA or the Federal Trade Commission, suits by state attorneys general (specifically authorized to enforce the CFPA's regulations),[54] and the inevitable class action lawsuits will have this effect. This is not a question of disclosure—making the risks and costs plain. Instead, it is a matter of denying some people access to these products because of their deficiencies in experience, sophistication, and perhaps even intelligence. The white paper notes: "Even if disclosures are fully tested and all communications are properly balanced, product complexity itself can lead consumers to make costly errors."[55]

This approach seems to be an unprecedented departure by the U.S. government from some of the fundamental ideas of individual equality that have underpinned U.S. society since its inception. Conservatives have long argued that liberalism reflects a paternalistic desire on the part of elites to control and limit others' choices while leaving themselves unaffected. The white paper seems to validate exactly that critique. Providers will be at risk if they offer some products to ordinary consumers but could feel safe in offering the same products to those who are well educated and sophisticated. In important ways, the administration's approach raises the issues in the famous Louis Brandeis statement, quoted by Milton and Rose Friedman at the beginning of their book, *Free to Choose:* "Experience should teach us to be most on our guard to protect liberty when the government's purposes are beneficial. Men born to freedom are naturally alert to repel invasion of their liberty by evil-minded rulers. The greater dangers to liberty lurk in insidious encroachment by men of zeal, well-meaning but without understanding."[56]

In addition, there are troubling questions about how determinations of sophistication or even mental capacity are going to be made, who is going to make them, and what standards will be followed. It appears that the provider must make this decision, but what kinds of guidelines will the CFPA provide to protect the provider against the inevitable legal attacks? Vague language in the legislation suggests the consumer can refuse to take the plain vanilla alternative, but this simply changes the nature of the provider's risk from the qualities of

---

54. *Consumer Financial Protection Agency Act of 2009,* § 1042.

55. U.S. Department of the Treasury, *Financial Regulatory Reform: A New Foundation,* 66.

56. *Olmstead v. United States,* 277 U.S. 479 (1928).

the product to the qualities of the disclosures that were made to the consumer about what such a waiver would mean. Finally, the elements of a plain vanilla mortgage can be quite arbitrary, forcing people into structures that are financially disadvantageous. How can anyone know, for example, whether a thirty-year fixed-rate mortgage is better than a thirty-year adjustable-rate loan with a reasonable cap on interest costs? If interest rates rise in the future, the fixed- rate mortgage is best, but if they fall, a variable rate should be preferred. Should a government agency have the power to determine whether a homebuyer is allowed to make this choice?

In contrast, the disclosure system has always seemed appropriate in our society because it does not require invidious or arbitrary discrimination between one person and another. As long as the disclosure is fair and honest, why should anyone be prohibited from buying a product or service? While it is apparent that everyone is not equal in understanding or sophistication, our national sensibility has been that these differences should be ignored in favor of the higher ideal of equality. Under this view, fraud and deception should be punished, but the government should not be involved in deciding whether one person or another is eligible to receive what our economy has to offer. Yet the white paper says: "The CFPA should be authorized to use a variety of measures to help ensure that alternative mortgages were obtained only by consumers who understood the risks and could manage them. For example, the CFPA could . . . require providers to have applicants fill out financial experience questionnaires."[57] If this sounds a bit like a literacy or property test for voting—ideas long ago discredited—it is not surprising. Both impulses spring from the same source: a sense that some people are not as capable as others to make important choices.

To be sure, the securities laws contemplate that some distinctions will be made among customers on the basis of suitability. A broker-dealer may not sell a securities product to a customer if the customer does not have the resources to bear the risk or the ability to understand its nature. This is the closest analogy to what the administration is contemplating for all consumers, but as a precedent it is inapposite. Owning a security is not a necessity for living in our economically developed society, but obtaining credit certainly is. Whether through a

57. U.S. Department of the Treasury, *Financial Regulatory Reform: A New Foundation*, 66.

credit card, an account at a food or department store, a car loan, or a lay-away savings plan at a local furniture dealer, credit is a benefit that enables every person and every family to live better in our economy. Denying a credit product suitable to one's needs but deemed to be beyond one's capacity to understand has a far greater immediate adverse effect on a family's standard of living than telling an investor that a collateralized debt obligation is not a suitable product for his 401(k). Moreover, investors tend to be customers of broker-dealers over extended periods, so their financial and other capacities are well known to the brokers who handle their accounts. This is unlikely to be true for various credit products, which are likely to be established in single transactions and with little follow-up. Any attempt to determine a customer's ability to handle the risks associated with, say, a credit card could also involve investigation into matters that the customer considers private. Neither the draft legislation nor the white paper suggests how the provider of a financial service is to determine suitability while still protecting the customer's privacy. As discussed below, simply determining what other credit products and obligations particular applicants might have—and thus whether they are able to meet their obligations—will be difficult and costly. These problems do not normally arise in the suitability inquiry that broker-dealers must undertake.

Other Effects

Several other serious problems arise out of the structure that the administration seems to have in mind. The decision on a particular consumer's eligibility for a product will not be made by the CFPA but by the provider of the product or service. Apart from consumers themselves, providers are the first victims of this legislation. They will have to decide—at the risk of a CFPA enforcement action or a likely lawsuit—whether a particular customer is suitable for a particular product. This will place them in a difficult, if not impossible, position. If they accede to a customer's demand, and the customer later complains, the provider may face a costly enforcement proceeding or worse, but if the provider denies the customer the desired product, the provider will be blamed, not the government agency. In not a few cases, the provider may be sued for denial of credit to someone later deemed suitable, rather than for granting credit to a person later deemed unsuitable. The white paper points out that the administration does not intend to disturb private rights of action and in some cases "may seek legislation to increase statutory damages."[58] As noted above, state attorneys general are specifically authorized to enforce the CFPA's regulations. Although the white paper offers the possibility that a provider might get a "no action letter" or approval of its product and its disclosure, the personal financial condition and other capacities of the customer are what will count, not the simplicity of the product.

The second victim will be innovation. Why should anyone take the risk to create a new product? Even if the CFPA will review it to determine whether it is accurately and fairly described—a process that may require the services of a lawyer and the usual expenses of completing applications and answering questions from a government agency—the developer will still have to decide whether the people who want it are suitable to have it. The suitability decision can be expensive; a provider's better choice might be to stay with plain vanilla products and give up the idea of developing new products to attract new customers.

The third victim will be low-cost credit. The tasks of getting approval for a product and investigating the suitability of every person who wants something more than a plain vanilla product—whatever that may be—will substantially increase the cost of credit and reduce its availability. Leaving aside the effect on economic growth generally, higher credit costs and the denial of credit facilities that are deemed to be unsuitable for particular consumers will seriously impair the quality of life for many people of modest means or limited education. Credit provided by stores to regular customers may become too costly to administer. As a result, small neighborhood establishments may simply abandon the idea of providing credit and small finance companies and other small enterprises engaged in consumer financial services may well go out of business or merge with larger competitors. Even large credit providers may find that the additional business they attract with this service does not compensate for the risk and expense. Withdrawal of these competitors from the market will not only mean that many customers will be deprived of any credit sources and other services, but also that the reduced competition will allow credit fees to rise.

Litigation will also be a factor in the decision of credit sources about whether to develop new products or offer the complex products and services that might lead to disputes with customers or the CFPA. Investor complaints about suitability in the securities field are handled through an arbitration process, so that

---

58. Ibid., 58.

an investor who claims that he was sold a product for which he was unsuitable must make his case to an arbitrator rather than a court. The current costs of a mistake in the suitability judgment are thus much smaller for the broker-dealer. The legislation would give the CFPA the authority to ban mandatory arbitration clauses in credit arrangements,[59] and the white paper recommends that the SEC consider ending the arbitration process for securities.[60] If the SEC decides to do this, litigation in the securities field will substantially increase the costs of broker-dealers and investment advisers.

Finally, inherent conflicts between consumer protection and prudential regulation will arise when consumer protection responsibility is moved from the bank supervisors to the CFPA. How these might be resolved has not been described in the legislation and, perhaps was not considered. For example, as noted above, the white paper suggests that prepayment penalties should be banned for certain types of products because they make loans too complex for the least sophisticated consumers. A prudential supervisor, however, might want prepayment penalties to be included in a prudently underwritten mortgage, since the ability of the borrower to prepay at any time without penalty raises the lender's interest rate risk. It is likely that the bank supervisors and the CFPA will have different policies on this and many other issues, and the banks will be caught in the middle.

The Community Reinvestment Act

One of the most astonishing elements of the administration's plan is its proposal to give the CFPA the authority to enforce the CRA. The white paper states: "Rigorous application of the [CRA] should be a core function of the CFPA. Some have attempted to blame the subprime meltdown and financial crisis on the CRA and have argued that CRA must be weakened in order to restore financial stability. These arguments are without any logical or evidentiary basis. It is not tenable that the CRA could suddenly have caused an explosion in bad subprime loans more than 25 years after its enactment."[61] This statement

---

59. *Consumer Financial Protection Agency Act of 2009,* § 1025.

60. U.S. Department of the Treasury, *Financial Regulatory Reform: A New Foundation,* 72.

61. Ibid., 69.

reflects a troubling ignorance about the CRA, how it works, and its significance in creating subprime and other nontraditional mortgages. For example, the following report appears in the National Community Reinvestment Coalition's 2007 publication entitled *CRA Commitments* and describes quite clearly how the CRA's requirements created leverage for the creation of huge numbers of subprime and other nontraditional loans:

> Since the passage of CRA in 1977, lenders and community organiza-
> tions have signed over *446 CRA agreements totaling more than $4.5
> trillion* in reinvestment dollars flowing to minority and lower income
> neighborhoods.
>
> Lenders and community groups will often sign these agreements
> when a lender has submitted an application to merge with another
> institution or expand its services. Lenders must seek the approval of
> federal regulators for their plans to merge or change their services. The
> four federal financial institution regulatory agencies will scrutinize the
> CRA records of lenders and will assess the likely future community rein-
> vestment performance of lenders. The application process, therefore,
> provides an incentive for lenders to sign CRA agreements with commu-
> nity groups that will improve their CRA performance. Recognizing the
> important role of collaboration between lenders and community groups,
> the federal agencies have established mechanisms in their application
> procedures that encourage dialogue and cooperation among the parties
> in preserving and strengthening community reinvestment.[62]

Thus, the CRA's requirement that banks show good CRA compliance records in connection with their applications for regulatory approval to merge has enabled interested groups to pressure them into making more than $4.5 trillion in loan commitments for loans—subprime and other nontraditional mort-gages—that would qualify under the CRA. CRA regulations provide that a bank earns a rating of "outstanding"—and thus can expect its merger or expansion applications to be approved—if it demonstrates "extensive use of innovative or

---

62. National Community Investment Coalition, *CRA Commitments* (September 2007), 4, available at www.ncrc.org/images/stories/whatWeDo_promote/cra_commitments_07.pdf (accessed July 6, 2009). Emphasis added.

flexible lending practices."[63] It is not clear what this administration thinks this language means, but there was no doubt in the mind of a banker who wrote the following to his shareholders in early 2009:

> Under the umbrella of the Community Reinvestment Act (CRA), a tremendous amount of pressure was put on banks by the regulatory authorities to make loans, especially mortgage loans, to low income borrowers and neighborhoods. The regulators were very heavy handed regarding this issue. I will not dwell on it here but they required [our bank] to change its mortgage lending practices to meet certain CRA goals, even though we argued the changes were risky and imprudent.

The loans made under these commitments—ultimately sold to Fannie Mae and Freddie Mac and to the Wall Street investment banks—are failing in unprecedented numbers and weakening all financial institutions that hold them. If we are looking for a primary cause of today's financial crisis, it is here. By advocating "rigorous application" of the CRA by the new CFPA, the administration is again setting up the conditions for flooding the financial markets with subprime loans. If the bank supervisors were not concerned about the effect of the CRA on prudent lending practices, it is highly unlikely that the CFPA will give any priority to this problem.

There is, finally, a serious contradiction between the administration's call for support for "rigorous application of CRA" and its view that only plain vanilla mortgages are suitable for borrowers who lack sophistication. Unfortunately, the "innovative or flexible lending practices" demanded by the CRA regulations require banks to make subprime and nontraditional loans in the communities they serve. This is because many borrowers in these communities have blemished credit, low FICO scores, insufficient funds for down payments, insecure employment, and low incomes. Subprime loans and nontraditional loans are not plain vanilla loans. They are the kinds of risky loans the CFPA is supposed to prevent because their high failure rate ultimately hurts the consumers who have taken them and the communities in which the borrowers live. If the administration believes that a "plain vanilla" loan can be subprime, then it is either not

---

63. Comptroller of the Currency Administrator of National Banks, "CRA Regulation—Appendix A: Ratings," available at www.occ.treas.gov/cra/cra-appa.htm (accessed July 6, 2009).

serious about creating simple loans without substantial associated risk or not serious about a "rigorous application" of the CRA.

Conclusion

The Consumer Financial Protection Agency Act of 2009 is one of the most far-reaching and intrusive federal laws ever proposed by an administration. Not only does it reach down to regulate the most local levels of commercial activity, but the act would also set up procedures and incentives that will inevitably deny some consumers an opportunity to obtain products and services that are readily available to others. It will be surprising if Congress—once it sees the legislation in this light—adopts it.

"Unnecessary Intervention: The Administration's Effort to Regulate Credit Default Swaps"

Originally published August 2009

The last element of the administration's effort to regulate the financial system—a new regulatory structure for derivatives like credit default swaps (CDS)—was sent to Congress this month. The legislation would impose capital and margin requirements on swap dealers and major nondealer participants in the swap markets. The idea underlying this new regulatory regime is that the failure of a large CDS dealer or market participant can create a systemic breakdown, but this is highly unlikely. The relevant default that can cause serious losses in the CDS market is not the default of the swap dealer or other market participant, but widespread defaults by the firms (known as "reference entities") whose debt is protected by CDS. Thus, there is no sound policy reason to impose the costs of regulation on a derivatives market that cannot create a systemic breakdown and that has functioned effectively without such regulation for over twenty-five years. Finally, the administration's attempt to force the trading of "standardized" CDS into a clearinghouse is also misplaced. Because of the incentives it sets up among its members, a clearinghouse is likely to become a place where risk for its dealer members is concentrated rather than reduced.

In the past few months, as the administration has rolled out successive portions of its regulatory reform proposal, it has headlined each new section with the statement, "The Administration's Regulatory Reform Agenda Moves Forward." As its plans have been drawn and quartered even by Democrats on the Hill, these statements have begun to look more aspirational than descriptive. The final piece of the plan, the regulatory regime for derivatives, was issued in early August with a new headline: "The Administration's Regulatory Reform

participants in that market: (i) there has been no market failure that justifies government entry into this field; (ii) even in the AIG case, where a major swap participant was rescued by the Fed, there is no evidence that AIG's failure would have resulted in a systemic event or even a serious disruption of the swap markets; and (iii) there is no reason to believe—even in theory—that the failure of a large CDS dealer or CDS market participant can cause a systemic breakdown unless that failure occurs before or contemporaneously with the failure of large numbers of reference entities.

Why Regulate Swap Dealers or Major Market Participants?

The most basic question anyone should ask about a new proposed regulation is this: "what problem is this proposal intended to solve?" Regulation is costly, suppresses innovation, and reduces competition, so before we impose these costs on yet another industry—and those who consume its products or services—we should at least ask why regulation is necessary.

The administration's short answer to this question would undoubtedly be "AIG"—the idea, firmly embedded in the media mind, that AIG had to be rescued because, as a major CDS market participant, its failure would have created a systemic breakdown. No one in a responsible position at the Federal Reserve ever said this publicly, and the story has now become a classic case of something having been repeated so often, in so many places, that it somehow becomes true, even though no one can trace it back to an actual fact. Perhaps the administration actually believes that regulation of CDS is necessary to prevent a systemic breakdown, but it is far more likely that the administration is proposing to regulate the swap markets because it can, following the precept of the president's chief of staff, Rahm Emanuel, who famously remarked at the outset of the administration that one "never wants a serious crisis to go to waste."

Even if Fed officials had confirmed that AIG's swap portfolio was the reason for the firm's rescue, there would still be a question as to whether that judgment was correct. Accordingly, this *Outlook* will start with the more basic question: could AIG's CDS portfolio—no matter its size—have caused a systemic breakdown (or even a major disruption) of the financial markets if AIG had been allowed to fail? As I will explain below, I think the answer to this question is no, and thus I doubt the need for any legislation that regulates this or any other part of the derivatives industry.

Can Credit Default Swaps Create Systemic Risk?

Despite their fancy name, credit default swaps are simply reimbursement or guarantee agreements, much closer to a bank's standby letter of credit (SLOC) than to an insurance contract. A simple example of how CDS work involves three parties. (In this hypothetical, I am not including the intermediary dealers, to be discussed later.) Let us assume that A has made a $10 million loan to B. A is now exposed to the risk that B will default on the payment of interest or principal on the loan. For a variety of reasons, A may want to hedge its exposure to B. For example, A may wish to diversify its portfolio or reduce its exposure to a credit that it believes may be weakening. A can accomplish this objective without selling the loan by entering a CDS with C. In this transaction, C promises to reimburse A for a specified sum (known as the notional amount) if B defaults on its loan obligation, and A agrees to pay a fee (known as a premium) to C over a predetermined period of years. A continues to hold the loan to B on its books, and to receive the payments of principal and interest B is paying. If C has a better credit rating than B, A has both diversified its portfolio and upgraded its quality.

Through SLOCs, banks have engaged in virtually the same transaction for years. SLOCs are routinely used to guarantee the obligations of companies and government entities that are borrowing money from third parties. In an SLOC transaction, a bank takes the credit risk of the borrower, and the lender makes the loan on the strength of the bank's credit rather than the borrower's. Thus, the SLOC serves much the same function as a CDS; it promises a lender that the bank will reimburse the lender if the borrower defaults on the loan. If the default occurs, the bank pays the lender and takes over the lender's position. The only difference between an SLOC and a CDS is that the bank's fee in the SLOC transaction is generally paid by the borrower (B in the hypothetical) instead of by the lender.

In other words, there is nothing mysterious or truly new about the standard CDS transaction. The fact that it is called a "swap" should not cause anyone to think this kind of transaction is impenetrable, strange, complex, or unusually risky. It does not even create any new "interconnections" that had never existed before in the financial system. SLOC transactions create interconnections, as do interbank loans, syndications, deposits, repos, reverse repos, warehousing agreements, joint ventures, under-writing agreements, and dozens of other contractual arrangements that create the web of interrelationships that allow financial institutions to do what they are supposed to do—move funds from places where they are not used productively to places where they are. Calling these arrangements interconnections does not change their character, and it is certainly wrong to claim that CDS suddenly created interconnections that never existed before.

Returning to our hypothetical example, let us suppose that C—which has written the protection for A—goes bankrupt. C's bankruptcy means that A has lost its protection against B's default. But what else has it lost? It is now once again exposed to the risk of B, but in our hypothetical example B has not defaulted: it is still paying principal and interest to A. In this sense, A has not suffered any serious loss. It certainly has not lost the $10 million of the original loan to B, since B is still current on the loan. If A still wants protection against B's default, however, A must go back into the market and contract with a new CDS counterparty. To put this in even simpler terms, if you are a homeowner and your insurance company fails, you have not lost anything unless you have already had a fire and have not collected from the insurer. If these things have not happened, you simply call your local insurance broker and get a new home-owner's policy from another insurer. That is basically what A would do if it still thinks it needs protection.

It could be, of course, that A has lost the value of a favorable contract with C. That would be true if B's credit had declined between the time when A bought protection from C and C's default. In that case, A would be (in swap jargon) "in the money"—it is paying much less for the protection than it would have to pay to buy the same protection today. Because the protection A has purchased is worth more than what A is paying, A can even "sell" its contract to another party not associated with B for a profit. In addition, if A still wants to hedge its exposure to B, the fact that B has weakened since the original CDS was entered with C means that A will have to pay more for the same protection against B's default than it had been paying C. This also represents a real cash loss to A, which may or may not be able to recover its loss from C's bankrupt estate. Obviously, however, a loss of this size is highly unlikely to cause the failure of A. But because of the way the CDS market works, A and the other counterparties of C are likely to be protected against this loss anyway. The typical CDS contract requires the party that is "in the money" to receive collateral to cover its risk of nonpayment by the other party. Thus, if B's credit has been weakening since the CDS was entered between A and C, A is in the money and C would be required to post collateral with A. In most CDS contracts, A is also entitled to receive more collateral from C if C itself is perceived to be weakening. By the time C has gone bankrupt, accordingly, A should have enough collateral to defray all or a substantial portion of the cost of a new CDS to cover its exposure to B. But even if the collateral is insufficient for this purpose, the loss A and others similarly situated have suffered is too small to cause a systemic breakdown.

Setting the Record Straight on AIG

At this point, it is useful to step back and recognize that the key default in the CDS market is not the failure of C—the party that wrote the CDS protecting A—but the failure of B. As long as B is current in paying its debt to A, the failure of C—the party that is in the position of AIG, having written protection on B—would not cause any major loss to A. In that case, A's only loss is the cost of buying a replacement CDS. To be sure, this could be costly, but it is clearly not of a size that might reasonably cause a systemic breakdown. On the other hand, if B had defaulted before C, A's loss of C's protection would have meant a real and substantial loss for A.

Now let us consider a thought experiment involving AIG and the hundreds of billions of dollars (in notional amount) of CDS protection that had been written by one of AIG's subsidiaries (with AIG's guarantee). What would have happened if AIG had been allowed to fail? As the A-B-C discussion above suggests, there would not have been a major loss to any of AIG's counterparties unless large numbers of the reference entities on which the CDS had been written had defaulted before or contemporaneously with AIG's default. As far as we now know, however, there were no widespread defaults anywhere in the world financial system before AIG defaulted, so AIG's default would not have resulted in its counterparties suffering any systemically significant losses. If these counterparties still wanted protection against the same reference entities, they could have gone out into the market and purchased replacement CDS providing the same coverage they had lost. In some cases, this might be costly, but even assuming that AIG's counterparties had not received sufficient collateral from AIG to reimburse them fully for their loss, the size of the loss would not have been large enough in each case to cause their default and thus a systemic breakdown of some kind.

This analysis is valid for all cases in which AIG's protection covered named reference entities, but much of AIG's protection is said to have been written on portfolios of collateralized debt obligations (CDOs). Because of the collapse of the market for CDOs based on subprime or other mortgages, it would have been virtually impossible for counterparties protected by AIG to obtain replacement coverage for those instruments. In that case, the risk that had been concentrated in AIG would in effect have returned to AIG's counterparties. This would have represented an accounting but not a cash loss, as these counterparties were required to put these assets back on their balance sheets. Nevertheless, the fact that AIG's failure would not have caused massive losses was demonstrated in mid-March this year when it was revealed that Goldman Sachs was the largest AIG counterparty, with total AIG protection of $12.9 billion. The others named were Merrill Lynch ($6.8 billion), Bank of America ($5.2 billion), Citigroup ($2.3 billion), and Wachovia ($1.5 billion). When media representatives asked Goldman how large its losses would have been if AIG had been allowed to fail, they were told that the losses would have been "negligible."[70] Consistent with the analysis above, Goldman had received collateral from AIG and had also bought CDS protection against AIG's potential default. If the firms named are indeed the largest AIG counterparties, the losses on whatever CDO protection AIG had written would not have been substantial in relation to their size—even if they had not obtained collateral from AIG before it was rescued. So it is highly unlikely that any systemic breakdown would have occurred if AIG had been allowed to fail. If this is true of AIG's default, it would also have been true of the default of any other CDS counterparty, no matter how large. The question, again, is not the number or the notional amount of the CDS that any such AIG-like market participant might have written, but whether the defaults of reference entities are so extensive or substantial that its counterparties suffer real cash losses.

The "Naked Swaps" Issue

In a sense, AIG was a special case. It was a major player in the CDS market, but not a dealer. It took on a lot of risk but did not appear to do much hedging. As such, it is a great example of the general proposition advanced in this *Outlook:*

---

70. Peter Edmonston, "Goldman Insists It Would Have Lost Little If A.I.G. Had Failed," *New York Times,* March 21, 2009.

a large, unhedged market participant can fail without causing any significant losses to its counterparties. In reality, however, most of the major players in the market are CDS dealers, and they are mostly hedged. The CDS market is a dealer market. The great majority of transactions go through dealers, firms that are in the business of buying and selling CDS for their own account. So in our A-B-C hypothetical example, A would have bought its CDS protection from D, a dealer, and the dealer would have hedged its own liability by purchasing protection from C. This refinement does not change the substance of the transaction. Instead of A being exposed directly to C, it is exposed to D, and D is exposed to C. When C went bankrupt, D (rather than A) would have had to find a new counterparty to hedge its obligation to A.

The fact that the most active participants in the CDS market are dealers is important for understanding two issues that come up frequently among critics of CDS: "betting" and "naked swaps." In the CDS market today, it is possible for two parties that have no connection whatsoever to a reference entity or its debt to enter into a CDS transaction. For example, a hedge fund, E, could sell protection against B's default, even though it has no interest in B's debt. It would do this because it believes B's credit will strengthen, and it hopes to profit from an increase in the value of the protection it has written if this occurs. The value of E's CDS will increase if B's credit strengthens because E is now receiving a premium that is larger than what protection on B now costs. Alternatively, if B actually defaults, E would have to pay the full notional amount of the CDS it has written. This kind of transaction is known as a "naked swap," and to some critics of the CDS market, it is simply betting on B's financial condition. Moreover, the argument runs, this creates risk in the market where none existed before and is thus unhealthy.

The answer on the creation of risk is easy. Yes, E is taking on the risk of B's default, but there is no net additional risk in the market as a whole. If B defaults and E has to pay its counterparty, E is a loser but its counterparty is a winner. Their respective risks net to zero. The notion that E is simply betting on B's default, however, requires more analysis. It is important to recognize that E has a counterparty that is betting exactly the opposite—that B will stay the same or strengthen. Could the CDS market perform its function without these "bets"—that is, without buyers or sellers who are willing to buy and sell protection with no interest in the underlying asset? The answer is that the market would not function efficiently without these bets, just as the equity markets would not function effectively without a constant supply of buyers and sellers speculating—or betting—that a stock will move up or down. Economists would say that all this speculation, in the equity markets as well as the CDS market, contributes to price discovery—determining the price that best reflects the market's judgment about an equity or debt security at any moment in time. Efficient price discovery makes it easier for transactions to occur because it narrows the difference between what the potential buyer of CDS protection is willing to pay and the price that the potential seller of protection wants to receive for taking default risk on a particular reference entity.

It is easier to understand this process in the equity market than in the CDS market, but the process is essentially the same. Say hedge fund E believes that B—the same reference entity in our earlier hypothetical—is actually a greater credit risk than was implied by the fee A is paying to C. E believes that it can profit if B's credit weakens, just as a short-seller in the equity market can profit from a decline in a stock price. So E contacts a dealer and says it wants to buy protection on B. Pursuing E's request, the dealer then attempts to determine what it will cost to buy protection on B, because the dealer will want to be sure that it can hedge its exposure to E if it agrees to E's request. The fact that someone is buying protection against B's default causes the price of protection (known as the credit spread) to rise in accordance with supply and demand. The opposite would be true, and the spread for writing protection on B would decline, if E had gone into the market to offer protection on B.

The price discovery in the CDS market is good enough to act as a guide to the credit condition of thousands of reference entities and conditions in the credit markets as a whole. In the fall and winter of 2008, when there was great anxiety about the stability of many financial institutions, there were over seventy references to CDS spreads in the press, all for the purpose of demonstrating that the risks in the credit markets were either rising or falling at a particular time. One of these statements was by Neel Kashkari, a Treasury official, in congressional testimony: "One indicator that points to reduced risk of default among financial institutions is the average credit default swap spread for the eight largest U.S. banks, which has declined more than 200 basis points since before Congress passed the [Emergency Economic Stabilization Act]."[71] The

---

71. Neel Kashkari (testimony, House Financial Services Committee, December 10, 2008), available at www.treasury.gov/press/releases/hp1322.htm (accessed August 25, 2009).

fact that spreads were declining was taken as an indication that the market was settling down. This was true of spreads as a whole and spreads on individual reference entities. In other words, CDS spreads were thought to reflect real market judgments on credit quality and effective price discovery. CDS spreads would be far less reflective of real credit conditions, and hedging transactions would be more costly in every case, if market participants were not allowed to speculate—through naked swaps—on whether reference entities were weakening or strengthening.

Thoughts on a Clearinghouse

The administration's proposed legislation provides for the creation of one or more clearinghouses—also known (and better described) as central counterparties (CCPs)—which would be regulated by the CFTC. As the name implies, a CCP takes on the role of counterparty for all CDS transactions brought to the clearinghouse by a clearinghouse member. As an example, in the hypothetical transaction we have been using, A seeks protection against B's default by purchasing protection from the dealer, D. In turn, D hedges this obligation by purchasing protection from C, a major market participant. Where a CCP is present, D, a clearinghouse member, in effect transfers to the CCP the obligation to pay A if B defaults, as well as the hedging CDS that D purchased from C. The CCP, in effect, stands in the shoes of D and has what might be called a matched book, just as D might have had if the clearinghouse did not exist.

This arrangement reduces the default risk of A, which now does not have to worry about the financial condition of D. If B ultimately defaults, the clearinghouse pays A and the CCP's loss is first taxed to D. If D and the collateral it has posted does not or cannot fully reimburse the CCP, the balance of the loss is shared by all the clearinghouse members. This makes hedging through a CCP a significantly less risky prospect for A, which now has the resources of the CCP to cover its exposure to B, instead of just the resources of D. In this sense a clearinghouse reduces the default risk of at least one of the counterparties. Another advantage of a clearinghouse could be a more efficient use of collateral. With a CCP, the members post collateral to cover all the risks that they have transferred to the clearinghouse, while in the OTC context collateral may have to be posted for each separate transaction. On the other hand, bilateral netting in the OTC context can allow collateral posted in a CDS transaction to be used in an interest rate swap or commodity futures transaction, so OTC transactions can also use collateral efficiently in some circumstances.

Since the rescue of AIG, clearinghouses have attracted a lot of interest, in part because they are said to offer a degree of transparency by exposing the CDS obligations of all the CCP members. The administration's proposal—correctly— does not require nonstandardized CDS to be cleared through a CCP, and this substantially reduces the usefulness of the CCP as a source of information about the overall risks of the members. Nonstandard swaps will still be handled OTC and will remain essentially invisible. Although a clearinghouse can reduce the default risk for hedgers, that is only true where, as discussed above, the reference entity has defaulted. In most cases, the costs of a CDS counterparty's default would be the cost of a replacement CDS and thus relatively small. The loss could be large for a hedger in the case of a default by the reference entity, but it is questionable whether the costs imposed by a clearinghouse, including the concentration of risks described below, are outweighed by the limited additional default risk mitigation that is provided to the protected party in these cases.

The administration has made clear that one reason, perhaps the major reason, for requiring a clearinghouse for standardized CDS is to reduce the chances that the default of a dealer or major market participant might cause a systemic breakdown. If it is true, as argued in this *Outlook,* that the failure of a large dealer or participant in the CDS market will create systemic risk only under very limited circumstances, then the relatively weak cost-benefit arguments in favor of a clearinghouse become decidedly weaker. Indeed, it is possible that by concentrating much of the market's CDS risk in one place, the clearinghouse itself could become another entity that the government will feel compelled to bail out in the event of financial trouble.

Risks could concentrate in a CCP because members' incentives will be different when they are taking on business that they will ultimately transmit to the CCP than when taking on business that they will have to hold themselves. Dealer members are likely to be far more prudent in the latter case than in the former. When D has the opportunity to pass along to the clearinghouse the risks of its CDS with A and its hedging transaction with C, D's incentive to evaluate the risk of B and C fully is likely to be substantially reduced. In the future it may be required to put up more collateral if B and C weaken as credits, but that is in the future, and may not actually happen. For this reason, the CCP will be taking on more risk than D would have agreed to assume for the premium it is being paid, and these risks now will be shared with the other members of the clearinghouse. To protect itself, the CCP must have a sophisticated enough model or pricing mechanism to evaluate the risks it is assuming from D and other members. If it cannot do this—and there is reason to believe its incentives for this purpose are far weaker than those who buy and sell CDS in the OTC market—the clearinghouse structure creates a kind of financial tragedy of the commons, in which it would be in each member's best interest to transfer more risk to the CCP than the other members are transferring.

Under these circumstances—and given the CDS market's history of stable operations over the current decade and even during the current crisis—it would not be good policy to force any CDS transactions through a clearinghouse. Because of the adverse incentives it creates for members, a clearinghouse could produce more aggregate risk than the bilateral OTC market that it would replace. Nor can it be shown that a clearinghouse will have any effect in preventing a systemic breakdown. Together, these elements suggest that the unintended consequences of requiring the establishment of one or more CDS clearinghouses seem to outweigh whatever limited benefits might be achieved by a CCP system.

"TARP Baby:
The Administration's Resolution
Authority for Nonbank Financial Firms"

Originally published September 2009

The Obama administration's proposal for a resolution authority to unwind large nonbank financial institutions is another example of its misplaced effort to expand the government's role in the economy. The plan's fundamental flaw is its failure to explain how this or any other government will distinguish in advance between companies whose failure would cause a systemic breakdown and those whose failure will cause only an economic disruption of some kind. Without a way to make this distinction, the resolution authority will simply become a permanent TARP (Troubled Asset Relief Program). Other conceptual flaws in the administration's plan are its effect in creating moral hazard, enhancing the competitive advantages of large nonbank financial firms, increasing the uncertainty faced by creditors of nonbank financial institutions, and adding yet another burden for the taxpayers. In the end, the existing bankruptcy system, which has done a far better job of resolving Lehman Brothers than the Fed has done with AIG, seems a superior policy choice to creating yet another government agency with wide-ranging but ill-defined powers.

One of the most remarkable things about Washington is the fact that poor performance by regulators is regularly rewarded with more funds and broader powers, both conferred by a grateful (and apparently forgetful) Congress. So, we see the Securities and Exchange Commission (SEC) receive more resources and staffing after failing to detect the accounting frauds in Enron and WorldCom and the same agency calling (without shame) for more staff and funding after failing to recognize that Bernard Madoff was running a Ponzi scheme; we have seen all the banking supervisors—the Comptroller of the Currency, the Federal Deposit Insurance Corporation (FDIC), and the Federal Reserve—obtain enhanced authority after the savings and loan debacle (when almost 1,600 banks also failed), and now being offered new authority by the Obama administration after failing to use the earlier powers to avert the near collapse of the banking system; and most remarkable of all, we watch in awe as the administration tries to make the Fed the regulator of virtually the entire financial system even though the agency—the closest thing we have had to a systemic monitor—abjectly failed to detect the housing bubble that ultimately caused the very kind of crisis the Fed is supposed to prevent in the future. I recently listened to a speech by Christina Romer, the chair of the administration's Council of Economic Advisers, who argued with a straight face that giving this new authority to the Fed would assure "accountability." Orwell would have been envious.

The point here is that Washington cannot seem to think of any response to a crisis except to increase the power and reach of the government's regulatory system, despite compelling evidence that it consistently fails to protect the public or maintain the health of the financial system. Many studies, in addition, have shown that regulation adds costs, suppresses competition, and reduces innovation; indeed, in the many areas of the economy in which deregulation has occurred—air travel, telecommunications, trucking, and securities brokerage, to name a few—it has uniformly produced innovation and lowered costs. It is time to think of something new, but imagination is not Washington's strong point.

The reigning liberal faith in the efficacy of regulation and government control is nowhere more clearly exhibited than in the proposals of the Obama administration for the regulation of the financial system. A number of earlier *Outlook*s have addressed the deficiencies and simple wrong-headedness of the Obama proposals,[72] but one idea has not received the extensive consideration it

---

72. See Peter J. Wallison, "Everything You Wanted to Know about Credit Default Swaps—but Were Never Told," *AEI Financial Services Outlook* (December 2008), available at www.aei.org/outlook/29158; Peter J. Wallison, "Regulation without Reason: The Group of Thirty Report," AEI *Financial Services Outlook* (January 2009), available at www.aei.org/outlook/29285; Peter J. Wallison "Risky Business: Casting the Fed as a Systemic Risk Regulator," AEI *Financial Services Outlook* (February 2009), available at www.aei.org/outlook/100006; Peter J. Wallison, "Reinventing GSEs: Treasury's Plan for Financial Restructuring," AEI *Financial Services Outlook* (March/April 2009), available at www.aei.org/outlook/100027; Peter J. Wallison, "Unfree to Choose: The Administration's Consumer Financial Protection Agency," AEI *Financial Services Outlook* (July 2009), available at www.aei.org/outlook/100056; and Peter J. Wallison, "Unnecessary Intervention: The Administration's Effort to Regulate Credit Default Swaps," AEI *Financial Services Outlook* (August 2009), available at www.aei.org/outlook/100065. (See pp. 223, 345, 361, 377, 396, and 409 in this book.)

warrants—the notion that we need a government-run mechanism for the "orderly resolution" of systemically significant nonbank financial firms when they fail.[73] Of all the Obama proposals for expanding government authority, this is the only one that seems now to have any real traction on Capitol Hill—probably because both the regulatory establishment and the big financial institutions can see benefits in it for them. The administration's argument—building on the aftermath of the Lehman Brothers bankruptcy—is that allowing a "systemically significant" nonbank financial institution to enter an ordinary bankruptcy proceeding will produce a "disorderly" collapse and thus contribute to a systemic breakdown. The proposal applies only to nonbank financial institutions because insured banks and other depository institutions are already covered by a resolution system run by the FDIC.

According to the administration, nonbank financial institutions that might be systemically important include bank holding companies, insurance companies, securities firms, finance companies, hedge funds, private equity firms, and any other financial-related firm that might—because of its "size, leverage or interconnectedness"—cause a systemic breakdown if it fails. The fact that none of those terms has any definitive content is a tip-off that what we are talking about is unfettered discretion.

This *Outlook* argues that while the terms "systemic risk" or "systemic breakdown" can be defined in words, they cannot be used as an effective guide for policy action. We have no way of knowing when or under what circumstances the failure of a particular company will cause something as serious as a systemic breakdown—as distinguished from a simple disruption in the economy. Government officials' inability to forecast or predict the effect of a particular company's failure will mean that the government will take over or rescue from bankruptcy many companies that should be allowed to fail in the normal way. As the late Irving Kristol observed, "it is politically impossible for any state to cope with the bankruptcies associated with economic risk taking."[74] Once the government takes responsibility for preventing systemic breakdowns, it will use that authority liberally to prevent mere economic disruption. The bailouts of General Motors and Chrysler make clear how this will work. Moreover, it will be

---

73. U.S. Department of the Treasury, "Financial Regulatory Reform: A New Foundation," FinancialStability.gov, www.financialstability.gov/docs/regs/FinalReport_web.pdf (accessed September 30, 2009).

74. Editorial, "Irving Kristol's Reality Principles," *Wall Street Journal,* September 19, 2009.

impossible to tell, after the government resolution authority has acted, whether the particular failure would actually have caused a systemic breakdown, making Congress's ability to oversee the use of this new power wholly ineffective. The result will be to introduce moral hazard into the financial system, as creditors come to believe that large financial companies will be rescued; the advantage this will confer on large firms will be competitively significant, driving small firms out of markets in which they could formerly compete and weakening the financial system as inferior managements and business models are saved from extinction by government action—all ultimately paid for by the taxpayers.

In addition, a resolution system for nonbank financial institutions is unnecessary to prevent a systemic breakdown. Such an event occurs when the failure of one financial institution causes such large losses to others that they are unable to meet their own obligations, thus causing losses to cascade through the entire economy. Losses of this kind, however, can only be caused by the failure of a large commercial bank, which deprives other banks of the funds they were expecting to be paid, deprives businesses of access to their working capital or payroll funds, and deprives individuals of the funds they use for their daily needs. The losses that occur when a nonbank financial institution fails are not of this character; they occur over time as obligations that come due are not paid and affect creditors and counterparties that are generally diversified and able to withstand an occasional loss. For example, a bank failure could deprive a business of the cash with which to meet its payroll, but it is highly unlikely that the failure of a nonbank financial institution will have a similar effect on the diversified lenders that are likely to be its counterparties.

Accordingly, there is no sound policy basis for providing the government with authority to resolve nonbank financial institutions, and granting such authority would be harmful to the financial system and the economy generally. Instead, failing nonbank financial institutions, both large and small, should be allowed to go into bankruptcy. This *Outlook* will show that the administration's proposal is both unnecessary and potentially harmful to the future stability of the financial system.

The Administration's Plan Compared to Bankruptcy

The administration's plan includes two possible scenarios—a conservatorship, in which the institution is managed back to viability, and a receivership, in which the institution is probably sold or liquidated. A conservatorship resembles a chapter eleven bankruptcy proceeding, in which the debtor remains in possession of its assets and continues to operate the business. In both cases, the objective is to return the firm to viability rather than to unwind it. However, in a government-mandated conservatorship, the firm is managed by a government agency, while in chapter eleven the operations of the company remain in the hands of its management. A receivership resembles a chapter seven bankruptcy, in which the debtor is simply wound up—its assets sold and creditors paid off based on their priority.

There are two requirements for a successful exit from chapter eleven—the necessary financing (known as debtor-in-possession, or DIP financing) to keep the debtor operating as a going concern, and the creditors' agreement to take less than they would get in a liquidation, in the hope that the debtor will eventually be able to pay them in full. In chapter eleven, the debtor prepares a plan for recovery, for approval by the creditors voting by class. If the creditors decide the company's prospects for eventual profitability are not sufficiently good to give them a chance to recoup their losses, they can vote down a plan for recovery, and the debtor will be liquidated.

Similarly, under the administration's plan, if the resolution agency (acting as a conservator) determines that there is no further danger of a systemic breakdown, it can liquidate the company—perhaps reimbursing itself for the funds it has extended—or return the company to financial viability if that is feasible and warranted by the circumstances. The administration's plan would, under most circumstances, assign the responsibility for resolving a failing financial firm to the FDIC and is thus another example of rewarding an agency whose performance has not been exemplary. In the last two years, the FDIC has resolved approximately 124 failing financial institutions. It does this under rules established in the FDIC Improvement Act of 1991, which empowered the agency to take over failing banks before they become insolvent. The purpose of this authority—called "prompt corrective action" (PCA)—was added to the FDIC's bank resolution arsenal so the agency could better protect the deposit insurance fund from the losses that occur when a failing bank's liabilities exceed the value of its assets. Nevertheless, the agency is seldom able to do so. The FDIC's average loss on the assets of the banks it has closed over the last two years is approximately 25 percent.[75] If this is the record with respect to banks, it is fanciful to

---

75. Federal Deposit Insurance Corporation (FDIC), "Failed Bank List," available at www.fdic.gov/bank/individual/failed/banklist.html (accessed September 21, 2009).

believe that the losses will be less for the much more complex and substantially larger nonbank financial institutions that the administration expects the FDIC to resolve—with no special expertise in the matter—in the future.

What Will Occur under the Administration's Plan?

Taking the administration's proposal at face value, an "orderly" resolution will begin as something like a conservatorship. This seems essential because—under the administration's assumptions—the failure of a systemically important company will, by definition, cause a systemic breakdown. In order to avoid that result, the company will have to be kept in operation for a period of time. Assuming that the necessary financing is provided by the government (an issue discussed later), the failed financial institution will be operated by the conservator, at least for a period of time necessary to assure there is no systemic breakdown when the institution is eventually closed. Under these circumstances, there are three possible outcomes for the failed institution's creditors.

Option One. If the objective of the orderly resolution is to avoid a systemic breakdown, then all creditors whose loans mature when the government controls the institution will likely be paid in full. This is because the establishment of a conservatorship for the failing company is likely to be an event of default under its loan arrangements, which normally accelerates the maturity of its obligations. It is unlikely that the FDIC or any other government agency that takes over a nonbank financial institution will immediately stop payments to these creditors. This could—under the rationale for establishing a resolution agency—cause the systemic breakdown that the entire resolution structure is supposed to prevent.

Option Two. Another possibility is that the institution's long-term creditors are paid a portion of what they are owed but advised that they will not be paid in full at the end of the government's control. This would presumably prevent the immediate losses that would occur if payments to creditors were stopped entirely. This option would not be available in bankruptcy, in which prebankruptcy creditors can be paid only in special circumstances.

Option Three. A third option might be to stop all payments to creditors. This would be closest to a bankruptcy, where the debtor in possession is not generally able to pay prebankruptcy creditors unless there is an exemption from the stay provisions that normally apply. However, this is highly unlikely, since it would vitiate the entire rationale for setting up a government agency to resolve a failing nonbank financial firm. For this reason, in the following discussion, we will assume that the administration's plan will involve the use of either option one or two.

Is a Resolution Authority Necessary?

What is the problem for which a resolution authority is the solution? The administration's argument is that the collapse of a large nonbank financial institution could cause a systemic breakdown; to avoid this outcome, the government should have the authority to take over any such firm and resolve it in an orderly manner. However, the administration's rationale for its proposal is highly questionable.

Systemic Breakdown versus Economic Disruption. Is it possible to know in advance whether the failure of a particular firm will cause a systemic breakdown, rather than simply an economic disruption of some kind? The failure of any large company will cause disruption—loss of jobs, losses to creditors, or perhaps the disappearance of an important intermediary. Although setting up a resolution system that would actually prevent a systemic breakdown might make sense, it would not be good policy to authorize a resolution system that, in practice, is used to prevent mere disruption. That would create extensive moral hazard and have the effect of preserving companies and managements that should be eliminated. If weak business models and bad managements are preserved by government action, that would weaken our economic system overall by preventing better business models and better managements from moving up to take their place.

The administration has not suggested how a systemic risk would be distinguished from a mere risk of economic disruption, and it is far from clear that it is possible to make such a determination in advance. Yet the distinction between the two is crucial; it provides the only limitation on the government's power to take over failing financial institutions. Without such limits, it is highly likely that the power will be used to prevent ordinary economic disruption rather than the far more dangerous systemic breakdown. The recent rescues of General

Motors and Chrysler are examples of government action to prevent economic disruption; no one has contended that the failure of either company, or both, would have created a systemic breakdown. Without clear limits, the resolution authority the administration is proposing will inevitably become a permanent TARP for the financial system.

What Causes a Systemic Breakdown? In advancing its various proposals, the administration has gotten a free pass on the question of what a systemic risk actually is and how a systemic breakdown might occur. Administration spokespersons regularly describe systemically important firms as those that are the "largest, most leveraged and most interconnected"[76] but never say how these factors might create systemic risk. Even assuming that the administration could describe how it would distinguish between a systemic breakdown and an economic disruption, it still would be necessary to explain how a nonbank financial firm would cause a systemic breakdown if it were to fail.

Pointing to the events that occurred after Lehman's collapse a year ago is not sufficient. Although many observers seem to assume that what followed the bankruptcy of Lehman was a systemic breakdown, this is far from clear. The term systemic risk usually refers to the possibility that the failure of a single large firm will cause the failure of others through a contagion-like process in which a cascade of losses flows through an economy. The administration's concern about systemically important firms seems based on this idea since the Treasury proposes to regulate all large firms as a way of preventing systemic risk. However, applying this standard, Lehman's bankruptcy did not seem to cause major or systemic losses. With the single exception of the Reserve Fund—a money market mutual fund that had invested heavily and imprudently in Lehman's commercial paper—no such Lehman-caused failures have been reported. In a market in which there was none of the panic that existed in September 2008, Lehman's failure would not have caused a freeze-up that many have identified as a systemic breakdown. It is noteworthy in this connection that when the large securities firm Drexel Burnham Lambert failed in 1990, there was no major

---

76. See, for example, House Financial Services Committee, "Timothy F. Geithner, Written Testimony on Financial Regulatory Reform," 111th Cong., 1st sess., September 23, 2009, 3, available at www.house.gov/apps/list/hearing/financialsvcs_dem/testimony_ -_sec_geithner.pdf (accessed September 28, 2009).

adverse effect on the markets, even though Drexel Burnham was as significant a firm at that time as Lehman was eighteen years later.

What happened after Lehman is better described as the result of a "common shock" to the market rather than a systemic breakdown. A common shock can occur as a result of any major event that creates widespread uncertainty about the future. Lehman was such a shock, largely because of the moral hazard created by the rescue of Bear Stearns six months earlier. After the Bear rescue, market participants were justified in believing that any firm larger than Bear would also be saved from bankruptcy. When that did not occur in Lehman's case, all market participants had to recalibrate the risks they faced in dealing with others, and the hoarding of cash began. Under this analysis, what followed Lehman's bankruptcy could have been provoked by the assassination of an important world leader, the collapse of the government of a major oil exporting country, or an earthquake in a major developed country. A common shock caused by any of these events would, of course, not be prevented either by regulating systemically important companies or setting up a special government authority to resolve them when they fail. For example, as Stanford University economist John B. Taylor's analysis has shown,[77] the global freeze-up in lending occurred several days after the Lehman failure, and was actually coincident with the Treasury-Fed request for what ultimately became TARP funds; it appears that there was a collapse of market confidence when the U.S. government appeared to be panicking, rather than a fear in the market that Lehman's collapse would cause losses to cascade through the world's economy.

If a systemic breakdown is the result of losses others actually incur because of the failure of a large nonbank financial institution, then the administration should explain the mechanism by which this contagion or cascading series of losses actually occurs. Indeed, it is not clear that there is a mechanism through which the failure of a nonbank financial institution—say, a bank holding company—would be able to transmit losses to other institutions. It is easy to see how such losses could be caused by the failure of a large depository institution such as a commercial bank. Bank borrowings—deposits—are withdrawable on demand. Businesses deposit payrolls in banks, individuals use bank accounts to

---

77. John B. Taylor, *Getting Off Track: How Government Actions and Interventions Caused, Prolonged, and Worsened the Financial Crisis* (Stanford, CA: Hoover Institution Press, 2009).

pay their daily obligations, small banks deposit funds in large banks and rely on large banks for access to the payment system. If a large bank fails, all these parties and many others suffer immediate cash losses and may be unable to meet their obligations, creating an expanding series of defaults through an economy. This is the classic systemic breakdown and why the FDIC has the power to step in and resolve a large commercial bank immediately.

Nonbank financial firms borrow for long and short terms, however, and their short-term borrowings are usually collateralized through repurchase (repo) agreements or asset-backed commercial paper. Both long- and short-term creditors of nonbank financial institutions are generally diversified and can take the eventual losses without becoming insolvent or illiquid themselves. In addition, the short-term or repo creditors have collateral that should enable them to recoup at least a substantial portion of their losses. Some observers argue that repo financing used by nonbank financial institutions can create conditions very similar to a bank run.[78] However, these discussions generally do not explain what is systemically harmful about a run of this kind on a nonbank financial institution. Repo lenders are very different from depositors; in addition to the collateral they hold, they are much more likely to be diversified and thus less affected by the failure of a nonbank financial institution to which they have lent funds. In other words, although a "run" on a nonbank financial institution has similarities to a run on a bank, it does not have—it probably cannot have—the same systemic effects as a depositors' run that causes a large depository institution like a commercial bank to close.

Thus, one can make a strong argument that systemic risk or a systemic breakdown cannot be created by the failure of a nonbank financial institution, and if so, there is no reason to create a special resolution authority to prevent the failure of such an institution. The same reasoning also nullifies the argument that a resolution authority would be more flexible in treating prebankruptcy creditors (option two above), since these creditors—which are largely diversified institutional lenders who would not be severely affected by the failure of large

---

78. See, for example, Gary Gorton, "Slapped in the Face by the Invisible Hand: Banking and the Panic of 2007" (presentation, Federal Reserve Bank of Atlanta's 2009 Financial Markets Conference: Financial Innovation and Crisis, Jekyll Island, GA, May 11–13, 2009), available at www.frbatlanta.org/news/CONFEREN/09fmc/gorton.pdf (accessed September 21, 2009).

nonbank financial institutions—do not need special treatment in order to avoid a systemic breakdown.

Additional Dangers from a Resolution Authority

Even if we concede that the failure of a nonbank financial institution could create systemic risk, there are still several reasons a government resolution agency for nonbank financial institutions would be bad policy.

Excessive Use. The existence of authority to take over a nonbank financial institution will make such takeovers more likely. As discussed above, once the authority is institutionalized through legislation, officials will use it to prevent disruptions in the economy, not just a systemic breakdown. Regulators will fear being criticized for the disruption that the failure of a large nonbank financial institution will cause—unemployment, a decline in stock prices, the temporary dislocations that occur to some counterparties or customers—but will be congratulated and treated as heroes if they step in to prevent these events. This is especially likely to occur because, as noted above, there is no effective way to distinguish in advance between a failure that will cause a systemic breakdown and one that will merely cause a temporary economic disruption.

Another important factor to consider is the ability of large companies and their managements to influence the government, and the ability of influential constituencies and powerful lawmakers to force government into granting special benefits and dispensations. This cannot be under-estimated. There will be pressure on regulators to rescue firms with influential managements, or from states or districts that are represented by influential lawmakers. If the resolution authority exists, it will be used to favor these companies, to the detriment of others, and probably the taxpayers.

Finally, as noted above, rescue of a firm that should otherwise have failed hurts the firms with better business models and better managements that might have moved up to take the place of the failed firm. Even in the unlikely event that a rescued firm is eventually liquidated, rather than simply returned to health under government control, the time between the takeover by the government, the introduction of government funds to keep the company operating and competing, and the prospect that the firm might one day return as a competitor will suppress competition from other, better-managed firms in the same market.

Moral Hazard and Competitive Advantages for Large Companies. The frequent use of the resolution authority will create moral hazard. A strong case can be made that the rescue of Bear Stearns did just this. After the Bear rescue in March 2008, creditors apparently expected firms larger than Bear to be saved. When Lehman was allowed to fail, this expectation was shattered, causing every market participant to reassess the safety and soundness of its counterparties.

So the danger is that as the resolution authority is used more frequently to prevent economic or financial disruptions, it will tend to create similar expectations for more and more firms, resulting in more moral hazard—and maybe even common shocks on a global scale—any time the authority is not used. The more moral hazard is introduced into the system, the greater the competitive advantage it will provide to the larger companies that will be eligible for resolution. This is because the potential of government support to prevent failure will encourage their creditors to believe they are less risky than other companies, weakening the usual restraints of market discipline. These apparently protected companies will be able to attract more capital and credit than their smaller competitors, which will gradually be forced out of contested markets.

Cost. As outlined above, the administration's concept of an "orderly" resolution must involve placing a failed or failing institution in a kind of conservatorship so that it continues operating. Otherwise, abruptly closing it down will cause what the resolution authority was supposed to prevent—a systemic breakdown. Accordingly, the agency in charge of the conservatorship will have to provide the necessary funding so the company can continue to operate under government control. This will entail paying off its creditors in whole or in part and retaining its employees and necessary offices and equipment. All of this will require the expenditure of taxpayer funds, unless there is another funding source. The FDIC administers a fund maintained by deposit insurance levies on all insured banks and uses that fund to finance the closing of failed banks and the compensation of the insured depositors. It then reimburses itself by selling off the assets of the failed institution. Any remaining funds are used to pay off the uninsured depositors and other creditors.

Where will the funds come from for the resolution of nonbank financial institutions? One source might be the industry in which the failed company operated while another might be all large nonbank financial institutions. In either case, it would be difficult to set up a fund similar to the bank insurance fund, because the amount necessary for a credible fund would be very high. The total government contribution to AIG exceeds $100 billion at this point. This is considerably more than the FDIC's bank insurance fund which was $52.4 billion at its highest point in 2007.[79] To collect a sum this large in advance or to recover it afterward would require a serious levy on the companies called upon to make the contribution, perhaps jeopardizing their health but certainly jeopardizing their ability to compete outside the United States with foreign companies not subject to such a cost. The likelihood, then, is that—if a resolution agency is established—the taxpayers will ultimately end up footing the bill.

Lack of Expertise. The administration does not propose to establish a new agency for resolving nonbank financial institutions, but rather to turn over the resolution responsibility to the FDIC. This is problematic: resolving a bank is nothing like resolving a failed nonbank financial institution. For one thing, most banks are small and are resolved over a weekend. There is almost always a buyer for the deposits, and unless the bank is so large as to create a danger of a systemic effect, the only creditors the FDIC has to be concerned about are the insured depositors; these are often made whole simply by transferring the deposits to a healthy institution. However, the institutions that will be covered by the administration's proposed resolution authority will be very large and complex. Because the objective of the resolution authority will be to make sure the failed institution does not cause a systemic breakdown (assuming it can), the resolution authority will have to be concerned about all its creditors, not just depositors. The FDIC will have no more experience in rescuing a large and complex nonbank financial institution than any other agency. If we want an example of what that will be like, AIG provides it. That takeover has resulted in a huge transfer of government funds to AIG with no end yet in sight. AIG's once-healthy subsidiaries have not yet been sold to reimburse the tax-payers, and the final status of AIG is not yet resolved—a year after it was taken over.

When Bankruptcy Is a Better Foundation. The absence of any expertise in resolving failed nonbank financial institutions anywhere in the federal government is one strong reason for relying on bankruptcy for most failures. If there

---

79. FDIC, "Statistics at a Glance: Historical Trends as of June 30, 2009," available at www.fdic.gov/bank/statistical/stats/2009jun/FDIC.pdf (accessed September 21, 2009).

is likely to be expertise anywhere in resolving failed financial institutions, it would be in the bankruptcy courts. Bankruptcy judges are appointed for terms of fourteen years and develop expertise in all aspects of insolvency and workouts. In large cities, bankruptcy judges, magistrates, and special masters are likely to have acquired the specialized knowledge necessary to resolve financial institutions—certainly more knowledge than government officials who have never seen an insolvent securities firm, insurance company, finance company, or hedge fund. Any deficiencies in the bankruptcy system for handling large nonbank financial institutions are beyond the scope of this *Outlook,* but in any event can be addressed by legislation if these deficiencies are identified with specificity.

Bankruptcy as the first choice for disposing of a failed nonbank financial institution would avoid many of the problems associated with creating a government resolution authority. It would assure that the prebankruptcy creditors take losses of some kind—avoiding moral hazard and maintaining market discipline—and the rules are known in advance, so creditors will be aware of their rights as well as their risks. Both the Drexel Burnham bankruptcy in 1990 and the Lehman bankruptcy show that very large nonbank financial institutions can be resolved by the bankruptcy courts without difficulty. Indeed, the bankruptcy system has done a much more efficient job in resolving Lehman Brothers than the Fed has done with AIG. Within a few weeks of Lehman's filing, the trustee had sold off Lehman's broker-dealer, its investment management, and its investment banking business to four different buyers. None of this dispatch has been present in the AIG case. Finally, bankruptcy provides a market-based judgment on whether a firm should return to viability. The creditors ultimately decide whether they should forgo the partial repayment they will receive in a liquidation, in the hope that they will eventually receive full repayment if the debtor is returned to viability. When a firm is taken over by the government, however, political pressures—by important members of Congress or powerful constituencies—are more likely to be the determinants of whether the company survives. Again, General Motors and Chrysler are examples of this phenomenon. Sending failed nonbank financial institutions to the bankruptcy courts is the resolution mechanism embodied in HR 3310 (The Consumer Protection and Regulatory Enhancement Act), introduced in late July by the House Republican leadership. This seems a sensible alternative to the administration's plan.

Uncertainty and Unpredictability. Finally, the existence of a government resolution authority creates uncertainty about when it will be invoked and which
creditors will be paid in what order. Although, as argued above, it is likely to
be invoked more frequently than it should—that is, to prevent disruption rather
than a real systemic breakdown—there will always be companies just on the
other side of the "disruption line" that will not be rescued. The unpredictability
about whether these borderline cases will be rescued will create moral hazard,
arbitrary losses as well as arbitrary gains, and otherwise pervert the incentives
of investors, counterparties, and creditors.

Other Special Cases

Bank Holding Companies. Although there is a procedure (through the FDIC)
for working out failed banks, there is no such procedure for resolving bank
holding companies (BHCs). There is no obvious reason why BHCs, which are
companies that control banks, should be treated any differently than other
nonbank financial institutions. All the points above about whether nonbank
financial institutions can create a systemic breakdown apply to BHCs. Banking
laws severely restrict transactions between banks and their holding companies,
so that the failure of a holding company would not have any adverse effect on
the condition of the bank and vice versa. There may be ways for holding companies to make it difficult for the FDIC to resolve failing banks (for example, the
FDIC has found cases in which the failed bank had no employees—they were
all employees of the BHC), but the FDIC has sufficient regulatory authority to
address minor issues like this. They are not an argument for a special regulatory
system for BHCs.

Ironically, the purpose of separating banks and BHCs has been to keep
the "safety net" for banks from extending to the riskier activities of the holding
company. Now, some in Congress and elsewhere who have always argued for
keeping holding companies from engaging in commercial activities in order to
"protect the safety net," appear willing to spread the safety net to the financial
activities of BHCs—such as securities and insurance—which are said to be
riskier than banking and not appropriate for safety net coverage. The administration's proposal for a resolution authority and other proposals to allow the FDIC
to take control of BHCs would now extend the safety net to BHCs, reversing
many years of congressional policy, putting much more pressure on the deposit

insurance fund, and raising doubt about the priority of BHC creditors. It is sometimes argued that BHCs should be treated differently from other financial institutions because they have an obligation to provide capital to their subsidiary banks, and if the holding company goes into bankruptcy, the FDIC will not have access to the capital that could be downstreamed to the bank. The idea that a BHC has an obligation to be a "source of strength" for a subsidiary bank is a Fed policy, not a law. It is one of those policies that the Fed uses to justify its continued authority to regulate and supervise BHCs. The Fed has asked Congress many times to enact this idea, and Congress has not done so. There is in fact no legal obligation for BHCs to support their subsidiary banks.

Complexity and International Operations. One other argument in support of a government resolution authority for nonbank financial institutions such as BHCs is that they are very complex and involve many different activities carried on all over the world. When such an institution fails, the many conflicts of laws and national interests make it difficult to unwind. That is certainly true, but the problem is not solved by turning it over to a government resolution authority. Resolving the many differences and conflicts among countries with jurisdiction over a failed financial institution is a task for diplomacy and intergovernmental organizations such as the International Monetary Fund and the Financial Stability Board. Whether the actual resolution of a company is handled by a government agency like the FDIC or through an ordinary bankruptcy proceeding will not make these problems more or less tractable.

Conclusion

The enactment of the administration's proposal to establish a government resolution authority for certain large systemically important firms would be a major policy mistake. The administration has not shown how a nonbank financial institution could cause a systemic breakdown, and in the absence of such a showing, there is no reason to create a special resolution authority. Moreover, even if a nonbank financial firm could create systemic risk, the administration has not made clear how officials will be able to determine in advance whether a particular company will cause a systemic breakdown—rather than merely a temporary economic disruption—if it fails. In the absence of a standard for making such a determination, it is likely that the authority will be used frequently to rescue companies that might only create economic disruption if they fail. This will be especially true with respect to firms with politically powerful backers. Frequent and unnecessary rescues will introduce moral hazard and be costly to the taxpayers, who will end up paying the bills.

Under these circumstances, it would be better policy to use the existing bankruptcy system for failing nonbank financial companies. Not only is there no reason to rescue nonbank financial firms from bankruptcy, but sending them through the bankruptcy system also provides a degree of certainty to creditors that would not be available in a government-run system, and the costs of a bankruptcy are borne by the failed company's creditors rather than the taxpayers. Most importantly, the bankruptcy system encourages creditors to monitor the companies they lend to, reducing moral hazard and enhancing market discipline.

"The Dodd-Frank Act: Creative Destruction, Destroyed"

Originally published July–August 2010

The dominant theme of the 2,300-page Dodd-Frank Wall Street Reform and Consumer Protection Act is fear of instability and change, which the act suppresses by subjecting the largest financial firms to banklike regulation. The competitiveness, innovativeness, and risk-taking that have always characterized U.S. financial firms will, under this new structure, inevitably be subordinated to supervisory judgments about what these firms can safely be allowed to do. But the worst element of this system is that the extraordinary power given to regulators—and particularly the Federal Reserve—is likely to change the nature of the U.S. financial system. Where financial firms once focused on beating their competitors, they will now focus on currying favor with their regulator, which will have the power to control their every move. What may ultimately emerge is a partnership between the largest financial firms and the Federal Reserve—a partnership in which the Fed protects them from failure and excessive competition and they in turn curb their competitive instincts to carry out the government's policies and directions. In addition, with the creation of the Consumer Financial Protection Bureau, the act abandons a fundamental principle of the U.S. Constitution, in which Congress retains the power to control the agencies of the executive branch. These wholesale changes in traditional relationships are hard to explain except as the triumph of a fundamentally different view—a corporatist political model more characteristic of Europe—of the government's role in the U.S. economy.

My mother always told me that what's done is done, and there's no sense worrying about decisions that cannot be changed. Still, it is useful to put down some markers about the recently adopted Dodd-Frank Act (DFA), which looks to be the most troubling—maybe even destructive—single piece of financial legislation ever adopted. The reason markers are useful is that they alert observers—especially those in Congress with the power to do something about it—to the problems they should be looking for in the future. And they might even alert regulators—charged with implementing the legislation—to the dangers of taking full advantage of what Congress has offered them. Given these objectives, this *Outlook* will discuss the most serious policy problems implicit in the DFA.

Regulation to Prevent "Instability"

This is probably the heart of the act, which was sold on the claim that it would prevent the recurrence of a financial crisis. As might be expected, one can find in the solution the germ of the putative cause. Some see this cause as the free-market system itself; others see it as a failure of regulators—with powers already in place—who did not take the necessary actions to prevent the crisis. The DFA comes down somewhere between the two. If the Democrats in Congress who wrote the law had believed that the cause was entirely regulatory failure, they would have revised the regulatory structure, not given yet more power to exactly the same regulators. The fact that they saw expanded regulation as a suitable remedy indicates that they believed the free-market system needed greater control.

My view has always been that the cause was 27 million subprime and other risky mortgages—half of all mortgages in the United States—that were largely a result of the government's housing policy.[80] When the housing bubble began to deflate, and subprime borrowers could no longer refinance or sell their homes at a higher price, an unprecedented number of defaults began. The resulting losses sank Fannie Mae and Freddie Mac as well as Bear Stearns and Lehman Brothers. The moral hazard engendered by the rescue of Bear led market participants to believe that the U.S. government's policy was to rescue all large firms. This made a crisis inevitable as soon as any large entity was allowed to fail. Lehman just happened to be that entity. This view, much simpler than the other two, would not have required any additional regulation of the financial system to prevent another financial crisis, only a determination to keep the government from distorting the housing market in the future. But this was not the narrative that drove the adoption of the DFA.

---

80. See, for example, Peter J. Wallison, "Ideas Have Consequences: The Importance of a Narrative," AEI *Financial Services Outlook* (May 2010), available at www.aei.org/outlook/100960. (See p. 273 of this book.)

Following the underlying principle that more regulation and less risk-taking are the keys to preventing another financial crisis, the act creates a Financial Stability Oversight Council, made up of all the financial regulators and chaired by the secretary of the Treasury. All twenty-six bank holding companies (BHCs) that have assets of more than $50 billion are made subject to "more stringent" regulation than smaller BHCs, and the council is authorized in its discretion to add an unlimited number of nonbank financial institutions of all kinds to the list of firms that the Fed will be empowered to supervise under the "more stringent" standard. In effect, this will enable the Fed, which already regulates banks and BHCs, to regulate and supervise all the largest nonbank financial institutions in the United States. Since most of these institutions—insurance companies, securities firms, finance companies, and hedge funds—are not regulated for safety and soundness by any agency at the federal level, there is no reason for the council to object to the Fed's request for greater regulatory reach.

The unprecedented nature of this authority is important to understand. Not only does the Fed, through the council, have the power to determine the scope of its own authority, but that authority is not limited by the rationale for imposing it. Banks, for example, are regulated for safety and soundness because government insurance for their deposits creates moral hazard—that is, depositors do not care what risks banks are taking because their deposits are insured. (It is not really clear why BHCs are regulated—they are not government-backed—but at least one can say that they have an intimate relationship to the insured banks they control.) Extending the same regulation to firms that are not in any way backed by the government, only because their activities or failure might be a source of instability, is something entirely new. If government regulation and supervision do not create moral hazard directly—and they probably do—they certainly imply that the government has an interest in the activities of these companies that has never before been legally recognized. We are embarking, therefore, on an entirely new path, not a mere extension of what has gone before.

The DFA's standard for making the important decision about whether to regulate a particular nonbank financial firm is so flexible as to be indistinguishable from complete discretion. The council can designate a firm for this especially stringent regulation "if the Council determines that material financial distress at the U.S. nonbank financial company, or the nature, scope, size, scale, concentration, interconnectedness, or mix of the activities of the U.S. nonbank financial company, could pose a threat to the financial stability of the United

States."[81] In effect, this gives the council and ultimately the Fed the power to regulate and supervise any financial institution in the United States if, in the judgment of the council (which effectively means in the judgment of the Fed), the company could under some circumstances yet to be imagined "pose a threat to the financial stability of the United States."

To put this in context: Bill Isaac, former chairman of the Federal Deposit Insurance Corporation (FDIC), reports in his recent book, *Senseless Panic,* that in 1982 he was asked by Fed chairman Paul Volcker to bail out the $500 million Penn Square Bank (a small strip-mall bank in Oklahoma City) because the bank had sold bad loans to bigger banks and its failure, in Volcker's view, would bring down the whole financial system. The story of Isaac's epic struggle with the weak-kneed Fed consumes seventeen pages in his book.[82] Similarly, Richard Breeden, former chairman of the Securities and Exchange Commission (SEC), told a June 2009 AEI conference[83] about a call he received from the Fed in 1990, when the securities firm Drexel Burnham Lambert, the fourth-largest Wall Street investment bank at the time, was headed for bankruptcy. Again, the caller from the Fed demanded that Breeden agree to bail out the firm, lest the whole market collapse as a result of Drexel Burnham's failure.

Both Isaac and Breeden successfully resisted the Fed's demands, with no adverse consequences for the financial system, but the point is that the first instinct of most regulators, and particularly the Fed, is to fear the worst about disruptions in the economy. Giving the Oversight Council the ability to designate financial institutions as "threat[s] to the financial stability of the United States" because of their "scope, size, scale, concentration, interconnectedness, or mix of [their] activities" is an invitation to subject most of the major financial institutions in the United States to banklike regulation. If the Fed asks—and it will—why would the council ever refuse?

Although it has not received as much attention as other aspects of the DFA, this may be the most troubling provision of this troubling act. To put it plainly, this provision alone has the potential to change the entire nature of our financial

---

81. *Dodd-Frank Wall Street Reform and Consumer Protection Act,* Public Law 111-203, 111th Cong., 2d sess. (July 21, 2010), §113(a)(1).

82. William M. Isaac and Philip C. Meyer, *Senseless Panic: How Washington Failed America* (Hoboken, NJ: John Wiley & Sons, 2010), 29–46.

83. Richard Breeden, "Addressing Systemic Risk" (conference, AEI, Washington, DC, June 3, 2009), available at www.aei.org/event/100061.

system. Once given supervisory power over a financial institution, the Fed can control its capital, liquidity, leverage, and activities, and with this authority can strongly influence the business decisions these firms will make. The focus for these companies will inevitably change from how they can beat their competition to how they can gain the Fed's approval for any new activity. The full-throated, unlimited competition that we are accustomed to in financial services will become a relic of the past. Our aggressive financial industry, which has come to dominate the world, will be tamed—much to the gratification of our trading partners, but not of the American businesses and American consumers who benefited from this competition.

But it gets worse. Can anyone imagine that one of these large financial institutions—securities firms, insurers, hedge funds, finance companies, and others—that will eventually come under the supervision of the Fed will ever be allowed to fail? A great deal of the debate about the act in Congress focused on the term "too big to fail"—the idea that an institution is so large that it cannot be allowed to fail. Congress went to great lengths to close off the opportunities for the FDIC to bail out the large financial institutions that could cause instability in the financial system if they failed. But all of it was probably directed at the wrong agency. Imagine, for example, a large securities firm in the future that is regulated and supervised by the Fed. The securities firm has been mismanaged, despite Fed supervision (yes, it does happen, see Wachovia), and it is on its way to failure, an event that would of course be embarrassing for the Fed. The Fed, however, because of the DFA, has the power of life and death over all the major BHCs, insurance holding companies, and other large financial institutions. So the Fed chairman calls the chairman of one of these firms and suggests that it would be a good idea if that firm acquired the failing securities firm: "No, we can't offer you any funding, of course, we don't have authority to do that, but there are probably a few other acquisitions you might like to make in the future. . . ."

This is not farfetched. Remember how the Fed and Treasury forced Bank of America to eat Merrill Lynch after its due diligence had revealed the losses involved? Or how the New York Federal Reserve Bank—not even the regulator of many of the financial institutions it called together—arranged for the largest New York financial firm to provide life-saving financing for Long Term Capital Management, a hedge fund that the Fed thought might bring down the financial system if it failed? So all the debate about the FDIC's bailout authority may have ailed to consider the Fed's ability to influence the actions of the firms it will be supervising. The real danger is that the Fed will implement "too big to fail" privately, outside public view, through its new powers under the DFA.

Sadly, this is just one example of the DFA's problems. Quietly covering up its own messes is one thing, but many other options are available to a financial supervisor that has so much power. Let's imagine that the largest U.S. banks hold large amounts of another country's debt. If the country fails to meet its obligations, the banks will be seriously weakened, with the possibility of financial instability in the United States. Worse, there could be—at least this is the fear—an international financial crisis. The Treasury secretary (the chairman of the Oversight Council, incidentally) is quite concerned and calls the Fed chairman, who wants to be cooperative. The solution to the problem, for both the U.S. banks and the international financial system, is to find some buyers for the troubled country's debt. What we need, they agree, are some patient institutional investors with big portfolios, willing to take this country's debt and hold it for a while, bailing out the country and the U.S. banks at the same time—investors, for example, like those insurance holding companies the Fed supervises. At some time in the future, of course, the insurance companies that had to take on this debt will suffer the consequences, but it can later be blamed on imprudent management. An example of exactly this is the blame cast on Fannie Mae and Freddie Mac for buying weak mortgages, when in fact they did so to comply with the government's affordable-housing requirements.

These examples can be multiplied endlessly. What we are talking about here is an incipient partnership between the government and the largest financial institutions in the United States, a partnership in which the big companies are protected against failure but are willing—in fact, eager—to do what the government wants. When we hear the CEOs of large financial firms praising their relationship with the Fed, or the stability that the DFA will bring about, we will know that the partnership idea has taken hold. That is not the financial system we had before the DFA was enacted.

Consumer Protection, Protected from Congressional Control

The DFA also created the Consumer Financial Protection Bureau (CFPB), whose director is also on the Financial Stability Oversight Council, and endowed it with broad regulatory powers. The CFPB probably has the widest reach into the U.S. economy of any agency in Washington. Although some people seem to imagine it is just an independent agency to regulate how banks treat their customers, it has a much broader jurisdiction than that. Below is the list of the business activities over which the CFPB will have jurisdiction, compiled by Davis Polk, a New York–based law firm. For brevity, I deleted the narrow exceptions that were listed as part of the broad activities outlined below:[84]

- Extending credit and servicing loans, including acquiring, purchasing, selling, brokering, or other extensions of credit;

- Extending or brokering leases of personal or real property that are the functional equivalent of purchase finance arrangements;

- Engaging in deposit-taking activities, transmitting or exchanging funds, or otherwise acting as a custodian of funds or any financial instrument for use by or on behalf of a consumer;

- Providing most real estate settlement services, or performing appraisals of real estate or personal property;

- Providing or issuing stored value or payment instruments, or selling such instruments, but only if the seller exercises substantial control over the terms or conditions of the stored value provided to the consumer;

- Providing check cashing, check collection, or check guaranty services;

- Providing payments or other financial data processing products or services to a consumer by any technological means;

- Providing financial advisory services to consumers on individual financial matters or relating to proprietary financial products or services, including providing consumer credit counseling or services to assist consumers with debt management, debt settlement services, modifying the terms of a loan, or avoiding foreclosure;

---

84. Davis Polk, "Summary of the Dodd-Frank Wall Street Reform and Consumer Protection Act, Passed by the House of Representatives on June 30, 2010," 104–105, available at https://www.davispolk.com/files/Publication/7084f9fe-6580-413b-b870-b7c025ed2ecf/Presentation/PublicationAttachment/1d4495c7-0be0-4e9a-ba77-f786fb90464a/070910_Financial_Reform_Summary.pdf (accessed August 24, 2010).

- Collecting, analyzing, maintaining, or providing consumer reports or other account information, including information related to consumer credit histories, used or expected to be used in connection with any decision regarding the offering or-provision of a consumer financial product or service, subject to exceptions; and

- Collecting debt related to any consumer financial product or service.

If we take just one of these services—say, check-cashing—we can begin to understand the scope of this agency's jurisdiction. There are check-cashing stores in virtually every city and town in the United States, and they are not big businesses. They do not generally operate interstate. If they are subject to regulation, it is by a state or perhaps a municipality. Under the DFA, they will be subject to regulation from Washington. We could assume this regulation will be light, maybe a few reports or an occasional visit by an examiner. But the likelihood is that these small companies will be required to comply with certain rules about disclosure, record keeping, personnel qualifications, hours of operation, advertising, signage, and maybe even their rates and products. What will that do to these thousands of small companies? It will force them to raise their prices, certainly, but also to consolidate with larger companies or leave the business. For those who use check-cashing services, this will make life just a little bit more difficult and expensive. Check-cashing services may require regulation, but state or local regulation is likely to be less intrusive and less bureaucratic than regulation from Washington.

But the worst thing about the CFPB is not the costs it will impose on the economy, the innovation it will stifle, or the small businesses it will eliminate. The worst thing about this agency is that it will operate independently, without any control by the Fed, Congress, or the president. The DFA states that even though the CFPB is lodged in the Fed, it is not subject to the control of the Fed. The autonomy language is clear: the Fed may not

A) intervene in any matter or proceeding before the Director, including examinations or enforcement actions, unless otherwise specifically provided by law; (B) appoint, direct, or remove any officer or employee of the Bureau; or (C) merge or consolidate the Bureau, or any of the functions or responsibilities of the Bureau, with any division or office of the Board of Governors or the Federal reserve banks. . . . No rule or order of the Bureau shall be subject to approval or review by the Board of Governors. The Board of Governors may not delay or prevent the issuance of any rule or order of the Bureau.[85]

The CFPB is also insulated from control by Congress. Under the U.S. Constitution, Congress exerts control over the executive branch of government through its power to appropriate funds. We all learned about this in grade school as "the power of the purse." Most regulatory and administrative agencies, including the cabinet departments, must go to Congress each year for appropriations to cover their operations in the following year. In this way, Congress can control executive-branch agencies by reducing funds, denying fund increases, or denying funds for specific purposes. Merely having to go to Congress hat in hand for the following year's appropriation is an important way for Congress to enforce its own policies—and some humility—on powerful agencies. The CFPB, however, is exempt from this process. Under the DFA, it is allocated up to 12 percent of the Fed's operating funds, a stipend that amounts to an estimated $600 million per year. The Fed's operating funds are not subject to appropriation—part of the special structure intended to keep the central bank independent of the political branches—so the $600 million that will be made available to the CFPB does not come with any necessary oversight or control, directly or indirectly, by Congress. The only way Congress will be able to control this agency is through amending its governing law.

Finally, the CFPB will be independent of the president, since the director is appointed for a five-year term by the president, with the advice and consent of the Senate, and can only be removed from office for cause.

The CFPB, then, is as independent as the Fed itself, but it has the power to control and regulate the consumer-related operations of companies from the largest banks to the smallest check-cashing stores. Moreover, all this power is concentrated in a single person, the director of the CFPB. Even the Fed, with all its independence, is ultimately governed by a board with a bipartisan membership. The establishment of an agency with this scope of authority, under the direction of a single person removable only for cause, outside the control of Congress or the president, is an unprecedented and—I might say—an irresponsible act, which Congress will eventually come to regret.

---

85. *Dodd-Frank Wall Street Reform and Consumer Protection Act,* §1012(c)(2)–(3).

Stability as the Goal

The structure and substantive elements of the DFA—and indeed all legislation—arise out of a combination of perceptions and ideology. The perceptions that guided the development of the DFA were that deregulation and a lack of regulation were largely responsible for the financial crisis. The underlying ideological notion, which both fed that perception and was driven by it, was that the unregulated market—because of risk-taking—will always create financial crises of this kind. Of course, if we ignore the government's role in creating the crisis, outlined above, our search for causes necessarily narrows to the deficiencies of the market.

True, free markets take risks; it is in their nature. Risk-taking in turn produces failure, disruption, and losses; it is supposed to, since the failures caused by risk-taking or incompetence take society's assets out of the hands of bad managers and put them in the hands of good ones. Innovation involves risk, as does entering new markets, cutting prices, investing for growth, and everything else that has brought material progress in the two centuries since the advent of the Industrial Revolution. As Raghuram G. Rajan observed in his recent book, *Fault Lines,* "We have to recognize that the only truly safe financial system is a system that does not take risks, that does not finance innovation or growth, that does not help draw people out of poverty, and that gives consumers little choice. . . . In the long run, though, that reinforces the incremental and thus the status quo."[86]

The drafters of the DFA feared risk-taking, innovation, and change, and the act shows it. The best examples are the Volcker rule and the draconian restrictions that the Fed can impose on large nonbank financial institutions that are considered important because they might, under some circumstances, create instability in the U.S. financial system if they fail. Adopted with fear of instability in mind, all of these new restrictions will make it difficult for competition and risk-taking to break out among banks, BHCs, and the large non-bank financial firms that will fall under the Fed's regulatory umbrella.

The Volcker rule prohibits any "banking entity"—which includes a bank, its BHC, and all subsidiaries of the bank and the BHC—from engaging in proprietary trading. Prop trading is the business of trading securities, loans, derivatives,

---

86. Raghuram G. Rajan, *Fault Lines: How Hidden Fractures Still Threaten the World Economy* (Princeton, NJ: Princeton University Press, 2010), 19.

or any other asset for the account of the banking entity itself and not as a service for customers. The fact that the restriction applies to the BHC and all BHC subsidiaries shows the extreme risk-aversion that animated this provision. First, there is no indication that prop trading had anything to do with the financial crisis; in fact, it is one of the activities that added significantly to the much-needed revenues and profits of the beleaguered banking system during the past few years. Second, because the BHC and the BHC's subsidiaries do not take deposits and have only very limited access to loans or other financing from the bank itself, a case cannot be made that the depositors' funds or the government's deposit insurance was being used to take substantial risks.

Nevertheless, these restrictions will take out of the financial markets a substantial number of participants that had added valuable liquidity. Without banks, BHCs, and their affiliates, vigorous trading that keeps spreads narrow and liquidity high in the U.S. market will substantially decrease. The likelihood is that foreign banks will become the dominant players in the business and world financial markets will move away from the United States.

This also raises a significant question about the future of the banking business. The development of an efficient securities market in the 1960s changed the relationship between banks and their corporate clients. Companies that had registered securities with the SEC found it less expensive and burdensome to meet their credit needs in the securities markets than through bank borrowing. As a result, banks have been concentrating increasingly on trading activities, private banking for high-net-worth individuals, small-business lending, consumer lending through credit cards, and commercial and residential real estate finance. The largest of these activities is real estate lending, through construction and development loans and commercial and residential mortgages.

This is not a healthy development. As noted in the November–December *Financial Services Outlook*,[87] bank lending to real estate in all its forms rose from less than 25 percent of all bank lending in 1965 to more than 55 percent in 2005. Real estate is a risky and highly volatile business, and banks are already too heavily involved in it. By taking away another profitable non-real-estate business from banks, the DFA forces them to concentrate even more heavily in

---

87. Peter J. Wallison, "Losing Ground: Gramm-Leach-Bliley and the Future of Banking," AEI *Financial Services Outlook* (November–December 2009), 4, available at www.aei.org/outlook/100925.

real estate financing. This makes it more likely that the deflation of the next real estate bubble will create another banking crisis.

The Volcker rule applies to all banks and BHCs, but the restrictions on large BHCs and nonbank financial institutions could extend much further than restrictions on prop trading. In this case, as noted above, the Oversight Council may authorize the Fed—the supervisor of those large financial institutions and BHCs that have been declared a potential danger to U.S "stability"—to impose "regulations that are more stringent than those applicable to other nonbank financial companies and BHCs that do not present similar risks to the financial stability of the United States."

The purpose of these more stringent regulations is to "prevent or mitigate risks to U.S. financial stability that could arise from the material financial distress, failure, or ongoing activities of large, interconnected financial institutions."[88] By classifying "ongoing activities" as a potential threat to stability, the act creates a license to curb and discipline the aggressive firms that might upset the stable, politely competitive environment that the act envisions for the future of the financial industry.

Efforts to curb bank activities because they are insured by the FDIC have been part of the political debate in Washington since deposit insurance was instituted. Most of the opposition to new or existing bank activities has grown out of competition between industries. For example, the realtors have fought the idea that banks or BHCs should be allowed to own real estate brokers. But the DFA is the first example since the passage of the Glass-Steagall Act in which restrictions on bank and BHC activities have been imposed solely because of the fear of risk-taking. In this sense, the Volcker rule may be the vanguard of further restrictions on bank activities and bank size.

One way out of this thicket was the solution in the Gramm-Leach-Bliley Act: to allow banks themselves to grow smaller voluntarily by shifting some of their capital to their holding companies, where more risky activities could be undertaken without risk to the deposit insurance fund. But by cutting off prop trading even at the holding-company level, the Volcker rule creates a precedent for BHCs to be as limited in their activities as banks. The irony is that the DFA also requires BHCs to be sources of strength for their subsidiary banks. How

---

88. *Dodd-Frank Wall Street Reform and Consumer Protection Act,* §115.

they are supposed to do that when their activities are restricted largely to what banks can do is not clear.

Acting out of the fear of change and "instability," those who voted for the DFA—mostly Democrats but also a few Republicans—have given the government extraordinary regulatory power, which it can use to prevent change, innovation, and economic growth. It is another sign that the modern proponents of corporatism—a partnership between big government and big financial institutions—won the day in the U.S. Congress, and that what they have done will be hard to undo in the future. Advocates of Joseph Schumpeter's "creative destruction," in which new and innovative companies displace old ones, had better look outside the United States for innovation and change in the financial markets—and they will.

"Is Obama's New Deal Better Than the Old One?"

Originally published July 2011

The New Deal failed to reduce unemployment, and the policies of the Obama administration and the Democratic Congress since the financial crisis look to be a repeat performance. These similar outcomes seem to rest on a similarity in policies. In both cases, the administration and Congress blamed the private market for the state of the economy when they assumed power, and in both cases they sought to impose needless and badly thought out regulations on private business activity. The result was to raise the private sector's perception of future risk and suppress the employment gains that come in a normal recovery.

When the new Democratic Congress convened in 2008, Representative Barney Frank (D-MA)—then the powerful chair of the House Financial Services Committee—exuberantly declared that what the public would see in ensuing months was a "New New Deal." For once, he was right. The policies of the Obama administration and the Democratic Congress bear an uncanny resemblance to the policies of Franklin D. Roosevelt (FDR) and the Democrats after the Democratic sweep of 1933, and the results for the U.S. economy have been much the same.

Yet the Democratic Party's left wing has unshakeable faith in the myth of the New Deal. To that group, it was a kind of golden age, a time when government showed its ability to improve the lives of the American people. The staying power of that myth—plus the realignment of the parties along conservative and liberal lines—has made the Democratic Party the party of government in the United States. Thus, when the Democrats took power after the 2008 financial crisis, their reflexive action was to use the opportunity ("Never let a good crisis go to waste," said the president's chief of staff) to increase the authority of government over the economy and the financial system. To make this work, it was necessary to argue that the crisis—like the Depression itself—was the result of faults in the private sector.

Despite the myth, and measured against its effectiveness in restoring jobs and a functioning economy, the New Deal was a failure. When FDR took the oath of office in March 1933, the unemployment rate in the United States was over 24 percent. It fell to 21.6 percent in 1934 and 19.97 percent by the end of 1935. Two years later, having hit 14.18 percent in 1937 after five years of New Deal policies, it rose again in 1938 to 18.9 percent before declining to 14.45 percent in 1940. Only in 1941, as the United States prepared for war, did the rate fall below double digits.[89] Yet before the New Deal, during the 1920s, the average unemployment rate in the United States was about 6 percent.[90]

The New Deal's eight-year failure to return unemployment numbers to the pre–New Deal rate is often ignored by the Left. Instead, FDR's policies are justified by the counterfactual and untestable claim that they "saved capitalism"—that conditions were so bad in the United States when FDR took office that, at the very least, his policies warded off a U.S. turn toward socialism, or worse. An echo of this claim is heard today, when the failure of Obama's economic stimulus policies of 2009 are challenged. In that case, it is argued that if the government had not intervened, unemployment would now be much worse. These issues can never be settled, but the question this *Outlook* will address is whether the similarities between the policies followed in the New Deal, and those followed by the Obama administration and the Democratic Congress elected in 2008, are responsible for the similar employment outcomes observed thus far.

Policies of FDR and the New Deal Congress

The New Deal was characterized by two key elements: substantial growth in government spending on public works and government job creation, and widespread intervention in the economy to keep wages and prices high and eliminate "cutthroat competition." From today's perspective, this prescription seems internally inconsistent—keeping wages and prices high would work against additional private-sector jobs—but it was based on a fundamental misreading of the causes of the downturn that began in 1929. FDR and his advisers apparently

---

89. Data are from US Bureau of the Census, *Historical Statistics of the US: Colonial Times to 1957* (Washington, DC, 1960), 70.

90. Infoplease, "United States Unemployment Rate," www.infoplease.com/ipa/A0104719.html (accessed July 1, 2011).

believed that the inherently competitive nature of a capitalist or free-market economy would eventually bring about financial collapse, manifested in falling prices. Accordingly, before there could be a recovery, the private sector's competitiveness had to be controlled.

In 1932, the last year of the Hoover administration, federal government spending was considerably higher than in 1931—6.9 percent as opposed to 4.8 percent of gross domestic product (GDP). But after the Roosevelt administration took over, spending moved to 8 percent of GDP in 1933, 10.7 percent in 1934, and over 9 percent on average through 1940.[91] The most significant and emblematic piece of New Deal legislation was the National Industrial Recovery Act of 1933 (NRA), which authorized industries to establish codes for managed or "fair" competition, including standards for preventing price and wage declines. The president was given authority to forbid specific companies from reducing prices and wages, and to require any company to apply for and receive a license to participate in any business.

This astonishing law, which the Supreme Court eventually struck down in 1935, was based on the notion that excessive or cutthroat competition had caused the financial collapse. A statement by the head of the National Recovery Administration at the time gives a sense of the thinking behind the legislation: "There is no choice presented to American business between intelligently planned and uncontrolled industrial operations and a return to the gold-plated anarchy that masqueraded as 'rugged individualism.' . . . Unless industry is sufficiently socialized by its private owners and managers so that great essential industries are operated under public operation appropriate to the public interest in them, the advance of political control over private industry is inevitable."[92] In other words, the competitive nature of private industry is not sufficiently devoted to public purposes; the invisible hand does not produce the public good. As might be expected, the NRA stimulated some economic growth, coming off the floor of the Depression, but efficient companies could not cut prices to gain market share and lacked incentives to expand and hire new employees."

---

91. Office of Management and Budget, *Historical Tables: Budget of the US Government Fiscal Year 2011* (Washington, DC, 2010), 24.

92. Arthur Schlesinger Jr., *The Coming of the New Deal: 1933–1935* (New York: Houghton Mifflin Books, 2003), 115.

A similar motive lay behind the Agricultural Adjustment Act (AAA), which attempted to keep farm prices high by creating artificial shortages. Again, the idea was to curb overproduction and return farmers' incomes to "parity"—their revenue in relation to their purchases of goods and equipment—which they had earned in the years before and during World War I. There seemed to be no recognition among New Deal policymakers that mechanization, global competition, and increasing agricultural productivity had been stimulating a decline in farm products and a steady move to the cities and industry well before the onset of the Depression—that the face of America was changing. The AAA was intended to improve the national economy by increasing the purchasing power of the 30 percent of the country that then lived on farms. It was a peculiar policy when so much of the country was ill fed and ill clothed, and like so many New Deal policies—and the echo these policies had eighty years later—it was based on unsound economic theories and assessments.[93] "At its core," said a monumental history of the time, "the thinking that underlay AAA derived from the same conviction about the salutary effects of scarcity that had produced the NRA industrial codes." The AAA was also declared unconstitutional in 1936.[94]

By 1939, so little improvement had occurred in the country's economic conditions that Treasury Secretary Henry Morgenthau noted in his diary: "We have tried spending money. We are spending more than we have ever spent before and it does not work. And I have just one interest, and now if I am wrong . . . somebody else can have my job. I want to see this country prosperous. I want to see people get a job. I want to see people get enough to eat. We have never made good on our promises. . . . I say after eight years of this Administration, we have just as much unemployment as when we started. . . . And an enormous debt to boot."[95] This was not the lesson the Democratic Left took from the New Deal experience.

---

93. David M. Kennedy, *Freedom from Fear: The American People in Depression and War, 1929–1945* (New York: Oxford University Press, 1999), 200–203.

94. Ibid., 203.

95. Burton Fulsom Jr., *New Deal or Raw Deal? How FDR's Economic Legacy Has Damaged America* (New York: Simon & Schuster, 2008), 2.

Policies of the Obama Administration and the Democratic Congress

When President Barack Obama took office in January 2009, the unemployment rate in the United States was 7.8 percent. It rose to 10.1 percent in October 2009, before declining to 9.9 percent at the end of that year and 9.4 percent at the end of 2010. In March 2011, twenty-seven months after Obama's inauguration, it stood at 8.8 percent. For a time, because of tax incentives and government spending, the economy seemed to recover, if slowly. For the three months ending in May 2011, net new jobs increased by more than two hundred thousand each month. But then the economy slowed and unemployment began to rise again, reaching 9.1 percent in May.[96] In June, only 18,000 net new jobs were created, and unemployment rose again to 9.2 percent. To be sure, the Obama administration has only had two and a half years to deal with the unemployment that developed in the recession following the financial crisis. Still, with unemployment rising again after a period of improvement, the New Deal recovery pattern seems to be setting in.

The Obama administration and the Democratic Congress elected in 2008 have pursued three major initiatives, which largely parallel the initial measures in the New Deal. The first was a package of substantial spending and tax cuts totaling over $780 billion, eventually enacted by Congress in February 2009 as the American Recovery and Reinvestment Act of 2009. This measure, together with the funds voted in 2008 for the Troubled Asset Relief Program (TARP), increased the percentage of GDP represented by government spending. This went from 19.6 percent in 2007 and 20.7 percent in the last two years of the Bush administration to 24.7 percent in 2009, 25.4 percent in 2010, and an estimated 25.1 percent in 2011.[97]

The other principal legislative initiatives were an expansion of federal health care coverage requirements through the Patient Protection and Affordable Care Act (PPACA), enacted in March 2010, and a sweeping regulatory measure for the financial system known as the Dodd-Frank Wall Street Reform and Consumer Protection Act (DFA), enacted in July 2010. Both acts are complex pieces of legislation that require substantial regulatory action before they can be fully implemented.

---

96. Bureau of Labor Statistics, "Databases, Tables, and Calculators by Subject," http://data.bls.gov/timeseries/LNS14000000 (accessed June 28, 2011).

97. Ibid.

In addition to these major initiatives, the Obama administration has intervened in the housing market to slow the decline in housing prices by providing tax credits for home purchases and keeping defaulting or delinquent homeowners in their homes. In February 2009, shortly after taking office, Obama announced a $75 billion plan to help as many as 9 million Americans avoid foreclosure.[98] The Department of the Treasury initially predicted that the Home Affordable Modification Program (HAMP) would help 3–4 million homeowners by modifying their mortgages so they could more easily meet their obligations. The funds for this program came from TARP and thus the program was overseen by the special inspector general for TARP, Neil Barofsky, who reported to Congress in March 2011 that in two years of operation HAMP had resulted in permanent mortgage modifications for only 238,000 home-owners. According to Barofsky, a similar program operated by the government-sponsored enterprises (GSEs) Fannie Mae and Freddie Mac modified about an equal number of mortgages.[99]

Possible Causes of the Slow Recovery

Attempting to assess the effect of similar policies in two different eras is potentially instructive in part because many scholars believe that the Fed followed overly restrictive monetary policies after the Depression began, tightening credit when it should have been easing. Thus, they argue, the Depression and its signal unemployment persisted despite substantially increased government spending. Federal Reserve chairman Ben Bernanke, as a scholar, was a student of the Depression and wrote about the errors of the Fed's monetary policy during that period. In a frequently cited speech in 2002, Bernanke expressed confidence that a combination of monetary and fiscal policy could revive the economy:

> In practice, the effectiveness of anti-deflation policy could be significantly enhanced by cooperation between the monetary and fiscal

---

98. Declan McCullagh, "FAQ: How Will Obama's Housing Plan Work?" CBS News, February 8, 2009, www.cbsnews.com/8301-503983_162-4811023-503983.html (accessed June 28, 2011).

99. *Home Affordable Modification Program, Before the House Committee on Financial Services, Subcommittee on Insurance, Housing, and Community Opportunity,* 112th Cong. (2011) (statement of Neil Barofsky, Special Inspector General of the Troubled Asset Relief Program), 2–3, http://financialservices.house.gov/media/pdf/030211barofsky.pdf (accessed June 28, 2011).

authorities. A broad-based tax cut, for example, accommodated by a program of open-market purchases to alleviate any tendency for interest rates to increase, would almost certainly be an effective stimulant to consumption and hence to prices. Even if households decided not to increase consumption but instead re-balanced their portfolios by using their extra cash to acquire real and financial assets, the resulting increase in asset values would lower the cost of capital and improve the balance sheet positions of potential borrowers. A money-financed tax cut is essentially equivalent to Milton Friedman's famous "helicopter drop" of money.

Of course, in lieu of tax cuts or increases in transfers the government could increase spending on current goods and services or even acquire existing real or financial assets. If the Treasury issued debt to purchase private assets and the Fed then purchased an equal amount of Treasury debt with newly created money, the whole operation would be the economic equivalent of direct open-market operations in private assets.[100]

In the last two and a half years, this has been the Fed's policy. Indeed, as suggested in this speech, the Fed has brought short-term interest rates down nearly to zero and has been purchasing Treasury and agency securities to bring down long-term rates. None of this activity, however, has stimulated significant GDP growth or had a significant effect on unemployment. So it can at least be observed that loose fiscal policy—in the form of substantial government deficit spending—accompanied by a stimulative monetary policy does not necessarily guarantee a return to economic growth. Something—perhaps many things—are still missing. What are they?

First, there is the possibility that increased government spending itself has a negative effect on employment. In an article published in early June in the *Washington Times,* Richard Rahn, a noted free-market economist, argues that, if anything, the data show an inverse relationship between government spending

---

100. Ben Bernanke, "Deflation: Making Sure 'It' Doesn't Happen Here" (remarks before the National Economists Club, Washington, DC, November 21, 2002), www.federal reserve.gov/boardDocs/speeches/2002/20021121/default.htm (accessed June 28, 2011).

and employment.[101] Citing recent scholarship, Rahn posits that government spending, by taking resources from the private sector, reduces the propensity of the private sector to hire additional workers.

In addition, there are numerous possible causes of the slow recovery that have not been adequately considered in the media, which have generally focused on the debate about whether the stimulus was large enough. Despite evidence that deficit spending per se, and now deficit spending plus significant monetary loosening, does not produce substantial economic growth, there has been little attention to less tangible causes of the extremely slow recovery. These possible causes include:

- Uncertainty in the business community about the costs of new Obama administration policies, particularly the PPACA and the DFA;

- A failure on the part of the administration and Congress to understand the causes of the financial crisis; and

- Administration intervention in the housing market to prevent foreclosures and declines in home prices.

These explanations for the slow recovery have gotten relatively little attention in the media or among scholars, principally because by their nature they are anecdotal and not susceptible to measurement or validation with numbers, tables, or charts. Like the "animal spirits" described by John Maynard Keynes as a way of explaining business activity that does not follow from any obvious stimulus, they are intangible but powerful features of human nature that can influence economic conditions. Like the drunk who searches for his keys not where he dropped them, but where the light is, it may well be that economists and other commentators, by focusing attention only on things that can be measured, are ignoring some important explanations for the slow recovery.

Business Uncertainty

"In terms of U.S. output contractions," wrote economists Gary Becker, Steven Davis, and Kevin Murphy eighteen months ago, "the so-called Great Recession

---

101. Richard W. Rahn, "How to Create Jobs," *Washington Times*, June 7, 2011.

was not much more severe than the recessions in 1973–75 and 1981–82. Yet recovery from the latest recession has started out much more slowly. For example, real GDP expanded by 7.7% in 1983 after unemployment peaked at 10.8% in December 1982, whereas GDP grew at an unimpressive annual rate of 2.2% in the third quarter of 2009. Although the fourth quarter is likely to show better numbers—probably much better—there are no signs of an explosive takeoff from the recession."[102] Becker et al. were correct about the fourth quarter of 2009, and their comment that there was still no sign of an explosive takeoff was an understatement. Figure 1 shows the record, thus far, of the recovery from the Great Recession of 2008.

Writing in 2007, before the financial crisis, Amity Shlaes, author of *The Forgotten Man,* explained the slow recovery from the Depression as the product of FDR's constant economic experimentation and changes in policy:

> NRA rules were so stringent they perversely hurt businesses. They frightened away capital, and they discouraged employers from hiring workers. Another problem was that laws like that which created the NRA—and Roosevelt signed a number of them—were so broad that no one knew how they would be interpreted. The resulting hesitation itself arrested growth. . .
>
> The trouble, however, was not merely new policies that were implemented but also the threat of additional, unknown, policies. Fear froze the economy, but that uncertainty itself might have a cost was something the young experimenters simply did not consider.[103]

Again, it is hard to escape the similarities between the current slow recovery and the seven years from 1933 to 1940 during which the U.S. economy failed to reduce unemployment below 14 percent. If uncertainty about policies and costs was a cause of business reluctance to hire in the Depression, the Obama administration's policies are subject to the same indictment. In terms of their propensity to cause uncertainty, there could hardly be two more troubling laws for business than the PPACA and the DFA. In a real sense, they are successors to the NRA and the AAA of the New Deal. Both embody enormously complex and costly

---

102. Gary Becker, Steven Davis, and Kevin Murphy, "Uncertainty and the Slow Recovery," *Wall Street Journal,* January 4, 2010.

103. Amity Shlaes, *The Forgotten Man* (New York: HarperCollins, 2007), 8–9.

FIGURE 1
THE UNSTABLE RECOVERY

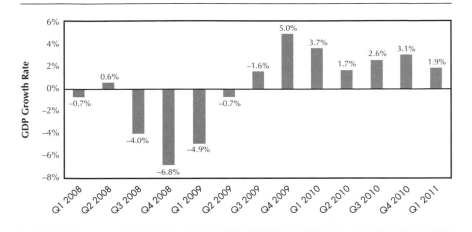

SOURCE: US Department of Commerce, Bureau of Economic Analysis, "Gross Domestic Product: First Quarter 2011 (Third Estimate); Corporate Profits: First Quarter 2011 (Revised Estimate)," news release, June 24, 2011, www.bea.gov/newsreleases/national/gdp/gdpnewsrelease.htm (accessed July 6, 2011).

requirements and have to be implemented by a vast number of regulations, most of which have not yet been drafted or proposed. Moreover, the DFA, like the AAA before it, tries to impose a U.S.-based straitjacket of regulation on a global industry that is changing rapidly under the influence of new communications technology.

The effect of all this on business is well illustrated in a May 2011 article in *Bloomberg* by Stephen L. Carter, in which the Yale law professor describes a conversation with a businessman who sat next to him on a recent airplane flight:

> The man in the aisle seat is trying to tell me why he refuses to hire any-body. His business is successful, he says, as the 737 cruises smoothly eastward. Demand for his product is up. But he still won't hire.
>
> "Why not?"
>
> "Because I don't know how much it will cost," he explains. "How can I hire new workers today, when I don't know how much they will cost me tomorrow?"
>
> He's referring not to wages, but to regulation: He has no way of telling what new rules will go into effect when. His business, although it covers several states, operates on low margins. He can't afford to take

the chance of losing what little profit there is to the next round of regulatory changes. And so he's hiring nobody until he has some certainty about cost.

It's a little odd to be having this conversation as the news media keep insisting that private employment is picking up. But as economists have pointed out to all who will listen, the only real change is that the rate of layoffs has slowed. Fewer than one of six small businesses added jobs last year, and not many more expect to do so this year. The private sector is creating no more new jobs than it was a year ago; the man in the aisle seat is trying to tell me why.[104]

The sense that this conversation reflected more than one businessman's opinion was reinforced by the news in early June and again in July that—after three months of employment growth—the economy stalled in May, with an increase of only 25,000 jobs and 18,000 in June, causing unemployment to tick up to 9.1 percent in May and 9.2 percent in June. The decline in new job growth has been a shock to forecasters, who had expected a confirmation of the jobs recovery that had seemed to be underway earlier in the year. There appear to be things going on in the economy—unmeasurable things, beyond the economists' models—that are at least as influential as fiscal and monetary policy.

As one example, by modifying the incentives for employers—perhaps unintentionally—the PPACA completely changed the traditional role of employer-paid health coverage in employee compensation. A survey by McKinsey & Co. published in June 2011 indicated that as many as 30 percent of employers were planning to terminate their health care coverage and allow their employees to buy their own health insurance after the new system becomes mandatory in 2014.[105] This contrasts with an initial estimate by the Congressional Budget Office that only 4 percent of employees would lose coverage when the new system goes into effect. According to McKinsey, the 30 percent figure increases to more than 50 percent among employers who have a thorough understanding of the new law. If the McKinsey study is correct, it could partly explain the reluctance of employers to hire new workers. Employers do not know whether they will be able to retain the employees they hire now if they are compelled to terminate

---

104. Stephen L. Carter, "Economic Stagnation Explained, at 30,000 Feet," Bloomberg.com, May 26, 2011.

105. Janet Adamy, "Study Sees Cuts to Health Plans," *Wall Street Journal,* June 8, 2008.

health coverage after 2014, nor do they know how much it will cost to continue to include health insurance in their employees' compensation packages.

In addition, the PPACA imposes numerous taxes and fees that are bound to increase the cost of coverage for employers who choose to retain it. Apart from the rising cost of medical care itself and excluding the new Medicare taxes on individuals with incomes over $200,000, the PPACA imposes new taxes on health insurance providers, fees on manufacturers and importers of branded drugs and medical devices, reduced health insurance tax deductions for certain employers, and other revenue raisers that will amount to approximately $400 billion over the next ten years.[106] Undoubtedly, the cost of employee coverage will increase, but by what amount is unknown and unknowable.

The most troubling of the new legislation from the standpoint of economic growth is probably the DFA, which strikes directly at the U.S. credit system and thus affects all businesses. The DFA is over 2,300 pages long and covers banking, securities, commodities, housing finance, rating agencies, derivatives, debit cards, proprietary trading by banks, insurance, investment advisers to hedge funds and mutual funds, resolution of failing financial firms, and all firms (to be named)—of whatever kind—that are considered to pose a threat to the stability of the financial system if they suffer financial distress. It also creates a new consumer protection agency with powers to prevent "abuse"—an undefined term that raises the potential regulatory cost profile for every firm that engages in financial transactions with consumers, from the largest banks to the smallest check-cashing stores. In a count by the New York law firm Davis Polk, there are 243 regulations required by the DFA, of which only twenty-four have been completed in the year since the law passed. Extensions of time to comment on major proposals have now been granted to affected industries and, according to the New York Times, twenty-eight statutory deadlines have already been missed.[107]

---

106. Joint Committee on Taxation, *Estimated Revenue Effects of the Amendment in the Nature of a Substitute to HR 4872, the "Reconciliation Act of 2010," as Amended, in Combination with the Revenue Effects of HR 3590, the "Patient Protection and Affordable Care Act ('PPACA')," as Passed by the Senate, and Scheduled for Consideration by the House Committee on Rules on March 20, 2010*, 112th Cong., 1st sess. (March 20, 2010), JCX-17-10, ww.jct.gov/publications.html?func=download&id=3672&chk=3672&no_html=1 (accessed June 29, 2011).

107. Louise Story, "Financial Overhaul Is Mired in Detail and Dissent," *New York Times*, June 8, 2011.

Even if a business is not in the financial industry, it must rely on credit. The costs of bank credit, derivatives, securities issuance and reporting, accounting, consulting and legal services, financial advice, commodity futures, insurance, pension fund management, or providing credit to customers cannot be known until these regulations are proposed, debated, and finalized. That could easily take five years at the pace it is going today. Again, here is Carter's seatmate, who has a business "somewhere in the Dakotas":

> My seat-mate seems to think that I'm missing the point. He's not anti-government. He's not anti-regulation. He just needs to know as he makes his plans that the rules aren't going to change radically. Big businesses don't face the same problem, he says. They have lots of customers to spread costs over. They have "installed base."
>
> For medium-sized firms like his, however, there is little wiggle room to absorb the costs of regulatory change. Because he possesses neither lobbyists nor clout, he says, Washington doesn't care whether he hires more workers or closes up shop.

Former Fed chairman Alan Greenspan has done some groundbreaking work in trying to find evidence that these increased risks are affecting the real (nonfinancial) economy. In a 2011 paper, Greenspan pointed to the unusually low level of corporate illiquid investment—for example, investment in plants or equipment with long useful lives. This kind of investment would be most susceptible to devaluation as a result of future events, and the allocation of liquid funds to an illiquid investment represents a risk in itself if liquidity is not readily available to the company in the future. He notes, "For nonfinancial corporate businesses (half of gross domestic product) the disengagement from illiquid risk is directly measured as a share of liquid cash flow they choose to allocate to long-term fixed asset investment. . . . In the first half of 2010, this share fell to 79%, its lowest peacetime percentage since 1940."[108] The only time it has been lower—perhaps not coincidentally—is during the period from 1932 to 1940. Greenspan attributes this decline to enhanced risk associated with "government activism." One element of that would be the DFA, which through new and far-reaching regulation of the entire financial market in the

---

108. Alan Greenspan, "Activism," *International Finance* 14, no. 1 (Spring 2011): 165–82.

United States raises serious questions about the availability of financing for the nonfinancial sector in the future. Given these facts, it is little wonder that legislation has been introduced in the Senate to repeal the DFA. The wonder is that anyone who worries about unemployment and a sluggish recovery continues to support the act.

Failure to Understand the Causes of the Financial Crisis

The precipitating cause of the financial crisis was, by common agreement, a mortgage meltdown that began in 2007. Congress never bothered to find out, before legislating on the subject, why this collapse in the housing finance system was so destructive. If it had done so, it would have realized that the financial crisis was not the result of deregulation or regulatory laxity but of government housing policies that fostered the creation of 27 million subprime and nonprime mortgages—half of all mortgages in the U.S. financial system—in an effort over two administrations to increase homeownership by reducing mortgage underwriting standards.[109] The desire to protect the government against challenge was so strong among Democrats (and, of course, in the government itself) that the Financial Crisis Inquiry Commission—set up by the Democratic Congress to find the causes of the financial crisis—refused even to acknowledge that this number of weak and risky mortgages existed in the financial system before the 2008 crisis. Instead, the commission sought to lay the blame for the financial crisis on private-sector risk-taking, greed, and regulatory laxity.[110]

The failure to acknowledge the number of low-quality mortgages in the financial system, and the refusal to look into the role of government policies in creating the weak and risky loans, distorted the response to the financial crisis

---

109. The causes of the financial crisis are discussed in Peter J. Wallison, "The Lost Cause: The Failure of the Financial Crisis Inquiry Commission," AEI *Financial Services Outlook* (January/February 2011), www.aei.org/outlook/101025. (See p. 312 of this book.)

110. Financial Crisis Inquiry Commission, *Final Report of the National Commission on the Causes of the Financial and Economic Crisis in the United States* (Washington, DC, January 2011), http://cybercemetery.unt.edu/archive/fcic/20110310173545/http://c0182732.cdn1.cloudfiles.rackspacecloud.com/fcic_final_report_full.pdf (accessed June 28, 2011); and Peter J. Wallison, *Dissent from the Majority Report of the Financial Crisis Inquiry Commission* (Washington, DC: AEI, January 2011), www.aei.org/paper/100190.

by the administration and the Democratic Congress in two ways. First, it encouraged the view—prevalent on the left—that the financial crisis was the result
of the normal operation of the U.S. financial system when it is not effectively
regulated. This ignored several facts, among them that this was the first financial
crisis of anything like this size in at least eighty years; that while deregulation
had taken hold in many parts of the U.S. economy there had been very little
deregulation in the financial sector; and that regulation of banks in particular
had been tightened substantially in 1991 with the enactment of the Federal
Deposit Insurance Corporation Improvement Act. If these points had been seriously considered, by Congress or the Financial Crisis Inquiry Commission, the
solution chosen—far tighter regulation of the financial system—would have
looked a lot less attractive.

Second, the sheer size of the low-quality mortgage problem—the fact that
so many homeowners were likely to default on their mortgages—might have
produced a legislative response that focused on the weakness in the mortgage
market rather than a lack of sufficient regulation in the financial system as a
whole. As it was, Congress spent eighteen months trying to adopt the DFA
rather than considering how to deal with the avalanche of mortgage defaults that
would inevitably come from the collapse of the 1997–2007 housing bubble. If
Congress had attempted to understand the size of the subprime mortgage problem, it might have been able to predict and address in advance the 30 to 40
percent decline in housing prices that ultimately occurred. This is not the place
to discuss what legislative actions might have been taken, but it is clear that by
focusing on strengthening and broadening regulation of the financial system
Congress entirely missed the real problem that would bring on and prolong the
recession—the unprecedented decline in housing values and the vast number
of delinquencies and defaults that ensued.

The results are plain to see in figure 2. After a short but disastrous decline in
prices, the market began an apparent recovery, stimulated in part by tax credits
for new home purchases, but it was not enough. The market was overwhelmed
by the vast number of foreclosures arising principally from the 27 million weak
and risky mortgages that had suffused the financial system before the financial
crisis, and it has now begun a double dip. If the administration and Congress
had paid more attention to the mortgage problem rather than the ideologically
driven desire for tighter regulation of the financial system, they might have
adopted policies to mitigate the resulting losses.

FIGURE 2
STANDARD & POOR'S/CASE-SHILLER HOME PRICE INDICES

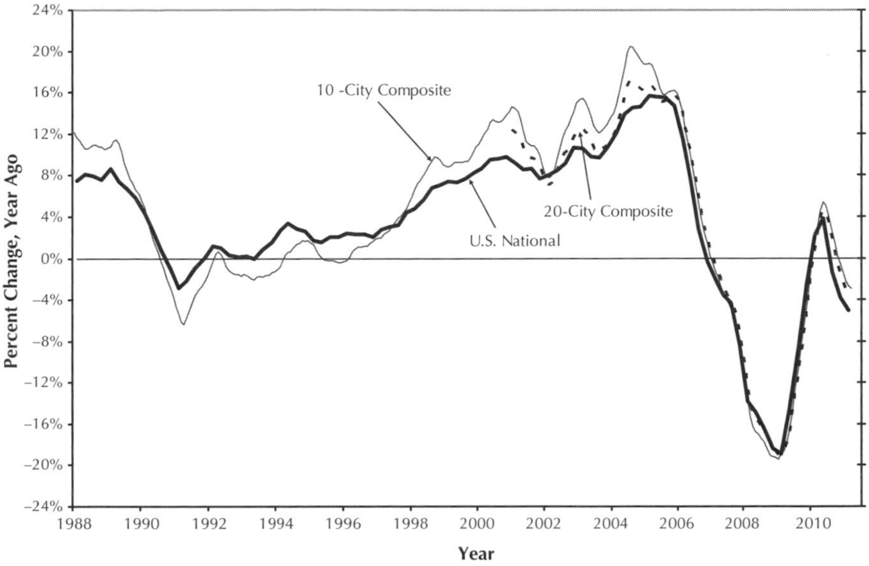

SOURCE: Standard & Poor's, "National Home Prices Hit New Low in 2011 Q1," press release, May 31, 2010, www.standardandpoors.com/servlet/BlobServer?blobheadername3=MDT-Type&blobcol=urldocumentfile& blobtable=SPComSecureDocument&blobheadervalue2=inline%3B+filename%3Ddownload.pdf&blobhead ername2 Content-Disposition&blobheadervalue1=application%2Fpdf&blobkey=id&blobheadername1 =content-type&blobwhere=1245305612764&blobheadervalue3=abinary%3B+charset%3DUTF-8&blobno cache=true (accessed July 6, 2011).

Tinkering with Housing Prices

The failure of the administration and Congress to recognize the dimensions of the impending housing price collapse and the weakness of almost half of all outstanding mortgages led to the adoption of policies that were doomed to fail. No one seemed to be aware that with a decline in housing prices that far exceeded anything that had happened previously, the usual policies that attempted to put a floor under prices or achieve widespread loan modification through HAMP would not work.

Of the 27 million subprime and other nonprime mortgages that were outstanding before the financial crisis, most were accompanied by little or no equity in the home before the price decline. This was because the Department of Housing and Urban Development (HUD), over the previous fifteen years, had been encouraging a decline in mortgage standards and particularly a reduction in down payments. Although less than one mortgage in two hundred involved a down payment of less than 3 percent in 1990, by 2007 that was true of almost 40 percent (80 in 200) of all mortgages. Because of the affordable-housing requirements imposed on Fannie and Freddie in 1992 and gradually tightened by HUD through 2007, the GSEs were required to buy increasing numbers of subprime and other deficient loans. The Federal Housing Administration, the Community Reinvestment Act, and a HUD program applicable to mortgage bankers such as Countrywide also contributed to a huge increase in the stock of lower-quality mortgages.[111]

Under these circumstances, tax credits and HAMP could never be effective to stanch the bleeding. Too many homes had too little equity to provide home-owners with incentives to hang on. The sheer number of defaults—strategic and otherwise—overwhelmed every government program that was attempted. In fact, these programs made things worse by preventing housing prices from falling to the bottom. If that had happened, buyers would have come in without tax inducements; the gradual recovery of housing prices would have encour-aged homeowners who were under water (with homes worth less than their mortgages) to stay with their homes in the hope that values would eventually recover. But the prolonged period of gradual decline has kept potential buyers out of the market until they are sure that prices have hit bottom and encour-aged others to walk away from what came to look like unrecoverable losses. It is likely that this process will be strung out until the government stops trying to mitigate the losses.

Conclusion

The New Deal failed because its supporters sought to address the weak econ-omy by substantially increasing government spending and imposing significant new regulations on the private sector. They thought, incorrectly, that the Depres-sion was caused by excessive or "cutthroat competition"—which they saw as

---

111. Peter J. Wallison, *Dissent from the Majority Report of the Financial Crisis Inquiry Commission,* note 20.

driving down prices and causing business failures and unemployment—and that government spending would restart the economy.

The polices of the Obama administration and the Democratic Congress— infatuated with the New Deal myth and following the New Deal pattern—sought to blame the financial crisis on the private sector, and to use it to take control of the financial system the way they have taken control of the health care system. Although the approach succeeded in attaining its ends, the risks and uncertainties these policies created suppressed the usual growth and hiring that pulls the country out of recessions. In addition, the failure to understand the dimensions of the mortgage problem—indeed a seeming intent to ignore it entirely in favor of more regulation—left the country without a policy to combat the effects of the mortgage meltdown that began in 2008 and accelerated in 2009.

"The Error at the Heart of the Dodd-Frank Act"

Originally published August–September 2011

The underlying assumption of the Dodd-Frank Act (DFA) is that the 2008 financial crisis was caused by the disorderly bankruptcy of Lehman Brothers. This is evident in the statements of officials and the principal elements of the act, which would tighten the regulation of large financial institutions to prevent their failing, and establish an "orderly resolution" system outside of bankruptcy if they do. The financial crisis, however, was caused by the mortgage meltdown, a sudden and sharp decline in housing and mortgage values as a massive housing bubble collapsed in 2007. This scenario is known to scholars as a "common shock"—a sudden decline in the value of a widely held asset—which causes instability or insolvency among many financial institutions. In this light, the principal elements of Dodd-Frank turn out to be useless as a defense against a future crisis. Lehman's bankruptcy shows that in the absence of a common shock that weakens all or most financial institutions, the bankruptcy of one or a few firms would not cause a crisis; on the other hand, given a similarly severe common shock in the future, subjecting a few financial institutions to the act's orderly resolution process will not prevent a crisis. Apart from its likely ineffectiveness, moreover, the orderly resolution process in the act impairs the current insolvency system and will raise the cost of credit for all financial institutions.

It is no exaggeration to say that the orderly resolution provisions are the heart of the DFA. Whenever someone in the administration or Congress is called upon to list the benefits of the act, the fact that a large financial institution can purportedly be resolved without triggering another financial crisis is always cited as one of its principal achievements. The orderly resolution process is also treated as a solution to the alleged problem that some institutions may be too big to fail—that is, they are so large that their failure will destabilize the financial system as a whole. With orderly resolution, we are told, all large financial institutions can be safely wound down and thus are not too big to fail.

However, the orderly resolution provisions of the DFA are another example of the misconceptions underlying this troubling legislation. These provisions, together with the special "stringent" regulation mandated for large, "systemically significant" financial institutions, are based on the assumption that the 2008 financial crisis was caused by the failure of a large financial institution and that future financial crises will stem from the same cause. Presumably, what the administration and congressional framers had in mind was that the failure of a large financial institution has knock-on effects, which drag down other "interconnected" institutions, creating a systemic event. If this were true, then it would be sensible to impose stringent regulation on large financial institutions, and perhaps even to provide for a special form of resolution or wind-down if such an institution failed.

But there is something wrong with this picture. The 2008 financial crisis was not caused by the failure of a single institution, but by a "common shock"—a weakening of all financial institutions because of a general decline in the value of a widely held asset. In this case, the asset was almost $2 trillion in mortgage-backed securities (MBS) held by financial institutions in the United States and around the world. When the unprecedented ten-year housing bubble collapsed in 2007, Bear Stearns, Wachovia, Washington Mutual, AIG, Lehman Brothers, and many other financial firms in the United States and around the world were all severely weakened, particularly because of mark-to-market accounting. Of these large financial firms in the United States, only Lehman was allowed to go into bankruptcy, but that event told us a great deal about what happens when a large financial institution fails. Contrary to the conclusions of the DFA's framers, it demonstrated that the failure of a large financial institution is very unlikely to cause a financial crisis. Even in a financial environment severely weakened by a common shock, Lehman's bankruptcy had virtually no knock-on effects. In other words, the collapse of Lehman showed that almost all financial institutions can survive the failure of a large firm even in the midst of a severe common shock.

This conclusion calls into question the need for both the stringent new regulations in the DFA's Title I and the orderly resolution provisions in Title II. If, as seems clear, the financial crisis was caused by the severity of the common shock rather than the Lehman bankruptcy itself, the proper policy response was to take steps to mitigate the likelihood of future common shocks. Given a severe common shock to virtually all financial institutions, the orderly resolution of one or even a few large firms will not mitigate its effects; in the absence of a severe common shock, on the other hand, it is unlikely that the failure of one or a few large financial institutions will cause a systemic breakdown.

Common Shock and the Financial Crisis

Most observers now recognize that the precipitating cause of the financial crisis was a collapse of the huge U.S. housing bubble in 2007. This was not just any bubble. It was almost ten times larger than any previous postwar housing bubble, and almost half of all mortgages in this bubble—27 million loans—were subprime or otherwise weak and risky loans.[112]

The reason for this was the U.S. government's housing policy, which—in the early 1990s—began to require that government agencies and others regulated or controlled by government reduce their mortgage underwriting standards so borrowers who had not previously had access to mortgage credit would be able to buy homes. The government-sponsored enterprises Fannie Mae and Freddie Mac, the Federal Housing Administration, and banks and savings and loan associations (S&Ls) subject to the Community Reinvestment Act were all required to increase their acquisition of loans to homebuyers at or below the median income in their communities. Often, government policies required Fannie, Freddie, and the others to acquire loans to borrowers at or below 80 percent, and in some cases 60 percent, of median income.

Of course, it was possible to find qualified buyers that met prime lending standards in these areas, but when all these agencies and institutions were trying to meet increasing government quotas for lending to low-income borrowers, mortgage underwriting standards had to deteriorate. Aggregate government demand, coupled with competition among the agencies trying to meet their quotas, not only built the housing bubble but loaded it up with subprime and other low-quality mortgages.

By 2008, before the financial crisis actually struck, two-thirds of the 27 million low-quality mortgages were on the books of Fannie and Freddie, other government agencies, and insured banks and S&Ls subject to the Community Reinvestment Act.

---

112. The data supporting these points are contained in Peter J. Wallison, *Dissent from the Majority Report of the Financial Crisis Inquiry Commission* (Washington, DC: AEI, January 26, 2011), www.aei.org/paper/100190.

FIGURE 1
THE U.S. HOUSING BUBBLE:
CASE-SHILLER NATIONAL HOME PRICE INDEX VALUES, 1987–2011 Q1

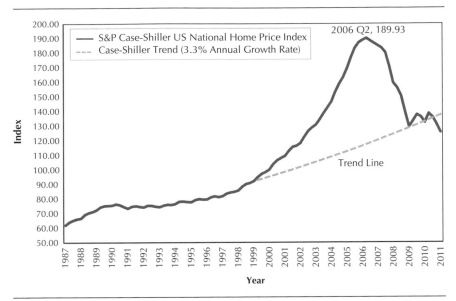

SOURCE: S&P Case-Shiller National Home Price Index.

As bubbles grow, they tend to suppress delinquencies and defaults, since borrowers can easily refinance their homes or sell them for more than they initially paid. So, to banks and other financial institutions, MBS issued against pools of these weak loans looked like good investments. They were paying high rates because the loans were high risk, but they were not showing the high levels of default normally commensurate with these risks. As a result, starting in about 2004, financial institutions around the world began to buy these instruments in large numbers, eventually acquiring MBS backed by pools of about 7.8 million mortgages—somewhat less than one-third of the 27 million low-quality loans outstanding.

But when the bubble began to deflate in 2007, the 27 million subprime and other weak mortgages started to default in unprecedented numbers, driving down housing values. Figure 1 shows the huge run-up and subsequent decline in real house prices during the bubble years 1997–2007.

FIGURE 2
THE MBS MARKET REACTS TO THE BUBBLE'S DEFLATION

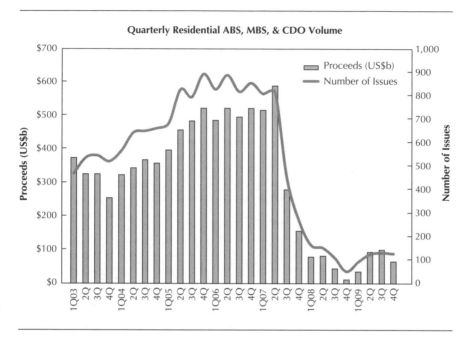

Quarterly Residential ABS, MBS, & CDO Volume

SOURCE: Thomson Reuters, *Debt Capital Markets Review* (New York, NY, fourth quarter 2008).
NOTE: ABS = asset-backed securities; and CDO = collateralized debt obligations.

With housing values falling precipitously, investors fled from MBS, making portfolios of these instruments unmarketable. Figure 2 shows the speed of the collapse in the MBS market. This had a devastating effect on the balance sheets of the large financial institutions in the United States and around the world that were holding these assets—a problem seriously aggravated by mark-to-market accounting, which required the writedown to market value of assets on which losses had not yet been suffered. With the market collapsed and moribund, these values were far lower than the capitalized values of the cash flows the portfolios were generating. As a result, at least in an accounting sense, the institutions holding these securities looked unstable or insolvent, triggering significant declines in their stock prices and general investor and creditor anxiety around the world. Panicky investors, fearful of insolvencies, began to withdraw their funds from financial institutions and place them in safer hands.

The rescue of Bear Stearns in March 2008 temporarily quieted the markets but created substantial moral hazard. Most market participants believed that the U.S. government's policy had been established: it would rescue all large financial institutions. On the evidence, it was not rational to believe otherwise. However, when Lehman was allowed to file for bankruptcy, market participants were shocked. Because of the decline in MBS asset values, it was unclear who was solvent and who was not—and now it really mattered. As a result, major financial institutions stopped lending to one another, creating the financial crisis.

Thus, the events of 2008 were the result of a sudden, generalized loss in value for a widely held asset—about $2 trillion in privately issued MBS—coupled with the effects of mark-to-market accounting and the moral hazard that flowed from the rescue of Bear Stearns. What happened in 2008, as mortgage asset values began to fall and investors fled from the MBS market, was a classic case of a common shock, described as follows in a 2003 article about bank failures by banking scholars George G. Kaufman and Kenneth E. Scott:

> Except for fraud, clustered bank failures in the United States almost always are triggered by adverse conditions in the regional or national macroeconomies or by the bursting of asset-price bubbles, especially in real estate. . . . Banks fail because of exposure to common shock, such as a depression in agriculture, real estate, or oil prices, not because of direct spillover from other banks without themselves being exposed to the shock.[113]

In other words, bank failures—and by extension, financial institution failures—are generally caused by declines in the values of widely held assets, not by spillovers from the failure of other banks.

The Theory of the DFA's Framers

However, the lesson of this history—that the financial crisis was caused by a common shock—was not absorbed by the framers of Dodd-Frank in the administration and Congress. From all indications, they diagnosed the crisis as

---

113. George G. Kaufman and Kenneth E. Scott, "What Is Systemic Risk and Do Bank Regulators Contribute to It?" *The Independent Review* VII, no. 3 (Winter 2003): 379.

the result of losses arising from the bankruptcy of Lehman Brothers, as though Lehman's failure had dragged down other financial institutions. This error is written boldly in their own statements, in their emphasis on the concept of "interconnections" among financial institutions, and in the DFA.

For example, in testimony before the House Financial Services Committee on October 1, 2009, Fed chair Ben Bernanke noted:

> In most cases, the federal bankruptcy laws provide an appropriate framework for the resolution of nonbank financial institutions. However, the bankruptcy code does not sufficiently protect the public's strong interest in ensuring the orderly resolution of a nonbank financial firm whose failure would pose substantial risks to the financial system and to the economy. Indeed, after Lehman Brothers' and AIG's experiences, there is little doubt that we need a third option between the choices of bankruptcy and bailout for such firms.[114]

This is a point repeated frequently by administration spokesmen—that the financial crisis came about because there was no choice but to allow Lehman to file for bankruptcy, and in effect that the bankruptcy itself caused the crisis.

Interconnections among financial institutions are also emphasized by the act's supporters, again to suggest that when one large financial firm fails it will drag down others. For example, Treasury Secretary Timothy Geithner, in a speech at New York University's Stern School of Business in August 2010, declared that "[t]he largest and most interconnected firms cause more damage when they fail." Although financial institutions are certainly interconnected to some extent, implicit in Geithner's use of the term is the argument that financial institutions are so critically interconnected that the knock-on effects of the failure of one could cause others to fail—in other words, a systemic collapse. A further illustration of this approach appears in a widely read speech in March 2011, by Federal Reserve governor Daniel K. Tarullo. Tarullo focused on the effects of a single firm's distress, outlining four ways in which that might cause general financial instability: a "domino effect" in which the failure of one large institution infects other firms; a "fire sale" effect in which a failing firm dumps assets and thus lowers asset values generally; a "contagion effect" in which

---

114. *Regulatory Reform, Before the House Financial Services Committee,* 111th Cong. 7 (October 1, 2009) (testimony of Ben Bernanke, Chairman of the Federal Reserve).

market participants conclude from one firm's distress that others are in similar straits; and the discontinuation of a critical function for which there are no substitutes.[115] None of these scenarios involves a common shock; it was an idea foreign to the framers of the DFA.

Thus, the DFA authorizes the Financial Stability Oversight Council to identify those financial firms which—if they fail—are likely to cause instability in the U.S. financial system. If it is in fact true that these knock-on effects can result in systemic breakdowns, the 2008 financial crisis would be the acid test; we are unlikely ever to see a case in which a firm as large as Lehman Brothers is allowed to fail when the solvency or stability of other large financial institutions is subject to such doubt among market participants. Yet, as discussed below, there is very little evidence of knock-on effects associated with the Lehman bankruptcy.

Finally, and most importantly, the DFA creates a new orderly resolution system for large *nonbank* financial institutions of all kinds, administered by the Federal Deposit Insurance Corporation (FDIC). In effect, the DFA extends to all financial institutions the FDIC's authority to resolve insolvent insured banks. Although there are some differences between the FDIC's authorities under the DFA and its authorities under the Federal Deposit Insurance Act, the authorities are essentially the same. It is important to note that these authorities can be extended to all financial institutions, and not just those designated by the Financial Stability Oversight Council as systemically important financial institutions (SIFIs).[116] As discussed below, this will have an important effect in creating uncertainty about the enforceability of creditors' rights among firms that are not initially designated as SIFIs and thus will raise the cost of credit to these firms, as well as their consumer and business customers.

All of this raises the question of whether Lehman's bankruptcy—the kind of failure the orderly resolution provisions were designed to prevent—caused the financial crisis, either through the disorderliness of its bankruptcy or the knock-on effects of its failure to meet its financial obligations.

---

115. Daniel K. Tarullo, "Regulating Systemic Risk" (remarks, Credit Markets Symposium, Charlotte, NC, March 31, 2011).

116. See §203(a) of the DFA, which authorizes the Financial Stability Oversight Council to make a recommendation to the secretary of the treasury for the orderly resolution of any financial company in danger of default.

Did Lehman's Failure Cause the Financial Crisis?

Contrary to the underlying assumptions of the DFA, the events that followed the failure of Lehman demonstrate the weakness of the interconnectedness and knock-on theories in explaining the financial crisis. With the single exception of the Reserve Fund, a money market mutual fund, there is no evidence whatever that any significant firm was caused to fail through the knock-on effects of Lehman's bankruptcy. Indeed, the case of the Reserve Fund is itself an example of the ill effects of the moral hazard created by the rescue of Bear. The fund could have rid itself of its Lehman holdings as Lehman was perceived to be weakening, but it likely held on to a large portfolio of the firm's commercial paper in the belief that Lehman, like Bear Stearns, would eventually be rescued and its creditors fully paid. AIG, one of the other high-profile failures around the time of Lehman, had virtually no exposure to Lehman. Nor is there any indication that the problems at Wachovia or Washington Mutual—the other institutions resolved in some way during the financial crisis—had any significant exposure to Lehman. In reality, all were victims of the same common shock that caused Lehman's failure. So in the absence of any evidence of knock-on effects from Lehman's failure, it is necessary to conclude that interconnectedness among financial institutions—as a theory for preventing a future financial crisis through tighter regulation—is invalid.

In the absence of any other examples, supporters of the interconnectedness theory have pointed to credit default swaps (CDSs) as a mechanism through which the failure of one financial institution could be transmitted to others. This is perhaps true in theory, but even in one of the greatest financial meltdowns ever, there is no evidence that the failure of Lehman or AIG—both of which were major players in the CDS market—caused any other financial institution to fail. Indeed, the CDS market continued to function effectively after Lehman and AIG (and through the entire financial crisis); losses on CDSs written on Lehman were resolved five weeks after its bankruptcy by the exchange of approximately $6 billion among hundreds of counter-parties.[117] The CDSs on which Lehman

---

117. Peter J. Wallison, "Everything You Wanted to Know about Credit Default Swaps—But Were Never Told," AEI *Financial Services Outlook* (December 2008), www.aei.org/outlook/29158; see also Peter J. Wallison, "Unnecessary Intervention: The Administration's Effort to Regulate Credit Default Swaps," AEI *Financial Services Outlook* (August 2009), www.aei.org/outlook/100065. (See pp. 223 and 409 of this book.)

was a counterparty were either terminated by its counterparties (who presumably bought replacement coverage) or continued in force by Lehman's trustee if they were favorable to the bankrupt estate. In other words, no great crisis developed in the CDS market as a result of Lehman's failure.

A particularly good summary of the outcome thus far with respect to Lehman's CDS portfolio is the following:

> While derivatives certainly lived up to their famous moniker as weapons of mass destruction in the view of the media and many policymakers, the fact remains that derivative transactions were terminated quickly and efficiently, although obviously settlement of claims and the ensuing fiduciary requirements of administration certainly slow the process, no major counterparties slid into bankruptcy, parties were eventually able to re-hedge their positions and quality collateral was fairly ubiquitous both before and after the meltdown in 2008.[118]

AIG, of course, was devastated by its participation in the CDS market, but this was because it had made the gross error of taking only one side of CDS transactions. It had sold protection against others' losses, but unlike other market participants it never hedged its bets by buying protection for itself. To use AIG's experience as a reason to condemn CDS activity as too risky to be carried on without regulation—the basis for the DFA's regulation of the CDS market—is like regulating all lending because one lender made imprudent loans.

Sometimes it is argued that the Troubled Asset Relief Program (TARP) prevented more failures. That seems highly unlikely. The first funds were made available under TARP on October 28, 2008, about six weeks after the panic following Lehman's failure. By that time, any firm that had been mortally wounded by Lehman's collapse would have collapsed itself. Moreover, most of the TARP funds were quickly repaid by the largest institutions, and many of the smaller ones, only eight months later, in mid-June 2009. This is strong evidence that the funds were not needed to cover losses coming from the Lehman bankruptcy. If there were such losses, they would still have been embedded in the balance sheets of

---

118. Kimberly Anne Summe, "An Examination of Lehman Brothers' Derivatives Portfolio Post-Bankruptcy and Whether Dodd-Frank Would Have Made Any Difference," in *Resolution of Failed Financial Institutions: Orderly Liquidation Authority and a New Chapter 14* (Palo Alto, CA: Stanford University, Hoover Institution Working Group on Economic Policy, Resolution Project, April 24, 2011), 3–28.

those institutions. If the funds were needed at all—and many of the institutions took them reluctantly and under government pressure—it was to restore investor confidence that the recipients were not so badly affected by the common shock of the decline in housing and mortgage values that they could not fund orderly withdrawals, if necessary. However, even if we assume that TARP funds prevented the failure of some large financial institutions, it seems clear that the underlying cause of each firm's weakness was the decline in the value of its MBS holdings, and not any losses suffered as a result of Lehman's bankruptcy.

The same is true of many other extraordinary actions taken by the government after Lehman's bankruptcy, including guaranteeing loans, purchasing commercial paper, and ring-fencing weak assets on the balance sheets of large financial institutions. These actions were made necessary by the effects of the common shock, not by the bankruptcy of Lehman. The fact is that even in their weakened condition, most financial institutions are so highly diversified that any losses suffered because of the failure of another firm are unlikely to leave mortal wounds, and that appears to be the lesson of Lehman.

This analysis leads to the following conclusion. Without a common shock, the failure of a single Lehman-like firm is highly unlikely to cause a financial crisis. This conclusion is buttressed by the fact that in 1990 the securities firm Drexel Burnham Lambert—then, like Lehman, the fourth largest securities firm in the United States—was allowed to declare bankruptcy without any adverse consequences for the market in general. At the time, other financial institutions were generally healthy, and Drexel was not brought down by the failure of a widely held class of assets. On the other hand, in the presence of a common shock, the orderly resolution of one or a few Lehman-like financial institutions will not prevent a financial crisis precipitated by a severe common shock. Resolving one institution, or even a few, will have little or no effect on the weakened condition of those still surviving. This question remains: even if the orderly resolution provisions of the DFA are not effectively designed to prevent a financial crisis, are they an improvement over the bankruptcy system? That issue is addressed in the rest of this *Outlook*.

Dodd-Frank and Insolvency Law

As long as they remain part of the law applicable to financial institutions, the orderly resolution provisions of the DFA will have important adverse effects on insolvency law. In effect, by giving the government the power to resolve any financial firm it believes to be failing, the act has added a whole new policy objective for the resolution of failing firms. Before Dodd-Frank, insolvency law embodied two basic policies—retain the going concern value of the firm and provide a mechanism by which creditors could realize on the assets of an insolvent firm that cannot be saved. The DFA, based on the view that Lehman's bankruptcy was a cause of the ensuing chaos, added a third objective—preserving the stability of the financial system by giving the federal government a role in any insolvency.

As this *Outlook* will discuss, there is a real question whether the orderly resolution of the DFA is any better than bankruptcy as a resolution process. But there is little question that orderly resolution leaves creditors' rights in a state of serious uncertainty. This is because the FDIC, which is the statutorily designated receiver for any firm placed into orderly resolution, is given virtually unlimited discretion to determine who among a firm's creditors gets paid and to what extent.

In the interest of preventing instability in the financial system, the FDIC as receiver can do almost anything it wants with the assets and liabilities of a covered firm. As outlined in the DFA, the orderly resolution process is invoked by the Federal Reserve, the FDIC, and the secretary of the treasury, acting separately. Each must decide that a financial firm is in default or "in danger of default" and that its failure might cause "instability" in the U.S. financial system. If they so decide, but the firm itself does not agree, the secretary can go to a federal district court in a secret proceeding for approval to place the firm involuntarily into the orderly resolution process.

Incredibly—I should probably say absurdly—the court has only one day to render its judgment, after hearing both sides. If it cannot decide in a day, then the orderly resolution process is automatically invoked and the FDIC becomes the receiver for the institution. Obviously, a court would have to be considerably outraged by what the government was trying to do before it would intervene. It would be far easier just to let the day pass. The right to a hearing, therefore, is essentially a nullity, and the idea that the government can at any time take over a financial firm it believes to be "in danger of default" is of questionable constitutionality under the "takings" clause.

There are two additional aspects of this process that are noteworthy. First, the DFA seems to assume that the regulators' approach to the firm, the dispute with the board and management, and the court proceeding can all be kept secret. This is wildly naïve. In our financial system, with its 24/7 financial news cycle, nothing can be kept secret. It might even be a violation of securities law for these discussions to be held and not revealed to the markets. Still, the DFA provides for criminal penalties—a fine of $250,000 or a prison term of up to five years—for anyone who "discloses a determination of the [Treasury] Secretary" to seek a takeover of a firm believed to be in danger of default.[119] So here, as a demonstration of the mindset and naïveté of the DFA's framers, we have our first Official Secrets Act for a matter not involving national security. It's a good thing for its sponsors that the act has a severance clause. A clearer and more meritless restraint on free speech can hardly be imagined.

In a paper published in early 2011, the FDIC argued that its examination of a prospective target would not attract the attention of the markets.[120] Such an examination, it said, would be regarded as "routine." That is a statement one would expect from an agency that has earned its stripes taking over small banks on Friday afternoon and reopening them under new ownership on Monday morning; it is a bit alarming that the FDIC thinks markets will not watch it closely as it goes about its business with firms that have billions of dollars in assets spread throughout the world. Once the rumors start, the markets and counterparties will react. There is a huge premium for those who can get out first. A firm that was stable one day will be unstable the next. Moreover, as its current creditors and counterparties desert it, no new creditors will be willing to come in—even as secured creditors—because the DFA leaves the ultimate discretion on payment of creditors with the FDIC. In the DFA's orderly resolution process, there is no stay and no debtor in possession financing. The assumption is that the government will provide the financing, recovering any losses from other large financial institutions—assuming they are not themselves in financial difficulty at the time—after the fact.

Second, to make the FDIC the statutorily designated receiver for any financial institution was—to put it plainly—a bizarre idea. During the few congressional hearings about the DFA, administration witnesses praised the FDIC as a highly successful agency in resolving insolvent banks. These statements were of questionable accuracy and clearly misleading. The FDIC is required by law

---

119. Wall Street Reform and Consumer Protection Act, HR 4173, 111th Cong. (2010), §202(a)(1)(C).

120. "The Orderly Liquidation of Lehman Brothers Holdings Inc. under the Dodd-Frank Act," *FDIC Quarterly* 5, no. 2 (2011).

to close down banks when their capital falls below 2 percent. If this process works, the agency should not suffer any losses because of bank failures, since the bank should have more assets than liabilities when it is closed. However, the FDIC has suffered losses averaging 25 percent on two-thirds of the banks it has closed in the last three years, and is itself currently underwater. With very few exceptions, the banks the FDIC closes are quite small, operating locally and not internationally, and the closure is done over a weekend, with accounts transferred to a healthy institution by the following Monday. The agency has no experience at all resolving nonbanks, or even bank holding companies. How it would resolve a trillion-dollar insurance holding company like AIG or a $600 billion securities firm like Lehman Brothers is anybody's guess. The only thing sure is that it would not happen over a weekend. It seems likely that the FDIC was selected and put forward as a qualified receiver because no one in the administration or Congress had any better idea.

Once the FDIC is appointed as receiver, it will have many of the extraordinary powers it already has under the Federal Deposit Insurance Act, but with very little of the judicial review available to creditors and others under bankruptcy laws. The agency's authorities as a receiver under the DFA include the power to:

- Transfer all or any portion of the assets and liabilities of a firm in receivership to any person—or merge the institution with any person—without any approvals.[121] Presumably, this would be for the agency's estimate of fair value, but even that would not be subject to judicial review.

- Cherry-pick assets and liabilities without creditors' consent or court review, even if it differentiates between creditors in the same class or treats junior creditors more favorably than senior creditors.[122]

- Set up a bridge institution and transfer to that institution any portion of the assets and liabilities of the firm in resolution.[123] If there is any doubt that the act allows the FDIC to protect creditors—which is really the meaning of a bailout—this provision should resolve

---

121. §(a)(1)(G).
122. §(b)(4).
123. §(h)(1).

it. Liabilities transferred to the bridge bank will be fully protected against loss. The DFA, despite the hoopla, has authorized bailouts instead of preventing them.

The net effect of these powers, and others, is to leave creditors' rights in a state of uncertainty. The FDIC has proposed a regulation that purports to limit its discretion in certain respects, but the statutory language can override that regulation in special circumstances the FDIC declares.

Uncertainty about the insolvency law applicable to a particular financial firm will continue to affect the US economy as long as the orderly resolution provisions of the DFA remain on the statute books. This is because *all* financial firms—not just the largest ones that have been designated for special regulation by the Fed—are potentially subject to this procedure. Section 202 of the act specifically confers authority on the secretary and the other officials noted above to cover *any* financial institution under the orderly resolution provisions. Accordingly, it will be difficult to tell in advance whether a financial firm in danger of failing will be resolved in bankruptcy—where one set of rules applies—or by the FDIC under the DFA's orderly resolution provisions. The key will be whether the Federal Reserve, the FDIC, and the secretary of the treasury determine that the failure of a particular firm at a particular point in the future is likely to cause instability in the financial system.

That decision, however, will be strongly influenced by the conditions when it is made and is unknowable when credit is advanced. If the financial system is stable when such a firm is in danger of failing, it will likely be allowed to go into bankruptcy. On the other hand, the same firm might seem to be a candidate for the orderly resolution process if the financial system is weak and investors are nervous.

The uncertainty about a firm's status will increase the cost of credit for any financial institution that might reasonably be subject to the DFA's orderly resolution rules. Ironically, this might not be true of the very largest firms that are eventually designated as SIFIs. These firms will in effect have been declared too big to fail, and their creditors are likely to believe that they will be better protected in lending to such a firm in the event of the firm's failure. After all, if a firm is designated as systemically important, it is because its distress could—at least in the view of the government officials then in office—cause instability in the financial system. Thus, its creditors could be reasonably confident that regulators will not allow such a firm to fail. In effect, then, the systemically important firms designated by the Financial Stability Oversight Council will have additional advantages over smaller competitors because the uncertainty about their status is much lower.

Finally, one of the key policies of bankruptcy laws is the preservation of the going concern value of a bankrupt institution; for this reason, bankruptcy laws allow the management of a failed firm to reorganize it and maintain it as a going concern. Liquidation is an option in bankruptcy, of course, but usually only when the management cannot persuade creditors that the firm has prospects for a return to profitability. Preserving the going concern value of a firm is especially difficult for financial institutions, because they are uniquely dependent on client relationships and the trust and confidence of their counterparties. But this possibility is cut short by the DFA, which requires the *liquidation* of any financial firm put into the orderly resolution process. Workout and reorganization are not an option.

The reason for this provision, which can only be described as punitive, seems to flow from the mistaken idea that unless a firm is liquidated its shareholders will be bailed out. Certainly this is not true of bankruptcy, where shareholders are generally wiped out and creditors work with the management to reorganize the firm. In contrast, under the DFA, the management of a firm taken over by the FDIC as receiver has to be immediately dismissed. So when the FDIC walks in, it does not know anything about how the firm really operates—who the key people are, where they are located, and how they carry out the successful and essential functions of the business.

To summarize, then, the orderly resolution provisions of the DFA will create uncertainty about which financial firms will actually be covered in the future, raise the financing costs of all financial firms that might be covered, destroy the value of going concerns by requiring liquidation and firing management, and turn over the resolution process for the largest nonbank financial firms to an agency—the FDIC—that has never resolved a nonbank and has not been particularly successful in resolving small banks.

Will It Work?

From the discussion above, it should be clear that the orderly resolution provisions of the DFA will have an adverse effect on the financial system and the economy generally. It is possible that this effect is already being felt in credit restrictions and the unwillingness of businesses to expand and hire new employees. Moreover, these provisions are not likely to help prevent a financial crisis: orderly resolution will not prevent or ameliorate the effects of a common shock, and is likely unnecessary in the absence of a common shock. Nevertheless, it is a legitimate question whether—simply by giving the FDIC the authority to replace the bankruptcy system under certain circumstances—the DFA reduced the likelihood of a financial crisis. In other words, if Lehman had been placed into the orderly resolution process of the DFA, rather than into bankruptcy, would that have reduced the chaos that followed Lehman's bankruptcy?

The answer to this question is fairly obviously no. As noted earlier, Lehman's bankruptcy filing was not itself the cause of the financial crisis; it was the fact that its filing upset the market's expectations—after the rescue of Bear Stearns—about the U.S. government's willingness to rescue all large financial institutions. The context is also important: at the time, because of the common shock associated with the mortgage meltdown and the collapse of the MBS market, virtually all large financial institutions were seen as unstable and possibly insolvent. The CDS market on Lehman's debt shows this confidence; it held steady for almost six months after Bear, blowing out only just before the last weekend when it became apparent that the government had run out of other options and was still refusing to support a Lehman rescue. When Lehman ultimately filed for bankruptcy, all market participants had to reevaluate their counterparties and hoard their cash, bringing lending—even among the largest banks—to a halt. Placing Lehman into the DFA's orderly resolution process would not have changed the fact that the government was not willing to do for Lehman what it did for Bear. The financial crisis would have proceeded exactly the same way as it did in 2008, and been just as severe.

But let's go one step further. Let's assume that Bear had not happened and Lehman was the first large financial institution to be threatened with default. Is there anything about the orderly resolution process that would have made the aftermath of the Lehman failure less chaotic? No, again. In fact, it would have been much worse. As Lehman's time began to run out, the FDIC and others would closely monitor the company, leading market observers to believe that the firm would be placed into the orderly resolution process. The DFA specifies that as far as possible the losses in any resolution should be borne by unsecured creditors. Accordingly, the unsecured creditors would not be hanging about doing nothing; they would be withdrawing whatever funds they possibly could, and the firm would be bleeding liquidity. It would have to be put into the resolution process quickly, before it lost any ability to operate.

What would happen then? Under the DFA, the management would be dismissed and the FDIC would try to run the firm as receiver—without any experience in operating a firm of this type or of this global size. In its 2011 paper,[124] the FDIC makes the claim that if it had had the authority conferred by the DFA before Lehman's failure, it would have been able to preserve Lehman's going concern value by transferring its assets and liabilities to a bridge bank. Let's consider this for a moment. What assets? What liabilities? Who makes this decision, and how fast could it possibly be made? A decision like this about a $600 billion global enterprise could not be made in days or weeks, or even months. Meanwhile, with no stay, creditors would be declaring defaults and insisting on payment. Congressmen and senators would be calling to make sure their favored constituents were at the top of the list for immediate payment or at least transferred to the bridge bank. Chaos would reign.

Is this any better than a bankruptcy filing, in which there would be a creditor stay, politicians would have no influence, and the Lehman management would get protection from creditors while they worked out a reorganization plan? There is much reason for doubt.

So what has the DFA wrought in this area? It has seriously disrupted the universality of the bankruptcy system for nonbank financial institutions, ensured the same chaotic wind-down that occurred with Lehman, and put an inexperienced political agency in charge of the resolution, all without actually addressing the true causes of the financial crisis.

---

124. "The Orderly Liquidation of Lehman Brothers Holdings Inc. under the Dodd-Frank Act."

"Magical Thinking: The Latest Regulation from the Financial Stability Oversight Council"

Originally published November 2011

The Financial Stability Oversight Council (FSOC), following directions in the Dodd-Frank Act, has been pursuing the idea that a financial crisis can be prevented by stringent regulation of large "interconnected" financial institutions. Its latest proposed regulation goes further than ever in establishing the importance of interconnectedness among financial institutions as the source of potential systemic instability. However, the events following the Lehman Brothers bankruptcy show that Lehman's failure had no significant knock-on effects, casting doubt on the idea that Lehman-like nonbank financial firms are too big to fail. The financial crisis was caused not by Lehman's failure but by a common shock to all financial institutions that were holding privately issued mortgage-backed securities based on subprime loans. The way to prevent future financial crises is to prevent future common shocks. The FSOC's pursuit of the bogus interconnectedness theory will, if it results in the designation of certain nonbank financial institutions as systemically important financial institutions, impair our competitive financial system while failing to prevent another financial crisis.

One of the key underlying ideas of the Dodd-Frank Act (DFA)—an idea that has gone viral in the community of financial regulators around the world—is that a goal of financial regulation after the financial crisis was to prevent "systemic risk." But there is a major problem with this idea: one can always imagine a systemic collapse, but identifying the factors that might cause it—that is, systemic risks—is quite another matter. Shortly after the financial crisis, the idea became popular among regulators worldwide—appearing first in a report by the Group of Thirty in January 2009—that large financial institutions such as Lehman Brothers could cause a systemic breakdown if they failed.

Little evidence existed to support this idea, but government officials suggested—and the media widely reported—that these and other institutions were "interconnected," so that the failure of one would cause systemic instability by bringing down others. This notion underlay the rescue of Bear Stearns in March 2008, and it gave rise to the idea that these firms—called systemically important financial institutions (SIFIs)—were too big to fail because their failure would cause another financial crisis. Accordingly, the argument ran, they should be identified and specially regulated and, if they still failed, wound down through a special resolution process outside the bankruptcy system.

That this would give regulators more power over the financial system as a whole should be duly noted; it clearly had a role in attracting support for the DFA, particularly at the Fed. In any event, the notion that that SIFIs existed became generally accepted, and the Obama administration quickly adopted the idea as it framed what became the DFA. However, as this *Outlook* will show, Lehman's failure cast a different and unfavorable light on these ideas. Despite the chaos that followed, the collapse did not result in any significant knock-on effects, providing robust evidence of the DFA's misplaced focus on designating and regulating SIFIs.

As the legislation that was to become the DFA moved through Congress, members of the Obama administration made grandiose claims about the promise of systemic risk regulation. For example, Michael Barr, then an assistant treasury secretary and still a believer in the idea, noted recently, "Today, while the regulatory infrastructure is far from ideal, with too many divided responsibilities, the Financial Stability Oversight Council (FSOC) is accountable to identify threats to financial stability and to address them."[125] The FSOC, in this view, would identify systemic threats in advance and take the necessary action to head them off.

Key sponsors of the DFA as it was being drafted made statements to the same effect. For example, Senator Chris Dodd (D-CT), the principal Senate sponsor of the DFA, said in a speech on the Senate floor on April 29, 2010, "We create an early warning system. . . . I think we all agree that to have the ability to watch and monitor what is occurring, both domestically and internationally, is very important. We have established what we call a systemic risk council that will allow us to observe what is occurring on a regular basis so we can

---

125. Michael S. Barr, "The Dodd-Frank Act: One Year On," Harvard Law School Forum on Corporate Governance and Financial Regulation, July 21, 2011, http://blogs. law.harvard.edu/corpgov/2011/07/21/the-dodd-frank-act-one-year-on (accessed November 14, 2011).

spot these problems before they metastasize and grow into, as we have seen, problems that created as much harm for our economy as the present recession has."[126] Again, the underlying notion was that systemic risk was something that could be recognized in advance, confronted, and eliminated.

These ideas now appear to have been abandoned, with the administration taking the position that the objective of the FSOC is simply to identify and shore up SIFIs against failure, through stringent regulation. This became clear in an exchange between Treasury Secretary Timothy Geithner and Senator Richard Shelby (R-AL), the ranking member of the Senate Banking Committee, at a committee hearing on October 6, 2011. Senator Shelby asked whether the FSOC had made progress in identifying the threats to the stability of the financial system that had been advertised as a purpose of the council during the framing of the DFA. Geithner responded that this was not what the FSOC was doing: "The basic strategy that underpins the design of this [systemic risk] framework is not a strategy that depends on the wisdom and foresight of government officials. It is a strategy that relies on building much stronger shock absorbers, safeguards in the system so that we are protected against a whole range of potential risk."[127]

In other words, the FSOC will not be seeking the scent of systemic risk but instead will simply be attempting to identify nonbank financial firms that are SIFIs and ensure that they are effectively regulated to prevent another systemic breakdown. Thus, the questions now are whether the DFA, with its focus on SIFIs, has created an effective structure for preventing a financial crisis in the future and, more particularly, whether the failure of a large financial institution can cause a financial crisis. Like so many other accepted ideas about the financial crisis, this idea has not been explored in any depth. In this *Outlook,* I will show not only that the interconnections theory is wrong, but that the absence of significant knock-on effects from Lehman's bankruptcy demonstrates that nonbank financial institutions—even those designated as SIFIs—are highly unlikely to cause a financial crisis if they fail.

This means that there is no need to identify SIFIs, no need for special regulation of nonbank financial institutions, and no need for a special resolution process to resolve large nonbank financial institutions, an idea explored fully

126. Senator Chris Dodd (D-CT), Senate floor debate, April 29, 2010.

127. Senate Banking Committee, Financial Stability Oversight Council, Annual Report to Congress, 112th Congress, October 6, 2011.

in my August–September *Outlook*.[128] For all practical purposes, these issues are relevant only for nonbank financial institutions, the focus of the following discussion. The DFA has already determined that any bank or bank holding company with assets greater than $40 billion will be considered a SIFI. (This is the magic number because every Federal Reserve Bank district contains at least one bank or bank holding company of that size. The fundamental impulses of the regulatory bureaucracy never change, lending credence to the idea that the SIFI notion is yet another way for regulators to enlarge their authority.)

The Notice of Proposed Rulemaking (NPR) the FSOC promulgated on October 11, 2011, is fully consistent with Geithner's statement about FSOC strategy. This NPR is the FSOC's second attempt to clarify the standards and criteria it would use to identify SIFIs. The first was figuratively hooted down because it did little beyond repeating the statutory language. The new version, while more detailed, still misses the mark. It makes clear that the FSOC has not fully understood, or even seriously considered, what happened after the bankruptcy of Lehman Brothers and how that aftermath should affect its analysis.

"Common Shock" and the Financial Crisis

The August-September *Outlook* fully addressed the causes of the post-Lehman chaos, but I will summarize them here. According to data gathered by Professor Robert Shiller of Yale University, a massive ten-year housing price bubble began to develop in the United States in 1997.[129] By 2007, when it began to deflate, the bubble was almost ten times larger than any previous bubble. Because of U.S. housing policy, which mandated that, by 2008, mortgage credit be made available to borrowers at or below the median income level, half of all mortgages in this bubble—27 million—were subprime or otherwise weak and risky loans.[130] As is true of all bubbles, this bubble's growth suppressed delinquencies and defaults; people who could not meet their mortgage obligations were able

---

128. Peter J. Wallison, "The Error at the Heart of the Dodd-Frank Act," AEI *Financial Services Outlook* (August–September 2011), www.aei.org/outlook/101077. (See p. 470 of this book.)

129. Robert J. Shiller, *Irrational Exuberance,* 2nd ed. (Princeton, NJ: Princeton University Press, 2006).

130. Peter J. Wallison, *Dissent from the Majority Report of the Financial Crisis Inquiry Commission,* January 14, 2011, www.aei.org/files/2011/01/26/Wallisondissent.pdf.

to refinance and extend their obligations or sell their homes for more than the principal amount of the mortgage.

By 2002, investors were beginning to notice that these high-yielding sub-prime mortgages were not showing the delinquencies and defaults normally associated with such low-quality loans. In other words, they had very favorable risk-adjusted returns, setting off strong investor demand, especially among banks and other financial institutions, for privately issued mortgage-backed securities (PMBS) based on these subprime and other low-quality loans. This demand resulted in the securitization and sale of about 7.8 million subprime loans, backing almost $2 trillion in PMBS and totaling slightly less than 30 percent of the 27 million subprime and other risky loans outstanding. The rest of the loans were on the balance sheets of U.S. government agencies such as Fannie Mae and Freddie Mac, which had made these loans in compliance with the U.S. government regulations noted above.

When the housing bubble began to deflate in 2007, the unprecedented number of delinquencies and defaults on both the government-induced and the privately securitized mortgages drove down the values of houses nationwide, as well as the PMBS backed by subprime mortgages on these now-devalued homes. Investors, shocked by the unprecedented number of defaults, fled the PMBS market, dropping PMBS prices to near zero. Mark-to-market accounting then came into play for banks and other financial institutions, requiring them to write down the value of their PMBS holdings to market values. This substantially reduced their regulatory capital, and because PMBS could no longer be used for financing purposes the liquidity of these firms was also impaired. No wonder the media dubbed these securities "toxic assets."

This produced what scholars know as a "common shock"—a condition in which a large number of financial institutions are hit by the sudden loss of value in a widely held asset.[131] In this case, many of the world's largest financial institutions were subject to this shock, and the writedowns in their assets required by mark-to-market accounting made them appear weak and unstable. The widespread instability among financial firms made it appear to investors and other market participants as though the whole financial system was disintegrating.

---

131. George G. Kaufman and Kenneth E. Scott, "What Is Systemic Risk and Do Bank Regulators Contribute to It?" *The Independent Review* 7, no. 3 (2003): 379.

In March 2008, with investors and other market participants unsettled and near panic, the U.S. government rescued Bear Stearns, the smallest of the large investment banks on Wall Street. This briefly calmed the markets, but it also caused enormous moral hazard by leading many firms to believe that they did not have to dilute their shareholders by raising significant amounts of additional capital. It also led many investors and other market participants to believe that the U.S. government had established a policy of rescuing any large financial institution in financial distress. When the government did not rescue Lehman in September 2008, investors and market participants were shocked; financial institutions, fearing that investors and depositors would seek return of their funds, began to hoard cash; banks stopped lending to one another. This is what we know as the financial crisis.

The Administration and Congress Get It Wrong

This brief history shows that three elements were at the heart of the financial crisis—a mortgage and housing price meltdown as the bubble deflated, mark-to-market accounting for financial institutions, and a resulting common shock to all financial institutions that held substantial amounts of PMBS. If the framers of the DFA had properly understood this sequence of events, the legislation would have been markedly different. They would have chosen to take steps to prevent another financial crisis by reducing the likelihood of common shocks and modifying mark-to-market accounting rules so as not to exacerbate any common shock that does occur. In a forthcoming paper, for example, Roberta Romano of Yale Law School posits that regulation itself, by reducing diversity among regulated institutions, could be a source of widespread breakdowns similar to a common shock.[132] Exploring ideas of this kind, rather than racing willy-nilly to impose new regulations, would have resulted from a more careful look at what happened after Lehman's bankruptcy.

The Obama administration and the framers of the DFA clearly did not see common shock as a cause of the financial crisis. Creating an agency (the FSOC) to designate certain nonbank financial firms as SIFIs and consign them

---

132. Roberta Romano, "For Diversity in the International Regulation of Financial Institutions: Rethinking the Basel Architecture" (forthcoming, Yale Law School, NBER and ECGI, October 30, 2011 draft).

to stringent Fed regulation makes sense only if the administration and its allies in Congress believed that the failure of Lehman was the cause of the financial crisis. To draw this conclusion, they uncritically accepted the idea—initially used to justify the rescue of Bear Stearns—that large nonbank financial institutions were interconnected and that the failure of one could drag down others.

Lehman—although unquestionably the kind of large nonbank financial institution that would be classified as a SIFI—did not cause any insolvencies among other financial institutions when it failed. The only institution that suffered serious losses was the Primary Reserve Fund, a money market mutual fund that continued to hold large amounts of Lehman's commercial paper, in the mistaken belief—probably induced by moral hazard—that the U.S. government would rescue Lehman as it had rescued Bear. The fund "broke the buck" (was unable to redeem its shares at the promised $1.00 per share) and in the panicky condition of the market at that time set off an unwarranted run on other money market funds.

Ironically, then, there was some real value in the catastrophe of the Lehman collapse. It provided strong empirical evidence that a large nonbank financial institution can fail without dragging down others. Previously, in cases like those of Bear Stearns and Long-Term Capital Management, the government—contending that the collapse of large financial institutions would bring on a financial meltdown—had taken or encouraged others to take steps to rescue large, failing financial institutions. The resulting severe moral hazard made the too-big-to-fail problem worse. It is worth noting at this point that the government's determination that a financial institution could not be allowed to fail is not evidence that this is true. Regulators are notoriously fearful that they will be blamed for chaotic conditions in the market they regulate and thus lean heavily in favor of bailouts and rescues.

Even the credit default swap (CDS) market—cited by many as the very "shadowy" heart of the interconnections problem—continued to function normally after Lehman's failure. Lehman was a major player in the CDS market, and at the time of its bankruptcy had 900,000 outstanding CDS contracts. Most of these were canceled by Lehman's counterparties—as provided in bankruptcy law—and the remaining ones became claims against the bankrupt estate. CDSs written on Lehman itself were settled five weeks after its bankruptcy by the exchange of less than $6 billion among hundreds of counterparties. As far as we know, no Lehman counterparty failed because Lehman failed or could not make good on its CDS obligations.

Some will argue that the steps the U.S. government took after the Lehman collapse prevented other failures. The Troubled Asset Relief Program (TARP) and the Federal Deposit Insurance Corporation's (FDIC) guarantee of loans to or from financial institutions are examples of this assistance; certainly they helped stabilize the financial system in that chaotic period. However, the goal and result of these efforts was not to shore up the finances of financial institutions weakened by Lehman's inability to meet its obligations, but rather to restore market confidence. This confidence had been lost in the common shock brought on by the mortgage meltdown and was further eroded by the government's irrational failure to rescue Lehman after it had rescued Bear.

That the government's actions were aimed only at restoring market confidence is shown by the fact that the first funds made available under TARP were not provided until October 28, 2008, about six weeks after Lehman's failure. By that time, any firm that had been mortally wounded by Lehman's collapse would have filed for bankruptcy. Moreover, most of the TARP funds were repaid by the largest institutions—with Fed approval—only eight months later, in mid-June 2009. If the firms that took these funds had needed them to cover losses on Lehman, they could not have recovered from those losses in only eight months. Similarly, the FDIC's guarantees allowed otherwise solvent firms to borrow but did not fill in holes in their balance sheets caused by losses on Lehman.

So the interconnections theory is simply wrong. Interconnections undoubtedly exist among financial institutions, but it appears that they are not so significant that the failure of a large nonbank financial institution like Lehman will drag others down. This evidence is especially robust because Lehman's failure occurred at a time when the entire financial system was in the midst of a widespread common shock, when the failure of one large institution like Lehman could have been expected to have the most devastating effect. If Lehman's failure did not have knock-on consequences then, it is highly unlikely that it would have any serious consequences during more stable times. From this, we can conclude that nonbank financial institutions are not as a general matter too big to fail and should be allowed to go into bankruptcy like any other insolvent institution.

Accordingly, if an agency like the FSOC is to have any value for preventing systemic risk, it would be to spot the cases where the risk of a common shock is developing. By recognizing these conditions, such an agency could take appropriate action. However, the latest NPR shows that the FSOC is barking up the wrong tree by pursuing its misguided interconnections theory.

The Magical Thinking of the FSOC

This is easily demonstrated by an analysis of the NPR, where the interconnections idea has a central role. The proposal creates a three-stage "determination process" for deciding whether a nonbank company is a SIFI and requires stringent Fed regulation. Stage 1 narrows the search to a smaller set of companies by using quantitative thresholds (for example, size) to identify the nonbank financial institutions that deserve further scrutiny. In Stage 2, "the Council will conduct a comprehensive analysis of the potential for the identified nonbank financial companies to pose a threat to U.S. financial stability."[133] The firms that remain after this "comprehensive analysis" will then be more thoroughly examined, with the use of "quantitative and qualitative information collected directly from the nonbank financial company" in Stage 3.

In Stage 3, the FSOC will apply what it calls an "analytical framework" consisting of six factors: size, interconnectedness, substitutability, leverage, liquidity risk and maturity mismatch, and existing regulatory scrutiny. It is immediately clear that in this framework only size, interconnectedness, and substitutability are important for the SIFI determination. The other three factors—leverage, liquidity risk and maturity mismatch, and existing regulatory scrutiny—are important only after size, interconnectedness, and substitutability set the institution apart as a potential SIFI. As the proposed regulation says, "leverage, liquidity risk and maturity mismatch seek to assess the vulnerability of a nonbank financial company to financial distress."[134] Thus, a firm that has fifty-to-one leverage would not be considered a SIFI—despite its excessive leverage—unless that leverage level might create some threat to the stability of the financial system, which would be realistic only if it had one or more of the other three defining factors: size, interconnectedness, or substitutability. For purposes of this analysis, however, we can leave out substitutability, which refers to the ability of an institution to provide a critical function or unique service to the market—by definition a limited category. If the lack of a substitute for an institution's services is a

---

133. Financial Stability Oversight Council, *Authority to Require Supervision and Regulation of Certain Nonbank Financial Companies,* 18–19, www.treasury.gov/initiatives/fsoc/Documents/Nonbank%20Designation%20NPR%20%20Final%20with%20web%20disclaimer.pdf (accessed November 10, 2011).

134. Ibid., 17.

problem, Congress could authorize the Fed to decide whether the market could function without these services, and if not, after appropriate safeguards such as court review, the Fed could impose the regulation it believes is necessary.

So we are down to interconnections and size. We know what size is, but what are "interconnections," and why are they important? This term clearly refers to mutual obligations of various kinds. These could be credit arrangements—with one institution a creditor of another—or counterparty arrangements, in which institutions are obligated or exposed to one another through a credit default swap or similar transaction. Exposure is important because the NPR posits only three "channels" through which a SIFI's "material distress" might be transmitted to the financial system as a whole: exposure, asset liquidation, and furnishing a critical function or service. Again, we can eliminate the final criterion and focus on exposure and asset liquidation as the two ways that a SIFI's material distress could affect the financial system at large.

The NPR argues that the material distress of a failing firm may cause losses to other firms because of the interconnections that are associated with exposure: "A nonbank financial company's creditors, counterparties, investors, or other market participants have exposure to the nonbank financial company that is significant enough *to materially impair those creditors, counterparties, investors, or other market participants and thereby pose a threat to U.S. financial stability*" [emphasis added].[135] This is the classic interconnections scenario but does not reflect in any way what actually happened when Lehman failed.

In describing the adverse effects of asset liquidation, the NPR outlines the following hypothetical situation: "A nonbank financial company holds assets that, if liquidated quickly, would significantly disrupt trading or funding in key markets or cause significant losses or funding problems for other firms with similar holdings due to falling asset prices."[136] In other words, a SIFI's material financial distress could cause it to liquidate assets. This in turn would have significant adverse effects on the value of the assets of other firms. Again, this is not what happened when Lehman was in danger of failing; if it did sell assets, its sales were not significant nor what caused PMBS values to decline. Indeed, it was the earlier decline in the value of these assets that caused Lehman (and others) to look weak, illiquid, and possibly insolvent.

---

135. Ibid., 53.
136. Ibid.

It is worth noting, however, that the asset liquidation scenario acknowledges that the loss of value in widely held assets can have a substantial adverse effect on other firms—the very definition of a common shock—but does not seem to recognize that a common shock arising out of the collapse of the PMBS market well before Lehman failed was the triggering event of the financial crisis.

Remarkably, the FSOC also recognizes that a SIFI's failure could be more destructive in an environment created by a common shock. "For purposes of considering whether a nonbank financial company could pose a threat to the U.S. financial stability," the NPR states, "the Council intends to assess the impact of the nonbank financial company's material financial distress in the context of a period of overall stress in the financial services industry and in a weak macroeconomic environment. The Council believes this is appropriate because in such a context, a nonbank financial company's distress may have a greater effect on U.S. financial stability."[137]

Yet, even though the Council apparently understands the significance of a "weak macroeconomic environment" in determining the likelihood that a failed or failing SIFI would create a financial crisis, it did not reach the obvious conclusion—that in the Lehman case, a SIFI had failed in the midst of a seriously distressed macroeconomic environment without any knock-on effects. Instead, it continues to pursue an idea based on nothing more than rank speculation. This is the very essence of magical thinking—pursuing an idea that has no evidentiary or empirical support while ignoring obvious facts that show it is heading in the wrong direction.

In summary, if we examine what actually happened after Lehman, we can see that neither the exposure of counterparties to Lehman nor its asset liquidation caused substantial losses to other firms—or, at least, losses that caused those other firms (with the exception of the Reserve Fund) to become materially impaired. Because Lehman's failure had no significant knock-on effects, the only conclusion we can reasonably draw is that nonbank financial institutions, even those large enough to be SIFIs, can be allowed to fail without danger to the financial system. They are not, therefore, too big to fail.

Nevertheless, the FSOC plunges ahead. If it continues on this course, it will make no contribution to preventing a future financial crisis while—for

---

137. Ibid., 54.

reasons outlined below—causing serious harm to the competitiveness of the U.S. financial system.

(Wrong) Ideas Have (Bad) Consequences

In September 2009, former Federal Reserve chairman Paul Volcker appeared before the House Financial Services Committee and declared his opposition to designating specific firms as SIFIs:

> The approach proposed by the Treasury is to designate in advance financial institutions "whose size, leverage, and interconnection could pose a threat to financial stability if it failed." Those institutions, bank or non-bank, connected to a commercial firm or not, would be subject to particularly strict and conservative prudential supervision and regulation. The Federal Reserve would be designated as consolidated supervisor. The precise criteria for designation as "systemically important" have not, so far as I know, been set out. However, the clear implication of such designation whether officially acknowledged or not will be that such institutions, in whole or in part, will be sheltered by access to a Federal safety net in time of crisis; they will be broadly understood to be "too big to fail."[138]

This testimony by the respected Volcker failed to dissuade the committee or Congress from empowering the FSOC in just this way. Volcker's principal concern expressed that day was that the designation of nonbank financial firms as SIFIs would extend the financial safety net beyond banks. He added, "What all this amounts to is an unintended and unanticipated extension of the official 'safety net,' an arrangement designed decades ago to protect the stability of the commercial banking system. The obvious danger is that with the passage of time, risk-taking will be encouraged and efforts at prudential restraint will be resisted. Ultimately, the possibility of further crises—even greater crises—will increase."[139]

---

138. Paul Volcker, Testimony before the House Financial Services Committee, September 24, 2009, 8, http://financialservices.house.gov/Media/file/hearings/111/volcker 9_24_2010.pdf (accessed November 13, 2011).

139. Ibid., 6.

However, a more important issue exists. Volcker is completely correct that the government's designation of certain nonbank financial institutions as SIFIs will mean that they will have been declared too big to fail. Despite the lack of obvious justification for such a policy, it will clearly signal to the world that the government will take steps to prevent the failure of these special firms. This will give them a funding advantage over their smaller competitors because creditors will immediately recognize that their loans to SIFIs are safer bets than loans to others, as government regulation will reduce their risk-taking and be more likely to bail out their creditors if they fail.

These funding advantages have already appeared in banking, where differences of fifty to eighty-nine basis points have already been found between the funding costs of large and small banks. If these large-firm advantages are spread to the other financial industries through the designation of insurers, finance companies, holding companies, hedge funds, and others as SIFIs, it will change the competitive nature of our financial system. We have seen this movie before. Because of their perceived government backing, Fannie Mae and Freddie Mac were able to borrow funds at rates that enabled them to drive all competition from the secondary mortgage market.

These competitive advantages can extend beyond funding. In the highly competitive insurance market, for example, many small and midsize property and casualty firms compete effectively with the largest companies. Imagine what the industry will look like if the FSOC declares that two or three insurers or their holding companies are too big to fail and subjects them to special regulation by the Fed. Customers will feel more secure buying insurance from these large, federally regulated and protected firms than from others, seriously distorting competition in the insurance market. The same insidious process will occur in every other market where the FSOC declares one or more companies a danger to stability if they fail.

Some will argue that the Fed's stringent regulation will actually be so costly to these large companies that they will get no benefit from the SIFI designation. Indeed, from all indications, large companies are busily making presentations to the FSOC, arguing that they are not too big to fail—certainly a signal that they do not see any advantages in the designation. Unfortunately, that is not very comforting. All firms would prefer to avoid regulation, especially regulation that the DFA terms "stringent," but if these firms are correct and the added regulation is actually more costly than the funding advantages, conditions could be even worse.

Then, these large, well-funded companies in every financial industry will gradually lose the competitive race to unregulated or more lightly regulated and nimble competitors. In the end, the government will have to resolve the so-called SIFIs, now unprofitable but essentially drifting hulks in the channels they have come to dominate, and it will likely find reasons to protect their creditors. The taxpayers may again be called upon to bail out these firms (think GM and Chrysler) because they have become such large employers and such important service providers that their wind-down and liquidation (as required by Dodd-Frank) would have a major adverse effect on the services provided for consumers.

The only way the regulatory costs imposed on SIFIs can turn out to be neutral in this scenario is if they exactly balance the funding advantage. That has not been true in banking, and it is unlikely to be true in the regulation of other kinds of financial institutions.

These are the likely consequences of the course that the FSOC is currently pursuing. If, despite the evidence of Lehman, it decides that large firms are interconnected in the way described in the NPR, competitive conditions in the financial services field will be forever changed, without any protection against the kind of common shock that can cause another financial crisis.

"Empty Promise:
The Holes in the Administration's
Housing Finance Reform Plan"

Originally published February 2012

In the year since U.S. Treasury Secretary Timothy Geithner announced the Obama administration's options for reforming the housing market, the administration has said and done nothing to indicate which option it prefers or how its plan will be implemented. In early February, however, Geithner reported to the Financial Stability Oversight Council (FSOC) that the administration wants to make progress on housing finance reform this year, winding down government-sponsored enterprises (GSEs) Fannie Mae and Freddie Mac and bringing private capital back into the market. For any such plan to be credible, it must do much more than wind down the GSEs. The Federal Housing Administration (FHA) creates competitive obstacles to the revival of the private securitization market that are at least as serious as the GSEs, and because of the Dodd-Frank Act a number of formidable legal obstacles now exist that must be cleared away before a private securitization market will come back. If the administration is serious, its plan must address all these issues.

In a report to the Financial Stability Oversight Council in early February, Geithner declared, "We also want to make progress this year in building the foundation for reforms to the mortgage market in the United States, including a path for winding down the GSEs. . . . Our plan will wind down the GSEs and bring private capital back into the market, reducing the government's direct role in the housing market and better targeting our support toward first-time homebuyers and low-and-moderate income Americans."[140] Unfortunately, for his statement to be credible, Geithner has to recognize that winding down Fannie and Freddie

---

140. U.S. Department of the Treasury, "Remarks by Treasury Secretary Tim Geithner on the State of Financial Reform," transcript, February 2, 2012, www.treasury.gov/press-center/press-releases/Pages/tg1408.aspx (accessed February 27, 2012).

will not in itself materially assist the revival of the private securitization market. Other steps are necessary, including reducing the role of the FHA and substantially changing the housing provisions incorporated in the Dodd-Frank Act.

Geithner's statement came almost one year to the day after he had announced a series of options for doing exactly what he just outlined—winding down the GSEs and reducing the government's role in the housing market. That original plan, announced on February 11, 2011, contained three options, (1) eliminating the government's role entirely, except for low- and moderate-income housing; (2) keeping the government as a backstop in case of another financial collapse; and (3) replacing the GSEs with a program in which a government agency would guarantee mortgage-backed securities issued by privately capitalized firms. It also proposed to limit the role of the FHA to providing loans for low-income housing. In the year that has passed, the administration has steadfastly refused to indicate which of these options it actually favored, and Geithner's most recent statement—except for the reference to reducing the government's "direct" role—does not provide any further guidance.

Shortly after Geithner's statement last year, Alex Pollock, Ed Pinto, and I released a white paper (the WPP white paper) that followed up on the administration's apparent willingness to consider a wholly private system of housing finance.[141] The plan detailed how a private market would work and how to eliminate Fannie Mae and Freddie Mac and reduce the role of the FHA while stimulating the revival of a private housing finance system. Political agreement between the House Republicans and the administration on a private housing finance system is a real possibility, but the administration must first express an interest in such a conversation, which it has not done.

The lack of any progress on housing finance reform in the past year was emphasized in late February when the Federal Housing Finance Agency (FHFA), the GSEs' regulator, issued what it called a "strategic plan" for their future.[142]

---

141. Peter J. Wallison, Alex J. Pollock, and Edward J. Pinto, *Taking the Government out of Housing Finance: Principles for Reforming the Housing Finance Market,* AEI White Paper, March 24, 2011, available at www.aei.org/papers/economics/financial-services/housing-finance/taking-the-government-out-of-housing-finance-principles-for-reforming-the-housing-finance-market-paper/.

142. Federal Housing Finance Agency, *A Strategic Plan for Enterprise Conservatorships: The Next Chapter in a Story That Needs an Ending,* February 21, 2012, www.fhfa.gov/webfiles/23344/StrategicPlanConservatorshipsFINAL.pdf (accessed February 27, 2012).

Given its subordinate position within the administration, FHFA's plan could not go beyond the terms the administration laid out a year ago, but it noted out that its limited recommendations were consistent with both the administration's year-old plan and the leading congressional proposals introduced to date. The FHFA cannot do much to move the ball forward until the administration and congressional Republicans come to an agreement about the major features of the housing finance system they want in the future.

Certainly, winding down the GSEs is an essential precursor to the revival of a private securitization market. However, it is not sufficient. The FHA is also a major player, especially for home purchase loans (as distinguished from refinances) and poses the same competitive problem as the GSEs for the revival of a private system. Between 2004 and 2010, the FHA has increased its market share in home purchase loans from 9 percent to 42 percent. Other government agencies—Veterans Administration and the Department of Agriculture (Rural Housing Administration)—had another 12 percent.[143]

In November 2011, under pressure from the National Association of Realtors, Congress increased to $729,750 the size of the mortgages FHA is permitted to insure. This gives the FHA an even wider scope of operations in the housing market than the GSEs, which are limited to acquiring mortgages no larger than $625,500. Accordingly, without FHA reform, including limits on its growth, the agency could take over the market now still dominated by Fannie and Freddie. Under those circumstances, winding down the GSEs will not substantially reduce either the amount of moral hazard in the U.S. housing finance system or the government's liability for housing losses. That would simply move it from the GSEs to the FHA.

The urgency of reviving the private-sector securitization system was emphasized in the FHFA's strategic plan, which noted, "No private sector infrastructure exists today that is capable of securitizing the $100 billion per month in new mortgages being originated."[144] Thus, an administration proposal to get housing finance reform moving is essential, but if the administration's plan for reviving the private securitization market is to have any credibility it must also provide a

---

143. Mortgage Bankers Association, "2004-2010 HMDA Home Purchase Owner-Occupied by Borrower Race," January 13, 2012 (draft).

144. Federal Housing Finance Agency, *A Strategic Plan for Enterprise Conservatorships,* 2.

mechanism for reducing the FHA's role, as well as that of the GSEs. Finally, and equally important, it will be necessary to change the regulatory landscape that now—after the Dodd-Frank Act (DFA)—is hostile to private securitization and the revival of a private securitization market.

This *Outlook* will address each of these issues.

Competition from the GSEs and FHA

The GSEs and FHA are serious competitors for a private housing finance system because they are subsidized by the taxpayers, who take much of the mortgage credit risk associated with their activities. Taxpayers have already invested more than $180 billion in the GSEs to keep them afloat, and the total loss on these two firms will most likely eventually reach $300 billion. As long as the taxpayers are required to take these risks, the presence of Fannie and Freddie in the housing finance markets will impede the revival of a private securitization market. No private securitizer can hope to survive when its competitors are backed by the government and, ultimately, the taxpayers.

The same is true of the FHA, which insures mortgages that are then securitized through Ginnie Mae, another government agency subsidized by the taxpayers. As described in a recent *Outlook,* if the FHA were subject to the accounting standards that are applied to private mortgage insurers, it would be deeply insolvent.[145] The only reason it is still able to function is that its insurance obligations are backed by the full faith and credit of the U.S. government. In other words, the taxpayers will eventually be required to recapitalize the FHA just as they have had to recapitalize the GSEs.

One obstacle to winding down the GSEs and reducing the FHA's role is the mistaken idea that, without a government guarantee of the credit risk, institutional investors will not be willing to buy mortgage-backed securities (MBS). The truth is very nearly the opposite; as long as the government continues to take the credit risk on mortgages, the institutional investors with the largest long-term investment portfolios—insurance companies and private pension plans—will

---

145. Peter J. Wallison and Edward J. Pinto, "Bet the House: Why the FHA is Going (for) Broke," AEI *Financial Services Outlook* (December 2011/January 2012), www.aei. org/outlook/economics/financial-services/housing-finance/bet-the-house-why-the-fha-is-going-for-broke/.

not be interested in acquiring these securities. Institutional investors are compensated for taking credit risk, allowing them to earn the higher returns they need to meet their obligations. Thus, insurance companies and private-pension funds buy corporate bonds and other fixed-income securities, which carry no government guarantee and in some cases involve substantial credit risk.

The data on this are very clear. According to the Federal Reserve's flow of funds reports, in 2006, at the height of the mortgage boom, these private institutional investors had total assets of $12.1 trillion.[146] Of this sum, $2.4 trillion, or 19 percent, was invested in corporate and foreign bonds. These instruments carry no credit support from governments and are attractive to institutional investors precisely because they earn the yields they need by taking credit risk. Financial instruments that do not involve credit risk—because the government is taking it—are not attractive because their yields are too low. Thus, of the $12.1 trillion invested by insurers and private pension plans in 2006, only $768 billion (6.3 percent) was invested in GSEs or other government-backed MBS.[147]

Similarly, as of the end of the third quarter of 2011, the same private institutional investors held assets totaling $12.3 trillion, of which $670 billion (5.4 percent) were invested in GSEs or other government-backed MBS, while $2.9 trillion (23 percent) were invested in corporate and foreign bonds.[148] In other words, the largest institutional investors in the United States have no significant interest in government-backed MBS. Instead, they prefer to bear the credit risk of corporate securities that produce the higher yields they need to meet their obligations over time.

This suggests that private institutional investors such as insurance companies and private pension funds would have a strong interest in a private market in mortgages and MBS, where they, rather than the taxpayers, could take the credit risk associated with mortgages. Indeed, this would be a rare win-win for the United States because it would allow these private investors to diversify their portfolios away from corporate debt, helping them achieve more financial stability while making large sums available to the housing market. And needless to say, it would remove from the taxpayers the burden of mortgage credit risk.

---

146. Federal Reserve Board of Governors, "Flow of Funds Accounts of the United States," December 8, 2011, 116, 117, 118, www.federalreserve.gov/releases/z1/Current/ (accessed February 27, 2012).

147. Ibid.

148. Ibid.

Another obstacle to winding down the GSEs is the idea that a government-backed mortgage is less expensive for homeowners than a private mortgage. However, this is true only because the taxpayers are taking the mortgage credit risk. If the government charged for the credit risk it assumes through the GSEs and FHA/Ginnie Mae system, its mortgages would cost roughly the same as private mortgages.

This also leaves unconsidered the unmeasured costs of the financial crises that occur when the losses that accumulate in the government's housing finance system finally come to light. This occurred in the late 1980s and early 1990s, when the savings-and-loan industry collapsed, causing a recession and many job losses, plus about $150 billion in taxpayer expenses in absorbing the losses of the savings and loans. It most recently occurred again when the 13.4 million subprime and other weak mortgages held or guaranteed by the GSEs defaulted in unprecedented numbers, driving down housing prices and causing both a worldwide financial crisis and a painful recession that continues in the United States. The cost to taxpayers thus far for bailing out the GSEs is $180 billion, with estimates of additional losses up to $300 billion.

High GSE and FHA Conforming Loan Limits. Winding down the GSEs and FHA is particularly important because their current conforming loan limits were set when housing prices were considerably higher. Over the last several years, these prices have fallen almost everywhere in the United States, with declines of 30 to 40 percent in some areas. As a result, the prior conforming loan limits, which still apply to Fannie and Freddie, now cover a much larger portion of the housing market than they did before the financial crisis. High conforming loan limits reduce the number of mortgages available for private securitization and thus restrict the scope of any developing securitization business. Reducing loan limits can be done in stages, perhaps over five years, but it must be outlined in a law so that private securitizers will have confidence that if they make the necessary investments to start a securitization business, the available private market will be large enough to make that investment profitable.[149]

In November 2011, Congress dealt a serious blow to the idea that the scope of government's housing finance activities could be reduced. When it was enacted in 2008, the Housing and Economic Recovery Act (HERA) provided that

---

149. Wallison, Pollock, and Pinto, *Taking the Government out of Housing Finance,* 36.

the conforming loan limits applicable to the GSEs and the FHA would be reduced from $729,750 to $625,500 on October 1, 2011. This step reflected a recognition that Congress had gone too far in bringing high-cost mortgages into the government's orbit. At the higher level, mortgages on homes costing almost $1 million would have been eligible for government backing by both the GSEs and FHA.

HERA's reduction of the conforming loan limit was a step in the right direction. If it had been left in place, the private market would have responded by moving into the areas from which the government had withdrawn, probably through the purchase of whole mortgages. Indeed, as the date approached, there were strong signs that the private sector was willing to increase its originations for mortgages above the new $625,500 limit. However, in November Congress returned the loan limit for the FHA to its previous level of $729,750, while leaving the GSEs' limit at $625,500.

This reversal sent a very ominous signal to the private sector; if Congress was willing to reverse itself on a limit already embodied in legislation, the risks of entering the field were even higher than anyone had anticipated. This action seriously set back hopes for a private market revival, a short-term victory for the realtors that will have a long-term adverse effect on home sales. To its credit, in this instance the administration had opposed the loan limit increase but was unable to persuade its Democratic allies in the Senate.

Even if the GSEs and FHA are substantially wound down, several provisions of the DFA—which the Obama administration designed and steadfastly defends—make a revival of the private securitization market highly unlikely, and these must be cleared away before a private securitization market can develop. Ironically, although many have remarked that the DFA does nothing to reform the GSEs, very few have noticed that it contains provisions that also effectively prevent the return of a private-sector securitization system. Accordingly, the administration's words about housing finance reform—insofar as they promise a revival of the private securitization market—are simply not credible unless it is willing to open the DFA for amendments in the areas I will discuss.

Dodd-Frank's Impediments to a Robust Private Securitization System

The DFA dramatically increases the competitive advantage the GSEs and FHA have over private securitization. The act substantially reconfigures the securitization process by creating the concept of a high-quality mortgage—called a qualified residential mortgage (QRM)—and requires the sponsor of the securitization to retain 5 percent of the risk if the mortgages in a securitization pool do not qualify as QRMs. This, in itself, will significantly impede private securitization, as I will describe, but the act contains additional provisions that will also impair the securitization process or discourage firms from entering the business.

Exemptions for FHA and the GSEs from Risk Retention. The act exempts the FHA from the risk-retention requirement, further widening the gap between privately securitized mortgages and those insured by the FHA. By creating a path for the securitization of mortgages without a 5 percent risk-retention requirement, the act also encourages the growth of a market in low-quality mortgages.

Although the DFA did not exempt the GSEs from the risk-retention requirement, the initial draft of the regulations under the act extended the exemption to Fannie and Freddie. This will have the same effect as the act's exemption of the FHA, widening the gap between GSE and private-sector prices and encouraging the securitization of lower-quality mortgages through the GSEs as well as the FHA. A private securitization market will not develop as long as these provisions remain in effect and the FHA and GSEs are able to insure or securitize any substantial portion of the mortgage market.

Risk Retention and Capital. The DFA provisions that mandate a 5 percent risk retention for mortgage securitizers were originally intended to penalize those who securitize low-quality mortgages. That idea has many flaws that go well beyond exempting the FHA and possibly the GSEs from the risk-retention requirement. Although minimum standards for mortgage quality make sense and some standards of this kind are included in the WPP white paper,[150] the risk-retention idea will make it difficult for any firm other than a large bank to carry on a private securitization business.

If a QRM is ultimately defined as a high-quality or bulletproof mortgage, most mortgages will not qualify, requiring securitizers to retain 5 percent of the risk. Under these circumstances, only large banks will have balance sheets and capital sufficient to carry the 5 percent retention amount for the maturity period of the loans, which could be thirty years. This will seriously impair competition and—if the largest banks are indeed too big to fail—again put

---

150. Ibid., 17–26 and appendix I.

the government's credit behind the mortgage market. A minimum standard for securitized mortgages should be retained, but the 5 percent retention requirement should be repealed.

Risk Retention and True Sale. Because it favors the largest banks, the 5 percent risk-retention requirement will impair competition. Yet, because of the "true sale" accounting requirements, it will not be effective in preventing the securitization of low-quality mortgages. Under true sale accounting, securitized assets are no longer considered to be assets owned by the securitization sponsor, and the sponsor can immediately recognize a profit on the sale. To get this treatment, the securitization must comply with accounting rules requiring that if the sponsor of a securitization retains any interest in a securitization pool, that interest must be proportional to the risks sold.

The financial regulators' initial proposal offered four options for how a sponsor might retain a required 5 percent interest; however, only a vertical slice through the pool—in which the sponsor takes a 5 percent share of each of the tranches—is clearly likely to clearly qualify for true sale treatment. Barring a huge loss in a pool, then, a 5 percent vertical slice does not represent a significant risk for a sponsor that will earn most of its profits from origination, distribution, servicing, and management of the mortgage pool.

Most of the risk in a privately issued securitization is rated triple-A, with only relatively small portions of the risk in the lower-rated tranches. Thus, if sponsors generally elect the vertical slice as a way of satisfying the DFA risk-retention requirements, this risk is unlikely to have much effect on the quality of the securitized mortgages. Accordingly, as recommended in the WPP white paper, it would be better to maintain mortgage quality in securitizations through a regulation that specifies the requirements for one or more categories of prime loans.[151]

SEC's Regulation AB. The Securities and Exchange Commission (SEC) has proposed an amendment to its Regulation AB that is intended to implement section 621 of the DFA. Section 621, among other things, prohibits securitization sponsors from engaging in transactions that involve a "conflict of interest" with investors in the securitization. The act requires that if there is a prohibited conflict,

---

151. Ibid.

the transaction must be rescinded. The provision was apparently intended to cover transactions in which a securitization sponsor sells interests in a pool and then bets against the pool by acquiring credit default swaps to protect against the possibility that the mortgages in the pool will default.

An inherent conflict exists in every transaction between a buyer and a seller—the seller always thinks the asset will decline in value, while the buyer thinks it will rise. The SEC has the unenviable task of defining and prohibiting some kinds of conflicts while permitting others. To do so, the SEC has proposed an amendment to its Regulation AB, which governs securitization transactions. The SEC's proposed rule is 118 pages long and asks for comments on 109 separate issues.[152]

Given the complexity of the rule, it may not be possible to know in advance whether a particular transaction will transgress the rule. Many firms that would otherwise enter the securitization business may, given the serious consequences of violating the rule, be deterred by the risk of overstepping the rule's complex elements, or by the cost of maintaining the expertise to advise on each transaction. Remedial legislation should make clear what specific transactions were meant to be covered, or section 621 of the DFA should be repealed.

Premium Cash Recapture. The DFA's requirements for premium cash recapture will also discourage securitization by substantially reducing the economic returns to securitizers. Some subprime securitizations during the housing boom involved a substantial spread between what the borrower paid and what the investor received. The existence of this spread, called the yield spread premium, has provoked concern that it was used to compensate originators for steering borrowers into riskier mortgages than they might otherwise have qualified for. To prevent this, section 1403 of the DFA authorized the Fed to prevent differences in originators' compensation that might create an incentive to steer borrowers into an unnecessarily high-risk loan. The Fed's regulation requires the entire spread on a loan to be retained until all proceeds have been paid to the investors. In this position, it amounts to a sizable risk retention that may limit the number of firms that can take on the business of securitization and jeopardize the availability of true sale accounting treatment.

---

152. Securities and Exchange Commission, *Prohibition against Conflicts of Interest in Certain Securitizations*, proposed rule, September 19, 2011, www.sec.gov/rules/proposed/2011/34-65355fr.pdf (accessed February 27, 2012).

Although intended to address predatory lending, this provision would prevent securitizers from realizing the economic benefits of the spread even when they are securitizing prime mortgages. If they try to make up this loss with a higher interest rate, they would be even less competitive with the GSEs and FHA. At the very least, this provision should be modified so that it does not apply to loans not properly categorized as predatory.

Volcker Rule. Although justified as preventing the use of insured bank deposits for risky trading, this rule, as enacted in the DFA, prohibits "bank-related entities" from engaging in proprietary trading and thus extends far beyond the insured banks it was intended to cover. The term "bank-related entities" includes bank holding companies and their subsidiaries, which do not have access to insured deposits. In addition, "proprietary trading" is so difficult to define that the most recent draft regulation covers almost two hundred pages and poses over one thousand separate questions to assist the regulators in drafting the final rule.

There are many concerns about the scope and effect of the Volcker Rule. One major adverse effect is its coverage of hedging transactions. Hedging is a regular and important element of every securitization because it is necessary to protect the issuer against a change in interest rates between the time a mortgage rate is locked in with the borrower and the time a complete pool can be assembled for a securitization.

Hedging transactions involve buying and selling securities for the issuer's own account and could be interpreted to be proprietary trading. It is unlikely that the complexities associated with proprietary trading can be adequately defined in a regulation. However, until a clear line distinguishes hedging from proprietary trading, many banks or bank-related entities likely will not want to take the risk of sponsoring securitization. Accordingly, the Volcker Rule may stand permanently as a serious obstacle to the development of a robust private securitization market.

There are two possible ways to solve this problem: repeal the Volcker Rule language in the DFA, or apply it solely to insured banks and not the broader "bank-related entities." This will enable bank holding companies and their affiliates to engage in securitization without fear of violating the highly technical Volcker Rule when it is ultimately finalized.

Qualified Mortgage. Section 1412 of the DFA also outlines a concept called a qualified mortgage (QM), defined roughly as a mortgage that a borrower can afford. A number of severe consequences exist for providing mortgage credit to a borrower who could not afford to meet obligations on the loan, but the most significant is that a violation of the QM requirements can serve as a defense to foreclosure. This penalty extends to the investor as well as the securitizer and, unless mitigated by a bulletproof safe harbor, will be a serious obstacle to private securitizations. Although the DFA has a provision described as a safe harbor, it requires compliance with so many qualitative elements that it offers no assurance of safety to either securitizers or investors. Without a clear and unambiguous safe harbor, this provision is a strong disincentive for anyone to securitize a mortgage or invest in MBS.

The FDIC's Safe Harbor. Although not specifically required by the DFA, a recent Federal Deposit Insurance Corporation (FDIC) rule has created another impediment to banks' entry into the securitization business. In 2000, the FDIC adopted a safe harbor to address legal uncertainty about when it would use its authority as a failed bank receiver to reacquire assets the bank had sold in a securitization. The investors in any securitization want to be sure they own and can dispose of the assets in the securitization pool. As receiver for a failed bank, however, the FDIC has the right under certain circumstances to reclaim property the bank has transferred.

In its 2000 safe harbor regulation, the FDIC promised that it would not exercise this right when the securitization met the accounting standards for a true sale. However, changes in accounting rules in 2009—stimulated by some of the events of the financial crisis—provided that under some circumstances assets previously sold to a trust could be consolidated with the bank's assets, vitiating the FDIC's 2000 rule. Accordingly, in September 2011, the FDIC adopted new standards for when a securitization would qualify for safe harbor. Many of these, such as adequate disclosure to investors, require qualitative actions that could, if not properly done, be the basis for repudiating a bank's securitization transaction prior to the bank's takeover by the FDIC. As a result, some investors may become reluctant to purchase securities in a pool put together by a bank, posing another obstacle to the revival of a robust private securitization market.

Basel III. Another impediment to bank participation in securitizations involves the treatment of mortgage servicing rights (MSRs) under Basel III. MSRs are an important part of the compensation that securitizers receive. Current accounting rules require that MSRs be capitalized and amortized over time. The new Basel rules on bank capitalization place a limit of 10 percent on the use of MSRs in computing tier one capital. This substantially reduces the value of MSRs to any financial institution covered by the Basel requirements. It also creates a number of other difficulties, the most important of which is an incentive on the part of any bank mortgage originator to sell its mortgages to the GSEs or FHA with servicing released.

This problem will be difficult to address because neither the accounting rules nor Basel III are easily changed. However, the loss of value of MSRs for capital purposes may not be an obstacle to securitization if the other impediments and disincentives I have described here are removed. Banks bound by Basel III may be able to sell the MSRs separately or make up the regulatory capital cost another way.

Conclusion

The impediments to the development of a robust private securitization system are serious. In general, the DFA creates so much complexity that it threatens to overwhelm the financial system. If Secretary Geithner and the administration are serious about reviving a private securitization market, they will have to do more than wind down Fannie and Freddie; they will have to rein in the FHA and open the DFA for amendment, both actions they have resisted thus far.

4

The Case for Reform

While political factors—special interest lobbying, social activist pressures, covering up of past mistakes—were probably behind much of the bill's architecture, economic analysis reveals that it also was based on a misdiagnosis of the financial crisis. As a result, the bill is riddled with deviations from sensible policy. The biggest factor contributing to the misdiagnosis is the presumption that the government did not have enough power to avoid the crisis. It most certainly did.

— John B. Taylor,
First Principles: Five Keys to Restoring America's Prosperity

As noted in the introduction, during the primary contest for the Republican presidential nomination, all the candidates agreed that the Dodd-Frank Act should be repealed. Mitt Romney made repeal of the act a central element of his subsequent presidential campaign, arguing that the act's excessive regulation was slowing the growth of the U.S. economy and delaying the recovery of the jobs lost in the recession. Repeal legislation was introduced by Republicans in both the House and Senate, with the Senate bill getting the support of the entire Republican leadership. The reasons for this opposition are reasonably clear: there are significant indications that, by creating uncertainty and reducing the availability of credit, the act bore important responsibility for the economy's slow recovery from the recession that ended in June 2009.

For his part, in the 2012 campaign, President Obama argued that without Dodd-Frank the American people would not be protected against a recurrence of the "the biggest, riskiest bets that crashed the economy."[1] By invoking the left's narrative about the financial crisis, Obama emphasized the intimate link between that narrative and the Dodd-Frank Act. Clearly, then, as long as the financial crisis is seen as a result of insufficient regulation and the irresponsibility of banks and other private financial institutions, efforts to repeal the act will be stalled. In effect, the true history of the financial crisis must be retold—with the central role of the government's housing policy clearly understood—before the act can be repealed. Nevertheless, as the relationship between the act and the economy's weakness grows stronger in Obama's second term and the act's internal contradictions become more obvious, there is a chance for bipartisan efforts to reform certain key provisions. These provisions are the focus of this chapter.

If the act were really necessary to prevent another financial crisis, the price in slow economic growth might be worth paying, but as I hope to have shown in this book, the financial crisis was not caused by inadequate regulation, an irresponsible private sector, or any of the other alleged causes that are part of the left's narrative. Dodd-Frank is a mirror image of the narrative on which it was based; nearly every major provision can be traced back to a corresponding provision in the left's narrative. Thus, if the narrative is wrong, the act is wrong. Indeed, on the analysis in this book, the act is illegitimate; it was supposed to prevent another financial crisis, but by failing to address the real causes of the 2008 crisis—the U.S. government's housing policies—it cannot achieve this purpose; instead, it simply imposes needless restrictions on the financial system that will not prevent—and indeed may cause—the next crisis.

In this chapter, I will try to show how certain major provisions in the act create serious potential harm for the financial system and the economy, while failing to prevent another financial crisis. This discussion will bring together and summarize many of the points made in the *Financial Services Outlooks* I wrote between 2004 and 2012.

---

1. Tamara Keith, "JPMorgan Loss a Gain for Campaign Positioning," NPR, May 15, 2012, http://www.npr.org/2012/05/15/152696746/jpmorgans-loss-a-gain-for-campaign-positioning, accessed July 15, 2012.

A Brief History of Financial "Deregulation"

With President Obama's statement in the 2008 presidential debates that the financial crisis was the result of "Republican deregulation," the idea that financial deregulation had a role in the financial crisis was added to the left's narrative. This remark was more uninformed than the usual partisan sally; since the Carter administration, both Democratic and Republican administrations had deregulated major sections of the economy, with great success. Air travel, freight transportation, communications, and securities trading, among others, had all been substantially deregulated, producing efficiency, economic growth, and lower consumer costs. The Clinton administration backed and signed into law both the Commodity Futures Modernization Act and the Gramm-Leach-Bliley Act, which have both been widely but wrongly blamed for the financial crisis. So even if financial deregulation had been a factor in the financial crisis, what deregulation occurred before 2008 had been broadly supported by both political parties for 30 years. Indeed, banking had largely been an exception to the deregulatory trend. Since the savings and loan crisis of the late 1980s, banking regulation had been tightened, especially by the FDIC Improvement Act of 1991, which enhanced regulatory authority and contained many significant penalties for banks and bank officials if they failed to follow applicable laws and regulations. At the time, many in Congress hailed this new and tighter regulation because it would, once and for all, prevent banking crises.

Obama's remark about "Republican deregulation" indicated that he would not be a supporter of deregulation; with his election, the modest era of deregulation that the United States had experienced (except for banking) since the Carter years has ended. And indeed, after the 2008 election, the Obama administration moved quickly to use the financial crisis as a reason to tighten regulation—not only for banks, but for the entire financial system. The DFA is a breathtakingly broad piece of legislation. More than eight hundred pages in its enrolled form, and requiring more than 400 separate regulations and studies, it covers every part of the financial system except insurance and extends the federal government's reach into areas that had previously been the province of state or local regulation. It is by far the most substantial financial regulatory regime ever enacted, far exceeding anything developed during the New Deal. Its complexity and scope are shown by the fact that—eighteen months after enactment—more than two-thirds of the regulations it requires for implementation have not yet been adopted by the agencies charged with the task. It says volumes about the haste with which this legislation was rushed through Congress that it has already taken longer for regulators to complete the principal regulations in each area than it took Congress to enact the law.

Among other things, the act provides for new and "stringent" (the statutory term) regulation on all nonbank financial institutions—including securities firms, finance companies, insurers, hedge funds, and possibly many others—that are deemed to be systemically important; allows the secretary of the Treasury to seize any financial firm and turn it over to the FDIC for liquidation if he or she believes that its failure will threaten the stability of the U.S. financial system; prevents banks and organizations affiliated with banks from trading securities for their own account, threatening to reduce market liquidity; adds serious new restrictions to the mortgage market that have stifled the private mortgage business and caused many banks to withdraw from residential finance; imposes new costs and regulations on the derivatives market and on hedge fund advisers, even though there is no evidence at all that unregulated derivatives or hedge funds had any role in the financial crisis; and sets up a Consumer Financial Protection Bureau with jurisdiction over every business in the U.S. economy (other than insurance and securities) that has financial dealings with consumers, from the largest banks to the smallest check-cashing firm.

There are also elements in the bill, as in Obamacare, that are of questionable constitutionality. The ability of the Treasury secretary to seize any financial firm if he or she believes that its failure might cause instability in the U.S. financial system is an unprecedented power in the hands of a government official. The seized firm has virtually no opportunity for judicial review. If the company objects, the secretary can apply to a court, but the court is not allowed to grant a stay or an injunction and must decide the issue in one day. Appeals are not permitted. If the court makes no decision in that day, the firm is handed over to the FDIC for liquidation. It's also a felony for anyone to reveal that the secretary has asked for a court ruling. These provisions are unlikely to pass a constitutional test. The same constitutional questions could be raised about the CFPB. This agency is established as a bureau within the Federal Reserve and is funded by allocating a portion of the Fed's revenues rather than appropriations from Congress. Virtually all other agencies of the government are funded by Congress, as the Constitution provides. In addition, the administrator of the CFPB is appointed by the president for a term of five years and cannot be removed from office except for "inefficiency, neglect of duty, or malfeasance in office." So one of the most powerful agencies ever established in the government is beyond the direct control of either Congress or the president. Even the Fed is prohibited from interfering in its activities.

By the time the Obama administration took office, the narrative about the financial crisis was almost fully developed. According to this story, the financial crisis was caused by the absence or inadequate enforcement of necessary regulations, reckless private-sector risk-taking, predatory lending by mortgage originators, and greed on Wall Street. In fairness, as described in the introduction, these ideas did not all originate with the Obama administration. President Bush's Treasury secretary, Hank Paulson, and Fed chair Ben Bernanke neither foresaw the mortgage meltdown nor understood the government's role in creating it. Their panicky reaction to the potential failure of Bear Stearns resulted in the first-ever government-financed rescue of a nonbank financial firm. The moral hazard created by this act was responsible for the chaos that followed the government's failure to rescue Lehman, and their invalid rationale for the rescue—particularly the notion that "interconnectedness" among financial institutions was a danger—became part of the Obama administration's narrative about the crisis.

In reality, deregulation—Republican or otherwise—had nothing to do with the financial crisis. In the rare cases where anyone actually asks what Republican deregulation had occurred, the administration and its allies on the left respond by pointing to the Gramm-Leach-Bliley Act of 1999 (GLBA), which repealed a portion of the Glass-Steagall Act. The fact that the GLBA was passed during a Democratic administration—backed by top officials of the Clinton administration and signed by President Clinton—does not, apparently, make it any less Republican deregulation.

In any event, as described in chapter 2, the Glass-Steagall Act's partial repeal was completely irrelevant to what happened in the financial crisis. The GLBA repealed a provision of the act that prohibited affiliations between commercial banks and firms engaged in underwriting or dealing in securities, which are generally called investment banks. The balance of the act, which prohibited banks from underwriting and dealing in securities, remained intact. JPMorgan Chase and Citibank are examples of commercial banks, while Merrill Lynch and Goldman Sachs are examples of investment banks. In the financial crisis, both commercial banks and investment banks got into serious financial trouble—and both for the same reason: they bought and held private mortgage–backed securities that were based on subprime and other risky mortgages. However, none of the commercial banks were affiliated with any of the large investment banks, so the fact that the affiliation prohibition in the Glass-Steagall Act had been repealed was irrelevant to the events of 2008.

Finally, in what is perhaps the ultimate irony, commercial banks that were heavily regulated by three specialized federal banking regulators (the Comptroller of the Currency, the FDIC, and the Federal Reserve)—and hundreds of smaller Insured and government regulated commercial banks around the country—suffered losses just as severe as the five large invest-ment banks that were only lightly regulated for prudential purposes by the SEC. As noted above, both got into trouble by acquiring and holding the same assets—PMBS backed by subprime or other risky mortgages. Regula-tion, and the degree of regulation, made no difference. Thus, the financial crisis could easily have been used to question the efficacy of regulation itself, which was no more effective in protecting insured commercial banks than uninsured investment banks; instead, the crisis became a rationale for even *more* regulation. Repealing the DFA and starting over with a clear-eyed view of what actually happened in the financial crisis—and whether additional regulation is a sensible solution—would be the most reasonable course, but in light of Obama's re-election, reform of Dodd-Frank's most damaging provisions is all that can be hoped for.

History suggests that more regulation is not the correct response to the 2008 financial crisis. The most apt example would be the panic of 1907. At that point, there was only a very weak regulatory structure for banks, and the Federal Reserve did not exist. It's not clear what caused the panic, but it strongly resembled what happened in 2008. As Phil Gramm and Mike Solon described in a 2012 article: "From beginning to end, [the panic of 1907] was a banking and financial crisis. . . . The stock market collapsed, loan supply vanished and a scramble for liquidity ensued. Banks defaulted on their obligation to redeem deposits in currency or gold. . . . The May panic triggered a massive recession that saw real gross national product shrink in the second half of 1907 and plummet by an extraordinary 8.2% in 1908. Yet the economy came roaring back and, in two short years, was 7% larger than when the panic began."[2]

The recovery from the panic of 1907 was quick and formidable, while the recovery from the crisis of 2008, during which the DFA was adopted, has been slow and halting. The precise role of the DFA in slowing the recovery is yet to be fully established and is beyond the scope of this book. Nevertheless, by showing that the left's narrative about the act is false—and that the most important provisions of the act flow directly from this narrative—it is possible to build a case for substantial reform.

In the following discussion—which addresses those major provisions of the act that were derived directly from the left's narrative—I will show not only that the narrative was in error but also that the provisions of the act that were based on the narrative are likely to cause substantial harm to the U.S. economy and the financial system if they remain in effect.

Title I. The Financial Stability Oversight Council

Although most of the principal provisions of the DFA are based on the idea that lack of regulation caused the financial crisis, two provisions are founded on additional false assumptions about the crisis. In a sense, these provisions, which appear in Titles I and II of the act, are the heart of the act because they purport to be the elements that will prevent another financial crisis. As discussed in the introduction and chapter 2, the first of these is based on the idea that the financial crisis occurred because large financial institutions are "interconnected," so the failure of one will bring down other large financial firms, causing a systemic event. This idea was first advanced by Secretary Paulson and Fed chair Bernanke to justify their rescue of Bear Stearns and became part of the left's narrative. It is the rationale for Title I of the act, which establishes the FSOC and authorizes it to designate certain

---

2. Phil Gramm and Mike Solon, "The 'Financial Recession' Excuse," *Wall Street Journal*, February 2, 2012, http://online.wsj.com/article/SB10001424052970204740904577193382 505500756.html?KEYWORDS=Gramm#.

large firms for special stringent regulation by the Federal Reserve. The purpose of the regulation, of course, is to prevent the firms' instability or failure, which—it is feared—will drag down others through the interconnections among them.

A similar idea is the claim—also originated by Paulson and Bernanke—that the chaos after the Lehman bankruptcy could have been prevented if the government had had the authority to take over and wind down large failing financial institutions like Lehman. This notion underlies Title II of the act. However, as discussed in the introduction, a close analysis of what actually happened when Lehman failed disproves both these ideas, indicating that Titles I and II will not prevent the next financial crisis. And since both will have affirmatively harmful effects on the financial system if they are left in place, they are major reasons why the act should be substantially reformed.

The FSOC is made up of the Treasury secretary, as chair, and all the federal financial regulators, including the SEC, CFTC, all the banking regulators (FDIC, Comptroller of the Currency, and the Federal Reserve); the CFPB; the regulator of the GSEs Fannie Mae and Freddie (the Federal Housing Finance Agency); and several others that are less well known. The council has two major functions—to watch for systemic risk that may be developing in the financial system and to designate certain firms as systemically important financial institutions, or SIFIs. The second of these authorities is very powerful indeed and, as outlined below, has the potential to change the nature of the U.S. financial system.

The DFA provides that a financial firm is considered a SIFI if its failure would create "instability" in the financial system. Under the act, banks are considered SIFIs if they have $50 billion or more in assets, but no numerical standards were set for nonbank financial institutions, such as insurance companies, financial holding companies, hedge funds, securities firms, and others. Under the act and the regulations published thus far, a nonbank financial firm can be designated as a SIFI if it is "interconnected" with other firms. The draft regulation defines interconnectedness as "substantial exposure"; thus, if firm A has substantial exposure to firm B, there is a danger that the losses on firm B will drag down firm A and others, setting off instability in the financial system and thus a systemic event. The DFA sets out no standards for how much interconnectedness will constitute a nonbank firm as a SIFI. The matter is left entirely to the discretion of the FSOC. This will provide grounds for litigation because a designation means that the firm is turned over to the Fed for stringent regulation. No one knows exactly what this means, although the Fed has now proposed a regulation that includes restrictions on such things as the degree of exposure that SIFIs can have to one another. Beyond that, the Fed has the authority to control a SIFI's liquidity, leverage, capital, and activities. Designation as a SIFI, therefore, puts the designated firm under the control of the Fed and can substantially reduce a firm's freedom of action.

On the other hand, SIFIs will have great advantages, particularly in funding their activities. Designation as a SIFI will in effect be a statement by the government that a firm is too big to fail. Under those circumstances, it is highly likely that the large firms designated as SIFIs will—because they will be seen as protected or even backed by the government—have lower costs of funds than their smaller competitors. This has been true in the banking industry, where the largest banks—because they are seen as TBTF—have a lower cost of funds than smaller banks. Providing credit to these large banks, accordingly, is seen as less risky, and carries a lower risk premium, than a loan to a smaller competitor that does not have this advantage. In addition, the fact that these large firms will be subject to "stringent" regulation is another inducement for creditors, who get no benefits from risk-taking. Stringent regulation will mean less risk-taking, making these firms much more attractive to creditors than firms that are subject only to "ordinary" regulation.

That this could happen in today's competitive financial markets should be very troubling. What it suggests is that at some future time, markets that are now highly competitive—with small firms able to compete with large ones—will come to be dominated by large firms that are seen as operating with government protection. Some proponents of the DFA argue that the stringent new regulatory requirements associated with Fed regulation will eliminate the cost advantage that may come from a SIFI designation, but a little thought shows that this is no solution. If regulatory costs are that much greater than the advantages of lower-cost funding, these large companies will be uncompetitive, becoming a burden on the financial system, and will eventually have to be liquidated—at some cost to the taxpayers and (under Title II) other financial firms. The only way this argument works, as I noted in chapter 3, is if the regulatory costs exactly balance funding advantages—a wholly implausible outcome.

If designating SIFIs were necessary to prevent a future financial crisis, the risk to the competitiveness of the financial system might be an undesirable, but unavoidable, consequence. However, as described earlier, there is no evidence whatever that the failure of a SIFI will have knock-on effects through interconnections with other large firms. With one exception discussed in chapter 3, these effects were not present after Lehman failed, even though all firms at the time were weakened by the common shock associated with the mortgage meltdown. This is strong evidence that the whole theory on which companies are designated as SIFIs and subjected to "stringent" regulation can be shown to be false. If no other major firm was dragged down by knock-on effects of exposure to Lehman—even when all the largest firms in the market were seen as weak and possibly insolvent—there is virtually no likelihood that there will be another financial crisis when another large firm fails in the future.

Some observers occasionally argue that there were no knock-on failures after Lehman's bankruptcy because the government took actions to prevent them. These actions consisted primarily of making liquidity available through the Federal Reserve, providing capital to the largest banks through TARP, and providing FDIC guarantees of bank loans. These were all confidence-building measures, which were put in place to calm the panic that hit the markets after the Lehman failure. Of these actions, only the TARP funding had the potential to prevent an insolvent firm from failing. However, the TARP funds were not made available to the large recipient banks until six weeks after the Lehman bankruptcy, by which time none of them had failed. All of these banks repaid the TARP contributions, with the approval of the Fed, by the end of 2009. The Fed would not have allowed repayment if the return of this capital would have left the firms without adequate capitalization. Thus, the assistance handed out by the government was designed only to build market confidence in the health of these firms, not to fill in holes in their balance sheets left by the failure of Lehman.

Accordingly, there is no sound basis for requiring the designation and special regulation of SIFIs; it will have no effect in preventing a future financial crisis but will in fact promote moral hazard. Moreover, the possibility that SIFI designations will impair competition in every industry in which a SIFI is designated far outweighs any benefit that might flow from the designation. For that reason, the provisions of Title I that authorize the designation of SIFIs should be substantially modified to eliminate the FSOC's authority to designate nonbank financial firms as SIFIs. Reform could also modify Title I so that banks and bank holding companies do not automatically become SIFIs when their assets reach $50 billion. That is a penalty for growth and enlarges the scope of moral hazard; moreover, there is evidence from the absence of knock-on effects from Lehman's bankruptcy that only the largest banks would have the potential to create instability in the U.S. financial system if they failed—and that is uncertain.

Shorn of the authority to designate SIFIs, the FSOC could be retained as a consultative body to assess whether systemic risk is developing in the financial system or to handle other questions that the administration in office may present. Nevertheless, the fact that the secretary of the Treasury heads the FSOC should be a cause for concern. Many members of the council are supposed to be independent regulatory agencies, and their independence could well be compromised by having to follow policies developed or heavily Influenced by the secretary of the Treasury.

There is a case for eliminating the Office of Financial Research (OFR), also authorized by Title I. The office has the power to command the production of data from the private sector, but the nature of the data it can request is not limited, and the provisions for confidentiality are not strong. Perhaps more important, the OFR is funded for its first two years by the Fed and thereafter by assessments on large banking institutions. There is no limit on the amount of funds it can demand. The OFR, in turn, supports the FSOC, so all these agencies bear some resemblance to the Consumer Financial Protection Bureau in the sense that they are deliberately insulated from congressional funding. Apparently, the OFR is also intended to be independent of the executive branch as well as Congress. The director is appointed by the president for a term of six years; there are no provisions for his or her removal; and the director is empowered to report to Congress on any subject without the approval of the president or the secretary of the Treasury. Congress and the president should call a halt to legislation of this kind, in which agencies are created that do not have any obligations to the political organs of government. The trend began with the Public Accounting Oversight Board in the Sarbanes-Oxley Act and seems to be continuing.

The constitutional structure of the U.S. government was designed so that Congress would have the power of the purse—the power to control the activities of the executive by limiting the funds the taxpayers are required to make available for government purposes. Putting assessments on banking organizations is simply an indirect form of taxation because all costs are ultimately passed along to consumers, who are taxpayers. In addition, the act's attempt to make the director of the OFR also independent of the president is another violation of the constitutional scheme. Accordingly, the funding of the OFR should be made subject to congressional appropriations, or at least congressional approval, and the director should serve at the pleasure of the president.

Title II. The Orderly Liquidation Authority

The proponents of the act argue that Title II eliminates "bailouts." This is a true statement only if one accepts their definition of a bailout, which appears to be a financial rescue outside bankruptcy that involves the use of taxpayer funds. That definition, however, is too narrow. The most troubling bailout is a bailout of the creditors—one that protects them from or reduces their losses. A bailout of this kind creates moral hazard; it causes creditors to believe that the risks associated with lending to large firms that might be bailed out are less risky than lending to small firms. Over time, that will create an unlevel playing field, reduce competition, and cause market consolidation. In addition, if creditors believe that they will be protected by the government, they are not wary of the risks associated with lending and do not exercise the control over borrowers that is called market discipline. Thus, the one group that really opposes risk-taking— a firm's creditors—is induced to be less vigilant. This, of course, is the story of Fannie Mae and Freddie Mac. They were able to take huge risks because their creditors believed that the two firms were ultimately backed by the government.

Unfortunately, Title II makes it possible for the FDIC to bail out the creditors. It allows the agency, acting as a receiver, to set up a new entity— sometimes called a bridge bank—and to transfer to it all the assets of the failed institution subject to whatever liabilities the FDIC chooses. This allows the FDIC to pick winners and losers among the creditors of a failed firm and to pay all of them off if it chooses to do so. The funds for a payoff of this kind can be borrowed from the Treasury, which is authorized by the act to treat the borrowing as a "public debt transaction." (section 210(n)). In effect, this means that the Treasury does not need a congressional appropriation to advance funds against the FDIC's note. In turn, the FDIC is authorized to borrow up to 100 percent of the value of the unencumbered assets of the failed institution. Thus, with Treasury funds, the FDIC can bail out all the creditors of a failed institution, recovering its losses from the other firms designated as SIFIs under Title I. It can sell the firm's assets to recover the funds it laid aside for the creditors, or it can reconstitute the firm by retaining the assets and recover its losses from designated SIFIs under Title I.

The most important question raised by Title II, however, is whether—in the context of a common shock—there is any significant difference between a bankruptcy and the FDIC's winding down of a failing financial firm. That is, is there any likelihood that the Treasury secretary's seizure of a firm and its winding down by the FDIC will have any different result in the markets than the Lehman bankruptcy?

Unless the idea is to bail out the creditors, and in that way prevent a panic, the answer to that question is no. If we assume that a common shock has occurred and that all firms look weak and possibly insolvent as a result, investors are going to be focused intently on all firms in danger of being seized by the Treasury secretary. If the FDIC begins to take a serious interest in a particular firm, the rumors will begin to fly, investors and creditors will run, and the firm will become illiquid—even if it is not insolvent—and will have to be taken over. This is exactly what happened in the Lehman case; investors began to run from Lehman as soon as rumors began to circulate that the government had no buyer and the firm would not be rescued. The same thing will happen if the market suspects that a particular firm will be seized and turned over to the FDIC. And if the seizure occurs, investors will run from other firms—just as happened in Lehman—for fear that their firm will be next. In other words, the OLA is unworkable as a substitute for bankruptcy in the context of a 2008-like common shock-induced panic.

The answer is no different if a financial firm is in danger of failing in a context in which there is no common shock. In that situation, as shown by the Lehman case, there is very little danger of a chaotic situation. This is true because Lehman's bankruptcy—even in the context of a common shock—did not have any significant knock-on effect on other firms. If large firms like Lehman have no knock-on effects even when other firms were thought to be weak or insolvent, it would certainly have no effect when other firms were considered healthy and stable. Accordingly, Title II suffers from the same deficiencies as Title I. It will impose significant costs on financial firms by creating greater risks for their creditors, but does not have any potential to produce a better outcome than bankruptcy for a failing financial firm. For this reason, Title II is one provision of the DFA that should probably be replaced. It creates significant and harmful moral hazard without Improving in any substantial way over bankruptcy—a resolution system where the rules are known and which does not create moral hazard or reduce market discipline. An addition to the bankruptcy code, designated as chapter 14 and specifically designed for the bankruptcy of a financial institution, has been developed by a group of financial experts and scholars. It accomplishes the objectives of Title II without creating moral hazard or reducing market discipline.[3] It would be a suitable substitute for Title II.

Title VI. The Volcker Rule and Other Restrictions

The most important provision in Title VI, which is principally devoted to technical matters relating to the regulation of bank and savings and loan holding companies, is what has come to be known as the Volcker Rule—a prohibition on proprietary trading that extends to holding companies and their subsidiaries as well as to all the bank and savings and loan subsidiaries of holding companies. Proprietary trading refers to trading securities for the account of the entity doing the trading rather than trading for the firm's clients or for some other purpose, such as hedging of risks or making markets. The idea that the banks got into financial trouble by making risky "bets" in their trading activities is what connects the Volcker Rule to the left's narrative about the causes of the financial crisis. Other parts of the narrative suggest that all these losses came about because of the "repeal" of the Glass-Steagall Act and that in engaging in proprietary

---

3. This is discussed in detail in Kenneth E. Scott and John B. Taylor, Eds., *Bankruptcy Not Bailout: A Special Chapter 14* (Washington, D.C.: Hoover Institution Press, 2012).

trading the banks were using FDIC-insured funds, which are ultimately backed by the taxpayers.

There are so many errors in this portion of the left's narrative that it's hard to know where to start. First, the idea that the banks were bailed out in the financial crisis springs largely from the fact that TARP was used to provide capital injections to the largest U.S. financial institutions in the wake of the panic that followed the bankruptcy of Lehman Brothers in September 2008. This is a bit of a distortion. None of these institutions, with the possible exception of Citigroup, actually needed TARP funds in order to stay solvent, so there was actually no "bailout" in any strict sense of the term. As noted earlier, all of them, except Citi, repaid the amount they'd received (with the approval of the Fed) within eight months from the time of the infusion. Citi had repaid Its TARP funding by the end of 2009. This shows that the capital injection was not filling a hole in their balance sheets, but was only a confidence-building measure at a time when market participants and investors were in a state of panic. Whether the capital injections were actually necessary for this purpose is an issue that will never be fully resolved, but it is clear that this action, plus guarantees of loans by the FDIC and the eventual publication in May 2009 of results from stress testing nineteen of the largest financial firms—showing that less than half had to strengthen their capital positions and none was insolvent—did contribute to a stabilization of market sentiment in mid-2009.

Second, there is no factual support for the idea that proprietary trading was responsible for the losses that the banks suffered in the financial crisis. As I made clear in the introduction, these losses came unambiguously from the banks' holdings of MBS backed by subprime or other nonprime mortgages. Indeed, proprietary trading was a source of badly needed earnings for banks, and prohibiting it in the future is not sound banking policy. It is not at all clear, for example, that trading fixed income securities is any riskier than making loans. The problem for banks now and in the future is not too much risk-taking but too few sources of profitable business. The idea that banks were making "bets" with depositor funds is also wrong and tendentious. The banks that got into trouble acquiring and holding MBS backed by subprime or other nonprime loans had purchased and were holding MBS that were rated AAA. These are the least risky securities of this type that they could acquire and, accordingly, produced the lowest yields.

If the banks had bought lower-rated tranches of the pools, one might argue that they were taking risks, and thus betting, but that's not what they did.

The Volcker Rule prohibits proprietary trading by bank holding companies and their nonbank subsidiaries as well as by the banks themselves. This shows that the rule was intended to do more than prevent the use of FDIC-insured funds for risky trading. Bank holding companies and their nonbank subsidiaries have no right of access to the Fed's discount window and do not receive insured deposits (bank regulations also tightly control and limit bank lending to affiliates like bank holding companies). Indeed, the Fed has always taken the position that bank holding companies are expected to be sources of financial support for their subsidiary banks. Eliminating a source of profit for bank holding companies—or limiting their activities only to the activities that are permissible for their FDIC-insured bank subsidiaries—runs entirely counter to this policy.

Prohibiting bank holding companies and even banks from engaging in proprietary trading also fails to recognize the changes that have occurred in financial markets over the last forty years. The rise of the securities markets as the principal source of financing for the real economy has left banks with limited sources of profitable activity.[4] Banks have been forced to find their customers among those firms that do not have access to the securities markets. As a result, most bank lending is now real-estate based—loans to developers and residential and commercial mortgages. Real estate is a highly volatile industry, which means that whenever the housing market sneezes, banks will catch a cold. Accordingly, restrictions on activities such as proprietary trading—activities in which banks are using their expertise to earn profits outside the real estate business—does not make policy sense.

Moreover, as an exception to the Volcker Rule, the act permits banks to engage in a number of activities that are almost indistinguishable from proprietary trading, including hedging and acting as market makers for fixed-income securities. Obviously, for risk management reasons, it is essential to

---

4. See. e.g., Peter J. Wallison, "Losing Ground: Gramm-Leach-Bliley and the Future of Banking," AEI *Financial Services Outlook* (November-December 2009), available at http://www.aei.org/outlook/economics/financial-services/losing-ground-gramm-leach-bliley-and-the-future-of-banking/; and Peter J. Wallison, "Does Shadow Banking Require Regulation?" AEI *Financial Services Outlook* (May-June 2012), available at http://www.aei.org/outlook/economics/financial-services/banking/does-shadow-banking-require-regulation/.

allow banks to hedge, and market-making by banks is important to creating and retaining liquidity in the markets for fixed-income securities. Congress appears to have recognized the importance of bank market-making by exempting Treasury securities from the Volcker Rule prohibitions on proprietary trading, but this has only sharpened the complaints of companies, other governments, and state and local issuers of fixed-income securities that restrictions on bank market-making will be harmful to the liquidity of the markets in their securities. Apart from these considerations, it may not be possible to draft a regulation that prohibits proprietary trading while still permitting hedging and market making; the two functions are too similar to draw a usable regulatory line between them. The danger implicit in the Volcker Rule, then, is that it will cause banks—fearful of violating the regulations—to abandon or significantly reduce their hedging or market-making activities. This, if it occurs, will further narrow the range of profitable activities available to banks, drive a perfectly good business—for which banks are eminently suited—overseas, increase bank riskiness by reducing hedging, and remove a substantial amount of liquidity from the global markets for fixed income securities.

It is possible to argue that there are good policy reasons to restrict insured banks themselves (although not their holding company affiliates) from engaging in proprietary trading. Deposit insurance provides banks with lower-cost funds that, arguably, were intended to be used solely for lending purposes. However, insured banks routinely engage in many other activities—advisory functions, funds transfer, currency exchange, and issuing letters of credit, to name only a few—that are not strictly lending. Where to draw the line is a question that is beyond the scope of this book, but at least there is a basis for limiting the scope of activities available to insured banks. None of this, however, applies to their holding companies and their holding companies' nonbank subsidiaries, which are ordinary corporations that do not have access to any special government support or backing. Accordingly, to the extent that the Volcker Rule continues in force, it should be limited only to insured banks and should not cover their holding companies. Finally, if there is any reason to retain the Volcker Rule for insured banks, it is not necessary to do it by regulation. The substance of the Volcker Rule can be supplanted with a requirement that it be enforced through supervision. This would enable regulators to inquire fully into the circumstances of a trade to determine whether it was done as a prohibited proprietary trade or for legitimate hedging or market-making purposes.

Another objectionable provision in this title is a restriction on bank holding companies making more than a minimal (3 percent) investment in hedge funds or private equity firms. As in proprietary trading, there might be a sensible policy argument that insured banks should not be allowed to control hedge funds or private equity firms, but this title goes further and restricts the ability of bank holding companies to control entities that are engaged in these activities. There is no reason to place restrictions such as this on bank holding companies, which are ordinary corporations that raise their financing in the public markets and are permitted to engage in a wide variety of financial activities, including underwriting insurance and underwriting and dealing in securities. Sections 23A and 23B of the Federal Reserve Act prevent banks from providing significant financing to their nonbank affiliates, so there is no basis for arguing that the risky activities of hedge funds or private equity will jeopardize the health of affiliated insured banks.

For all these reasons, the Volcker Rule and other provisions in Title VI that restrict the activities of bank holding companies should be substantially reformed. Although there is a basis for repealing the Volcker Rule in its entirety, Congress may conclude that it wants to draw a line on the permissible activities of insured banks and exclude proprietary trading from that list. Accordingly, the reforms to the Volcker Rule that seem most likely to assist—or at least not interfere excessively with—economic growth are: eliminate the application of the Rule to bank holding companies and their nonbank subsidiaries, and apply the limitation on proprietary trading to insured banks through supervisory activity, not through a regulation.

Title VII. Regulation of the Derivatives Markets

The "repeal" of Glass-Steagall was not the only way in which the left's narrative identified supposed "deregulation" as a cause of the financial crisis. The claim was also made by the administration and many on the left that by approving the Commodity Futures Modernization Act of 2000 (CFMA), the Clinton administration had made it possible for the trading of over-the-counter (OTC) derivatives to contribute to the crisis. The CFMA, some claimed, prohibited the CFTC and its chair, Brooksley Born, from regulating derivatives, and the abuse of derivatives was said to be a major cause of the financial crisis. It has become an article of faith on the left that losses in the derivatives market almost—in the oft-repeated phrase—"brought the financial system to its knees." Credit default swaps, or CDSs, were singled out as a particular example of deregulatory mischief when AIG was rescued by the Fed in 2008—with an infusion of more than $130 billion—because of its dealings in CDSs.

It is certainly true that AIG suffered major losses in its CDS trading, but the evidence for any significant additional losses by any other firms that were dealing in CDSs is, to say the least, scant. Indeed, AIG turned out to be the only firm—of the hundreds that participated regularly in the CDS market—to have any solvency-level losses from trading activity. That was largely because AIG was probably the only firm that took only one side of a series of CDS transactions—it only sold protection against the default of private MBS—but, in order to increase its profits, it did not hedge these obligations.

The FCIC, because of Brooksley Born's membership, was particularly focused on this issue, but after extensive efforts to demonstrate a significant role of CDSs and derivatives generally in the financial crisis, the commission could only say that derivatives "facilitated" the accumulation of subprime mortgages (by protecting holders against losses), enabled Wall Street to meet investor demand by creating synthetic instruments known as collateralized debt obligations (even though this *reduced* the number of subprime mortgages that had to be created to meet investor demand), and "added to uncertainty and escalated panic."[5] The FCIC's reference to collateralized debt obligations (CDOs) is derived from the fact that some of the securities sold by Wall Street before the crisis were synthetic CDOs—that is, they used CDSs to replicate the performance of actual pools of subprime mortgages. In reality, this actually reduced the demand for "real" subprime mortgages, but in any case it makes no sense to blame an instrument or a technique for things that happen when it is misused. The left's narrative did the same thing with securitization, blaming it for distributing MBS based on subprime mortgages. CDSs and securitization, like lending itself, are only a means of financing; they can be misused by incompetently managed firms,

---

5. Financial Crisis Inquiry Commission, *Financial Crisis Commission Report*, xxv.

just as incompetent lending results in bank failures. Although yet more regulation is the left's all-purpose cure for private-sector losses, there is no evidence that bank regulation prevented banks from buying the MBS that ultimately caused their losses.

The FCIC's inability, despite a diligent effort under Brooksley Born's guidance, to show that CDSs—let alone the much larger markets for interest rate or currency swaps—caused any significant losses to firms other than AIG (or, possibly, those who had bought protection from AIG) demonstrates the weak foundation for the regulation imposed by Title VII. This is an important fact. Regulation is justified where there has been a market failure. Despite a diligent inquiry, the FCIC was never able to find anything more than the failure of a single firm. The most that could be said about the unregulated derivatives market was that it was not "transparent"; this is true, a result of the fact that the market was diversified among a large number of players—dealers and major swap participants that took speculative positions for profit. This can be seen as a good thing for market stability and resulted in the spreading of risks and losses over a large number of market participants. The regulation that was authorized by the DFA would do the opposite, as discussed below, concentrating the risk in a few clearinghouses. When market participants want more transparency, they can achieve it, as they have in the past, through private agreements on clearing, exchanges, or reporting facilities. The government's intervention in markets frequently has unintended consequences that reduce or eliminate such values as the stability that diversity provides.

The fact that the only one firm—AIG—faced difficulties because of its activities in the derivatives market should tell us that regulating the entire derivatives market for this reason is a vast overreach. Would it make sense to regulate how loans are made if one lender among thousands made imprudent loans? In reality, the demand for regulation was based on the left's ideological commitment to more regulation of the economy rather than anything that happened in the financial crisis. The left's narrative, which refers to derivatives as a major element of the financial crisis, has been widely accepted and repeated in the media, but has little basis in fact.

As discussed in the introduction, the Lehman case also shows that the left's narrative about derivatives and CDSs was grossly overstated. Lehman was a major player in the derivatives market and at the time of its bankruptcy had more than 900,000 contracts outstanding. There were also billions of dollars of CDSs written on Lehman itself, protecting Lehman's creditors. All the CDSs written on Lehman were settled five weeks after its bankruptcy by the exchange of $5.2 billion among hundreds of counter-parties. There is no known example of a firm failing because it had written protection against the failure of Lehman. This is because almost all partici-pants in the market—unlike AIG—hedged their obligations. Those firms that had purchased protection from Lehman against the failure of some other party had to purchase new protection after Lehman's bankruptcy, probably requiring them to pay a higher premium, and since the market for CDSs remained open and functioning throughout the financial crisis it was possible to buy new protection—just as it is possible to buy new insurance protection if your Insurance company goes out of business.

Thus, we begin the analysis of Title VII with two main points. First, the left's narrative about the role of derivatives in the financial crisis is false; derivatives were not a significant cause of the financial crisis. The immedi-ate cause was the common shock to most financial institutions from the collapse of values in the U.S. housing market—a result of U.S. government housing policies. Second, if the derivatives market had no significant role in the financial crisis, and it has functioned effectively without regulation for many years, there is no principled basis for imposing regulation on that market now; the only justification for regulation, after all, is market failure. The fact that the market is not transparent enough for some is not a market failure. If more transparency is warranted, that can be required by regula-tion. Indeed, much can be achieved along these lines by existing bank regu-lation, since banks are the major players in the derivatives markets.

The most significant and controversial part of Title VII is the "swaps push-out rule," which prohibits FDIC-insured banks from participating in CDS transactions unless they are cleared through a clearinghouse. These activities, however, can continue in affiliates of the bank that are separately capitalized subsidiaries of the bank's holding company. When it was in development, this provision was opposed by the Fed and the FDIC because it would have prevented banks from hedging their risks through the use of CDSs. The final language of Title VII allowed the use of CDSs for hedging transactions, but exactly what a hedging transaction is—as in the Volcker Rule—has not been determined and will be very difficult to work out in a rule. Whatever hedging transactions are, the push-out rule deprives the CDS market of the enormous amount of capital that was supplied by the participation of U.S. banks. This will probably mean that most CDS business will move to foreign banks outside U.S. jurisdiction, but even more important, the decline in the amount of capital available to the CDS market will increase spreads and reduce the availability of hedges for end-users that are trying to limit their risks. U.S. banks can continue to write CDSs for transactions that are cleared through clearinghouses. Some CDS transactions cannot be cleared in this way, however, because they cannot be tailored to meet the risk-management needs of particular end-users. In these cases, banks will be excluded from the market. These transactions can be handled by their affiliates, but the more limited capital resources of bank affiliates will reduce competition and widen spreads so that these hedging and risk-management activities will become more expensive for end-users.

Another important provision of this title is an effort to push as many transactions as possible into clearinghouses. The act authorizes the CFTC and the SEC to determine whether a particular form of swap transaction must be cleared through a clearinghouse. Once that determination is made, all swaps of the same class must be cleared in that way. This requirement is derived from the portion of the left's narrative that blames the financial crisis in part on the lack of transparency in the derivatives market. This is highly unlikely. There are two ways in which lack of transparency could have contributed to the crisis. First, uncertainty among investors and depositors about the CDS or other derivatives liabilities of banks and other financial firms might have contributed to the panic. However, any such contribution was minuscule compared to the effect of mark-to-market accounting as housing and mortgage values plummeted in late 2007. Another effect might have come through the fears of policymakers about CDS liabilities. These instruments were not completely understood in the early stages of the financial crisis, as shown by the claim—originating with Secretary Paulson and Chairman Bernanke—that they had created "interconnections" among financial firms that justified the rescue of Bear Stearns. This was not true, as shown by events after Lehman's failure, but by that time the idea had become embedded in the left's narrative about the causes of the financial crisis. It should be obvious that regulators' ignorance about the nature and extent of swap liabilities is not a good reason to regulate a market; it is far more efficient to educate the regulators. The costs in time and money to obtain a determination of whether swaps must be cleared through a clearing facility will discourage innovation and act as a bar to new entry into the market.

In addition, there is the likelihood that clearinghouses themselves—now required to clear trillions of dollars in trades—will become TBTF. The drafters of the DFA were aware of this possibility, so clearinghouses were made eligible for financial support from the Fed if they are designated as financial market utilities (FMUs) by the FSOC. In July, 2012, the FSOC voted to designate eight clearinghouses as FMUs, giving them access to the Fed's support in case of financial difficulties. Providing that clearinghouses have access to government backing will make it more likely that one or more clearinghouses will become TBTF and eventually fail, triggering a need for government funds. Before the clearinghouse requirement was enacted, most clearing was done by banks. In that case, the trading parties had to be confident about the financial condition of the clearing bank. The same was true when the trading parties chose a clearinghouse—both parties had to have confidence In the financial condition of the clearinghouse. However, now that clearinghouses have access to government support, the counterparties to a swap do not have to be concerned about the clearinghouse's credit. As a result, clearinghouses will no longer have to compete on the basis of their financial strength; instead, they are likely to compete on other measures, such as market share or rates, taking more risks to win more business. Thus, despite expressed concern by the framers of Dodd-Frank about moral hazard and taxpayer liability for too-big-to-fail institutions, they have made matters worse. By requiring that most swaps go through clearinghouses, the act has gone a long way toward introducing moral hazard into the derivatives market and thus increasing the likelihood of taxpayer liability when clearinghouses fail.

If the left's narrative about the role of the derivatives market in the financial crisis were correct, these costs and likely consequences would perhaps be acceptable, but there is no evidence that derivatives, or the lack of transparency in the derivatives market, had any role in the bringing on the 2008 financial crisis. The regulation authorized by the DFA will certainly achieve greater transparency, but it will also add to the cost of risk management for financial institutions and others, reduce both innovation and diversity and increase the likelihood that one or more clearinghouses—made TBTF by government policy—will require a taxpayer-financed bailout.

The CFTC has been the most active of all the regulatory agencies in implementing the act, primarily exercising its authority to fill out the Dodd-Frank mandate for the regulation of derivatives under Title II. By the fall of 2012, most of its regulations were finalized, while other agencies were far behind. In a sense, the result provides an early warning to the financial markets that when others complete their work the outcome will be a highly burdensome regime that will drive businesses out of U.S. jurisdiction where they can leave, and impose heavy regulatory costs on those that cannot.

Indeed, the CFTC's swap regulations have proved to be so costly, and have created such uncertainty about how they will enforced, that by the fall of 2012 the industry was moving to escape the new swap rules entirely by substituting futures for swaps. For example, the Intercontinental Exchange, a major international trading platform, proposed in September 2012 to convert its cleared swap contracts to futures or option contracts, noting that "Our customers are seeking regulatory certainty amid the continued evolution of new swap rules and how those rules might impact their operations."[6] And CFTC commissioner Scott O'Malia observed, "Given the inconsistency in the commission's interpretation of its own rules, the lack of regulatory certainty and the increased cost of compliance with the commission's swaps regulations, including the complicated and controversial swap dealer definition rules, swap customers have turned to the futures markets for regulatory certainty."

This is an untenable situation. There is some value in achieving transparency in any market, but not at the price exacted by the DFA. The regulations that have thus far been imposed have unnecessarily increased costs, created uncertainty about the future, and raised the possibility that clearinghouses will eventually have to be rescued with taxpayer funds. In addition, like all regulation, the new regulations imposed on the derivatives market will suppress innovation and stifle competition by foreclosing entry to smaller firms. Given the fact that derivatives had little if anything to do with the financial crisis, it is difficult to argue with the Clinton administration's

---

6. Peter Madigan, "Ice Move from Swaps to Future Unlikely to Be Last, Says O'Maila," *Risk*, September 28, 2012, http://www.risk.net/risk-magazine/news/2208965/ice-move-from-swaps-to-futures-unlikely-to-be-last-says-o-malia.

judgment that the derivatives market did not require regulation. Sensible reform in this area would repeal the clearinghouse requirement, allow banks to continue to trade derivatives of all kinds, and achieve transparency by requiring more reporting of positions by all market participants.

Title VIII. Payment, Clearing, and Settlement Supervision

As noted above, Title VIII provides that the FSOC may designate clearinghouses and other financial institutions as systemically important and authorizes the Fed to provide funds for FMUs that require financial assistance. In July 2012, the FSOC designated eight clearing organizations, among them Chicago Mercantile Exchange, ICE Clear Credit LLC, and National Securities Clearing Corp., as FMUs.[7] These entities may receive advances from the Fed in "unusual or exigent circumstances." The FSOC can also designate as an FMU any financial institution that is engaged in payment, clearing, and settlement functions in connection with a financial transaction, if it believes that the activity "is, or is likely to become, systemically important" (section 804(a)(2)). There has been almost no discussion of this provision, but it appears to give the FSOC the authority—through designating a financial institution as an FMU—to provide any financial firm with access to the Fed's financial support. This provision seems to provide a route around the general prohibition, in section 1101 of the act, on the Fed's use of section 13(3) of the Federal Reserve Act to assist a particular financial institution, limiting that assistance to programs of "broad-based eligibility." If Congress was serious about restricting the Fed's ability to bail out individual firms with taxpayer funds, this section should be modified or repealed.

Title IX and Title XIV. Housing Finance Reform

As outlined earlier in this book, the financial crisis was caused by the collapse of a huge housing bubble that developed between 1997 and 2007. This bubble, far larger than any in U.S. history, was fed by substantial

---

7. Donna Borak, "Financial Utilities Are First to Get 'Systemic' Label," *American Banker,* July 18, 2012.

government investment, primarily through Fannie Mae and Freddie Mac, in subprime and other weak and low-quality loans. These investments were the result of government housing policies, led by HUD over two administrations, that were designed to reduce mortgage underwriting standards and increase the availability of housing finance credit for low-income borrowers. By 2008, these policies had produced a housing finance market in which half of all mortgages—28 million loans—were subprime or otherwise low quality. Of these, 74 percent were on the books of government agencies like Fannie and Freddie or entities that were regulated by the government.

The remaining 26 percent were on the books of private financial institutions which held them primarily in the form of private mortgage-backed securities (PMBS). When housing values fell with the collapse of the housing bubble in 2007, PMBS lost substantial value as investors fled from the PMBS market. Although most PMBS were still paying at near expected rates at the time, financial institutions were required by mark-to-market accounting to write down the values of these assets to the minimal or distressed prices they were then receiving in the market. The sharp decline in asset values caused serious erosion in the capital and liquidity positions of many of the largest financial institutions in the United States and Europe, creating anxiety among investors. When Lehman Brothers filed for bankruptcy, a panic ensued, with banks hoarding cash that might be needed to meet withdrawals and refusing to lend to one another.

Given these facts, one would suppose that the first priority of the act's drafters would be to reform government housing policies so that similar disasters would not occur again. But it was not to be. The left's narrative about the financial crisis, as exemplified by the FCIC report, regarded Fannie and Freddie as only marginal players in the housing collapse. Even less responsible was government housing policy, since Fannie and Freddie's activities were chalked up to profit-seeking rather than government requirements. Instead, the left's narrative blamed the greed and irresponsibility of the private sector and focused its attention on predatory lending and securitization—particularly what was called the "originate to distribute" securitization system—as the housing finance system's contribution to the crisis. The fact that the government had created the demand for the mortgages that had eventually crashed the financial system was never recognized as inconsistent with the left's narrative about the role of the private sector.

With this narrative guiding the drafting of the act, it was inevitable that restrictions and restraints would be placed on the private sector and that the government's role would remain untouched or even enlarged. That is the story of Titles IX and XIV of the DFA.

The DFA attempted to address the originate-to-distribute idea by requiring that securitizers have some "skin in the game." Accordingly, the act requires that securitizers retain 5 percent of the risk in any pool of mortgages that they securitize—unless all the mortgages in the pool were high-quality loans that the act referred to as qualified residential mortgages (QRMs). FHA/Ginnie Mae, the government mortgage insurer and securitizer, was exempted from the risk retention requirement. The key elements of a QRM were to be defined by the regulators in the implementing rules.

This approach had two major flaws. First, it heavily favored banks that have large balance sheets—necessary to hold those 5 percent retentions indefinitely—and virtually excluded securitizers that could not do so from the business of securitization. In addition, by not defining the terms it expected to see in a QRM, the act left the regulators in an impossible position. A narrow standard specifying a bulletproof mortgage would be consistent with the apparent intention of the act—to discourage the origination of risky mortgages—but would then encourage most non-QRM mortgages to go to FHA/Ginnie Mae, cutting out private securitizers and preventing recovery of the private market. On the other hand, a broad interpretation of QRM would defeat the idea that most securitizers have "skin in the game."

When the proposed rule came out in March 2011, the QRM was defined to include a 20 percent down payment; in addition, the regulators who drafted the proposal further suggested that Fannie and Freddie should be exempt from the 5 percent risk retention requirement, along with FHA/Ginnie. The 20 percent down payment requirement stunned the industry, which had become accustomed to 5 percent down payments, and brought complaints from both the industry and Congress. Strong comments, opposing the draft rule, were filed during the comment period. As this is written, 18 months later, the regulators have not been able to publish a final rule or put out a second draft proposal. The housing finance market, as a result, is in the grip of uncertainty about the laws under which it will be operating in the future.

A parallel problem, even more severe, is how the act dealt with the other main element of the left's narrative—the notion that predatory lending accounted for a large portion of the millions of subprime and other low-quality mortgages in the financial system before the financial crisis. Since this was blamed on greedy originators that forced these mortgages on unwitting borrowers, the act's solution was to penalize the lender if it turned out that a borrower could not afford the mortgage. This idea gave rise to the so-called qualified mortgage (QM), which specified that if a mortgage originator were to make a loan that the borrower could not afford, the borrower—among other things—would have a defense to foreclosure. This is an extraordinary penalty and penalizes not only the originator, but also the securitizers and investors in pools of mortgages that include one or more non-QM loans.

Few people are likely to make mortgages under this rule without some kind of legal protection, but the act leaves this question unclear. Without choosing between them, it contains a provision that describes both a safe harbor, in which a lender could avoid liability by taking specific steps, and a rebuttable presumption, in which the lender would have a presumption of correctness that could be overcome by the substantial evidence produced by the borrower. Lenders want the safe harbor, and consumer advocates want the rebuttable presumption. The decision will be made by the CFPB. In the early fall of 2012, the CFPB reopened the comment period on this question, which conveniently took its decision past the election, but it is likely the decision will be made before the end of the year. No matter what the decision, some originators will leave the business because of the potential liability. Because of the uncertainties surrounding the QRM, however, a resolution of the QM issue will not resolve the problems created by the DFA for the housing finance system.

Risk retention, the exemption of FHA/Ginnie and Fannie and Freddie from risk retention and the QM requirements are impediments to the recovery of a robust private securitization system. This is problematic because banks and S&Ls do not have sufficient funds themselves to support the U.S. mortgage market. Unless the taxpayers are to take on mortgage risk, other investors must be brought into the market, and for that a private securitization system is essential. The collapse of Fannie Mae and Freddie Mac shows the vulnerability of government-backed securitization systems to political exploitation and moral hazard. Other provisions in the act that also impede the development of a private securitization system are restrictions on the release of the yield spread premium—a higher spread than normal between what the borrower pays and the investor receives—until all proceeds have been paid to investors; the Volcker rule, which may make hedging difficult when it is promulgated in final form; and the SEC's Regulation AB, which purports to prevent conflicts of interest between sponsors and investors in securitizations. Even if the QRM and QM issues are eventually resolved, these additional elements will prevent the recovery of a robust securitization system.

Accordingly, to begin the process of reviving a private securitization system and end the uncertainties that are now holding back the recovery of the housing market, the housing finance provisions of Title IX and Title XIV should also be substantially reformed. First, the impediments to the revival of a private securitization market have to be removed. These include the specific elements of the DFA outlined above and the risk retention requirement for securitizers. The idea behind the QRM—that securitized mortgages should meet a minimum quality standard—is a good one, but it cannot be achieved by requiring securitizers to retain a portion of the risk. A better idea would be to enable private mortgage insurers to price Insurance for mortgages based on the risks they perceive. That would provide the "skin In the game" that the QRM was seeking without excluding some smaller competitors from the market. The QM would be workable with a sufficiently clear safe harbor, but unless this can be devised the QM should be repealed. Finally, as all these things are done, the conforming loan limits of Fannie and Freddie should be gradually reduced over, say, five years, and FHA's authority should be limited to insuring mortgages for low-income borrowers. As Fannie, Freddie, and FHA are gradually withdrawn from the market, private-sector securitization will revive. Eventually, most of the housing market—with the exception of low-income borrowers who will have access to FHA—will be financed by the private sector and the distortions introduced by the government's Involvement will be eliminated.

Title X. The Consumer Financial Protection Bureau

Another provision of the DFA that is derived directly from the left's narrative is the Consumer Financial Protection Bureau, which was given authority under Title X of the act to police all financial relationships between consumers and firms of any kind—not just financial firms. A consumer's charge account at a local grocery store, for example, would come within the jurisdiction of the CFPB at the federal level. The CFPB fits into the left's narrative because of the left's belief that predatory lending was a significant cause of the financial crisis. This idea was also explored by the FCIC, which recounted many anecdotes about predatory lending but—despite my repeated request for data on numbers—was never able to estimate how many mortgages were the result of predatory lending. To be sure, there was widespread evidence of mortgage fraud, and even some estimates of how much of this contributed to the financial crisis, but mortgage fraud refers to deception by borrowers, not lenders. In a period when stated income was accepted on mortgage applications, it is highly likely that predatory borrowers were more of a problem than predatory lenders. Predatory lending is certainly a reprehensible activity, but there is no reason to believe—based on the FCIC's work—that it was a significant cause of the financial crisis.

The agency's jurisdiction is broad—perhaps the broadest of any federal agency—and extends from the biggest banks to the smallest check-cashing firm on Main Street. Its regulations will cover many small firms that have never been subject to regulation before. The added costs of regulation for many small firms will certainly result in consolidations as firms try to economize on regulation by merging with one another or selling out to larger firms. For example, on July 10, 2012, the agency published a proposed rule that was intended to implement the terms of a simplified disclosure document that will inform borrowers about mortgage costs. It would be funny if it weren't so sad, but the proposed rule for the simplified disclosure form is more than one thousand pages long.[8] This symbolizes the enormous regulatory burden that will fall on all mortgage firms—a burden that will certainly drive many of the smaller ones out of the mortgage business and reduce competition and the services available to borrowers. The same effect will be visible in other areas of the economy, as the additional costs required by CFPB regulation are felt by smaller firms.

---

8. Consumer Financial Protection Bureau, Integrated Mortgage Disclosures under the Real Estate Settlement Procedures Act (Regulation X), and the Truth in Lending Act (Regulation Z) (proposed rule), July 10, 2012. http://files.consumerfinance.gov/f/201207_cfpb_proposed-rule_integrated-mortgage-disclosures.pdf

Apart from the costs to the economy, the principal problem associated with the CFPB, as noted earlier, is the power that the DFA lodges with the director—a single administrator appointed by the president for a five-year term and only removable from office for cause. A director appointed by an outgoing president could serve through the entire first term of the new president, no matter what the elected president's mandate might be. That not only places a great deal of authority in one person but also seems inconsistent with the constitutional structure that is supposed to subject the government to political controls. In the U.S. constitutional structure, for example, Congress has the power to appropriate funds for the operations of the executive branch. However, the DFA provides a unique funding mechanism for the CFPB, granting it a direct statutory allocation of funds from the Federal Reserve. So Congress has no power to control the scope of the agency's activities through appropriations. Finally, although the CFPB's funds come from the Fed, the DFA forbids the Fed to exercise any control over the agency. In other words, the CFPB, alone among federal agencies (except for the Fed itself), is free of any political or policy controls. This is very troubling in a democracy and was obviously intended by the framers of the DFA to prevent the elected organs of the government from interfering with the agency's actions.

These factors have raised questions about the constitutionality of the CFPB. A lawsuit has been filed on the issue, and in 2012 Senate Republicans refused to confirm a director until the administration agreed to convert the CFPB into an ordinary multiheaded commission like the SEC, CFTC, and other bipartisan regulatory bodies. In response, the president made a recess appointment that is itself of doubtful constitutionality. A repeal of the DFA would eliminate this questionable structure, after which Congress could decide whether to reconstitute the agency as a multiheaded regulatory body subject to congressional appropriations or to return the consumer protection functions to the bank regulators or to a new regulatory structure for financial services generally.

Practical Considerations

Although this chapter recommends reform of the Dodd-Frank Act in several major respects, there are practical reasons to consider repeal. The most significant elements in the bill must be filled out in detail through regulation before they can be operative, and the regulations have encountered so many obstacles—and so much industry opposition—that by the fall of 2012, they were very far behind schedule. The most important ones, covering housing finance, prudential regulation of systemically important firms, proprietary trading under the Volcker Rule, and the regulation of derivatives, have not been completed as this is written, and it appears that in some areas—the Volcker Rule and the definition of the QRM—the regulators assigned to the task appear to be awaiting new guidance from Congress. Many economists believe that the uncertainties and costs created by the act, and the delay in getting the regulations approved, is a major cause of the slow recovery from the 2008 financial crisis. Alan Greenspan, among others, has argued that the uncertainties caused by the DFA have reduced the long-term investments in such items as physical plant that businesses customarily make as the economy recovers from recessions. For that reason, the act bears a great deal of responsibility for the continuing slow recovery in economic growth, particularly in construction.[9]

Furthermore, it is likely that every one of the major regulations, when they are finalized, will be challenged in the courts by the industries and firms that are subject to them. The act is extremely general in the authority it lays down; it is more a direction to the regulatory agencies to make major policy decisions under general statutory guidance rather than a series of policy directions by Congress itself, and for that reason it is already being challenged as an unconstitutional delegation of legislative authority. Finally, many of the initial draft rules are strongly opposed by the industries to which they will be applied. As a result, many very specific challenges are likely once the regulations are finalized. These challenges will be specific to the terms of the rules themselves and are likely to be based on grounds that the regulatory agency exceeded its vague statutory authority, was arbitrary or capricious in its rule making, or failed to do a thorough cost-benefit analysis. Legal challenges could mean that the regulations will not go into effect for several years, even after they are adopted. Again, the uncertainties associated with these delays will have an adverse effect on the economic recovery, growth, and jobs.

For these reasons, repeal of the act could be the most sensible course.

---

9. Alan Greenspan, "Activism," *International Finance* (March 2011), infi_1277_rev6(1).pdf.

Index

About the Author

Peter J. Wallison is Arthur F. Burns Fellow and a codirector of AEI's program on financial policy studies. He researches banking, insurance, and securities regulation. As general counsel of the U.S. Treasury Department, he had a significant role in the development of the Reagan administration's proposals for the deregulation of the financial services industry. He also served as White House counsel to President Ronald Reagan and is the author of *Ronald Reagan: The Power of Conviction and the Success of His Presidency* (Westview Press, 2002). His other books include *Competitive Equity: A Better Way to Organize Mutual Funds* (2007); *Privatizing Fannie Mae, Freddie Mac, and the Federal Home Loan Banks* (2004); *The GAAP Gap: Corporate Disclosure in the Internet Age* (2000); and *Optional Federal Chartering and Regulation of Insurance Companies* (2000). He also writes for AEI's *Financial Services Outlook* series.